THE AGE OF IDEAS

THE AGE

from
reaction
to
revolution

OF IDEAS

in
eighteenth-
century
France

GEORGE R. HAVENS

HENRY HOLT AND COMPANY
NEW YORK

TO LOUISE

first and best of readers

TABLE OF
CONTENTS

CONTENTS

PART III

EXPLOSION

INTRODUCTION

IDEAS LIVE ONLY IN PEOPLE—THE MEN AND WOMEN WHO EXPRESS them in cogent form or who, listening to the spoken word or attentively reading the printed page, re-think for themselves the thoughts which are the most precious heritage of the past. For this reason, it is natural not to separate in this book the course of ideas from the vivid personalities who gave them birth.

The eighteenth century in France was above all notable for its literature of ideas. The abuses of this pre-Revolutionary society were many and blatant. In angry protest against the crying evils of injustice, oppression, and torture, there arose a brilliant corps of writers wielding their pens with a vigor and an originality rarely equalled. The leaders of thought at this crucial time were masters of a style which compelled the attention even of their enemies. Seldom has literature been forged into a more potent weapon in the slow battle for progress. These were authors who never forgot that the war in behalf of the unknown future must be won or lost first of all in men's minds.

In an age of repression and censorship, the ablest writers of the day learned to beat the government's game with wit, allegory, clever fiction, or surreptitious publication. The general public, in turn, eagerly patronized the contraband peddlers of forbidden books or manuscripts. As the century wore on, the French authorities themselves, half-conniving, often looked discreetly the other way, tacitly permitting the circulation of whatever seemed not to threaten too loud an uproar.

This book proposes to tell the story of these ideas in terms of the varied and colorful men who gave them expression. In doing so, however, we have at no time had recourse to "novelized biographies." The facts, as authenticated by the *Notes* in the back of the book for the benefit of those interested, speak sufficiently for themselves. To present these vivid personalities, there is no need of succumbing to the easy lure of fiction.

INTRODUCTION

We shall endeavor here to relive the past as far as is possible, to view the places and the people as they then appeared to contemporary eyes, to feel for ourselves something of the alarms, fears, and doubts which beset the eighteenth century. Since we, too, are human, these same alarms, fears, and doubts, remain to a remarkable degree our own anxious concern today. The past, whether we wish it or not, is prolonged into the present and offers us our only guide toward the future.

For we must not allow ourselves to forget that the chief ideas of the eighteenth century are by no means of historical interest only, in the narrow sense of that term. The writers of this great period were above all ardent humanists, inspired by the vital literature of Greece, Rome, and Judea; they were the heirs both of classicism and Christianity. Though they often revolted impatiently against the fixed dogmas of the past, they cherished a warm interest in whatever affected human happiness or welfare. Their violent hostility to war, their battle against arbitrary imprisonment and torture, their active campaign for freedom in all its forms, their lively debate over material versus moral progress, are but a few of the basic human problems presented vividly by them in a language which we continue to enjoy and to understand. What they so boldly began, remains still, to our keen regret, "unfinished business." We also are deeply involved in the final success of their battle. For us, as it did for them, "the bell tolls." It is conceivable that we might even be unfortunate enough to lose in our day what they at least partly won.

But the story which we have to tell should speak clearly for itself. Let us, then, without more ado, get on with the telling.

PART I

TRANSITION

CHAPTER I

HOW ABSOLUTE GOVERNMENT FAILED

I

I T WAS MID-OCTOBER IN THE YEAR 1685.

In the vast one-storied château which sprawled grandly over one side of the huge park situated in the smiling countryside of the Seine valley some forty miles south of Paris, an impressive figure strode majestically into the conference room. A large wig fell in curls around his shoulders, framing the august face in jet black. His flaring knee-length brown coat of the latest fashion, brilliant-colored vest, and spotless white hose drew the eyes of contemporaries. A man born to command, he was about to take the grave step which had been long meditated and long urged upon him.

Nearly a quarter of a century ago, on coming of age, he had promptly given the astonished public a taste of his firm mettle by declaring, after the death of crafty Cardinal Mazarin, that he would henceforth rule directly himself, without the usual aid of a prime minister. Through the passing years there had been no lack of zealous counselors pressing him for instant action on one supremely important issue, but with silent calm the King—for he was King of France— had firmly refused to be hurried. During the agreeable month of the Court's annual autumn residence in the magnificent castle of Fontainebleau, he had, however, at last made up his mind. The eight-page quarto document, entrusted to the Marquis de Châteauneuf for final drafting, would be read with varied emotions of joy or despair by all the French people.

The exact proceedings of this great occasion have not been preserved. But Wednesday, the 17th of October, was the day for a regular meeting of the Council of State. It is also the official date of the fateful edict expressing the royal decision. The brief ceremony of signing would therefore naturally have taken place at this important session.

CHAPTER I

As the King, according to custom, presided solemnly in the high-backed chair at the head of the table in the gilded salon of Fontainebleau, there was revealed no outward sign of hesitation in his grand manner. Indeed, if ever he felt special excitement of any sort, he had early schooled himself to conceal it beneath an air of unruffled dignity. He was ordinarily a man of few words and given to knowledge of his own mind. Henceforth he had resolved to reign over a kingdom forcibly united around the royal person. No longer should a stiff-necked Protestant minority continue to flaunt its unsmiling opposition to his divinely-appointed will. "I am the State" was his declared policy, if not the precise words which expressed his thought. Unity had at length been established in government. From an absolute king all authority stemmed. Why not a similar unity in religion also? *Hors de l'Eglise, point de salut.* "Outside of the Church, no salvation." Such was the belief held by a great majority of his loyal subjects. It was a simple creed, and it was clear.

Too long, no doubt, as it seemed to him, had these Protestants, these Huguenot rebels, a veritable nation apart within the very body of the French nation, been tolerated in their heretical thoughts! It was true they had remained quiet and docile throughout the abortive revolt of the Fronde around the middle of the century, while the supple Mazarin still ruled during the King's minority, but those youthful days beset by fierce fighting in the streets of Paris and by insolent defiance of royal authority had nevertheless been dark and troublous. The boy king and his mother had actually been forced to flee in haste from the capital and to sleep almost on bare straw in their refuge at Saint-Germain. Bitter memories not easily to be forgotten! And could one ever be sure of these dour Protestants? Did they not constantly offer a vague threat of insurrection, renewed civil war, or even of insidious plotting with foreign enemies of like heresy?

For eighty-seven long years, certain liberties of worship had indeed been permitted by the government, though more and more reluctantly, since that far-off time in April of 1598 when they had been first promulgated by the King's great ancestor, him whom people were pleased to call the "good Henry." But had not this conciliatory Edict of Nantes, as it was called, been extorted from Henry IV and signed only for reasons of state? So at least it appeared, readily enough, to his autocratic successor.

With the brief, firm scratch of his quill pen on the paper, the strong-willed man of forty-seven was at last putting an end to what he considered an unhappy state of political uncertainty and religious dissidence. Besides—as he had often been assured—few of these recalcitrants were left in France by this time. Most of the miserable heretics had managed somehow to flee abroad, had been persuaded by eager missionaries, or else had yielded to the practical arguments of the rough dragoons whom unfortunately it had been necessary to quarter upon them in the very interest of their immortal souls. Nearly all, it was now reported, had been converted to the true faith. Almost daily there poured into the Court enthusiastic accounts of abjurations by the thousands in Poitou, Languedoc, Dauphiny, Béarn, and other French provinces. The royal action this day, as the lengthy document itself stated, merely gave official recognition to the new religious unity, already so completely established. Henry IV's old-time proclamation of tolerance seemed no longer needed in the new age. It was a dramatic moment, a turning point in history. Quickly, boldly, with habitual confidence in the rightness of his judgment, the King, with a flourish, signed the potent word "Louis" at the end of the eighth and final page. The signature was witnessed by the son of the great Colbert.

Thus on Wednesday, the 17th of October, 1685, Louis XIV approved the Revocation of the Edict of Nantes.

The next day, as the eighty-two-year-old Chancellor, Le Tellier, countersigned the edict with a hand shaking from desperate illness, he joyfully quoted from the Latin version of Luke the well-known exclamation of the aged Simeon, greeting the infant Jesus: "Lord, now lettest thou thy servant depart in peace, according to thy word: for mine eyes have seen thy salvation." The Chancellor had good reason to rejoice—within his lights. He had played an important part in shaping this unfortunate text which completely undid King Henry's forward-looking work. Indeed, the actual date of the Revocation is said to have been advanced nearly ten weeks in order to permit the dying Le Tellier to welcome the event with his own eyes.

The Great Seal was next affixed to the edict with green wax upon red and green silk cords. Copies of the historic document were immediately rushed to all parts of the country, though it was necessary to wait over the week end until Monday, October 22nd, for this decisive state paper to be officially recorded by the King's Procurator

General on behalf of the vacationing Parlement of Paris. Only then was it made public. Mobs quickly began to tear to the ground those Protestant temples which still remained. Hardly more than a week later, Chancellor Le Tellier was dead, and, on the 25th of January, the great Bishop of Meaux, Bossuet, in characteristic tones of thundering eloquence, delivered a commemorative oration, lauding Le Tellier and the King for having in one bold stroke wiped out heresy in France.

Except among the persecuted Protestant minority, the sentiment of the nation was at first almost universally one of joy and satisfaction. Few could foresee the gloomy future. That famous writer of vivid letters, Madame de Sévigné, comfortably remote from the terror which stalked through the provinces, cried out happily: "The dragoons have so far been very good missionaries. . . . You have no doubt seen the edict by which the King revokes that of Nantes. Nothing is so good as its contents, and never has any king done or will do anything so memorable." Similarly the great author of fables, the genial La Fontaine, and even Jean de La Bruyère, in spite of biting criticism of the Old Régime in his book, *The Characters,* hailed the extinction of religious dissent.

2

While it is evident that, under an absolute government, opposing voices hardly dared to make themselves heard within the country, yet approval of Louis's action was natural enough in an age when the very idea of tolerance was incomprehensible to most minds, fanatically bound down as they were to a single narrow and exclusive conception of truth.

Nor was such intolerance peculiar to any one group or belief. Not much over a hundred years previously, Servetus, because he was an anti-trinitarian, had been marched to the stake and burned alive as a dangerous heretic in Calvin's Protestant Geneva. He would probably have been treated with equal cruelty in many other parts of Christendom. Only seven years before, in 1678, England under Elizabeth was stirred to panic against Catholics at Titus Oates's charges of "papist" plots. Soon, even amidst the relative freedom of Holland, to which Pastor Jurieu had fled from the persecutions of Catholic France, this combative Huguenot would attack passionately the tolerant and, as it seemed to him, the too independent Protestantism of his former friend, Pierre Bayle. And three quarters of a century later, Jean-Jacques Rousseau, too radical in his beliefs to satisfy the orthodox either among Catholics or Protestants, too inherently religious for his one-time comrades of the philosophic party, would call down upon his unhappy head the wrath of all three powerful groups, condemning himself to years of persecution and wandering.

In 1685 Church and State were nearly everywhere closely linked together in men's minds; they would continue thus in alliance for centuries; in many instances they remain so today. By most people political and religious unity were regarded as inseparable. Passions ran as high as convictions. To coerce thought was generally considered a clear duty.

Although Madame de Maintenon, who had been secretly married the year before to Louis XIV, recognized that the so-called "conversions," made almost daily in the thousands by dint of brutality, threats, and torture, could not be sincere, she nonetheless consoled herself with the reflection that "the children will at least be Catholics, even if the parents are hypocrites!"

Saint-Simon, the great contemporary writer of memoirs, and many historians who follow his testimony, have indeed claimed that Madame de Maintenon, though originally a Protestant herself, was primarily responsible for determining Louis XIV in favor of the Revocation. There is no positive evidence, however, to support this charge. Other advisers, secular and religious, had long been urging the King toward action. Besides, from the very beginning of his personal rule in 1661, he had declared his firm intention of checking the expansion of Protestantism. It was only a step to go further and attempt to abolish it completely. In any case, his increasing devotion to the external forms of the established Church, his own unwavering belief in unity, even though extorted by force, were pushing him toward the annihilation of dissidence. Deeply suspicious of any attempts to influence him, Louis XIV could be led only by the most discreet and covert of suggestions. Voltaire and later authorities appear justified in saying that Madame de Maintenon was too unsure of her position to take any open part in bringing about the Revocation. Following her prudent custom, nevertheless, she may have worked through secret hints dropped to other counselors, or perhaps succeeded in bringing the King himself actually to request her humbly-expressed opinion. At any rate, it is probable that Louis XIV, with or without her encouragement, would have come in the end to the same decision.

Yet, plausible and indeed righteous though it undoubtedly seemed to the King, the Revocation of the Edict of Nantes was a grievous error, political, economic, and religious. It was a long step backward, toward repression and reaction. Of the something like a million and a half Protestants out of a total French population at that time of about twenty millions, it has been conservatively estimated that no less than two hundred thousand fled the country during the next fifteen years. An equal number left France during the following half-century down to 1750.

Those who thus risked life and worldly fortune to maintain their beliefs were naturally the men and women of strongest character and most fervent faith. Since, by law, all professions and all government posts had little by little been barred to Protestants, these refugees were for the most part hard-working artisans, successful manufacturers, businessmen, small farmers, energetic and generally well-educated pastors, or else country noblemen of a type less easily converted against their real convictions than the too pliant courtiers. Nine thousand of them were much-needed sailors; twelve thousand, soldiers; six hundred, officers in the army. The great Marshal Schomberg, who with his family refused to be won over to Catholicism, was, because of his distinction, reluctantly given permission to emigrate. His contemporary, the Marquis de Sourches, observed in his *Memoirs* that he departed "to the great regret of all France, who lost in him the best and most experienced of her generals." By one of fate's ironies, Marshal Schomberg afterwards commanded the troops of the Stadtholder of the Dutch Republic, William of Orange, and contributed to the latter's successful invasion of England in 1688, thus driving from the throne James II, Louis's Catholic ally.

In spite of the many obstacles placed in the way of the refugees to prevent them from carrying property abroad, Vauban, the King's expert in fortification and a realistic observer in his travels over the country, estimated that the fleeing Protestants succeeded in exporting sixty million livres in five years. This was a huge sum for the time. So much money entered with these Huguenots into Holland that it was well-nigh impossible to invest it, and the interest rate fell to the then low figure of two per cent.

But, aside from money, what was lost to France in stalwart, virtuous citizens of firm convictions and independent thought, of solid economic achievement, was gained by Louis's foreign enemies, Holland, Germany, England. Many vigorous and enterprising Huguenots, braving cramped, foul-smelling quarters, unpalatable diet, seasickness, and the dreaded scurvy, sooner or later embarked upon the long, painful, and dangerous voyage in tiny sailing vessels across a stormy ocean to far-off America.

It was no easy task for the unhappy refugees to tear up their roots from the native soil of France and choose deliberately the rough path of exile. Frontiers by land and sea were for a time closely guarded until at length these constant patrols became tiresome to the government itself and in fact a serious drain upon the country's weakened economy. Except for some of the pastors, considered to be dangerous leaders, better kept separated from their flocks, and a few other distinguished individuals, who were privileged because of their rank or position, members of the "Pretended Reformed Religion," as it was called, were forbidden even the desperate resource of flight, on pain of imprisonment for women, and death or the galleys for men. And death itself was preferable to the frightful daily misery of the vermin-ridden slave chained to a bench, nearly starved, half-clothed, and condemned perpetually to row under the broiling Mediterranean sun and the cutting lash in the King's galleys. Many unfortunate fugitives were shot in their attempts to escape over the frontier. If some Huguenots did contrive to carry funds with them or send money in advance abroad, more of them landed in poverty to begin life anew in a country of strange customs and unknown language. In spite of welcoming friends and the organized charity of co-religionists, such forced emigration was a test to the very limit of moral stamina.

Still Protestantism stubbornly refused to die in France. After the first simulated conversions under the terror of the fearful "dragonnades," the burning of the soles of the feet, the suspensions from rafters, the keeping of whole families awake for weeks by wanton noise until they were driven into hysteria by relays of mocking soldiers, the pillage and complete economic ruin which fell upon peaceful households with the sudden descent of these terrible "booted missionaries," and the worse crimes of licentiousness and torture which hardly bear narration, the bolder spirits began to go "underground." With the destruction of their churches, many Protestants held their secret meetings in the "desert," as they called it, that is, in the woods, the hills, or the remote countryside. Pastors caused themselves to be smuggled back from safe exile, risking death or the awful galleys as the price of again guiding their flocks. During the next century, in spite of continuing persecution and emigration, the number of French Protestants gradually returned to nearly the figures of the years preceding the Revocation. Thus, once more, it was proved that thought, in the face of the courageous human spirit, can hardly be permanently coerced.

3

Such insistence upon unity of belief, which we have just seen so cruelly invoked against Protestants, is one of the inevitable maladies of absolutism.

This same passionate desire to dominate the mind brought about repeated measures to suppress those Catholic dissidents, the Jansenists, followers of doctrines advanced by the Dutch bishop Jansen, for they, since early in the King's reign, seemed likewise to offer a stubborn challenge to the royal will that all should be as one. The religion of the Jansenists was a devoted and austere faith, somewhat resembling Calvinist beliefs in predestination and original sin. Moreover, Pascal's widely-read *Provincial Letters* (1656-57), the ablest polemical expression of their thought, had attacked with potent irony their Jesuit rivals, who, through his confessors, so strongly influenced the King. In their high moral integrity the Jansenists were naturally suspected, moreover, of censuring Louis's long succession of adulterous love affairs. In this complex situation, abstruse theology, legalistic quibbling, all the political schemes of individuals and groups intriguing for power, became inextricably mingled together.

The great stronghold of Jansenism was the famous convent of Port-Royal-des-Champs and its appendages. This solitary retreat was situated in the country about fifteen miles southwest of Paris in the damp Chevreuse valley. The then undrained marshes made the spot unhealthy with malaria. Nevertheless, the ardent Jansenists had succeeded in developing there an influential educational center.

From it came their most distinguished pupil, the famous writer of tragedies, Jean Racine. It was a center also for study and meditation to which withdrew many of the noblest spirits of the age. The fervent personal religion of Port-Royal had been for a while a powerful moral force in the seventeenth century.

Yet Jansenism was an anachronism, in spite of its admirable qualities of earnestness and sincerity. It remained too deeply rooted in the past, too inflexible, to meet the needs of a constantly-changing world. That it should ultimately disappear was no doubt inevitable, but not the cruel manner of its passing.

In 1699 Louis XIV declared categorically that "he abominated Port-Royal." Ten years later, he issued an order to close the convent and disperse the few nuns who remained there.

So it was that, early on October 29, 1709, the King's Lieutenant of Police at Paris, the elder Marquis d'Argenson, arrived in the peaceful valley with his officials and a large body of archers to execute Louis's command. Desiring to avoid local scandal and the embarrassing approach of curious or indignant peasants, the Marquis prudently posted three hundred of his soldiers in military fashion to block all roads for a mile and a half around. At half past seven in the morning, he knocked at the convent door and asked for the Mother Superior. On his request, the nuns were assembled and he read to them the King's order of dispersal. Each of the sisters was assigned to a different and widely separated convent. The arrangements for hurried departure took up much of the day. At length, the nuns with their little bundles of personal effects mounted two by two into the carriages which D'Argenson had provided in advance for the purpose. In their immaculate white robes with the bright red cross sewn on the scapular, they made a striking contrast to the gruff soldiery. Desirous of being conciliatory in his disagreeable duty, the Lieutenant of Police enjoined his officers:

"Take good care of these ladies, make the journey by easy stages, and see that they lack nothing they need."

The Mother Superior remained throughout the day to hearten the others in their painful separation from friends and long-familiar scenes. She refused even to grant herself time to eat, and departed fasting. Finally, last of all, as she thought, at five o'clock, the head of the convent stepped into her carriage. It was only later discovered that, in the confusion of departure, an unfortunate paralytic, a nun of eighty-six years, lying helpless on a stretcher, had been overlooked. By that time, it was too late for her to set forth and she was therefore kept over night. The next morning at six she, too, rode away, along the road to Nantes, accompanied by the wife of an officer. Thus, twenty-two Sisters, ranging from fifty to far over eighty years of age, were forcibly dispersed by the King's agents, and the convent was officially closed.

In June of the following year, 1710, on orders of Louis XIV, most of the buildings of Port-Royal-des-Champs were razed and the very cemetery itself was destroyed. Stray dogs tore savagely at the decayed flesh and bones of the heaped-up corpses, exhumed with indifference by careless workmen. When these painful happenings at Port-Royal were shortly bruited about Paris, they shocked even the undeveloped opinion of that age still thoroughly imbued with the concept of absolute government. Yet no open protest dared stir. The King had won another victory over the weak and unprotected, though at a price which would only later become evident. No one then could foresee the brutal rifling of the royal tombs of France which was to take place at Saint-Denis in 1793 during the Revolution, as the mills of the gods with rough poetic justice ground out their slow revenge.

In the end, the most fervent among the Jansenists, like the Protestant refugees before them, followed the road of freedom into exile, establishing themselves in Holland where with their leader Quesnel they formed a small independent Church. Others elected to remain in France, a dissident group throughout the eighteenth century.

Along with these unhappy disputes over Jansenism and Port-Royal, there raged another quarrel within the body of the Church, that over Quietism. This belief in a supreme state of divine love, in contemplation, in ardent prayer of communion, in mystical oneness with God, had been taught in an extreme form by Molinos, a Spanish priest living in Rome. The doctrine came into France with a certain widowed Madame Guyon. The famous Abbé Fénelon, soon to be Archbishop of Cambrai, greatly impressed by her piety and zeal, lent his ardent support to the new movement. For a time even the secret wife of Louis XIV, Madame de Maintenon, at the very Court of Versailles, was drawn to Quietism. Not so, however, Bishop Bossuet of Meaux, firm for the things of reason and the established forms rather than for those of feeling. Soon there was public controversy between these two great leaders of the Church in France,

Bossuet and Fénelon. Both at length appealed to Rome. Finally, the Pope condemned Quietism, but without severity toward Fénelon.

If, in these bitter doctrinal quarrels, unity in Church and State seemed at first to triumph, both royal government and official religion came out in the end with lessened prestige. The sight of intrigue after intrigue, of fanatic intolerance, of persecution even within the body of Mother Church herself, could only arouse or strengthen skepticism in many minds regarding all constituted authority. While Louis XIV grew more and more devout in the external practices of his ceremonial piety, many courtiers scarcely veiled their protective hypocrisy. When at last death took the aged King in 1715, frank debauch characterized the Regency of the Duke of Orleans. Yet it was not so much a veritable social change as an outward reaction after the removal of repression.

These long years of doctrinal quarrels were also years of increasingly open criticism of a king who ruled for what he called his personal "glory," and not for the welfare of his subjects. They were years moreover of a developing "libertinism," signifying primarily at the time freedom of thought in religion, though often indeed accompanied by that unrestrained immorality which is associated with the modern meaning of the word. Free-thinking, free-loving Ninon de l'Enclos, as a wrinkled octogenarian, was struck by the pert, mobile features of a young schoolboy named Arouet, who in the unseen future was destined both to charm and shock contemporaries under his chosen name of Voltaire. In her will Ninon left him 2,000 francs "to buy books." Thus the underground free-thinking of the seventeenth century joined hands with that of the eighteenth as new, bolder spirits came up into the light for a more direct attack upon ancient abuses.

4

Added to such fierce internal struggles over unity of religious belief were the King's numerous and unprovoked wars. In May of 1667 Louis set his armies in motion to enforce the claim of the French Queen upon certain districts of the Spanish Netherlands. This was called the two-year "War of Devolution." It was shortly followed in the years from 1672 to 1678 by the "Dutch War." Both these wars were momentarily successful. But ten years later came the

"War with the Grand Alliance," which brought together Austria, Holland, Spain, and England in a powerful league against France. For nine long years this war dragged on. To raise money and to offer a needed example to his harassed subjects, Louis even melted down his marvelous array of silver plate and varied furnishings. In the end no one was victorious; France and her enemies were alike exhausted.

Finally, an even longer war, that of the "Spanish Succession," from 1701 to 1713, darkened the closing years of Louis's reign. In the midst of this war, during the terrible winter cold of 1709, hunger stalked the streets of the cities and spread utter misery over the bare countryside. The eighteenth-century historian, Charles Duclos, reports that as a boy in those difficult times he saw conscripts chained together like criminals and driven off by press gangs to fill the rapacious maw of the dwindling armies.

France herself was invaded, seemed about to fall. Her troops fled in disorganized rout. Nothing remained between the enemy and a rapid march upon Paris. In this desperate situation the once glorious reign stood on the brink of an inglorious end. Yet the King, great in his hour of defeat, bore himself with his usual calm dignity. Only sheer good fortune and the lack of decisive action by the attacking forces averted complete disaster before peace was at last made in 1713.

From these years of almost constant wars or preparations for wars France had gained nothing and lost much. Financial and economic ruin, exhaustion, poverty, wounds, and death were the dire results of the King's insistent pursuit of military "glory."

In contrast to these mad foreign adventures, the great Finance Minister Colbert in the early part of the reign had dreamed dreams of encouraging French agriculture and industry. He dug canals, built roads, and improved transportation generally; he interested himself also in manufactures. A descendant of tradesmen himself, Colbert knew instinctively that thriving business, factories, and farming meant a prosperous France. Unfortunately he believed with his times that detailed regulation from the central government was necessary. So he weighed the people down with burdensome and unworkable restrictions on the size and quality of goods. He supposed that his country would most benefit from exports without imports, not seeing that trade must be a two-way enterprise. His control of grain production and the limitations on exchange from province to province brought repeated famine instead of that abundance of which the fertile soil of France was capable. The royal persecutions of Protestants, which Colbert opposed, sent many successful industries and manufactures to exile in Holland, England, or Germany. Thus these rival countries became still stronger competitors of a weakened France. After Colbert's death in 1683, his successors pushed even further the excesses of his isolationist policy, while wars and the King's extravagant building at Versailles and Marly caused the royal deficits to mount ever higher. Because the nobles and the clergy were "privileged classes" and largely exempt from taxation, the cruel load of government contributions bore grievously upon those least able to pay, the great masses of the people.

When the Reverend James Fontaine landed in England as a Protestant refugee early in December of 1685, six weeks after the Revocation of the Edict of Nantes, he was at once struck by "the extreme cheapness of bread." Large biscuits, he wrote, cost but a fourth of their price in France. This fact is the more significant in view of the essential place of bread in the French diet.

A black picture of peasant misery at the end of the century under him who was known grandly as the "Sun King" is given by Jean de La Bruyère in his famous book entitled *The Characters.*

"We see," says La Bruyère, "certain wild animals, male and female, scattered about the countryside, black, leaden in color, and deeply tanned by the sun, bound to the soil, which they dig and till with unconquerable persistence: they have, as it were, an articulate voice, and when they rise to their feet, they show a human face; and they are in fact men. At night they withdraw into dens, where they live on black bread, water, and roots: they spare other men the labor of sowing, plowing, and harvesting in order to live, and deserve thereby not to lack themselves, the very bread which they have planted."

The accuracy of this dark picture has been contested, for, in any country, in any age, it is not difficult to find cases of sordid poverty and to generalize them into proof of universal misery. Yet there is abundant testimony to support the essential truth of La Bruyère's dramatic paragraph and to justify the sympathy expressed in his final words.

Using as his authority the actual official reports of the King's own Intendants, the American historian, James Breck Perkins, offers confirmation in almost identical terms of La Bruyère's fierce indictment.

"In 1675," says Perkins, "the inhabitants of Dauphiny had for their diet only roots, and bread made from acorns, and when this failed they were driven to eat grass and bark. In Poitou, in 1686, they had been without bread for two years. In 1692, seventy thousand people in Limoges were living on rotten chestnuts, with begging as the only means of livelihood left to them. In Normandy, in 1693, the peasants were dying of hunger; convoys of provisions were attacked and plundered by starving men and women, in whom one could hardly recognize the appearance of humanity."

Toward 1694 the great Fénelon wrote a surprisingly blunt letter to Louis XIV, which, because of its dangerous frankness, was doubt-less never intended to be delivered. "Your people," he wrote the King, "are dying of hunger. Cultivation of the fields is almost abandoned; city and country are losing their inhabitants; all trades languish and no longer support their workmen. Commerce has been wiped out. . . . Instead of drawing money from these poor people, you ought to give them alms and feed them. The entire land of France is but a huge poorhouse, desolate and without resource."

Vauban, who traveled over the country planning the King's fortifications, had his eyes open to still larger questions and recognized sympathetically the increasing misery of the overburdened peasant. He was a keen observer and in no way to be suspected of special pleading. The economist Boisguillebert, toward the end of the century, painted an equally gloomy picture of revenues decreased at least by a half within the last thirty-five years. Even the great dramatist Racine, at the request of Madame de Maintenon herself, drew up a statement on the woes of the oppressed people. One day Louis XIV surprised her reading it. At his demand she had the weakness to reveal its author but not the courage to defend him. From that time on, the heart-broken poet found he had lost the King's favor.

The wages of the artisan, too, were pitifully low in proportion to the cost of food. As the seventeenth century ended, a pound of wheat was worth on the average one cent in Normandy. A good weaver at that time could earn fifteen cents a day, an ordinary worker, only ten. Others less skillful received not more than eight, six, or even four or five. "That's not much," admitted the King's Intendant himself, "when they have to pay high prices for food and meet their taxes."

According to Vauban again, agricultural laborers gained on an average eight or nine cents a day, but worked only a hundred and eighty days in a year. The cost of living rose steadily from 1693 on, and the real value of wages decreased, to the consequent accompaniment, among the workers, of suffering, conflicts, and strikes.

5

In the midst of such economic distress and bad administration, it was natural that absolute rule should offer no real opportunity for protest, criticism, or improvement. The King, humanly, welcomed flattery, but would not brook censure. Surrounded as he was by deferential courtiers, Louis, even had he wished to do so, could hardly penetrate beneath the surface to the truth. If he did catch a glimmer of the real situation, he was ill-disposed to apply the essential remedies of peace, economy, and sound government. By avoiding the possible turbulence of Paris and establishing the royal residence in the rarefied atmosphere of Versailles, he further isolated himself from his toiling subjects.

No individual was secure against the suspicions of the King. The *lettre de cachet* was always there awaiting the royal signature. By it, anyone could be arbitrarily ordered to prison in Bastille or elsewhere, to remain within grim walls until it suited the caprice of an all-powerful ruler to release him. There were no charges, no hearing, no opportunity to present evidence, no trial by jury, no term of sentence. Voltaire, twice in his early career, was to experience this capricious tyranny of the Old Régime. What wonder that the sight of English civil and political liberty in the years 1726 to 1729 at once struck him with admiration? In England, already, the writ of *habeas corpus,* with its protection against unjustified imprisonment, had become a great conquest in behalf of human liberty.

Even the thoughts of the individual were supposed to be guarded against religious or political heresy. So all books or pamphlets during the seventeenth and eighteenth centuries had to be submitted to censorship. Before publication in France, an official "approbation" and a "privilege" were necessary. This practice continued, though with some increase in tolerance, down to the Revolution in 1789.

Of course, there developed various devices to elude the censor. Pierre Bayle, the Protestant philosopher and critic, sought to hide his dangerous thoughts by means of interminable footnotes, hard to follow in their fine print and loaded down, as they were, with learned Greek and Latin references. That popularizer of science and rationalism, Fontenelle, like Voltaire later, resorted to wit, irony, and clever subterfuge. Writers who were critical of beliefs or conditions under the Old Régime became adept at meaning more than they seemed to say, at inviting the public to read between or behind the lines. "Strike and conceal your hand," wrote Voltaire. The literature of this period, whenever it is hostile to contemporary abuses, must be read with the mind awake to the fact of censorship and the punishment always in wait for him who overstepped prescribed bounds.

Often there were passages which had to be deleted or toned down before the authorities would permit them to appear. Such *cartons* or "cancels" in the form of substituted pages pasted in are not infrequently a distinguishing mark of important early editions. Often, too, books were published with false indications of place or date on the title page, and of course anonymously or with the name of a fictitious author. Still others were printed abroad, in Amsterdam or Geneva, then smuggled contraband into France and distributed *under the mantle,* as the expressive saying went. Some appeared with a "tacit permission," which could at once be revoked by the government if a book made too much noise. A book-seller in those days had to be a hardy soul, an adventurer ready to take big personal risks. If successful, he might make a fortune, but oftener than not he found himself haled away to prison in the dark of the early morning, lucky indeed if he could be soon released to hazard another try at his dangerous business, ignoring his humble and profuse promises of future good behavior. Such were the difficulties and perils under which ideas little by little fought their way toward freedom.

6

What kind of a man was Louis XIV, who thus shaped the destiny of his time?

The King was admittedly a majestic and awe-inspiring figure. Even Saint-Simon, the famous writer of *Memoirs,* though a high-ranking noble himself and fanatically jealous of his prerogatives, confessed that it required long practice and the utmost firmness to support Louis's keen glance unflinchingly during a private audience. The famous portrait by Rigaud shows forth the royal personage in all his trappings of consummate splendor.

Louis XIV was always polite, raising his plumed hat slightly to all women, including chambermaids in the palace. His disciplined courtesy prevailed even over his wrath. Once, angered at a nobleman who had the temerity to accuse him of breaking his word, the King suddenly threw his cane out of the window, exclaiming that he would not let himself be tempted to strike a man of noble blood.

As a rule, Louis spoke little and listened attentively. When he did speak, it was briefly, judiciously, and to the point. He was very industrious, observing regular hours daily for conference with his different ministers, even twice a day in later years. No amusement, no dissipation the night before, no ordinary illness could prevent him from following his usual schedule. During his old age, he often worked in the evening also, going over official papers with one of his cabinet ministers while his secret consort, Madame de Maintenon, sat quietly with her reading or embroidery, never venturing her own opinion, characteristically prudent though it was, unless directly asked.

Through all his long royal life, only once or twice, when with the Army, did Louis XIV fail to attend mass daily. In the external practices of religion, he became, as time went on, increasingly devout, but without visible benefit to his character.

Of a strong constitution and generally of robust health, the King was basically self-centered and inconsiderate of the weaknesses or ills of others. Sick or well, the ladies of his intimate circle had to make frequent trips with him by carriage to Marly, Fontainebleau, or wherever the Court moved. Even Madame de Maintenon was forced to call upon all of her great will power to appear constantly smiling and cheerful in the midst of sorrow or illness. How the penalties of high position wearied and bored her in the end!

The King himself had no lack of fortitude. In spite of repeated bereavement, the loss of successive heirs to the throne, humiliating defeats and even near-disaster in the later wars, Louis remained throughout calm and self-contained. In his bearing at least, he was to the last the Great King.

His keen eye, moreover, never failed to note those present or absent from his court. Not to be in frequent attendance at Versailles meant prompt loss of favor. Of such a delinquent, the King would say with cutting brevity: "I do not know him. He's a man whom I never see." And these verdicts, once given, were irrevocable. Thus the great Sun King completed the process, begun under previous reigns, of reducing the pliant nobility to unproductive idleness in the ceremonial life of his majestic palaces. Courtiers became mere satellites in his grandiose orbit, submissive pursuants of the royal bounty. Such subservience was naturally most unhealthy for the country at large.

Louis went to the point of having letters opened by his postal employees, and caused extracts and summaries of them to be made for his perusal; on important occasions he even read the original letters himself. Until the belated discovery of this secret censorship, people marveled at the King's all-embracing knowledge and the quick descent of his devastating wrath.

No doubt the times were not yet ripe for democracy. The King needed to rule, and for that purpose had to have entire confidence in his royal mission. A leader torn with doubts would be the worst of heads in storm or crisis. But with all his qualities of grandeur and majesty, his extraordinary ability to evoke respect and even fear, his hard-working sense of responsibility, Louis had no insight to perceive that in Colbert's forgotten dreams for the welfare and consequent strength of the people as a whole lay real glory for the King and for France herself. His narrow spirit fed too complacently on a heady diet of power and constant flattery. He was unable to move with changing times and to adapt himself, ever so little, to the tide of freedom which, slowly and almost imperceptibly, was already beginning to rise in men's minds. He was a last great heritage of the past, not a harbinger of the future.

The superficial glories of Versailles and the royal court blinded all but a few among his contemporaries to the hidden weaknesses of the King's rule.

Over modern minds also, the magnificent literature of seventeenth-century classicism casts a justifiable glamor. Yet most of the remarkable galaxy of writers whom we read with continued admiration today possessed talents already formed when Louis began to reign by himself in 1661 or before he had been long in power. From the time of the Revocation of the Edict of Nantes in 1685, the greatest writers of the earlier period except Boileau, Bossuet, and La Fontaine had died or, like Racine, slipped into retirement and loss of favor. The last thirty years of Louis's reign are years of military reverses and increasing misery among the people. They are years, too, of criticism by men like La Bruyère, Bayle, Fénelon, and Fontenelle. What we now call the eighteenth century was already beginning to dawn in the field of ideas. From reaction under Louis XIV it would lead at length, through the sorry reign of Louis XV, to violent revolution under the latter's well-intentioned, but inept successor, Louis XVI.

As Louis XIV lay dying in late summer of 1715, he called to his bedside the five-year-old boy who, as his great-grandson, Louis XV, was so soon to ascend the august throne. There are several versions of what the old King said. The most accurate seems to be the transcript made by a secretary, Gilbert.

"My dear child," observed the enfeebled monarch, "you are about to be the greatest king in the world. Never forget your debt to God. Do not imitate me in wars; try always to maintain peace with your neighbors, something which, unfortunately, because of reasons of state, I have been unable to do." Saint-Simon adds also to the King's final counsel a word of regret for the mad extravagance of the royal buildings at Versailles and elsewhere. Whether this prudent addition is in accordance with the facts or not, it is evident that the King, in spite of his divine concept of office, had become wise, like many a more ordinary human, too late.

On September 1st, at a quarter past eight in the morning, after a brief two weeks of illness, inexpertly treated by his physicians, Louis XIV was dead. In four more days he would have been seventy-seven. He had ruled for seventy-two years, fifty-four of them after his personal assumption of power in 1661, the longest recorded reign in European history. After him the weakened monarchy was destined to endure for only another almost equal period of seventy-four years. In that significant fact lies the clear proof of his grievous misrule.

"I observed in my youth," wrote realistically the eighteenth-century historian Duclos, "that those who had lived longest under his reign were the least favorable to him."

CHAPTER II

THE CRITICAL SPIRIT OF
PIERRE BAYLE

I

W HERE THE FIRST OUTPOSTS OF THE PYRENEES TOWER A THOU-
sand feet above the high Garonne plain of southwest
France, there lies a tiny region quite forgotten except by the most
detailed of modern map-makers. Not far beyond in the direction of
Spain, a lofty range looms to three times the height of these sentinel
peaks, forming thus a majestic backdrop to a beautiful and picturesque scene. Densely wooded slopes, roaring *gaves,* or torrents,
precipitous gorges, dark grottoes, snow-capped summits, hurrying
storm-clouds, characterize the landscape. It is the County of Foix,
today the department of the Ariège, a remote and long an almost
independent little country.

During the Middle Ages, the Counts of Foix had been among the
freest of French feudal nobles. Indeed, not until the coming to the
throne of Henry IV in 1589 was the region finally annexed to France.
Amid these mountain defiles lived a hardy and self-reliant people
stubbornly determined to think their own thoughts. The country
had been cruelly ravaged by fire and sword in the wars which suppressed the Albigensian heretics during the thirteenth and fourteenth centuries. Two hundred years later, Protestantism took firm
root there and grimly held its ground, in spite of bitter persecutions,
until nearly exterminated at last by the inhuman dragonnades of
Louis XIV.

Here, in the distant country village of Le Carla, far from the seat
of the central government at Paris, where only four years previously
the boy king, Louis XIV, had begun his long rule, Pierre Bayle was
born on November 18, 1647. Today, in honor of him, its most illustrious son, the place is fittingly named Carla-Bayle. His father, Jean,
and his older brother, Jacob, were both Protestant pastors and the
boy was of course brought up in that individualistic faith. Most of

his time the studious youth spent poring eagerly over his books. When he did have occasion to trudge the country roads or trails, his thoughts were turned within and he appears to have been quite unmoved by the too familiar mountain grandeur to which modern spirits are so vividly attuned. But, in such seeming indifference to outdoor nature, he was very much of his time.

Bayle's alert mind was quickly open, however, to the sharp clash of opposing ideas. Intellectual debate was to become, and remain, the passionate interest of his life. From infancy, he began to manifest the independent temper of his rugged countrymen. With lively curiosity, the precocious boy plied his parents with question after question, ceasing only when he had clearly grasped their repeated explanations. Bayle was never one to be put off with mere words.

Latin, when he was still a child, and Greek from the age of twelve, young Pierre learned at home from his well-educated father. At nineteen, since the pastor, busy with sermons and calls, no longer had time to direct the more advanced education of his son, the boy entered the Academy of Puylaurens, some forty miles away to the north. Indifferent to the normal recreations of his age, Bayle studied like mad, even during a vacation visit to his family the following September. Successive illnesses, the natural result of this overwork, kept him out of school during the next year and a half, but he returned to Puylaurens for a few brief months in 1668 and 1669. The great moralistic biographer Plutarch and the keen skeptic Montaigne became his favorite authors, leaving a deep impress on his later thought.

His family next sent him to the celebrated University of Toulouse, then directed by those great educators, the Jesuits. Such a step was by no means unusual for the Huguenots of the time. A small minority in the country, confident in the firmness of their faith, and eager to give their sons the best of educational advantages, they were naturally limited in their choice of opportunities and frequently sent their students to the Catholic higher institutions of learning. In this case, however, the experience was to bring consequences most painful to these pious parents. Through the skillful arguments of a priest who lived in the same house, the immature youth, hearing for the first time the other side to what he had been taught at home, soon became converted to the dominant religion. For the next seventeen months of his stay at Toulouse, Bayle was a Catholic. Indeed, in a long, mysterious, embarrassed letter, he even tried vainly to win over his elder brother and through him his father. In this instance, as during his entire life, there seems no doubt of his utter sincerity. He had been convinced, momentarily, and had acted courageously in abandoning the ancestral religion in accordance with the dictates of his new-found convictions. As time passed, however, he felt he had been hasty. His family handled the delicate situation tactfully, and at length the young man indicated a wish to return to the Protestant fold.

But now, at twenty-three, Bayle was a relapsed Catholic, and as such found it dangerous to remain in the France of Louis XIV. His father therefore hurried his son off secretly from Toulouse to Calvinist Geneva where he arrived in September, 1670. Yet the experience of having been a Catholic, if only for a brief time, had weakened the intensity of his native Protestantism, opened his eyes to other points of view, and rendered his religious attitude more tolerant and more universal.

Bayle remained nearly four years in Geneva, drinking in the new philosophy of the great Descartes, forming scholarly friendships, studying, as always, intensely, and debating earnestly the claims of various thought-systems. But he was eager to return inconspicuously to his native France. At the first opportunity, therefore, he went to Rouen in the northern province of Normandy, and soon after to that Mecca of the intellect, Paris. In this great metropolis, the rich libraries, the lectures on all kinds of subjects, the active ferment of ideas, drew him like a magnet. But alas! poverty still chained him to the daily drudgery of tutoring two noble scions whose least of all interests was learning. Impatiently Bayle chafed at the lack of time for reading as he felt himself week by week slipping down to the level of the ignorant, unruly boys in his charge. Happily, there suddenly came an invitation to present his candidacy for a professorship of philosophy at the Protestant Academy of Sedan. Here was the possibility of longed-for release from the slavery and humiliation of his almost menial position at Paris. After some months of eager study, Bayle was successful over his two competitors in the public defense of a thesis on the assigned subject of *Time*. He began his courses at Sedan on November 11, 1675.

The engraved portrait of Bayle, now the frontispiece of the third edition of his famous *Dictionary*, shows him at twenty-eight, as he entered on this new and important phase of his career. We can see him there, wearing a scholar's black gown, relieved only by white cuffs and a broad, flat collar, which is also white and hooked together closely in clerical style at the neck. The oval face is grave and thoughtful, framed to the shoulders with wavy black hair, after the fashion of the time. The dominant feature is the long nose, straight and strong. A softer note is in the lips, hinting at a reserved smile on occasion and that charm which even his future enemy, Pastor Jurieu, found irresistible during the years of their warm friendship as colleagues on the faculty at Sedan.

In this position Bayle remained for six years, until Louis XIV ordered the closing of the Academy in 1681, thus presaging by a definite measure of repression the unhappy Revocation of the Edict of Nantes four years later. In face of new uncertainty, Bayle considered for a moment possible emigration to England. It was to Rotterdam, however, that he was soon called and there, with his friend Jurieu, he established himself as professor of philosophy and history at the Ecole Illustre, a school illustrious, as it chanced, in name only. He was destined to spend the rest of his life in Holland.

For the first three years in Rotterdam, he lived modestly in a little room on the Geldersche Quai, close to the busy port. At Sedan, Bayle had had every week twenty classes, the subject matter of which he dictated by dull rote to his students. Here at Rotterdam, he had a favorable weekly schedule of seven with several days free. Each week he was to give three public lectures and four hours of private courses. His salary was soon fixed at five hundred florins annually "in recognition of his good services to youth." Thus he was no longer a mere elementary teacher. He was now a scholar with leisure to pursue his own study and writing. It was in many ways an ideal position for a man of his reflective temperament and distinguished talents. In rapid succession important publications followed.

In spite of his slight aptitude for teaching, Bayle held the post of professor at the Ecole Illustre for twelve years. Gradually, however, his former friend Jurieu, ultra-conservative and dogmatic in theology, by nature inquisitorial and domineering, grew more and more enraged at Bayle's tolerance and breadth of view, perhaps also not a little jealous of his Europe-wide reputation. In 1693, Jurieu "the injurious," as even his uncle called him, succeeded after much wire-pulling in forcing Bayle's removal under the dangerous charge of atheism.

At first the philosopher, without property or regular income, was naturally disturbed at the sudden loss of his salary. The receipts from his learned books can hardly have been great and, since postage on letters was then paid by the recipient, Bayle's very popularity entailed much additional correspondence and expense. There is some mystery about how he managed even his meager subsistence. But he was unmarried and had no dependents; he was temperate in all his tastes; his personal needs were of the simplest; and he slept and worked in a single room, though changing his lodgings frequently, probably under pressure of high living-costs in Holland. An occasional pause in the crowded streets of Rotterdam to watch the popular puppet shows, so representative of the way Fate shapes the course of human action, the weekly evenings with a small group of close friends, or the visits of travelers from abroad, eager to seek out the famous exile,—these, outside of his beloved reading, were his sole recreations. Indifferent, it seems, to the picturesque canals and animated streets of the busy city, as he had been to the familiar mountain grandeur of his boyhood valleys, Bayle, unlike the later nineteenth-century poet Gautier, was a man for whom "the external world did *not* exist." The reader today is appalled at the sheer physical labor involved in covering with ink the double-columned pages of Bayle's huge folios. Working away persistently fourteen hours a day in his solitary chamber, he was indeed a veritable monk of modern thought.

In spite of weak lungs, a constant cough, recurring fevers, and almost weekly headaches, Bayle drove himself calmly on with intense and unremitting toil. Finally, on December 28, 1706, at the age of fifty-nine, he died peacefully one morning in the little room to which he had moved some years before on West Nieuwland Quai, after having worked as usual the whole of the preceding day and dispatched a last manuscript to the printer. It was a fitting death for the quiet and industrious scholar.

2

Seven months before leaving the Academy at Sedan, Bayle had begun a first important book, his *Miscellaneous Thoughts on the*

Comet. It appeared anonymously at Rotterdam, though under the fictitious imprint of Cologne, during the month of March, 1682. There was also a new two-volume edition only a year and a half later. In spite of its length and its rambling composition, this is a most remarkable work, laden with what was, for the times, thinly-concealed intellectual dynamite.

In December, 1680, many people had shuddered fearfully at an unusually brilliant comet. A German writer of the day describes vividly the awe which it inspired. "I tremble," he says, "when I recall the terrible appearance it had on Saturday evening in the clear sky, when it was observed by everybody with inexpressible astonishment. It seemed as though the heavens were burning, or as if the very air were on fire. The star itself was not larger than an ordinary star of the first magnitude. . . . But from this little star stretched out such a wonderfully long tail that even an intellectual man was overcome with trembling; one's hair stood on end as this uncommon, terrible, and indescribable tail came into view."

If we smile today at such exaggerated terror, we may humble our false superiority by seeking out the latest newspaper horoscope, and reading the sage advice: "Let your birthday star be your daily guide." Old superstitions die hard! Astrologers still ply their trade, sometimes even in circles apparently sophisticated.

With his quiet, but cogent pen Bayle set out to disabuse his readers of the persistent belief that comets were a foreboding of dire ills to come. This idea that comets presage evil rests on no sound reasons, he says. Poets, historians, and philosophers who have maintained such a notion are without real authority. Scientifically, we can find no support for the supposition that comets influence the earth's inhabitants through their light or by the emanations which they give forth. General credence in the malign effects attributed to comets has no value as evidence, for we know only too well, says the author, that the great mass of people still believe in astrology and all sorts of other marvels. If we consider the comets of the past, we can argue from history that numerous evils took place before their appearance and that several fortunate happenings, like the Treaty of Aix-la-Chapelle, occurred afterwards. "How ridiculous it is to seek the cause of what does not exist!" exclaims Bayle in a forceful chapter, forerunner of a like passage in Fontenelle's famous *History of Oracles* only a few years later. The superstitious fear of eclipses, observes the writer, is similar to the present seventeenth-century awe regarding comets.

Turning next to the field of theology, Bayle, in his leisurely and thorough-going fashion, argues that there too we can find no support for such beliefs. Then, in a characteristic digression, he maintains that atheists are less reprehensible than idolaters, that in fact lack of religious belief does not necessarily lead to bad conduct. There have been philosophical atheists whose lives were exemplary, he asserts, drawing on his wide reading of history. Indeed, he observes, choosing his words with artful prudence, "the detestable Vanini, who was burned at Toulouse for his atheism in the year 1619, had always been quite upright in his conduct, and whoever undertook to bring suit against him for anything else than his doctrines would have run great risk of being convicted of calumny."

How can this be? It is due to the fact, Bayle argues, that man rarely acts according to his principles, but according to his passions. There are indeed some Christians who, through God's grace, are good Christians, but from the majority we must expect conduct quite different from what they profess to follow. Christians, for instance, do not hesitate to wage war. Soldiers, though often filled with religious zeal, lay waste whole countries with fire and sword. At the King's Court there are few atheists and many who are both orthodox in belief and punctilious in their ceremonial observance, yet the conduct of courtiers is notoriously corrupt. Could a society of atheists exist and maintain itself successfully? Yes, believes Bayle, provided it were governed by strict laws. But what country can be found with no need of being so governed? Is not this the only way that even Christian countries preserve order?

After reiterating these arguments at great length and with a multitude of other examples, Bayle returns in his conclusion to the comets with which he had started. They are not by any means, he points out, miraculous manifestations, signs of war, pestilence, or famine. "They are bodies as old as the world, which, by the laws of motion through which God governs the vast machine of the universe, are made to pass from time to time within our sight, and to reflect the light of the sun modified in such a way that we perceive a long trail of rays in front of them or behind them—on which one may consult the gentlemen of the Royal Academy of Science," concludes the author slyly. "For the rest, their passage through our world is of no consequence for good or evil, no more than the coming of an inhabitant of India to Europe."

Even as late as 1857, the poet Oliver Wendell Holmes remarked humorously to those who feared the comet of that day: "I should have felt more nervous about the late comet, if I had thought the world was ripe. But it is very green yet, if I am not mistaken; and besides, there is a great deal of coal to use up, which I cannot bring myself to think was made for nothing!"

Bayle's calm, serried arguments were much read. There were four editions of the *Miscellaneous Thoughts on the Comet* in French during his lifetime, and five others before the middle of the eighteenth century. An English translation appeared in 1708. Thus Bayle became at a stroke one of the most famous writers and thinkers of Europe. It was this work which ten years later was to explode like a delayed-action bomb and serve as a pretext for Jurieu's charges of heresy. At first, however, this "Protestant Inquisitor" appears to have seen nothing wrong in Bayle's book and instead hailed it with favor.

Only a few weeks after this initial success, Bayle composed in the short space of a fortnight during the first half of May, 1682, his *General Criticism* of the *History of Calvinism by Father Maimbourg*. The latter, with his argument for the suppression of heresy by force, was a fervent advocate of intolerance, a dire forerunner of the Revocation of the Edict of Nantes, which was to come only three years later. That such an attitude was not peculiar to Catholics is shown by the violence of the reply to Maimbourg made by Pastor Jurieu the year following. This Protestant theologian had likewise strongly attacked toleration, especially as applied to unbelievers. "It is a dangerous principle," he asserted, "leading unquestionably to indifference in religion."

Bayle's refutation of Maimbourg rests on quite other grounds than Jurieu's. Calm, impartial, Bayle rises above party spirit. He does not hate, he does not insult, his enemies. He speaks in the interest of truth and human freedom. Making no effort either to defend the details of Protestant doctrine or to attack point by point the assertions of Father Maimbourg, Bayle proceeded easily and courteously to expose the passion and prejudice of his adversary, a passion and a prejudice which cast great doubt on the accuracy of his historical interpretations.

CHAPTER II

Religion, Bayle holds, should not use force against its opponents. Otherwise, it must itself expect to be suppressed by violence whenever it is not in the majority. If Catholics may use their power to exterminate Protestants in France, then why should not the Protestants similarly persecute Catholics in England? Bayle's appeal is to the rights of humanity in general, above those of any one sect or party. In this, he is far in advance of his century, ahead even of our own time where the spirit of intolerance still savagely persists. "It is assuredly an attack against the rights of divinity to wish to force conscience," says Bayle.

Such moderation, courtesy, and reasonableness appealed to the more tolerant among orthodox French Catholics as also to those Jansenists who were themselves under attack. The very cogency of Bayle's arguments, however, only angered Maimbourg the more. He moved heaven and earth to suppress this dangerous refutation, but without success until he had appealed directly to Louis XIV himself. Finally, in March of 1683, Bayle's criticism was ordered torn to pieces by the hangman and was burnt in the Place de Grève at Paris. Anyone venturing to sell the book in France was to be put to death. Such was the potency of the challenge presented by this calm scholar, scratching away with diligent pen in his peaceful study at Rotterdam.

By now repressive measures against the Protestants, the persecutions and the dragonnades, were rising in France to a more and more terrible crescendo. In May of 1685, Bayle received word of the death of his aged father. At the end of June, a letter brought further sad news that his brother, Jacob, pastor at Le Carla, had been imprisoned for his faith. This measure of vengeance against the surviving relative of the exiled author of the famous *Criticism of Father Maimbourg* had been ordered by the cruel Louvois himself, minister of Louis XIV. Transferred to Bordeaux, Jacob died there in the dungeon on November 12th, ten days before the arrival of an order for his release. About three weeks earlier had occurred that decisive action against French Protestants, the Revocation of the Edict of Nantes. Thus, in his private, as well as in his public feelings, Bayle was struck to the quick. This fact accounts for the concentrated indignation of his next work, *What Wholly Catholic France under the Reign of Louis XIV Really Is,* published in early spring of 1686.

With a restrained anger, which nevertheless remains thoroughly rational, Bayle wrote the strongest of indictments against Louis XIV's religious policy. The pretense that the Protestants in France have been treated with kindness is indeed but pretense. How reconcile the claim that the Huguenots are recalcitrant and stubborn in their heresy with the further assertion that merely by gentle persuasion they have been converted wholesale? Is it gentleness to be eaten out of house and home by soldiers, to be kept continually awake by horns blowing in your ears, to have one's property confiscated, to be deprived of all livelihood, or to be condemned to the galleys on trying to escape? "And after that can you pride yourselves on having hanged no one?" Bayle demands ironically.

Such conduct discredits all positive religions. It can lead only to skepticism or deism. "The name Christian," says Bayle, "has become justly odious to infidels. . . . If I knew a corner of the world where these persecuting maxims are not carried, how gladly would I go there tomorrow!"

At the end of this vigorous book, Bayle had forecast the appearance of another anonymous work, attributed to a fictitious John Fox in England. It is entitled: *A Philosophical Commentary on Christ's Words, "Compel Them to Come In."* This extensive volume was published late in 1686, with a third part early in 1687.

In Jesus's famous parable of the guests who with one excuse or another refused an invitation to supper, we read in Luke xiv, 23, that the Lord commanded his servant to "go out into the highways and hedges and compel them to come in." From the time of Saint Augustine, a literal interpretation of these Scriptural words had often been employed to justify the application of force to convert heretics.

Bayle's opposing treatise is a masterpiece of sound reasoning in regard to the Bible. His basic principle in exposition of the Scriptures is that "any literal interpretation which contains the obligation to commit crimes is false." Thus the individual conscience itself must be the final judge in these matters. Moral and humane values constitute the supreme test. The supposed right to use constraint is contrary to reason. It can only produce hypocrites or out-and-out unbelievers. Nothing in the long run can be more harmful to religion itself. Protestant persecution, like Catholic, Bayle condemns. Moreover, if we allow the appeal to force in favor of one religion, we must forthwith grant it to all, since others are just as sure of the unique rightness of their belief as we are of ours. Hence they, too, will persecute when they are in the majority. Instead of this, the only sound principle is universal tolerance. Is it objected that such an attitude will permit a multiplicity of religions within a state? No matter, if all are tolerant. Only intolerance is dangerous. The best that can happen in a country is a multiplicity of religions, each vying with the other in good works. Even the so-called *erring* conscience must be tolerated, for no one has the right to decide for another. In the realm of religious belief, no outside force may intervene. Says Bayle: "If we had been born in China, we should all be of the Chinese religion, and if the people of China were born in England, they would all be Christians."

In 1763, Voltaire, speaking of his own *Treatise on Tolerance*, called Bayle's work much bolder, though it had been allowed to pass because longer and more abstruse. The great *Encyclopedia* of Diderot and D'Alembert about the same time said that Bayle's *Commentary* "exhausts the subject." The historian Lecky considered it "the foundation of modern rationalism."

More unequivocably even than his famous English contemporary John Locke in a similar work, Bayle urged universal tolerance. Only aggressive intolerance, dangerous to the stability of the state, he holds, cannot be tolerated.

3

When Bayle lost his professorship at the Ecole Illustre in 1693 through the persecuting zeal of Jurieu, he did not know at first which way to turn. Shortly, however, as he found himself able to solve with his writing the problem of his meager needs, he rejoiced quietly at the complete leisure now left him for his scholarly work.

As early as 1690, he had made announcement of tentative plans for a critical dictionary, correcting the numerous errors of its predecessors. In fragmentary form, the prospectus for such a dictionary, accompanied by a group of articles, came out two years later. Free at length of other demands on his time, Bayle threw himself ardently, in spite of crippling headaches which made him lose several days each month, into an enterprise for which he was ideally fitted. The first volume of his great work is said by Bayle's biographer, Des Maizeaux, to have been printed as early as 1695. In any event, the original edition of the famous *Historical and Critical Dictionary* was first published under date of 1697. It appeared in two so-called tomes, comprising four huge and imposing folios.

Among predecessors of Bayle's *Dictionary,* the most recent and notable had been that of Louis Moréri, a pious and learned Jesuit. Since its first appearance in 1674, this important reference work had already gone through seven editions, several of them after the author's death in 1680, and other revisions were to come during the course of the eighteenth century.

With his hard-headed insistence on facts, Bayle set out to correct the carelessness, credulity, and theological bias of Moréri. In spite of a constant lack of needed books, Bayle would take no opinion second-hand if he could possibly get access to the original source. Often he had to stop work and sally forth to borrow some rare volume from one of the private libraries of Rotterdam. A scholar by very instinct, Bayle filled the *Notes* of his *Dictionary* with innumerable quotations, many of them in Greek or Latin, and carefully cited his authorities, listing volume and page references in the margin. With his constant distrust of Moréri's inaccuracy, Bayle used him only when other sources were unavailable. No one but a man of his intense singleness of purpose and entire freedom from distractions or the need of diversion could have accomplished in a few years, notwithstanding ill health, so enormous a task.

Bayle's *Dictionary,* it should be remembered, is *historical* and *critical.* Although the titles of its articles are most frequently biographical, the chief subjects actually dealt with are history, philosophy, and religion, but not natural science, one of the few great gaps in Bayle's wide learning. In this broad sense, the *Dictionary* is *historical.* It is *critical* in that the author takes nothing on trust. He confronts authorities one with another, exposes their contradictions and discrepancies, estimates their relative value, and often suspends conclusions where a final judgment would be doubtful or theologically dangerous.

A remarkable peculiarity of the *Dictionary* must be indicated. The *Notes* are much more extensive and also more important than the so-called text. Sometimes the generally orthodox and seemingly innocuous text consists only of one or two or three lines stretched across the top of the huge folio page while the *Notes* in double column and fine print fill the rest. There are two reasons for this curious procedure. In the first place, such an arrangement fitted in completely with Bayle's discursive genius, allowing him to utilize in rambling fashion whatever he had turned up over the years in his wide and miscellaneous reading. Above all, this system permitted him to hide away in these closely-printed notes amid the learned references his dangerous thoughts and queries, hoping that the censor would nod his head wearily and approve by default what otherwise was sure to be forbidden. In addition, Bayle trickily used cross-references to other articles in the effort to elude or wear down all but sympathetic readers. Such tactics were not wholly successful, even in relatively tolerant Holland, but they helped. In Paris, however, permission to print the *Dictionary* was promptly refused. It had to be smuggled into France and distributed surreptitiously as contraband.

If we set one of Bayle's big folios on a convenient bookrack and slowly turn these pages yellowed by time, our thoughts fly back to the bitter doctrinal disputes of more than two hundred and fifty years ago. Three articles were particularly condemned by the Walloon Consistory of Bayle's church in Rotterdam: those on David, the Manicheans, and Pyrrho. Hence these articles at once introduce us to the explosive ideas buried away by the author in his innocent-seeming volumes. Only the theologically-minded are today equipped with knowledge and patience to follow closely the details of Bayle's serried arguments, but the attentive reader can quickly note and enjoy the methods of his wily attack.

The question involved in the article on the Manicheans, as in several others, was that of the age-old problem of evil in the world. If God is good and all-powerful, it was reasoned, how can He permit evil? One answer had been given in the early centuries of the Christian era by the Manichean heretics, followers of Manes, who alleged the existence of two spirits, one the source of good, the other of evil. With this solution, Bayle had indeed a certain historical connection through the persecuted Albigensians, his remote forebears in the County of Foix. At the same time, his realistic sense of the appalling dominance of evil throughout the history of mankind made the Manichean doctrine seem to him no doubt the most logical of intellectual attempts to explain this baffling problem. Naturally, however, Bayle had to treat it with at least the appearance of orthodoxy.

So he refers ironically to Manicheanism as an "infamous sect," which taught the "most horrible things." It is a "false dogma, . . . indefensible if we admit the truth of Sacred Scripture in whole or in part, yet rather difficult to refute. . . . Happily, Saint Augustine . . . abandoned Manicheanism, for he would have been able to remove the grossest errors and make of it a system which in his hands would have embarrassed the orthodox." Since, in spite of such condemnatory terms, some keen-eyed readers not unnaturally thought Bayle secretly favored this heretical teaching, he promised an explanatory addition at the end of the *Dictionary*. To the Consistory he replied slyly that he "would meditate further on the doctrine of the Manicheans" and, if he "found any replies, or if the ministers of the Consistory would be good enough to furnish him with some," he "would be glad to put them in the best form possible!"

The article on Pyrrho deals with an ancient Greek thinker whose name has become synonymous with complete skepticism. Such skepticism, suggests Bayle, is not dangerous to the state or to morality, but only to theology. Besides, there are few who are capable of being misled by the reasons of the skeptics. The grace of God among the faithful, the force of education among others, and, if you like, even ignorance and the natural human tendency to hold decided opinions, constitute an impenetrable buckler against the Pyrrhonians. We should note, too, observes the author, that Pyrrho himself was a man of exemplary life, even helping his sister with the prosaic task of housework. Thus the central theme of the *Miscellaneous Thoughts on the Comet* returns. Man's conduct, good or bad, does not depend on metaphysical belief.

The most shocking article of all to Bayle's pious contemporary critics was that on David. This ancient King of Israel was customarily called, in the Biblical phrase, "the man after God's own heart." His conduct, however, had often been cruel, barbarous, and immoral. Yet, with a stronger feeling for orthodoxy than for ethics, many people defended him as a great saint, one who was therefore justified by God even when his actions by modern standards would not be justifiable.

Such an unreasonable position Bayle frankly rejects. No doubt David was "a sun of sainthood in the Church, . . . but he had his spots."

"I shall not indicate many faults in Monsieur Moréri," says the author with dry humor; "only five!"

Not only must we note David's admitted sins of adultery with Bathsheba, his murder of Uriah, the forbidden numbering of the people, but many others also. And Bayle enumerates. Indeed, he adds ironically: "The history of King David may reassure several crowned heads against the fears inspired in them by severe casuists who maintain that it is almost impossible for a king to be saved!" No wonder the *Dictionary* could not be authorized in France during the lifetime of Louis XIV!

In this article, Bayle clearly too little understands the relativity of human morals. He does not take account of the barbarism of the times when David lived, the legendary character of his biography, or the mingling of contradictory traditions from different historical periods. Only modern Biblical scholarship has been able to see the sacred books in this light. Moreover, the Bible itself often condemns David with severe realism. But Bayle's error was the error of those who defended this King of Israel with a similar lack of allowance for the slow evolution of ideals. On grounds of his supposed saint-hood, they did violence to sound morality. Conscience, believed Bayle, must be superior to such casuistry. He poses the ethical stand-ard as supreme. This is his great achievement, so little perceived in his time, even by some who most welcomed his bold attack.

Though the Walloon Consistory forced a revision of this article in the second edition of the *Dictionary,* the publisher met popular demand by reprinting the original text and distributing it separately. Thus, as so often happens, censorship increased its vogue. In Eng-land, the article provoked much discussion pro and con. In France, Voltaire and others cited it joyously. It remained during the period before the Revolution a powerful weapon against orthodoxy.

Bayle, it has been said, became "the Bible of the eighteenth cen-tury." His work was an arsenal of fact, argument, and calm irony much used by his successors, often without acknowledgment. He taught men to doubt and to think. He wiped out an enormous mass of gross superstition and archaic scholasticism which still cluttered the human mind. At the very time of the Revocation of the Edict of Nantes, he preached a much-needed tolerance. Montesquieu, Vol-taire, and Rousseau, all used him assiduously. Bayle was a most important ancestor of the great *Encyclopedia* of Diderot, D'Alembert, and their colleagues. He was much admired by Frederick the Great. Within less than fifty years, there were nine French editions of his big folio volumes, which no publisher could venture to print without an assured sale. There were also two English translations and one in German.

Shortly after the death of Louis XIV, during the early Regency, students stood in line before the doors were open in the morning at the Bibliothèque Mazarine along the Seine in Paris for the privilege of reading Bayle's *Dictionary*. Of all the works published during the first half of the eighteenth century, Bayle's was the one most often found at the time in the private libraries of France. In this dramatic way, the ideas of the exile returned to the land of his birth. Such was the impact of this quiet scholar upon his age!

CHAPTER III

FÉNELON, CRITIC OF
LOUIS XIV

I

FÉNELON, IN THE WORDS OF HIS GREAT CONTEMPORARY, SAINT-Simon, "was a tall spare man of good figure, pale, with a prominent nose, eyes from which fire and intelligence poured like a torrent, and a face such as I have never seen elsewhere, and which once seen, you could never forget. . . . It was difficult to take one's eyes off him."

François de Salignac de la Mothe-Fénelon was the thirteenth of the fifteen children who were the offspring of his father's two marriages. The future archbishop first saw the world amid the fortress walls of the medieval château of Fénelon, close by the little town of Sarlat in the smiling southwestern region of Périgord. He was born on August 6, 1651, four years later than his Protestant contemporary, Pierre Bayle.

The family stemmed from the most ancient nobility, tracing their lineage proudly back to the far-off tenth century and not unmindful of a notable record of service in war, diplomacy, and the church. Fénelon himself, in later years, showed always the calm assurance, as well as the easy and distinguished bearing, of the authentic *grand seigneur,* and remained besides intensely devoted to the public welfare. Noble though it was, this huge family was poor, and the impressionable child knew from infancy the simple and austere life which he later preached so fervently in books and sermons. Early destined for the church, the gifted boy, after completing his theological education at the Seminary of Saint-Sulpice in Paris, was ordained to the priesthood at about twenty-four.

Influenced by his strong classical training, Fénelon first dreamed romantically of missionary work in exotic Greece. "The Sultan recoils in terror," he exclaimed with playful exaggeration. "Already the Peloponnesus breathes the spirit of liberty; the Church of Corinth revives; and there the voice of the Apostle will once more be heard." Thus he joked about his juvenile ambition, fearing with his natural delicacy even the appearance of taking himself too seriously. Three years of more prosaic service followed in the home parish of Saint-Sulpice.

Soon the brilliant Abbé Fénelon was promoted to become Superior of the Convent of New Catholics, an institution in the heart of Paris on the Rue Sainte-Anne intended for converting and confirming in the faith girls recently separated from Protestantism. By his ability, tact, and above all by personal magnetism, the eager young priest with the flashing eyes and strong, yet winning and expressive features was admirably fitted to charm his feminine hearers. He held this important position for nearly twelve years, from 1678 to 1689.

A more arduous duty awaited him. In December of 1685, hardly six weeks after the unfortunate Revocation of the Edict of Nantes, Abbé Fénelon was chosen, on the recommendation of the famous Bossuet, Bishop of Meaux, to head a preaching mission for the conversion of Protestants in Saintonge and Aunis, the region surrounding the ancient Huguenot stronghold of La Rochelle on the western Atlantic seaboard. There he remained, not too happily, for some seven months until July, 1686, and returned for a briefer period the year following. It was on the whole a thankless and ungrateful task.

The eighteenth-century philosophic party later cherished something of a legend about the supposed tolerance of Fénelon. He was, however, definitely of his time and hence in full sympathy with the declared purposes, if not the methods, of the Revocation. As a loyal priest, he yearned with all his heart for renewed unity of the dissident Protestants within the Catholic fold. "It is important," he wrote, "for the authorities to support our work and make the people feel the advantage of being instructed gently." Thus force was to be held menacingly over the heads of those whom he could only regard as arrant heretics. Although Fénelon recognized that, "where the missionaries and troops are together, the new converts go in crowds to communion," he was too sincerely religious not to recoil from the use of such pressure for the purpose of hastily performing "a superficial work which might appear impressive from afar," as he said frankly in a letter to the King's minister, Seignelay. Unlike many of his contemporaries, he did not rejoice in fake converts. Yet, while excoriating the trapped Huguenots as "cowardly and self-interested," Fénelon was human enough to be indignant against those who resisted and contemptuous of them when they yielded. So it was impossible for these unfortunates to please him either way. On the other hand, he counseled a less rigorous exercise of authority and a restoration of the attractiveness of life in France so that the harassed Protestants might lose their natural urge to emigrate. Instead of reliance on force, he wisely preferred the slower, but sounder policy of gentleness, patience, and persuasion. Who in his time and in a similar position would have done more? In the end, the experience of this ill-fated mission, for a man of Fénelon's keen insight, seems to have been largely disillusion, though it was no doubt a profound lesson in human nature not to be lost in the future.

In March of 1687 Fénelon published an influential *Treatise on the Education of Girls,* the fruit in part of his experience at the Convent of New Catholics. In his insistence on making education attractive, the author was in many ways and in sounder fashion a forerunner of Rousseau's *Emile* seventy-five years later.

The year following, the brilliant young priest was honored by presentation to Madame de Maintenon, who had recently become the secret, but influential wife of the all-powerful Louis XIV. This event brought Fénelon already at the age of thirty-seven very close to the ear of the throne. It was an illustrious acquaintance, destined to have decisive consequences, first for the meteoric rise, then for the startling fall of Fénelon's favor at Court.

Later, on the 4th of October in this same decisive year, an even more significant meeting took place. The Abbé was in the country at Beynes, the château of the Duchesse de Béthune. Here he was introduced to a woman with a long, oval, pock-marked face, prominent eyes, but expressive and not unpleasing features. This was Madame Guyon. She was then forty, some three years older than Fénelon himself, and the ardent exponent of a mystical movement known in France as Quietism. Behind her were sad memories of an unhappy marriage entered into at family behest. With her widowhood, however, she had found solace in an intense religious fervor. While the two new acquaintances with another companion jogged along together in a carriage on the road back to Paris, Madame

Guyon was at once drawn to Fénelon, though with feminine intuition she recognized that "this first interview," as she wrote afterwards, "left him unconvinced" of her mission. A week later all was changed.

Eager to enrich his inner life, Fénelon was deeply impressed by Madame Guyon's conviction, her unusual ability to lose herself in prayer and meditation, her devotion and unworldliness. The eccentric, even hysterical aspects of her enthusiastic nature did not long repel or alarm him as they shortly excited the fears of the more matter-of-fact Bossuet. Fénelon evidently passed over these external traits for the sincere inspiration which he found beneath.

Madame Guyon, supported by Fénelon, for a time won the favor of Madame de Maintenon also and zealously preached Quietism to teachers and pupils of the school for girls which the latter directed at Saint-Cyr near Versailles. Into the dull, heavy air of the formalized Court swept for a moment a breath of exuberance, aspiration for perfection, and complete union with the divine spirit.

It was soon over. Madame de Maintenon began to have qualms about the orthodoxy of the new doctrine, perhaps even a kind of jealousy of the marked influence of this feminine missionary on the brilliant Abbé. Her confessor likewise put her on guard. In any case, Madame de Maintenon's prudent, rather self-centered character, hardened by the bitter lessons of youthful poverty, a loveless first marriage with the crippled, pain-racked novelist Scarron, and finally all the perils and disillusionments of her precarious position in the very center of court intrigues, was ill-adapted to abandon itself whole-heartedly to Quietism. When she read to Louis XIV Madame Guyon's *Short and Easy Means to Prayer,* the King, interested only in the outer forms of religion, contemptuously dismissed the book as "foolishness." Presently this quarrel over doctrine became more violent and Madame de Maintenon later admitted that she had never been "so near disgrace." She dared not, even if she had wished, stand out against the royal master.

Saint-Simon has charged Fénelon with over-weaning ambition. No doubt the Abbé, like most men of spirit and ability, was ambitious, ambitious for advancement, prestige, and above all for influence. No doubt he hoped, in Church and State, to leave his constructive mark on the shape of things to come. What more legitimate and normal? Yet, if ambition without scruples had guided him, his quick penetration could hardly have failed to warn of utter ruin if he persisted in supporting Madame Guyon against the invincible league of Bishop Bossuet, Madame de Maintenon, and ultimately the King himself. Fénelon's correspondence shows clear premonitions of loss of favor with Louis's secret consort, but he refused to sacrifice conscience to expediency.

Between Bossuet, the opponent of Madame Guyon, and Fénelon, her firm defender, opinion has long been divided. In recent years the latter appears in a more favorable light. Fénelon insisted that he would not impugn the character and motives of Madame Guyon when he felt certain she had done no wrong. If the language of her books was often too emotional, slightly puerile at times, even dangerous in some cases to sound doctrine, Fénelon believed that Quietism in its essence was in the tradition of the great mystics of the past, who were already accepted by the orthodox. He knew that it had relieved the occasional barrenness of his own former religious life, had enriched his faith as by the influence of a saint. Moreover, *noblesse oblige!* As a gentleman through and through, Fénelon, come what might, would not abandon Madame Guyon or her teachings merely to curry favor. Right or wrong, his conduct in this whole unhappy controversy, which divided France and the Church, seems proof both of his courage and sincerity.

2

But, before the final outcome of this quarrel, many honors were yet in store for Fénelon. In August of 1689, Louis XIV named him Preceptor to the Duc de Bourgogne, the King's grandson, heir once removed to the throne. The Duc de Bourgogne, observed Saint-Simon, was a spoiled royal child, utterly willful and subject to blind tantrums of rage, even against inanimate objects, until it seemed, as the great writer of memoirs said, that passion "would tear his body to pieces." Nevertheless, little by little, Fénelon, by a rare combination of firmness and tact, won the respect, then the affection, and finally the entire devotion of this difficult pupil. Though Fénelon had to leave the Duke at fifteen long before his education was complete, though some historians question whether the priest may not even have gone too far in breaking the will of this scion of royalty, other writers still speculate as to the devoted King the boy might have become if his sudden premature death in 1712 had not opened the way instead to the undisciplined and conscienceless child, Louis XV.

In March, 1693, Fénelon was further honored by election to the French Academy. On the 4th of February, two years later, Louis XIV approved his nomination as Archbishop of Cambrai. It was a princely, if difficult and remote post on the northeastern frontier. He was consecrated in the chapel of Madame de Maintenon's Saint-Cyr by Bishop Bossuet himself on July 10, 1695. Fénelon, at forty-four, had reached the pinnacle of royal favor.

At this time church dignitaries by no means always imposed on themselves the duty of residence in their ecclesiastical posts. Fénelon, however, at once decided to pass no less than nine months of each year at Cambrai. He also voluntarily abandoned the rich revenues of the Abbey of Saint-Valéry which the King had granted him the year before. Such scruples astonished and indeed embarrassed less conscientious colleagues. The newly-appointed Archbishop continued to direct the education of the Duc de Bourgogne, though for the most part now at a distance.

But the dispute between Bossuet and Fénelon over Madame Guyon and her teachings grew bitter. Book and pamphlet followed book and pamphlet in sharp rejoinder. Bossuet was self-confident, dogmatic, not always just; Fénelon showed himself unyielding, subtle, tricky perhaps, accused in any event of bad faith. The King grudgingly permitted the latter an appeal to the Pope, but did not allow him to plead his cause personally at Rome as he had ardently wished. At length, in 1697, Louis imperiously ordered the too-independent Archbishop into complete exile at Cambrai. Fénelon departed promptly on the 2nd of August never to return. The next eighteen years remaining to him of life, he spent, barring short trips, in his diocese. To a seventeenth-century noble, who for years had enjoyed royal favor, it seemed at first to be ruin, utter and complete. For a long time, except for a few unshakeable friends, courtiers avoided him like the pest.

Yet, though Fénelon, in his sensitive nature, was wounded to the quick, and if a lesser man, with his frail and ardent physique, would certainly have succumbed to this almost mortal blow, the indomitable Archbishop was too deeply and sincerely religious not to find hidden springs to sustain him in these long years of lonely trial.

"God opens a strange book for our instruction, when he teaches us to read our own hearts," he wrote later with searching frankness.

In spite of taut nerves and sleepless nights, he threw himself devotedly into the absorbing work of his diocese, jolting over the deep ruts of the muddy roads, preaching in village churches, hearing confession, making the constant decisions incumbent on an able administrator, winning the respect and even the affection of these half-hostile Flemings so recently annexed to a foreign France. Fénelon built important additions to the episcopal palace at Cambrai. Moreover, he ruled his huge establishment with all the firmness, judgment, and calm urbanity of a perfect great noble. By contrast, the administration of Bishop Bossuet, in spite of his otherwise extraordinary gifts, appears inefficient, lax, almost slovenly. Even Abbé Le Dieu, Bossuet's private secretary, when he visited Fénelon after his master's death, was deeply impressed by the order and the polite distinction he saw around him.

At length, in early March, 1699, the Pope, torn between two great French dignitaries of the Church, reluctantly gave his decision condemning Fénelon's book on the *Maxims of the Saints,* but treating the author with leniency. The committee of examination, which had been evenly divided five to five, seemed thereby to demonstrate the legitimacy of differing opinions on these complex issues of doctrine.

"The Pope understands my book better than I do; to that I submit," wrote Fénelon in a private letter with perhaps a touch of irrepressible irony, but the context shows his firm conviction that he had meant no heresy in his thoughts, whatever interpretation men might put upon his words.

As the overwhelming news of the Pope's Brief came to him shortly before he was to preach on the Festival of the Annunciation, March 25, 1699, the tall, spare, impressive Archbishop at once changed the subject of his intended sermon and, after a period of meditation, mounted into the high pulpit to announce in moving terms his complete submission to the Church. If Bossuet, in appearance, had triumphed, it was Fénelon who gained prestige in the end. The former indeed complained bitterly: "Monsieur de Cambrai continues in the most arrogant fashion to play humble." But the Pope himself is said to have expressed the opinion of many. "The

Archbishop of Cambrai," he remarked, "has sinned by excessive love of God; the Bishop of Meaux by lack of love for his neighbor."

During the years of almost continuous war which, provoked by the great King, beset this exposed frontier city of Cambrai, Fénelon won the esteem of friend and foe alike. Repeatedly he bedded down in straw on the polished floors of the episcopal palace hordes of peasant refugees, fleeing in helpless fear with their pitiful bundles before the fierce onrush of the invading armies, which century after century have ravaged this open corridor of battle. Lowing cattle and draught animals often covered his courtyard with litter. At other times, the splendid residence was turned into an impromptu hospital, crowded with wounded officers and men from both sides, while Fénelon heartened them with daily visits and quiet words. The Duke of Malborough and Prince Eugene of the attacking forces treated the distinguished Archbishop with the greatest consideration, allowing him to transport necessary supplies of grain from the surrounding countryside, as Fénelon at his own expense fed all who came. At a time when chivalry, in the midst of war, was not yet completely dead, these foreign generals even offered him safe-conduct, which he for patriotic reasons refused, in his trips through the diocese. He had become an international figure, admired certainly for his winning character and imposing position, but still further enhanced in prestige and courted no doubt abroad because of the very hostility with which Louis XIV was known to have treated him.

Yet Fénelon remained no less faithful to war-torn, impoverished France. Voluntarily he taxed himself to supply the hungry French armies, spending without stint his own funds and stored-up grain for the purpose. Indirectly, even the stubborn King deigned to recognize this act of unselfish patriotism.

While, through the troubled nights, long trains of siege guns and military wagons rumbled heavily over the ancient cobblestones of Cambrai, Fénelon slept but lightly in his plain little room, avoiding by preference the show-place of the great episcopal bedchamber with its furnishings of crimson damask. He awoke early, devoted himself to his multifarious tasks, answered numerous letters, and continued to correspond with the Duc de Beauvilliers, who still remained in charge of the education of the Duc de Bourgogne and in spite of Louis XIV loyally refused to abandon his old friend in disfavor.

At the Archbishop's well-served table in the princely palace, there was always a goodly number of a dozen, sometimes a hundred and fifty or two hundred guests. Fénelon himself, eating abstemiously, never failed to be the gracious host, talking with seeming leisure and easy dignity to old friends and new. Here came the cosmopolitan Scottish deist, the Chevalier de Ramsay, to be converted to Catholicism and to devote himself to the first biography of Fénelon. Here came the young English Pretender to discuss the principles of how to govern with tolerance a hostile Protestant country, should fate ever relent and bring him to the coveted throne. So far as Fénelon was concerned, the lessons of the unfortunate Revocation of the Edict of Nantes and his own mission to the harassed Huguenots had not gone for naught. He would not urge conversion by force.

In the latter part of November of 1714, Fénelon was riding in his coach, going the rounds, as usual every year, about his diocese. With habitual industry, even in his carriage, he made use of the idle moments, reading, his glasses on his long nose, book and pencil in hand. His feet were tightly wrapped in a bearskin robe, a welcome protection against the autumn chill. Without warning, as the episcopal party clattered across a little country bridge, one of the lead horses took fright at the noise and motion of a mill wheel. Behind the glass of the inclosed coach, Fénelon, occupied as he was, could not hear the excited cries of attendants urging him to jump. His feet in any case were encumbered in the heavy blanket. The little bridge had no guard rail and the three rearing horses plunged to death in the river below. Only the pole of the carriage, catching in a hole in the bridge floor, prevented the imminent crash of the vehicle and its distinguished passenger. Though none of the people had been hurt, the loss of the horses and the narrow escape had been a great shock to Fénelon's frail and sorely-tried physique. After a brief illness, he seemed to recover, but the premonition of early death was strong upon him.

On January 1, 1715, Fénelon was back in bed with a high fever. On the 6th, he dictated to his secretary a final letter to be given to Louis XIV by Le Tellier, now the royal confessor, expressing once again the sincerity of the Archbishop's submission in the affair over Quietism and renewing his respect and attachment to the aged King. He requested only the appointment in his place of a "pious, regular, and good successor, firm against Jansenism," and the establishment at Cambrai of the seminary which he had worked for over the years and hoped to organize under the direction of the priests of Saint-Sulpice, the seat of his own far-off youthful training.

"I wish Your Majesty a long life of which Church and State have great need," he wrote.

The death of the Dauphin in 1711, of the Duc de Bourgogne in 1712, had wrecked Fénelon's last ardent hopes for the future. The welfare of the whole kingdom, in its desperate plight, had thus been put in jeopardy and seemed now more than ever dependent on the experience and continued reign of Louis XIV in spite of his grave faults.

On January 7, 1715, in the early morning, the Archbishop was dead. He had left the troubled scene at the age of sixty-four, only eight months before the great King himself. So wisely and so generously had Fénelon administered his princely revenues that he died with no large balance of money and without debts.

3

"As for *Télémaque*," said Fénelon, "I wrote it at a time when I was delighted with the marks of kindness and confidence with which the King overwhelmed me. I should have had to be, not only the most ungrateful, but also the most foolish of men to think of including in it satirical and insolent portrayals of real people. . . . The more one reads this work, the more clearly he will see that my intention was to speak frankly without depicting anybody in connected fashion." Thus the author denied charges of a direct attack on Louis XIV.

The narrative had been written, probably between the end of 1694 and the beginning of 1697, while the author, as he said, was still enjoying favor at Court. It was composed for the combined entertainment and instruction of Fénelon's royal pupil, the Duc de Bourgogne. Nevertheless, in April, 1699, when the first volume of the little novel appeared in an unauthorized edition, Fénelon, who had hardly yet recovered from the Pope's condemnation, a month before, of his book on Quietism, here received a new blow. *Télémaque* was widely interpreted as an open criticism of the great "Sun King."

The book tells in story fashion the adventures of Telemachus, traveling through the ancient Mediterranean world in search of his father, the long-absent Ulysses. The boy is accompanied by the Goddess Minerva under the guise of the wise Mentor, who helps him to learn by his youthful mistakes and by his observation of men and events. The work was written for a son of royalty. It has become indeed a childhood classic, one of the books in the French language long most widely read by young and old. It has gone through numerous translations in many languages, and, during the eighteenth century particularly, its prestige and influence were immense. It became exceedingly popular in America, even giving the name Ulysses to General Grant.

Though Fénelon was no doubt sincere in protesting, as we have just seen, against accusations that he was deliberately holding up to scorn before the royal grandson the august figure of the great King, the author could not but disagree almost wholly with the ruinous policy which Louis XIV was following in the latter half of his reign. If the Duc de Bourgogne was destined some day to mount the throne, Fénelon hoped to make of him a man very different from France's present ruler.

"'Happy,' said Mentor, 'the people guided by a wise king! Such a people enjoys abundance, lives in happiness, and esteems him to whom it owes its good fortune. Thus,' he added, 'O Télémaque, you must reign and bring joy to your people, if ever the gods bestow upon you your father's kingdom.'"

The wicked king, Pygmalion, obviously represents too great an extreme of evil to be compared for a moment with Louis XIV. Pygmalion lives in constant threat of treachery and perishes at last by the very poison which he has so fearfully sought to avoid. The lesson is pointed up by the good Baléazar who succeeds him and needs no protection other than the love of his devoted people.

An ideal society is first depicted by Fénelon in the latter half of Book VII under the guise of the fictitious country of Bétique, reminiscent geographically of Andalusia in southern Spain. Here the charmed eighteenth-century reader, tired of bitter reality, could enjoy in imagination the delights of the mythical Golden Age, which had been set alluringly before the eyes of humanity ever since the days of the ancient Greeks and Romans, indeed since the story of the Garden of Eden itself. The author also drew on fond memories of his own frugal, but happy youth amidst the pleasant hills, valleys, and ravines of his native Périgord.

In this idyllic land of Bétique, "the inhabitants, simple and happy in their simplicity, do not deign even to consider gold and silver among their riches." Self-contained, with little foreign trade, they need no money. They are "almost all shepherds and farmers." These Utopians eat little meat, eschew wine (strange anomaly to a Frenchman!), build no permanent houses in their mild climate, live on "the necessary" without coveting "the superfluous." They do not divide their lands into private properties, but practice a kind of idealistic rural communism. The people of Bétique are "all free and all equal." They marvel at mankind's strange admiration of conquerors. For themselves, they never go to war except to defend their liberty. Individually and collectively, they dwell in virtue and innocence, wisely and happily following "right Nature." Forestalling skeptical criticisms of his dream of perfection, the author concludes: "So degenerate have we become that we can scarcely believe this natural simplicity possible!"

Thus, more than half a century before Rousseau, who, incidentally greatly admired Fénelon, the author of *Télémaque* sang the praises of simplicity and a back-to-nature primitivism in order to wean his royal pupil from attachment to court luxury and the engrossing complexities of modern life. It is certain, however, that Fénelon had no serious thought of turning the clock of time back to this legendary Golden Age. Under the heavy hand of censorship, he set up his imaginary state to be approached as nearly as might be, not to be taken literally.

In contrast to the happy idyll of remote Bétique, the Archbishop's hope for modern times is better typified by the kingdom of Salente, which is treated at length in Books X and XVII. Here Idoménée rules. Unfortunately he has fallen into the all-too-human error, so characteristic of Louis XIV, of feeding his pride on the construction of grandiose buildings. Idoménée is wise enough, however, to listen to Mentor who shows him that the real strength of his country lies in widespread and thriving agriculture.

Even Télémaque in his youthful inexperience is at first shocked at the striking change which greets him on his return to Salente. The former magnificence of gold, silver, and precious stones has yielded to simplicity in buildings and dress. But outside of the diminished cities, lands which once were waste are now cultivated and fertile. Everywhere he sees farmers bent industriously over their tasks. Food is consequently abundant. Luxury for the few has given place to prosperity for the many. Telemachus, too, as well as Idoménée, has to learn the needed lesson of esteeming solid economic strength instead of the deceitful façade of glory.

But Fénelon did not neglect to encourage trade also. Unlike Louis XIV's finance minister, Colbert, Mentor counseled against hampering restrictions. Foreigners must be attracted to do business with Salente. Commerce should be allowed free rein. It is "like certain springs: if you impede their flow, you make them run dry." The commerce of this prosperous city resembled "the ebb and flow of the tides. . . . All that came in was useful; all that went out left behind other riches in its place." Characteristically, however, remembering his own frugal past, Fénelon opposed the importation of luxuries as weakening to the moral fibre of the people.

Constantly and vigorously Fénelon attacked wars of aggression and conquest, painting a realistic picture of the terrible carnage of battle. Télémaque is torn with pity at sight of the wounded, the dead, and the mangled bodies of the dying. This seventeenth-century priest is contemporary with us in his compassion for suffering humanity. Nevertheless, he is not blind to the need of military preparedness for defense and urges the importance of maintaining the nation strong, alert, and economically sound in time of peace. The nobility, he said, should learn the art of warfare by fighting at the side of their country's allies and keeping invasion, if possible, far from the home land. Télémaque himself proves his courage in many a spirited and dangerous action. In real life, Fénelon's own nephew, the "Little Marquis," carried to his grave a painful limp from a wound received in battle. Later, in his letters, the Archbishop exhorted the Duc de Bourgogne never to spare himself the inevitable risks of combat. So this idealistic prelate showed a hard-headed realism regarding the unhappy necessities of defensive warfare.

The history of one brief passage in *Télémaque* offers proof of the book's extraordinary prestige in the eighteenth century. Defining the authority of the ideal ruler, Fénelon had written that the king's freedom of action should be specifically limited by law. "He has absolute power to do good, but has his hands tied the moment he wishes to do evil," said Mentor. When the Duke of Orleans rose to speak before the Parlement of Paris on the afternoon of September 2, 1715, the day after the death of Louis XIV, he made a telling point in favor of his desire to be chosen Regent by exclaiming that he wished to be independent to do good, while consenting to be bound as much as the Counselors might wish in order to prevent him from doing evil. In similar terms, Fénelon himself had spoken to the young English Pretender on his visit to Cambrai about 1709. Voltaire in 1734 also echoed this cogent phrase in his widely-read *Philosophical Letters*. Finally, Thomas Jefferson, looking back on his experience as American Ambassador at Paris during the early days of the French Revolution, expressed regret that Louis XVI had not, by a wise constitution, been given "powers so large as to enable him to do all the good of his station, and so limited, as to restrain him from its abuse." Jefferson, too, though so long afterwards, evidently had not forgotten Fénelon's epigrammatic words. Thus *Télémaque* entered the field of action in behalf of a constitutional monarch, properly restrained by law.

"Remember," warned the farsighted Fénelon forcefully, "that countries where the domination of the sovereign is the most absolute are those where he is least powerful. . . . At the slightest blow, the idol falls, is broken, and trampled under foot." In another passage, the Archbishop observed succinctly: "Nothing offers so great a threat of a fateful crash as authority pushed too far."

If, as has been reported, Louis XIV did contemptuously call Fénelon "the most intelligent and at the same time the most chimerical spirit" in his kingdom, the Grand Monarch was the one who was wrong in the second half of his statement, not Fénelon. After all, it was the hard-working, but unimaginative "Sun King" who unconsciously laid the basis for the French Revolution; the keen-eyed Archbishop, given a ruler willing and able to put the constructive ideas of *Télémaque* into action, might, more perhaps than any one else, have prevented it. One of the neglected lessons of history is that the most idealistic thinkers, if their feet are firmly planted on the ground, are in the long run the most practical.

4

About the time he was beginning the composition of *Télémaque* in 1694, or possibly a year earlier, Fénelon wrote a startling letter to Louis XIV himself. There is a mystery about this letter. Was it, or was it not, ever delivered? Opinions differ. Very likely, because of its blunt frankness, it was not intended actually to be shown to the King, at least in that form. Perhaps it was meant as an indication to Madame de Maintenon and to the Duc de Beauvilliers of the lines along which they should try to guide the self-willed sovereign away from his fatal policy.

The *Letter to Louis XIV* was unknown to most of the eighteenth century. It was referred to by the famous Encyclopedist, D'Alembert, in the *Eulogy of Fénelon* which he read before the French Academy in 1774 and again at a special meeting attended by Emperor Joseph of Austria three years later. At this time Voltaire heard of it, without, however, believing in its authenticity. In 1785 the *Letter* was first published in a posthumous edition of D'Alembert's *History of the Members of the French Academy*. That it had actually been written by Fénelon was conclusively demonstrated at last by the discovery, in 1825, of a manuscript copy in the Archbishop's own hand.

In this daring letter, the author was obliged to adopt the cloak of anonymity. The King, so accustomed to obsequious flattery, must not be astonished, he says, at his frankness, for "truth is free and strong." Though born just and equitable, Louis XIV, continued Fénelon, has been ill-trained in the science of government, filled with "suspicion, jealousy, hostility to virtue, fear of all outstanding merit, and a taste for people who are compliant and servile. He is given to haughtiness and attention to narrow self-interest." During the last thirty years, his ministers have turned everything in the direction of absolutism. While the King thought he was governing, "each minister has actually been the master within the limits of his administration." They have "rendered your name odious," charges Fénelon bluntly, "and the whole French nation intolerable to its neighbors."

The unjust war imposed on Holland has been the starting point of all the others. "So many frightful troubles which have afflicted Europe for more than twenty years, so much blood which has been shed, so many provinces ravaged, so many cities and villages reduced to ashes, are the dire consequences of this war of 1672, undertaken for your glory."

Like a modern Jeremiah, Fénelon lashes out at the King's formalistic religion. He does not mince words. "You do not love God," he says: "you fear him merely from dread of eternal punishment; it is Hell, and not God, that you fear. Your religion consists only of superstition, of little superficial practices. You are like the Jews of whom God said: 'Forasmuch as this people draw near me with their mouth, and with their lips do honor me, but have removed their heart far from me.'"

Then Fénelon condemns point-blank the Archbishop of Paris, François de Harlay, who died in 1695—a fact which thus dates approximately the composition of this letter as written while the author was still in favor and before his grandiose exile as Archbishop of Cambrai. Fénelon also indicts vigorously the King's confessor at that time, Father La Chaise. They are "blind leading the blind," he says. At least, he continues, "Madame de M[aintenon] and Monsieur le D[uc] de B[eauvilliers] ought to have used your confidence in them to undeceive you, but their weakness and timidity are a public scandal. France is at bay. What do they wait for to speak frankly to you? Until all is lost? Do they fear your displeasure? Then they do not love you; for we must be ready to anger those we love rather than to flatter or betray them by our silence. . . ."

"You will perhaps ask, Sire, what they should tell you. Here is what they should say. They should urge you to humble yourself beneath the powerful hand of God, if you do not wish him to humble you; to ask for peace and expiate by this humiliation all the glory which you have made your idol; to reject the unjust counsel of your political flatterers; in short, to restore at once to your enemies, in order to save the state, conquests which you cannot in any case hold without injustice."

"The person who speaks these truths to you, Sire," concludes Fénelon, "far from being contrary to your interests, would give his life to see you as God wishes you to be, and for you he never ceases to pray."

So ends this extraordinary letter whose words seem almost to scorch the paper. In an age of rigid censorship, Fénelon sought means to brush aside, for himself at least and his closest friends, the inherent weakness of absolute government, the suppression of that open criticism which alone might have brought about the timely correction of abuses. He could speak thus frankly only under the protective veil of anonymity. For a moment he perhaps vainly hoped that Madame de Maintenon or the Duc de Beauvilliers, softening the bluntness of his words, would yet have the courage and prestige to convey their substance to the King. It may well be that the autocratic Louis, knowing at least the general lines of the Abbé's thinking, was for this reason glad, a year or two later, to find a pretext for removing him from Versailles and the Little Dauphin to the splendid isolation of the archbishopric at Cambrai. In any event, Madame de Maintenon thought the letter "well expressed," but too harsh and fitted only to "irritate" and "discourage" the King.

This letter is revealing of the intensity, the power, and even the bitter violence of Fénelon's style on occasion, so different from the cloying sweetness too often associated with the author of *Télémaque,* which was written hurriedly for the moral and political instruction of the little Dauphin. The letter shows the rugged honesty which Fénelon commanded as confessor and spiritual director. The priest was to a degree protected by his robe. With revolutionary thoroughness he goes to the core of Louis XIV's grievous faults. That the letter remained for nearly eighty years unknown and without influence is one more evidence of the basic weakness of despotic government. "All power corrupts," said Lord Acton, "and absolute power corrupts absolutely."

5

Fénelon did not, however, limit himself merely to thinking behind the scenes of the wrongs the Grand Monarch was unintentionally inflicting on his country. He offered a definite program to succeed that of Louis XIV.

His most important contributions to this end are two: the *Examination of Conscience on the Duties of Royalty* and the so-called *Chaulnes Tables,* or *Plans of Government,* both intended to arouse the young Duc de Bourgogne to his grave responsibilities and a clear understanding of the urgent needs of the hour.

Like a true confessor, the Archbishop, in the first of these works, presses his ideas home in question after searching question. "Have you not given to your ministers, or allowed them to take, excessive profits which their services have not merited? . . ." he asks. Have you not tolerated impressment of soldiers or sailors,—a policy only permissible during just and unavoidable wars and then only under conditions which disrupt as little as possible family and economic life? "Have you been scrupulous about releasing each galley slave at the expiration of his sentence? The condition of these men is frightful; nothing is more inhuman than to prolong it beyond its term. . . . Do you pay your troops enough so that they can live without pillage? . . . Have you not committed some injustice against foreign nations? Society hangs a poor unfortunate for stealing a doubloon on the highway, out of extreme need, and treats as a hero a man who conquers, that is to say, unjustly subjugates, the territory of a neighboring state! . . . Have you carefully examined to see whether a projected war was necessary to your people? . . . Have you executed treaties of peace punctually? Have you never violated them under fine pretexts? . . . Have you not neglected to become acquainted with mankind, either out of inertia, a desire to be alone, a haughtiness which leads you to withdraw from society, or a taste for details which are but trifles in comparison with this study of people, in short out of the amusements of solitary reading under the pretext of work of a confidential character?" This last criticism was pointed at one of the young Duke's greatest shortcomings, his timidity and an unfortunate tendency to retire within himself instead of mingling freely with life and learning to know humanity at first hand.

But this practical idealist, Fénelon, sorrowfully recognizes the seeming inevitability of power politics. "We must expect that in the long run," he says, "the strongest nation will prevail and overcome the others unless they unite to form a counterbalance. We dare not hope among men that a strong power will remain within the limits of exact moderation, and that in its strength it will desire only what it could obtain in the greatest weakness. Even if a prince were sufficiently perfect to make so remarkable a use of his prosperity, this marvel would end with his reign. . . . We must, then, count on what is real and characteristic of daily experience; namely that every country seeks to triumph over the others around it. Each nation must, therefore, as a measure of its own security, watch constantly to prevent the excessive aggrandizement of any of its neighbors." Amid the long-drawn-out wars of Cambrai, Fénelon had had full opportunity to observe life among nations as it is so tragically lived. Without losing his ideals, he did not delude himself with vain hopes of rapid improvement. He would not counsel the young

Duc de Bourgogne to stake the whole future of his people on a too naïve trust in human nature.

But the Duc de Bourgogne died prematurely in 1712. The *Examination of Conscience on the Duties of Royalty* was to have been published posthumously by the Marquis de Fénelon, nephew of the author, along with a new edition of *Télémaque,* in 1734. It was suppressed on the insistence of the timid, cautious, and conservative Cardinal Fleury, then directing the government. Twelve years later an edition in French and English appeared in London. Numerous other reprintings abroad followed until at last, in 1775, King Louis XVI requested that it be published in France. Unfortunately, Louis XVI, with all his good intentions, was ill-adapted to carry out the bold and searching program indicated by Fénelon. To have put such a program into action would have required a ruler as keen, courageous, and steadfast as the author himself.

The second work in question, the *Chaulnes Tables,* is named after the little town in the northern province of Picardy where Fénelon, for several days in November, 1711, discussed with his friend, the Duc de Chevreuse, plans for the possible government of the Duc de Bourgogne after he had briefly become Dauphin and direct heir to the throne with the sudden death of his father. These proposals are detailed and specific. They are arranged succinctly in outline form with heads and sub-heads. The first and most important of all, in the opinion of Fénelon, close to the disastrous fighting around Cambrai, is the urgent necessity of peace. This long and fatal war must be brought to an end at once for the safety and preservation of France. If peace unfortunately proves impossible, then the struggle should be prosecuted under the most able generals, in the interest primarily of defense. Should worst come to worst, let the weakened army go down, if need be, fighting gloriously.

But, once peace is made, there should be numerous internal reforms. The army ought to be reduced to a hundred and fifty thousand men. The number of fortified places and the size of garrisons will have to be limited for the purpose of economy. Another general war with all Europe must be avoided. France has no real quarrel with the English. Peace with Holland should be easy to negotiate. At the Court, all unnecessary pensions ought to be eliminated. Luxury should be curtailed, economy and a balanced budget must be the rule. A less centralized government with more authority given to the provinces, reform of the inefficient and iniquitous system of farming out the taxes, re-establishment of the Estates General, are all urged by Fénelon. The temporal and spiritual powers should be independent and should cooperate within the state. Fénelon opposes granting patents of nobility except in return for distinguished service to the nation. Nobility of birth should be maintained, but the aristocracy should be allowed to enter commerce or the magistracy without losing caste. Simplification of laws and procedure, a better administration of justice, are proposed by Fénelon with specific recommendations. Liberty of commerce is a cardinal tenet, as in *Télémaque*. Manufactures should be established to produce better goods than foreign countries, but without exclusion of competing articles—a remarkably liberal and farsighted proposal.

With his austere opposition to luxury, however, Fénelon does unwisely insist on sumptuary laws and rather ridiculous prescriptions as to the dress to be allowed within each rank of society. Yet, while occasionally reactionary in the sense of reverting to an older France as it existed before the establishment of an absolute king, Fénelon remains on the whole farsighted and forward-looking.

Would Fénelon have made a great prime minister, a more Christian Richelieu or Mazarin, if he had in the end come to power under the Duc de Bourgogne as King? His firm, able, and enlightened administration of the difficult diocese of Cambrai gives earnest of his possible success in a larger sphere. But more than that we do not know.

At any rate, it was not to be, and the proposals of the great Archbishop remained merely the hopeful suggestions of one of the keenest minds of his time. Following the early death of the Duc de Bourgogne in February, 1712, Louis XIV unhesitatingly burned such of Fénelon's papers as came to hand. The autocratic King recognized a spirit sharply clashing with his own. The phrase attributed to Louis after Fénelon's death, "We shall miss him in time of need," is hardly in the royal character and is unsupported by contemporary testimony. Madame de Maintenon is said to have observed coolly: "I am sorry for the death of Monsieur de Cambrai; he was a friend I lost over Quietism, but they claim he might have done good work in the Council if things are carried that far." The sun was setting on what was called the "Grand Reign." Fénelon had been one of the few to see the demands of this critical period and to prescribe definite and on the whole workable remedies.

To have been idealistic without being chimerical, realistic without cynicism, high-minded yet practical, such was the art which Fénelon had largely learned from his long and penetrating observation of men and events. It remains a rare achievement in his, or any age.

LOUIS XIV French Embassy Press and Information Division

Portrait by **Rigaud** (1701). See page 19.

Tel fut l'illustre Bayle, honneur des beaux esprits
Dont l'élégante plume, en recherches fertile,
Fait douter qui des deux l'emporte en ses écrits,
De l'agréable ou de l'utile ? D. L. M.

PIERRE BAYLE at 28

Original engraving used as frontispiece to his *Historical and
Critical Dictionary*, third edition, Rotterdam (Geneva?), 1715.
See page 25.

ses (*K*) sur les éditions des Oeuvres de St. Augustin. Plusieurs de ses traitez ont été traduits en nôtre langue.

AU-

semblable que St. Augustin ne se tint pas tellement assujetti à cette regle qu'il ne la passât quelquefois entre ses amis, & ceux qu'il prioit de manger à sa table Episcopale. (*s*) *Fesim & mihi illud concedi; non minus probabile; non ita hunc regulæ illi addictum vixisse, ut non cum vini modum nonnunquam inter amicos, & mensæ episcopalis hospites bibendo excederet.* Car autrement il faudroit conclure qu'il ne vivoit que d'herbages, & de lard, (*t*) ce qu'on ne pourroit penser sans une folie monachale.

Voïons que Mr. Cousin a répondu à cet (*m*) étrange paradoxe de Mr. Petit: c'est ainsi qu'il comme ce sentiment. Il veut qu'on lise (*n*) le chapitre entier des *Confessions* d'où le passage a été tiré. On verra, *Que saint Augustin y represente sa disposition où il s'étoit à l'égard du boire & du manger, & qu'il declare qu'il s'est appris de Dieu à ne rechercher les alimens que comme il avoit recherché les remedes, & à user de la mesme sorte des uns & des autres.* Il dit que suivant ce principe il est toujours en garde contre le plaisir, lors qu'il satisfait aux besoins de la nature; qu'il se fait une guerre continuelle, *Que les sensues & par l'abstinence; qu'il reduit souvent son corps en servitude, & entend sans cesse la voix de Dieu qui lui crie: Ne graventur corda vestra in crapula & ebrietate.* Mr. Cousin demande, *si un Evêque qui a vécu de la sorte peut estre soupçonné d'avoir pu quelquefois avec excés?* Il assure qu'il n'y a point ici de distinction à faire, que St. Augustin n'a jamais bu qu'autans que la necessité le demandoit, & (*p*) qu'ainsi quand il dit, *crapula autem nonnunquam obrepit fervo suo; il prend le mot crapula dans un autre sens, Outre celui d'Ariste, auquel il signifie la chaleur de la chaleur causée par le vin pris avec excés, il en prend à un autre encore au delà deux autres, selon l'un desquels il est pris pour l'excés du manger, & selon l'autre pour le plaisir mesme de manger, & de boire. Ce n'est pas un premier que saint Augustin l'a pris; car s'il estoit aussi éloigné de manger avec excés que de boire avec excés. Il n'a donc pu le prendre qu'au second, & expliquant que bien qu'il s'essoyast de resister continuellement à la tentation du plaisir qui se met comme en embuscade au passage des alimens necessaires pour appaiser la faim & la soif, pour entretenir la santé; neanmoins il s'y laissoit quelquefois surprendre. Cette surprise arrive à tous pas parfaits, & à ceux qui refusent tout à leur corps; qu'il est vray partisans que sa jeunesse & d'abstinence.* Mr. Cousin confirme ceci en indiquant plusieurs choses que Possidius a raportées touchant la sobrieté de St. Augustin. Je crois qu'il n'eut pas mal fait de donner de bonnes preuves des deux significations du mot *crapula* qu'il a jointes à celle que Mr. Petit a si bien prouvée.

C'est à mes lecteurs à prononcer sur cette dispute: je me contente de leur indiquer les raisons des deux partis. J'ajouterai seulement que j'ai consulté plusieurs Dictionaires sans y trouver la moindre trace de la signification que Mr. Cousin veut que l'on donne au mot *crapula* dans cet endroit-ci. J'ai même trouvé qu'il n'y a des Medecins qui soutiennent que l'ivresse & la *crapula* le signifient la même chose, & que (*a*) ceux qui y cherchent des differences s'amusent à des disputes de mots. Il est certain que dans Ciceron les termes de (*b*) *crapulam edormire, crapulam exhalare,* veulent dire la mesme chose que les mots François *cuver son vin.* Plaute emploie dans le même sens (*c*) *crapulam amovere,* (*d*) *crapulam edormire,* (*e*) *crapulam edormiscere.* On s'est aussi que presentement notre mot *ivresse* dans un sens odieux que celui d'*ivresse,* qui signifie le degré le plus excessif de l'ivrognerie. C'est, comme le remarque Furetiere, *une vilaine & continuelle débauche de vin, ou d'autres liqueurs qui enyvrent.* Crapuler, ajoute-t-il, veut dire *boire sans cesse, & s'enyvrer salement & continuellement.* Le Dictionaire de l'Academie Françoise confirme ces definitions. Mais il n'y a point de consequence à tirer d'un siecle à un autre quant au sens des termes. L'usage le fait varier prodigieusement. La distinction entre l'ivresse & la crapule étoit certaine au tems d'Ariste, & au tems de St. Augustin. Cela est encore plus clair par le passage de ce Pere de l'Eglise, que par celui de ce Philosophe. La question est de savoir en quoi consistoit cette diference au tems de St. Augustin. Si Mr. Petit avoit (*f*) répliqué à Mr. Cousin, il auroit débité sans doute beaucoup de literature, & je pense qu'il n'auroit pas oublié ceci, c'est que les Auteurs qui comme Ariste traitent dogmatiquement un sujet, défendent dans le detail des genres, & des especes, & observent la proprieté des termes destinez à signifier les diferences des especes, ou les diferens

degrez d'une même qualité; mais les Poëtes & les Orateurs quittent bientôt cette exactitude; ils introduisent un usage plus degagé, ou bien ils s'accommodent à l'usage plus public, qui fait prendre indiferentment les uns pour les autres en mille rencontres les termes que les Docteurs avoient distinguez.

(*K*) *Sur les éditions des Oeuvres de St. Augustin.*] Mr. du Pin (*g*) en a donné une liste qui n'est ni aussi ample, ni aussi exacte que celle que les Journalistes de Leipsic (*h*) en ont donnée. Or comme il est très aisé de consulter ces Auteurs-là; il seroit bien superflu de les copier ici. Je dirai donc seulement que la meilleure édition des Ouvrages de ce Pere est celle qui a paru à Paris par les soins des Benedictins de St. Maur. Elle est divisée en dix volumes in folio comme quelques autres, mais elle a donné un nouvel arrangement, ou une nouvelle œconomie dans chaque tome. Le premier & le second furent imprimez l'an 1679, le 3. fut imprimé en 1680. le 4. en 1681. le 5. en 1683. le 6. & le 7. en 1685. le 8. & le 9. en 1688. le 10. en 1690. Ce dernier volume contient les Ouvrages que St. Augustin composa contre les Pelagiens, il a paru une lettre (*gg*) de l'Abbé D * * * aux RR. PP. Benedictins de la Congregation de saint Augustin. L'Auteur de cette lettre prétend qu'ils ont, ou pour but de favoriser le Jansenisme, & que les preuves qu'il en aporte sont convaincantes. J'ai oui dire que cette lettre embarrassa d'autant plus les Benedictins, qu'il y a quelques Evêques qui leur demandent compte de leur conduite; & qui les menacent de faire defendre dans leurs Dioceses la lecture de cette édition de St. Augustin. Ces sçavans Peres ont donné des éclaircissemens là dessus, & ont satisfait le public à l'égard de ce reproche. Voïez la lettre d'un Théologien à un de ses amis sur un libelle qui avoit pour titre *lettre de l'Abbé * * *,* &c. Elle fut achevée d'imprimer le 22. de Fevrier 1699. & contient 88. pages in 12. Mais elle n'a point terminé le different. Il a paru un (*h*) *Memoire d'un Docteur en Théologie adressé à Messeigneurs les Prelats de France, sur la responce d'un Theologien des PP. Benedictins à la lettre de l'Abbé Allemand,* & l'on soutient dans ce mémoire que sous les reproches qui avoient été faits aux Benedictins sont justes, & que ces Peres y ont très-mal répondu. On remarque (*i*) qu'ils ont envoié de Rouën à Paris une seconde réponse à l'Abbé Allemand, & que le Pere de sainte Marthe souffre mesme, disent-ils, *volontiers qu'on la luy attribuë.* Ces Benedictins ne repliquez, & n'ont point fait taire leurs antagonistes. Il a paru d'autres écrits pour & contre, dont je ne sçaurois donner le detail, puis que je n'en ai vu qu'une petite partie. J'ai vu le livret intitulé, *La conduite des Moines au tems des Peres Benedictins depuis qu'on a arrangé leur Edition de S. Augustin.* Il contient 29. pages in 11. & il a été imprimé l'an 1699. On y aprend entre autres choses 1. qu'avant qu'ils eussent rien publié pour leur defense, (*k*) un Incunu ... *leur affirme les Ecrits, qu'il eut soin de debiter afin que tout Paris, avant que de leur en envoyer étant Exemplaire.* 2. Qu'il avoit donné pour titre à son ouvrage: *Lettre d'un Abbé Commendataire aux Reverends PP. Benedictins de la Congregation de S. Maur.* 3. Que comme celle que l'Abbé Allemand avoit écrite contre ces Peres s'étoit apellée *la Benedictine Allemande,* on appella celle-ci, *la petite Benedictine,* & tout le monde disoit que la cadette valoit bien l'aînée. 4. Que (*l*) l'Auteur fait personage depuis le commencement jusqu'à la fin, & ne parle le langage des Jansenistes que pour mieux le faire entendre des BB. 5. Que (*m*) la petite Benedictine piqua & reveilla les gens du parti; qu'ils songerent dès lors à soutenir le nouvel Augustin, & que Mr. l'Abbé du Guay alla à l'Abbaïe offrir sa plume à la Congregation de S. Maur. 6. Que (*n*) la petite Benedictine n'avoit pas encore été vuë de tout le monde, qu'une autre plus petite & plus agreable le mouru tout-à-coup. Elle etoit intitulée, *Lettre d'un Benedictin non reformé aux Reverends Peres Benedictins de la Congregation de S. Maur,* & venoit de la même source que la petite Benedictine. 7. Que (*o*) les Benedictins deliberarent encore quand on vit prendre l'effort à une quatrième Benedictine, qui étoit d'un serieux à faire croire qu'elle seroit veritablement d'un Cloistre. Elle avoit pour titre. *Lettre d'un Benedictin Reformé de S. Denys, pour servir de Réponse à l'Abbé Allemand, & à l'Abbé Commendataire, & au Benedictin non reformé.* 8. Que (*p*) la premiere reponse

Left margin notes

(*s*) *Petine ibid.*

(*t*) Quod putare cucullatæ esset dementia. *Id. ib.*

(*l*) Quod *putare cucullatæ esset dementia. Id. ib.*

(*m*) Journal des Savans du 27. Juin 1689. pag. 416. édit. de Holl.

(*n*) *Ibid. pag.* 417.

(*o*) *Ibid.*

(*p*) *Ibid. pag.* 428.

(*a*) Qui differentiam inter crapulam & ebrietatem fingunt Λεγομαχχσι. Poël. pag. 353. Dict. n. 475. Jacob. Pancratius *Brunn in Lexico Medico p. m.* 385.

(*b*) Viez la 2. Philippique de Ciceron fol. m. 247. D. & la 2. Fevrier fol. 53. B.

(*c*) Plaut. in Pseud. act. 5. sc. 1. v. 35.

(*d*) Id. in Mostell. act. 5. sc. 2. v. 1.

(*e*) Id. in Rud. act. 2. sc. 7. v. 28.

(*f*) Il n'a pu le faire; il étoit mort avant que son Nependes eus vu le jour.

Right margin notes

(*g*) Voïez la Nouvelle Bibliotheque des Auteurs Ecclesiast. to. 3. pag. 157. édit. de Holl.

(*h*) Dans leur mois de Janvier 1683. pag. 2.

Quelques circonstances du démêlé des Benedictins & des Jesuites au sujet de l'édition de saint Augustin.

(*gg*) Imprimée l'an 1699. elle contient 72. pages in 12.

(*h*) Imprimé l'an 1699. il contient 128. pages in 12.

(*i*) Pag. 121.

(*k*) Pag. 24.

(*l*) Pag. 25.

(*m*) Pag. 28.

(*n*) Pag. 29.

(*o*) Pag. 31.

(*p*) Pag. 35.

FÉNELON

Portrait by Vivien (Munich). See page 38.

CHAPTER IV

FONTENELLE AND THE SPIRIT OF MODERN SCIENCE

I

THE GREATEST MASTERPIECE OF FONTENELLE WAS HIS LIFE. BORN February 11, 1657, a little later than Fénelon but in the same decade, he died very literally "full of years" on January 9, 1757. He had lived out a century lacking only one month.

Moreover, already famous in young manhood, Fontenelle succeeded in that rare *tour de force* of moving forward open-mindedly with the advancing ideas of his time until on the whole, in spite of occasional criticism by Voltaire and other partly hostile voices, he attained the end of his extraordinary career with increased, not diminished prestige. From far and near, people sought him out as one of the marvels of his age. "What! you can't tell me where Monsieur de Fontenelle lives!" indignantly exclaimed a foreigner to a custom's officer at the gates of Paris. "What ignorance! A man known to the whole universe!"

So feeble was the sickly infant at birth that his very life was despaired of. He was consequently at once baptized at home and not taken to the church for the customary christening until three days later. Even at sixteen a game of billiards was too violent an exercise for him and any extreme activity or excitement made him spit blood. In spite of this weakness, or more likely because of it, he learned to husband his meager strength with such astonishing prudence that only once and at the age of fifty did he actually fall ill and, except for the gradual failing of his faculties of hearing, sight, and memory, he kept general good health right up to his very last days. Frail lungs offered a convenient excuse for sparing his thin voice and he became that miracle of brilliant conversationalists, an attentive listener, never impatient to interrupt and place his own *bon mot*. An excellent stomach, moreover, supreme resource of the inveterate diner-out, permitted him the daily pleasures of the table even to excess. Resultant attacks of gout, the characteristic eighteenth-century malady, caused him merely to rest his foot quietly on a chair for a few days without pain. So kind a fate watched over him!

Free from passions, free from vices, with just enough shrewd ambition to ensure success, able to win fame and wealth, yet without impatience, excitement, or worry, Fontenelle dropped off into calm unconsciousness at the end of the day as soon as his head touched the pillow and regularly slept the whole night through. In him dwelt that most uncommon of humans, one who never took work or troubles to bed with him. When incendiaries threatened to burn down the Palais-Royal in vengeance for the crash of John Law's financial "System," Fontenelle, housed there through the hospitality of the Regent, Duke of Orleans, firmly refused to move even for a few days in spite of persistent urging. Instead, he retired at his customary hour, and slept uninterruptedly as usual. On awaking the next morning, he remarked calmly: "They didn't set it on fire after all!"

With such a passionless character, Fontenelle, quite naturally, never showed any desire to marry. Like Bayle, he was a bachelor born, but, unlike the great Protestant scholar, Fontenelle had brilliant social gifts, charming the men and women of his time. In a sense, he was always without age, eternally old in his youth, eternally young as an old man.

In such a nature, there are grave limitations, obviously. Fontenelle acknowledged that he had never laughed out loud. But he was spontaneously gay, and smiled readily. In conversation, he was witty and intelligent, a delightful story-teller even acting out on occasion his brief anecdotes. Thus he easily became the lion of successive salons of Madame de Lambert, Madame de Tencin, and Madame Geoffrin. His constant and sincere devotion to his friends never turned, however, into intensity of feeling or grief. Fontenelle was prudent with money, yet without the avarice which is often the besetting sin of old age. Indeed, examples of his unhesitating generosity are not rare. Although he had no high regard for humanity in general, he was kindly and tolerant of individual shortcomings. In all things Fontenelle showed himself sensible to the extreme, not least in his calm refusal to read hostile criticisms or to answer them.

One of his famous hostesses, Madame de Tencin reproached him for his lack of feeling. Laying her hand on his chest, she said: "That's not a heart you have there; it's a brain as in your head!" It was true, and Fontenelle had no wish to deny it. He was intelligence personified.

Literally, Fontenelle was a living and direct link between the "Great Century" of Louis XIV and the eighteenth which followed it. In 1753, for example, at the age of ninety-six, he could remark casually of a time some seventy-five years before: "I was at Madame de La Fayette's. I saw Madame de Sévigné come in." But, if he knew the past intimately, he was no sour detractor of the present. After all, the modern age had been kind to him, and he was not one to sing the praises of "the good old days." He could himself recount the story of the dragonnades and the Revocation of the Edict of Nantes, though of course with no claim to a martyr's role. Thirty-two years older than Montesquieu, Fontenelle nevertheless survived him. He was thirty-seven years the senior of Voltaire, yet lived past the middle of the next century into its turbulent second half, witnessing exactly three-fourths of the great Patriarch's own long career. More than fifty years separated him from those revolutionary children of another age, Rousseau and Diderot, but Fontenelle was present as the first years of fame came noisily to them also. He was indeed, as he himself said, the Nestor of his time.

In later years deafness grew upon him, taking away his greatest pleasure, that of conversation. So he had to keep an ear trumpet handy on his lap or suspended from a chair arm. In spite of this infirmity of hearing, he continued to frequent the salon of his good friend, Madame Geoffrin. At times when he saw the faces about him light up with particular animation, he would inquire what was the subject under discussion. Once he had been set right on the "Chapter," as he put it, he would again subside and converse silently with himself in accordance with a habit of long standing. Later, on request, he would tell the respectful circle the gist of the exchange of ideas which had just taken place between Fontenelle and Fontenelle, while his hearers eagerly compared his summary with their own previously-expressed opinions. And he could slyly put his indispensable ear trumpet to other uses also! For years he had lived with his disputatious second-cousin, Richer d'Aube. When the latter shouted dogmatically: "And *I* say, . . ." Fontenelle placidly turned away his ear trumpet, remarking drily: "Ah! you say?"

Yet the aged Fontenelle lost none of his early gallantry. To a young and pretty woman, the near-centenarian bowed his witty compliment: "Ah! if I were only eighty now!" According to tradition, the great jurist, Oliver Wendell Holmes, in more recent days, once made a similar response. Had he, too, read Fontenelle, or was it merely the natural, joking reaction of great age to a like situation?

In any event, Fontenelle took his increasing physical limitations philosophically. As he felt death making its inroads little by little, he would say: "I am sending my heavier baggage on ahead." Yet life was still sweet. When the even more aged Madame Grimaud, at a hundred and three, came to see him six months before his death and remarked: "It seems, Monsieur, as though Providence has forgotten and left us on earth," Fontenelle put his finger to his lips and said quietly: "Ssh!"

If Fontenelle lacked the qualities of enthusiasm and warm affection, those he did possess of gaiety, patience, and calm resignation are not to be despised. He had at least what was required for his own happiness and that of his friends around him.

The details of his life can be quickly summarized. Born in the historic old Norman town of Rouen on February 11, 1657, Bernard le Bovier de Fontenelle was educated there in the Jesuit school. As the nephew of the famous dramatist, Pierre Corneille, and his lesser, but more genial brother, Thomas, Fontenelle made several early trips to Paris and was promptly introduced into the literary circles of the capital. His attempts at poetry, tragedy, opera, and a vapid prose work dealing with love revealed the author's complete lack of profound emotion, his affected style, and his want of the qualities needed for great creative literature. Even as late as 1694, when Fontenelle was already deservedly famous, the hostile La Bruyère satirized him unmercifully in his *Characters* under the name of Cydias, but merely demonstrated thereby how completely even a penetrating observer can go astray when, through blindness or prejudice, he gives the truth, but not the whole truth. In the end, Fontenelle was to prove La Bruyère so far wrong in his total estimate that the passage is cited as a literary curiosity today.

While still spending most of his time in Rouen, Fontenelle began to devote his pen to clear and popular discussions of modern science and ideas. Here he was at once successful. In the short space of five or six years from 1683 to 1688, he became a celebrity before he was thirty. Four times he presented himself as a candidate for the French Academy. Largely on account of the unyielding hostility of those great figures, Racine, Boileau, and La Bruyère, four times he was rejected. Finally, on a fifth attempt in 1691, he was elected and in his reception address angered his opponents still more by boldly praising the dramatic work of his uncle, Pierre Corneille, at the expense of the latter's younger rival, Racine. In 1697, Fontenelle became Secretary of the newly-reorganized Academy of Science, a post which he held until, at the age of eighty-three in 1740, he at length insisted on being allowed to resign. With his *History of the Academy* and his penetrating *Eulogies* of the great men of science as their work came to an end in death, he made his most important contributions to the popular spread of the scientific spirit. These *Eulogies* manifest also his remarkable ability, not to remain intellectually static, but to grow and move forward with his age.

As the late afternoon waned on January 9, 1757, Fontenelle's death came peacefully in Paris, after only a day's illness. His disappearance from the scene was overshadowed by popular excitement at the mad attempt of Damiens four days before to assassinate the King, Louis XV. Fontenelle had experienced no special suffering, merely the gradual wasting away of his immense age. "I feel no pain," he said to his physician, "only a certain difficulty in existing."

2

At the very beginning of 1683, when Fontenelle was still in Rouen and was not quite twenty-six, he brought out a little book entitled *Dialogues of the Dead*. By March, it was already in a second edition. Not many weeks later, in a third edition, the author felt encouraged to double the number of dialogues by adding a second volume containing eighteen more. Obviously, the work had become immediately popular. Pierre Bayle praised it highly in his *News of the Republic of Letters*. It was widely imitated and by the following October had been translated both into English and Italian.

Fontenelle's point of departure lay in the famous *Dialogues of the Dead* by the ancient Greek writer, Lucian, but from his predecessor the young Frenchman borrowed little beyond the general device of using such striking conversations to give dramatic expression to ideas. In piquant contrast, Fontenelle brings together the world-conquering Alexander and the courtesan Phryne; the love poet Anacreon and the staid philosopher Aristotle; Homer, the epic author of *Iliad* and *Odyssey,* and Æsop, popular writer of children's fables; the Greek Socrates and the sixteenth-century French essayist, Montaigne;—and many more. In general, the dialogues come to unexpected and seemingly paradoxical conclusions, yet these conclusions find support in the foibles and follies of human nature, so generally governed more by emotion than by reason.

"If we wish only to make a noise in the world," Phryne reminds the proud Alexander, "it's not the most reasonable people who are best adapted to that end." The effeminate Sybarite Smindirides deflates the strong-man Milo with the embarrassing question: "Don't you think that boasting of having lifted an ox is the same as boasting of being a good deal like an ox?" So much for pride in mere athletic prowess! When Aristotle grows a bit vain over his clear definition of the passions, Anacreon, the singer of love, retorts from sure knowledge: "What folly! We're not concerned with defining the passions, as they say you have done, but with controlling them." Homer warns Æsop: "You imagine that the human mind is looking only for truth! Don't believe it! Man gets on admirably with the false." To Joan of Naples, Saint Anselm laments: "If man is as you think he is, he's born to aspire to everything and enjoy nothing, to keep constantly moving and get nowhere." Why will Molière's comedies continue to live when the metaphysical speculations of Paracelsus are forgotten? Because "he who would write for immortality should depict human folly." Such a man will never run out of material!

Fontenelle's method may especially be watched in the famous dialogue between Socrates and Montaigne. The latter, overflowing with admiration for antiquity, enthusiastically greets his illustrious predecessor in the after-life.

"How is the world going?" asks Socrates. "Isn't it very much changed?"

"Extremely," replies Montaigne. "You wouldn't recognize it."

"I'm delighted at that," says Socrates. "I had always suspected it would have to become better and wiser than in my time."

"What do you mean?" exclaims Montaigne. "It's crazier and more corrupt than ever. That's the change I wanted to speak about, and

I expected to learn from you the story of your times in which such integrity and uprightness reigned."

"And for my part," responds Socrates, "I hoped on the contrary to learn marvels of the century in which you have just been living. What! men of the present haven't given up the follies of antiquity? . . . I thought at last things would go on more reasonably, and that men would profit from so many years' experience."

"Ah! do men learn from experience?" asks the skeptical Montaigne. "They are like birds always getting caught with the same nets in which a hundred thousand birds of the same species have already been taken. There is no one but enters brand-new into life, and the mistakes of the fathers are lost upon their children. . . . Men of all centuries have the same propensities over which reason has no power. So, wherever there are men, there is folly, and the same kinds of folly."

"And on that basis," retorts Socrates, "how could you expect antiquity to be better than today?"

Montaigne, surprised and a bit crestfallen, sees too late that he has been neatly trapped in his own reasoning and led by Socrates to a conclusion quite different from what he had anticipated. Thus he learns that a romantic admiration for "the good old days" can be just as foolish as to suppose that the modern world has either greatly improved deep down underneath or on the other hand quite gone to the dogs. And the *Dialogue* concludes:

"Clothes change, but that is not to say that the shape of the body changes also. . . . The outside of man changes, but the heart of man does not change, and all of man is in the heart. . . . The general order of nature appears very constant."

Thus, the only significant progress is moral progress, and that, alas! moves on laggard feet. Fontenelle was never the naïve and uncritical partisan of so-called modern progress that he has too often been considered. A conversation he once had with his friend and biographer, Abbé Trublet, confirms the sage conclusion of this famous *Dialogue*. Another acquaintance called him the patriarch of a sect to which he did not belong!

If the *Dialogues* are generally more clever than profound, they remain agreeable reading today, inculcating without bitterness their skeptical and disillusioned picture of human folly. In the clear and entertaining presentation of ideas under the guise of conversations,

Fontenelle had found his true way. With him, as with many of his successors, the salon makes its significant contribution to French literary form. To the general public, these *Dialogues* demonstrated that anything can be said, provided it be done with skillful regard for clarity and interest. *Il y a la manière.* "The chief aim of an author must be to please," said Molière. In this art, Fontenelle became at once a master.

During these gloomy years when relations between Catholics and Protestants were growing more and more bitter, Fontenelle seems to have written three or four brief pages satirizing under the transparent anagrams of Mréo and Eénegu the rival claims of Rome and Geneva. The title of this little skit was *Relation from the Island of Borneo* and the date, probably fictitious, November 27, 1684. The serious-minded Bayle actually took this for a *bona fide* narration from the East Indies and, in January, 1686, printed it solemnly as such, under the incriminating name of Fontenelle, in his widely-read *News of the Republic of Letters.* Coming less than three months after the Revocation of the Edict of Nantes, this untoward publication almost landed its rash author in the dreaded Bastille. Only Fontenelle's fame and the promptness with which he made his submission by issuing, in the *Triumph of Religion under Louis the Great,* some verses laudatory of the unfortunate Revocation, saved him from imprisonment. It was deeply humiliating to have thus to bow completely and disavow one's opinions before despotic power, but Fontenelle needed no repetition of this disagreeable lesson in the hard facts of seventeenth-century life. Henceforth he would be prudent. "If I had my hand full of truths, I would take good care not to open it," he said later.

3

In January, 1686, appeared one of Fontenelle's most successful and famous works, his *Conversations on the Plurality of Worlds.* Here the author enters definitely upon his characteristic role as a popularizer of science. For the most part the general public of the time still believed the earth to be the center of the universe with the sun and the planets turning around it—in short the Ptolemaic theory handed down from far-off antiquity. The more modern Copernican interpretation was yet unknown to most readers.

The work contains two characters, a beautiful Marquise, Fontenelle's friend, Madame de La Mésangère, and himself. Their extended conversations are held on successive evenings in the grounds of the Marquise's château near Rouen. Each of the five original chapters is appropriately entitled an "Evening." A sixth "Evening" was added and published the year following. When the author first read his book to the heroine, her maid, recognizing the vaguely described locale and the characters, smiled at being in this way let behind the scenes of literature. Thus forewarned, Madame de La Mésangère made Fontenelle change her fictional portrait from brunette to blond and so prevent the embarrassment of easy identification by contemporaries.

To appreciate the *Plurality* today, the reader must forget for a moment any school course he may have had in the elements of astronomy and endeavor to approach the subject matter as if it were entirely new. Then he can admire the skill with which Fontenelle has succeeded in making his complex material clear and interesting.

The book starts with a brief description of the setting in the park of the château. "It was a delightful cool evening after a hot day. . . . The moon had been up for about an hour, and its rays, filtered through the branches of the trees, made a pleasant mingling of the vivid silvery white on the upper side of the leaves with the green which appeared black by contrast beneath. Not a cloud in the sky, and the brilliant gold of the stars stood out clearly against their background of blue." With these few, but concrete details, we see that Fontenelle was not, as writers of the seventeenth century have generally been represented, wholly devoid of a sense of visual beauty in nature.

"Don't you think," asked the Marquise's companion, "that the day itself is less beautiful than a fine night?"

"Yes," she replied, "the beauty of the day is like a blond who is more brilliant, but the beauty of the night is a brunette who is more attractive."

"You are very generous," answered Fontenelle, "to give this advantage to brunettes when you are not one yourself." Thus the author underlines his slight disguise of the heroine. More than half a century later, Voltaire, in his little philosophical tale of *Micromégas*, would rather unjustly poke fun at his ninety-five-year-old contemporary for these "blonds" and "brunettes" who had aided him in popularizing astronomy.

Like a successful laboratory lecturer, Fontenelle clarifies his explanations with simple concrete comparisons and lightens his exposition with occasional little jokes or graceful badinage. The universe, he says, resembles a watch whose carefully regulated movements are dependent upon the skillful arrangement of all its parts. The rotation of the earth on its axis and its annual circuit about the sun may be illustrated by the double motion of a ball rolling along a path in the park. The earth glides through space like a boat on a river. How do we know the boat moves? By the changing banks. But there are no banks to show the earth's motion. Oh yes, there are! The banks are the fixed stars which reveal to the scientist by their changed position in relation to the earth that the latter is no longer where it was. The moon is probably inhabited just like the earth, suggests Fontenelle to the astonished Marquise. If a group of Parisians on top of the tower in Notre-Dame Cathedral should conclude there were no people in neighboring Saint-Denis just because they could not see any, even though everything else, houses and streets, looked much like Paris, wouldn't they be illogical in their reasoning? But no! Perhaps the moon isn't inhabited after all. Fontenelle has thought of a grave difficulty. No atmosphere! So the author presents the pro and the con, teaches his neophyte Marquise a scientific suspension of the judgment when evidence is contradictory or inconclusive, at the same time playing lightly with the new ideas. Another example. The sun is gradually growing weaker. In mock terror, the Marquise retorts: "Instead of looking at my mirror in the morning to see if I am pale, I think I shall have to look at the sun!"

All of this, though pleasant joking, may seem unnecessarily frivolous today. It was not so in the seventeenth century when such knowledge was still new to most readers. Voltaire criticized this banter later while himself popularizing Newton, but Fontenelle did much to make Voltaire possible.

Indeed, even here, the author of the *Plurality* was not spared theological difficulties. Toward the end of his *Preface,* he pays his respects with delicate irony to those "scrupulous people who may imagine there is danger to religion in supposing inhabitants elsewhere than on the earth." He continues with a protective fooling, which was to become characteristic of his eighteenth-century successors. "When you are told that the moon is inhabited," says Fontenelle, "you at once imagine men there like ourselves, and then, if you are a bit of a theologian, you find yourself in the midst of difficulties. Adam's posterity cannot have extended to the moon or sent colonies to that country. The men in the moon are therefore not sons of Adam. Now, it would be embarrassing in theology if there were men who did not descend from him. There is no need of saying more. . . . The objection turns, in consequence, entirely on the men in the moon; but it's those making this objection who are pleased to put men in the moon. As far as I am concerned, I don't put any there; I put inhabitants there who are not in any sense men. Who are they, then? I haven't seen them. It's not for having seen them that I speak of them. And don't imagine this is a mere trick to elude your objection," concludes the author slyly.

Thus, in matters which, thanks to Fontenelle and his co-workers, seem innocuous today, the heavy hand of a traditional orthodoxy still lay in wait for the unwary scientist. It was disturbing to suggest that man was not the center of the universe. The unimagined distances of the immense solar system inspired fear and skepticism in many a reader. Under Fontenelle's light touch, the old order of an intimate tight little world was breaking up, giving place to a new and awesome vastness in which man, in Voltaire's later words, had become but "an insect on a ball of mud."

Then, there was the question of the great age of the universe. "The ancients were young compared with ourselves," observed Fontenelle in an epigrammatic and quotable phrase. Suppose the roses, who live but a day, had written histories and memoirs. "We have always seen the same gardener," they would say. "In the memory of roses, no one has seen anyone else but him; he has always been as he is; assuredly he does not die as we do; he does not even change." And the author asks: "Would the reasoning of the roses be good? . . . Should we establish our life, which is but an instant, as the measure of anything else? . . . One is not so easily eternal."

Simple, clear, concise, and interesting, such was the style of Fontenelle at its best. He thought his material out carefully in advance and, when he wrote, he wrote rapidly, without that painful labor which has driven many an author to distraction. In this too, fate was kind to him.

4

Hot upon the heels of the successful *Plurality of Worlds* there appeared anonymously in December of this same year, 1686, Fontenelle's equally famous *History of Oracles*. Three years before, a learned Dutch physician named Van Dale had published two long dissertations proving the fictitious character of pagan oracles. But Van Dale was heavy, prolix, difficult to follow, and he wrote in Latin. For all these reasons, his erudite work was closed to the general public. Fontenelle abridged, rearranged, made Van Dale's material simple, direct, and clear, spiced it occasionally with penetrating irony, and out of this forbidding volume created another popular and influential work.

To attack pagan oracles might seem indeed quite innocent. Christian theologians, however, had traditionally attributed these oracles to demons, hence accepted them as real, and had used their supposed existence as one of the proofs of Christianity, since they were thought to have ceased at the coming of Christ. But such was not at all the case, said Fontenelle. In fact, the oracles continued for centuries. Only, they were not in any sense due to supernatural or miraculous manifestations, but rather to the trickery of the pagan priesthood and the credulity of their followers. Indirectly, therefore, Fontenelle's book is leveled against all belief in the marvelous or the supernatural. By implication, it seeks a rational and scientific explanation for whatever is not readily understood. It was a powerful weapon against human stupidity and gullibility. Only the extremely guarded manner in which the author presented his argument protected him from dangerous censure. As it was, a refutation by a certain Father Baltus did finally appear twenty years later in 1707. Fontenelle thought an effective reply to Baltus would be easy, but he prudently refrained, and even avoided temptation by closing the book, he says, and refusing to read more of his adversary. In 1713, however, Le Tellier, Louis XIV's confessor, tried to suppress Fontenelle's pensions and have a *lettre de cachet* issued against him, alleging as proof of atheism the *Relation from the Island of Borneo* and the *History of Oracles*. Fortunately, according to Voltaire, the timely intervention of the King's respected Police Lieutenant of Paris, the elder D'Argenson, saved the author from imminent disgrace and ruin. Fontenelle seems to speak discreetly of this debt to D'Argenson at the end of his *Eulogy* of that great man.

One of the high spots of Fontenelle's *History of Oracles* is the famous page in which, at the beginning of Chapter IV of the First Part, he narrates the "Story of the Gold Tooth."

Is the explanation of pagan oracles as the work of demons correct? asks the author. "Let us assure ourselves thoroughly of the fact before troubling about its cause. It is true that this method is very slow for most people who run naturally to the cause and jump over the question of the truth of the fact. But after all, in this way, we shall avoid the ridiculous result of discovering the cause of what does not exist," concludes the author succinctly, repeating almost verbatim an effective chapter heading in Bayle's *Miscellaneous Thoughts on the Comet.*

"This misfortune happened so amusingly toward the end of the last century to a number of German scholars that I cannot refrain from speaking of it here," continues Fontenelle.

"In 1593, the rumor spread that, a seven-year-old child in Silesia having lost his teeth, a gold tooth had come in to take the place of one of his molars. Horstius, Professor of Medicine in the University of Helmstad, wrote in 1595 the history of this tooth, and claimed that it was in part natural, in part miraculous, and that it had been sent by God to this child for the purpose of consoling the Christians afflicted by the Turks. Imagine what a consolation and what a relationship between this tooth and either the Christians or the Turks! In the same year, that this tooth might not lack historians, Rullandus also wrote its history. Two years after, Ingolsteterus, another scholar, wrote against Rullandus's opinion of the gold tooth, and Rullandus at once drew up a fine learned reply. Another great man named Libavius gathered up all that had been said about the tooth and added his own particular opinion. In all these splendid works nothing was lacking except that the tooth should really be of gold. When an expert had examined it, he discovered that gold leaf had been most skillfully applied to the tooth. But people began by making books, and afterwards they consulted the goldsmith!"

"Nothing is more natural than to do the same in all sorts of matters. I am not so much convinced of our ignorance by the things which exist, though we do not know why, as by those which do not exist, but for which we find a reason. That is to say, not only do we not possess principles which lead to the truth, but we have others which get on very well with what is false."

The lesson is clear. Where the learned scholars with their Latinized names ending in *us* all failed because they argued from prejudice and opinion without a hard-headed study of the facts, so we too may fail. Even the specialist is rarely objective and impartial outside of his own field, if indeed there. In political or social controversy, for example, he may be as naïve as the proverbial man in the street. So Fontenelle speaks as pertinently to our own time as to his own.

While the *History of Oracles* was being read and discussed, another and quite different question was very much to the fore. Since the rebirth of learning in the Renaissance, the Ancients had been deservedly admired and imitated. Indeed the great literary achievements of the Greeks and Romans had done much to fix the form and content of French thought and style during the preceding two centuries. But some people were now beginning to chafe under what seemed to them excessive deference toward the past. Could the Moderns not surpass or at least equal the Ancients, they asked? Thus little by little over the years there had been taking shape the famous "Quarrel of the Ancients and the Moderns," which has most important connotations for the idea of progress.

On the 26th of January, 1687, Charles Perrault read before the French Academy a poem entitled the *Century of Louis the Great*. In this poem he set the contemporary period in parallel with the age of Augustus, showed the scientific superiority of the Moderns, emphasized the supposed weaknesses of Homer, and praised the literary achievements of his own time. Curiously enough, the greatest writers of the day, Boileau, Racine, La Fontaine, and La Bruyère, conscious of their own debt to the Greek and Roman classics, were ardently on the side of the Ancients. Fontenelle, at least in the field of science, tended toward the camp of the Moderns. In fact, this was one of the reasons for the opposition which so long blocked his election to the French Academy.

In 1688, the year following Perrault's poem, Fontenelle, in a brief essay of some twenty pages entitled *Digression on the Ancients and the Moderns*, stated his position with his usual remarkable clarity. He begins with a striking comparison.

The whole question of preëminence between the Ancients and

the Moderns, he says, "comes down to knowing whether the trees formerly in our countrysides were bigger than they are today."

"Let us explain this paradox," continues Fontenelle. "If the Ancients were more intelligent than we are, that must be because the brains of that time were better, formed of stronger or more delicate material, filled with more animal spirits. But why should the brains of that time be better? The trees would in consequence have been bigger and finer also, for, if nature was younger and stronger then, the trees, as well as the brains of mankind, would have had to reflect this youth and vigor." But physical science does not accept all these fine phrases about the superiority of the Ancients. Indeed, "nature has in her hands a certain substance, always the same, which she ceaselessly turns and re-turns in a thousand fashions. . . . Certainly, she has not formed Plato, Demosthenes, or Homer of finer clay than our philosophers, orators, or poets of today."

"There, it seems to me," says Fontenelle, "is the answer to the great question of the Ancients and the Moderns. . . . We are all perfectly equal." In fact, "enlightened by the discoveries of the Ancients, as well as by their mistakes, we need not be surprised if we can surpass them."

"But, for the Moderns to surpass the Ancients, it must be in fields where this is possible. Eloquence and poetry . . . depend on vividness of imagination, . . . which does not require long experience . . . to reach perfection. But physics, medicine, and mathematics are made up of an infinite number of ideas and rely upon accurate reasoning, which is constantly and very slowly being perfected. . . . It is evident that all this goes on endlessly and that the latest physicists and mathematicians must be the best."

Choosing a famous comparison already made by Francis Bacon, Pascal, and others, Fontenelle likens the long history of humanity to the life of an individual man, who, young at the time of the Ancients, in full vigor and maturity today, will in truth never grow old. That is to say, man, in the opinion of the author of the *Digression,* will not degenerate. Knowledge constantly increases, but nothing is a greater hindrance to progress than excessive admiration for the Ancients, a crude prejudice which reason will certainly overcome. Indeed, men of the seventeenth century, he suggests, will become Ancients themselves some day, and, who knows?—may be unduly respected by the Moderns of that time, looking down contemptuously on their own men of genius, "who will perhaps be Americans!" Of course, it is the American Indian whom Fontenelle in imagination puts thus wittily in parallel with his own age of Louis XIV.

So the question of progress offers three aspects. In science, the advance is infinite, believes Fontenelle. There, limitless vistas stretch before the wondering eyes of humanity. In the field of literature, on the other hand, the Moderns cannot perhaps surpass the highest achievements of the Ancients, but they may hope at times to equal them in genius. As for the problem of moral progress, it is not discussed in the *Digression*. We must not forget, however, that the author of the *Dialogues of the Dead* had not changed his views in five years. In regard to this, the most vital problem confronting the human race, Fontenelle, like his fictional mouthpieces, Socrates and Montaigne, remained skeptical. Experience with mankind gave him no encouragement. In spite of the scientific enthusiasm of the *Plurality of Worlds* and the *Digression on the Ancients and the Moderns,* Fontenelle was no blind and undiscriminating believer in complete and all-embracing progress. On man's too persistent selfishness and folly he continued to look with realistic eyes.

5

From the time Fontenelle assumed the secretaryship of the Academy of Science in 1699 to his resignation at the age of eighty-three in 1740, he delivered from year to year his famous *Eulogies* of the departed great. There are seventy-one of these *Eulogies* in his published works. Through this succession of biographical studies, given with remarkable factual precision and regard for truth, we follow the course of scientific achievement during more than forty years. The author's style is clear and sober without the irony or flowery ornament which sometimes characterize his more youthful works.

In his discussion of Newton, for example, Fontenelle showed himself by no means chauvinistically wedded to the vortex theory of the universe proposed by his great countryman Descartes. He is scrupulously fair to both Newton and Leibniz in the dispute as to which held the primacy in the invention of differential calculus. Fontenelle unhesitatingly gives the palm to Newton, yet without injustice to the achievements of the German mathematician and philosopher. It is to be noted that he had taken exactly the same impartial stand in 1716 when speaking of Leibniz as he did regarding Newton in 1727. He did not shift positions with the person who happened to occupy the center of the stage.

The *Eulogy* of Du Fay gives a vivid picture of the ex-soldier and man of action who, turning to the field of science, manifests a remarkable practical ability to get along with people. By his patience, tact, good humor, and persistence, he wins from indifferent or hostile governmental ministries the necessary funds for developing the neglected Botanical Gardens, bringing them during his short lifetime to a position of European supremacy from which, on his death, he passed them on to his successor, the even greater Buffon.

In his tribute to the elder D'Argenson, Fontenelle portrays, not a scientist this time, but a distinguished police commissioner, keeping order in a big city like Paris, honest, fair, indefatigable, and unsparing of time and energy in his devotion to the public service.

Fontenelle possessed an exceptional ability to understand the different mathematical and scientific developments of his day and to express them in language so simple and clear that it could be grasped by the general public. In the *Eulogies*, he manifested, too, an unusually open mind and a rare capacity to grow and move forward with his time.

In 1724, with a new edition of his works, appeared a brief fifteen-page essay by Fontenelle entitled, *On the Origin of Fables*. It has extraordinary significance. Long withheld from publication out of prudence, this little work had been composed, according to the author's eighteenth-century biographer, Abbé Trublet, during the decade of the 1690s. A thorough modern student of Fontenelle, Mr. J.-R. Carré, is inclined to date it still earlier, even before 1680. If the ideas here expressed had perhaps taken definite shape from the very beginning of the writer's maturity, the simplicity and lack of frivolous ornamentation of style suggest that the work may have been rewritten after the *Dialogues of the Dead* and the *Plurality of Worlds,* during a period contemporary with the plain, unvarnished clarity of the *Eulogies.*

This short discussion is more than a kind of introduction to the *History of Oracles,* as it has sometimes been called. It has important implications for the understanding of the human mind in general.

How does it come about, asks Fontenelle, that the early history of nations is a mass of absurdities? "Could these fables have been thought true? With what purpose could they have been composed if considered false?" The ignorance and barbarism of primitive peoples must have been great to a degree inconceivable today. In fact, the Kaffirs, Laps, and Iroquois, whom we now know, have attained a level of civilization superior to that of these early men. Clearly, Fontenelle, unlike Rousseau later, was no admirer of primitivism, no worshipper of the supposed joys of the Golden Age.

How have these fables and myths been formed? Exactly in the same way as when modern man reasons from the known to the unknown. How does it happen that rivers run inexhaustibly? The primitive mind concluded there must be some mysterious figure at the source continuously pouring in water from a jug. What of the young man whose body, drowned in a stream, could never be recovered? He was no doubt kidnapped by water maidens, nymphs of the river. The pagan gods? They manifest the characteristics of men, of men who are simple and gross in habits and ideas. The chief trait of the heathen gods is power, because power is what is understood and respected by these early men. Wisdom and justice? Such concepts can come into being only with developing civilization. The gods grow better as men do.

All peoples, says Fontenelle, have formed myths remarkably similar—the American Indians like the ancient Greeks. This shows the uniformity of the human mind. Not trickery, not deceit, are the fundamental bases of these manifestations. Thus the *Origin of Fables* is even broader in scope and more scientific in conception than the *History of Oracles*. With its sure understanding of the relativity of thought, its changing aspects in different ages, the *Origin of Fables* transcends Voltaire and touches hands with our own time. Fontenelle lays a sound foundation for an understanding of primitive sociology and an unbiased study of comparative religions. Prudently, he exempted ancient Judaism and orthodox Christianity from the implications of his bold reasoning, but it is evident that these were only the restrictions of a man well acquainted with the persecuting habit of mankind. "Let us seek nothing else in these fables," he concludes, "but the errors of the human mind."

A great modern student of these matters, Andrew Lang, observed: "Fontenelle's paper . . . requires little but copious evidence to make it adequate. . . . A better and briefer system of mythology could not be devised."

Fontenelle's century-long life was also a potent factor in his influence, an influence, however, not to be exactly measured. Who could come into the presence of this extraordinarily lucid mind without being impressed! How much daring thought must have been encouraged by mere hint or suggestion! Could credulity or conservatism stand out before his skeptical smile? What Fontenelle did not say counted as well as what he said. His was the fine art of teaching to read between the lines, to link together startling conclusions intentionally scattered in widely different parts of his work, to develop the bold consequences of his simple, matter-of-fact remarks. In this ageless man, the very spirit of scientific rationalism appears personified. "Man is only a reed, but he is a thinking reed," said Pascal. Fontenelle's mind is the distilled essence of unprejudiced thought, unswayed by sentiment or emotion. If man is ever destined to come under the rule of reason, he will find in Fontenelle a true ancestor.

PART II

CRITICISM, FERMENT, REPRESSION

CHAPTER V

THE SORRY REIGN OF LOUIS THE «WELL BELOVED»

I

SOON AFTER THE DEATH OF THE AGED LOUIS XIV EARLY ON THE morning of Sunday, September 1, 1715, there appeared on the balcony of the great palace at Versailles an officer in uniform, a black plume waving from his hat. In measured, sonorous tones, he proclaimed the solemn news: "The King is dead!" Then, abruptly, the herald withdrew, to return a few moments later wearing a sparkling white plume. Three times he called loudly: *Vive le roi Louis XV!* "Long live King Louis XV!"

On both sides of the gallery and succession of apartments within, the royal guards snapped into position, "forming the hedge," as the French phrase goes, in two lines facing each other at attention. Striding with infant dignity between the impassive ranks of soldiers, a pale-looking five-year-old boy came out on the balcony to show himself to the waiting throng in the courtyard below. The traditional hopeful cries rose to his hardly comprehending childish ears: *Vive le roi Louis XV! Vive le roi Louis XV!* Ushered in with all the formal trappings of the Old Régime, another fateful reign had begun.

The next day, at six o'clock in the morning, members of that august judicial body, the Parlement of Paris, were already assembling in the Grand Chamber of the Palais de Justice on the ancient Ile de la Cité. They were to decide the pressing question of who was to govern during the minority of the young King. Under the guise of doing honor to the occasion, Philip, Duke of Orleans, insistent on being chosen Regent, had taken the significant precaution of throwing a strong cordon of over three thousand French and Swiss guards around the Place Dauphine, the Quais, the stairway to the Sainte-Chapelle, and all the approaches to the Palace. Two days before, it was said, there had been issued to these soldiers more than ten rounds of powder and bullets for use in emergency. Privately, the Duke had presented to leading members of Parlement, as early as the day before the King's death, a written outline of his intended program, including restoration of the cherished parliamentary right of remonstrance to royal edicts. Thus the way had been discreetly prepared.

In the lower seats of the Chamber near the central rostrum, the scarlet robes of these legal dignitaries made a brilliant splash of color. Gradually, after the termination of the early-morning discussions, the dukes, leaders of the Church, and other notables filed in and took their places on benches in the assembly hall. At a quarter to nine, word came that the Duke of Orleans was attending mass in the adjacent Sainte-Chapelle. A delegation was thereupon sent to escort him to the Chamber. His rival, the Duc du Maine, legitimatized natural son of Louis XIV and Madame de Montespan, entered, "bursting with joy," as Saint-Simon put it, bowing with exaggerated courtesy to right and left and basking fatuously in the knowledge that he alone was especially favored in the royal will.

After a tenacious dispute over precedence between Parlement and the dukes as to which should first doff their hats in addressing each other, this matter was at length successfully shelved for more important business. The Duke of Orleans, dressed in solemn black, next rose, looked calmly over the assembly for a few moments, raised his hat politely in salutation, then replaced it in accordance with the forms befitting a grandee of France. He read forcefully a brief speech of four or five minutes urging his right to the Regency by virtue of his birth as nephew of the late King. It had been carefully ghost-written for the occasion. Anticipating the hostile clauses of the will, Philip declared that Louis XIV had personally told him: "I have made such arrangements as I thought wisest, but, since it is impossible to foresee all, if there is anything which is not right, you will change it." This of course was complete nullification in advance.

The will was next ceremoniously brought in; its numerous seals were inspected, and found unbroken. The document was then read, "seven or eight pages in the King's own rather bad handwriting," as was observed. The will prescribed various privileges for the Duc du Maine with severe limitations on his rival, who was to be subject to control by a majority vote of the Council. Brushing these stipulations aside with every appearance of astonishment at their tenor, the Duke of Orleans boldly called upon Parlement to decide at once upon his rightful claim. The way had been so well prepared that this was done by acclamation. The members forthwith declared the Duke of Orleans, Regent as he had wished. The morning session thereupon adjourned.

At three in the afternoon, the Parlement once more assembled. Confident in his newly-established position and anxious to avoid possible criticism, the Duke of Orleans had tactfully dismissed the surrounding troops, now no longer needed. As Regent, he again addressed the assembly, invoking in favor of his untrammeled power, as we have previously seen, the well-known and expressive words of Fénelon's *Télémaque*. The members enthusiastically applauded the appropriate reference. By his momentary energy and decision in this crucial session, Philip had completely triumphed. The inept Duc du Maine was shorn of all but token influence upon the education of the boy king; the Duke of Orleans received full command over the military; and the Regent was thus to be, during the eight years' minority of Louis XV, the sole depository of royal authority.

2

But the most striking figure of the Regency was one neither King nor Parlement could foresee. John Law of Lauriston was a Scotchman, born in Edinburgh, three years before the Duke himself, in 1671. The French called him "Jean Lass." This extraordinary man was tall and handsome, with easy manners. He was moreover dashing and self-confident, a man of many feminine conquests. During his early twenties he had been obliged to flee from England after killing his antagonist, Beau Wilson, in a duel over a love intrigue. For years he had wandered about the Continent, studying the intricacies of banking, particularly in prosperous Amsterdam, and gaining his living by nerve and mathematical acumen at the gaming table. He spent, too, with a gambler's prodigality. In 1708, during the hard years of war, he had made the acquaintance of the pleasure-loving Duke of Orleans at Paris. But Louis XIV, solemn and conservative, would have none of Law's unorthodox financial wizardry. He was, besides, a foreigner and a despised Huguenot. Now at last in the autumn of 1715, with his old friend in power as Regent, John Law again sought out France as a promising field of activity.

CHAPTER V

The immediate problem before the harassed country was the immense debt left by Louis XIV. France owed 2 billion, 400 million livres. The annual gross receipts amounted to some 165 million of which not more than 70 actually reached the Treasury because of the vicious system of tax farming. Each collector took his "cut" and found it therefore to his interest to squeeze out of the oppressed public as much as possible. Interest and current expenses required, in round numbers, 150 million. Thus there was a deficit of about 80 million livres annually. The Regent, well-intentioned, was anxious for financial reform. He rejected Saint-Simon's proposals for bankruptcy. Who more fitted, in the opinion of the Duke of Orleans, to work the necessary miracle than this gay, intelligent Scotchman, so like himself in age and voluptuous tastes, so familiar with all the abstruse complexities of banking, so clever at finding his way through mazes of figures—John Law?

Law's first proposal was sound. He urged the establishment of a bank. On May 2, 1716, such an institution was authorized at Paris under his management. It was capitalized at 6 million livres and all its functions were strictly and judiciously regulated. This Banque Générale, as it was called, soon proved its worth. In the face of a currency which had been capriciously subjected to more than twenty up-and-down modifications within fifteen years, Law's new bank notes remained stable and soon became a preferred medium of exchange. Manufactures, commerce, business in general, began to boom.

In December, 1718, Law's bank was changed from a private to a public enterprise. Under proper conditions, this might have been a source of added strength. But to tie his successful bank to the uncertain policies of the debt-ridden and decrepit Regency was a fatal error. Bills were now no longer issued in accordance with the business needs of the country; they were poured out at the whim of ignorant and unscrupulous rulers.

John Law had already floated a new scheme. It was the organization of a "Company of the West" in August, 1717, to develop the great Louisiana territory which stretched vaguely through all the unknown heart of the rich North-American continent. The following year New Orleans was founded and named in honor of the Regent. This city of an ultimately brilliant future was for long merely a collection of wretched huts in the midst of a damp, low, malaria-infested country. To populate the distant colony, the King's archers impressed young men and women at random, emptied prisons or asylums, and deported girls of whom the Manon of Abbé Prévost's novel and of opera fame is but the idealized type. This operation, naturally, was not overly successful. Many of those thus carried away by force in carts or marched in chains along the highways fled at the first opportunity before taking ship. Some were shot as they tried to escape. Relatives and friends in many instances led revolts against the hated archers who were indiscriminately paid so much a head for whoever was brought in. It was one more of the hated tyrannies of the Old Régime.

Law's new creation, expanded to the Company of the Indies, was soon popularly called the "Mississippi Company." Shares were issued to the value of 500 francs each, forming a total of 100 million livres. Next the privilege of coinage was granted to the company. Then it took over the profitable operation of collecting the taxes. Finally it offered to assume and refund the national debt. More shares were put out to the amount of a billion and a half livres. The road to speculation was open.

A few squares east of the Central Markets of Paris, in a quarter teeming with life, is a short, narrow street with the resounding name of the Rue Quincampoix. In the absence of a modern stock exchange, the activities of the get-rich-quick centered here, entirely unregulated. Throngs from all classes of society squeezed their way in, noblemen and grand ladies, bourgeois, peasants, market women, valets, and lackeys. The lower classes generally entered "the Street," as it was called, from the northern end by the Rue-aux-Ours; aristocrats or the newly-rich descended from their carriages two blocks south in the Rue Aubry-le-Boucher. Rents for tiny stalls, cellars, space in coffee houses or on roof tops, soared. In the fever of speculation, no story seems incredible. A hunchback is said to have collected fees for the use of his hump as a desk for recording the hurried transactions! People were trampled to death in the milling, sweating crowds. Residents of the area complained that they could not sleep because of the noisy cries which went on for twenty-four hours around the clock. The government then set up grilled barriers and posted guards at each end of the street to close it down and prevent entrance at night. Servants, who had been sent to sell their masters' shares, found the price gone higher within minutes and slyly pocketed the difference. One lackey waited two days before making the required sale and thus enriched himself too.

In November of 1719, the price of shares, from their original 500 francs, reached 10,000. They soon rose further to 12,000, 15,000, and even on January 5, 1720, to 18,000. For those who had come in at the beginning, this was nearly 4,000 per cent profit—on paper. The modern term "millionaire" dates from these hectic days.

The population of Paris increased rapidly with the rush of eager speculators from the provinces or foreign countries. An estimate more conservative than some puts the number of newcomers at 300,000, which still appears a hardly credible figure in proportion to the city's total population of less than a million! Naturally there was an acute housing shortage. Rents mounted to unheard-of heights. Prices of everything, necessities and luxuries, climbed with this flood of easy money. As always, the needy suffered. Various kinds of cloth sold for twenty-five, thirty, and forty-two livres a yard; cabs rented for as much as forty livres a day, three livres an hour. In terms of normal purchasing power, it is probably no exaggeration to liken the eighteenth-century livre to the dollar of our own times. Bread brought four and five cents a pound although total daily wages were still measured in *sous*. Yet the workingman, eating a pound and a half a day as almost his sole food, considered his bread very literally to be "the staff of life."

Under the mirage of something for nothing, corruption honeycombed all classes of society. Easy come, easy go. Blatant luxury and wild spending became the rage of the hour. Robbery and murder were rampant, unprevented by the customary penalty of savage torture or the terrible breaking on the wheel in the presence of morbid sightseers. Those who were shrewd among the speculators cannily transferred their quick winnings into land, gold, or diamonds, seeking hard and permanent values, in spite of laws which sought vainly to prevent this natural tendency. The over-greedy and the naïve stayed in the venture till the end and lost everything with the terrific crash when the Mississippi Company became at last the "Mississippi Bubble," and burst. As what had gone up, finally came down, it swept all before it, mingling every class of society in a common *débâcle*. The unfortunate John Law was nearly torn to pieces in the streets by a rabid populace. With the permission of the friendly Regent, he fled into exile abroad, arriving at Brussels in late December of 1720.

3

That Law had not been dishonest and had himself, from beginning to end, been a firm believer in his "System," as it was called, is shown by his having made no protective foreign investments of his winnings. Of the millions in wealth which he had brought into France on his arrival in 1715, he took only a few hundred livres with him on his departure, and died poor in Venice nine years later. John Law had been in some respects a financial genius, but an unregulated one. He had inaugurated the use of paper money and credit. He had forecast some successful characteristics of the modern age, and the dangerous ones also. Both wild inflation and deflation tormented this brief span of years known as the Regency. Unwittingly, Law had given a further downward push to the France which Louis XIV had ruined. Financially and morally, he left the country even worse than he had found it. In many ways the Regency set the tone for the rest of the eighteenth century.

Yet there had been compensations. If the aristocracy lost in reputation and influence, showing itself fully as avid for lucre as the most arrant bourgeois, industry and trade did boom; new classes of society threw their energy and business acumen into the fray, and began to demand for themselves a share in the national prosperity.

The Regent had a mind in many ways keen and brilliant. Completely indifferent in religion, he for that very reason inclined toward a return to the Edict of Nantes and a consequent toleration of the hated Huguenots. He would have liked to emulate the reputation of Henry IV, the "good" father of his people. He rejected proposals for out-and-out bankruptcy and hoped vainly for successful financial reforms. Unfortunately, he had no persistence to carry these measures through to fruition or to resist hostile advice. He succumbed to the lure of Law's facile optimism. His notorious daily debaucheries weakened both his prestige and his physical stamina. It is said he rarely, if ever, went to bed sober. The eight years of the Regency have become the synonym for corrupt morals, irreligion, financial turmoil, and a mad reaction against the boring, if superficial, decorum of the last decades of Louis XIV. If, as La

Rochefoucauld had said in his famous *Maxims*, "hypocrisy is the homage which vice renders to virtue," the change from one age to the next was more apparent than profound. In open and shameless defiance of convention it was nevertheless a shocking change.

The Regency ended suddenly with the death of the Duke of Orleans on December 2, 1723, at forty-nine. In the presence only of his latest mistress, Madame de Falary, he fell back in his chair, rigid, and slipped heavily to the floor. In response to Madame de Falary's frantic search for help, doctors at length rushed in. The sovereign remedy of the time, bleeding, proved of no avail. At seven in the evening, the Regent was dead, of apoplexy, without regaining consciousness or uttering a word. Technically, during the last few months since the death of Cardinal Dubois, he had acted only in the capacity of Prime Minister. Louis XV, crowned at Reims in October, 1722, and declared of age at thirteen the February following, was now officially King of France.

4

The Duke of Bourbon, "Monsieur le Duc," as he was called, offered himself as Prime Minister immediately upon the death of the Regent, and on the advice of the King's influential preceptor, Abbé Fleury, former Bishop of Fréjus, was accepted. Bourbon was then thirty-one. Along with his ambitious mistress, Madame de Prie, he ruled for three years, until 1726, completely unintelligent and inept.

The most important act of the new Prime Minister was no doubt his arrangement for the King's marriage. The Regent, in 1721, had brought to Paris as Louis XV's future wife the three-year-old Infanta of Spain. Bourbon, however, had no desire to continue this policy of his predecessor. He urged the dangers of the long delay until the child Infanta became of age. If the King should chance to die without an heir, a new successor would probably at once remove Bourbon from power. Moreover, he and Madame de Prie hoped to maintain their influence upon the youthful Louis through a wife of their own choosing, one who would be appropriately grateful to them for her elevation. The Infanta was therefore sent back with little ceremony to Spain and this neighboring, jealous ally was humiliatingly affronted.

After long search among the eligible princesses of Europe, choice fell in a most unexpected quarter. Maria Leszczinska, the pious but rather homely daughter of the poverty-stricken ex-King of Poland, Stanislas Leszczinski, was then living with her father in a dilapidated château in Alsace. When the letter came bearing the incredible offer of marriage to the greatest monarch of Europe, Stanislas gathered his wife and daughter together and called upon them to fall upon their knees in a prayer of thanksgiving.

"Ah, father!" exclaimed Maria, "have you been called back to be King of Poland?"

"No, Heaven has been even kinder to us," replied Stanislas, "you are Queen of France!"

In spite of her many bourgeois virtues, poor Maria Leszczinska was to be a most unhappy and unqueenly queen. Probably no one could have been less fitted to guide or dominate the self-willed, but irresponsible King than she. The marriage was celebrated, however, with royal pomp at Fontainebleau in early September, 1725. Louis was still only fifteen years of age.

At the same time, the lawyer Marais noted in a contemporary letter: "The public misery continues to be very great; bread sells for eight *sous* a pound, and is not fit to eat!"

Fleury, while not unwilling for Bourbon to remain as Prime Minister, contrived always to be present at consultations between the King and the Duke. The latter was naturally irked at this supervision and resented the preceptor's great influence. When Bourbon finally succeeded in holding a conference to which Fleury was not invited, the aged priest withdrew from the Court and sent a letter of farewell to the King in explanation. Just as the Abbé had expected, Louis at once forced the Duke of Bourbon to recall Fleury. On June 11, 1726, in the middle of the afternoon, the King left, as usual, for the one amusement of which he was passionately fond, the chase. To the Duke of Bourbon, who had been invited to spend the night with the royal party at Rambouillet, he remarked with seeming casualness: "Don't keep me waiting for supper." After he had gone, a *lettre de cachet* informed the astonished Duke: "I command you, on pain of disobedience, to repair to Chantilly, and to remain there until further orders." It was signed in accordance with the simple autocratic forms: "Louis." With this exile to his château twenty-five miles north of Paris, Bourbon's rule came to a sudden end.

Fleury, at seventy-three, had triumphed. He was to govern France, in spite of his great age, for nearly seventeen years until his death in 1743 as a feeble old man of ninety.

With his customary prudence, Fleury did not assume the formal title of Prime Minister. Instead he encouraged Louis XV in the fiction that the young King, like his famous predecessor, would himself rule. Within two months, however, Fleury saw to it that he was named cardinal and the prestige of his red robe and hat, as well as his own dogged will for dominance, insured him the unquestioned authority over the other ministers which he wished.

Fleury was no Richelieu or Mazarin. Yet he was honest and economical. He sought, without always attaining it, peace. With the natural caution and love of tranquillity of his great age, he endeavored to avoid rash military adventures. Voltaire judges him with the disillusioned severity of a close contemporary. He remarks ironically that Fleury, "incapable of being an office clerk," was nevertheless "able to govern the state!" At a time lacking in great political leaders, Fleury did at least outshine his sorry rivals. With his desire for a quiet and orderly administration, he checked such corruption as he could. On the whole, the condition of the people improved slightly during his long rule in spite of the unhappy wars of the Polish and Austrian successions into which he weakly allowed himself to be drawn. During his last years, as great age and feebleness weighed heavily upon him, his grasp of government little by little relaxed while he yet stubbornly refused to yield his place to a successor. The hard-headed lawyer, Barbier, comments in his *Journal* that the Cardinal had lived "two years too long for the reputation of his ministry." In spite of a good supply of wheat, he was unable, with the senseless restrictions then in force on trade from province to province, to secure adequate distribution. Hunger continued to torment the country and impaired what little of Fleury's popularity remained.

5

On January 29, 1743, the aged Fleury finally tottered into death. Louis, then thirty-three, decided not to choose a successor to the Cardinal, but to govern directly himself. Of such a course, however, the young King was completely incapable. It is true he was not

FONTENELLE

Portrait by Aved.

MONTESQUIEU'S CHÂTEAU OF LA BRÈDE, NEAR BORDEAUX

See page 98.

MONTESQUIEU'S AUTOGRAPH LETTER

Supporting the candidacy of J.-J. Bel to membership in the Academy of Bordeaux (June 10, 1736).

MONTESQUIEU

Portrait attributed to J.-B. Lemoyne. See page 126.

To the Friends of Literature in North-America.

BOSTON, *October* 12, 1772.

P R O P O S A L S

For Re-Printing by Subfcription,

An *American* Edition of the fearned M. DE SECONDAT, Baron de MONTESQUIEU's celebrated

Spirit of Laws,

[Which ought to be in EVERY MAN's Hands.]

Tranflated from the French Original, and which has been tranflated and publifhed in moft of the civilized Nations of EUROPE.

To which will be prefixt, a larger Account of the Life and Writings of the AUTHOR, than is in the European Editions.

Of this WORK the Monthly Reviewers publifhed a very juft, though extenfive Character, in *July*, 1749, of which the following is an Abftract. " The Title of the Work fufficiently denotes the defign of it,---the Author affures us, it coft him 20 Years labor, and hopes it will be judg'd by its Merit, in the Complex, and not be partially condemned for a few Errors, unavoidable in fuch a length of complicated difquifitions." The whole Matter is divided into thirty-one Books, fub-divided into Chapters. The following Table of the Titles of the Books, will give a general Idea of the Performance.

Book.
1. Of laws in general.
2. Of laws directly derived from the nature of government.
3. Of the principles of the three kinds of government.
4. That the laws of education ought to be relative to the principles of government.
5. That the laws given by the legiflator ought to be relative to the principle of government.
6. Confequences of the principles of different governments with refpect to the fimplicity of civil and criminal laws, the form of judgments, and the inflicting of punifh-ments.
7. Confequences of the different principles of the three go-vernments, with refpect to fumptuary laws, luxury, and the condition of women.
8. Of the corruption of the principles of the three govern-ments.
9. Of laws in the relation they bear to a defenfive force.
10. Of laws in the relation they bear to offenfive force.
11. Of the laws that form political liberty, with regard to the conftitution.
12. Of the laws that form political liberty, with regard to the fubject.
13. Of the relation which the levying of taxes, and the great-nefs of the public revenues have to liberty.
14. Of laws as relative to the nature of the climate.
15. In what manner the laws of civil flavery are relative to the nature of the climate.
16. How the laws of domeftic flavery have a relation to the nature of the climate.

Book.
17. How the laws of political fervitude have relation to the nature of the climate.
18. Of laws in the relation they bear to the nature of the foil.
19. Of laws in relation to the principles which form the ge-neral fpirit, the morals, and cuftoms of a nation.
20. Of the laws in relation to commerce, confidered in its nature and diftinctions.
21. Of laws relative to commerce, confidered in the revolu-tions it has met with in the world.
22. Of laws in relation to the ufe of money.
23. Of laws in relation they bear to the number of inhabi-tants.
24. Of laws as relative to religion, confider'd in itfelf, and its doctrins.
25. Of laws as relative to the eftablifhment of religion, and its external polity.
26. Of laws as relative to the order of things, on which they determine.
27. Of the origin and revolutions of the Roman laws on fuc-ceffions.
28. Of the origin and revolutions of the civil laws on fuc-ceffions.
29. Of the manner of compofing laws.
30. Theory of the feudal laws among the Franks, in the rela-tion they bear to the eftablifhment of the monarchy.
31. Theory of the feudal laws among the Franks, in the rela-tion they bear to the revolutions of their monarchy.

THAT the Reader may have fome view of the character of this illuftrious Author, the following paragraph is taken from his Elogik, Monfieur DE ALEMBERT, who fays, " That which ought to render this Author dear to all nations, that which would ferve to cover far more and greater faults than are in (the Spirit of Laws) is that fpirit of *patriotifm* which actuated it. The love of the public good, a defire of feeing men happy, difcovers itfelf in every part of it ; and had it no other merit but this, which is fo rare and fo valuable, it would be worthy on this account alone, to be read by na-tions and Kings. We already perceive, by happy experience, that the fruits of this work are not confined to ufelefs fenti-ments in the minds of its readers. Though Monfieur de Montefquieu furvived the publication of the Spirit of Laws, but a fhort time, he had the fatisfaction, in fome meafure to forefee thofe effects which it already begins to produce amongft us, namely, the *natural love of Frenchmen* for their country turned towards its *true object* : that tafte for commerce, for agricul-ture, and for ufeful arts, which infenfibly fpreads itfelf in our nation ; and that *general knowledge* of the *principles* of *govern-ment*, which renders people more attached to *that* which *they ought to love.*

C O N D I T I O N S.

I. The celebrated Spirit of Laws is to be printed in two hand-fome Octavo Volumes, on a fine Paper, and a neat Type, of which thefe Propofals are a Specimen : And a pecu-liar attention will be paid to the correctnefs of the Matter.

II. Each Volume will contain about 400 Pages.

III. The Price of the two Volumes to Subfcribers, will be *Ten Shillings* and *eight Pence* Lawful Money, fewed in blue Boards,---although the Englifh Edition is fold at *Twenty Shillings.*

IV. Thofe that fubfcribe for *Six* will be allow'd *One* gratis.

V. As foon as the Names and refidence of 500 Subfcribers are collected, the Work will be immediately put to the Prefs, and completed with all expedition.

VI. No Money expected till the delivery of the firft Volume, ----at *Five Shillings* and 4d.

VII. If any of the Subfcribers fhould choofe them bound and lettered, they are defired to fignify it at the Time of fub-fcribing, and the Publifher will have them done in the neateft Manner,---only adding *One Shilling* to the Price of each Volume.

VII. The Names of the Subfcribers will be printed in the fe-cond Volume.

SUBSCRIPTION will be gratefully received by JOHN BOYLES, the Publifher, next Door to the Three Doves in Marlboro'-Street : EDES and GILL, Printers in Queen-Street : and HENRY KNOX, Bookfeller, Cornhill, BOSTON. And by moft Printers and Bookfellers in *America.*

Proposal to publish Montesquieu's *Spirit of Laws* in America, October 12, 1772. See page 142.

unintelligent. He was far from deficient in penetration or political judgment. Some have said he had basically a better mind than his predecessor, Louis XIV, but, unlike his awe-inspiring great-grandfather, Louis XV had no will to rule. The details of administration bored him to extinction. Indifferently, he signed documents without reading them. He permitted the several members of his ministry to make their own decisions, often contrary to each other. His government, observed the Marquis d'Argenson, was a "chaos" of conflicting policies. The one thing which the King insisted on controlling was his daily sport of the chase. He meticulously laid out as much as a year in advance the employment of his numerous packs of hunting dogs!

The King had one royal quality, physical courage. As the useless War of the Austrian Succession dragged on, Louis XV resolved to appear in person at the front and inspire his troops to combat. "I have a strong desire," he wrote on July 24, 1743, "to familiarize myself with the trade in which my forefathers have been proficient." Three weeks later, he said: "I cannot look on while our cities are captured and our frontiers ravaged."

But this tour of the armies, urged on by the ambitious reigning mistress, Madame de Châteauroux, was more royal than military. In the spring of 1744, the King proceeded, followed at a day's distance by the impressive train of the favorite and other ladies of the Court, all attended by the luxury to which they were accustomed. It is proof of changing public opinion that this royal camp-follower, who would have excited hardly a ripple of surprise under Louis XIV, now aroused wide condemnation. Monarchy was no longer too sacred for criticism. All letters from the army were ransacked and censored to prevent scurrilous remarks on Madame de Châteauroux from getting back to Paris. Naturally this was without avail, for the news traveled nevertheless by word of mouth.

When the King suddenly fell ill at Metz, there was wide-spread alarm, accompanied by the feeling, which Louis himself shared, that Heaven's judgment was upon him. Filled with fear and remorse, he vowed reform and dismissed Madame de Châteauroux. As his health quickly returned, prayers for his recovery became prayers of rejoicing. Paris gleamed with festive lights, fireworks pierced the blackness of the sky, broke, and fell in gay clusters, *Te Deums* were sung solemnly in the cathedrals, bread was given in the streets to the hungry, wine ran freely. Louis was hailed as "the well beloved," and the title remained in spite of the little he had done, or would do, to earn it. Needless to say, the King who, when sick, had so earnestly promised reform, soon backslid, like many another human, once health was restored. He recalled Madame de Châteauroux to favor. But death almost immediately removed her from the Court at only twenty-seven. She was, however, to have many successors.

The following year, Louis again joined the armies campaigning in the Low Countries. It was at Fontenoy, near the Belgian frontier, that a famous battle was fought on May 11, 1745, against the allied armies of the English and Dutch. The commander of the French forces, Maurice de Saxe, was a brilliant foreign soldier who had taken service under Louis XV. In spite of serious illness and a body so swollen with dropsy that he had to be carried groaningly from point to point in a litter, Maurice out-generaled the opposing leaders headed by the Duke of Cumberland, and by mid-afternoon had won the stubbornly-contested battle.

A famous incident of the day has been often recounted. The English troops marched forward from the Barry wood, converging toward Fontenoy. At fifty yards from the French lines, they halted smartly at command. The English officers gracefully doffed their hats in salute. The French officers did likewise. Lord Hay called out: "Gentlemen of the French Guards, you fire first." Count d'Auteroche replied: "Give the order to fire yourselves; we never begin!" Saluting again, the two officers turned sharply and rejoined their respective ranks. In a fierce blast, the rolling fire of the English rang out, as the trained battalions discharged and loaded their guns in relays. The French lost more than six hundred men, it is said, killed or wounded, in these murderous volleys and were thrown for a time into great disorder. Misplaced Gallic chivalry? Or were these merely the well-tried tactics of Marshal de Saxe, who had little confidence in the uncertain muzzle-loaders of the time and believed that the side which was first drawn into shooting, instead of relying upon a resistless charge with cold steel, was most likely to lose the engagement? There is still dispute.

The King himself, who had been unmoved under occasional fire and had shared the risk of near-defeat, now received from the public his meed of enthusiastic acclaim. He had wisely maintained confidence in Maurice's abilities in spite of the murmurs of his officers, jealous of their general's fame or fearful of the effects of his illness. "When I chose you to command my army," said Louis firmly, "I intended that you should be obeyed by every one, and I myself will be the first to set the example."

In a courtier's poem on the battle of Fontenoy, Voltaire sang without stint the praises of the King and the prowess of the French nobility.

"How great are the French when guided by their master!" he exclaimed rapturously. The Marquis d'Argenson, present at the battle as a civilian Minister of Foreign Affairs, shuddered at the "frightful butchery," honestly admitted that he felt faint, and trembled at the roar of the cannon. Voltaire himself, when in less epic and more realistic mood, fully shared his friend's horror of war as it actually was.

This day of victory at Fontenoy was no doubt the high-water mark of glory for Louis XV. It was short-lived. Capable only of a brief burst of energy and the mere appearance of action, the King soon glided back into the old ways. Since he himself had so little urge to govern, power was shortly grasped by a new mistress.

Jeanne-Antoinette Poisson, shortly to be known as Madame de Pompadour, was born in 1721. She was therefore in 1745 twenty-four years old and at the height of her alluring beauty. Married to Monsieur d'Etioles, the nephew of a rich farmer-general of the taxes, this young woman, when she entered the government by the back door, so to speak, represented the rising prestige of the financial circles of the kingdom. For nearly twenty years, she was to be the center of court intrigue and influence. Too often the fate of France was to be decided in a palace boudoir.

Loveless marriages of convenience, the traditions of power without responsibility, had sapped any pretense of morals on the part of King and nobility. The flaunting vice of the Regency had set the tone for the rest of the country. Absolutism without the check of public opinion was too great a temptation for weak human nature. To become the royal mistress was a distinction as openly sought after as any title at Versailles. So it was no matter for remark that Mademoiselle Poisson had been deliberately trained in all the charms and social graces by which it was hoped she would play a great role. The one count against her among the haughty aristocracy was that she was a mere bourgeoise in origin, and therefore in their opinion by no stretch of the imagination eligible for the high position she aspired to occupy.

Dressed as a picture-book huntress in blue and riding in a pink carriage, or, on another day, reversing the colors to a costume of rose and a phaeton of deep azure, this new beauty easily drew the eye of the King on his way to the chase. He was soon enraptured. Two months after the death of Madame de Châteauroux, her successor was installed at Court in February, 1745. She was granted the title of Marquise de Pompadour and the following autumn was presented officially to the King and Queen. The latter, schooled in adversity, was obliged to treat her with ceremonious politeness and even, ten years later, to accept her as Lady-in-Waiting.

Madame de Pompadour, though an accomplished musician, a graceful actress in the little theaters of the Court, a patron of the arts and of literature, quite naturally showed no hint of greatness in her policy, domestic or foreign. Her chief thought, amid the shifting quicksands of the royal circle, was to retain power. Men and women openly sought her smile of favor, but her externally gracious rule, seconded as it was by inefficient ministers, could only drag the government of Louis XV still lower.

In 1749, the Marquis d'Argenson, no longer in the Cabinet, wrote in his *Memoirs:* "The King works a good deal less than in my time, and every day his taste for work appears to diminish. The meetings of the Councils are shorter; the work of the ministers still more so. In a word, nothing is done, nothing is finished." The next year, the same author remarked that "a desire for a republican form of government is winning the support of thoughtful people every day." Whatever exaggeration there may have been in this opinion of a caustic critic, it is a fact that ugly riots in the streets so alarmed the King that he dared not take the direct route across Paris, on his way to Compiègne, for fear of attack. His prudent, roundabout course skirting the turbulent city was realistically termed "the road of revolt." In 1754, revolution seemed already in the air, and many were surprised that it did not break out at once. "After us the deluge," exclaimed Madame de Pompadour cynically in 1757 after the defeat of the French by Frederick the Great at Rossbach. The year following appears this startling sentence by Abbé de Mably: "Choose between revolution and slavery; there is no middle course."

It is true these bold words, buried in the mass of the author's undistinguished prose, were not actually published until the more appropriate days of 1789. Indifferent to the black future, the King is said to have observed: "This will last through my time; let my successor make out as best he can."

The Treaty of Aix-la-Chapelle, which brought the War of the Austrian Succession to an end in 1748, had been unpopular because of diplomatic set-backs. "Stupid as the peace," was the contemptuous cry in the streets of Paris.

6

Late in the afternoon of Wednesday, January 5, 1757, the King was descending one of the smaller staircases in the château of Versailles to get into his carriage in the Marble Courtyard and return to the nearby Trianon Palace. There were few people present and, in the early dusk of a winter evening, few torches to furnish light. As he paused a moment to chat with the Duke of Richelieu, a tall man in black suddenly pushed his way past a guard, laid his hand on the King's shoulder and struck him in the right side. As Louis instinctively touched his hand to the spot, he felt the blood of a stab wound and cried out: "I am assassinated." Pointing out his attacker, he added: "That's the man. Arrest him, but don't do him injury." The King feared a poisoned dagger, but the wound, made with a light penknife, proved merely superficial and not dangerous. The assassin, a man named Damiens, seems to have been excited by the hostile measures taken against Jansenism, not by political motives. He was horribly tortured and slowly put to death by being torn asunder by horses while people watched curiously from streets and windows.

In 1763, the Seven Years' War came to an end with the Treaty of Paris. Again France lost ground in the European and world struggle. Her colonies in Canada fell definitely to the English. The following year the Jesuits in France were suppressed. The province of Lorraine was annexed in 1766 with the death of the Queen's father, Stanislas, and two years later the island of Corsica was bought from Genoa. By this last event it came about that a child born in 1769 grew up on French, not Italian soil and thereby changed the course of history. The infant boy was destined to become famous as Napoleon I.

Meanwhile, Madame de Pompadour, prematurely exhausted by the years of long struggle to retain her uncertain position, died in 1764 at forty-three. She was soon succeeded by Madame du Barry, of even more plebeian origin and tarnished past. Without the distinction which surrounded Madame de Pompadour and without her ambition to play a role in government, she was nevertheless forced to intervene in order to maintain her footing in the midst of court intrigue. "Madame la Comtesse du Barry" was to perish miserably under the guillotine in the Terror of '93.

In 1770, a fifteen-year-old girl, full of life and gaiety, appeared in the midst of the sordid court. She was Marie-Antoinette, the child wife of the lumbering youth for whom destiny reserved the sorry jest of becoming Louis XVI. Marie-Antoinette turned a cold shoulder toward Madame du Barry and remained reserved with the old King in spite of his obvious pleasure in her carefree vivacity. The further decline in dignity on the part of Louis XV, his nameless amours of the so-called Parc-aux-Cerfs, cast still darker shadows over the King's last years. Only the firmer and more capable ministry of the Duc de Choiseul from 1758 to 1770 and his efforts to strengthen the army and the navy raised France from the reverses of the Seven Years' War. It was during these years that the naval power and tactics were developed which bore important fruit against England during the following decade and vitally aided the young American colonies in their successful battle for independence.

A long struggle between King and Parlement culminated in the suppression of the latter in 1771. It had been a center of Jansenist and political resistance, but unfortunately was inspired by no higher principle than conservatism and a desire to protect its own prerogatives. It had not possessed the vision to raise the issue to the plane of popular freedom and liberation of the nation from a blind and outworn absolutism.

Louis XV's eldest son, the first Dauphin, who had aroused forlorn hopes of a better reign than his decadent father, died in 1765; the unhappy Queen, Maria Leszczinska, three years later. At length, on May 10, 1774, the King also died suddenly after a short illness from that scourge of the Old Régime, smallpox, which was still widespread in spite of the ardent efforts of Voltaire and other forward-looking thinkers in favor of inoculation. With mingled contempt and fear of contagion, people hurried the royal corpse unceremoniously off to burial.

Louis XV had rendered his own semi-frank judgment on his unfortunate reign. In his will, we read: "I have ruled and administered badly, which comes from my lack of talent and the way in which my efforts have been ill seconded." In fact, he had hardly made even an effort to assume his grave responsibilities. But what could have been expected from a king orphaned at three, set on the throne at five, and flatteringly told by an obsequious preceptor that he alone was the master of his people?

A society rises or falls with its leaders. The crowning weakness of the French government in the eighteenth century was the lack of any constitutional method by which a feeble or inefficient king could be replaced. The unhappy country must play out its role to the tragic end. Only revolution, it seemed, could bring about the inevitable change. After the death of Louis XV, the Old Régime was to endure but fifteen troubled years more.

A caustic epitaph went the popular rounds, as a bitter wag exclaimed:

> Here lies Louis the Fifteenth,
> Second of the name of «Well Beloved»:
> God preserve us from the Third!

CHAPTER VI

MONTESQUIEU AND THE SATIRICAL
PERSIAN LETTERS

I

SOME TEN OR TWELVE MILES SOUTH OF THE BUSY PORT OF Bordeaux rise the crenelated towers and thick walls of the half-medieval château of La Brède. Its weathered gray mass dominates the smiling green countryside. Even now the wide protective moat of a former day remains filled with water which turns into sudden rippling circles as the voracious carp break the smooth surface and greedily gulp the bits of bread tossed down to them by the idling tourist. Although humanity has since eaten copiously of the dangerous Tree of Knowledge and, to its misfortune perhaps, far outgrown the old castle's primitive system of defense, the ancient atmosphere of times past lingers on. Only on foot can traveler or proprietor make his way across the broad moat to the gravel-covered inner court, passing over a succession of light bridges too frail and narrow for even the smallest vehicle. Something of the remoteness and suspicion of the turbulent Middle Ages emanates still from these dark and well-worn stones, since within their confines the valued books and manuscripts of their illustrious eighteenth-century owner, too jealously guarded by his descendants, have, until the recent sale of some of them, been kept from all but a very few modern scholars. Yet the world at large, as well as the former master of La Brède, could only gain by fuller knowledge of his life and thought.

Here, on the 18th of January in 1689, a full hundred years before the outbreak of the French Revolution, was born an infant whom his parents named Charles-Louis de Secondat. He was destined to become famous one day as Baron of La Brède and of Montesquieu. So it happened that the first great artisan of change and reform in France during the eighteenth century was a member of the ruling aristocracy. The child was in fact to grow into no hidebound partisan of prejudice and reaction. Instead, he developed the rare independence to look upon the grave shortcomings of his age with keen eyes and had the courage to speak his mind with startling frankness.

In harmony with a widespread tradition of the time, symbolic of the common human bond between rich and poor, the newborn baby, in spite of all his imposing inheritance of nobility, was held over the baptismal font in the humble arms of a chance beggar who also bore the name of Charles. Following custom also, the boy was early put out to nurse and passed his first years among peasants in the adjoining village of La Brède. When his parents took him back home again, he had become almost a peasant himself with dirty face and running nose. But, with the unlearning of these crudities, his natural democracy remained.

Moreover, in spite of the strong pull of many years in Paris, boy and man clung with stubborn affection to the marked provincial accent of his Gascon speech. Indeed, as a prosperous country gentleman, he loved to clump about his wide acres in rough costume and heavy wooden sabots, carrying on his shoulder a long vine-prop instead of swinging an aristocratic cane in his sun-tanned fingers. He often paused to chat freely with his peasant workmen in their salty rustic dialect and appeared hardly distinguishable from a peasant himself to visiting strangers who used to ask him patronizingly where they could find the great Montesquieu.

A deep instinct rooted him firmly to his native soil amid the fruitful sunny vineyards of southwest France. While attending the royal court at Versailles or frequenting Paris salons, he was generally content to look on from one side in aloof silence, a willing provincial, indifferent to bystanders who whispered to each other in half-contemptuous amusement: "Monsieur de Montesquieu is composing his book." Among intimate circles of his friends, however, he was urbane and genial, a well-loved and respected figure.

At seven the boy lost his mother. Four years later, his father sent him far away to the college of the Oratorians at Juilly, twenty miles northeast of Paris. It was a sharp change in climate and surroundings for the young native of the warm south.

Less narrow, intense, and austere than the somber Jansenists, more progressive for the time than the influential, supple Jesuits, the Oratorians gave their due place to modern languages as well as to the well-worn classics of the ancient world. They even made bold to carry on their classroom teaching in French rather than in the traditional Latin of other schools. With a true forward-looking spirit, they taught history, particularly that of France, then so generally neglected or taken for granted. They also introduced the first timid beginnings of the natural sciences, which elsewhere had not yet entered the curriculum. Discipline among the Oratorians was firm, but kindly, and corporal punishment was rare. The young boy spent five important years at Juilly, probably happily enough, from 1700, when he was eleven, to 1705, when he was sixteen. His general education had been good and astonishingly liberal for the age.

Back in his native Bordeaux, the eager youth plunged into the study of law. This was natural, for he belonged by inheritance more to the parliamentary Nobility of the Robe than to the military aristocracy of the Sword, as the expressive phrases went. We know little or nothing, however, of the details of these legal studies. Montesquieu himself later commented on them scornfully: "When I left college, they put law books into my hands; I tried to discover the spirit behind them; I worked, but accomplished nothing worth while."

In 1708, on receipt of his law degree, he was admitted to practice before the august Parlement of Bordeaux, not a legislative body, as English-speaking people might think, but one of the higher regional courts of the Old Régime. Now events came crowding rapidly one after another: five years more of study in Paris, the death of his father at the time of the son's second return to Bordeaux in 1713, admission as an actual counselor or judge of Parlement the year following, a marriage of convenience, not of love, and strangely enough to a Protestant, next the honor of election to the Academy of Bordeaux, and finally, through the death of his uncle, elevation to the post of President or Chief Justice of the Bordeaux Parlement and to the title of Montesquieu in 1716 at the early age of twenty-seven. These were decisive years.

But Montesquieu lacked enthusiasm for law as a daily profession; he had no stomach for the monotonous round of civil or criminal procedure. What he sought, as he later remarked, was the spirit behind established law, its inner meaning, its slow development, its variations from country to country, its relations to manners, customs, and institutions, its inherent justice or injustice—in short, the great basic principles of jurisprudence itself.

Montesquieu, in sum, was eager to study the philosophy of law.

He had no desire to be a practicing lawyer or to continue in the arduous role of judge. His moderate wealth, his extensive holdings in land, and his high rank in society permitted him in the end to follow his deep-rooted preferences. He was able wisely to use his fortune, and not be used by it. At length, ten years later, when already famous as a writer, he sold his post as President of the Bordeaux Parlement, a practice sanctioned by the customs of the time, and joyfully turned his back forever on what was for him only the dull slavery of day-by-day legal administration. Henceforth, he would set himself the difficult task of trying to think his way through to the very foundations on which civilized society rests.

But already, in his late twenties, he had learned to employ his leisure productively in other ways also. These were years of amateur research in the rising field of natural science. The results of his experiments were recorded in ambitious papers read before fellow-members of the Academy of Bordeaux, papers on the *Causes of the Echo*, the *Functions of the Kidneys*, the *Principles of Weight*, on the *Tides*, on *Fossil Oysters*. There was great variety in his interests. Uncertain yet of his real destiny, Montesquieu even announced a huge *Project for a Geological History of the Earth*, soliciting correspondents to send him relevant information from all over the world. But this grandiose plan came to nothing. It was not for him to become another Buffon and succeed in putting these vague dreams of natural history into numerous imposing volumes written, with the aid of an organized corps of assistants, in the grand manner.

Montesquieu did, however, observe under the microscope the striking effect of cold in contracting, and of heat in expanding, animal tissue. From these experiments he drew the significant deduction that differences in climate have a concrete physiological basis for their profound influence upon people. Later he raised this conclusion into one of his fundamental explanations of the wide divergencies noted between human character and institutions throughout the earth. Climate, he held, is actually a decisive factor in shaping law!

So, what seems at first sight only an interlude in Montesquieu's development, was not without its meaning for his later career. Although he was not destined to continue his work in the natural sciences, he would strive to apply something of their exact methods to the infinitely more complex and unpredictable field of the social sciences. He would try to study man in relation to his environment of organized society.

2

During these same formative years young Montesquieu carried, along with his scientific explorations, a quite different project up his sleeve; in a lively fictional narrative he would contrive to criticize by implication the society around him. Like many another reader, then and since, he had plunged with enthusiasm into the colorful narratives of the *Arabian Nights,* which had recently been translated for the first time into French by Antoine Galland. Montesquieu had also made a pleasant armchair voyage from his château at La Brède to the Near East with the aid of the popular *Travels in Turkey, Persia, and the Indies* by the seventeenth-century writer, Tavernier. The *Account of a Journey through Persia and the Orient* by Jean Chardin was likewise one of his favorite books, highly esteemed for its sober accuracy. Already, moreover, a certain Marana had depicted a *Spy of the Great Mogul in the Courts of the Christian Princes.* Still another minor author, Charles Dufresny, had published a feeble effort entitled *Serious and Comical Amusements of a Siamese at Paris.* It is not certain whether this book influenced Montesquieu. But, if Dufresny's writing lacked vividness, his basic idea evidently was excellent. Here was the piquant entry of a far-off exotic traveler into the midst of conventional French society. How strange everything seemed to this astonished Oriental! What an admirable opportunity for slightly veiled, entertaining, and yet, if need be, bold satire of the manners, beliefs, and institutions of contemporary France!

Inspired in greater or less degree by these and other predecessors, Montesquieu conceived the plan of bringing two fictitious Persians of his own creation to Paris. In their brief, compact, incisive letters —and in default of modern methods of rapid communication, it was still an age of leisurely and distinguished letter-writing—these foreign travelers would reveal their amazement and their implied criticism of what they saw. There would be some characterization of these Persian spokesmen; there would be a slight element of *risqué* plot in the realistic portrayal of the oriental harem and its tragic manifestations of jealousy back in the distant homeland; there would be just enough of a story to whet the appetite even of the superficial reader; and meanwhile this reader, shallow or profound as he might chance to be, would be brought, perhaps in spite of himself, face to face with the broad panorama of multiplied abuses which were slowly undermining the Old Régime.

No one knows when Montesquieu began writing his book. At the head of the first "letters" appears the date 1711. If we may take this date seriously, the obvious conclusion is that he must have been occupied with the little work for nearly ten years. However that may be, it is a fact that ideas matured slowly and deliberately in his mind. He was always one of those fortunate people who work with no pressure of haste, and his few books, like fine wines, are but the better for their long aging.

At length, in 1721, when he was in the full maturity of young manhood at thirty-two, Montesquieu published anonymously his famous *Persian Letters*. Although actually printed secretly at Amsterdam, the two small, russet-leather volumes appeared, following a frequent custom in this day of censorship, under the intentionally misleading rubric of Cologne. They were immediately snapped up by an avid reading public. Nothing quite so vivid, quite so piquant, quite so startling, had yet been seen along this line.

"Write me some more *Persian Letters*," urged Paris publishers upon their only too eager authors. So, little by little over the years, there were printed *Turkish Letters, Iroquois Letters, Peruvian Letters,* and all sorts of similar hopeful efforts to cash in on this brilliant idea of the foreign observer criticizing in original fashion a strange land. Alas! all that they lacked, these struggling writers, was that one essential, the trenchant genius of another Montesquieu. But a new literary vogue had been launched which was to endure past the middle of the century.

By a lucky stroke, Montesquieu had chosen his time well. When the *Persian Letters* burst upon the French public toward the beginning of 1721, people were still bitter over the financial crash which, just a few months before in December of the preceding year, had tumbled the paper fortunes of mad speculators by the thousands and had driven the unhappy John Law into exile and poverty. Nor had the French had time to forget the gloomy close of Louis XIV's grandiose reign in 1715. And now, six years later, the Regent, the debauched Duke of Orleans, continued his chaotic rule. The time was ripe for satire of society as it existed then in France.

And what could be more effective, interesting, and thoroughly up-to-date than an oriental setting? Right at the moment when these fictional letters appeared, the eyes of Paris and the court were fascinated, from March to July, 1721, by the colorful visit of the Ambassador of the Grand Turk who, long before the trumped-up wiles of modern advertising, seemed to have been dispatched to France by a kindly destiny expressly to create a vivid background for Montesquieu's initial work. In the first year of its publication there were ten editions of this little book, which is recognized today as the outstanding literary product of the hectic Regency.

As we read Montesquieu's rapidly-moving pages, we come, in an early chapter or "letter," upon an oft-quoted passage of apt human satire. Irked at the excessive curiosity aroused by his exotic Persian costume, one of the foreign travelers, Rica, decides at last to give it up for conventional European dress. An unexpected disillusion awaits him. He, who had just been the center of all eyes, suddenly falls into embarrassing obscurity. Nobody any longer pays the slightest attention to him. Upon what flimsy externals does man's fame often depend! But, if someone in the company happens to learn that the stranger is a Persian, Rica hears a quick hum of surprise.

"Ah! ah! Monsieur is a Persian? How extraordinary! How can one be a Persian?"

So much for the naïve hundred-percenters, French, American, or what you will, who can conceive of nobody different in nationality or customs from themselves. Montesquieu's irony hits playfully at all such unimaginative creatures fenced in by the narrow confines of town, province, or native country. No effort will they make to become citizens of the world. They have not even a wish to understand other members of the human race, diverse in so many ways, yet so alike too under their light or swarthy skin. Nevertheless, a real movement toward cosmopolitanism was characteristic of eighteenth-century French thought as of Montesquieu himself.

One whole aspect of the *Persian Letters* deals entertainingly with light social satire. There is the mad rush of people through the crooked streets of the busy Paris metropolis. Coming from their quiet Oriental life, these astonished foreign travelers find themselves continually on the go.

Strange to relate, as Montesquieu's astonished Persians report in their letters to the folks back home, "Paris is as big as Ispahan! The houses are so high that one would swear they were inhabited by astrologers." Imagine! these sky-scrapers are really six or seven of the one-storied Persian houses, each on top of the other! What traffic jams! Frenchmen run, they. fly, through their narrow, crowded, ill-paved streets. Their reckless carriages splash the unwary pedestrian with mud from head to foot—a common complaint of the day in Paris as in London. Almost as irksome, the leisurely foreigner is jostled rudely by the hurrying natives whose sharp elbows do not spare his sensitive ribs. All is relative, and the smaller Paris of that day seemed to the wandering Persians—no doubt also to Montesquieu himself coming from his tranquil southern countryseat of La Brède—a veritable New York of modern times. Our Persian sometimes becomes "as angry," he humorously observes, "as a Christian!"

Coffee-houses appear as very much *à la mode* in eighteenth-century France. Some are centers for the latest news or gossip. Others draw the enthusiasts for chess. Various type figures in the society of the times are mirrored with "oriental" wonder: the rich farmer-general of the taxes, the fashionable preacher, the accommodating father-confessor, the old warrior, who is continually boring his audience with the repeated story of his long-past campaigns. There is the perennial Don Juan, proud of his many feminine conquests. The Capuchin friar with his long beard, gray robe, and bare feet seems to the wandering Persians a most extraordinary "dervish" indeed. The well-worn joke over women's age is once again refurbished in lively dialogue. Gambling, notes the more serious of the two travelers, Usbek, is not merely a game, it is a profession. Even women play wildly for high stakes, sometimes ruining the fortunes of their husbands in the process. Luckily, our Holy Prophet, observes the Persian complacently, has forbidden wine and games of chance; he has wisely preserved his people from these Christian dangers!

The Persian Rica quotes from a letter written by a French traveler abroad. Nobles in Spain, the latter comments prudently, while the initiated reader quietly substitutes France, do not deign to work. "It is by sitting on chairs that nobility is acquired," he remarks in a piquant phrase leveled at the fashionable idleness of European aristocracy. "A great noble," says Usbek, "is a man who sees the King, speaks to his ministers, and who possesses ancestors, debts, and pensions!" In Persia, however, he writes, with human pride in the assumed perfections of his far-off homeland, the only great men are those to whom the monarch grants governmental responsibility. Here in France, continues the Persian, there are people who are great through their birth, but they are without power or real prestige.

It was true that Louis XIV in the previous century had reduced the hereditary nobility to the passive role of mere satellites about the brilliant royal sun. Montesquieu, as a noble himself, felt keenly the slight to his aristocratic order, and conscientiously yearned to see the *grands seigneurs* again play an important part in the rule of the country as they had once done in the distant Middle Ages. But the time for that had long since passed. Moreover, the nobility as a whole constituted no *élite* of vigor, intelligence, devotion, and character. There were few Fénelons, few Montesquieus, inspired by a deep sense of duty to the nation; and the boy king, Louis XV, absolute even in his weakness and futility, still barred the way.

3

These mordant comments of Rica and Usbek on aristocracy show how easily the realm of social satire merges into serious criticism of government. Many of the *Persian Letters* are occupied with this question of politics which was always one of the deepest of Montesquieu's concerns.

The author's irony plays readily on the grave shortcomings of the late ruler, Louis XIV. "He has often been heard to remark," observes Usbek slyly, "that, of all the governments in the world, he would prefer the Turkish or the rule of our august Sultan, so highly does he esteem the oriental system." So much for Montesquieu's hatred of tyranny.

In the eyes of the travelers, what a mass of contradictions the strange character of the old French king presents! He has a cabinet minister of eighteen and a mistress who is eighty! Louis XIV had indeed named the seventeen-year-old Marquis of Barbesieux Secretary of State in 1685. It was a fact also that in 1713, the ostensible date of this "Persian" letter, Madame de Maintenon, only secretly the king's wife, was seventy-eight and three years older than the aged Grand Monarch himself.

Louis XIV, continues Usbek, clings fervently to his religion, but cannot stomach those who tell him to observe it strictly. Although at Versailles he avoids the commotion of cities like Paris, and is anything but talkative, he is busy from morning till night with getting himself talked about. He likes trophies and victories, but fears a good general at the head of his troops as much as one in command of a hostile army. Never has any one been so rich, and yet at the same time weighted down with a governmental poverty such as no private individual could support without bankruptcy. He rewards the idleness of his courtiers as generously as the hard-fought campaigns of his military generals. Often he grants preferment to an obsequious noble who helps him dress or undress or who hands him a napkin at table, rather than to one who wins his battles. There are more statues in his palace gardens than citizens in a great city, remarks Usbek with piquant exaggeration.

This king is "a great magician." He makes his subjects think what he pleases. "If he has only a million crowns in his treasury and needs two, all that is necessary is to persuade people that one crown is worth two, and they believe him!" So Montesquieu attacks devaluation of the currency. "If the king has a difficult war on his hands," continues Rica, "and he is without money, he has only to put it into men's heads that a piece of paper is money, and they are immediately convinced." After the tragic fiasco of John Law's alluring financial schemes, it is easy to understand Montesquieu's prudent skepticism regarding the uncontrolled use of paper money, whose convenience everyone today admits, whose dangers, in the light of modern experience also, nobody can deny.

In a series of early letters, Montesquieu had recounted the story of a mythical people, the Troglodytes. The tale is a brief apologue, somewhat in the manner of Fénelon's *Télémaque*.

The first Troglodytes, in their Arabian home, followed their bent completely. Selfishness was their motto. "Every man for himself, and the Devil take the hindmost!" Each farmer cultivated his own field with no thought for his neighbor. If wool was scarce, the producer of wool doubled his price and profiteered without conscience. When an epidemic ravaged the country, a doctor came from the neighboring territory and skillfully cured the sick with appropriate remedies, but, once they were well again, they refused to pay. The fearful malady returned. This time no physician would hurry to their rescue. So the unscrupulous Troglodytes perished from their own wickedness. Of them all, only two good families survived.

These virtuous Troglodytes led "a happy and tranquil life." They knelt before their altars only to request "the health of their parents, union with their brothers, the affection of their wives, the love and obedience of their children." Herds were held in common. The people vied with each other in good deeds.

But, when predatory neighbors sought to invade their territory and carry off their possessions as booty, the virtuous Troglodytes rose in righteous wrath and drove the enemy out by a just exercise of force. War of self-defense, Montesquieu never failed to believe, is an unfortunate necessity of human life as it is lived.

As the nation grew in population, the inhabitants finally sought to choose a king. The old man whom they selected for his justice and virtue accepted the task most reluctantly, casting his eyes longingly back toward simpler days of freedom and independence.

The lesson is plain. The first Troglodytes were destroyed by their own unbridled evil. Their successors rose and flourished through their virtues. Society, in the long run, Montesquieu maintained, can endure only if based on at least a minimum of good conduct and mutual fair dealing. A king appears to him a regrettable essential of an all-too-human community. If he is conscientious, he assumes his grave responsibilities with a heavy heart. Like Fénelon's ideal king, he should rule, not for personal glory, as Louis XIV did, but for the welfare of his people.

From this simple apologue, we may conclude that virtue, in Montesquieu's opinion, requires no divine revelation or supernatural sanctions. It has its own *raison d'être*. Virtue is deeply rooted in the necessity of human cooperation. It is indispensable to a healthy and enduring society. Selfishness and isolation will not work for long. Virtue is alone practical. "Honesty," in Ben Franklin's homely words, "is the best policy."

Many are Montesquieu's observations in the field of politics and government. We need a business-like administration, he remarks, an ideal far from attainment under the Old Régime and still rare today. In contrast to the torture and the whole cruel penology of the time, he advocates moderate and just punishments as equally effective in controlling crime. The Inquisition came particularly under attack in the eighteenth century. "In Spain and Portugal," says Montesquieu in a biting sentence, "there are certain dervishes who will take no fooling, but burn a man like straw."

The great Italian criminologist, Cesare Beccaria, acknowledged, in a letter to his French translator, Morellet, the decisive influence on him of Montesquieu's *Persian Letters.* Beccaria's treatise, *On Crimes and Punishments,* first appeared in 1764. It had a surprising success and, in eighteen months, went through six editions. The book was esteemed in America by Thomas Jefferson. Two years later, it was translated into French with an introduction by Voltaire himself. Many penal reforms among European nations are directly due to Beccaria, but it was Montesquieu, here as often elsewhere, who furnished the powerful original stimulus, both on author and public.

In vigorous terms, Montesquieu attacks slavery. Christians have abolished slavery, he remarks, where it suited their economic interest, alleging the ideal of human equality, but have hypocritically maintained or established it where it seemed to their advantage. The widespread French practice of dueling, he considers, is a ridiculous abuse. "Because a man was more adroit or stronger than another," wrote Usbek, "it did not follow that he had the best reasons." In esteem for the ability of women, Montesquieu was also far ahead of his time. The sexes would be equal, he observed, "if they had equal opportunities for education." The decisive effect of climate upon mankind was one of his basic tenets. Like most of his French contemporaries, he was conservatively opposed to foreign colonies, believing that they merely drew economic strength away from the mother country. It was due to such a generally-held viewpoint, in part at least, that France lost out in America and India before the vigorous colonial enterprise of England in the eighteenth century.

Moderate and simple governments are best, thought Montesquieu. There are three main types of government in the world: tyranny, controlled chiefly by terror; monarchy, motivated by love of glory; and the republic, which can succeed only through the civic virtue of its citizens. Thus, already in the *Persian Letters,* Montesquieu sketches out the basic principles to which he will return in almost identical terms twenty-seven years later in his master-work, the *Spirit of Laws*.

Although he had not yet seen England at first hand he had talked and read much about the little-known country across the Channel, which was already becoming through its free institutions a potent challenge to thinkers on the Continent. "But, if a prince, instead of making his subjects happy, oppresses them, all basis for obedience ceases," remarked Montesquieu of English radical political beliefs. Indeed, this forthright people had beheaded the too arbitrary Charles I in 1649. Thus the theory of the right of revolution was boldly brought out into the open long before the fateful advent of 1789.

In a sentence of extraordinary concision and vigor, Montesquieu summed up the strikingly independent English character, so shocking to monarchists on the Continent who clung to an out-worn belief in the "divine right of kings." In England, wrote Montesquieu trenchantly, "we see liberty rising ceaselessly from the fires of discord and sedition, a prince constantly trembling on an unshakeable throne, a nation which is impatient, wise in its very madness, and, mistress of the seas (a thing hitherto unheard of), mingles commerce with empire." Who, in so few words, could say so much, analyzing the balanced clash of opposite traits in the complex English people? From his assiduous reading of Latin, Montesquieu seems to have imbibed something of the laconic brevity of ancient inscriptions.

In two letters, the author of the *Persian Letters* raised a most vital modern question. "I constantly tremble," he said, "lest man discover some secret which will provide a quick means of destroying men and even entire nations." Perhaps the sciences and the arts have been too much cultivated. "Happy the ignorance of the children of Mahomet!" exclaims another of the Persians, Rhédi, complacently. The same question was to be posed and similarly answered in a famous essay by Jean-Jacques Rousseau in the middle of the century.

But Montesquieu remained more optimistic than Rousseau over moral progress. He left the final word to Usbek. "No," the latter replied with assurance. "If a fateful invention should chance to be discovered, it would soon be prohibited by international law." Thus, as happens not infrequently to men of good will, Montesquieu, generally so hard-headed and realistic, was for once betrayed by a too naïve confidence in human nature. He had not yet encountered the dangers and difficulties of international agreement over the exploding atom. He did not seem to realize that law among nations can have only the power conferred on it by the general will, backed by mutual esteem and trust. "It is in men's minds," as has been said, "that the battle for peace must be won." Law can only register the majority decision and must be maintained, in the event of resistance, by effective force.

4

Religion was another great question which challenged eighteenth-century thought.

Vigorously Rica attacks the illogical evil of religious wars. We have already noted his onslaught against the Inquisition. "Other judges presume that the accused is innocent," he adds; "these always assume his guilt." Then, with effective irony, he preaches tolerance and freedom from persecution. "Happy the country which is inhabited by the children of the Prophets!" he exclaims. "These sad spectacles are unknown there. The holy religion brought by the angels is defended by its very truth: it has no need of these violent means to maintain itself." While the supposed tolerance of Mohammedans had been a cherished illusion, or perhaps merely a shrewd tactic, since Pierre Bayle, the lesson for Christianity was clear. Let it defend itself by truth, not by oppression of dissidents or heretics.

Significantly, these multiplied religious disputes do not produce good conduct. People argue, but "seem to vie with one another to see who will observe his religion the least!" Yet we must assume that God loves mankind. Hence charity, humanity, and obedience to law should be the first duties of religion. "By these virtues we are much more sure of pleasing God than by observing such and such a ceremony: for ceremonies have no value in themselves," says Usbek. Thus it is the essence of religion, not its external forms or complicated creeds, which is vital—an obvious truth, yet still how difficult of general acceptance!

With almost incredible hardihood in the midst of Catholic France, Montesquieu in a simple sentence rushed full-tilt at the very head of the Church at Rome. "The Pope," wrote Rica, "is the chief of the Christians; he is an old idol worshipped out of habit." A dozen years later, even Voltaire was to exclaim in astonishment at the startling boldness of the *Persian Letters* and the fact that their author had been so little molested by the government. No doubt, in addition to Montesquieu's noble rank, it was the skepticism and indifference of the free-and-easy Regency which protected him. The Duke of Orleans and many of his contemporaries felt much as he did. The reaction against the narrow-minded intolerance of Louis XIV had been well-nigh complete. Moreover, the dispute over the Pope's condemnation of Jansenism in the Bull Unigenitus had sharply divided the French clergy as recently as 1713. At the same time, a nationalistic Gallicanism or pro-French rule, even in religion, was in revolt against the very idea of an ultramontane dominance over France from Italy. Thus, once again, the stage was happily set for Montesquieu. But, when the aged Cardinal Fleury became head of the government in 1726, he would quite naturally think otherwise. The temper of officialdom had changed and Voltaire with his ironic *Philosophical Letters* of 1734 was beset by much greater difficulties than Montesquieu in 1721.

The idea of relativity was one of Montesquieu's leading principles. Rica observes to Usbek that "we seem never to judge of things except by an unconscious throw-back to ourselves." Like Anatole France's dog, Riquet, we appear each of us to stand in the center of the universe. "I am not surprised," continues Rica, "that negroes depict the devil of a dazzling whiteness and their gods black as charcoal; . . . or in short that all idolaters have represented their gods with a human face and their own inclinations. It has been well said that, if triangles created a god, they would give him three sides." After this pointed attack upon anthropocentric or man-made concepts, the author, many years later near the close of his life, added a brief paragraph to another letter emphasizing the immensity, spirituality, and infinitude of God. But "we know him well," he said, "only through his precepts." Montesquieu was always practical, never inclined to metaphysical speculation or theological hair-splitting.

In his mind, there remained, however, one concept which was absolute. "Justice is eternal and does not depend upon human conventions," he observed, pushing forward the never-ending campaign for the rights of man. Believing constantly in tolerance, he attacked the iniquitous Revocation of the Edict of Nantes. The Armenians, he said, had been foolishly and wrongfully expelled from Persia. "By proscribing the Armenians, the government in a single day almost destroyed all the merchants and artisans of the kingdom." The parallel with the French Protestants extends obviously to the economic argument also.

"If we are to reason without prejudice," says Usbek, "I do not know whether it is not a good thing to have several religions in a state." So, with the sly prudence of his indirect statement, Montesquieu insinuates his opposition to the prevailing fallacy of unity obtained by force. "It is not the multiplicity of religions which has produced wars," continued the author of the *Persian Letters,* "but the spirit of intolerance on the part of that religion which considered itself dominant." Like Bayle before him and Voltaire later, Montesquieu held firmly to the necessity and justice of freedom of thought. He had no fear of difference of opinion, unaccompanied by persecution.

All religions are good, he thought, if they make men better. "I believe that the best way to please God," said Usbek, "is to live as a good citizen in the country where God has placed me and as a good father in the family he has given me." Once again, Montesquieu insists on the ultimate test of right conduct.

The *Persian Letters* expressed vividly the skeptical spirit of the Regency. The times would no longer willingly tolerate Louis XIV's self-confident absolutism, either in government or religion. An atmosphere of independence and bold criticism of abuses was abroad in the land. Montesquieu early absorbed this inquiring attitude and gave it the attractive form of his youthful genius. Light in their literary style and external appearance, yet extraordinarily meaty in content, the *Persian Letters* ushered in a new age. In social satire of follies and foibles, in piquant criticism of established government and orthodox religion, they sketched out in brief compass a whole broad program of needed reform. Montesquieu prepared the way for Voltaire and his revolutionary successors.

CHAPTER VII

MONTESQUIEU'S QUESTION: WHY DID ROME FALL?

I

WHEN, IN THE AUTUMN OF 1727, MONTESQUIEU FOR THE second time in two years offered his candidacy for membership in the historic French Academy, he found himself in an embarrassing position.

"If you did write the *Persian Letters*," it was objected to him ironically, "one of them is directed against the Academy and its members. If you didn't write them, then what have you written?"

The question was pertinent. For six years it had been an open secret that Montesquieu was the unavowed author of these incriminating *Letters* with their biting criticism of Church and State so much more dangerous to the established order than his quite conventional satire of the not too august Academy. Obviously, the *Persian Letters* were his real, and only, title to fame. Montesquieu's other works so far were negligible. Yet could the French Academy under the patronage of an absolute king and during the ministry of a cardinal of the Church like Fleury elect the writer of a book which, from their standpoint, was so clearly subversive?

Voltaire recounts that Montesquieu fooled the aged Cardinal by bringing him a special edition hurriedly printed up in a few days and expurgated of its bold sallies. The anecdote, however, appears improbable. Such action was hardly in the author's straightforward character; the risks in the case of failure would have been great; and Fleury, in spite of his easy-going tolerance, could scarcely have been so naïve as to have swallowed this crude trick without investigation.

The facts seem to be that Montesquieu refused to disavow the *Persian Letters*, but willingly stated that he made no public claim to being their author. This bare compliance with the forms apparently satisfied the conciliatory Cardinal, although, according to the

Marquis d'Argenson, Fleury in some quarters was reproached with having shown a dangerous weakness in granting his consent.

In any event, Montesquieu was finally elected. On January 24, 1728, he gave the required Reception Discourse, praising his obscure predecessor, Monsieur de Sacy, according to long-established custom, and along with him Richelieu, the original founder of the Academy, next Cardinal Fleury, and finally even Louis XIV, whom the author had so scathingly criticized in the *Persian Letters*. Such flattery was the humiliating price of official favor under the Old Régime.

But it was hardly worth it. Montesquieu's sensitive pride was wounded by the director of the Academy who, in his Reply, hinted blandly at the insufficiency of the new member's anonymous title to election and slyly urged him "to make his works public!" The Baron de Montesquieu, in the end, paid little attention to this formal honor and, it is said, attended the Academy's meetings only three times in all his life.

Barely more than two months later, on April 5, Montesquieu set out on an important journey. He wished to study at first hand governments and conditions in the neighboring countries of Europe. The next year and a half he spent in Austria, Venice, Rome, Naples, Switzerland, the small German states along the Rhine, and finally in busy, commercially-minded little Holland. At length, on October 31, 1729, he left The Hague and set sail in the yacht of his friend, Lord Chesterfield, for England.

Of all the numerous countries visited, England was by far the most instructive for a man of Montesquieu's reflective stamp. It alone at the time had succeeded in establishing a large measure of political and religious freedom. Hardly nine months before the Baron's arrival, his contemporary, Voltaire, had departed from London after over two years and a half of a similarly important voyage of discovery. The impression made upon both great French writers was profound.

In England, Montesquieu was honored by election to the Royal Society for scientific study, was initiated into deistic Free Masonry, was received in audience by the King and Queen. He attended sessions of the House of Commons and observed with amazement the outspoken criticism of the government by that admirable institution of a freedom-loving country, "the King's loyal opposition," as it was later to be called. Montesquieu formed wide acquaintances among the leaders of the nobility, scientists, and men of letters. He improved his ability, if not to pronounce and speak English, at least to read it fluently.

On his return to Bordeaux in the spring of 1731 after a year and a half in England and three whole years away from his native country, Montesquieu remarked in one of those broad generalizations which he so much loved: "Germany is good for travel, Italy for a short stay, England for thought, and France to live in."

While in Italy, Montesquieu, like many another visitor among the august ruins of ancient civilization, had been led to meditate on the great drama of the rise and fall of Rome. As a schoolboy with the Oratorians at Juilly, he had slowly parsed his way through the chief Latin historians. Later in England, he began to read eagerly everything he could get hold of bearing on this impressive subject. Years later he wrote to a friend: "Rome *antica e moderna* has always enchanted me."

Among the Ancients, Montesquieu had read Plutarch, Tacitus, Livy, Polybius, Suetonius, and many others. He was familiar with the oratorical phrases of Bossuet, the great Bishop of Meaux, who had written for the education of the young Dauphin a famous *Discourse on Universal History* in which the rise of Rome to world power played a dominant role. Bossuet paid little attention, however, to its fall. Montesquieu probably knew also many other works, now largely forgotten and unnecessary to mention here.

Who in that day could ignore Rome? Every educated Frenchman then was brought up from early childhood on the Latin classics of the schools. In addition, for long years a patient band of scholars had been slowly establishing authentic texts of the ancient authors. After them, another group of research workers set themselves to dig out little by little the proved facts, as distinguished from the legends, of Roman history. So there was keen interest in the Eternal City on the part of the reading public.

Unfortunately, Montesquieu seems to have made little or no use of these exact and erudite studies. The too-confident Baron clung to the traditional fables and legends of Rome's early years and made no significant revisions in later editions of his work. He had first learned his Roman history from the Oratorian fathers. Their early teachings had cut deep and continued to shape his thought. *J'y suis, j'y reste,* seems to have been unconsciously his attitude. Like the majority of his contemporaries, he took his ancient history as he found it. Seldom did he go behind the books he read to criticize their value. This, as Voltaire liked to point out, always remained one of Montesquieu's weaknesses. But along with this serious shortcoming went, happily, great qualities also.

2

Montesquieu's *Considerations on the Causes of the Grandeur of the Romans and their Decadence* was printed anonymously at Amsterdam in 1734.

The key word in this lengthy descriptive title is *causes*. Unlike the modern Henry Adams who, after years of study, could see in history only one disconnected event after another, Montesquieu, in the narrative of the past, sought and found meaning. In this little book, he was not interested in telling again the detailed story of Roman history, already so familiar to his contemporaries. He wished rather to discover its underlying significance. By what means did Rome become great? Why, after attaining the pinnacle, did it gradually fall?

"It is not fortune which dominates the world," said Montesquieu in his eighteenth chapter. "There are general causes, either moral or physical, which are active in each monarchy, increase its power, maintain it, or precipitate it to destruction. All happenings are due to these causes; and, if the hazard of a battle, that is to say, a particular cause, has brought about the ruin of a state, there was a general cause which predestined it to perish by a single battle."

Bossuet, the great churchman, had seen in the broad sweep of history the grand design of Providence guiding and overruling the affairs of men. Montesquieu for his part remains purely secular. He seeks no supernatural explanations, but places his faith entirely in reason. The author of the *Considerations* approaches history in the spirit shown years before in the scientific experiments of his youth when he had inquired diligently into the *Causes of the Echo,* the *Functions of the Kidneys,* or the *Principles of Weight.* Can history, too, though so much more complex and uncertain, become, at least in some degree, a science? Can man learn from the successes or failures of the past, or must we each individually burn our own fingers in defiance of what has gone before? "Those who ignore history," George Santayana is said to have remarked, "are condemned to repeat it." Montesquieu wished neither to ignore nor repeat history. Could eighteenth-century France, after the decline of the aged Louis XIV, the blunderings of the debauched Regent, and the indifference of the cynical Louis XV, learn in time the lesson of Rome's greatness and of its cataclysmic fall? Such, by implication, must have been the question in Montesquieu's mind as he looked with foreboding at the chaotic present and the ominous future. The same question confronts the modern reader in our own or any other nation. How does a people rise to greatness? Why, once at the top of its power and influence, is it seemingly unable to maintain itself there? Can humanity by taking thought break the tragic cycle of the past?

What, in Montesquieu's opinion, are the causes of Rome's greatness? He finds in the Romans a willingness to learn from other nations. He comments on their probity, their warlike spirit, their ability to overcome obstacles, the riches they gained from wars, and the fear they aroused in other nations. Above all—and in this we may see a lesson for modern times—their government was so organized that it could be modified to correct abuses.

But why did Rome fall? Its very success, believed Montesquieu, was its ruin. When the republic expanded beyond the narrow confines of Italy, the soldier was no longer a citizen familiar with, and taking an important part in, the affairs of government. More and more he tended to give his allegiance to his general, the Imperator, on whom his daily fate depended. From these rival generals and their lust for power sprang the ruinous civil wars. The Epicurean philosophy of happiness, thought Montesquieu, weakened the Roman character. While the Republic had maintained its strength by constant wars, the Empire took its ease in a long peace. Yet the basic fierceness of the Romans continued to manifest itself in the tyranny of the emperors, while the common people detested commerce and preferred to be supported by the state. "The warlike virtues remained," said Montesquieu of the Romans, "after they had lost all the others." The lesson should be clear for the eighteenth-century nobility of France, lounging grandly at Versailles and reduced to unprofitable idleness by the blind absolutism of Louis XIV. Finally, the Romans were torn apart by the ruinous division of the

Empire into East and West, and the barbarian invasions sent crashing to the ground the imposing statue with its feet of clay.

"Here in a word," summarized Montesquieu with his constant search for bold generalization, "is the history of the Romans. They conquered the world by their maxims, but, when they had succeeded, their republic could no longer continue to exist. They needed to change their government, and, in their new government, principles contrary to those first employed, brought about the fall of their grandeur."

Like Fontenelle in his fictitious *Dialogue between Socrates and Montaigne,* Montesquieu saw in human nature a constancy in folly with which we must still reckon. "As men in all times have had the same passions," he says, "the occasions which produce great changes are different, but the causes are always the same." Thus the lesson of experience lies before us if only we have the wit and the will to learn.

Montesquieu's little book abounds in thought-provoking sentences. "It has been said," he remarks, "that Hannibal made a great mistake in leading his army to Capua where it became soft: but people fail to consider that this does not bring us to the real cause. Would not the soldiers of this army, grown rich after so many victories, have found a Capua anywhere?" The basic explanation, thought the author of the *Considerations,* lay in human nature itself.

"Conquests are easy to make," wrote Montesquieu, "because they are made with all one's forces; they are difficult to keep because they are defended with only a part of one's strength." Frederick the Great, reading this little book with the interest of one keen mind ready to learn from another, applied the lesson in a marginal comment to Louis XIV's rapid conquest of Holland and his equally precipitate retreat from the Dutch cities he had so recently won.

"It is the folly of conquerors," observed the author of the *Considerations on the Romans,* "to wish to impose their laws and customs on all other peoples. In that there is no advantage, for, under any sort of government, people are capable of obeying." So much for uniformity exacted by force.

"The government of England," wrote Montesquieu in the first edition with undue boldness, "is one of the wisest in Europe, because it has a body—the Parliament—which is constantly examining the government and itself. Its errors consequently are never of long duration, and, by the spirit of vigilance they arouse in the nation, are often useful." Such was the result of his firsthand observations of the House of Commons in session. It was proof of the extreme sensitiveness of French authorities, even to merely implied criticism, that the author prudently softened his statement almost at once in the *Errata* of 1734.

Montesquieu found in the early Roman government a division of powers among a great number of magistrates, in short, the salutary system of checks and balances which he had recently admired in England and which he was to make one of the key principles of his influential *Spirit of Laws* later. Rome's subsequent ruin was facilitated, he believed, by the unhappy concentration of control in the hands of a small group or of a single emperor. The liberty-loving Baron opposed tyranny wherever he saw it, whether in Rome or in eighteenth-century France.

Sometimes Montesquieu ran the inevitable risk of embracing too much territory in his sweeping generalizations. In the first edition of his work, he had declared that "in civil wars great men are *always* developed." The keen French critic, Gustave Lanson, accused him here of obvious exaggeration. It was Lanson himself, however, the usually impeccable scholar, who, using an unauthoritative text, generalized too hastily, and failed to notice that Montesquieu early discovered his mistake, or had it pointed out to him, and quickly changed his dangerous "always" into a more prudent "often."

With a profound understanding of human nature, Montesquieu observed in another place: "We never offend men more than when we attack their ceremonies or usages. An attempt to oppress them is sometimes a proof of esteem; to shock their customs is always a mark of contempt." It is frequently the little things that count.

"The faults committed by statesmen are not always freely chosen," wrote Montesquieu keenly. "Often they are but the inevitable consequences of the situation in which one finds himself. Difficulties beget difficulties." As the great English statesman, Lord Morley, out of his long experience of public life, observed: "In politics the choice is constantly between two evils; and action is one long second best." The ideal is rarely possible. Not what one would, but what one can, imposes the framework of our action. The mere observer often forgets the harsh limits which confront the man of affairs, judging him, not practically, but according to an unattainable standard. It was an error Montesquieu did not make.

"There is no nation," says the author of the *Considerations,* "in which taxes are more needed than in those which are becoming weaker, so that it is necessary to increase the burdens in proportion as people are less able to bear them. Soon, in the Roman provinces, the tributes levied grew intolerable." Thus financial difficulties multiply and feed on one another. They are like a man in quicksand whose frantic efforts to escape only leave him deeper buried.

One of the greatest errors of the eastern empire, wrote Montesquieu, "was the project it conceived of reducing all men to the same opinion in matters of religion." Clearly France could have applied this thought with advantage to the calamitous Revocation of the Edict of Nantes, or indeed to the persecution of Protestants which still continued in the eighteenth century. Church and State, believed the author of the *Considerations,* should always remain separate. "This great distinction, the basis of the tranquillity of nations, is founded," he concluded, "not only on religion, but also on reason and nature."

Montesquieu "always thinks, and makes others think," observed Voltaire.

3

But, it is natural to ask, how do Montesquieu's explanations of Rome's rise and fall compare with those of later historians?

The classic example chosen from the eighteenth century itself is of course that of the great Englishman, Edward Gibbon. His majestic *Decline and Fall of the Roman Empire* came before the public in six volumes beginning with 1776, the year when the American Colonies declared their Independence, and concluding in 1788, on the eve of the French Revolution. Gibbon's was a massive achievement which offered food for reflection to many succeeding generations.

Young Gibbon was sixteen in 1753 when his angry father sent him to Lausanne to be reconverted to his native Protestantism. The choice of Lausanne was a happy one. The boy remained there six years. Living in the home of a Calvinist pastor of intelligence and tact named Pavilliard, the youthful exile soon learned to think, speak, and read in French. He worked assiduously ten to twelve hours a day in his host's excellent library. During the latter part of his stay, Gibbon even fell in love with the attractive daughter of another pastor and, but for his father's unbending opposition to a foreign bride, would probably have married beauteous Mademoiselle Curchod and perhaps established himself permanently abroad. Destiny, however, had other plans. The girl later became the wife of the Swiss banker, Monsieur Necker, future finance minister of Louis XVI, and the mother of that distinguished woman of letters, Madame de Staël. As for Gibbon, he wrote unhappily: "After a painful struggle, I yielded to my fate; I sighed as a lover, I obeyed as a son," thus bowing before the threat of disinheritance.

After long residence in this Swiss environment, Gibbon was naturally permeated with French thought. Indeed, his first work, *An Essay on Literature,* was actually written in French. "My delight," he says, "was in the frequent perusal of Montesquieu, whose energy of style and boldness of hypothesis were powerful to awaken and stimulate the genius of the age." Like Montesquieu also, Gibbon observed: "The knowledge of history is to the philosopher that of causes and effects." Later, he says: "Let us carefully preserve every historical fact. A Montesquieu may discover, in the most trivial, connections unknown to the vulgar." A few pages further, Gibbon writes: "What a wide field opens itself to my reflection! The theory of general causes would, in the hands of a Montesquieu, become a philosophical history of man. He would display these causes operating in the rise and fall of empires." In another passage, Gibbon becomes more precise: "The corruption of all orders of men among the Romans was owing to the extent of their empire and was itself productive of the greatness of the republic." This was exactly Montesquieu's position.

In the *Decline and Fall* itself, Gibbon frequently quotes, or refers to, Montesquieu. He often does so to disagree with him, but it is evident that the Englishman had the work of his French predecessor constantly in mind. Even so, the general analysis of the reasons for Rome's fall is strikingly similar in the two historians. Like Montesquieu also, Gibbon uses his study of ancient times for comparison with contemporary events, emphasizing the element of constancy in human passions through the centuries. Thus Montesquieu guided Gibbon on that long chain of thought regarding the causes of

Rome's decline and fall which was to become his life's work.

When we turn from Gibbon to modern historians of Rome, we find among some of them a new stress upon economic causes. Tenney Frank, indeed, indicates this orientation by his very title, *An Economic History of Rome*. The soil of Italy, says Frank, was in the beginning remarkably fertile, enriched by volcanic ash, but thin. By intensive cultivation, it was capable of supporting a large population. Gradually, however, Italy became more and more a country of great estates farmed by slave labor. "During the century of the fall of the Roman government, neither the population nor the natural resources of the Empire were exhausted," it has been said in summary of Frank's position, "but there was a lack of intelligence and spirit in the effective employment of these resources which resulted in confusion and ill-will." Thus the "economic causes" appear in the end to be basically human causes, not material or external, but moral.

Another historian, William E. Heitland, concludes: "To improve your citizens and to interest them in their own real welfare, is the only course that offers a possible means of avoiding the Roman fate." There is no permanent remedy, therefore, in absolutism or even in the idea of the "beneficent despot," dear to some thinkers in the eighteenth century, but only in more democracy or self-government, the correction of one mind, or a few minds, by the many. Once again, no doubt, Montesquieu with his hatred of tyranny would have agreed.

A modern economist, Simkhovitch, in a challenging essay, advances the idea that the basic cause of Rome's fall may have been the failure to use proper methods of restoring organic elements in the soil by rotation of crops. This is an explanation notably different from any given by Montesquieu. Other recent historians have contested it. While no doubt an oversimplification, Simkhovitch's theory does, however, stress the inescapable relation between a sick agriculture and a sick national life.

Like Montesquieu, like Gibbon also, who gave it a provocative discussion, Edward Lucas White puts special emphasis on the weakening of Roman military and civic fibre which he attributes chiefly to Christian teachings of pacificism and otherworldliness. The Romans were no longer willing to serve in the army and fight in their own defense, but preferred to leave that unpleasant task to hired soldiers from among the barbarian immigrants. In addition, their attention to salvation after this life drew their minds away from the urgency of solving the civic, political, economic, and social problems around them. These were the paramount internal causes. The chief external cause in White's opinion was the progressive drying-up of central Asia which drove the barbarian hordes of the steppes toward the fertile and alluring West. Though Montesquieu did not propose this latter explanation himself, he would no doubt have welcomed such emphasis on the role of climate in the affairs of men.

The historian Rostovtzeff does not favor the single-cause type of economic or climatic explanation like those advanced in part by Frank or by Simkhovitch. He does, however, in spite of his recent attack upon use of the word *decay* without exact definition in connection with the ancient world, find a real decline of initiative, ambition, and originality due apparently to the absence of struggle which came with the centuries of peace, luxury, and easy living for the higher classes under the early empire. Pleasure and material advantage occupied their minds. The creative powers of the aristocracy were in this way undermined without corresponding gains to the classes below. "In the case of the Roman Empire," Rostovtzeff concludes, "a steady decline of civilization is not to be traced to physical degeneration, or to any debasement of blood in the higher races due to slavery, or to political and economic conditions, but rather to a changed attitude of men's minds." The difficult question of the reason for this change still remains. Shall we say with Rostovtzeff that the goal of an easy life which man so naturally seeks is in itself self-defeating for the individual and for the nation, resulting finally only in fatal weakness?

It is obviously impossible in brief space to seek a definitive answer to this great problem which has puzzled so many historians over the centuries. Each has his own explanation or explanations in which probably lies at least some grain of truth. It is sufficient to point out that Montesquieu's question and indeed many of his answers still stand. None of his points were developed in detail. What he wrote, as he said, consisted only of "Considerations." He aimed primarily to think, and to set others to thinking, about these continuing problems of the rise and fall of nations which the Englishman Toynbee has recently again raised. Montesquieu lived too early to reflect upon the possible role of the soil itself, of agriculture, and of complex economic forces in this great *débâcle*.

Which come first, in such a catastrophe, the outer, material causes or the inner failures of intelligence or character? We have seen how even a small group of historians may differ. The answer, with nations as with individuals, remains obscure. Is man entirely molded by environment or, grappling with it, can he in turn overcome unfavorable surroundings and shape them to his ends? In the last analysis, this is no doubt an insoluble question. But belief itself is a force, and a man or a nation is defeated, it seems, when the will weakens before the impact of external events. Why does the will weaken? Like Montesquieu, we are still in search of the answer. But the question which he posed about the fall of Rome remains vital to the welfare, possibly even to the survival, of humanity itself. Perhaps to ask it is to take the first step toward a solution.

CHAPTER VIII

MONTESQUIEU'S
SPIRIT OF LAWS

I

FOR TWENTY YEARS AND MORE, IN THE LONG LIBRARY OF LA BRÈDE, Montesquieu wrote away on the great work of his lifetime, the *Spirit of Laws*. Many an hour one might have seen the Baron's tall, spare frame in the big chair before the blazing wood fire with a notebook on his knee as he jotted down the results of his endless reading or slowly, little by little, with long pauses, shaped his incisive sentences in his mind and then dictated them to a secretary. Perhaps it is true that the worn depression in the ancient stone on the side of the fireplace does in fact represent, as guides like to tell us, the spot where the author rested his foot as he sat with one leg crossed over the other. His face was thin, his nose large, his eyes alert and full of life, though increasingly tired and weak as the years wore on, his profile strong and sharp in outline like a Roman medallion.

From the far-off time when, leaving school, Montesquieu returned to Bordeaux in 1705, he had earnestly sought the meaning of laws and institutions, at first with no success. The same basic question haunted his inquiring mind as he toured continental Europe and studied the widely different governments and civilizations presented to his view. He brought the problem back with him from liberty-loving England to his native Gascony in 1731. The profitable interlude spent analyzing the causes of Rome's rise and dramatic fall could hardly have failed to clarify his thinking on this great subject.

But there were many discouragements. For years the riddle escaped him. "I have many times begun and many times abandoned this work," he wrote as he mused over the piled-up hours of seemingly fruitless labor. "I pursued my object without plan," he continued elsewhere; "I knew neither rules nor exceptions; I found the truth only to lose it; but when I discovered my principles everything

I sought came to me; and, in the course of twenty years, I have seen my work begin, grow, advance, and come to an end."

Yet, even in a man of his patient application, the long-continued tension of thought had taken its heavy toll. "I confess that this work has almost killed me," he wrote sadly to a friend in 1749; "I am going to rest; I shall work no more." He was only sixty (a youngster beside the ninety-two-year-old Fontenelle), but he was worn out and his sight was already growing dim with cataracts. During the five or six years which remained to him, he would vigorously defend his book and would stand on his well-earned laurels. His important creative work was over.

The *Spirit of Laws* was at last published anonymously in two volumes at Geneva in November of 1748. It reached Paris toward the beginning of the following January. Almost immediately a new printing came out "furtively," as one writer put it, in the French capital. Within a year and a half, more than twenty editions appeared. The demand was keen. Everybody had to read Montesquieu's latest work, or must at least be able to talk as though he had read it. The long-established reputation of the author, the great importance of the subject matter, and the unique form in which the book was cast ensured its vogue.

"There is no study so neglected in France as that of jurisprudence," wrote the journalist Raynal. "The few works we have on this subject," he continued, "are very bad and, even if they were good, they would not be read. It took a very great man and, in addition, one *à la mode,* to change in that respect the taste of a nation. Monsieur le Président de Montesquieu has just brought about this change. His book, entitled the *Spirit of Laws, . . .* has turned the heads of the whole French people. We find this work in the libraries of our scholars and on the dressing tables of our ladies and our fashionable young men."

For his work, however, the author seems at first sight to have chosen a curious form. The thirty-one "books" consist of numerous "chapters", which would not in itself be strange, were it not that these so-called chapters often comprise only a page or two, sometimes a single paragraph, not infrequently a mere few lines, or indeed a single brief sentence. The obvious result is in many cases to break the continuity and to give the book, for the modern reader, an unfortunate effect of "choppiness."

But this arrangement was by no means a disadvantage when the work first appeared. To many a lady and *grand seigneur* of the day, it offered a chance to dip into the book here and there with frequent convenient resting places. Moreover, the titles of the "books" and "chapters" listed in the *Table of Contents,* constituted then, as they still do, a detailed analysis of the subject matter itself. Thus the inevitable heaviness of the material was considerably lightened for the superficial reader by the form of presentation.

"Have you read the *Spirit of Laws?*" people asked. And many a man or woman, after galloping through the chapter headings of the *Table of Contents* could no doubt glibly say "yes," and defend the assertion by showing a rather convincing familiarity with the main outlines, if not the details, of Montesquieu's book. The author knew his public and he wrote his work to be read. Moreover, his method added emphasis to certain ideas by making them stand out, isolated in the spotlight. Finally, it corresponded also with his own tendency, in literary style, toward an extraordinary concision and the suppression of most connectives. In some cases, it permitted him to empty the contents of his note books, with the minimum of composition, into his gradually growing manuscript. It was not a perfect form, certainly, but it was effective.

So the book became immediately popular. It was admired, studied, attacked, and defended. The more than twenty years during which Montesquieu read, took notes, and reflected on his theme did not go for naught. The *Spirit of Laws* became one of the great literary landmarks of the eighteenth century. It remained a guidepost of government for nearly a hundred years thereafter, in America as in Europe. Even the modern world might find in it many an important political truth which can be neglected only at one's peril.

Madame du Deffand remarked in her *salon,* with a clever, if malicious, play on two meanings of the French word *esprit,* that the book, instead of being the *Spirit of Laws,* consisted of "some wit on the laws." But she could not so easily demolish the work of Montesquieu's lifetime. At one stroke, he had brought into general literature the great field of political and social science.

2

What does Montesquieu mean by "laws"? Like a wise and careful thinker, he begins with a definition. "Laws," he says, "in their widest signification, are the necessary relationships which derive from the nature of things."

These relationships are, then, inherent. They exist in the complex fields of government and institutions as in the more concrete world of science. Montesquieu brings to bear on the difficult and little understood realm of human relations something of the results of his wide study and observation of facts and conditions everywhere.

Laws, he believes, are human reason in action. They must be adapted to each people for whom they are made and there is little chance that those developed by one nation will prove suitable also for another. Laws must be related to the basic principle of the government where they are established. They vary with the "physical characteristics of the country, with its climate, frigid, hot, or temperate, the nature of the terrain, its situation and extent, the kind of life led by its inhabitants." The religion, inclinations, wealth, numbers, commerce, manners, customs, and morals of a people all exert their influence. The analysis of these and other factors that may be discovered constitutes what Montesquieu calls the "Spirit of Laws."

One fundamental consequence of this approach is the development of a broader and more open-minded attitude toward the peoples of the world. In contrast with the attempt in the seventeenth century to emphasize fixity, Montesquieu sees diversity as natural and desirable. All truth is not to be found at home. If other nations have different manners and customs, a different civilization, this is to be expected since they live under different conditions and have behind them a different history and experience. Montesquieu is like his great sixteenth-century compatriot, Montaigne, in being interested, not shocked, by the infinite variety of human manifestations. The result of this viewpoint is a new cosmopolitanism which will gradually open the mind to curiosity regarding the strange and exotic. In literature, it will lead to Romanticism and a breakdown of the exclusive domination of the classic unities in tragedy; in government and politics, to the objective study of foreign civilizations. So Montesquieu is here a great liberating influence.

There are three main types of government, observes Montesquieu: the republican, the monarchical, and the despotic. Each of these operates from a basic principle which supplies its motive force.

Popular democracy, to function successfully, must rely on the civic virtue of the majority of its citizens. Unless they, for the most part, are devoted to the general welfare of the state, it will in the end fail, or change its form.

Monarchy, on the other hand, depends upon the principle of honor. The king wields his power by means of the recognition he confers upon the different gradations of the noble hierarchy established around him.

Despotic government is based crudely upon fear.

Already in the *Persian Letters,* nearly thirty years before, Montesquieu had recognized these same principles under slightly different terms. He had in the meantime carried his analysis further, but not changed his fundamental viewpoint. It goes without saying that such a classification, if taken literally, is too rigid. Civic virtue, desire for honor, fear are found in varying degrees in all effective governments. The lines of demarcation, as always in human affairs, overlap; they are not clearcut in their separation. But Montesquieu should be interpreted as laying down what he understands to be the dominant and essential trait in each case, the one without which the government in question cannot continue to endure in its present form. Taken in this sense, his distinctions are valid and fruitful.

It follows that education in each country should be shaped according to the principle required to maintain its form of government. The laws likewise should follow this principle. In a democracy, Montesquieu believes it necessary to maintain frugality and relative equality. Without these, civic virtue will degenerate and the government will in the long run fail. Excessive wealth or poverty are threats to democracy. Respect for laws, good morals, and obedience to paternal authority, are, in Montesquieu's opinion, all helpful to the maintenance of a democratic state.

Monarchy, intermediate between democracy and despotism, has certain advantages, according to the *Spirit of Laws.* It has moderation, it has stability, and it has a promptness in action which the democracy, subject to many minds, with difficulty attains.

As for despotism, Montesquieu's hatred and scorn are sufficiently shown in a single "chapter" of two sentences in which he says trenchantly: "When the savages of Louisiana wish to get fruit, they cut the tree at the base and gather the fruit. That is despotic government."

But despotisms exist. Montesquieu therefore analyzes them. Other thinkers of the eighteenth century, like Helvétius and Voltaire, in their legitimate desire for reform, did not in all cases appreciate the strong realistic strain in Montesquieu, which led him to explain what he by no means always approved. He sought an objective study of things as they are, but the trend of his preferences and basic sympathies is sufficiently clear to any reader who takes his work as a whole.

One of the important problems of society, any society, is its penology. In the eighteenth century, as in the modern world, where torture still exists, though without being openly recognized, the question continues vital. Montesquieu remarks succinctly: "It would be easy to prove that, in all or nearly all of the states of Europe, punishments have lessened or increased in proportion to the rise or fall of liberty." We have seen that the great Beccaria, whose *Treatise on Crimes and Punishments* first appeared in Italian in 1764, admitted his important debt to Montesquieu. The reforms of the French Revolution and those of the nineteenth century undoubtedly stem from the strong current of opinion partly set in motion by the *Persian Letters* and the *Spirit of Laws*. Torture is not necessary, observed their author. It has been abandoned without disadvantage by a powerful nation. In this remark he of course meant, though he discreetly did not name, England.

One of the questions much debated for centuries since the days of ancient Rome was that of luxury and its effect upon nations. The traditional attitude considered luxury harmful. It was held to produce physical and moral softness, bringing about decadence and ruin. A modern eighteenth-century school, however, influenced by growing world commerce, tended toward a new view: namely, that luxury was natural and desirable, that it led to the increasing comfort and welfare of mankind, and consequently to the greater economic and military power of those nations who developed their manufactures and trade. Voltaire belonged to this affirmative group, Rousseau to the traditional and orthodox negative. Montesquieu hesitated between the two.

In a republic, dependent for its continued existence, in Montesquieu's opinion, upon frugality and equality, luxury is deadly. It must be suppressed, he thought, by rigorous sumptuary laws. Such had been the attempt of that austere Geneva from which Rousseau sprang. In eighteenth-century England and in France, the author of the *Spirit of Laws* believed there was a sufficient balance between agriculture and industry to permit the superfluous without serious danger. Luxury, however, he held, had been fatal to China. Certainly, Montesquieu, with his strong Stoic proclivities and his natural simplicity, tended to revolt against excessive and blatant display such as that of the French court at Versailles, and to fear its consequences. Let him who would, therefore, heed the lesson of what had happened in far-off China. In a country of censorship, a word to the wise must be sufficient.

3

All three of these forms of government, democracy, monarchy, despotism, Montesquieu observed, may become dangerously corrupted. Democracy may degenerate into a popular excess of equality. The mob may become king as was to be fearfully proved during the French Revolution. On the other hand, there is the obvious danger of rule by one man or by a single aristocratic class.

Monarchy, too, may commit the error of infringing upon the prerogatives of the nobles or interfering with the local self-government of cities. It may degenerate into a mass despotism or into the tyrannical rule of the king alone. The author of the *Spirit of Laws* observes: "What caused the ruin of the Tsin and Soüi dynasties, said a Chinese author, is the failure to limit themselves, like the ancients, to a general oversight, the only one worthy of a sovereign; the princes decided to govern everything directly themselves." Let the descendants of autocratic Louis XIV take note in time. That no one may miss the prudent lesson to be learned from China on the other side of the world, Montesquieu comments further: "The Chinese author here gives us the cause of the corruption of almost all monarchies." It is clear that, when Montesquieu discusses monarchy, he is expressing no admiration for absolutism, but only for a monarchy with established constitutional safeguards.

What of despotism? The answer is simple. "The principle of despotic government is constantly becoming corrupted because it is corrupt by nature." Always on the verge of ruin, it may be maintained by accidental circumstances which favor its continuance. But its fundamental nature does not change. "Its ferocity remains," even though for a time tamed.

A republic, believes Montesquieu, can subsist only in a small territory; a monarchy, in one of medium size, no doubt like France; a despotism befits a state of large extent.

These statements must of course be understood in the light of the slow methods of communication at the time. It required a week then for news to travel from Paris to Geneva. When the nineteen-year-old Lafayette landed in America, it took him a full thirty days to make his painful way on horseback, by carriages, constantly breaking down over execrable roads, by boat, and even at times afoot from Charleston, South Carolina, to Philadelphia! Under such circumstances, obviously, public opinion could develop but slowly, if at all. This is the explanation of Montesquieu's dictum that a democratic or republican form of government could exist only in a small territory. Up to Montesquieu's time, there had been as examples of such popular government only the Greek city states, early Rome of limited extent, and the tiny Helvetic or Swiss confederation. The weight of experience was in favor of his position. Aristotle had said that a democratic government was limited by the size of territory in which the voice of the leader could be heard. In his time, clearly, this was the Greek city with the free citizens grouped about the market place or amphitheater. Today, the railroad, the automobile, the airplane, the telegraph, the telephone, the radio, and television have altered the situation completely. News girdles the civilized earth almost instantaneously. For good or ill, the immense slow-moving world of past centuries has shrunk to a tiny globe in which friends and enemies constantly rub elbows. This greatly expands the possible area of popular government based upon free opinion. At the same time, it increases the need for reliable news gathering, for intelligence in dealing with the infinitely complex problems of the day, for good will and firmness of character; it multiplies the dangers of false information, wrong interpretation, and propaganda.

If Montesquieu had reason in his day to limit a republic to a small territory, experience had already taught him an important compromise. The federated republic, he saw, offered the possibility of local self-government over small areas combined with national union over a larger territory. The early leaders of the infant United States, in their constitutional debates, did not forget the value of Montesquieu's solution to their problem.

Montesquieu, like his leading contemporaries, attacked war. The spirit of the monarchy, he believed, was one of expansion, aggrandizement, and war; that of the republic, of moderation and of peace. Nevertheless, he held there were occasions when a freedom-loving nation, menaced with invasion, must attack first in its own defense. Voltaire saw the dangers of abuse in this doctrine and ridiculed it forcefully. Any nation, bent on conquest, could pretend it had moved only to forestall aggression. In modern days, we have seen strong nations impudently accuse the weaker of hostile designs which strain credulity to the limit. At the same time, small nations have been ruthlessly occupied by an enemy while strong friendly nations stood by hesitant. With the disappearance of formal declarations of war in advance of attack, with the multiplication of means of sudden aggression without warning, it is clear that the problem of survival has become more, not less, complicated. There is here in Montesquieu an element of bitter realism which Voltaire, hard-headed as he was, in this instance failed to recognize, which we ourselves might have overlooked only a few years ago, but which facts now compel us to face, however regretfully. The law of the jungle threatens to prevail over the last vestige of international law. The way of the complete pacifist is still belied by unscrupulous human nature. Montesquieu, on the contrary, was an idealist who sought to keep his feet on firm ground.

A most important chapter in the *Spirit of Laws* is Chapter 6 of Book XI, "On the English Constitution." Here we see the significant results of Montesquieu's journey to England twenty years before, of his extensive reading and reflection later.

"In each state," he observes in a momentous declaration, "there are three kinds of powers: the legislative power, the executive power which deals with international affairs, and the executive power which has to do with civil law." The author continues: "When in the same person or magistracy the legislative power is united with the executive power, there is no liberty, because we may then fear that the same monarch or the same senate can make tyrannical laws in order to execute them tyrannically. There is no liberty, moreover, if the power of judging is not separated from the legislative and executive powers. If it were joined to the legislative power, the power over the life and liberty of citizens would be arbitrary; for the judge would be legislator. If it were joined to the executive power, the judge could have the force of an oppressor."

This is the famous doctrine of the "separation of powers," which Montesquieu had found, partly in the ancient government of Rome, partly in Locke and the English theorists, partly in his own experience with the supposed independence of judges in the French parlements. In England, above all since the Revolution of 1688, the judiciary was not really separate and, with the diminishing power of the King and the Prime Minister, the executive and the legislative powers were already beginning to merge. But much of the theory and, to some extent the practice, were there, and Montesquieu gave them wide currency, especially in America.

The idea of governmental checks and balances to prevent one man or group of men from excessive power over another still has much to commend it in an imperfect world. Cumbersome often, inefficient, as it may be, and slow-moving, the separation of powers can nevertheless expose and stop abuses. In time of crisis and imminent danger, it may have to give way to centralized authority for the period of emergency. The swift onrush of perils borne on the wings of science threatens the continuance of this safety-valve handed down from the eighteenth century. Yet the alternative would seem to be the old, well-known abuse of power by a single man, body, or class. "Eternal vigilance is the price of liberty," as has been so well said.

"It is not for me to examine whether the English do now enjoy this liberty, or not," wrote Montesquieu toward the end of his chapter. "It is sufficient for me to say that it is established by their laws, and I do not seek further." Here he distinguishes clearly between theory and practice. Anxious no doubt to see the French monarchy liberalized, he laid down the constitutional lines of possible reform. England offered the ideal, even if, human-like, it did not perfectly attain it. Montesquieu saw more than his critics, then or since, have always been willing to grant. For reasons of prudence or tactics, he did not, however, completely expose his hand.

4

"Important maxim: one must be very circumspect in prosecuting magic or heresy." There is the warning, in clear language. Next is the palliative—to escape the censor. "I did not say here that we must not punish heresy; I say that one must be very circumspect in punishing it." Montesquieu's prudence was necessary, in his time. It was indeed barely sufficient, at best. His book appeared anonymously, and entered France only after protest.

Book XIV introduces a well-known idea, closely associated with Montesquieu's name. It is entitled: "Laws in their Relation to the Nature of the Climate." Once again, as throughout his work, the key word is *rapport,* relationship, for this idea of "relativity" is predominant in Montesquieu's thinking. It destroys the old idea of fixity and absoluteness. Institutions vary with conditions. Here the influence studied is that of climate. The thought is of course not wholly new. Aristotle, among the Greeks, had expressed it. The Frenchman, Jean Bodin, in the sixteenth century, and others had seen something of its possibilities. But Montesquieu gives it emphasis and wider currency.

His thought goes back to his early experiments with the microscope at Bordeaux. He recalls how he had seen the tissues of a sheep's tongue shrink when frozen, the protuberances reappear clearly when again thawed out. This confirms his feeling that the sensations of mankind are dulled by cold, stimulated by heat. People react to weather, good or bad, hot, cold, or temperate. Climate is only continued, or changing, weather. Gaiety or gloom may be induced by weather, sluggishness or activity. What we become in the long run is very much determined by the climate to which we are predominantly accustomed. Hence the distinction between the peoples of the North and those of the South, to be applied later to literature by Madame de Staël at the beginning of the nineteenth century.

The colder climates of the North stimulate activity and movement. Hunting is a popular sport. In the South, people are more likely to loll comfortably in the shade. The men of the North are said to be more liberty-loving, those of the South appear more likely to be enslaved. Such, at any rate, are some of the striking generalizations toward which Montesquieu's mind leans.

No doubt there is exaggeration here. We still know too little of human geography to be sure of our ground. Tentative experiments seem to show that more work is done in a temperate, but changeable climate than in one which is relatively pleasant and equable all the year round. Perhaps in too good weather man takes his ease. In any case, Montesquieu has raised an interesting and important question. We may not yet fully accept his answers, but we have still to find our own.

In Book XV, Chapter 5, Montesquieu, in a brief page, treats of negro slavery. A recent writer, incredibly, misreads this chapter as a defense of slavery! As a matter of fact, never was the author's irony more plain and bitter. In a series of short sentences, each made to stand out in a separate paragraph, Montesquieu lashes out against this terrible abuse.

"If I had to support our right to render the negroes slaves, here is what I should say":

"The Europeans, having exterminated the peoples of America, were obliged to enslave those of Africa, in order to clear the land."

"Sugar would be too dear if we didn't cultivate with slaves the plant which produces it."

"Those in question are black from head to foot, and have such a flat nose that it is impossible to pity them."

"We can't imagine that God, who is very wise, has put a soul, especially a good soul, in a body which is all black."

*   *   *

"It is impossible to suppose that those people are men, because, if we supposed them men, one would begin to think that we ourselves were not Christians."

Arguments from expediency, economics, color, are all fiercely brushed aside in favor of humanity. Who can claim to be a Christian if he is not humane? Montesquieu could hardly be clearer, except to the too literal-minded, nor his irony more devastating and completely unanswerable.

A similarly bitter irony in Book XXV, Chapter 13, attacks the Inquisition of Spain or Portugal for burning Jews as heretics. It is noteworthy that Montesquieu's indignation in these two cases rises to its height. But he has seen too much of human nature to delude himself with the belief that his onslaught will be quickly effective. "When we are concerned with proving things that are so clear, we may be sure of not convincing," he observes pessimistically. The human mind yields only grudgingly to logic.

There is much more in the *Spirit of Laws* than we have been able even to refer to here. If all of a great book could be put into a few pages, it would be unnecessary to read the book itself. But there is profit too in a quick survey. We can better see the highlights in brief space. If such a summary whets our appetite for the author himself, that is a real gain. If we perceive more clearly what remains true over the years and what our modern age may still learn from the past, that too justifies our turning back for a time to Montesquieu. Wisdom is a slow growth. With all its vaunted scientific progress, humanity advances toward civilization at a snail's pace. We need all the help of a great political thinker like the author of the *Spirit of Laws* to win, recover, or preserve our liberties.

5

In the middle of 1748, a few months before the appearance of the *Spirit of Laws,* Montesquieu published at Paris a new and definitive edition of his famous *Considerations on the Romans.* As we know, the slight changes he made did not extend to revision of the fabulous history of early Rome. But it was a great year for the illustrious author and brought to a well-deserved climax his growing fame.

On Christmas Day, 1754, according to one of his last letters, Montesquieu still lingered amid the familiar and well-loved surroundings of La Brède. Soon after, toward the end of December or the beginning of the new year, he left on what was to prove a final journey to Paris, returning once again to the house which he continued to rent on the Left Bank of the Seine at former Number 27 of Rue Saint-Dominique in the aristocratic Faubourg Saint-Germain.

Montesquieu's eyes had grown steadily worse and cataracts threatened him with a complete blindness about which he joked stoically. Late in January a sudden illness with the danger of pneumonia, forced him, on the advice of his doctor, to take to his bed. The malady proved serious and, two weeks later, on February 10, 1755, the great author was dead, surrounded by a few friends, but far from his family and his native Bordeaux. He had recently passed his sixty-sixth birthday.

Louis XV had honored himself, as well as Montesquieu, by sending the Duc de Nivernais to inquire after him during his illness. The King was not, however, wise enough to profit by the Baron's three great books. Of the men of letters of the day, only Diderot, according to Grimm, attended his funeral at the church of Saint-

Sulpice. Voltaire was far away in exile at Geneva, Rousseau outside of Paris in the country.

The *Spirit of Laws*, said the contemporary Raynal, "was made for all times and all nations." Montesquieu wrote first of all for France, but he was also, in the best sense of the term, a citizen of the world.

CHAPTER IX

MONTESQUIEU AND AMERICA

I

As early as 1750, hardly two years after its publication in France, the Library Society of Charleston, South Carolina, offered on its shelves an English translation of the *Spirit of Laws*. Benjamin Franklin possessed a copy of Montesquieu's work as also did the influential John Adams, James Wilson, and others. The first collection of books owned by Thomas Jefferson was burned and unfortunately no record remains of its contents. Jefferson was almost unique, among the great Americans of the time, in becoming violently opposed to Montesquieu in later life, but during his formative years he made an extensive abstract in French of the *Spirit of Laws* and evidently studied it closely. Indeed, a recently-discovered bill for books shows that he acquired a three-volume French edition of Montesquieu's works in mid-December of 1769 when he was twenty-six years old and probably read the *Spirit of Laws* shortly afterwards. In 1790, Jefferson wrote to Thomas Mann Randolph: "In the science of government, Montesquieu's *Spirit of Laws* is generally recommended." It is beside the point here that, with his newly-developed hostility, the future President continued: "It contains, indeed, a great number of political truths, but also an equal number of heresies, so that the reader must be constantly on his guard." By this time, Jefferson had begun to fear Montesquieu as a dangerous influence in support of English monarchy and of a strong centralized government according to the ideas of Hamilton. His very fear, however, is proof of Montesquieu's remarkable prestige.

John Adams had early read the *Spirit of Laws* systematically, writing in the margin "a sort of index to every paragraph." Although in his choleric independence, he by no means agreed fully with his predecessor, Adams was whimsically glad to entrench himself behind numerous authorities, among them Montesquieu.

James Madison, rightly known as the "Father" of the American Constitution, was from his early days at Princeton a diligent student of Montesquieu. Mr. Paul M. Spurlin, the authority on the vogue of Montesquieu in eighteenth-century America, points out that "the *Spirit of Laws* was repeatedly and consistently advertised, north and south," in booksellers' catalogues.

On April 18, 1763, the *Boston Gazette,* alarmed by the appointment of the Lieutenant-Governor to the post of Chief-Justice, invoked against this action "the admired writer of the *Spirit of Laws,*" adding "there is no liberty, 'says this writer,' if the power of *judging* be not separated from the *legislative* power." This discussion over the separation of powers continued vigorously throughout the formative period of the government, and indeed afterward down even to the present day. Adversaries, as well as supporters of the famous principle, cited Montesquieu as a respected, or feared, authority.

Both John and Samuel Adams quoted Montesquieu's celebrated description of the English Constitution. He appealed to them strongly as a concise expositor of their own inherited political background. Among the citations taken from Montesquieu in the colonies during the fifteen years before the American Revolution, "there were approximately three times as many references to Book XI" of the *Spirit of Laws,* observes Spurlin, "as all other references combined. And out of some twenty-five references to Book XI, eighteen were to the Constitution of England. In that chapter the point most cited was separation of powers; next in order of frequency was its definition of political liberty; and then came two citations of the prediction that England would lose her liberty when the legislative became more corrupt than the executive body."

Many political scientists now hold that Montesquieu either failed to perceive the English tendency to fuse the executive and the legislative powers in the concept of ministerial responsibility to Parliament, or at least oversimplified the separation. Yet as great an authority as Sir Frederick Pollock maintained, against his distinguished American friend, Justice Oliver Wendell Holmes, that Montesquieu, for the eighteenth century, was substantially right. "No one," writes Pollock, "thought of the King as a cogwheel: certainly not the fathers of the American Constitution, who knew a good deal more than they read in Blackstone." Certain it is, in any event, that Montesquieu's interpretation was widely and consciously accepted in America as accurate. His very emphasis upon the theory of a clear-cut separation of governmental powers, which was adopted in so much more thorough-going fashion in the United States than in England, offers further evidence of his influence.

On October 19, 1772, a full-page advertisement appeared in the *Massachusetts Gazette and the Boston Post Boy and Advertiser,* proposing to print by subscription an American edition of the *Spirit of Laws,* "which ought to be in every man's hands," as the sponsor enthusiastically said. The *Pennsylvania Gazette* made a similar proposal on December 28, 1774, in behalf of the masterpiece of "the great and immortal M. de Secondat, Baron de Montesquieu (so honorably mentioned by the Continental Congress)." But nothing came of either of these advertisements. Evidently, the relatively small group of Colonial leaders already possessed their own copies of the *Spirit of Laws* in French or English editions and had no need of more. In spite of his prestige, the reading public was still too limited to support a republication. The first American edition did not finally appear until 1802.

Through the critical period of the first and the second Continental Congress, the Revolution, and the Confederation, Montesquieu continued to be invoked frequently, with emphasis constantly on the separation of powers. The *Maryland Journal* on July 3, 1776, stated: "The justly celebrated Montesquieu observes that a complete tyranny is established by such a combination of powers." James Madison, in June 1784, attacked the Virginia Constitution as "defective . . . in a union of powers which is tyranny," according to "Montesquieu."

By the time the Constitutional Convention opened in the middle of May, 1787, the *Spirit of Laws,* observes Paul M. Spurlin, "had become an American classic." It was already a textbook at "the College of Philadelphia," at Yale, and at "the College of New Jersey," the later Princeton. Indeed, at Princeton, the great President Witherspoon gave a large place to Montesquieu in his lectures on political theory. James Madison, so decisive in the development of the American Constitution, learned his Montesquieu under Dr. Witherspoon. "Madison's knowledge of Montesquieu's *Esprit des lois* was so accurate," it has even been said, "that twenty years after he left Princeton he could quote it freely without error." Whatever exaggeration there may be in this statement, based, it seems, on a letter of Madison to Jefferson mentioning a single instance of such quotation, there is no doubt of Madison's remarkable familiarity with Montesquieu or of the esteem in which he held him. There were twenty-five college graduates in the Constitutional Convention. Nine of these were from Princeton and six bore diplomas signed by that rugged Scotchman, Dr. Witherspoon, who promptly after his arrival in this country had become an influential American citizen, taking a prominent part in public affairs as a member of the New Jersey Legislature, of the Continental Congress, and of the Congress of the Confederation. There is no doubt of the great influence of Montesquieu on President Witherspoon, and through him on his students.

2

Just a few squares west of the Delaware River, in the midst of the checker-board streets of early Philadelphia, stood the beautiful Georgian brick building of the Pennsylvania State House, not yet known as Independence Hall. The name was, however, already sometimes given to the small white-paneled council chamber where the revolutionary signers of the famous Declaration had met and voted in 1776. Now, eleven years later, this substantial colonial edifice situated between Fifth, Sixth, Walnut, and Chestnut Streets was again to be the scene of decisive debate and action. Although the second city in size at the time in the infant country, Philadelphia still had a population of less than 28,000 and the distances within its limits were not great. Except for the bustle along the busy waterfront, the general atmosphere was one of leisure and tranquillity in sharp contrast to the rush and roar of modern traffic.

On Sunday afternoon of May 13, 1787, General Washington drove into Philadelphia after a five-day journey in his carriage over rough roads from his home at Mount Vernon, some one hundred and fifty miles away. He was then fifty-five and in the full flower of his prestige after the successful conclusion of the Revolutionary War. His chief longing, however, was for retirement from the strain of public life to the peaceful quiet of his beautiful country estate on the Potomac. Yet, in spite of grinding pain from rheumatism in the shoulder, he had consented, under urging, to abandon his personal preferences and to serve his country again, this time as a delegate from Virginia to the Constitutional Convention. Somehow the brave attempt must be made to establish a stronger and more effective national government than the feeble Confederation. In that effort, forlorn as it might appear in the midst of sharp clashes of contemporary opinion, Washington above all must show confidence, lending to the cause his incomparable reputation for strength, integrity, and devotion. "Let us raise a standard," he said, "to which the wise and honest can repair."

The next day, Monday, the 14th of May, the Constitutional Convention met in its first session. Nothing could be done, however, as most of the delegates, under the slow conditions of travel which prevailed, had not yet arrived. Not more than eight or ten men were probably present. Franklin, if he came, had to be carried about the city in a sedan chair. His sufferings from gout and the stone were so intense as to prevent him from riding in a conventional carriage. Franklin was by a full twenty years the oldest of the delegates. The youngest, Alexander Hamilton of New York, was only thirty. Gouverneur Morris of Pennsylvania was thirty-five, and James Madison of Virginia was but a year older than Morris. Thomas Jefferson, many weeks away across the Atlantic in succession to Franklin as American Minister to France, was not in close touch with the Convention.

Finally, about ten days later, on Friday, the 25th of May, seven states, a majority of the thirteen, were represented and a first formal meeting was held. Twenty-nine delegates were present, the number from each state, however, not being equal. Because of a pouring rain, the aged Franklin, with his infirmities, did not attend, but Robert Morris moved, in his absence and at his suggestion, that Washington be elected to preside. Before so obvious a choice, there was no debate and he was at once unanimously voted in as chairman.

Of the thirteen original states, Rhode Island sent no delegates and was not represented; New Hampshire did not name anyone until the end of June. Altogether, there were finally a secretary and fifty-five delegates who attended, though several of these straggled in late during the summer, while others departed, and it is probable there were rarely more than thirty present at an average day's session. It was a small, intimate group, suitable for momentous discussion, which thus came together in the beautiful East Room, hardly forty-feet square, to the left of the main entrance to the State House. The place was one adapted to reasoned, factual argument, not to the grand oratorical flights, imagined by a recent French writer, remote from the American scene.

On Tuesday, May 29th, it was voted to conduct the debates in complete secrecy. Jefferson, far away in Paris, when he finally heard about this decision, revolted vigorously at "so abominable a precedent as that of tying up the tongues of their members" and this "ignorance of the value of public discussions," but none of the many wise and judicious men present objected to what they evidently regarded as a desirable provision against misunderstanding and distortion. Moreover, this procedure permitted members to speak frankly and to change their opinions later without too great embarrassment or "loss of face." Madison, the best informed and most influential man in the Convention, still believed forty-three years later that no agreement would have been reached if the debates had been public. In the end, the final conclusions were of course fully made known and were widely discussed in each state before adoption. Only the uncertain and difficult route by which they were arrived at was for the time being withheld from the public.

Armed sentries outside the State House and in the corridor near the closed chamber, where the sessions were held through the long, humid summer of 1787, enforced this rule of secrecy. On one occasion, a careless delegate dropped outside the meeting hall his copy of the famous Virginia Plan, which ultimately became the basis of the Constitution. It was found and turned over to Washington. The presiding officer kept it silently in his pocket until the end of the session. Finally, before putting the motion to adjourn, Washington in measured words sternly rebuked the assembly. "I must entreat Gentlemen to be more careful," he said, "lest our Transactions get into the News Papers, and disturb the public repose by premature speculations. I know not whose Paper it is, but there it is, let him who owns it take it." Throwing the missing paper down on the table, Washington bowed coldly, picked up his hat, and strode from the room with that severe dignity which only he could command. No one in the awed meeting ever dared admit his ownership of the offending document. So much for the rule of secrecy which effectively proved its value by the ultimate results.

Fortunately for posterity, several of the delegates kept records of the momentous assembly, the most important being the one by Madison. "I chose a seat," he said later, "in front of the presiding member, with the other members on my right hand and left hand. In this favorable position for hearing all that passed I noted in terms legible and abbreviations and marks intelligible to myself what was read from the Chair or spoken by the members; and losing not a moment unnecessarily between the adjournment and re-assembling of the Convention I was enabled to write out my daily notes during the session or within a few finishing days after its close. . . . It happened also that I was not absent a single day, nor more than a casual fraction of an hour in any day, so that I could not have lost a single speech, unless a very short one." In a number of instances also, Madison's fellow members gave him copies of their remarks which thus survive in his indispensable notes.

James Madison of Virginia not only made the most complete record of the deliberations of the Convention; he played a decisive part in it. Before the meetings began, he had prepared himself in scholarly fashion for what was coming. He had drafted an analysis of the *Vices of the Political System of the United States,* that is, of the abortive Confederation, and he had written an extensive study entitled, *Of Ancient and Modern Confederacies.* Thus he sought, in every way possible, to learn from the experience of the past. This latter article has been found, moreover, among the papers of Washington, copied in his own hand, striking evidence of his desire to inform himself in advance from the best possible source.

Madison had much to do also with drafting the famous "Virginia Plan" for a new national government. The "New Jersey Plan" was rejected except for one important point; those drawn up by Hamilton and by Pinckney were not seriously considered. It was the Virginia Plan, as gradually amended, which became the basis for the federal Constitution.

3

Major William Pierce, delegate from Georgia, noted down on the spot his impressions of James Madison. "Mr. Madison," wrote Pierce, "is a character who has long been in public life; and what is very remarkable every Person seems to acknowledge his greatness. He blends together the profound politician, with the Scholar. In the management of every great question he evidently took the lead in the Convention, and tho' he cannot be called an Orator, he is a most agreeable, eloquent, and convincing Speaker. . . . From a spirit of industry and application which he possesses in a most eminent degree, he always comes forward the best informed Man of any point in debate. The affairs of the United States, he perhaps has the most correct knowledge of, of any man in the Union. . . . Mr. Madison is about thirty-seven years of age, a Gentleman of great modesty,—with a remarkable sweet temper. He is easy and unreserved among his acquaintance, and has a most agreeable style of conversation."

Washington's character and prestige carried great weight, but, as the presiding officer and by inclination he spoke little in debate. Franklin's renown was world-wide. His age and his infirmities, how-ever, prevented him from taking a leading role in the Convention. The few proposals he made were listened to with respect, but generally not accepted by the other delegates. It was by his occa-sional humorous anecdotes, which relieved tension, and by his calm, conciliatory attitude that Franklin most helped to bring about ulti-mate agreement. Madison's part was more positive. He it was who, more than any other, by his knowledge, his logic, and his poise, shaped the form of the final decisions.

On June 30, for example, Madison pointed out that Mr. Ellsworth of Connecticut, arguing for equal representation of the small states, "had erred in saying that no instance had existed in which con-federated States had not retained to themselves a perfect equality of suffrage." He "reminded Mr. Ellsworth of the Lycian confederacy, in which the component members had votes proportioned to their importance, and which Montesquieu recommends as the fittest model for that form of Government." This question of representa-tion was basic and involved a sharp disagreement between the large and small states which was only resolved in the end, as we know, by a compromise, with numbers proportional to population in the House of Representatives and fixed representation of two for each state in the Senate. Montesquieu clearly lent his authority in sup-port of one half of the compromise, proportional representation, which was an important modification of the existing feeble Con-federation.

On Tuesday, July 17th, in a crucial discussion, Madison observed in regard to the separation of governmental powers: "Why was it determined that the Judges should not hold their places by such a tenure? Because they might be tempted to cultivate the Legislature, by an undue complaisance, and thus render the Legislature the virtual expositor, as well as the maker of the laws. In like manner a dependence of the Executive on the Legislature, would render it the Executor as well as the maker of the laws; and then according to the observation of Montesquieu, tyrannical laws may be made that they may be executed in a tyrannical manner."

Alexander Hamilton, on June 18th, in a long, able speech, cited Montesquieu in favor of the form of the British Constitution and against the dangers of domestic factions and standing armies. James Wilson of Pennsylvania referred to Montesquieu in support of a confederated republic. This was on June 1st in the early period of the debates as the fundamental plan of government was beginning to take form. Speaking in favor of a regular national census so that proportional representation could be properly carried out, Edmund Randolph of Virginia said: "What relates to suffrage is justly stated by the celebrated Montesquieu, as a fundamental article in Republican Governments." On September 6th, James Wilson remarked: "Montesquieu says, an officer is the officer of those who appoint him. This power may in a little time render the Senate independent of the people." On June 23rd, Pierce Butler of South Carolina had spoken on an amendment to curb the eligibility of the legislative body to other offices at the same time. He said: "The proposed amendment does not go far enough. . . . The great Montesquieu says, it is unwise to entrust persons with power, which by being abused operates to the advantage of those entrusted with it."

While abroad as Minister to England, John Adams published a carefully documented defense of the system of checks and balances as against Turgot's attack, nearly ten years before, on the form of the American government in favor of a strongly centralized national power. In support of his position, Adams reproduced without comment of his own nearly a third of Montesquieu's important chapter on the Constitution of England.

Montesquieu was likewise cited in the conventions which were called in the different states for the decisive purpose of ratifying or rejecting the new Constitution. In Pennsylvania, James Wilson addressed himself to an often-repeated objection. Montesquieu had said that a democratic government was suited only to a small territory. With the slow means of communication in those days, it is easy to understand his position, which was based on the experience of history up to that time. But Montesquieu had also pointed out the value of a federative republic to combine the advantages of local democracy with a strong national government over a large territory. "The definition of this form of government," observed Wilson, "may be found in Montesquieu, who says, I believe, that it consists in assembling distinct societies which are consolidated into a new body, capable of being increased by the addition of other members—an expanding quality peculiarly fitted to the circumstances of America." This was a crucial point, involving a union of all the existing states in spite of their twelve-hundred mile extent along the Atlantic seaboard and permitting likewise the admission of new states as they should chance to be created in the unknown future. Many men at the time argued for the necessity of three or four regional confederacies because of this very difficulty of slow communication and differences of interest over an immense territory. Thus Montesquieu was cited against the possibility of union by those who knew him incompletely, in behalf of union by those who had read him better. In Massachusetts, James Bowdoin, Jr., developed the same point, also quoting Montesquieu in favor of ratifying the Constitution. Hamilton took a similar stand in the New York Convention.

In Virginia, Edmund Randolph, though he had wavered and refused to sign the Constitution as a delegate to the Convention, now came out for adoption against George Mason and the eloquent Patrick Henry. Randolph referred to the "definition of a republican government, as laid down by a man who is highly esteemed," and proceeded to quote "Montesquieu, so celebrated among politicians." As Patrick Henry thundered his fiery, but ill-informed opposition, Edmund Pendleton, with cogent logic, argued the necessity of a strong government to protect liberty: "What say the most respectable writers—Montesquieu, Locke, Sidney, Harrington, etc?. . . . They recommend making the ligaments of government firm, and a rigid execution of the laws, as more necessary than in a monarchy, to preserve that virtue which they all declare to be the pillar on which the government and liberty, its object, must stand."

4

Most important as an exposition of the principles of the new Constitution was that remarkable series of essays written by Alexander Hamilton, James Madison, and John Jay, and known as the *Federalist*. These eighty-five essays first appeared in New York newspapers from October, 1787, to April, 1788. They were gathered together into book form during March and May of the latter year in two small volumes. Though nothing of course could influence prejudiced partisans in the opposition or the purely political maneuvers on either side in the various ratifying conventions, these essays did carry conviction to the thoughtful and the open-minded. Washington for example praised them highly. They remain to this day one of the most penetrating discussions ever made of the problem of combining government with freedom. "In framing a government which is to be administered by men over men," wrote Madison with hard-headed realism, "the great difficulty lies in this: you must first enable the government to control the governed; and in the next place oblige it to control itself."

From the *Federalist* as from other sources, it is clear that one of the questions confronting the delegates to the Constitutional Convention was, as we have seen, the enormous extent of territory which made national union doubtful. It should not be thought today that the thirteen states easily came together into one government. In fact, "we already hear it whispered," wrote Hamilton, "that the thirteen States are of too great extent for any general system, and that we must of necessity resort to separate confederacies of distinct portions of the whole." Montesquieu was, with a semblance of truth, quoted on both sides, but Hamilton pointed out that, when the author of the *Spirit of Laws* spoke of a small territory for a democracy, he was thinking of a size even less than that of the large states of the existing confederation. Thus the argument, if pressed, would suggest the inefficacy even of the state governments themselves. Hamilton then cited Montesquieu on the advantages of a Confederate Republic. "I have thought it proper," he concluded, "to quote at length these interesting passages, because they contain a luminous abridgment of the principal arguments in favor of the Union." But the spectre was not easily laid. Madison, too, had to combat "the prevailing prejudice with regard to the practicable sphere of republican administration," draw clearly the distinction between representative government and pure democracy, and emphasize the changes to be brought about in the rapidity of communication through improvement of roads and canals.

Another object of attack in the new Constitution was the representation in proportion to population accorded in the House of Representatives in contrast with the equal votes of the states under the feeble Confederation. The small states insisted on equality; the large ones wished influence based on number of inhabitants. Hamilton, like Madison in the earlier debates, cited Montesquieu in support of this latter principle in the Lycian confederacy.

A further troublesome issue was the question of states' rights. Some degree of local independence must evidently be given up if a strong union was to be formed. "Among the advantages of a confederate republic enumerated by Montesquieu," observed Madison in the *Federalist* with an eye no doubt to Shays's recent rebellion in Massachusetts, "an important one is, 'that should a popular insurrection happen in one of the States, the others are able to quell it. Should abuses creep into one part, they are reformed by those that remain sound.' "

Most important of all was the theory of checks and balances with the separation of governmental powers. Few men at the time were inclined to question its validity, but the question was: How to apply it in practice? Aristotle had hinted at the principle. Polybius had spoken of it with favor in Roman antiquity. The Englishman Locke nearly a century before had observed that it may be "too great temptation to human frailty, apt to grasp at power, for the same persons who have the power of making laws to have also in their hands the power to execute them." But Locke remained in many instances ambiguous in his phraseology, he believed in the supremacy of the legislative, and he did not set off clearly by itself the judicial power. The Swiss Burlamaqui, in his *Principles of Natural Law* (1747), made this latter distinction, was widely read, and was certainly known among others to Madison, Hamilton, Jefferson, James Wilson, and John Adams, but Burlamaqui was less precise and more fragmentary than Montesquieu; he seems not to have been often quoted to clinch an argument, and must therefore have lacked general appeal. "The oracle who is always consulted and cited on this subject is the celebrated Montesquieu," as Madison so well said. "If he be not the author of this invaluable precept in the science of politics," continued the great authority on the formation of the Constitution, "he has the merit at least of displaying and recommending it most effectually to the attention of mankind."

CHAPTER IX

"There can be but one supreme power, which is the legislative, to which all the rest are and must be subordinate," Locke had written confidently in 1690, flushed with the importance of recent successful Parliamentary resistance to the English King. But experience with this predominance in the States during the Confederation had not been happy. "The legislative department is everywhere extending the sphere of its activity, and drawing all power into its impetuous vortex," observed Madison in the *Federalist* with vigorous condemnation. "The founders of our republics," he continued, "seem never to have recollected the danger from legislative usurpations, which, by assembling all power in the same hands, must lead to the same tyranny as is threatened by executive usurpations." Thus oppression by the many was seen to be possible as well as oppression by the few. Hamilton repeated the criticism: "The tendency of the legislative authority to absorb every other, has been fully displayed and illustrated by examples in some preceding numbers. In governments purely republican, this tendency is almost irresistible." In another passage, he commented: "The propensity of the legislative department to intrude upon the rights, and to absorb the powers, of the other departments has been already suggested." Even Thomas Jefferson, in spite of his strong democratic sympathies, had remarked in his *Notes on Virginia*—and Madison quoted him—that a mere declaration in favor of the separation of powers in the state constitution had been of no effect. "All the powers of government, legislative, executive, and judiciary, result to the legislative body. The concentrating these in the same hands," said Jefferson, "is precisely the definition of despotic government."

This position is clearly in accord not with Locke, but with Montesquieu. Indeed, Madison quotes the latter directly to this effect. "The reasons on which Montesquieu grounds his maxim are a further demonstration of his meaning," wrote Madison in the *Federalist*. " 'When the legislative and executive powers are united in the same person or body,' says he, 'there can be no liberty, because apprehensions may arise lest the same monarch or senate should enact tyrannical laws to execute them in a tyrannical manner.' Again: 'Were the power of judging joined with the legislative, the life and liberty of the subject would be exposed to arbitrary control, for the judge would then be the legislator. Were it joined to the executive power, the judge might behave with all the violence of an oppressor.' "

Fear of legislative rashness was one thing; fear of a strong executive was another. There was a clear memory of the numerous abuses of autocratic power in history and particularly of recent acts by George III. The state of Pennsylvania for this reason had given the direction of affairs to a plural governing body. But Montesquieu had said: "The executive power . . . is better administered by one than by several." Likewise, Hamilton observed: "Those politicians and statesmen who have been most celebrated for the soundness of their principles and for the justice of their views, have declared in favor of a single Executive and a numerous legislature." Hence the decision, ultimately, after much discussion, in favor of one man as President with broadly defined powers.

But, if in early America there was fear, equally, of legislative and of executive tyranny, Montesquieu had said and Hamilton cited him: "Of the three powers above mentioned, the judiciary is next to nothing." So Hamilton, fortified by Montesquieu and by his own conservative leanings, expressed no fear of the possibility of judicial tyranny. "It is far more rational to suppose," he said, "that the courts were designed to be an intermediate body between the people and the legislature, in order, among other things, to keep the latter within the limits assigned to their authority. . . . Nor does this conclusion by any means suppose a superiority of the judicial to the legislative power. It only supposes that the power of the people is superior to both." In fact the courts of justice have the duty, he had already stated more specifically, "to declare all acts contrary to the manifest tenor of the Constitution void." Thus Hamilton supported the theory of judicial review by which the judges determine the constitutionality of a legislative act.

But adversaries of the new Constitution argued that in this plan of government the three powers were not sufficiently "separate and distinct." In rebuttal, Madison explained: "Montesquieu . . . did not mean that these departments ought to have no *partial agency* in, or *control* over, the acts of each other. His meaning . . . can amount to no more than this, that where the *whole* power of one department is exercised by the same hands which possess the *whole* power of another department, the fundamental principles of a free constitution are subverted." Madison then, without defending the form of the existing state governments, observes that "there is not a single instance in which the several departments of power have been kept absolutely separate and distinct." Some indeed may have "too great a mixture, and even an actual consolidation of the different powers." Jefferson, in his *Notes on Virginia,* had already pointed out that, although tripartite separation of powers was decreed by the state constitution, there was a fatal weakness because "no barrier was provided between these several powers," and Madison concluded: "A mere demarcation on parchment of the constitutional limits of the several departments, is not a sufficient guard against those encroachments which lead to tyrannical concentration of all the powers of government in the same hands."

Since a simple prohibition on paper is no firm guarantee against abuse, what, then, is the remedy? "But the great security against a gradual concentration of the several powers in the same department," answered the *Federalist,* "consists in giving to those who administer each department the necessary constitutional means and personal motives to resist encroachments of the others. . . . Ambition must be made to counteract ambition." This is the theory of powers which are separated, but to some extent overlapping, so that the different authorities must either concur or else prevent action in certain cases, the famous principle of checks and balances.

5

Many political writers have criticized Montesquieu's idea of the separation of powers, and hence its application in the American government, as a cumbersome block to changes sought by the majority. "This is a useful theory for those who have something to guard," says Herman Finer, "but a wasteful obstacle to those who have urgent wants." The system has generally been favored by conservatives; it has been opposed by liberals or radicals desirous of prompt reform. Particularly, the theory of judicial review and the role of the "nine old men" of the Supreme Court has in modern times come under scathing attack. "The Constitution," said Charles Evans Hughes, no doubt half facetiously, but no less realistically, "is what the judges say it is." In the long run, however, necessary changes do tend to take place, though less rapidly and perhaps in some cases less rashly, than if determined at once under popular pressure by Congress or the Executive. "The Supreme Court too," it has been observed, "reads the election returns." But in human affairs it is always men who have to decide moot questions, and it is sometimes forgotten that the majority, like the minority, is not always right or wise. " 'There is safety in numbers,' " it has been said, "is the maxim of the foolish; 'there is ruin in numbers', of the wise." Thus complete truth lies certainly with neither side. It was the feeling of the founding fathers that slow change concurred in by three different divisions of government was in the long run safer than the perhaps impulsive action of a single man or of a popular majority. This too was Montesquieu's opinion which they held in high esteem.

What the authors of the Constitution in the United States chiefly feared was tyranny. They had witnessed the long, bitter battle for liberty in England; they had seen the struggle for freedom hardly even begun in most parts of the world; they felt keenly the need for effective law and order after the chaos of the feeble Confederation; they had also a profound experience of "the ordinary depravity of human nature," as Hamilton put it. "Are not popular assemblies frequently subject to the impulses of rage, resentment, jealousy, avarice, and of other irregular and violent propensities?" he further asked. "Is it not time to awake from the deceitful dream of a golden age?" he urged. "Why has government been instituted at all? Because the passions of men will not conform to the dictates of reason and justice, without constraint." And again: "The idea of governing at all times by the simple force of law . . . has no place but in the reveries of those political doctors whose sagacity disdains the admonitions of experimental instruction," concluded Hamilton. Thus, in practical affairs, as Madison observed, "ambition must be made to counteract ambition."

"The doctrine of the separation of powers was adopted by the Convention of 1787," as the late Justice Brandeis has well stated, "not to promote efficiency, but to preclude the exercise of arbitrary power. The purpose was, not to avoid friction, but, by means of the inevitable friction incident to the distribution of the governmental powers among three departments, to save the people from autocracy." The separation of powers was intended as a brake upon oppressive or unwise action.

With the threat of totalitarian tyranny renewed in the world today, the safeguard of the separation of powers, with all its delays and imperfections, becomes understandable in a way that it was not so easily comprehended a generation ago when humanity was fondly thought to be moving rapidly toward greater understanding and peace. The authors of the Constitution were far from claiming that their system was perfect. "I never expect to see a perfect work from imperfect man," said Hamilton succinctly. But the delegates agreed with Montesquieu when he said: "Constant experience shows us that every man invested with power is apt to abuse it, and to carry his authority as far as it will go. . . . To prevent this abuse, it is necessary from the very nature of things that power should be a check to power." The founding fathers sought to be safe rather than sorry.

It would be a mistake to suppose that Montesquieu was the sole author of this theory of the separation of powers, which went back in part to Aristotle and Polybius in ancient times, in part to the judicial parlements in France, in a greater degree to the English system, to Locke, and to firsthand experience with the colonial charters and governments in America. But it is clear after the evidence cited here how much the great French writer meant from the standpoint of support and clarification of what Madison called "the sacred maxim of free government." Without the aid of Montesquieu's *Spirit of Laws*, the uncertain task of drawing up the new constitution would certainly have been more difficult, perhaps even impossible, in the midst of the violent struggle between divergent opinions. The battle throughout was keen, the issue doubtful, until the final ratification in close votes by a majority of the states. If these early debaters so frequently drew upon Montesquieu, it is evidently because they set great store by his prestige and authority, and because they found his reasoning conclusive.

CHAPTER X

VOLTAIRE AND THE BOMBSHELL
OF THE *PHILOSOPHICAL LETTERS*

I

IT WAS A FRAIL CHILD INDEED WHO WAS BORN IN THE HEART OF Paris on November 21, 1694, in the midst of what are still the narrow twisting streets of the old parish known as Saint-André-des-Arts. Who, in this feeble infant, could have foreseen a long, combative, and colorful career of nearly eighty-four years?

His father was a business-like notary of some distinction, what we should call a lawyer engaged in civil practice. The boy, François-Marie Arouet, as he was baptized the next day—the name Voltaire was to come later—belonged therefore to the prosperous upper *bourgeoisie* or middle-class. By his extraordinary wit, acumen, and literary ability, he was to step over the dividing line which sharply separated noble and commoner, getting himself more or less accepted as a member of that aristocracy to which his merit, if not his birth, entitled him. But the ascent was difficult, and the young man, if he easily acquired a graceful and exquisite courtesy, lost none of his natural impudence on occasion or his mordant, critical spirit in regard to snobbery and ancient abuses.

The child's mother, Marguerite Daumard (or D'Aumard), was a descendant of the lesser nobility from the old province of Poitou in west-central France. From her the boy inherited, it seems, his keen taste for literature; from his father came that practical hardheaded business sense which is not often combined with authorship. But the mother died prematurely when the boy was seven, and we can only speculate in vain as to whether his life would have been notably different if he had longer enjoyed her vivid companionship and guidance.

Three years later the father, a busy man of affairs, unable no doubt longer to supervise effectively the upbringing of his precocious and self-willed son, placed him in the near-by Jesuit *collège* of Louis-le-Grand, adjacent to the Sorbonne in the ancient Latin Quarter of Paris. The institution still exists under the same name today as a state-supported *lycée*. Young Arouet was ten in 1704 when he entered the famous school; he was sixteen when he left it in 1711. Many sons of the nobility were to be found there. The D'Argenson brothers, D'Argental, Cideville, were among those who remained his lifelong friends. Their acquaintance encouraged and facilitated his ambition.

The Jesuits formed the boy's literary taste, stimulated his interest in history, drama, and poetry, taught him Latin, which was of course then the backbone of the curriculum, and a little Greek. The legend is that he already manifested an instinctive skepticism and a mocking disrespect for established authority. But the stories are unproved and may well have been invented after the fact in order to show forth the boy as completely father to the man. In any case, Arouet never lost his esteem for some of his able instructors at Louis-le-Grand, Father Porée, Father Tournemine, and willingly acknowledged his great debt to their skillful and patient teaching. It was a good, though not profound classical education which the Jesuits gave him. The future author was to furnish a striking example both of its excellencies and of its limitations.

As he finished school in 1711, the question naturally came up of his plans for a career. With the self-confidence of youth, he replied: "I want none but that of a man of letters." All-too-conscious of the many uncertainties besetting such a profession, his practical father retorted: "That's the position of a man who wishes to be useless to society, a burden to his parents, and to die of hunger." With the advantage of our present hindsight, we can easily perceive now how wrong his father was on all three counts, but, in view of the unpredictability of genius and the hand-to-mouth existence of many a struggling writer in the eighteenth century, it did not look so then. The brash young boy was put to the study of law.

Like many another author, before and since, Arouet was infinitely bored by legal terminology and technicalities. He wanted none of what was to him a humdrum profession. Yet experience with the law sharpened his business sense, armed him with courtroom forms and procedure, made certain that he would be well able to increase and protect his later wealth—for he was by no means "to die of hunger," as his father had so sourly predicted.

Meanwhile, a freethinking, deistically-minded ecclesiastic, Abbé de Châteauneuf, had introduced the lively youth to what was known as the "Society of the Temple," a group of men gathered about the Duc de Vendôme, Grand Prior of the Knights of Malta. It was a circle of distinguished *débauchés* whose irreverent wit played gaily over all the seeming follies of Church or State. If Arouet's frail physique left him little taste for the drinking bouts of these boon companions, he could soon vie with the best of them in quip, epigram, or light society verse. "Are we all princes or all poets?" he was to say later at supper to the Prince de Conti. His first classical tragedy of *Œdipus* was here read aloud and respectfully polished under the counsel of these arbiters of literary fame. The young author took eagerly to this worldly schooling, so different from the Jesuit *collège,* so fitted to his taste. We can sympathize, too, with the long-suffering father, sure that his riotous son was going completely to the dogs.

For a change of scene, the notary snatched up his troublesome offspring and packed him off in haste to Holland. It bespeaks the elder Arouet's considerable influence that he was able to put him under the charge of the French ambassador at The Hague. But the busy envoy had little time, no doubt, to watch over and check the rising ardor of youth. The boy promptly imagined himself in love with a certain Mademoiselle Dunoyer, "Pimpette," as she was nicknamed. With a useful veneer of piety he plotted the conversion of this girl of a dubious Protestantism, even planned an elopement to Paris. The harassed ambassador returned his disturbing protégé home, where the angry father thought of banishing the son to "America," that is, to the far-off islands of the French West Indies. What a different and probably obscure career if this hot-tempered impulse had been followed! But the father relented and some kind of a treaty of peace was made. Young Arouet went back by day to the musty law office of Maître Allain, while continuing his gay career by night with the dangerous *habitués* of the Temple. With such a compromise, neither side could be happy, but the son had the better of the arrangement, for he managed still to neglect the law to his heart's content, while devoting his plentiful leisure to literature and the roistering companions who pleased him.

In 1715, the irrepressible boy burst forth with satirical verses against the then well-known author La Motte. The much-tried father sent his nuisance of a son into prudent exile at the château of Saint-Ange with the elderly noble, Monsieur de Caumartin. This was a most important experience, as it turned out, since the memory of Monsieur de Caumartin was well stored with significant and interesting anecdotes direct from the preceding seventeenth century. Here, at first hand, young Arouet was unconsciously preparing himself for what became his long-famous epic poem on Henry IV and his much more important history of the *Age of Louis XIV*.

Back in Paris, the son of the notary went on his merry way. But this time he aimed his shafts too high. A new satirical poem was leveled audaciously at the Regent of France, the dissolute Duke of Orleans himself. The result was prompt imprisonment in the gloomy fortress of the Bastille which, until the Revolution, continued to frown menacingly over the teeming eastern quarters of Paris. For eleven dragging months in 1717 and 1718, the young man remained behind these thick walls. The experience was not exactly painful, but it was boresome, an unhappy contrast to the joyous, varied life outside. There is a tradition that the budding poet contrived to write much of his future epic, the *Henriade,* between the lines of a book he had managed to get hands on in default of paper. In the eighteenth century, such imprisonment in the Bastille for political, religious, or other defiance of censorship, was generally not too harsh and carried with it indeed a certain distinction. Nevertheless, we can be sure that young Arouet was not loath to be at last released. Wittily, he paid his court to the Regent in that best of coins at the time by begging him gaily in the future to provide his board, if he wished, but not his lodging!

A successful series of performances of his play, *Œdipus,* at the Comédie-Française made the young author famous at twenty-four. He was hailed widely as the promising successor to the great Sophocles and Corneille. It was a heady diet for one in no way noted for prudence or restraint. The time seemed appropriate to adopt a new and more distinguished name. The dramatist signed himself Arouet de Voltaire. Of the different theories as to the origin of this name, perhaps the most plausible is that it comes from inverting and respelling the syllables of Airvault, a little village in the province of Poitou where the family owned property. This is the theory proposed by Mr. Ira O. Wade. In any event, it was to be some time before the emerging writer could get his aristocratic name completely accepted by society.

2

Several uneasy years followed. The young author was not able immediately to duplicate the striking success of his tragedy of *Œdipus*. His next plays were failures. In 1722, Voltaire returned to Holland, this time in his greater maturity to be much impressed by the prosperous world trade and the extraordinary freedom which the little country enjoyed. The experience was a kind of preparation for the more important journey to England a short while later.

In 1725 the young man's new name and his self-assurance again got him into trouble. The Chevalier de Rohan-Chabot belonged to a haughty and illustrious family. Deciding no doubt to take down the upstart young author with a bit of studied insolence, the nobleman eyed him contemptuously one evening at the Opera and, alluding to his unauthorized change of name, addressed him with obvious sarcasm: "Monsieur de Voltaire, Monsieur Arouet, what is your name anyway?" Voltaire's exact reply is not certainly known. Perhaps he said, as was reported many years later by Abbé du Vernet, who is supposed to have drawn much of his information from Thieriot, the friend of Voltaire, that he did not dishonor a great name, and that he knew how to honor the one he did bear; perhaps he observed that he was beginning his line while on the contrary the Chevalier de Chabot was bringing his to a close. Little doubt that Voltaire's ready wit did not leave him at a loss.

Two days later at the Comédie-Française, the Chevalier renewed the quarrel. Voltaire answered that he had already made his reply at the Opera. The nobleman raised his cane as though to strike down this impudence, whereupon the celebrated actress, Mademoiselle Lecouvreur, conveniently fainted and, by thus diverting attention, put an end to the dispute for the moment. Two or three days later, Voltaire was dining in distinguished company at the table of the Duc de Sully. A lackey brought a message that someone was inquiring for him below. The author went downstairs, suspecting nothing. Outside the door, three lackeys promptly began belaboring him on the back and shoulders with rods, while the Chevalier de Rohan-Chabot, it is said, directed the affair from a neighboring carriage.

CHAPTER X

There is a story from the diary of the contemporary Marquis d'Argenson that the brave Chevalier called out: "Don't hit him on the head; something good may come out of that yet!" Onlookers exclaimed ironically: "Oh, the kind nobleman!"

In this outrageous assault, the Duc de Sully refused to intervene. The Prince de Conti, who had praised the author of *Œdipus* as worthy to rank between Corneille and Racine, dismissed the blows as "well received and badly delivered." Even Abbé de Caumartin, of the family with whom Voltaire had been so intimate at Saint-Ange, observed: "We should be most unfortunate if poets had no shoulders." The lawyer Marais reported simply and brutally: "The poor recipient of the blows shows himself, as much as he can, at the Court and in the city, but no one sympathizes with him, and those whom he thought his friends, have turned their backs on him."

It was a bitter lesson in the great gulf which still yawned between noble and commoner. In spite of his witty sallies and striking success as a dramatist, in spite of his seeming equality at table with dukes and princes, Voltaire found himself relegated to the position of a clever entertainer with no rights which a degenerate scion of a noble house was bound to respect. In the effort to restore his wounded honor, the poet took lessons in fencing to prepare himself for a duel. But the Chevalier de Rohan-Chabot had no great reputation for courage. Besides, he would not lower his noble self to fight with a mere *bourgeois,* who if beaten by lackeys had received only his just deserts! The powerful Rohan family no doubt spoke a word to the government. An order was given for Voltaire's arrest and, during the night of April 17, 1726, he was hustled away a second time to the Bastille. More schooling in the capricious tyranny of the Old Régime!

While in the Bastille, Voltaire had English books brought him by his friend Thieriot. Since the imprisonment this time lasted but two weeks, they are significant, however, only as an indication of the way his mind was turning. Shortly the offended author received permission to exchange his walled cell for exile in England. Early in May he was released, on the fifth he was at Calais, and sometime during the month he arrived in London. His stay in the country across the Channel is a very important period in his life. Perhaps he would have gone there sooner or later, anyhow, perhaps not. In any case, the Rohan-Chabot quarrel had far-reaching consequences. The empty-headed Chevalier had started a chain of events the ultimate importance of which he little knew. Voltaire was to become an important medium for the spread of ideas of English liberty over the Continent.

The Revocation of the Edict of Nantes in 1685, as we have seen, had driven large numbers of Protestant refugees into difficult exile in England. Many of them were educated pastors who, in their new-found asylum, made themselves into journalists eager to write in French periodicals about English liberty, English tolerance, and English literature. These periodicals generally circulated from Holland, thus avoiding censorship. Louis XIV, with his ill-conceived aim of religious unity based on force, had thus unwittingly set in motion forces destined to further the rise of the very freedom which he so much feared and hated.

It was no accident therefore that Voltaire chose in 1726 to go to England as the condition of his release from the Bastille. England was the one country, at the time, which could best contribute to his education and experience. With all its human imperfections, the known bribery of many members of Parliament at the time, the violence of its political quarrels, England nevertheless offered the rare spectacle of a large measure of religious tolerance, of free debate over government policies, of arrest only on a warrant showing cause, of an early trial by jury guaranteed by the famous writ of *habeas corpus*. What a contrast to Voltaire's own two arbitrary imprisonments in France! Who better prepared than he to appreciate the lesson and its meaning!

Wisely, Voltaire set himself promptly to learn English. With many of the aristocracy and his literary confrères in Britain, he could of course have made shift to converse in his native French. Lord Bolingbroke, indeed, whom Voltaire had known in France since 1722 and at whose house he spent part of his time in London, had a French wife and spoke her language with a vigor and facility which astonished his guest. But Voltaire saw how much is closed to a traveler confined to his own tongue in a foreign country. He wished to be able to enjoy the theater, to read the literature of the past and present, to understand people in the street, to witness Parliamentary debates, to follow the course of events in the daily newspapers, in short, to steep himself to the full in English life.

In pursuance of his goal, Voltaire withdrew to the country for a period of quiet study at Wandsworth in the company of a distinguished merchant, Falkener. At the startling performances of Shakespeare, so different from the classic Racine, Voltaire sat with text of the play in hand, prepared to some degree in advance for the bold flights of Elizabethan poetry and vigorous action on the stage. He even argued baptism with a young Quaker, Edward Higginson. Legend has it that, when reviled in the street as "a French dog," Voltaire, in an impromptu speech regretting that he did not have the honor to be born an Englishman, quickly won the cheers of his hostile audience.

Thus Voltaire learned English well, even came soon to write it with force and a high degree of correctness as is evidenced by his unrevised letters to his friend, Thieriot. Naturally, however, since he was thirty-two years old at the time of his arrival across the Channel, he always retained a strong foreign accent and never quite mastered the intricacies of prepositions, those little demons which in all languages lie in wait for the unwary. Like a good Frenchman, for example, he spoke of obeying "to" the laws. Yet thirty-five years after his return to France he could still speak English with a readiness which amazed the visiting Boswell at Ferney. He even "swore bloodily as was the fashion when he was in England," commented the young interviewer as his aged host let fly with the out-of-date oaths of a former generation.

3

One of the chief results of this important voyage was a little book known as the *Philosophical Letters,* sometimes called also more accurately *Letters on the English.* The adjective "philosophical" was itself provocative as it would not be today. It carried with it an idea of freethinking, of radicalism, of hostility to the conventional in government, religion, science, or literature. Moreover, it was the first work of Voltaire to be written in his characteristic prose with its short, crisp sentences, its brilliant concision, its biting irony, its effective challenge to the Old Régime. No wonder the work fell like a bombshell, as Gustave Lanson says, among the reading public of the day! No wonder it was officially burned by the hangman while the author, back in France since 1729, found it convenient for a time to remain away from Paris in the far-off South!

Fittingly, by August of 1733, the book had appeared first in English translation at London. The French version came out in Paris during the last week of April, 1734, Fearing the uproar it would create, the author had the work printed surreptitiously at Rouen, prudently withheld it for a time, and trickily denied responsibility for its final release. Making war upon governmental censorship and repression, Voltaire was never overscrupulous about the means used. He fought fire with fire. Stratagem and brash denial of authorship were his ready weapons against arbitrary force and tyranny. The government in turn often half-cooperated by pretending to believe such assertions. Printers and booksellers used similar methods in the effort to escape imprisonment or financial ruin. It required a bold spirit to spread new ideas under the Old Régime.

The *Philosophical Letters* begin with four essays on the Quakers. This is more than on any other subject, an indication of the piquant challenge presented by this sincere, but, to the eighteenth century, strange sect. Voltaire writes his first letter in the form of a vivid dialogue between an unnamed Quaker and himself.

The Quaker, he says, "was a healthy old man who had never been sick because he had never indulged in passions or intemperance. . . . He was dressed, like all those of his religion, in a coat without pleats at the sides and without buttons on the pockets or sleeves, and he wore a large hat with turned-down brim like our ecclesiastics. He received me," observed the author, "with his hat on his head and advanced toward me without making the slightest bow; but there was more politeness in the open, friendly expression of his face than there is in our usage of drawing back one leg behind the other and holding in the hand what is made to cover the head!"

Thus Voltaire effectively reduces French ceremonial courtesy to its lowest common denominator of a merely conventional physical action, a low bow and a wide, graceful sweep of the plumed hat, while the Quaker is more truly polite with his hat on his head and a sincere welcome in his face. Here the author's irony plays frankly on himself and his compatriots.

"Sir, I said," continues Voltaire, "bending my body and slipping one foot toward him according to our custom, I flatter myself that my just curiosity will not displease you and that you will be good enough to do me the honor of instructing me about your religion."

CHAPTER X

So the writer again makes fun of his own exaggerated forms of politeness.

Under the Quaker's tutelage, the Frenchman changes to a sudden brusqueness, beginning, he says, "with the question which good Catholics have more than once addressed to the Huguenots." Thus he paid his respects to the infamous dragonnades and the Revocation of the Edict of Nantes.

"My dear sir, I said to him, are you baptized?"

"No, the Quaker replied, and my fellow Quakers are not either."

"Zounds!, I retorted, then you are not Christians?"

"My son, he rejoined gently, don't swear; we are Christians, and we try to be good Christians; but we do not think that Christianity consists in throwing on the head cold water mingled with a little salt."

Ceremonies are but ceremonies, the Quaker suggests. It is the spirit and conduct which count. By his vivid dialogue and original expression Voltaire has renewed an old preachment.

After a few pages of more serious discussion of Biblical teaching on baptism, fruit of Voltaire's argument with the young Quaker, Edward Higginson, the author turns to the most characteristic trait of the sect, their unwavering hostility toward war.

"We never go to war," said the Quaker. "It is not that we fear death; on the contrary, we bless the moment which unites us to the Being of beings; but it is because we are neither wolves, nor tigers, nor bulldogs, but men, but Christians. Our God, who has commanded us to love our enemies and to suffer without murmuring, doubtless does not wish us to cross the sea and slit our brothers' throats because murderers dressed in red coats with bonnets two feet high enlist the citizens by making a noise with two little sticks on an ass's skin stretched out taut."

So much for that martial music which intoxicates the blood! The stirring roll of drums is only the beating of two little sticks on a piece of hide! Three times in this letter Voltaire has followed the effective technique of reducing external politeness, religious ceremony, or military ardor to its components of mere physical action. Thus a sentence replaces pages of reasoning, and, besides, pierces through into the reader's mind.

"And when, after the battles have been won, all London gleams with lights, the heavens are enflamed with fireworks, and the air resounds with the noise of thanksgiving, with bells, organs, and cannon, we groan in silence over these murders which cause the public joy." Thus the letter ends, as befits the gravity of the subject, on a tone of complete seriousness. Voltaire is at one with the Quaker in his condemnation of war. He reduces war to what it is, the organized murder of one man by another. The Quakers are amusing eccentrics as portrayed by Voltaire; they are strange heretics in conduct and belief; but, underneath, he suggests, they put us all to shame by their unvarnished goodness and give us much to think about. Is Christianity something from within or is it only a veneer on the outer surface of action or manners?

Turning from the Quakers to the Anglican Church, Voltaire wrote two immortal sentences. "This is the country of sects," he observed of England. "An Englishman, like a free man, goes to Heaven by the road that pleases him." Knowing the keen aversion of France to sects, we can see in the first sentence a special bite which it would not have with us, accustomed as we are to such diversity. The multiplicity of religions was itself a marked characteristic of England and by implication, as so often in the *Philosophical Letters*, struck a backhanded slap at the author's own country. The second sentence dispenses with reams of argument in favor of tolerance. "An Englishman, like a free man, goes to Heaven by the road that pleases him." The open-minded reader cries: Why not? and is convinced, without more ado.

The letter on the Presbyterians ends with a no less pungent sentence. "If there were only one religion in England," writes Voltaire, "we should have to fear despotism; if there were two, they would cut each other's throats; but there are thirty, and they live in peace and happiness." James Madison, it is said, deeply imbued with French thought, liked to cite this sentence, so in harmony with the varied religious patterns of America, so in accord with his own insistence and that of Jefferson on the separation of Church and State. If the Puritans of Massachusetts, the Dutch Lutherans of New York, the Catholics of Maryland, the Quakers of Pennsylvania, the Episcopalians and Methodists of Virginia, were ever to come together into union, it could only be on a basis of live and let-live, of the absence of any religious test for the holding of office, in short, on the broad English principle expressed here so succinctly and vigorously by Voltaire.

4

Letter VIII turns from questions of religion to government. It is entitled "On Parliament." Referring to the long years of successful struggle against royal tyranny, the author observes: "The English nation is the only one on earth which has managed to regulate the power of kings by resisting them, and which from effort to effort has finally established this wise government in which the prince, all-powerful to do good, has his hands tied against doing evil." The last part of this expressive sentence, it will be remembered, had appeared in Fénelon's widely-read *Télémaque,* had been repeated by the great Archbishop as advice to the young English pretender at Cambrai ten years later, and had been effectively used by the Duke of Orleans as he seized the power of the Regency in an incisive speech before the Parlement of Paris in early September, 1715. Voltaire gave it added currency. Finally, even Thomas Jefferson, as we have seen, was to echo it in France during the Revolution.

It was customary at the time of the *Philosophical Letters* for conservatives on the Continent to shudder at the thought of the supposed violence of English history. Voltaire disposes of this argument.

"To establish liberty in England has been costly, no doubt; the idol of despotic power has been drowned in seas of blood; but the English do not think they have purchased good laws too dearly. Other nations have had no less troublous times; but the blood they have shed for the cause of their liberty has only cemented their servitude. . . . The French think that the government of this island is more stormy than the sea surrounding it, and that is true; but it is when the king begins the tempest, it is when he seeks to make himself master of the vessel of which he is only the chief pilot."

"The greatest reproach which the French address to the English," Voltaire continues, "is the execution of Charles I, who was treated by his conquerors as he would have treated them if he had been successful."

"After all, look on one side at Charles I beaten in pitched battle, taken prisoner, tried, condemned at Westminster, and on the other at Emperor Henry VII poisoned by his chaplain at communion, Henry III assassinated by a monk, minister of the rage of a whole party, thirty plots on the life of Henry IV, several of which were carried out, and the last successful at length in depriving France of this great king. Weigh these attacks and judge."

Who could present the case as effectively in so few words?

In Letter IX, the author points out that "this happy mixture, . . . this harmony between commons, lords, and king, did not always exist." It was a gradual growth from the time of Magna Charta on. With a new-found democracy, which will not always remain with him, Voltaire refers to "the people, the most numerous, the most virtuous even, and consequently the most respectable part of mankind." Continuing, he says: "It has taken centuries to do justice to humanity, to perceive that it was horrible for the many to sow and the few to reap." Thus the author echoes the Old Testament prophet Micah, in a passage which he had perhaps heard quoted in Bible-reading England.

As the letter comes to an end, Voltaire again characteristically gives his eighteenth-century French compatriots something to think about by way of clearly-implied contrast. "Here a man, because he is a noble or because he is a priest," he says in a passage perhaps, as the wording suggests, actually written in England before his return to France, "is not exempt from paying certain taxes. . . . Each man contributes, not according to his rank (which is absurd), but according to his income. There is no *taille,* no arbitrary poll-tax, but a direct tax on land." Thus the author attacks the abusive exemption from taxation of "the privileged classes" in France. "The peasant," continues Voltaire, "does not have his feet pinched by wooden shoes, he eats white bread, he is well dressed, he is not afraid to increase the number of his cattle or to cover his roof with tile for fear that his taxes will be raised the next year," a fear which greatly impressed young Jean-Jacques Rousseau in 1731, as he stopped at a peasant's house after a long day's tramp across the country and found himself at first taken for a government spy seeking to ferret out the countryman's concealed wealth.

The next letter discusses English commerce. Voltaire was perhaps one of the first admirers of big business. No doubt his residence at Wandsworth with the successful merchant, Everard Falkener, who later became English ambassador to Constantinople, forerunner of many similar American appointments later, played a role in what was in any case a natural viewpoint on the part of the son of Monsieur Arouet.

CHAPTER X

"In France," writes the author with a fine scorn, "anyone who wishes is a marquis; and whoever arrives in Paris from the provinces with money to spend and a name ending in *ac* or in *ille* can say: 'A man like me, a man of my rank,' and look down with sovereign contempt on a businessman." Voltaire's humiliation by the Chevalier de Rohan-Chabot, though not the sole cause of his attitude, was certainly too recent to be forgotten. He continues: "The merchant so often hears his profession spoken of with disdain that he is foolish enough to blush at it; I do not know, however, which is more useful to a state, a well-powdered nobleman who knows exactly the time when the King gets up or goes to bed, and gives himself an air of grandeur while playing the role of a slave in the antichamber of a royal minister, or a businessman who enriches his country, dispatches from his office orders to Surat and Cairo, and contributes to the happiness of the world." Following a suggestive technique of his predecessor, Montesquieu, in the *Persian Letters,* Voltaire writes with a pretense of caution, "I do not know." Of course, no one doubts that he does know very well, and the reader knows too. In France, the idle and increasingly useless nobility were not allowed to demean themselves in trade. "It is on chairs that nobility is acquired," had remarked Montesquieu in a piquant phrase. It was otherwise in England where the younger sons of the aristocracy, particularly, were pushed out to make their way in the world. Hence business followed the flag, or led it, and the course of empire went its way. Voltaire was keenly conscious of the rising tide of economic forces.

A letter follows on inoculation against smallpox, forerunner of modern vaccination. In the eighteenth century, this terrible disease ravaged Europe. Many perished from it, and those who escaped remained generally pock-marked for life. It was no respecter, naturally, of prince or princess, and Louis XV was destined to die of smallpox in 1774. Voltaire himself had barely survived after coming down with the malady in 1723. No wonder, then, that he appreciated the importance of the radical new remedy, brought to England by Lady Mary Wortley-Montaigu from Constantinople. But the theologically-minded Sorbonne and the hide-bound physicians of the time, devoted to the traditional bleeding and purging, registered violent opposition. It took Voltaire and many of his contemporaries long years of protest to overcome their blind resistance.

Other letters on Locke, Francis Bacon, Descartes, Newton's system of gravitation, also had their great importance for the eighteenth century. Voltaire inherited something of Fontenelle's lively interest in the developing role of science in the modern world.

5

One of the most striking, most false, and at the same time most characteristic of the *Philosophical Letters* is that dealing with English tragedy. To the classically-minded Voltaire, brought up on Corneille and especially on Racine, himself the successful author of plays based on the principle of the famous three unities of time, place, and action, Shakespeare appeared as "a barbarian of genius." Thus the Frenchman mingled admiration for the English author's originality with severe criticism of his failure to follow the regular forms established in France. Shakespeare, he said, "had a genius full of force and fecondity, of naturalness and sublimity, but without the slightest spark of good taste and without the slightest knowledge of the rules."

"You know," continues Voltaire, gaily echoing the Englishman Thomas Rymer, termed by Macaulay the worst critic who ever lived, "that in the tragedy of the *Moor of Venice,* a very touching play, a husband strangles his wife on the stage, and, when the poor woman has been strangled, she cries out that she is dying most unjustly." So much for *Othello.* Now let us take *Hamlet.* Here "grave-diggers shovel out a grave, while drinking, singing comical songs, and uttering, over the skulls they unearth, jests suitable to men of their profession."

We hardly agree with Voltaire today, yet recently the great Shakespearean actor, Maurice Evans, mindful no doubt of popular taste, omitted the gravedigger scene because he considered it "not needful to the plot" and "the humor of it strange to modern ears." David Garrick in the eighteenth century held a similar view. Voltaire revolted likewise against the rough jokes of the carpenters and shoemakers in *Julius Caesar* in such shocking contrast, as it seemed, to the high tragedy of Brutus, Cassius, and the Roman dictator. The Frenchman, limited by his classic background, could not accept these scenes which accorded with the turbulent, outspoken populace of Elizabethan times, as no doubt with the plebeians of Rome also; he could not see how the great issues of the play came out intensified when refracted through common minds in all their unvarnished humanity. For him, as for most educated Englishmen of the age, classical unity must prevail. When the drunken porter of *Macbeth* staggered about the tragic stage, it was as though he had blundered into the august, gilded corridors of Versailles in the midst of all the splendor and grandiose dignity of a court function. He ought of course to be thrown out forthwith. Why had Shakespeare tolerated such intrusion? It could only be because of the crude "groundlings" to whom he played. It was doubtless because of his "ignorance of the rules."

If we are inclined to smile at Voltaire in superiority now, we must not forget, however, that in the eighteenth century, not only Frenchmen, but most cultivated people in England also thought as he did. The poet Milton objected to the mingling together of tragic and comic elements in the same play, opposed "introducing trivial and vulgar persons," as he called them, into Shakespeare's tragedies, considering their presence due to a desire to "gratify the people," and clung to the unity of time in its rigid twenty-four-hour limitation. Even Dryden, who on the whole warmly admired his great predecessor, said that "the times were ignorant" in which Shakespeare lived and that "the fury of his fancy often transported him beyond the bounds of judgment."

Thomas Rymer, now regarded with merriment or contempt, was quoted with deference in the England of Voltaire's time. Pope, according to Spence, referred to Rymer as "on the whole one of the best critics we ever had,"—quite different from Macaulay! Dryden likewise observed: "How defective Shakespeare and Fletcher have been in all their plots, Mr. Rymer has discovered in his criticisms." On *Othello*, Rymer concluded: "There is in this play some burlesque, some humour, and ramble of comical wit, and some mimicry to divert the spectators: but the tragical part is plainly none other than a bloody farce without salt or savour." Shakespeare's *Julius Caesar* fared no better. John Dennis, though he admired Shakespeare's "beauties," charged him with having "introduced things into his tragedies, which are against the dignity of that noble poem, as the rabble in *Julius Caesar*." Addison objected to what he termed "pompous phrases" in the Elizabethan dramatist, said there was too much killing on the stage, and though he esteemed him, on the whole, as much as Dryden, perhaps more, wrote his own tragedy, the pale and ineffective *Cato,* according to the classic "rules."

Nicholas Rowe defended Shakespeare, but Charles Gildon attacked the gravedigger scene as out of place in *Hamlet,* believed that the English author "would have given us far more noble plays if he had had the good fortune to have seen but any one regular performance," and concluded: "Shakespeare is indeed stored with a great many beauties, but they are in a heap of rubbish!"

Alexander Pope was in many ways the great and typical poet of the England which Voltaire visited. Pope's *Preface* to his edition of Shakespeare appeared in 1725, only a year before the young Frenchman's arrival. "Of all English poets," said Pope, "Shakespeare must be confessed to be the fairest and fullest subject for criticism, and to afford the most numerous, as well as most conspicuous instances, both of beauties and faults of all sorts." Pope praised Shakespeare for the individuality and reality of his characters, for his power to move our emotions either to laughter or tears, but blamed him for including in his plays "tradesmen and mechanics," for bombast, "thundering versification, . . . mean buffoonery, vile ribaldry, and unmannerly jests of fools and clowns," and of course for his deviation from the rules. These defects, however, were those of his age, admitted Pope by way of excuse, and were due in great part to the necessity of pleasing an uncultivated populace. Bolingbroke, Voltaire's first patron in England, agreed with Pope. Obviously, England itself was then strongly under French influence in literary taste.

Such was the *milieu* into which the young and intellectually curious Voltaire came in May of 1726. It would be unreasonable to expect him to abandon his own classical background and actually combat the opinions of cultivated Englishmen of the day about their own greatest dramatist. These attitudes may surprise us now, but, without idolatry toward Shakespeare, we must admit that even in the modern theater many scenes of his plays are often cut or rearranged. Voltaire, like most of his contemporaries in England itself, failed to give Shakespeare his due. Yet, though he was extreme, he was not entirely wrong in his criticisms. He saw that the English dramatist possessed a great and original genius. If Voltaire could not divorce himself from his classical background and personal experience, he nevertheless admired the vigorous Shakespearean action which he had seen on the stage, felt there was too much mere talk in French tragedy of the time, and was inspired to imitate, though but timidly, Shakespeare's vivid use of history in dramatic form. Bold as Voltaire was in attacking religious, social, and political abuses of the Old Régime, he was curiously conservative in literary matters. The *Philosophical Letters* offer us clearly a contrast which was deeply imbedded in his nature. The Jesuit fathers at the College of Louis-le-Grand had successfully molded his taste in drama and poetry, if not in religion.

The *Philosophical Letters* are Voltaire's first masterpiece in prose. They may still be read with pleasure and profit today. Voltaire's wit, his irony, his incisive brevity, have never been surpassed except in his own immortal little novel of *Candide* twenty-five years later. Jean-Jacques Rousseau, in his *Confessions*, tells how the *Philosophical Letters* first inspired him to think. They did indeed offer him most varied material on which to exercise his slowly maturing mind. If the particular style of Voltaire would of course never be his, the little book showed him how effectively a great author can wield his pen. When Rousseau burst forth from his obscurity in the middle of the century, he still recognized Voltaire as his literary "master." Certainly, the Genevan was already going in a direction very different from that of his illustrious predecessor, yet the early stimulus had evidently come from Voltaire, and to a degree difficult to estimate today. Along with Rousseau, we can only bow in admiration before a work which remains inimitable and unimitated, still unique as it was in its own time.

CHAPTER XI

VOLTAIRE THE HISTORIAN

I

WHILE IN ENGLAND, VOLTAIRE WAS OCCUPIED NOT ONLY
with the material which went into the *Philosophical
Letters;* he had also turned his attention to the writing of history—
not the traditional history of ancient Rome, thought-provoking as
it was shortly to become in the hands of a Montesquieu and so
familiar in its main outlines to every schoolboy brought up on his
daily Latin. Instead, Voltaire cast his eyes toward the unfamiliar
North to tell the story of Charles XII of Sweden who had been
killed suddenly in battle a scant ten years before. This was contemporary history, and was therefore still clouded with the uncertainties
of what is near and hotly disputed. In England, the author talked
directly with men who had witnessed the events described, consulted
all the documents he could lay hands on, endeavored with bold
skepticism and keen insight to penetrate to the hidden truth. His
method of research, in short, was essentially modern and in its broad
results sound. Only nineteenth-century historians with access to the
archives of Sweden itself have been able to make significant corrections in Voltaire's narrative.

Why tell the story at all? "There are very few sovereigns whose
private history should be written. . . . The princes who have the
greatest right to immortality," observes Voltaire, "are those who
have done some good to humanity. Thus, as long as France exists,
men will recall the affection of Louis XII for his people; they will
excuse the great faults of Francis I in favor of the arts and sciences
he fathered; they will bless the memory of Henry IV who won his
inheritance by dint of conquest and pardon; they will praise the
magnificence of Louis XIV who protected the arts originated by
Francis I. For a contrary reason, men will keep in mind the lives
of bad princes just as they remember floods, fires, and pestilence."

Thus there is a moral side to history and mankind should be able
to learn from its teaching.

"But," continues Voltaire, "such is the miserable weakness of men that they look with admiration on those who have done evil brilliantly, and they are often more ready to speak of the destroyer than of the founder of an empire."

Where, then, does this King of Sweden come into the picture? The author replies: "We thought the reading of his story might be useful to certain princes if the book should chance to fall into their hands. Certainly, there is no sovereign who, after reading the life of Charles XII, ought not to be cured of the folly of conquests." In his *Philosophical Letters* only three years later, Voltaire was to re-echo significantly the last words, heightened with a carefully chosen adjective. They became "the *brilliant* folly of conquests," thus underlining effectively man's unhappy fascination for the mad lure of power and the abuse of force. It was too late for Louis XIV to learn the unpopular lesson. Could young Louis XV perhaps take it to heart? No doubt Voltaire hoped so, even though the hope was destined to prove vain.

"We have composed this history," says Voltaire, "from the narratives of men well known, men who passed several years by the side of Charles XII or of Peter the Great, Emperor of Muscovy, men who, having settled in a free country [England] long after the death of these princes, had no interest in disguising the truth. . . . We have not advanced a single fact without consulting irreproachable eyewitnesses. . . . If any princes or ministers should find disagreeable truths in this work, let them remember that, being public men, they are accountable to the public for their actions; that this is the price they pay for their grandeur; that history is a witness and not a flatterer; and that the only way to oblige men to speak well of us is to do good."

The point of view is what we are pleased to call modern, yet how far from being generally accepted in our propaganda-ridden world! Even in the midst of democracy, we have much still to learn in the matter of respect for unpopular or painful truth. Voltaire's lesson, no doubt, will always be pertinent.

In simple, direct, factual sentences, the author tells the story of how Charles XII fell suddenly by a bullet as he exposed himself unduly at a point where a communication trench joined the lines dug parallel with those of the enemy. Voltaire narrates what he has been able to discover "of truth about the event."

"Thus perished," writes the historian, "at thirty-six and a half years of age, Charles XII of Sweden, after having experienced the greatest prosperity and the most cruel adversity, without being weakened by the one or a moment shaken by the other. Almost all his actions, even those of his uniform private life, have gone far beyond the average. He is perhaps the only man, and up to the present the only king, who has lived without weaknesses; he carried all the virtues of a hero to an excess which made them as dangerous as their contrary vices. His firmness, which turned into stubbornness, gave rise to his misfortunes in the Ukraine and kept him five years a prisoner in Turkey; his liberality, degenerating into extravagance, ruined Sweden; his courage, pushed to the point of rashness, caused his death; his justice sometimes became cruelty, and, in his last years, the maintenance of his authority was near to tyranny. His great qualities, of which a single one might have rendered another prince immortal, brought misfortune to his country. He never attacked anyone; but he was not as prudent as he was implacable in his vengeance. He was the first to have the ambition of being a conqueror without a desire to increase his territory: he wished to gain empires in order to give them away. His passion for glory, for war, and for revenge, kept him from being a wise statesman, a quality without which there has never been a real conqueror. Before battle and after victory, he remained modest; after defeat, firm: harsh toward others as to himself, counting for nothing the sufferings and life of his subjects as he did his own; a man who was unique rather than great; a man to wonder at rather than imitate. His life should teach kings how much a pacific and happy government is superior to such glory." This is the conclusion to which the book brings us.

The *History of Charles XII, King of Sweden,* appeared in 1731, two years after the return of Voltaire from England. In contrast to the dull narratives of mediocre chroniclers, Voltaire bore his learning easily. With the same swiftness of movement and apparent simplicity which he was to give later to the prose tale, the author carried his story along. People could hardly believe they were reading history. Was not history something erudite and heavy, unhappily associated with the schools? But this was a modern biography, an astounding hero of one's own time. And there was a lesson to be drawn from it also. If rulers would not learn it, the general public had a direct stake in the author's hatred for war, his debunking of conquest. "The paths of glory lead but to the grave," the English poet, Thomas Gray, was to write a generation later. But Napoleon, in the midst of his own fateful Russian campaign, spoke contemptuously of Voltaire's work. Obviously, the "man of destiny" did not relish the unwelcome conclusion, pointing toward defeat, exile, and death on Saint-Helena. Hitler, in our own day, was no doubt too egocentric even to read such a book. But the work remains, after would-be conquerors have fallen.

2

Since the brief exile with Monsieur de Caumartin at Saint-Ange in 1715, Voltaire had had a special reason to be interested in the reign of Louis XIV. His host had entertained him with a store of firsthand reminiscences of the Great Century. The young man himself had passed the first twenty-one years of his life under the Grand Monarch, and, besides, the literary period of Boileau and Racine appealed to him with all the prestige which came from the remarkable achievements of French classicism, already admired throughout Europe. Quite naturally, Voltaire looked back affectionately at this as the Golden Age of French letters. Why not write the history of these times, so close to the living present and yet soon in danger of slipping partly into forgetfulness? Again there were direct oral sources for the author as there had been for the *History of Charles XII*, the vivid recollections of older contemporaries. There were also many manuscript volumes of memoirs, not destined to be published until the early nineteenth century. There were the useful chroniclings of Villars and Dangeau, later the passionate eyewitness impressions of Saint-Simon. Voltaire had access to much material which was still secret.

He wrote to friends or acquaintances who might help him. "If, Sir, you happen to have anecdotes on the reign of Louis XIV, worthy of philosophical readers, I beg you," he asked Lévesque de Burigny, "to inform me about them."

"It is not simply the life of this prince that I am writing," Voltaire told his fellow historian, Abbé du Bos, "it is not the annals of his reign, it is rather the history of the human mind taken from the century which has brought it the most glory. . . . What characterizes this century, what has caused revolutionary changes, what will be important in a hundred years, that is what I wish to write about today."

"I am tired of the histories which deal only with the adventures of a king, as if he existed alone or nothing else existed except in relation to him," Voltaire wrote to Lord Hervey. "In a word, it is rather the history of a great century than of a great king that I am writing." Thus Voltaire early turned away from a simple biographical story such as that of Charles XII which he had so recently published. He now sought a broader canvas. It would be "Louis XIV and his Times," or "the Age of Louis XIV."

Moreover, Madame du Châtelet, the woman with whom Voltaire fell in love, who became his mistress, and who shaped much of his life during the next fifteen years, did not like history. She saw in it only the dull recital of wars and battles, the long listing of the reigns of successive kings. Like many a modern schoolboy or girl, she was familiar only with a foreshortened history from which the textbooks in their brevity or lack of genius had squeezed out all the sap of human life. What meaning had history for human experience or human thought? Madame du Châtelet did not see. For her, mathematics, science, philosophy, had meaning, but not history. Voltaire, then, sought to convince his companion that history could be "philosophical," could have significance for the human mind. He would try to show this through a depiction of all the broad panorama of civilization during the "Age of Louis XIV."

So for nearly twenty years, while he engaged also in numerous other literary enterprises, Voltaire worked away on his great task, reading widely, taking many notes, consulting numerous authorities. From the forty volumes of Dangeau, "I have extracted forty pages," he observed dramatically, emphasizing his tireless effort toward concision.

Even the rather insignificant recollections of Louis XIV himself were communicated to him. Voltaire read also some two hundred volumes of printed memoirs. Finally, after he became royal historiographer in 1745, the author had the privilege of access to state archives. True, his work lacks much of the color which only the Romantic period would bring into the too analytical style of the eighteenth century. Voltaire had no desire to write for the eyes; he did not attempt to make people see the men and women of the time, the costumes, the grandiose pageantry of court functions, which were after all familiar enough to most readers then; he wrote rather for the mind, the intelligence. True it is also that Voltaire, for once too discreet, conceals from view many of the shortcomings of Louis's reign, which his documents could not have failed to reveal to him. On the one hand, he admired the preceding century too much to be completely impartial; on the other, he sought to offer a useful lesson in greatness to the disappointing Louis XV, and would not therefore criticize the former age too severely. Moreover, as a patriotic Frenchman, Voltaire no doubt could not but vibrate with sympathy toward a century which was still the avid center of European eyes.

But, in spite of such human defects as we can see from the calm perspective of today, Voltaire's history had notable qualities also, which made it deservedly popular in its time. He studied the authenticity of documents, weighed with a wholesome skepticism the relative value of his sources, and tried in many instances with great care to establish the truth. He endeavored to penetrate behind the famous mystery of the "man with the iron mask," talked "with men who had served him." Voltaire examined the memoirs of the provincial intendants in the effort to establish the economic history of the reign, sought to borrow a "political diary on Louis XIV," written by Abbé de Saint-Pierre. He wished to follow "the march of the human mind in philosophy, eloquence, poetry, criticism; to trace the progress in painting, sculpture, music, gold and silver work, tapestry, mirrors, cloth of gold, and clock-making." It was a broad picture of a whole rich culture, too comprehensive no doubt for a single author, especially one so busily occupied with multifarious activities as Voltaire, but, even where it did not fully succeed, it set a program and an ideal for the future. Henceforth, historians would be less ready to limit their interest to mere political questions, in the narrow sense; they would endeavor to embrace also the intellectual, artistic, and religious life of an age.

"The reader must not expect to find here, more than in the picture of preceding periods," wrote Voltaire, "the numerous details of wars, attacks on cities taken and retaken by arms, yielded and given back by treaties. Many circumstances interesting for contemporaries are lost to the eyes of posterity and disappear before the great events which have determined the destiny of empires. All that was done does not deserve to be written about. We shall include in this history only what merits the attention of all ages, only what will serve to depict the genius and the manners of mankind, only what will be instructive, will encourage love of virtue, of the arts, and of one's country."

History must be selective. One cannot, like the child Anatole France, dream of writing the account of his country "in fifty volumes with all the details." Limits of space, of the reader's time and interest, impose a choice. Voltaire sought what seemed to him significant; he wished to learn and to pass on to posterity whatever lesson history might teach. We may at times disagree today with his selection or his emphasis, but we nonetheless ignore at our peril the experience of the past. The alternative is the pain of repeating outworn mistakes. To point a moral is dangerous. There is risk of preaching or propaganda, and Voltaire did not escape completely these pitfalls. On the other hand, there is risk also in having no goal, no purpose, no ideal, in seeing in history only one meaningless event after another. As always, it is a struggle to preserve the sound middle course, to aim at an impartial portrayal of events, but not to avoid or obscure such meaning as may be there. Voltaire's effort, in its successes and in its failures, shows us what to seek and what to shun.

The *Age of Louis XIV* appeared finally in 1751 when its author was in Potsdam at the court of Frederick the Great. Like Montesquieu's *Spirit of Laws,* it represented the attainment of a goal pursued through twenty years of effort, though less slowly, painfully, and exclusively than in the case of Voltaire's great predecessor. Nevertheless, the *Age of Louis XIV* marked an epoch. After its publication, history too would be clearly recognized as worthy once again, after the great historians of Greek and Roman antiquity, to occupy the attention of a man of genius. History could call into play all the qualities of knowledge, understanding, and interpretation of the most penetrating minds. It could demand to be couched in the best of narrative styles for the benefit of the general reading public. In short, history also could combine erudition with art.

3

During these busy years of success as a dramatist, poet, and prose writer, Voltaire was turning his attention, moreover, to a subject of even broader scope. Ambitiously, he dreamed of enlightening

CHAPTER XI

Madame du Châtelet and the world at large in regard to what he first called *Universal History*. He aimed to take as his province mankind itself. He would not, it is true, go again over the ground so well covered by Bossuet for the story of the Roman people or the ancient history treated by Rollin and others. Voltaire would begin with Charlemagne and come down to the period studied in his *Age of Louis XIV*. He would deal especially with medieval times, but would extend his interest even to remote China which was beginning to appear in the narratives of missionary travelers, usually as an object of wonder at the complex civilization so early developed there. Thus Voltaire's gaze went beyond the conventional horizon of Europe and the Mediterranean basin in the effort to embrace, to some degree at least, the whole round globe itself.

To Madame du Châtelet, particularly, he addressed his *Preface*. If he could enlist her interest, that of the general public would no doubt follow also.

"You are at length willing," he wrote, "to overcome your disgust at modern history, from the time of the decadence of the Roman empire, and form a general idea of the nations which inhabit and devastate the earth. In this immense field, you are seeking only what deserves to be known: namely, the spirit, the manners, the morals, and the customs of the leading nations, supported by those facts of which it is hardly permissible to be ignorant. The aim of this work is not to know in what year a prince unworthy of our attention succeeded another barbarous prince in an uncivilized nation. If we could crowd into our heads the chronological list of all the dynasties, we should have nothing but words. Just as we ought to know the great actions of those rulers who have made their peoples better or happier, we can pass over the common run of kings who only burden the memory. Of what use to you would be the details of so many petty interests which no longer subsist today, of so many extinct families which fought over provinces swallowed up since that time by great kingdoms? Almost every city today has its history, true or false, which is more ample, more detailed, than that of Alexander. The mere annals of a monastic order contain more volumes than the Roman empire."

"In all these immense collections which exceed our grasp, we must pick and choose. It is a vast storehouse from which you will take what is useful."

Thus the principle of selection in this broad field becomes even more necessary than in the case of the *Age of Louis XIV*. Voltaire will choose only what is interesting, what is significant, for the modern reader. The general procedure is of course not open to discussion. Every writer must follow it. Only the method of application may be debatable.

In the case of the medieval church, for example, Voltaire could not divorce himself from the lack of sympathy and comprehension imposed by his eighteenth-century rationalism. Voltaire "is like the monks," observed the shrewd, if hostile, Montesquieu, "who write, not for the subject they are treating, but for the glory of their order. Voltaire is writing for his monastery."

Similarly, Voltaire could never understand Joan of Arc, who relied on miracles in a miracle-believing age. For him, she must have "feigned" a miracle, just as her enemy, Bedford, "feigned to believe her a sorceress." Yet she was a "heroine," admits Voltaire, and "worthy of the miracle which she had feigned." Thus the author's attitude combines admiration with a complete inability to comprehend the mind of an unscientific period. The same limitation prevented him from grasping the real spirit of Christ and the New Testament era. He could not project his imagination beyond the skepticism of his time.

Yet there was reason also in his viewpoint. With the superstition and ignorance, which he saw in the Middle Ages, went a fanaticism "which has been the malady of nearly all centuries." It was fanaticism and its cruelties that he feared. This was the cause of the burning of Joan of Arc. It was also the source of persecution and torture, the foe of the beneficent tolerance which he preached.

"Let the citizens of a huge city where the arts, pleasures, and peace reign today, where reason even is beginning to appear, compare these different times and complain if they dare. Such is the reflection which must be made on almost every page of this history," concluded Voltaire. Thus, in spite of the long annals of the folly and wickedness of mankind, the author saw some progress through the slow spread of enlightenment. It was a slight gleam, no doubt, and hard to keep constantly in full view. Yet if reason is "only a torch," as Voltaire himself said elsewhere, it is our soundest guide and not to be unwisely extinguished. Imperfect as reason is, it is much to be preferred to ignorance, and less likely to afflict humanity with terror.

Voltaire's *Universal History* appeared first as a few trial fragments in a monthly periodical, *Le Mercure de France,* during 1745 and 1746. Seven years later, two volumes were published under his name but apparently without his consent, and the author complained of many errors. In 1756 an authentic edition was released under the imposing title of *Essay on Universal History and the Manners and Spirit of Nations from Charlemagne to our own Day.* It was, in short, a bold attempt at a history of modern civilization throughout the world. Not until 1769 did the work receive its final title, *Essay on the Manners and Spirit of Nations.*

In this title, Voltaire's basic purpose is revealed. "I should like to discover," he wrote, "the nature of human society at that time, how people lived within their families, what arts were cultivated, rather than to repeat so many misfortunes and combats, baneful objects of history and commonplaces of human wickedness."

He occupied himself with artisans and merchants, mechanical inventions, the use of glasses for the eyes toward the end of the thirteenth century, the development of windmills in Italy about the same period, how earthenware took the place of porcelain. Window glass was still very rare and expensive. It was carried into England by the French, says Voltaire, about 1180 and was regarded there as a great object of luxury. The Venetians alone knew the secret of manufacturing mirrors. There were a few tower clocks in Italy; the one at Bologna was famous. The chance discovery of the compass had already been made, but was still of little value because of the limitations on geographical knowledge. The production of paper out of linen came with the beginning of the fourteenth century, Voltaire observes. Almost all houses in French, German, and English cities were still roofed with thatch. Protection from cold through a modern fireplace remained to be developed. Entire families continued to shiver around a smoky circular hearth with only a tube of pipe extended through the ceiling. Candles were luxuries; people had recourse to torches of dry wood for light. Table-linen was little used in England. Silver vessels, money, knives and forks, were scarce everywhere. There was no room yet for a strong middle class whose trade could form the basis of national prosperity.

In short, from this brief summary of his work we can see that Voltaire was interested in what we call cultural history. He awakened his contemporaries to the significance of these seemingly commonplace aspects of daily life through the ages. He made mistakes, of course. The field was too vast for a single mind, especially for a pioneer who had to explore nearly everything for himself, alone or with uninspired secretaries. But, since his time, no comprehensive historian can neglect such important phases of the past. The manners and morals, the arts, sciences, inventions, and literature, the little comforts which add to human civilization, these, too, comprise the stuff of history, and are of intense interest to the human mind. To Madame du Châtelet and her contempt for mere dull chronicles, we today are greatly indebted. She provoked Voltaire to devote his talents to a broader picture, to show "the Manners and Spirit of Nations," the march of human civilization through the centuries. Hume, Robertson, and Gibbon, the great eighteenth-century English historians, recognized Voltaire as a master, and the remarkable development of historical studies during the nineteenth century owes much to his epoch-making work. In England and America, as well as in France, Voltaire's histories were among the most popular of all his voluminous writings.

CHAPTER XII

TAKING COUNSEL WITH CANDIDE

I

FOR THE SPREADING OF IDEAS, WHAT COULD BE BETTER THAN THE so-called philosophic tale? No technical philosophy, of course. Instead, under the agreeable guise of fiction, the reader would be swept along, while beneath the sugar-coating of a novel he absorbed, almost unconsciously, its author's most characteristic thought.

Voltaire probably began composing his first philosophic tale at the age of forty-five during the years 1738 or 1739. The story seems to have lain unfinished, however, and did not appear until long afterward when its author was in Berlin at the court of Frederick the Great. We know it today as the little masterpiece of *Micromégas*. Meanwhile, there had been published in 1746 a short piece entitled *Babouc or the World as It Is*, the main thesis of which brings out the lesson that, if there is much bad in the world, there is some good too, and we should be prepared to accept things realistically as they are. Clearly, the close friend of Madame du Châtelet at the rejuvenated castle of Cirey, the recently elected member of the French Academy, the royal historiographer, the proud "Gentleman in Ordinary of the King's Bedchamber," was finding life rather more to his liking than would be the case only a few years later. *Babouc* lacks the sharp "bite" of the better known stories which followed.

The writer had evidently been slow to take up the popular literary genre of the philosophical tale, but lost nothing in the end by waiting. He came to it with his brilliant prose style already formed, and with notable achievements behind him in the tragedy of *Zaïre*, the *History of Charles XII*, the irony of the *Philosophical Letters* on England, the epic poem of the *Henriade,* and other varieties of light or serious verse. Perceiving finally the extraordinary possibilities of this new type of literature for reaching a large audience, Voltaire easily made himself a master in its use. *Zadig, Micromégas,* and

Candide are each pre-eminent in the rapidly-moving narrative art. They are read with the same keen pleasure today as when they were first welcomed by an eager public nearly two centuries ago.

Zadig or Destiny dates from 1747 and 1748. It bears the further subtitle of *An Oriental Story*, thus capitalizing on the remarkable vogue created in part by Montesquieu's famous *Persian Letters* more than twenty-five years before.

The rich, young, and generous Zadig lived happily in Babylonia, the author tells us, "during the time of King Moabdar." He possessed all the qualities of goodness, "knew how to moderate his passions, was without affectation, did not always wish his own way, and respected the weaknesses of mankind." Like Voltaire himself, he enjoyed the advantage of an excellent education, was instructed in the existing natural sciences, and "knew of metaphysics what people have known in all ages, that is to say, very little!" The author's satire always plays willingly on reason's inability to penetrate the deep mystery of life. The enigma of the universe eludes us.

Zadig experiences the fickleness of women, the double-talk of charlatan doctors, the intrigues of envy, and is obliged to flee for safety to Egypt. As he guides himself over the trackless sands with the aid of the constellation of Orion and the bright star of Sirius, Zadig is oppressed by the greatness of these distant orbs in contrast to the littleness of man's cupidity. "He then imagined men as in fact they are, insects devouring each other on a tiny atom of mud." These derogatory metaphors were to become favorites of Voltaire, destined often to be repeated with only slight variation. As with Fontenelle in his popular *Conversations on the Plurality of Worlds,* the vast new reaches of astronomy underlined the pettiness of humanity, no longer master of a flat little world or the respected center of a universe.

Arriving at last in Egypt, Zadig suddenly comes upon a woman being angrily beaten by a man to the accompaniment of her loud outcries. "Help me," she begs between sobs, "free me from this barbarian, save my life!" After a furious struggle, Zadig finally has to kill the Egyptian to protect himself. As he advances toward the woman, expecting gratitude for her deliverance, he is astonished to receive only bitter reproaches. The woman would have preferred her jealous tyrant back again even at the price of being cruelly beaten once more. Amazed at the illogic of passion, Zadig goes on his disillusioned way. In the future, he will know better than to mix in lovers' quarrels. Voltaire has renewed a well-known scene from the dramatist Molière.

Convicted of involuntary manslaughter, the unhappy Zadig is sold into slavery and, being less robust than his servant, he brings a lower price. His master, Sétoc, looks upon Zadig as only an inferior beast of burden. But Zadig finds an opportunity to advise Sétoc on a problem involving a considerable sum of money. The latter has formerly lent five hundred ounces of silver to a man who now impudently refuses to pay, taking advantage of the fact that the two witnesses to the transaction are dead.

"Where did you lend your five hundred ounces to this trickster?" asks Zadig.

"On a huge stone, near Mount Horeb," replies the merchant.

"What kind of a disposition does your debtor have?" inquires Zadig.

"That of a rogue," answers Sétoc.

"No, I am asking you whether he is quick or phlegmatic, prudent or imprudent."

"Of all bad debtors," replies Sétoc, "he is the most impulsive that I know."

"Very well," says Zadig, "let me plead your case before the judge."

The judge asks if he has witnesses.

"No, they are dead, but there is a big rock on which the money was counted out, and, if it pleases Your Honor to order someone to go get the stone, I hope that it will testify. We'll stay here, . . . until the stone comes. I'll send for it at the expense of Sétoc, my master."

"Agreed," says the judge, and proceeds to other cases.

At the end of the session, the judge inquires of Zadig: "Well, hasn't your stone come yet?"

The debtor, laughing, answers: "Your Honor will remain here until tomorrow and the stone will still not be here; it is more than six miles away, and it would take fifteen men to move it."

"Ah, ha!" cries Zadig. "I told you the stone would testify. Since this man knows where it is, he admits that it was on the stone that the money was counted out."

As Sétoc thus won his case, he began at last to alter his first unfavorable estimate of brain versus brawn.

After many other apologues, which follow from chapter to chapter, Zadig at last encounters an ancient Hermit "whose venerable white beard descended to his waist."

"What is the book you are reading?" asks Zadig curiously.

"It is the book of destiny," replies the Hermit. "Would you like to read some of it?"

Versed though he was in several languages, Zadig could not make out a single character!

As the two travelers went on together, they came to a magnificent castle. Although they were well served and fed, master and lackeys treated them with disdain. After their departure the next morning, Zadig discovered to his surprise that the strange Hermit had stolen a gold basin decorated with precious stones. This was his way of endeavoring to teach the vainglorious rich man a needed wisdom. The Hermit then gave his plunder to a miser with the purpose of making him hospitable. At a philosopher's house, Zadig and the Hermit conversed together of the passions.

"How dangerous they are!" says Zadig, echoing the conventional viewpoint.

"They are the winds which fill the sails of the vessel," replies the Hermit, repeating an expressive passage from Pope's widely-read *Essay on Man* or perhaps from one of Pope's French predecessors going back to the great Montaigne. "The passions sink the boat sometimes, but without them it could not sail. The bile makes one angry and sick, but without bile, man could not live. Everything is dangerous here below, but everything is necessary."

So it is that the Hermit expounds the popular doctrine of Optimism, as it was then taught by Alexander Pope and the German Leibniz, that everything in the World has its purpose and must be as it is.

Departing before dawn from their hospitable host, the Hermit, in "testimony of esteem and affection," puts a torch to the pleasant house, too quickly for the horrified Zadig to prevent him! Next, at the home of a charitable and virtuous widow, the pair meet her attractive fourteen-year-old nephew. The following morning, as the boy guides them on their way over a ruined bridge, the graybeard suddenly pushes the unhappy youth to his death in the raging torrent below, thus "paying his debt of gratitude," as the Hermit claims, "to the aunt!"

CHAPTER XII

"Monster! wickedest of men!" cries out Zadig in angry protest.

"You promised me more patience," replies the Hermit, interrupting him. "Under the ruins of this house which Providence burned down, the master has found an immense treasure. The boy whom Providence killed would have assassinated his aunt within a year, and you within two."

"Who told you so, brute?" exclaims Zadig, "and even if you had read this event in your book of destiny, are you permitted to drown a child who has done you no ill?"

Even as Zadig was speaking, he saw that the old Man's beard had vanished from his face, and, instead of the Hermit, a youthful angel with four wings stood before him, gleaming with majesty and light.

"Oh, envoy of Heaven, oh, divine angel!" cried Zadig, throwing himself on his knees. "Did you come down from above to teach a feeble mortal to bow before the eternal commands!"

"Men," said the angel Jesrad, "judge of everything without knowing the first word about it."

"But," objected Zadig respectfully, "wouldn't it have been better to correct this boy and have made him virtuous instead of drowning him?"

Jesrad replied: "If he had been virtuous and had lived, his destiny was to be himself assassinated with the woman whom he was to marry and the child who was to be born."

"But what!" said Zadig, "must there be crimes and misfortunes, and must these misfortunes fall on the good?"

"The wicked," responded Jesrad, "are always unhappy: they serve to test a small number of the just who are spread over the world, and there is no evil which does not give rise to some good."

"But," said Zadig, "suppose there were only good and no evil?"

"Then," replied Jesrad, "this earth would be another earth, the chain of events would be another order of wisdom, and this order, which would be perfect, can exist only in the eternal dwelling of the Supreme Being whom no evil can approach. . . . Men think this child who has just perished fell into the water by chance, that by this same chance the house burned down, but there is no such thing as chance. All is testing, punishment, reward, or foresight. . . . Feeble mortal, cease to dispute against what you ought to adore."

"But . . . ," said Zadig.

"As he was saying 'but,' the angel was already in flight toward the tenth sphere. Zadig, on his knees, worshipped and submitted himself to Providence."

On the surface, before these insoluble age-old problems of Providence, Chance, and Destiny, Voltaire seems to remain orthodox and conservative along with the Angel, but this is clearly only appearance. In reality, the author hints at the dilemmas which torment mankind in every answer proposed. It is the "philosophic *but*" of Zadig which gives the final word. Zadig is in no way satisfied with the facile reasoning of Jesrad, spokesman for Pope and Leibniz. He would continue to interpose objections. But the Angel conveniently flies away. Voltaire knows from experience that metaphysical arguments are never ended. He will not bore the reader; he will only try to make him think. Would it be better if man knew the future? No, it might indeed be worse. To know the future, bad or good, would paralyze all action in the present. The paradoxical conduct of the Hermit serves to reduce such foreknowledge to absurdity.

Zadig is at first sight entirely safe from the objections of the censor. As a matter of fact, Voltaire discreetly turns away from the so-called philosophy of Optimism. Babouc's doctrine of acceptance of things as they are will no longer satisfy him any more than it does in general modern man. And in his next prose tales, the author goes further still.

2

In 1752 Voltaire was at the court of Frederick the Great in Potsdam. Here he evidently turned over some old papers one day and came back to a story he had partially written some thirteen or fourteen years before. He gave it a new name, *Micromégas*, from the two Greek words meaning "little" and "great," for its hero, the giant Micromégas, though huge in physical size, remains limited and finite in his feelings like the human beings of earth. He is, to put it briefly, the "Little Great Man." In writing this tale, the author clearly preserves a keen memory for Swift's *Gulliver's Travels*, which he first read and enjoyed on his arrival in England more than twenty-five years before. Gulliver had been the giant in Lilliput, the tiny Lilliputian in Brobdingnag. Voltaire repeats such piquant contrasts. He also recalls the "extraordinary voyages" of Cyrano de Bergerac to the sun and moon, which had been rather popular in the second half of the seventeenth century. And he naturally does not forget the well-known *Conversations on the Plurality of Worlds,* written by his famous predecessor, Fontenelle. Out of these different elements and his own vivid imagination, Voltaire created both the immense Micromégas and another smaller giant, but one of enormous size as compared with infinitesimal man, who shows a remarkable resemblance to the still living, ninety-five-year-old Fontenelle.

The great Micromégas, "eight leagues tall," coming from the planet Sirius, decides to broaden his experience by making a journey to "our little anthill" of Earth. He is accompanied by the "dwarf" from Saturn, Secretary of the Academy, as Fontenelle had once been, who stands a mere "six thousand feet" high. After Micromégas has stretched out on the ground so that his small companion can speak into his ear—an obvious reminiscence of Gulliver' and the tiny inhabitants of the sands of Lilliput—there is a little spoofing of the "blonds" and "brunettes" who had served to entertain the readers of Fontenelle's *Plurality of Worlds.* Voltaire finds them altogether too frivolous, rather unjustly refusing credit for what his predecessor had done nearly seventy years before to make popularization of science easier.

Micromégas asks his companion from Saturn how many senses the inhabitants of his globe have.

"We have seventy-two," replied the Academician, "and we are constantly complaining of possessing so few. Our imagination runs beyond our needs; . . . and in spite of our curiosity and the rather large number of passions which are the result of our seventy-two senses, we have all the time in the world to be bored!"

"I should think so," answered Micromégas, "for in our globe we have nearly a thousand senses, and yet we still have a kind of vague desire, a strange disquiet, which constantly tells us of how little consequence we are and that there are other beings much more perfect. I have traveled about a little; I have seen mortals far inferior to us; I have seen some who are greatly superior; but I have seen none who did not have more desires than real needs, and more needs than satisfaction. Perhaps I shall arrive some day at the land where nothing is lacking, but up to the present nobody has brought me any positive news of that country."

Everything is relative and, in spite of the contrast between these remarkable beings with their myriad senses and the poorly endowed inhabitants of Earth who have a mere five, the same feeling of dissatisfaction remains in both. Each is more conscious of what he wants than of what he has. Man is finite; the more he possesses, the more he desires, and rare is he who knows the secret of that contentment which lies within. The problem is the same for the "Little Great Man" from Sirius, for the traveling Saturnian, or for the feeble insect, Man, on his "little ball of mud."

Micromégas and the Secretary of the Academy of Saturn arrive at last on Earth. As they stride together across the Atlantic Ocean, the water comes only to the knee of the panting "dwarf." The giant Micromégas barely moistens his heel! Mountains are merely little pointed grains of sand which hurt their feet! Try as they may, their huge eyes give them at first no hint of inhabitants, but the man from Sirius, wiser than his hasty comrade, will not jump too soon at conclusions.

Finally, the Saturnian picks up an infinitesimal object with his little finger and, putting it on his thumbnail, shows it to Micromégas who laughs aloud at the microscopic size of Earth's people. It is a whale! Next, the traveler from Sirius very carefully takes hold of a ship from the Baltic and, most cautiously for fear of accidentally crushing it, sets the tiny thing likewise on his nail. The frightened passengers and crew, sure that they have been shipwrecked by a storm, swarm out with their cargo upon the giant's enormous hand. One of these little beings actually tickles Micromégas with an iron pike driven a foot into the latter's forefinger! At length, with an improvised microscope, the man from Sirius is able to examine these atoms in detail and discover that they are talking to each other. Within a few hours even, the superintelligent Micromégas manages to understand French, using a cunningly extemporized ear trumpet to catch their diminutive voices. The Saturnian does the same, though with more difficulty. After infinite precautions to prevent their huge cries from deafening the mites, the two giants succeed in conversing with them. A geometer among these atoms even amazes Micromégas by determining, with a system of triangulation, his exact height of 120,000 feet.

How happy these tiny beings must be to combine such intelligence with so little base matter!

"We have more matter than we need," replies one of Earth's franker philosophers, "to do a great deal of evil if evil comes from matter, and too much mind if evil comes from intelligence. Do you know for instance that, at this very moment while I am speaking to you, a hundred thousand fools of our species, covered with hats, are killing a hundred thousand other animals, wearing turbans, or else are being massacred by these latter, and that, almost all over the Earth, men have been doing the same from time immemorial?"

The Sirian shuddered and asked what could be the cause of these horrible quarrels between such feeble creatures.

"It's a question," answered the philosopher, "of a few bits of mud as big as your heel. It's not because any of these millions of men who get themselves slaughtered care a straw about these bits of mud. It's only a matter of determining whether they will belong to a certain man named Sultan or to another called, I don't know why, Caesar. Neither of them, Sultan or Caesar, has ever seen the little corner of Earth in dispute, and almost none of these animals, who are slaying each other, has ever seen the animal for whom he is being killed."

"Ah! wretches!" cried the Sirian indignantly. "Can anyone imagine such an excess of madness! I feel like taking three steps and stamping out this whole ant-hill of crazy assassins."

"Don't take the trouble," someone answered. "They're working fast enough toward their own ruin. . . . Besides, they're not the ones to punish; it's those sedentary barbarians who, from their desks while they're digesting their dinner, order the massacre of a million men and then go and solemnly thank God for it."

Voltaire never misses a chance vigorously to condemn war.

Next the traveling giants are astonished at the accurate knowledge the tiny thinking atoms of Earth show of mathematics and the natural sciences.

"Since you understand so well what is outside of you," observes Micromégas, "no doubt you know still better what is within you. Tell me what your soul is and how you form ideas."

The Philosophers speak all at once just as before, but this time each is of a different opinion, citing Aristotle, Descartes, Malebranche, Leibniz, or Locke. In the opinion of Micromégas and the Saturnian, the partisan of Locke with his philosophy of sense impressions appears by no means the least reasonable.

So the author hints at his own strong preference for the modest English thinker.

But a little animal in a scholar's medieval bonnet breaks in on the other philosophers. Invoking the *Summa Theologica* of Thomas Aquinas, he confidently asserts that all the universe, Sirius, Saturn, their suns, their satellites, and the rest, were created solely for the sake of man. At this strange thought, the two giant travelers from other planets let go in a loud burst of Homeric laughter. Their shoulders and their sides shake wildly. In the midst of their convulsions of merriment, the vessel falls off the Sirian's nail into one of the Saturnian's pockets. After a long search, the two at last find it again, and carefully repair the damage. Then Micromégas once more speaks kindly to the mites "although at bottom he was somewhat angry to see that these infinitely tiny beings had a pride almost infinitely great."

He promises to make them a little book on philosophy, written very small so that they can read it. In this work, they will find the riddle of the universe explained. In fact, he does give them the volume before his departure. And they carry it off to the Academy of Science at Paris, but, when the old secretary opens it, he sees nothing but a book which is entirely blank.

"Ah!" says he, "I suspected as much!"

Thus the short tale of a mere twenty pages ends. The Secretary of the Academy of Saturn has finally exchanged roles with the Secretary of the Academy of Science at Paris, who, until his resignation in 1740, had actually been the aged Fontenelle. In this manner Voltaire's irony plays mildly upon his famous predecessor both in his fictional and his real capacities. Before the unexplained and unexplainable mystery of the universe, Voltaire himself remains no less skeptical than his century-old rival and forerunner. Zadig's prudent objections to the Angel Jesrad become even clearer and more pointed with the blank pages of Micromégas. At Berlin, seated intimately at table with the freethinking Frederick, the author could be far bolder than under Louis XV at Paris.

3

Much happened in the next few years. Voltaire quarreled with the autocratic Frederick and, after some difficulty and much uneasiness, was happy in the end to escape from "the claws of the lion." Where should he now go? Paris was closed to him by his apparent defection from King and Court. After months of wandering along the frontier, he finally secured permission to enter Geneva. Curiously enough, the gates of this little Protestant stronghold in the midst of its powerful Catholic enemies were not this time, as usual, shut at sundown, but were held open until six o'clock on this December day to await the carriage of the distinguished Monsieur de Voltaire! In contrast, the same clanking gates had barred the laggard return of the sixteen-year-old Jean-Jacques Rousseau and sent him into vagabond exile more than a quarter-century before!

Soon the celebrated French writer was allowed to acquire a home and property in the Protestant "Zion" through the forms of a long-term rental which amounted practically to a sale. So he established himself at Saint-Jean which he immediately christened "Les Délices," a pleasant countryseat located beyond the then city limits with a magnificent outlook over the swift-rushing Rhône and the varied rooftops of Geneva to the distant snowcapped range of Mont Blanc. It was indeed, as he had named it, a haven of "Delight."

But Geneva, in its Protestant hostility to Voltaire's favorite diversion of the theater, had its disadvantages, too. There were stiff-necked objections even to what, with tongue in cheek, he prudently called "dramatic readings." The author thereupon secured a freer winter home at "Mon Repos" in neighboring Lausanne. Soon, moreover, he acquired a thick-walled medieval château complete with moat at Tournay along the lake shore, a place at that time outside of Genevan jurisdiction. A little later he was master also of the castle of Ferney only a mile away down in the Jura valley just across the French frontier. "Philosophers should have two or three holes underground" in which to hide, observed Voltaire sagely. Henceforth, he would pay obeisance, if he could avoid it, neither to Louis nor Frederick nor the strait-laced Swiss citizenry. Rich and independent, he would at last live life pretty much as he willed it. If bothered in Geneva, he could be quickly over the convenient border into French territory; if menaced by the remote and slow-moving monarchy at Versailles, he could step into his carriage and in a half-hour find himself safe across the frontier in the heart of the tiny republic. It was indeed a strategic position! Voltaire had finally become a king himself, a King of Thought. In one way or another, he would speak his mind.

At sixty-five, in 1759, the author was at the height of his powers. There was no hint of "retirement" for him. Indeed, for nineteen years more, his multiple literary activities would continue hardly abated. Behind him were the instructive journeys to Holland, England, and Germany; his mind was stored with incident and anecdote gleaned from long years of reading for his histories, the *Age of Louis XIV* and the *Essay on Manners;* he knew at first hand both the charm and the disillusion of court life, whether at Versailles or Potsdam; his very success, as well as his own sharp practice, had exposed him to much intrigue and envy; he had said his say about delicate matters of religion and government, but often at the price of exile, persecution, and some compromise on his part; he had meanwhile early perfected his prose style, so that briefly, easily, it seemed, yet with a biting irony, it would do his bidding.

So it was that early in 1759, he published his greatest and still most widely read work, the rapidly-moving little novel *Candide.* It appears to have been largely written in a short three weeks at Schwetzingen, the castle of Charles-Theodore, Elector of the Palatinate, the year before. Tales that it was composed in three days, however, do not bear credence, even for the facile Voltaire!

In spite of his success, he was hardly conscious of the little masterpiece he had written. His fondest thoughts went to his histories, his classic tragedies, or his short philosophical poems. With details on them, the many pages of his brilliant correspondence are filled; about *Candide,* there is practically nothing. It seemed to him only a bagatelle, the easy offshoot of brief moments of leisure, with nothing of the long preparation or careful workmanship which went into what he considered his major writings. *Candide* was only the happy product of a practiced pen, racing with extraordinary sureness over the paper. An author, too, can be blind about the true value of his work. The reader now knows better.

Still Voltaire saw there was dynamite in his little book. Playing the usual, accepted game with the censor, he published the novel anonymously, denied any possible connection with it himself, and palmed it off on other authors, real or fictitious "I have finally read *Candide,*" he remarked facetiously in a letter! No one was fooled of course—who else could write like the far-off magician of

Ferney?—but the forms of deference were met, and the easy-going authorities were satisfied. There were thirteen or more printings in 1759 alone. For the rest of the eighteenth century, *Candide* vied with Rousseau's *Nouvelle Héloïse* for popularity. Jean-Jacques's novel has fallen now by the wayside, but Voltaire's remains untouched by the passage of time, as fresh today as it was yesterday.

The story begins with the author's usual directness and simplicity. "There was in Westphalia, in the castle of Baron Thunder-ten-tronckh, a young man to whom nature had given the gentlest manners. His face reflected his soul. He had fairly good judgment accompanied by complete simplicity of spirit. That is why, I think, he was named Candide."

So the naïve, the innocent, the candid young man makes his way through the trials of life. The story is the story of the impact of these tribulations upon his frank and simple nature, a gradual learning of a hard lesson. In the process, it is the so-called philosophy of Optimism which falls before Voltaire's keen shafts, a philosophy which had already been at least dented by passing blows in *Zadig* and *Micromégas*.

Optimism had come in for quite a vogue in the eighteenth century. Voltaire's mistress, Madame du Châtelet, until her sudden death in September of 1749, had been an eager student of its teachings. She had managed to enlist Voltaire's attention to these beliefs, but his adherence had been far from complete, although some passages in his work did lend color to his being classed as an advocate of the popular philosophy. Several minor writers openly hailed him as a real disciple of Pope and Leibniz. Voltaire was irked. The acceptance of things as they are, the doctrine that "God's in his Heaven, all's right with the World," while comforting, could easily degenerate into fatalism, and with such an attitude the author of *Candide* in the end would have nothing to do. Instead, he would work untiringly for necessary change, for improvement, for reform. He would not accept a viewpoint, well-meant though it might be, which would tend to make man content with the *status quo*. It would have been easy for him to sit down tranquilly in his comfortable surroundings of wealth, but he would not. Voltaire's impatient spirit was always ready for revolt. The philosophy of a misnamed Optimism must go down before the open ridicule of *Candide*.

So, in the story, the candid youth is whisked through an astonishing series of adventures for which he had been prepared only by the empty words of the "great" philosopher Pangloss, "All-Tongue"—Wind-Bag, *par excellence*.

"It is demonstrated," observed Pangloss solemnly, "that things cannot be otherwise, for, all being fashioned for a certain end, all is necessarily for the best end. Note well that noses have been created to support glasses; therefore we have glasses. Legs have clearly been intended for breeches, and we have breeches. Stones have been formed to be cut into blocks and built into castles. So My Lord has a very fine castle. The greatest baron of the province ought to be the best housed. And, pigs being made to be eaten, we eat pork throughout the year. Consequently, those who have said that all is well have been talking nonsense; they should have said that all is for the best." Thus Voltaire gaily makes fun of the so-called "argument from design" in the universe. If everything is conceived of as having a purpose, how about all those which clearly do not fit into any ordered scheme, and yet are usually left out of account?

But this chapter of the novel ends with the unhappy Candide being literally kicked out of the château for falling in love with Mademoiselle Cunégonde, his superior in social station, and "all was in consternation in the finest and pleasantest of possible castles!"

Suddenly, he finds himself a "volunteer," per-force, in the Bulgarian army! They teach him right-face, left-face, to draw out and push in his ramrod, to aim, fire, do a double-quick, and reward him with thirty blows with a stick. The next day, he does the drill a little less clumsily, and receives only twenty blows. The third day they give him only ten, and he is regarded by his comrades as a "prodigy." But when, tired of being a "hero," he decides to exercise his freedom of the will, by making off across the country, he is quickly recaptured, compelled to run the gauntlet of the whole regiment, and beaten into a pulp until he is ready to ask the kind favor of having his head bashed in once for all. As they are about to accord him this favor, the King of the Bulgars, who represents Voltaire's erstwhile friend, now his enemy, Frederick the Great, happens to pass by. "As this king had a penetrating genius, he understood, by all that he learned about Candide, that the latter was a young metaphysician very ignorant of the world, and the king pardoned him with a clemency which will be praised in all the newspapers and down through the centuries."

A good doctor cured Candide. "He had recovered a little of his skin, and was able to walk, when the King of the Bulgars gave battle to the King of the Abars." We have here a clear reflection of the Seven Years' War in the midst of whose horrors Voltaire's novel was written.

"Nothing was so fine, so gay, so brilliant, so well drilled as the two armies. The trumpets, fifes, oboes, drums, and cannon formed a harmony such as there was never seen anything like it in Hell." Thus Voltaire's sentence rises and then suddenly cascades to an astonishing, but effective anti-climax. "Candide, who trembled like a philosopher, hid himself as well as he could during this heroic butchery" of battle. In this last sentence, the idealistic adjective intentionally clashes with the realistic noun, once again revealing Voltaire's bitter hostility to war. Over the heaped-up piles of the dead and the dying, Candide made his way to a neighboring village, burned to ashes by the Bulgars, "according to the principles of international law," thence to another village, which the Abar "heroes had treated in the same way." Finally, he escaped to Holland where he re-encountered Pangloss, now in even worse case than himself.

The two sailed off for Lisbon, but had the misfortune to arrive just in time for the terrible earthquake of November 1, 1755. The earthquake, the tidal wave, the ensuing fire, ravaged the unhappy city and took some thirty thousand lives. Pangloss and Candide, however, escaped the disaster, the philosopher of Optimism continuing to maintain stoutly that "things could not be otherwise, for all is for the best." This seems heresy to a spy of the Inquisition, who was listening to the learned doctor's words. Could it be that Pangloss believed neither in the Fall nor the Damnation of Man, or, if he did, how about Free Will? Pangloss, untroubled, actually set out to reconcile Free Will and Determinism, but without being able to satisfy his orthodox hearer. Pangloss and Candide are therefore hurried off to "apartments of an extreme coolness in which they were never inconvenienced by the sun!" From these dank dungeons, they are taken a week later and find themselves principals in an *auto-da-fé* at which Pangloss is hanged, instead of being burned according to custom, and Candide is beaten "in cadence to the accompaniment of hymns." In spite of this religious "act of faith," the earth trembles again the same day worse than ever!

Later, Candide meets once more "the beautiful Cunégonde," who had been a horrified spectator of the *auto-da-fé* at which Candide was beaten while "refreshments were served to the ladies between the mass and the execution." Candide, having killed an Inquisitor, flees by ship to Buenos Aires. He is accompanied by Cunégonde, an old woman, and a South American native servant, a clever fellow by the name of Cacambo, whom he had found at Cadiz.

At Buenos Aires, Candide would fain have married Cunégonde, but the Governor, Don Fernando d'Ibaraa y Figueora y Mascarenes y Lampourdos y Souza, "twirling the points of his mustache," moved by a pride befitting his long string of Spanish names and with a fondness himself for Cunégonde, would have none of it. Comes a dispute with a Jesuit, the brother of Cunégonde—how these West-phalians do turn up as Voltaire satirizes, not only Optimism, but the incredible coincidences of the popular adventure novel as well!—and Candide is forced in self-defense to run the cleric through with his sword. This time Candide and Cacambo escape to a neighboring tribe of "Big-Eared" Indians. "Let us eat some Jesuit, let us eat some Jesuit!" exclaim the cannibals, joyously, at the sight of the robe in which Candide is disguised.

"Tell them," cried Candide, "how inhuman it is to cook a man and eat him, and how unchristian!"

Cacambo, more realistically, secures his companion's release on the ground that he is a friend who, instead of being a Jesuit, has just killed a member of the order! What an astonishment to Candide that the pure life of nature, so much admired by Jean-Jacques Rousseau, could be as it is! Candide was not eaten because he had had the fortune to run his sword through the body of a Jesuit!

Next the two travelers arrive at the idyllic country of Eldorado, the one place where everything seems to be for the best. There one finds no persecution, no tyranny; the religion is one only of worship and adoration; gold, diamonds, and precious stones have no mean-ing; they are merely the yellow mud and glittering pebbles which children pick up in their play. Men have what they need. Here, at last, is the ideal land which Candide has been seeking. Here is the foil to things as they unfortunately are in the rest of the earth. But, alas! Candide and Cacambo, human-like, are unwilling to remain where everything is perfect. They prefer to take their "yellow mud" and precious "pebbles" back to a world which will make them millionaires. Unable to dissuade the pair from their folly, the leaders of Eldorado regretfully aid them to depart.

On their way back to Europe, they lose or are tricked out of most of the great wealth which they have loaded onto the sheep or llamas of Eldorado. The two witness the anomalies of life in Paris, they see Admiral Byng courtmartialed and shot in England for having lost a sea battle in the Mediterranean just a few years before. "It is a good thing to kill an admiral from time to time in order to encourage the others," an Englishman ironically explained to Candide in a phrase which has become memorable. Voltaire had, indeed, vainly endeavored to save the life of the unhappy Byng. This was one more of many episodes from reality transferred directly to the pages of his rapidly-moving novel.

"Do you think men have always massacred one another as they are doing today?" Candide in despair asks his new companion, the pessimistic Martin. "That they have always been liars, cheats, traitors, ingrates, brigands, weak, fickle, cowardly, envious, gluttons, drunkards, misers, ambitious, fanatical, hypocrites, and fools?"

"Do you think," replies Martin, "that hawks have always eaten pigeons when they found them?"

The Jesuit brother of Cunégonde had not been killed, after all, only wounded! Pangloss had been very "badly hanged" and had recovered! The two are found again as slaves rowing the galleys in the Mediterranean. So Voltaire, with tongue in cheek, makes fun of the improbable novels of adventure which often form the escape literature of our age as of his. But the philosopher of Ferney does not ask us to regard the plot of his story seriously. It is the philosophy behind the tale which concerns him. The rest is only sugarcoating for the bitter pill of ideas which most readers would otherwise take unwillingly.

Cunégonde, too, turns up in Constantinople, washing dishes and ugly as can be after her checkered career. Her brother, the Baron, still haughtily insistent upon rank even after Candide has kindly ransomed him from the galleys, persists in opposition to a commoner's marrying his sister. "If I listened to my anger, I'd kill you all over again, I'd *re*kill you," shouted Candide in a phrase vivified by Voltaire's skill in the use of words.

But Candide marries Cunégonde in spite of her ugliness and bad temper, egged on as he is by the Baron's impertinence and his sister's urging. The troublesome brother is sent back to the galleys to get rid of him. Candide, Cunégonde, the old woman, Pangloss, Cacambo, and Martin, all settle down to a peaceful life near Constantinople where, in the cool of the evening outside their door, they can watch the dervishes pass and the ambitious muftis rise and fall.

"I should like to know which is worse, to be attacked a hundred times by black pirates, to run the gauntlet among the Bulgars, to be whipped and hanged in an *auto-da-fé,* to be dissected, to row in the galleys, in short to experience all the misfortunes through which we have passed, or to remain here doing nothing?"

"That's a great question," said Candide.

Pangloss, however, maintained the same opinion as at the beginning. "For, after all, I am a philosopher," he said, "it's not becoming for me to contradict myself." He admitted indeed that "he had suffered horribly, but, having once asserted that everything was excellent, he kept on in his assertion, without believing a word of it." Pangloss too must "save face."

They went to consult a dervish who had the reputation of being the best philosopher in Turkey.

"Master," Pangloss said to him, "we come to beg you to tell us why so strange an animal as man has been formed."

"What business is that of yours?" replied the dervish.

"But, my reverend Father," said Candide, "there is a horrible amount of evil in the world."

"What difference does it make," said the dervish, "whether there is evil or good?"

"What must we do, then?" asked Pangloss.

"Be silent," said the dervish.

"I flattered myself," said Pangloss, "that I might reason a little with you about effects and causes, about the best of possible worlds, the origin of evil, the nature of the soul, and about pre-established harmony."

At these Leibnizian words, the dervish "closed the door in his face," thus putting an abrupt end to all metaphysical argument.

Returning to their little farm, Candide, Pangloss, and Martin, came upon an old man, enjoying the cool air of the evening under a bower of orange trees.

Pangloss asked him the name of the mufti who had just been strangled and done away with.

"I haven't the least idea," replied the good man, "and I have never inquired the name of any mufti or any vizir. . . . I never bother to inform myself what's going on in Constantinople. I'm satisfied to sell there the products of the garden which I am cultivating."

"You must have a magnificent estate," said Candide to the Turk.

"Only twenty acres," replied the Turk. "I cultivate them, along with my children. Work saves us from three great evils, boredom, vice, and want."

"I know too," said Candide, "that we must cultivate our garden."

"Let's work without philosophizing," said Martin. "That's the only way to make life bearable."

And so they did.

"All events are connected in the best of possible worlds," the irrepressible Pangloss observed to Candide, "for, in short, if you had not been kicked out of a magnificent château for love of Mademoiselle Cunégonde, if you had not been tried by the Inquisition, if you had not made your way all over America afoot, if you hadn't run your sword through the Baron, if you hadn't lost all your sheep from the good country of Eldorado, you wouldn't be sitting here eating candied fruit and pistachio nuts."

"That's well said," replied Candide, "but we've got work to do in our garden."

Philosophical reasoning proves fruitless. Who can agree on what is true about life, man, and the universe? All, however, can agree on the value of productive work. "Work," had said the Turk, "saves us from three great evils, boredom, vice, and want." Who should know this better than Voltaire, reading, writing, waking his secretaries in the middle of the night, always in an enthusiastic fever of fruitful activity? At the château of Cirey, Voltaire and Madame du Châtelet slept sometimes but two or three hours, then were up and at work again with unconquerable persistence. Even during a brief call on Madame de Graffigny in 1738, Voltaire could not be prevailed upon to sit down, but exclaimed: "It's frightful the amount of time lost in just talking; we shouldn't lose a minute; the greatest expenditure we make is that of time." The result in the end was fifty big volumes of published works, more than fifteen thousand letters, with many others lost, and withal an active concern for contemporary victims of tyranny or abuse. For Voltaire would not carry out literally the old Turk's indifference to mufti or vizir. These were only the passing words of a man tired of royal courts and the affairs of an ill-run world. Actually, he would never give up the courageous effort to ameliorate life.

At Ferney, Voltaire established a productive watch-making industry, planted trees, crops, studied improved methods of farming. His writings, his letters, his clever pamphlets, never failed to have bearing on what was going on about him. He never ceased to keep himself informed. His philosophy in *Candide* is one of active work against all the man-made evils about us. No more acceptance of things as they are, no slightest tinge of fatalism, no false Optimism. Voltaire, in little over a decade, has moved far from Babouc and the "World as It Is." *Candide,* too, presents the world as it unhappily is, today as yesterday, but with a wit, an incisive irony, an intentional piling up of horrors, which are a challenge to complacency. And the final word is one of work in "our garden" where we happen to be, a motto which Voltaire would follow to the last. Such was Candide's counsel.

CHAPTER XIII

THE PHILOSOPHER OF FERNEY

I

HOW EASY IT WOULD HAVE BEEN FOR VOLTAIRE TO SIT QUIETLY beneath the shelter of the Jura Mountains, watching the hectic world go by, planting his trees and cabbages, selling his clocks and watches to the crowned heads of Europe, declaiming the roles of his tragedies on his little stage, receiving like a royal potentate distinguished visitors of many nationalities! But the author of *Candide* was no indifferent cynic. He was a satirist, and a satirist is a reformer whose ideals force him to lash out at human folly. The woes of mankind would not let him rest. In the philosophical tales, Voltaire's attack had been general; now, in these later years, it would in certain cases become specific.

Since the Revocation of the Edict of Nantes in 1685, Protestants remained without legal standing in France. To practice the learned professions, a "certificate of Catholicity" was required. In the southern city of Toulouse, religious passions ran high. The Protestant merchant, Jean Calas, was accused of having murdered his son to prevent his conversion to the dominant faith. It did no good to show that young Marc-Antoine Calas was melancholy, had been given to reading the "To be or not to be" monologue of *Hamlet,* was discouraged over not being allowed to become a lawyer, had probably committed suicide, and could hardly in any case have been forcibly hanged by his less vigorous father, who was a man past sixty years of age. The elder Calas was broken on the wheel, was put to death after horrible torture, yet made no confession of guilt. All this happened in 1762.

Voltaire, in his pleasant countryseat near Geneva, heard of the affair, was convinced at length of the innocence of Calas, and began to move heaven and earth for a *post-mortem* reversal of the conviction. To this end he enlisted the aid of Monsieur de Beaumont, celebrated lawyer of Paris, and aroused public interest by letter after letter to his numerous friends. Finally, the Parlement of Paris re-

versed the decision of the Parlement of Toulouse, decreed a rehabilitation of the memory of Jean Calas, and caused an indemnity to be
paid to his family. They had made such restitution as was possible.

The facts of the Calas affair still remain in dispute among Protestants and Catholics, and perhaps will never be put completely
beyond the scope of argument. It seems clear at least that Jean Calas
was far from having an entirely fair and unprejudiced trial. Feeling
at Toulouse ran too high for that. It should be added that Voltaire's
condemnation of religious fanaticism wherever he found it, as for
instance in the ancient case of the Protestant Calvin burning the
Anti-Trinitarian heretic Servetus at the stake, shows his impartial
stand in favor of liberty of the human spirit.

Voltaire's most important contribution to the Calas case was his
Treatise on Tolerance, published in 1763. The first chapters present
in simple, direct language the sequence of events at Toulouse. Then
the author turns to more general considerations. Is tolerance dangerous? How is it that it causes no trouble in England, Germany, or
Holland? Indeed, the multiplicity of sects is an advantage, believes
Voltaire, renewing a page from the *Philosophical Letters* of thirty
years before. "Do not what you would not have others do to you,"
says the author, giving in negative form the Golden Rule. "The right
of intolerance is absurd and barbarous; it is the right of tigers. . . .
I say it with horror, but truthfully: it is we Christians who have
been persecutors, executioners, assassins! And of whom? Of our
brothers?"

"If you wish to be like Jesus Christ, be martyrs, not executioners."

"The less you have of dogmas, the less disputes; and the less disputes, the less misfortunes. If that is not true, then I am wrong,"
writes Voltaire succinctly.

"No great art is needed, no refined eloquence, to prove that
Christians should tolerate each other. I go further. I maintain that
we must regard all men as our brothers. . . . 'Love God and your
neighbor,' " enjoins the author of the *Treatise on Tolerance.*

Voltaire concludes with a *Prayer to God.*

"Thou has not given us a heart to hate or hands to slay each
other. Grant that we may aid one another to bear the burden of a
painful and transitory life, that the slight differences between the
garments which cover our feeble bodies, between our inadequate
languages, our ridiculous customs, our imperfect laws, our senseless

opinions, between our stations, so different in our own eyes, so equal before Thee, that all these little differences which distinguish the atoms called *men* shall not be signals for hate and persecution, that those who light candles to worship Thee at midday may bear with those who are content with the light of Thy sun, that those who cover their robes with white linen to testify their love for Thee shall not scorn those who say the same thing from beneath a cloak of black wool, that it make no difference whether we adore Thee in a jargon formed from an ancient language, or in one which is more recent, that those whose garb is dyed red or violet, who dominate a tiny bit of the little heap of mud of this world and who possess a few round pieces of a certain metal, enjoy without pride what they call *grandeur* and *riches,* and that others look upon them without envy, for Thou knowest that in these vanities there is cause neither for envy nor pride."

"May all men remember that they are brothers! May they look with horror on tyranny exercised over souls just as they execrate the brigandage which steals by force the fruits of work and peaceful industry. If the scourge of war is inevitable, let us not hate one another, not tear one another to pieces in the midst of peace, and let us use the moment of our existence to bless, in our thousand different languages from Siam to California, Thy goodness which has granted us this moment."

To a world still torn with religious, racial, and national intolerance, Voltaire's preachment continues to speak with a needed eloquence. Unfortunately, humanity has not yet outgrown the *Treatise on Tolerance* any more than it has outgrown the varied irony of *Candide.*

2

Since 1751, the great *Encyclopedia* of Diderot and D'Alembert had been going its ponderous way at the rate of one folio volume a year until by 1757 seven huge tomes had appeared. Two years later, however, the work was suppressed by the censor. The other volumes, held in reserve by the irrepressible Diderot, were to come out finally together in 1766, under the cover of anonymity and a false place of publication.

In 1752 while still in Berlin, Voltaire, according to his secretary

Colini, had conceived the idea of what he called a *Portable Philosophical Dictionary*. It was to be a small, inexpensive volume, handy for the pocket, presenting important ideas under a convenient alphabetical arrangement. Such a volume did at last appear in 1764, the year after the *Treatise on Tolerance*. Little by little, it has grown by accretions from other similar works of his, until now it is no longer "portable," but nevertheless is said to be still much in demand in the public reading rooms of France, and has been reprinted in modern English translations.

One of the key articles in the *Philosophical Dictionary* is that entitled "Government." Voltaire does not yield to Montesquieu in his admiration for the government of England. "Has not the love of liberty become the dominant characteristic of the English as they have grown more enlightened and more prosperous?" What is it to be free? "To be free," replies Voltaire, "is to be governed only by laws." No capricious tyranny, no government at the whim of men, but the equal rule of all under the same established principles.

"It is probable that a constitution which has regulated the rights of the King, of the nobles, and of the people, and under which each is protected, will last as long as human institutions can endure. It is probable also that all states not founded on such principles will have revolutions." So Voltaire sounds the ominous tocsin of 1789.

"Here is what English law has at last attained to. It has restored each man to all the rights of nature of which he has been deprived in most monarchies. These rights are: full liberty of his person, of his goods; freedom to speak to the nation by the pen; freedom not to be tried under any criminal charge except by a jury formed of independent men; freedom not to be tried in any case except according to the precise terms of the law; freedom to profess peacefully any religion he wishes, on condition of renouncing those employments open only to Anglicans. These are called prerogatives. And, in fact, it is a very great and happy prerogative to be sure on going to bed that you will awake the next morning with the same fortune you possessed the evening before; that you will not be torn from the arms of your wife or your children, in the middle of the night, to be lodged in a dungeon or exiled to a desert; that, on opening your eyes from sleep, you have the right to publish all you think; that, if you are accused, either of acting or speaking or writing ill, you will be judged only according to law. This prerogative extends to everyone landing in England. A foreigner there enjoys the same liberty of property or person, and, if he is accused, can require that half of his jurors shall be foreigners."

"I dare to assert that, if the human race should assemble to make laws, it is so they would make them for their own protection."

Even today, almost a hundred and eighty years after our Declaration of Independence, Voltaire's words have a modern ring. They still sound a call to oppressed peoples in all countries of the world. There is indeed no country where democracy is so perfectly established as not to leave room for further advance.

Another important article of the *Philosophical Dictionary*, as might be expected, is that on "War." A prince, says Voltaire, "finds forthwith a host of men with nothing to lose; he dresses them up in heavy blue cloth at a hundred and ten cents a yard, runs a thick white cord around their hats, teaches them to turn to the right and to the left, and marches to glory." The author's sentence of course applies particularly to the mercenary armies of the eighteenth century. "The marvelous part of this infernal enterprise is that each chief of the murderers causes his flags to be blessed and invokes God solemnly before going out to exterminate his neighbor." Hardly a preacher, laments the author of the *Philosophical Dictionary*, ventures to attack "the malady which tears us into a thousand pieces." In that respect, there has been a great change. The converse appears true today. Indeed, are not many ministers more or less pacifist, even though the tough facts of life belie all wishful thinking? Then Voltaire turns to belabor sharply the position of "the celebrated Montesquieu," who stated the necessity of sometimes attacking first in the interest of effective defense. "If there were ever a war clearly unjust, it is the one you propose," charges the philosopher of Ferney; "it is to go out and kill your neighbor for fear your neighbor (who is not attacking you) might be in a position to attack you." The argument is cogent. We should all have admitted it readily a few years ago. Yet, in our modern age of undeclared war, the issue presents itself ever more urgently. To attack first is repugnant to all democratic peoples, hating the butchery of war with a bitter hatred. The alternative seems, however, under certain circumstances to be bombed into submission like sitting ducks. Voltaire perceived the danger of each side's pretending to have been threatened with attack first. We have seen that, too, in recent years—the strong claiming to have been threatened with destruction by the weak! But Montesquieu, in this instance, was more realistic than his usually realistic rival. In a world dominated by lack of moral scruples even more than in the eighteenth century, the problem remains unsolved and can never be completely settled on an idealistic basis until ideals themselves prevail among the strong on both sides of the lines.

Yet Voltaire, in his article "Man," remains hopeful about humanity's possessing a degree of inherent goodness. "If the human race had been under the rule of the Devil, there would no longer be a person on earth," he says. What is man, however, in the state of pure nature? "An animal far below the first Iroquois discovered in North America," the philosopher answers. "More than half the habitable earth is still peopled by two-legged animals living in that horrible state which is close to that of pure nature, possessing scarcely food and clothes, scarcely enjoying the gift of speech, hardly conscious that they are unhappy, living and dying almost without knowing it." Let Jean-Jacques Rousseau take note. Voltaire is no admirer of "the goodness of nature." He is a realistic partisan of as much civilization as possible. His picture of the way in which a majority of the human race live is still applicable to much of the modern world in spite of the march of science. Unless the problem of population in relation to food is solved, the situation could become worse rather than better.

"*Liberty and property* is the English motto," cries Voltaire. "It is certain that the possessor of a piece of land will cultivate his own inheritance much better than that of another. The spirit of private property doubles the force of a man." The master of Ferney sees the value of ownership as a stimulus to self-interest and initiative; Rousseau, on the contrary, underlines the abuses of possessions, though he became conscious of another side, too, as he grew older.

There was also the problem of torture, which remained the common eighteenth-century procedure even in the case of persons merely accused, not yet convicted, of crime. Voltaire re-echoes an effective sentence in Diderot's *Encyclopedia* of a few years before, a sentence found previously in La Bruyère, Montaigne, or, more distantly, in Cervantes. "It has often been said that torture was a means of saving a guilty man who is strong and condemning an innocent man who is too weak." The so-called "third degree" still remains an abuse in many supposedly civilized communities. A confession elicited by force is obviously a test, not of guilt, but of endurance.

3

What of religion, always the key subject associated with the name of Voltaire? The author of the *Philosophical Dictionary* devotes a special article to it. Traveling in a dream through the other world, he sees great heaps of bones, the myriad victims of man's numerous religious wars.

"I saw a man of gentle and simple mien," continues Voltaire, "who seemed about thirty-five years old. From afar he cast glances of compassion on these heaps of whitened bones through which I had been obliged to pass in order to reach the dwelling of the sages. I was astonished to find his feet swollen and bleeding, his side pierced, and his back scarred with the lashes of a whip."

"Ah, my good Lord!" I said to him, "is it possible that a just man, a sage, is in such a state? . . . Have you also been treated so cruelly by bad priests and bad judges?"

"He replied *yes* with much kindliness."

"And who were these monsters?"

"They were hypocrites. . . ."

"You sought to teach them a new religion?"

"Not at all; I simply told them: 'Love God with all your heart and your neighbor as yourself, for that is the whole duty of man.' Judge whether this precept is not as old as the universe; judge whether I brought them a new cult. I never ceased to tell them that I had come, not to abolish the law, but to fulfill it; I had observed all their rites; circumcized as they all were, baptized like the most zealous among them, like them I paid the consecrated tax.". . .

"What! these wretches couldn't even reproach you with breaking their laws?"

"No. . . ."

"But didn't you once say that you had come to bring, not peace, but a sword?"

"That was the error of a copyist; I told them I was bringing peace and not a sword. I never wrote anything. It was possible to change my words without evil intention."

Thus ingeniously, Voltaire alters the clear meaning of the text in favor of his own hostility to military strife, particularly wars of religion.

"I besought him simply to teach me in what true religion consists," continued Voltaire.

"Haven't I already told you? Love God and your neighbor like yourself."

Thus no fasting, no ceremonies, no particular observances, are of moment, only good conduct and love of God.

"If this is so, then I take you for my only master," concludes the author.

So Voltaire stresses the essence of Christianity, going behind the long-established forms of the different churches to the heart of Christ's teaching. He appeals over the heads of ecclesiastical authorities to Jesus himself. It was an effective and frequent tactic of the philosophers of the eighteenth century.

In his article "God," Voltaire emphasizes "the necessity of believing in a Supreme Being." His "remunerative and avenging God" is, as has often been pointed out, not a very high conception of deity, but a "policeman God," sanction of virtue, punisher of crime. Voltaire finds neither the existence nor the non-existence of God provable. "We reason in metaphysics," he says, "only on the basis of probabilities." Is it religion which has produced these millions of crimes? Say rather that it is "superstitution" and "fanaticism." "To be a disciple of God is to show a gentle heart and a tranquil spirit." The articles "Theism" and "Theist" develop the author's ideas further. "What is a true theist? He who says to God: 'I worship and serve you.' He who says to the Turk, to the Chinese, to the man of India, to the Russian: 'I love you.'" Thus once again, Voltaire restates the Golden Rule. The theist believes that all men are brothers. "He holds that religion does not consist in unintelligible metaphysical opinions or in vain show, but in worship and justice. To do good is his cult; to be submissive to God, his doctrine."

Two years later, in 1766, Voltaire underlined his consciousness of the deep mystery of life which no philosophy has succeeded in penetrating. Significantly, the new work was entitled *The Ignorant Philosopher*.

"Who are you?" begins the author. "Where do you come from? What are you doing? What will later become of you? These are questions which we must address to all the beings of the universe, but which no one can answer." Before the mystery of plant or human life, Voltaire remains ignorant. How does man think? Are we two, matter and spirit, or are we somehow one? What can we know of the world except through experience? What is this mysterious thing which we glibly call "matter"? Do we act according to the philosophical notion of Free Will or are our acts determined for us from without? Our acts follow our will, our choice, believes Voltaire, but our will is shaped by what has gone before. After all, without such a belief, man's conduct would be merely capricious, without continuity of character. "Train up a child in the way he should go, and when he is old he will not depart from it," is a very effective and indeed encouraging form of determinism. All education, for good or ill, rests upon a similar concept. Freedom of the Will emphasizes the wholesome effect of assuming individual responsibility. Determinism indicates the possibility of shaping our predominant choices in advance, not fatalistically, but for better or for worse as our training or environment may decide.

Voltaire believes in universal principles of morality and, in the midst of hydra-headed fanaticism, sees a dawning glimmer of reason to enlighten the world. "Shall we remain idle in the darkness, or shall we light a torch even though envy and calumny, too, will take their fires from it? For myself, I believe that truth should no more hide itself before these monsters than one should refrain from taking food for fear of being poisoned." Let us go forward courageously in the light of reason, says Voltaire.

4

Voltaire's thought is much too complex for any brief summary. On the one hand, we see the old war horse, lashing out violently against abuses wherever he found them. "Crush the infamous thing," he cried out constantly in his letters, abbreviating the phrase into a slogan and a rallying cry which we may transliterate into: *Cr. the inf.* What is the *infamous* thing? Some have said it was organized religion itself, the Church and its hierarchy. And, in so far as the Church was responsible for persecution, for the death of the Protestant, Jean Calas, the exile of Sirven, whose flight alone protected him from a similar fate, the execution of young La Barre, after conviction of not baring his head before the procession of the Holy

Sacrament and of giving other evidences of disrespect, there is no doubt that Voltaire was angrily against it, revolting with every fibre of his being. He was bitterly opposed also, as we have seen, to all elevation of creeds, of ceremonies, into the first place, before good conduct and brotherly love. Yet it was not the religion of the Golden Rule which he attacked. Rather it was what he clearly called superstition or fanaticism. Much of the violence, the irreverence, of the traditional Voltairean criticism of the Bible came from the literal-minded narrowness of his adversaries. Voltaire had only to reproduce mockingly what naïve writers like Dom Calmet advanced in their Biblical commentaries with all seriousness. No informed Biblical scholar would follow Dom Calmet today, any more than he would accept Voltaire's hostile rebuttal. The philosopher of Ferney, moreover, was too deeply enmeshed in his own somewhat narrow rationalism to be able fully to understand Jesus or Jeanne d'Arc who spoke in terms of an unscientific age. Yet Voltaire's often unsympathetic criticism swept away the dry bones of the past and made a more penetrating modern interpretation possible. In place of a literal-minded view of oriental imagery or allegory has come an insight into the spirit, of which Voltaire, no doubt, enlightened by the passage of time, would be the first to approve. After all, in his calmer moments, he, too, admired the spirit of Christ, he, too, put forward the Golden Rule as humanity's best guide to conduct, he, too, preached that all men are, or should be, brothers.

Did he always follow this inner light in his own life? No. He was passionate, impulsive, violent in his hates as in his loves, tricky, guilty at times of sharp practice, ready to lie like a trooper when it was necessary to "fight fire with fire" and, outwitting the government in its warfare against freedom of thought and speech, live to fight again another day. The often repeated quotation attributed to Voltaire—"I disapprove of what you say, but I will defend to the death your right to say it"—is an attractive legend, but with no demonstrated basis in fact. It can only be paralleled in much less striking form. Courageous as Voltaire often was in his protests, he by no means sought a martyr's role. Moreover, Voltaire's eye was turned out upon the world, not within toward himself. Unlike his contemporary, Jean-Jacques Rousseau, there was with him no thought of sin. He was not dissatisfied with himself, experienced no tormenting self-conflict. In a certain sense, he was less profound, perhaps. Yet his thoughts and his acts were constantly directed toward combating abuses, toward righting wrongs. Wealthy as he was, he could easily "have passed by on the other side." But for the urge which drove him on, he could have remained safely silent, enjoying his comforts and his honors, sparing his excitable nerves the fear of renewed imprisonment or persecution. Unlike so many of us in similar case, he did not do so. This was his honor and his glory. This it is which still makes his works live today, speaking to us with a clear voice which the world, unhappily, has not yet become good enough or wise enough to heed.

5

To the pleasant château of Ferney in the Jura valley across the French frontier, the world came for years to pay its court. So many lingered on as uninvited guests that Voltaire remarked sarcastically one day to Abbé Coyer: "You don't want to be like Don Quixote; he took every inn for a castle, and you take castles for inns!" James Boswell was astonished at the vigor and expressiveness of Voltaire's English after thirty years. "He had bold flights. He had humour," writes Boswell. "Then he talked of our constitution with a noble enthusiasm. I was proud to hear this from an illustrious Frenchman." The master of Ferney led the English traveler, Martin Sherlock, out into his garden, showed him the distant Alps, the Lake, the city of Geneva, and the smiling country around. "It is a beautiful prospect," said the aged author in the language of his guest and with a fairly good pronunciation. He went on to talk animatedly of Shakespeare and a host of other English writers.

Voltaire commonly wore a long coat reaching to the knees, gray shoes and stockings, a large wig falling about his shoulders, and on his head a small hat of black velvet. "It is impossible to describe the light in his eyes or the charm of his face. What an enchanting smile!" exclaimed Madame Suard. "Not a wrinkle which is not attractive," she continued enthusiastically. "How surprised I was when, in place of the decrepit figure I expected to see, there appeared this vivid and expressive face; instead of a bent old man, I saw a figure erect, noble, though natural, with a firm and even a quick step, and a manner, a courtesy which, like his genius, is his alone!" This was in 1775, when Voltaire was already eighty-one!

He loved to play the roles of aged men in French tragedies on his own stage at Tournay or Ferney. Chabanon and Gibbon remarked his declamatory style with the sonorous lines, his own or those of Racine. It was old-fashioned, but somehow pleasing and impressive. His ardor for work or study inspired his auditors with a similar fire. When Boswell, with the brash insistence of the born interviewer, pressed him for his views on religion, Voltaire replied with an intensity, a passion, which left him for the moment nervously exhausted in his chair. Ideas crowded in upon him at all hours. In the midst of his light sleep, he would awake to call upon his hardworking secretary and dictate while the inspiration was hot. Yet this same secretary, Wagnière, remained devoted to his master and, unlike some modern servants of the great, spoke of him always with admiration, respect, and affection. Voltaire even dictated while riding in his coach across the country. Not a day passed without its several pages of writing, year after year, as time wore on. It was in this way that the fifty big volumes of his published works little by little were gathered together. "You don't go down to posterity with so much baggage," he lamented, as editors avidly snatched up every bit of prose or verse they could lay hands on from the facile and expressive pen. Some of it was ephemeral, of course, written for immediate influence on contemporary events, but it is astonishing how much has remained. New editions of his voluminous works poured from the busy presses. On the eve of the Revolution, the dramatist Beaumarchais directed and financed still another complete collection, the famous Kehl edition, which climaxed the eighteenth century and formed the basis for those editions to come after. For many, Voltaire was the greatest man of his time, the vivid, active, all-embracing personality of his age, the ruler of his mile-square little realm of Ferney, the very King of French literature and thought.

At length, in February of 1778, Voltaire was persuaded by his fat, bustling niece, Madame Denis, to go back once more to Paris. It was twenty-eight years since he had last visited the alluring capital. He had a new play, *Irène*, which he wished to see performed at the Comédie-Française. The timid Louis XVI, only four years seated on his uncertain throne, looked aghast at the idea of the radical's return, but found no easy way to prevent it without unpleasant uproar. Voltaire, in his carriage, appeared at the gates of the city. "Have you any contraband?" asked the customs officer. "There's only myself," answered the lively old man with his usual double-edged facetiousness.

Benjamin Franklin, representative of the infant American states to Paris, brought his grandson to receive the great man's blessing. "God and Liberty," exclaimed Voltaire in his still serviceable English, "that's the only benediction which is suitable for the grandson of Mr. Franklin." At the public session of the Academy of Science, the crowd applauded, insisted that these famous men of the two worlds should embrace, hailed them as the lawgiver Solon, the tragic dramatist Sophocles, of their time.

Active as ever, Voltaire threw himself eagerly into the composition of the *Letter A* for the new *Dictionary* of the French Academy, attended a public performance of his latest tragedy, *Irène,* at the Comédie-Française—then temporarily located for the past eight years in the Tuileries Palace—where his bust on the stage was enthusiastically crowned with laurel, mercilessly whipped his aged frame on with cup after cup of his favorite beverage, coffee. "They want to kill me with flowers," he lamented in his wiser moments. "You don't transplant a tree which is eighty-four years old unless you want to make it die," observed the famous Dr. Tronchin. The faithful secretary, Wagnière, sought unsuccessfully to get his master out of the tumult back to the wholesome quiet of Ferney. But Voltaire's strength broke down. He went to bed, was bled according to the prevailing medical practice of the time, seemed momentarily to recover, plunged back into the maelstrom. He was received with respect by the Masonic Lodge of the Nine Sisters. But it was all too much, as Tronchin had realistically said. Voltaire was bled again, finally had to take once more to his bed, and died during the night of May 30, 1778, less than five weeks before the death of his great younger rival, Jean-Jacques Rousseau.

During his last days, priests endeavored to extract from Voltaire a confession and renunciation of past attacks upon the Church. He had long feared desecration of his body after death. To insure, as he hoped, burial in consecrated ground, he signed a statement "that he wished to die in the Catholic religion in which he had been born, that he asked pardon of God and the Church if in any way he had offended them," but he refused to acknowledge the divinity of Christ. What seems the most authentic expression of his last opinions he had dictated to his secretary, Wagnière, at the time of his

À Mad. la présid. de Bernières rue de Baune.
août 1726

On doit me conduire demain, ou après demain
de la bastille droit a Calais. pouvez vous madame
avoir la bonté de me prêter votre chaise de poste
celuy qui m'aura conduit vous la ramènera roit
demain mercredy ceux qui voudront me
venir voir, peuvent entrer librement. je me
flatte que j'aurai la consolation de vous
assurer encor une fois en ma vie de mon
véritable et respectueux attachement
venez je vous en prie avec madame du deffens
je me flatte que je verrai notre ami tiriot

VOLTAIRE'S LETTER TO MADAME DE BERNIÈRES

On the eve of his leaving the Bastille for exile in England.

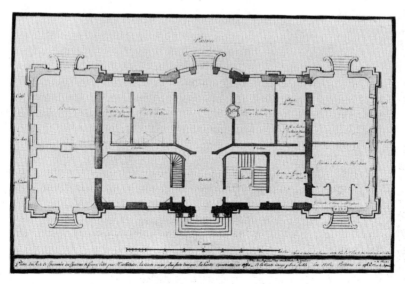

FLOOR PLAN OF VOLTAIRE'S CHÂTEAU, AT FERNEY

SIECLE

DE

LOUIS XIV.

CHAPITRE XXV.

Particularités et anecdotes du règne de Louis XIV.

Les anecdotes font un champ refferré où l'on glane après la vafte moiffon de l'hiftoire ; ce font de petits détails long-temps cachés, et de-là vient le no public quand il illuftres.

Les vies des g font un recueil c certaines : comm fidèles de la vie Il y a dans la p dans la bouche morale que de v

L'hiftoire fec eft une fatire dic que la vengean fatire , qui con *Procope*, ne para

Il faut fe défier des anecdo-

CHAPTER OPENING, *Age of Louis XIV*
VOLTAIRE, Portrait by Largillière

ESSAI

SUR LES MOEURS

ET L'ESPRIT DES NATIONS.

CHAPITRE CLXXIX.

De l'Angleterre, jusqu'à l'année 1641.

Si l'Efpagne s'affaiblit par *Philippe II*, fi la France tomba dans la décadence et dans le ... uccès ... échut ... fuc- ... ence ... à la ... epen- ... uccef- ... cette ... 'elles ... mpte ... ment ... e : et ... mmé ... dont

Décadence paffagère de l'Angleterre.

1603.

Columbus Gallery of Fine Arts, Columbus, Ohio.

CHAPTER OPENING, *Essay on the Customs and the Spirit of Nations*
MADAME DU CHÂTELET, Portrait by Largillière, about 1736

Caterogue des Livres de la bibliotheque

ıˢ Raÿon En Entrant agauche j'usqu'au Poêle.

Volumes.

1. Loix Ruang mss.
2. Corpus juri Romani.
1. Coutume de Bourgogne.
8. Oeuvres de Pasquier.
1. Compilation des Edits Et Ordonnances.
1. Chronique de Monstrelet.
1. Recherches de Dutillet.
2. Théatre d'honneur.
1. L'Etat Militaire de l'Empire Ottoman.
1. Armorial de la ville de Paris.
1. Alsatia jllustrata.
5. histoire de Languedoc.
1. Descrip.ⁿ géographique de la Suisse par Sougrue
1. Déffence de la Reine mère de Louis 13.
4. guerre de 1740. mss.ᵗ
1. Sot poury mss ou se trouve Legouvré.ᵗ la musique.
1. Annales des Provinces unies ban que
1. Baile dict:
1. Dictionnaire de Bayle
1. L'abrégé de Bayle mss sous la fenêtre 3 vol: dépareillés

First page of manuscript catalogue of Voltaire's library at Ferney (now in Leningrad).

first illness on February 28th: "I die," he said, "worshipping God, loving my friends, without hatred of my enemies, and detesting superstition."

In pursuance of his desires, his inert body was supported upright in a carriage which was driven post-haste to the Abbey of Scellières near Troyes in the province of Champagne. There, under the jurisdiction of his nephew, Counsellor Mignot, Voltaire was buried, barely in advance of an order from the Bishop of Troyes refusing the usual rites. In 1791 his remains were exhumed and transferred with enthusiastic procession and honors to the Pantheon at Paris.

The great career was at an end, but much of his work lives on.

6

Voltaire's popularity in France during the nineteenth century was enormous. The proof lies in the numerous editions or reprintings of his voluminous works, which publishers do not undertake without a sure demand. Wherever liberalism was militant against opposition, there Voltaire was to the fore. During periods of reaction or conservatism, his popularity temporarily waned. With Montesquieu and Rousseau, he prepared the way for the French Revolution and it was no accident that the two latter were especially honored at that tragic but fruitful time. He also stimulated anti-clericalism in France and created the type of the rather narrow skepticism typified by the notorious Homais in Flaubert's novel of *Madame Bovary,* an unintelligent skepticism quite unlike the fiery, passionate doubts of Voltaire himself, who was never indifferent, but always up in arms to correct abuses. His Biblical criticism has been superseded by the more understanding viewpoint of modern liberal theologians, but his attacks were necessary to sweep away the dead wood and compel a more reasonable revaluation.

In America, Voltaire was read and quoted by Madison. Jefferson had some of the same points of view, tempered by the greater moderation which was generally in the English tradition. Franklin appears to have been a deist not greatly different from Voltaire in many respects, but of course calmer, more self-contained. Voltaire undoubtedly contributed to the insistence of the shapers of the government of the United States upon the separation of Church and State; but many other factors were also at work in the same direction, and no case can be made for an exclusive influence of Voltaire in this respect. Lincoln read Voltaire in his youth and was probably stimulated by him in his opposition to dogma and orthodoxy, though he remained friendly to the aims and general teaching of the Church. Robert Ingersoll, in his lectures on Voltaire himself, on the "Mistakes of Moses," and other similar topics, continued most closely, though superficially, the narrower side of Voltaire's Biblical criticism with its unsympathetic mockery. This it is which has come to represent the popular conception of Voltaire and his work. Ingersoll may thus have helped somewhat in causing the abandonment of certain untenable theological positions, in calling forth more emphasis upon moral and ethical issues, but, if at all significant now, reaches only the less informed public to whom such ideas are still new.

On the other hand, Voltaire's work for freedom of thought and tolerance, against war, brutality, and torture, continues valid for our time as for his. Unfortunately, the world has not yet caught up with his teaching in these crucial matters, still needs to heed his sharp challenge. His wit, his straight-faced irony, the whiplash of his brief, incisive sentences, lay bare hypocrisy and call for the establishment everywhere of a civilization free from false propaganda, devoted to the true interests and welfare of humanity. If no new Voltaire has arisen in our day, the old Voltaire still speaks to us with the same potency as when he first wrote. To hear his clear voice, we have only to read again the pages of his *Philosophical Letters,* his histories, above all the rapidly-moving narrative of *Candide.* In most respects, Voltaire remains a contemporary.

CHAPTER XIV

ROUSSEAU AND MODERN PROGRESS

I

ENEVA, IN THE EIGHTEENTH CENTURY, WAS STILL VERY MUCH a tiny Protestant Zion set down dangerously in the midst of powerful Catholic enemies, France on the one side, the Italian territories of Savoy and the King of Sardinia on the other. With its thick zigzag walls from which to enfilade assaulting forces, its heavy gates prudently closed each night at sundown, its huge chains blocking the harbor entrance from the Lake into the swift Rhone which flows through the city, it had successfully repelled the sudden treacherous attempt at an "Escalade" by the Duke of Savoy and his troops back in 1602, and continued to maintain its cherished independence by an alert watch against foreign invasion. Such measures intensified Geneva's proud patriotism. Moreover, stern sumptuary laws sought to prohibit fine clothes and various forms of luxurious display. So the little city expressed its old-time convictions in favor of the virtues traditionally associated with simplicity and austere living. It opposed vigorously the corruption attributed to the proposed establishment of a theater. In this small republic of some 20,000 inhabitants, only a minority who were entitled "citizens" governed the much larger number of the unfranchised. The frank theocracy founded in the sixteenth century by the strong-willed Calvin persisted, though somewhat weakened by the inroads of wealth, a traveled aristocracy, and a less fervent belief in the somber doctrine of the "natural perversity" of man.

It was in such a strict environment that Jean-Jacques Rousseau, the son of a watchmaker, was born on Tuesday, June 28, 1712, in the house of his grandparents high up the steep slope of the Grand' Rue in the heart of the old walled town. His mother he never knew; she died nine days after the infant's birth. The father, easy-going and undisciplined, naturally could not transmit to the bright-eyed and passionate boy the needed self-control which he himself so much lacked. Till all hours of the night the two would sit up together, reading, both of them oblivious of time, the precocious Jean-Jacques drinking in as literal truth the romantic novels of love and adventure into which he was too early plunged. When at last the elder Rousseau slowly closed the book and hurried off his still wide-awake son to a reluctant bed, he used to remark in shame-faced apology: "I'm more of a child than you are!"

In the beautiful Swiss country of neighboring Bossey, the youngster spent two happy years in the pious home of Pastor Lambercier and his conscientious sister. The boy's quick-tempered father, meanwhile, in a violent quarrel wounded his adversary with a sword and found it convenient to decamp from Geneva, at the same time relieving himself of responsibility for his son's upbringing. At Bossey, young Rousseau listened attentively to the daily reading aloud of the Bible at family prayers, took into his being the sonorous rhythm of the oriental phrases with their mysterious imagery, heard the resounding oratory of sermons on Sunday vigorously excoriating sin or exhorting earnestly to good conduct, and so little by little formed the basically moralistic outlook which, if it did not suffice to steel his weak, untrained will against grievous lapses encouraged by his vagabond existence, nevertheless remained with him throughout life as a bright ideal. It was an ideal which led to bitter self-condemnation on the one hand, mingled with a curious feeling of confidence in his self-righteous intentions on the other. While Voltaire's gaze, untroubled with his own shortcomings, turned outward in attack upon the misbehaving world, Rousseau tended first of all to look deep down into his own heart, and strange things indeed his day-dreaming introspection found there. His probing remains often a very human revelation, even to modern psychology.

In 1725, Jean-Jacques was apprenticed to an engraver, Monsieur Ducommun. In this work, the boy was unhappy. The idyllic days of Bossey were too soon gone. For pilfering of food and other peccadillos, he was roundly whipped by his harsh master. There was solace, however, in the eager reading of books, good and bad, which fell into his hands. And, on Sunday afternoons in fine weather, he could escape for long, carefree tramps with other boys of his age across the rolling green countryside. Slow to start, but difficult to stop, Rousseau always went further than the rest. Twice he dallied too long and came lagging back to see the great city gates clank shut in his face at sundown. A pleasant night outside under the stars was no great hardship to him, keen lover of nature that he was, but his sensitive spirit revolted against the certainty of a hard beating the next morning. In spite of good resolutions, a third time ensued. As he tells the story in his *Confessions*, perhaps with some dramatic exaggeration, there was a certain Captain Minutoli who seemed to take a malicious pleasure in shutting his gate and raising his drawbridge a half-hour before the others.

"About half a league from the city, I heard retreat sounded," writes Rousseau. "I doubled my pace; I heard the tattoo beat, and ran with all my might. I arrived out of breath and bathed in perspiration; my heart pounded; from a distance I saw the soldiers at their posts; I rushed up and cried out with a voice half-choked. It was too late! Twenty paces from the outposts, I saw the first bridge raised. I shuddered when I saw those terrible horns rising in the air—a sinister and fateful omen of the inevitable destiny which that moment was opening before me."

In vain he threw himself in despair on the smooth slope of the glacis which stretched in front of the moat; the bridge remained up; the gates did not open. On the spot, Rousseau resolved never to return to his brutal master. It was Sunday night of March 14, 1728. Jean-Jacques was not quite sixteen years old. The next day the boy said good-bye to his devil-may-care companions who re-entered the city, and he set forth blithely on his uncertain wanderings.

Always happy when striding freely across the country on foot, Jean-Jacques went gaily on, enjoying what seemed his new-found independence, reliving scenes from the romantic novels which he had devoured years before. No doubt a castle awaited him! No doubt a beauteous lady would be leaning out the window to welcome the young stranger! No doubt a glamorous future lay ahead, quite different from the humdrum life of the apprentice engraver which he was leaving behind! Thus he dreamed his rosy day-dreams. The reality of course was quite different.

In the neighborhood of Geneva, there appears to have been a kind of "underground" for refugees from the Protestant stronghold. In any event, the boy Rousseau seems not to have hesitated long as to what he should do. Within a few days, he went to a Catholic priest, Monsieur de Pontverre, who in turn shortly packed him off to a certain Madame de Warens, not many miles away in the picturesque Savoy town of Annecy.

Madame de Warens herself had behind her a strange history. "Born with the century" in 1700, she was only twenty-eight years old, and beautiful indeed she appeared to Jean-Jacques at least, when he saw her for the first time on Palm Sunday, March 21, 1728. He had imagined a devout old woman, far from attractive. Now he was sure that a religion preached by such a charming missionary could not fail to be true. He was converted in his heart forthwith. Madame de Warens herself had abjured Protestantism some years before and was now playing an anomalous role which has never become entirely clear. Was she a kind of spy or secret agent for the King of Sardinia? Was that why she received a pension from him? Was she placed in Annecy to make converts from Geneva? What lay back of her occasional mysterious journeys to Paris? Whatever her purpose, it was to her that the priest, Monsieur de Pontverre, promptly sent the young Rousseau. Three days later, she in turn sped Jean-Jacques on his way afoot to Turin beyond the Alps in the sunny Italian valley of the Po.

2

At the end of his long jaunt across the border, the homeless youth was admitted on April 12th into the Hospice of the Holy Spirit. There, amid a sorry group of unwashed tramps and professional converts, this unsuspected genius was quickly instructed in the rudiments of Catholic doctrine. Writing many years later in his *Confessions* and anxious to put as good a face as possible on a conduct of which he had afterwards become ashamed, Rousseau's wishful thinking pictures a prolonged struggle of tough theological argument between the priests and himself before at last he yielded. But this sixteen-year-old boy, whatever his native gifts and miscellaneous background of unguided reading, could certainly have been no match for his experienced teachers. Moreover, he was entirely without resources either in money or occupation. He had been sent to be converted and he was converted—forthwith. An able scholar, Pierre-Maurice Masson, has searched the archives for evidence. There the dated documents show that actually Rousseau abjured his Protestantism nine days after his entry into the Hospice. He was then promptly baptized but was allowed to linger on some weeks more before being finally dismissed with a meager collection of a little over five poor *lire* in his pockets. It was a real vagabond existence which he was now beginning.

Rousseau tramped the streets of Turin, found a cheap bed at a penny a night, learned at first hand "how the other half lives." The experience was to color his whole character and system of ideas. He became for a time a lackey waiting on table in a noble family, learned a bit of Latin and some Italian, showed flashes of an intelligence and an occasional knowledge beyond his humiliating station. Other happenings, more pitiful or more sordid, comprise the rapidly-moving narrative of the next twelve months.

But finally Rousseau tired of Italy. Swinging one foot gaily ahead of the other, he was off across the Alps again to Madame de Warens at Annecy. She hardly knew what to do with her new-found and embarrassing charge. But the boy read eagerly among the books in her small library. Madame de Warens still held to some of her former Protestant ideas and talked much of Pierre Bayle. In this way, Rousseau made the acquaintance of the *Historical Dictionary*, dipping into the closely-printed pages of the huge folios with their strange mingling of antiquarian learning and sly skepticism. Did the boy perhaps have in him the stuff for a village priest? Some of Madame de Warens's friends wondered.

Then there was music at Annecy; Jean-Jacques knew little of it, but he drank in its rhythm and tones with all the enthusiasm of his ardent temperament. Indeed, he even set himself up as a music teacher and composer. In Lausanne, with brash assurance, he undertook, without experience, to conduct an orchestra! "No, not since the days of French opera, did anyone ever hear such a shivaree of clashing sounds!" comments Rousseau himself in his *Confessions*. "Poor Jean-Jacques!" he goes on. "In this cruel moment, little did you think that one day, in the presence of the King of France and all his Court, your music would excite murmurs of applause and astonishment." More incredible than fiction, the true novel of Rousseau's life was in the end to reveal him as the successful composer of a delightful operetta, *The Village Magician*, which, if he had wished, would have made him the center of Court attraction and the recipient of a royal pension.

In 1731 Rousseau again set off on foot, this time for Paris nearly three hundred miles away. Filled with his rosy day-dreams, he tramped along the roads, never so happy as when out of doors with the air blowing against his cheeks and his hardened muscles carrying him steadily across the open country. But Paris in the end belied his hopes. Instead of the glories of the French metropolis of which he had read so much in books, he saw only, as he entered the city from the south, "the dirty, foul-smelling, narrow streets of the Faubourg Saint-Marceau," the beggars, the dingy houses, the loud criers of their wares, the teeming, jostling life of sordid poverty and filth. "This, from the outset," he wrote, "struck me so forcibly that all the real magnificence I have since seen in Paris has been unable to destroy my first impression, and I have always retained a secret dislike for residence in this capital." His lively imagination outran the disillusioning reality. Indeed, the whole experience of Paris was a disappointment. There was no opportunity in this busy center for the untrained country boy to make his way. Back he turned again toward Sardinian Savoy and Madame de Warens.

One day, at the end of a long journey afoot, hungry, tired, and parched with thirst, he stopped at a solitary peasant's hut along the road. It was not much to look at, but the only house in sight. Could Rousseau pay for something to eat and drink? The peasant, suspicious of government spies seeking out his income for tax purposes, doled out some skimmed milk and coarse barley bread to the stranger. But the weary youth devoured the poor meal with such avidity that the peasant, his confidence restored, opened a trapdoor into the basement and returned with a loaf of wheat bread, a piece of ham, and a bottle of wine to which he even added a substantial omelet.

"He gave me to understand," continues Rousseau, "that he hid his wine on account of the excise, that he hid his bread on account of the tax, and that he was a lost man if anyone had a suspicion that he was not starving. All that he said to me on this subject, of which I had not the least idea, made an impression upon me which will never be forgotten. It was the germ of the inextinguishable hatred which subsequently grew up in my heart against the oppression to which these unhappy people are subject, and against their oppressors." It was one more laboratory experience for Jean-Jacques in the lamentable system of tax-farming under the Old Régime.

Back in the familiar province of Savoy, on the edge of the Alps,

Rousseau returned to spend much of his time again with Madame de Warens. She was no longer in delightful Annecy, but was less pleasantly situated, in Jean-Jacques's view at least, in the populous city of Chambéry. A few miles out from the busy provincial capital lay the simple country-house of Les Charmettes which Madame de Warens, concerned about the ill health of her protégé, rented for a few years beginning in 1736. With its orchard, its fine view down the hillside into the valley, it offered a pleasant oasis of green after the hot pavements and crowded streets of the city. It was a delight for Rousseau to live there. The house, which still stands today, substantially as in the eighteenth century, preserves for us one of the important scenes of Jean-Jacques's youth. There he fell in love with Madame de Warens. There, with her curious unmoralism, she became briefly his mistress. There she transferred her affections again and aroused his jealousy and grief. There he threw himself for solace into an ordered system of reading and study. At twenty-five, Rousseau realized at last that he was only an ignoramus and, in default of a formal education, set out to teach himself. A self-education is likely to have many gaps and shortcomings as compared with the education of the schools, but it has one great advantage: it is ardently desired by the student and it is retained. The books which Rousseau read at Les Charmettes he read with all the eagerness of one seeking a revelation of the truth. When he found them contradictory, he learned gradually to evaluate, to pick and choose, to form his own opinions, to develop, not the thought of others, but his own. At Les Charmettes, we may truly say in modern parlance, Rousseau went to college, but to a college in which he was himself at the same time both professor and student. He learned by that surest of all roads, the teaching to himself of what he intensely wanted to know.

Among the many books which interested and guided Rousseau, he makes brief, but special mention of Voltaire's *Philosophical Letters*. More than any other work by that author, he says, it inspired him to study. No doubt the way Voltaire's rapid pen touched incisively on a whole host of subjects roused the curiosity of the young provincial and impelled him to fill the void of his ignorance. Voltaire's works, besides, different as they were from those later produced by Rousseau, first stirred Jean-Jacques with ambition to become a writer himself. And for some fifteen years, Voltaire remained his literary master, one to whom he looked up in respectful emulation.

3

Leaving Les Charmettes behind him, after several unsuccessful attempts to establish himself somehow in life, Rousseau went on to Lyons in France. Here, for a year in 1740, he became tutor of the two sons of Monsieur de Mably. Hardly educated yet himself, unschooled in dignity and self-control, the young man was totally unfitted for such a position. The chief result of this ineffectual effort was to pose for him more clearly than ever the inner problem of education, which he saw primarily, after his own hard experience, to be the development of character more than of the intellect. Twenty years later these ideas were to receive definitive expression in his widely read book *Emile*.

Next came a second journey to Paris with a numerical system of musical notation for which Rousseau had high hopes of adoption. Musicians, however, saw more practicality in the established graphic method of notes placed visually higher or lower on a staff. Again he met disappointment in the great capital. But he made the acquaintance of the future Encyclopedist Diderot, a young man obscure, though ambitious, like himself. Later Diderot was to become one of Rousseau's closest friends. Soon the latter was off to Venice where he had been recommended to a post as private secretary to the French ambassador, Monsieur de Montaigu.

Monsieur de Montaigu, it appears, was no great marvel of intelligence. But Rousseau himself made little effort at tact, and, according to his own story, could not resist the malicious pleasure of openly manifesting contempt for his master, who hemmed and hawed, vainly seeking the right word to dictate to his literary-minded secretary. Jean-Jacques probably exaggerated his own abilities at the time and may likewise have underestimated those of Monsieur de Montaigu. Whatever the unvarnished truth, it is clear that under such unhappy circumstances a break ultimately was inevitable. It is only remarkable that it was delayed for a full year. Indeed, Rousseau in his *Confessions* remembers his stay in Italy erroneously as lasting eighteen months. The records show otherwise. In the end, the discharged secretary returned to Paris smarting under what he considered a rank injustice. Society, he found, favored a noble over a commoner, the strong over the weak. This bitter disillusionment was one more source of his later violent attack upon what he calls "our foolish civil institutions." At the same time, his experience with diplomacy in Venice offered him an inside view of the Doge's auto-cratic oligarchy and set him to thinking about the problems of government. On the positive side, he developed a keen admiration for Italian literature and the singing melody of Italian music.

It was 1744. The next five years in Paris were to pile disappoint-ment upon disappointment. Rousseau, on request, tried his hand at adapting a drama of Voltaire's to music, but the famous composer Rameau denied him credit for his work. Jean-Jacques then wrote a light play for the Opera, but, foreseeing ultimate rejection, with-drew his manuscript and gave up for the time being all hope of literary success.

Meanwhile, he had drifted into a sad liaison with a poor servant girl, Thérèse Levasseur, who was too ignorant to offer him either understanding or intelligent companionship. His desperate poverty actually led him, irresponsible like his father and further corrupted by long years of half-vagabond life, to put into a Foundling Asylum the five children who were born to them. There these children, with the careless records of the time, disappeared forever. Only later did Rousseau experience a remorse which cast a black shadow over the rest of his life. Besides all this, as secretary to Madame Dupin, wife of a Farmer General of the taxes, he again chafed under that infe-riority of position which had so much galled him in Venice. What bitterness to feel superior genius surging up within him, yet all at the whim of a woman, wealthy indeed, but of wholly undistin-guished talents! Several bits of verse from his pen showed merely his continuing aspirations toward literature; they brought him no fame and no improvement in his fortunes. His one solace was his close friendship with Diderot. Although poor like himself, Diderot was acquainted with publishers and was already beginning to figure as a radical thinker even while he supported himself and his sharp-tongued wife by dull hack-work. Diderot, too, was interested in music. He was enthusiastic in temperament and encyclopedic in knowledge, a happy foil, it seemed, to Rousseau's natural timidity and hard-won fragmentary education.

Finally, in early October of 1749, an event occurred to shake Jean-Jacques unexpectedly out of his long obscurity.

Since the 24th of July Diderot had been imprisoned for his agnostic publications in the somber fortress of Vincennes, a few miles east of Paris. For a full month he had been in solitary confine-ment high up among the thick walls of the towering Donjon. It was a grievous trial for anyone as talkative and companionable as Diderot. Finally, the humbled philosopher saw no way out but to yield to arbitrary pressure. So he signed a retraction and made a promise of good behavior in the future. He was thereupon transferred from the Donjon to the more agreeable neighboring château and was granted the privilege of books, of continuing his interrupted work on the *Encyclopedia,* of taking walks in the surrounding park, and of receiving visitors. On the 25th of August therefore, Rousseau, Diderot's closest friend, hastened out to see him. Generally, for lack of money, except when he went in a cab with Madame Diderot, Rousseau made the long trip every other day from central Paris on foot. He was lodging at the time in a single room in the old Rue Jean-Saint-Denis, which has since disappeared. It was a good six-mile walk each way.

The summer of 1749 had been insufferably hot and this heat, as often happens, continued on into the autumn. With his nervous, impetuous temperament, Rousseau was inclined to rush madly over the intervening miles, arriving exhausted and all of a sweat at Vincennes. To calm this undue haste, he formed the habit of putting in his pocket something to read. Thus he had an excuse to throw himself down from time to time along the road and rest.

One early autumn day, he set out about two in the afternoon, taking with him the October number, just published, of the well-known literary periodical, the *Mercure de France.* Leaving behind him the great edifices of the Louvre and the Palais-Royal, he swung down the teeming Rue Saint-Honoré past the gloomy black mass of the Bastille, out into the sparsely built-up Rue du Faubourg Saint-Antoine. On his right, after a half-hour or so, he passed the Foundling Asylum where, already, he had left two unacknowledged children. We do not know whether, at the sight, any qualms yet stirred in his slowly awakening conscience.

The widely-spaced trees and the rare houses of the open country offered almost no shade. The near mid-day sun beat down upon him as the thirty-seven-year-old pedestrian strode along at a pace much too fast for the unseasonable heat. He pulled out his copy of the *Mercure de France.* His eyes fell on the announcement of the coming 1750 prize essay contest of the provincial academy of Dijon. The question proposed for discussion was startling. "Had the Renaissance in the Sciences and Arts contributed to purify morals?" In the answer, the whole of the eighteenth-century's smug pride in contemporary progress was at stake. It would be possible, obviously, to make the banal affirmative reply: "Yes, of course." But what if one responded "No" and thus challenged the entire march of human civilization?

Quickly he took fire. Pencil and paper flew out of his pocket. At white heat, he scribbled rapidly an eloquent address to the austere early Roman Consul, Fabricius. What would this ancient sage have thought if by chance he had returned to see the degenerate, luxury-loving Rome of a later century? What would he think of the imposing surface splendor of Paris today?

Ideas crowded in upon Rousseau. His head swam with the dizziness of excitement. Breath came in rapid gasps. In the friendly shade of a tree along the highway, he sank limply to the ground. During the half-hour of emotional agitation which followed, tears poured unnoticed down the front of his jacket. If he had been able to get on paper a fourth of the wild tumult of ideas which then surged up in his mind, he afterwards felt, how vividly he could have exposed the terrible weaknesses of contemporary society, how clearly he would have shown man's instinctive goodness corrupted by the ill-ordered institutions of modern times! Such was the author's perhaps over-dramatic, but seemingly essentially true, account of this moment of extraordinary inspiration.

When the still obscure Jean-Jacques finally arrived at Vincennes to visit his friend Diderot, he naturally poured forth the emotional flood of his recent experience and read him the invocation to Fabricius which he had just dashed off on the way. Diderot enthusiastically urged him to compete for the Dijon prize. He certainly encouraged Rousseau to persist in his criticism of the Old Régime. A vigorous attack was much more likely to challenge the attention of both judges and public than a conventional defense of the joys of modern progress. Besides, Diderot himself, after a month of solitary confinement in the grim fortress of the Vincennes tower, and another month of modified imprisonment in the château, was in no mood to praise excessively the government, institutions, and capricious tyranny of the increasingly unpopular Louis XV.

4

In the following months Rousseau wrote for the competition his brief *Discourse on the Sciences and the Arts,* the famous First Discourse. According to the rules of the contest, it had to be in the hands of the Dijon Academy by April 1st, 1750. With little hope of success—in his checkered career he had already suffered so many disappointments!—the author dropped his manuscript in the mails. Four months or so later, Rousseau received an agreeable surprise. He had won, after all! On July 20th, he carefully and respectfully indited his letter of grateful acknowledgment. The prize was awarded on Sunday afternoon, August 23rd, in a public ceremony at Dijon which Rousseau, remaining in Paris, did not attend. During the latter part of November, the *Discourse* appeared in print, the proofs having been corrected by Diderot during the author's illness. It was the friendly Diderot also who, better known at this time than the obscure Jean-Jacques, had obtained him a publisher—without royalties.

Soon there was an unexpected uproar of discussion with numerous refutations of this bitter indictment of modern "progress." Rousseau had touched a sensitive nerve. The wounded pride of many readers slapped back. But the author discovered himself a forceful debater and was at no loss for a plausible, if sometimes specious, defense. His published joust with the ex-King of Poland, Stanislas, Duke of Lorraine and father-in-law of Louis XV, brought him added fame.

The historical arguments of Rousseau in favor of humanity's degeneration are weak. Who can maintain successfully that the "good old days" were uniformly better, regretfully as we may sometimes look back toward the simpler times of a remote past? The abuses of a bygone age are too easily forgotten in the face of its seeming virtues. A man's youth, and similarly the youth of the race, are readily idealized in retrospect. Rousseau's eloquence is often hollow, more fervent than convincing.

Yet all is not mere empty rhetoric in this brief *Discourse* of only a half-hour's reading. Not for nothing did it challenge and exasperate Rousseau's too complacent contemporaries. His Encyclopedist friends, Diderot and D'Alembert, who had thought it simply a clever piece of prize eloquence, were astounded when they saw the author take it seriously, defend it with unexpected vigor, endeavor to put it into practice in his own life, even make it largely the basis of his whole thought-system.

For Rousseau had seized upon an important truth, obvious enough if one stops to think about it, but uncomfortable for easy-going humanity, which prefers to look the other way. Jean-Jacques had pointed out that, unhappily, increase in knowledge, luxury, and material comfort are not synonymous with the only progress which really counts, moral progress. Man does not necessarily grow better as he learns more. Rousseau agrees with Fontenelle in his famous *Dialogue between Socrates and Montaigne.* Science and invention may go forward with rapid strides, but the problem of man's choices between good and evil remains. Indeed, these choices have become, in the midst of modern complexities, even more difficult for mankind than in the past. As Dr. Albert Schweitzer observes: "We venture to face the truth that with so much progress in knowledge and power true civilization has become not easier but harder." Never, it seems, has brutality become more scientifically organized, more widespread, than in the world today.

This is the vigorous "sermon" which Rousseau, avid reader of Plutarch, Seneca, and Montaigne, precocious child of his austere Genevan heritage, sitting all-ears as a boy on the hard benches of the Protestant cathedral in Calvin's little Zion, was preaching here in his First Discourse to his proud and reluctant contemporaries. His own bitter struggle for knowledge and fame on the one hand, for an intermittent moral progress on the other, had burned deep into his soul. More than in the case of most writers, his life explains his work.

Rousseau's caustic words carry down insistently to our own day. Inequality, luxury, vain ambition, love of money, cynicism, loss of liberty, political and moral corruption, beset humanity in all times, modern as well as ancient. If we are unable with Rousseau to look back longingly to an idyllic Garden of Eden or an imagined Golden Age, we can with him reject any tendency to think complacently of our existing civilization.

No doubt the new atomic dangers of the present have already hammered this unwelcome truth home. Science and knowledge are clearly what we make them. The airplane carries serums to relieve or devastating bombs to kill. It is men themselves who make war, not shells or guns or guided missiles. Modern inventions merely sow destruction more widely and with more terror than the primitive club, arrow, or flint-lock of the past.

These are obvious and hackneyed truths, no doubt. Yet man is loath to face them. There is momentary comfort in turning the eyes away. Rousseau, however, came back to the conclusion gained from his painful effort to teach the children of Monsieur de Mably at Lyons. Better "a well-formed head," had observed the sage Montaigne, "than one well filled." It is judgment and character that man lacks, more than faster automobiles, jetplanes, or three-thousand-mile bombs. Without intelligence, moral stamina, and devotion to justice, it seems, we can hardly hope to escape disaster.

As Rousseau, echoing Plutarch and Montaigne in a favorite contrast between ancient Athens and Sparta, said in an oratorical conclusion to his *Discourse:* "Let us try . . . to observe this distinction which was formerly noted between two great peoples, that one knew how to speak well, and the other to do well."

On that sunny October day in 1749, Rousseau had sounded a vigorous warning. It is no wonder that, overcome with emotion, he fell in a daze by the Vincennes roadside. As long as man is fallible and human, we can never find, no doubt, the complete and fully satisfying answer to his challenge. But we do need, it is evident, to discover at least a partial answer, a better answer than in the past, if humanity is to avoid the destructive fate unleashed in the form of the incredible developments of recent scientific discovery.

Lay sermons are never popular. Rousseau's was widely read, but it was not relished. It is not good form to preach. Cassandras and prophets of doom are unwelcome in society. Their doleful warnings break in on the pleasant round of "life as usual." It is more comfortable, like the traditional ostrich, to bury one's head in the sand! Yet the eighteenth century ended in the tragic violence of the French Revolution.

In the late autumn of 1750, Rousseau published his brief *Discourse* which so unexpectedly had won the prize. It made him famous overnight. "Has the Renaissance in the Sciences and the Arts contributed to purify morals?" The question of the Academy of Dijon still echoes in our ears. The issue of moral progress, difficult as it is, appears to bear within it the ultimate fate of civilization and of humanity itself. While the details of Rousseau's argument are superficial and have fallen by the wayside, the central core of his First Discourse remains.

"Why did Rome Fall?" asked Montesquieu. "Why has man himself, while increasing his material knowledge, not grown happier and better?" demanded Rousseau. These questions are two important aspects of the same basic problem.

CHAPTER XV

ROUSSEAU AND THE PROBLEM
OF INEQUALITY

I

Iт was November, 1753.

The shifting lights and shadows danced among the fallen leaves as the autumn sun sifted down through the ancient oaks of Saint-Germain less than fifteen miles northwest of Paris. Wandering here alone on the winding paths, the forty-one-year-old Rousseau easily imagined himself in the depths of a primeval forest. Far from the muddy cobblestone streets, far from the cries, the clatter, the splashing vehicles, and the mad pressure of life in the great metropolis, he could enjoy to the full the quiet delight of a week's vacation. Since his youthful days at Geneva, Annecy, and Les Charmettes, long, solitary tramps in the country had always intoxicated him. Now, as the *Confessions* tell us, a season of fine weather favored his outdoor rambles, and he could muse undisturbed on the fortunate lot of primitive man while an idyllic picture of early times welled up from his varied reading and from the pleasant daydreams which were evoked by these enchanted surroundings.

The present age was corrupt. Anyone could see so plain a fact by merely looking about him at the bitter struggle for place and power in the grandiose capital where shameless luxury and sordid misery obtruded their sharp contrasts. Indeed, along the imposing colonnade of the Louvre near Rousseau's own quarter, the wretched dealers in old clothes loudly hawked their cast-off wares while the gaily dressed nobles dashed past, unheeding. Then, there were Jean-Jacques's own rankling memories of forced subservience to Monsieur de Montaigu at Venice, to the wealthy Madame Dupin at Chenonceaux and Paris. There were years of humiliating want and of disappointment piled on disappointment. He himself had witnessed at first hand the peasant hiding his humble food for fear of the government's prying tax collector, had drunk his wine and eaten with relish his appetizing ham and the good wheat bread brought up furtively out of the dark cellar. Rousseau's growing hatred of the rich had been nourished, too, by his boresome work as secretary and cashier in the families of the great Farmers General. Speciously, he even blamed the putting away of his own children in the Foundling Asylum, in spite of Thérèse's resistance, on the grinding poverty to which society seemed to have condemned him. Inner remorse, which would not down, gnawed away at his heartstrings and constituted one more bitter count against the inequalities of the Old Régime. "It is a misfortune for which you must pity me, not a crime to charge against me. . . . It is the rich, it is your class," he had written harshly to Madame de Francueil, the wife of a financier, two years before, "who rob mine of the bread of my children!"

Much of this violent revolt against society had already been poured into the *Discourse on the Sciences and the Arts* and into the several refutations directed against his adversaries. With new-found eloquence, he had indicted man's conspicuous failure to progress in morals and happiness. Now, unexpectedly, he found himself famous and his brain was in a ferment of ideas tumbling over each other for forceful expression. Could he not convince humanity of its fateful errors and set it at last upon the right way?

In the November number of the *Mercure de France* in 1753, the Academy of Dijon had once more proposed a challenging question: "What is the origin of inequality among men? Is it authorized by Natural Law?" Already, in a passing sentence of his First Discourse, Rousseau had touched upon this important problem. Now he again took fire.

Accompanied by Thérèse Levasseur and two of her friends, Jean-Jacques had left behind for a few days the modest lodgings furnished for him by Madame Dupin in the Rue Grenelle-Saint-Honoré north of the Louvre in the busy heart of Paris, and set forth on a happy excursion to the beautiful forest of Saint-Germain-en-Laye. There he could meditate in peace over the contrast between the hubbub of the great city and the repose of a sylvan setting. No noise in this country retreat except the crunching of a fallen twig, the occasional chirp of a late autumn bird, or the swish of his feet among the masses of dead leaves.

Had man not in fact been happier in an earlier, simpler period? Rousseau himself, stimulated by this crisp November air three hundred feet above the winding Seine, improved in health by his long walks among the trees, relieved momentarily from the fever of life in the hurrying capital, was sure of it. A host of writers from ancient Greece and Rome down to Jean-Jacques's own times had pointed up the supposedly happy contrast between the equality and innocence of former ages and the complex civilization of a later day. Montaigne, in a famous essay, had sung the praises of the so-called "cannibals," and Rousseau had eagerly thumbed the pages of Montaigne. Numerous explorers and missionary travelers to the New World had painted a similarly glowing portrait of the "noble savage." The Biblical Garden of Eden and classic dreams of a Golden Age still beckoned alluringly to a tired and disillusioned humanity.

Joining the women only at meal times, Rousseau buried himself the rest of the day in the forest. There, he says, "I sought and found the picture of those primitive times of which I boldly sketched the history. I demolished the pitiful lies of mankind; I dared to expose their nature in all its nakedness, to follow the progress of time and of the things which have disfigured this nature; and, comparing man, as man has made him, with natural man, I showed him, in his pretended perfection, the true source of his misery." The Second Discourse is thus a natural sequel to the First.

The Academy of Dijon prudently rejected the *Discourse on the Origin of Inequality*. Technically, under the rules of the contest, it was much too long, but, above all, it was too shockingly bold to win the prize. The unhappy Academicians had already been criticized severely for awarding first honors to Rousseau in 1750. This time they would play safe; they would not commit the same mistake again. But Jean-Jacques had now no need of their support; he could make his way without such artificial aid. His *Discourse* finally appeared during the summer of 1755, printed by Marc-Michel Rey at Amsterdam with a striking title page half in red and half in black ink.

2

Rousseau has often been attacked for supposedly not recognizing that men are in fact grossly unequal in ability, industry, and character, and that no amount of argument can talk away these basic differences. Such reproaches come, however, from a careless reading of his work. At the very beginning of his *Discourse,* the author clearly distinguishes between two kinds of inequality: "one, which I call natural or physical," he says, "because it is established by nature and consists of differences in age, health, strength, and the qualities of mind or spirit; the other, which may be termed moral or political inequality, because it depends on a sort of convention and is established, or at least authorized, by the consent of mankind."

Thus there exist a *natural* inequality and an *artificial* inequality. It is of the latter only that Rousseau speaks. Why is one man a prince, duke, or baron, and another a serf or downtrodden peasant? we might ask in terms of eighteenth-century hierarchies. Why does one man have the advantages of wealth and education while another enjoys none of these assets? Although, to some extent, a man may be able to create his own opportunities, it is evident that there are stern limits to this possibility and that some societies are much less favorable in this respect than others. Whatever the natural inequalities among men, no one would be rash enough to maintain that each receives all that his abilities may justly entitle him to. So it is the unfair organization of society which Rousseau condemns, the inequality of race, rank, education, or economic outlook which might be improved by the removal of prejudice or of purely artificial barriers. It is clear also that, if all these unnatural inequalities could conceivably be eliminated, if each person could have every possible advantage of good food, medicine, education, freedom from want and slums, much of what we today consider inherent differences, though not of course all, would tend to disappear. This, then, is what is implied by Rousseau's *Discourse.* It calls, basically, for a revolutionary reorganization of society.

"Let us begin by putting aside all the facts, for they have no bearing on the question," cries Rousseau. Here, indeed, is a startling sentence which, as the reader will readily imagine, has brought down many a sarcastic comment upon the author's head. Once more, however, we must be sure that we fully understand his meaning. As a matter of fact, Jean-Jacques was about to embark upon the difficult history of early man. But that story had already been told officially in the first two chapters of *Genesis.* How could anyone in the eighteenth century venture to recount the slow evolution of humanity along purely natural lines and not clash sharply with established orthodoxy? It was the "Biblical facts" which Rousseau had in

mind and, with tongue in cheek, he must perforce tip his hat politely
to the censor or else have no circulation of his book in France. He
was but following an old tactic known to Descartes, Bayle, Fontenelle, and many others.

Moreover, in the infancy of anthropology and the lack of scientific
studies of primitive man, the writer of the *Discourse* was obliged to
relie upon travelers' tales and his own imaginings of the probabilities
as he pictured them under the spreading trees of Saint-Germain.
He himself lamented the unreliability of much of the information
available in his day, emphasized the need of investigations made by
the best and most impartial minds of the age. Rousseau was attempt-
ing to justify, discreetly, something not unlike a kind of pre-
Darwinian theory of man's slow development from humble beginnings. In fact, if men were to be held naturally unequal because so
created by God, then it was obviously impossible to discuss the
proposed question at all and the debate would be over before it
was begun.

Rousseau, however, pushes aside speculation, such as that of Aristotle, about an early animal stage of mankind when he was hairy like
a bear and equipped with long claws or perhaps with hands like an
orang-outang. "Comparative anatomy has still made too little progress," he observes, to give us sound information. The author begins,
then, with man as we know him, so far as his physical aspect is
concerned, standing erect, walking on two feet, using his hands as
he does today. The point of view of the *Discourse,* though written
without the advantages of modern research, is to a considerable
degree scientific, at least in purpose.

Like himself in the forest of Saint-Germain, Rousseau depicts
early man as solitary, a nomad without fixed work, free from the
trammels of civilization. Such a man was robust, he believes, made
so by the hard law of survival, relatively healthy, because of his
vigorous, outdoor life, timid, rather than warlike, a light sleeper,
endowed with feelings, but hardly troubled by ideas. It is clear that
this picture is much influenced by the easy-going natives whom the
Spaniards encountered in the tropical West Indies, not by the fierce
Indian tribes of North America.

Only gradually did this "ingenious machine" of man unfold his
"perfectibility" and form a more and more complex society. The
author muses interestingly on the slow development of language and

its profound significance for the human mind. What long ages must have been required to progress from the mere "cry of nature" to abstractions like matter, spirit, substance, figure, or movement! In the end, Rousseau remains perplexed as to whether society could have come into being without language, or language without society!

Early man, believes Rousseau, was neither bad nor good, but rather neutral. The main advantage of the natural life lay, as it seemed to him, in offering fewer temptations to wickedness. Man was better and happier only in the sense that his simpler environment was less dangerous and less corrupting. Like Bayle, Jean-Jacques saw that reason exerts little hold upon most men. It was their feelings and passions which, in his opinion, have played the decisive role in human conduct. A natural pity for his fellows gave mankind some semblance of developing morality.

3

With the *Second Part* of his *Discourse,* Rousseau launches abruptly into an eloquent, if rhetorical, attack upon the institution of private property. "The first man," he exclaims belligerently, "who, after fencing in a piece of ground, took it into his head to say: *This is mine,* and found people simple enough to believe him, was the true founder of civil society. How many crimes, wars, murders, how many miseries and horrors would not have been spared the human race by him who, pulling up the stakes or filling in the ditch, had cried out to his fellow men: Take care not to listen to this impostor; you are lost if you forget that the fruits belong to all and the earth to no one!"

When this violent passage fell under the flashing eyes of Voltaire, the newly-established owner of Les Délices snatched up his pen and scribbled angrily in the margin opposite Rousseau's first sentence: "What! he who planted, sowed and fenced in has no right to the fruit of his labors!" Beside the second half of the passage, the patriarch vented his spleen with equal vigor: "What! this unjust man, this thief, would have been the benefactor of the human race! That's the philosophy of a beggar who would like to see the rich robbed by the poor!"

Voltaire's indignation still comes quivering down the centuries to our own time. No socialism or communism for him! His passion is equal to Rousseau's, but in sharp conflict with it. Inspired by the natural conservatism of wealth, he sees the constructive side of property; Jean-Jacques, a semi-outcast from society, and a willful outcast, underlines the oppressive aspects of ownership. Obviously, use and abuse cannot be discussed in such simple terms. It is sometimes forgotten that, without sure protection for at least limited rights of private property, individual livelihood and life itself may be endangered by an all-embracing society. Indeed, Rousseau himself, when confronted later in *Emile* and the *Social Contract* by the difficult practical problems of existence, would not always hold to the unrestrained theoretical view on property expressed in his inflammatory *Discourse*.

In the somewhat vague state of nature, the present inequality among men seemed hardly perceptible to Rousseau. He was far from having invented such a view. Indeed, he was rather the last and the most striking of a long line of writers. It was a commonplace handed down from remote classical antiquity. Early travelers in the New World mostly supported the same attitude. Ignorant of Indian languages or customs, unable to see differences in clothes or wealth between the naked chieftains and their savage followers, eager besides in many cases to offer an alluring contrast between the "noble redman" and the glaring evils of existing European society, they nearly all concurred in the idyllic picture. If these conclusions were based only on conjectures, as Rousseau freely admitted, they seemed to him plausible. In the then elementary phase of science, it was at any rate difficult to do better.

Mankind, in Rousseau's opinion, found his greatest happiness in an intermediate period between complete barbarism and a too complex civilization. This was the true Golden Age. But the discovery of metallurgy and the development of agriculture brought about a dangerous evolution. "Iron and wheat," said Jean-Jacques forcefully, "ruined mankind!" With the growth of power and acquisitiveness, the scourge of inequality increased. Avarice, ambition, crime, followed in its train. War, too, was a natural consequence. The state of master and slave, the clamping fast of the bonds of despotic rule, was the fateful term of this long history. Whether this was actually man's story, Rousseau admits that we cannot positively know. "Such was or must have been the origin of society and law," he believes.

This development culminated in an "adroit usurpation" which riveted the chains of property and inequality upon mankind.

"I have tried to explain the origin and progress of inequality," he states, "the establishment and the abuse of our political societies, as well as these things can be deduced from the nature of man by the sole light of reason and independent of the sacred dogmas which give sovereign authority to the divine right of kings." Once more he is at pains to explain his neglect of the "Biblical facts."

In a caustic conclusion, closely imitated from Montaigne's striking essay *On the Cannibals,* Rousseau exclaims: "It is manifestly against the law of nature, in whatever way one may define it, that a child should command an old man, that an imbecile should conduct a sage, and that a handful of men should be gorged with luxuries while the hungry multitude lacks what it needs!"

Here is the sharp condemnation of child kings, foolish kings, kings by divine right rather than because of ability or merit. Here is the wild call to "the revolt of the masses" against the red-heeled aristocracy, sated with wealth and pursuit of pleasure. To some minds, revolution already in 1754 seemed imminent. No wonder that the members of the Academy of Dijon, though they had rashly offered this provocative subject, shuddered at Rousseau's incendiary answer. They would have none of it and, turning their faces deliberately the other way, gave the prize to the safe and sane—and still today obscure—Abbé Talbert! No wonder that Voltaire, when he received the complimentary copy of the *Discourse* sent him by Jean-Jacques, contented himself, so far as the public was concerned, with a politely ironical letter of acknowledgment which carefully avoided the subversive theme of social inequality. Instead, he gaily made fun of the state of nature and the supposed dangers of the sciences and arts so vigorously attacked by Rousseau in the First Discourse five years before.

"I have received, Sir, your new book against the human race," wrote Voltaire on August 30, 1755. "I thank you for it. You will give men pleasure by telling them well-deserved truths, but you will not correct them. It is impossible to depict in stronger colors the horrors of human society from which our ignorance and weakness promise such consolation. Never has anyone used such wit to reduce us to animal stupidity. One feels like walking on all-fours while reading your work. However, as it is now more than sixty years since I have lost this habit, I feel unfortunately that it is impossible for me to resume it, and I leave this natural gait to those more worthy of it than you and I. Neither can I take ship to seek out the savages of Canada: first, because the maladies with which I am afflicted retain me near the greatest physician in Europe and I should not find the same help among the Missouris; in the second place, because war has been carried to those countries and the example of our nations has rendered the savages almost as bad as ourselves. I limit myself to being a peaceful savage in the solitude which I have chosen near your country where you ought to be."

There follow two or three pages of more serious refutation, but of the first *Discourse on the Sciences and the Arts* rather than of the second on *Inequality*. Then Voltaire concludes gracefully with a witty thrust at Rousseau, the alleged admirer of the country and primitive life, who still lingers amid the tumult of Paris.

"Monsieur Chappuis tells me that your health is very bad. You must come and regain it in your native air, enjoy liberty, drink with me the milk of our cows, and browse on our herbs."

"I am very philosophically and with the most tender esteem, Sir, your very Humble and very Obedient Servant, Voltaire."

This is telling irony on the part of the master of Les Délices, mingled shrewdly with the external forms of politeness. It is a style in which Voltaire was never excelled and rarely equalled. He shows clearly that he does not take seriously Rousseau's admiration for primitivism among the North American Indians, now "corrupted" by civilization and become, through our example, "almost" as bad as ourselves! At the same time, he prudently overlooks the central theme of the Second Discourse, the glaring inequality which, in Rousseau's opinion, called for a new social organization.

But, if Voltaire's letter offered clever mockery of Jean-Jacques's ideas, the latter was by no means at a loss for a courteous and at the same time effective reply:

"Embellish the asylum you have chosen," wrote the Citizen of Geneva from Paris, and the very choice of the word "asylum" was fitted to remind Voltaire painfully of his forced exile within the borders of the Protestant Zion, far from his native Paris. "Don't try to fall back on all-fours; no one in the world would be less successful at it than you. You teach us too well to walk erect on our two feet, and should not cease to stand on your own. . . . I am grateful for your invitation," he concludes, "and, if this winter leaves me well enough, in the spring, to go and live in my native country, I shall take advantage of your kindness. But I should rather drink the water from your fountain than the milk of your cows, and, as to the herbs in your orchard, I very much fear finding only the lotus, which is not good food for animals, and the magic moly, which prevents men from becoming brutes."

So Jean-Jacques closes with a reference to Homer's tempting food of the lotus, which it was almost impossible for men to abandon, and the moly, which protected Ulysses from the dangerous enchantments of Circe. Such, Rousseau politely suggests, would be the result of a stay under the captivating charm of Voltaire's rare genius and flashing wit.

This exchange of letters was shortly published by the patriarch of Les Délices with the ready permission of Jean-Jacques. The latter was no doubt proud of having successfully crossed swords with his famous antagonist. Relations between the two writers continued for the time being amicable in spite of their profound intellectual differences. Indeed, about a year later, Voltaire courteously half-apologized for his "bad pleasantries," as he called them, and "everything remained for the best in the best possible of worlds."

4

The *Discourse on Inequality* constituted a flaming attack on existing injustice. Rousseau's was the voice of a Samson in desperation pulling down the pillars of the temple upon himself as well as upon his enemies. The prosperous can afford to wait patiently for slow and safe reforms; those who dwell in misery at the bottom of society, easily believe that they have "nothing to lose but their chains." Disillusion comes too late when the whole great edifice of the state comes crashing down upon their heads.

Later, after his unhappy break with Diderot, Rousseau attributed to his friend's influence the harsh, bitter tone of this second work. It may indeed be that Diderot, known himself for similar fierce tirades on occasion, did contribute some fruitful suggestions on the idleness of the rich, the grinding toil of the poor, the surfeit at the top and the hunger in the lower ranks of humanity, the murders, battles, and wars which make mankind shudder. Diderot was perfectly capable of writing similar passages, as some later works show, but with his mercurial temperament such views represented only one of many moods. In the case of Rousseau, on the other hand, the attitude, if not the tone, was substantially that of his whole mature life. Diderot probably greatly stimulated and encouraged Jean-Jacques, gave him helpful examples to support his violent onslaught, and instructed him on scientific theories of human evolution, but it is unlikely that the Encyclopedist in any way originated his friend's deep-rooted hostility toward society which, as we have seen, sprang naturally out of so many painful experiences.

It is evident with the Second Discourse, as with the First, that the reader can by no means accept Rousseau's fond admiration for earlier ages in contrast with the unhappy present. "Say not thou, What is the cause that the former days were better than these? for thou dost not enquire wisely concerning this," is a little-known, but thought-provoking Biblical text. Man's natural tendency to look back longingly toward his youth and the youth of the race must be resisted. Modern study shows that the "noble savage" was rarely noble. He was dirty; he was the helpless victim of many maladies; he was uncertain about his food; he was constantly surrounded by danger from man and beast; he was fearful, superstitious, credulous about charms, magic, and incantations. But to say that we no longer wish to turn the clock of time back towards an overidealized past does not free civilization from Rousseau's fierce attack. Injustice, prejudice, inequality, crime, war, all the multiple evils of man's life, unhappily persist and call continually for reform. Once more Rousseau had preached an eloquent, if harsh, sermon, and once again to unwilling listeners.

Yet it is also true that, on vacation, many a man or woman delights in the opportunity to don few or old clothes and "get back to nature," seeking temporary release from the heavy pressures of a too complex society. In this way, one can fish or hunt or swim or perhaps merely bask idly in the sun. For a time, the happier aspects of life in Tahiti return. The "mystic isles of the South Seas" hold their legitimate lure. Rousseau rightly saw in the simple life an unescapable charm. "Most of the luxuries, and many of the so-called comforts of life," wrote Thoreau later, "are not only not indispensable, but positive hindrances to the elevation of mankind." It is not simplicity of living, but grinding want, which holds great masses of humanity down. Jean-Jacques's *Discourse* implicitly suggests both aspects of this unsolved problem. The increasing materialization of life entails its obvious, but often unperceived dangers.

With all his glaring errors and too facile generalizations, the author of the *Discourse on Inequality* had laid bare the running sores of an unjust society; he had cut ruthlessly to the very roots of human nature; he had cried out savagely for revolutionary change. Unhappily, to disclose the problem is easier than to solve it. A complete regeneration of society demands also the regeneration of humanity itself. But some good can gradually be accomplished by wise change. How to approximate "the life of nature" in the very midst of society was the next great question to which Rousseau would turn his thought.

CHAPTER XVI

NOVELIST, EDUCATOR, AND POLITICAL THEORIST

I

IT WAS ON A FRIDAY, THE 9TH OF APRIL, 1756. ABOUT TEN IN THE morning, Madame d'Epinay, Rousseau's obliging patron, drove up before his simple lodgings in the Hôtel du Languedoc, Rue de Grenelle-Saint-Honoré, in the busy quarter of Paris north of the Louvre. She was there to transport him from the city to the pleasant little place in the country which he had just recently so much admired. Already that morning her peasant farmer had come on ahead in his heavy wagon to move the necessary household goods. Now, with little or no further baggage to bother about, Jean-Jacques and Thérèse could assist the latter's aged mother to make her slow way down the six flights of stairs from their seventh-floor apartment to the street.

When they had all settled back comfortably in the cushioned carriage, the coachman picked up the reins and, with a quick word to the horses, started the little party clattering off over the rough pavement toward the northern limits of the capital. Soon the crowded metropolis thinned out behind them, the alluring countryside opened up ahead, and they jogged along through the village of Saint-Denis, ancient burial place of kings. Finally, however, after five or six miles more, they were obliged to pull up at the edge of the forest of Montmorency. The narrow muddy trail through the woods in the early springtime was no longer passable for the big coach. All but Madame Levasseur, the infirm mother of Thérèse, stepped out. The aged woman, well past seventy and walking with difficulty, had unexpectedly to be carried the rest of the way, it is reported by Madame d'Epinay, in an armchair hurriedly attached to two strong poles. Nevertheless, they must have arrived before noon at the little cottage which Rousseau's friend had recently had repaired and fitted out expressly for their use. Abbé de Linant, preceptor of Madame d'Epinay's son, was there to welcome them, having already ridden out in advance at her behest to arrange the furniture. Rousseau's famous sojourn at "The Hermitage" had begun. It was only then, he wrote some years later, that he really "started to live."

The uncertain April weather was rather cold still and there were even occasional patches of late snow on the ground in shady places, but the buds were opening on the trees and bushes and the grass was showing a fresh green, while here and there violets and gay primroses pushed up confidently toward the warm sun. That evening, from a neighboring wood, a nightingale sang his best spring song, to which Rousseau, from his window, listened with delight. When he awoke the next day from a fitful sleep, his first half-conscious thought as he lay in bed was of being back as usual in the old apartment of the Hôtel du Languedoc high above the noisy city streets. But no, there once again rang out the clear notes of the nightingale rising joyously in the early morning.

"At last all my wishes are fulfilled!" exclaimed Jean-Jacques rapturously to himself in the perfection of his new-found happiness. The calm country life of Les Charmettes seemed to have returned after twenty years of bitter struggle, which had culminated recently in a troubled and uneasy fame. Rousseau could finally put the hectic air of Paris behind him and revel to the full in this agreeable solitude.

There was no pressure of haste to unpack his few belongings. For the next several days, Jean-Jacques gave himself entirely to eager explorations of every path, copse, and thicket nearby. Who could believe that this happy retreat was barely twelve miles from the rush and clamor of the crowded city!

After having gratified his first curiosity, Rousseau began slowly to sort out his mass of papers and to turn his wandering thoughts back toward various literary projects which had been long germinating in his mind. Mornings he gave over systematically to the dull trade of copying music by which, for some years now, he had elected to earn a meager living. But, in the afternoons, he was pleasantly free for unconfined rambles under the great chestnuts of the Montmorency forest, while with notebook and pencil in hand he jotted down ideas just as they occurred to him. Never, he says, had he been able to think easily except in the open air. Jean-Jacques felt himself to be no professional author bound down to the slavery of a study table. Instead, the calm exercise of walking, the blood stirring in his veins, the quiet solitude, and the beautiful country surroundings favored his independent meditations as nothing else did. Only Madame d'Epinay, his kindly patron, visiting occasionally at her neighboring château of La Chevrette, soon intruded unduly on his freedom, he felt, with well-meant interruptions and invitations to dinner. Not without reason had she long since jokingly nicknamed him her "Bear." His native timidity and the obsequious politeness noted by the hostile Grimm had in fact easily turned, after his fame, into a gruff boorishness which broke out impatiently on slight provocation. It was merely a defensive shell which covered a deeply sensitive spirit. He was in truth quite unsuited to the solitude which he so much sought.

As Rousseau, in long tramps alone through the forest, traveled back in revery over his vagabond life, how utterly strange it seemed to him that he, so eager for warm friendship, so fitted to enjoy the intimate communion of love, had nowhere met the reality of his fond dreams! He was nearly forty-four now, yet he had never known these glorious heights of happiness. Certainly, he could not count his brief interlude with Madame de Warens in that category. She had been twelve years older than Jean-Jacques, and appeared more like a kind mother to him, a curiously unmoral mother, separated from the young man, too, by all the profound differences of age and experience. Nor, obviously, could he include his sorry liaison, already of more than ten years' standing, with Thérèse, devoted and faithful as he always considered her to be. The poor woman was startlingly illiterate, as is evident from two extraordinary letters of hers which have been published in their original form. So striking was her ignorance, not only of spelling, but even of word divisions, that these letters almost require "translation" into ordinary French to make them intelligible! Also, according to Rousseau himself, she could hardly even learn to tell the time of day on a sundial! However that may be, she evidently was in no way prepared to share the confidences of an original genius like Jean-Jacques. All the subtle life of the mind and the spirit was barred to them. Nor could the other passing love affairs which are narrated so frankly in the *Confessions* be numbered among the ideal any more than the disappointing experiences with Thérèse or Madame de Warens. "I saw myself approaching the portals of old age," remarked Rousseau sadly, "and dying without having lived."

But there always remained the dream world, the happy life of his vivid imagination! The hermit of the Montmorency forest harked back now in memory to a single idyllic day many years ago on a chance picnic with two young girls, Mademoiselle Galley and Mademoiselle de Graffenried. It was in the beautiful lake and mountain country near Annecy in far-off Savoy on the borders of Switzerland. Rousseau, as so often was his habit even then, had been out for an early morning hike. When the girls' horses balked at fording a small stream, Jean-Jacques waded in to his knees and led one of the animals across by the bridle while the other followed docilely after. Gratefully, the girls invited him to come along with them. So it happened that he rode double on the horse with Mademoiselle de Graffenried, his arms timidly around her waist. They had picked cherries together, had shared lunch, and later, with Rousseau perched on a stool and the girls seated on benches in the farmer's kitchen, they had eaten a dinner fit for a king. There had been gay laughter and the vibrant joy of youth. That was all, but it was enough to linger happily in the mind through these many crowded and disillusioning years! It was enough to people his solitary thoughts in the forest of Montmorency and to make out of his memories a developing novel.

So Jean-Jacques pictured himself as a young, romantic hero to whom he gave the name of Saint-Preux. There was of course a charming girl, light-blond like Madame de Warens, beautiful like Mademoiselle Galley, whom he called Julie d'Etange. Her friend and confidante, Claire d'Orbe, sprang largely from recollections of Mademoiselle de Graffenried. As a setting, Rousseau chose the beautiful Swiss country which he had revisited only two years before at Vevey on the northern shores of Lake Geneva. Soon he was composing at white heat passionate letters between Saint-Preux and Julie, letters which, after the manner of the popular English novelist, Richardson, told a kind of story and all of it vividly in the first person. Thus Jean-Jacques, who had first startled the public as the austere writer of the two Discourses, so moralistically critical of existing civilization, now found himself drawn by circumstances into an unexpected new career as a novelist of romantic love.

VOLTAIRE IN OLD AGE

Statue by Houdon, Foyer of the Théâtre-Français in Paris

VOLTAIRE'S CHÂTEAU AT FERNEY

SECONDE PARTIE.

LE premier qui ayant enclos un terrain, s'avisa de dire, *ceci est à moi*, & trouva des gens asſés ſimples pour le croire, fut le vrai fondateur de la ſociété civile. Que de crimes, de guerres, de meurtres, que de miſéres & d'horreurs n'eût point épargnés au Genre-humain celui qui arrachant les pieux ou comblant le foſſé, eût crié à ſes ſembla-bles. / Gardez-vous d'écouter cet impoſteur; Vous êtes perdus, ſi vous oubliez que les fruits ſont à tous, & que la Terre n'eſt à perſonne :) Mais il y a grande apparence, qu'alors les choſes en étoient déjà venües au point de ne pouvoir plus durer comme elles étoient; car cette idée de propriété, depen-dant de beaucoup d'idées antérieures qui

G 5   n'ont

[Voltaire's handwritten marginal notes:]

quoy celui qui a planté ſemé, et enclos n'a pas droit au fruit de ſes peines

quoy cet homme injuste et voleur auroit été le bienfaiteur du genre humain ! voyla la philoſophie d'un gueux

qui voudroit que les riches fuſſent volez par les pauvres.

Voltaire's marginal comments on Rousseau's *Discourse on In-equality* (1755). See pages 240-241.

ANNECY

Street in Annecy, Savoy, where Rousseau first met Madame de Warens in 1728. See pages 223-224.

GENEVA

The walled city of Geneva in the 18th century. Map by Nicolas Chalmandrier in 1776. See pages 196, 221, and 223.

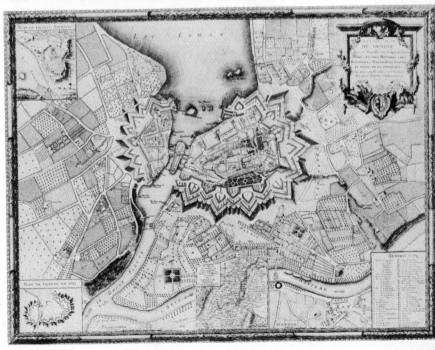

ancor mieu re mies quan geu ceures o pres deu vous, e deu
vous temoes tous la goies e latandres deu mon querque vous
cones ces que getou gour e rus pour vous,. e qui neu finiraes
quotobocs ces mon quere qui vous paleu ces paes mes le vre
gapire leu moman pour vous reugoidre geu neutien plues
arien qua vous mon cher amies, ge sui avestous lamities e
la reu cones caceu posible e la tacheman mon cher bonnamies
votreu enble e bon amies theress le vasseur.

(P. S.) Geu vous asure que geunous blires games deu ma
vies Monsieu leu maréchaleu et madame la marichal deu

LETTER OF THÉRÈSE LEVASSEUR

FRENCH TRANSCRIPTION:

Mais il [mon esprit] sera encore mieux remis quand je serai auprès
de vous, et de vous témoigner [?] toute la joie et la tendresse de mon
cœur que vous connaissez que j'ai toujours eue pour vous et qui ne
finira qu'au tombeau; c'est mon cœur qui vous parle, c'est pas mes
lèvres. J'aspire le moment pour vous rejoindre, je ne tiens plus à rien
qu'à vous, mon cher ami. Je suis, avec toute l'amitié et la reconnais-
sance possibles, et l'attachement, mon cher bon ami, votre humble et
bonne amie, Thérèse Levasseur.

ENGLISH TRANSLATION:

But it [my mind] will be still more at ease when I am with you and
can express to you all the joy and affection of my heart which you
know I have always had for you and which will end only with the
tomb; it is my heart that speaks to you, not my lips. I long for the
moment when I can again be with you, I no longer care for anything
but you, my dear friend. I am, with all the friendship and gratitude
possible, and all the attachment, my dear good friend, your humble
and good friend, Thérèse Levasseur.

LES CHARMETTES

Near Chambéry, in
Savoy. Rousseau's
home in 1736 and in
the years immediately
following. See pages
227-228.

2

Amid the absorption of such thoughts, Rousseau met from time to time in the neighborhood a slight acquaintance of former times, Madame d'Houdetot, the sister-in-law of Madame d'Epinay. Madame d'Houdetot was in the mid-twenties, some two decades younger than Jean-Jacques. She was not beautiful, certainly, and her face was pitted with smallpox, that wide-spread eighteenth-century malady, but she was gay, vivacious, and bubbling over with natural charm. The customs of the time had condemned her to an unhappy marriage of convenience, as it was called, to an uninspiring husband, otherwise unknown to history. She herself was quite frankly acknowledged to be in love with an absent army officer, Saint-Lambert, whom, curiously enough, destiny had also interposed between the famous Monsieur de Voltaire and Madame du Châtelet only seven or eight years before.

Finally, it came about, on a Sunday or Monday afternoon, January 30th or 31st, 1757, after Rousseau had been nearly ten months at the Hermitage, that the Countess d'Houdetot made a first dramatic visit to the plain little cottage. Her coachman, pulling his horses off the road at the turn, had unwisely attempted to cut directly across from the mill at Clairvaux. But the wheels ploughed deep into the winter mud of the valley and the heavy carriage lurched suddenly to a stop. Unable to proceed as she had planned, Madame d'Houdetot impetuously jumped out and tried to make the rest of the way on foot. Soon she, too, was caught in the soft ooze, her light party slippers were filled with water, and her servants had all the difficulty imaginable in pulling her safely from the mire. At last, decked out in boots, wet and dirty, yet filling the air with peels of gay laughter, she walked up to the door of the Hermitage. At sight of the grand lady's bedraggled appearance, Rousseau joined heartily in the merriment, Thérèse trotted out with dry clothes, the informality of the occasion broke down all the usual barriers of rank, they sat down together for a jolly rustic meal, and then, as the winter darkness early came on, the countess took her departure. The whole incident was indeed a kind of episode from a novel, as Jean-Jacques himself later wrote.

In the spring Madame d'Houdetot made a second unexpected visit to the Hermitage from the neighboring countryseat which she had rented at Eaubonne near Montmorency. She was on horseback this time and dressed in riding breeches, a costume rarer and more striking in the days of widespreading hoop skirts than today. Suddenly, all the imaginary ardor which Rousseau had been breathing into the pages of his epistolary novel was caught up and fused into real experience. Jean-Jacques was in love as, up to that time, he had never been.

There were long walks together in the forest, there were warm kisses in the grove under the moonlight at Eaubonne three miles away, there were letters—actual letters this time—addressed to his dear Sophie, there was an eloquence, all the eloquence of Rousseau's rare genius, such as Madame d'Houdetot had never heard before and no doubt would never hear again. Who, when self-consciousness had for a moment left him, could talk of love like Rousseau? Who could match his mobile, sensitive face, the light in his eyes? Madame d'Houdetot listened, and she too seemed carried away. But it was only early June madness, and the lady had not after all forgotten Saint-Lambert. There were jealous talebearers too, perhaps Thérèse, perhaps Madame d'Epinay, to stir the suspicions of the absent lover. Jean-Jacques's strange dream of a fervent friendship to be maintained peacefully between the three broke down before stern reality. Shortly, there were no more intimate confidences, no more walks together in the forest, no meetings under the moon at Eaubonne, and Rousseau's letters were less regularly addressed to Sophie, but respectfully and formally to Madame la Comtesse d'Houdetot! His last and most ardent idyll was at an end.

But what was lost to Jean-Jacques's life was gained to literature. Into the writing of his novel he now poured all the feeling, all the romantic passion, which had just been so sharply cut off in reality. The Julie of fiction is separated from the commoner, Saint-Preux, and married by her autocratic father to an estimable gentleman of her own station in life, but much older, Monsieur de Wolmar. It is easy to recognize echoes of the situation between the author, Madame d'Houdetot, and Saint-Lambert. But, in spite of Julie's respect for her kindly, if rather prosaic husband, her love for Saint-Preux unconsciously persists, and in the end only death intervenes to save her perhaps from herself. The novel is more dramatic in its conclusion than the brief happenings in the forest of Montmorency, but it is evident that reality itself held the author's pen, dictated the course of the action, added a new fire of passionate feeling, even at times chose the very words which gave it expression.

No wonder that, when the novel first appeared in Paris at the end of 1760 or early in the following year, lines formed before the rental libraries to secure one of the rare copies! One lady, it is said, was reading Rousseau's story, the *New Heloïse,* as he entitled it, after the famous love of Heloïse and Abelard, during the night of a ball at the Opera. At midnight, she ordered the horses harnessed to her carriage. Servants told her when the coach was ready, but she made no reply and continued absorbed in her reading. At two o'clock, they returned. "There is no hurry yet," she answered, and kept on with her book. Some time later, noticing that her watch had stopped, she rang to ask what time it was. "Four o'clock," an attendant informed her. "Well, in that case, it is too late to go to the ball; unharness my horses," she commanded, and, slipping into bed spent the rest of the night deep in the *New Heloïse.*

Such wild enthusiasm is hard, at first sight, to understand today. Too many other novels of love have come along since, inspired or quickened by Rousseau's and closer to the spirit of our own time. Although by the outbreak of the French Revolution over fifty editions of the *New Heloïse* had appeared, while it ran neck and neck with Voltaire's *Candide* for popularity with the reading public, the latter alone still lives, leaving its great rival to enjoy only historical interest. It is surely impossible to conceive of anyone missing a dance now in order to gallop madly through the pages of Jean-Jacques's romance!

Yet in the eighteenth century it was not so. Who, before the author of the *New Heloïse,* had dipped his pen in such passionate ink? Who seemed so completely, not to be writing a mere work of fiction, but rather to be telling the whole ardent story of his own life—as indeed he very nearly was? Who, like Rousseau, had been able to transport his readers out of the perfumed boudoir or the talkative salon and make them see the dark fir trees on the slopes of the Swiss Alps, look down from the heights upon the deep blue of Lake Geneva and across the green hills of the Vaudois country to the magnificent backdrop of the Jura mountains, watch the slow-moving grinding glaciers, note the crystal flash of the waterfall, and catch the swift rush of the hurrying torrent? Or, if Jean-Jacques, because he was nearsighted, did not himself perceive these things exactly in all their color or detail, he keenly sensed their mood in harmony with his and imparted his own feelings to the many enchanted readers. With Rousseau, outdoor nature enters the pages of the novel, becoming significant and interesting like the characters themselves. His successors would learn to follow in his footsteps. If Voltaire wrote cogently for the mind and the intellect, Jean-Jacques here spoke directly to the eyes and the emotions. Though his work has now lost its earlier power and freshness, it still lives vicariously through the new element which it added to the novelist's art. Many a writer today, without knowing it, remains a distant disciple of Rousseau.

We should not forget, moreover, that there were significant ideas expressed in the *New Heloïse*. Jean-Jacques, too, had written a "philosophical" novel. His was not indeed like Voltaire's tales with their clever puppets, pulled by the author's strings through the fast-moving action. Rousseau's people, though they seem emotionally exaggerated today—torrents of tears are no longer in fashion—are of three dimensions, not mere silhouettes flashed on a screen.

Julie was utterly frank in confessing to Monsieur de Wolmar her previous guilty fault with Saint-Preux. It is only so, Rousseau believes, that she could regain her integrity. Complete sincerity wipes out the past and establishes her life on a new basis of mutual confidence and esteem. Even Saint-Preux is to be readmitted to the Wolmar household as tutor to the children, just as the author had vainly hoped to live as a friend with both Madame d'Houdetot and Monsieur de Saint-Lambert. It was not destined to work out thus in real life, as we have seen. Rousseau's lack of tact and his failure to fathom certain depths of human nature are only too apparent in the novel. The death of Julie, while she is forced to admit that her love for Saint-Preux still burns beneath the surface and might have betrayed her in the end, shows how reality took the course of Jean-Jacques's pen out of his hands and made his fiction truer than if guided solely by arbitrary theory. Exaggerated or not, Rousseau's characters nevertheless live in the plane of the real.

In the *New Heloïse,* we see the education which will be given to Julie's two children. It will be a natural process, linked to direct observation of the world about them, pleasant, stimulating, a drawing-out of the mind, not a harsh cramming with ill-digested facts. Rousseau is already giving a brief preview of what will shortly be developed more fully in his educational treatise of *Emile*.

Christianity also figures in the novel. Julie's religion, as might be expected, is little concerned with complex dogma. It is rather a mystic reaching-out of the soul toward God, seeking a strength and an inspiration through prayer. Prayer overcomes the moral weakness of which Julie, like Jean-Jacques himself, is only too conscious. Even the agnostic Wolmar is touched by the depth of her feeling, and his ultimate conversion to this religion of love, worship, and humility is clearly forecast at the end. One of the unattained aims of Rousseau was to bring the philosophic party and the devout together in a religion which should be simple, tolerant, and helpful to humanity.

On Julie's country estate in company with Monsieur de Wolmar, we witness, finally, the life of nature by which the author proposed to cure the moral degeneration, the unhappiness, and the inequality of which he had so fiercely accused society in the First and Second Discourses. It is admittedly no longer possible to turn the course of humanity back to a primitive Golden Age, but, with wisdom, the natural life can again be created, under favorable conditions, in the midst of modern civilization. Julie and her husband live in honesty and mutual understanding. Even the marriage of convenience is sanctified by integrity. The two enjoy their home and the natural beauties which surround it. They bring up their children in the ways of nature. The servants, the laborers, the peasant farmers, who work daily for Monsieur and Madame de Wolmar, are treated like human beings. There is concern for their recreation and happiness. These people are recognized as men and women, not mere "hands," paid for an unremitting toil. Once more Rousseau speaks to the modern world as well as to his own century. The "life of nature" remains a call to strip off the artificialities, which constantly encroach upon mankind, and to rediscover those first principles which are alone essential to his welfare. The *New Heloïse* is not only a novel of romantic love; it is an attempt also to express the author's philosophy on a living canvas.

3

Rousseau's next, and again very different publication, *Emile*, appeared in Paris toward the end of May, 1762. He had begun this educational treatise at the request of the young wife of Monsieur de Chenonceaux, son of Madame Dupin, Jean-Jacques's former employer. This was the immediate motive for composition, but the difficult and basic problem of education had filled his thoughts ever since his own struggle for self-instruction at Les Charmettes and particularly since his abortive effort to teach the two sons of Monsieur de Mably at Lyons in 1740. Already at that time, moral principles appeared to Rousseau as more basic than intellect. Not having himself gone through the conventional training of the schools, he could think about the questions of aim and method along unorthodox lines.

Characteristically, Jean-Jacques opens his book with a challenging phrase. "Everything is good," he says, "when it springs from the Creator of all things; everything degenerates in the hands of Man." Following the position taken in the First and the Second Discourse, Rousseau thus blames humanity for society's supposed fall from the idyllic Garden of Eden or the early Golden Age. Nevertheless, what man has ruined, he can also change for the better. A natural education will produce the natural life. *Emile* offers a logical sequel to the philosophy presented in the *New Heloïse*.

In form, *Emile* appears as a kind of novel. It is not as vivid a personal narrative as the ardent romance which tries the souls of Julie, Saint-Preux, and Monsieur de Wolmar, nor is it on the other hand a mere abstract treatise. There are two principal characters, the boy Emile, who is to be educated, and his tutor, who is to direct the process. Later, a girl, Sophie, appears, named obviously after Madame d'Houdetot, to typify the education of women and to become the ideal helpmeet for the young man. Often, an effective dialogue or a swiftly-recounted scene shows Rousseau's own exceptional talents as a teacher, at least within the pages of a book. Like other great French authors of the eighteenth century, Jean-Jacques knew how to win the interest of the general reader by dramatizing his ideas.

Emile has sometimes been criticized as utterly impractical because it portrays a single pupil who is guided in all his waking moments by a single devoted teacher. Evidently, this is an education available only to the very rich or to children of a royal family. But, while plausible at first sight, such criticism is not really valid. Intentionally, Rousseau sets his goal so high that it will never be completely attainable. Education, in his opinion, is of such importance that we should focus our attention, ideally, on a single boy and a single teacher. In actual practice, we shall have to be content with less, much less, but we ought constantly to hold before us a perfect mark at which to aim. The author reminds his readers, by implication, that great schools are not made from marvelous buildings, lavish equipment, or complex organization, helpful as all of these adjuncts may be. Good teaching and effective learning come only from able teachers and eager pupils. "Mark Hopkins on one end of a log and a student on the other" still epitomize the problem. The human elements are more significant than the setting. It is a lesson too frequently ignored!

Rousseau's first objective for his pupil is a vigorous, healthy body. The child should run, jump, play, grow strong by exercise in the open air during all sorts of weather. The injunction was more needed in the eighteenth century and in France than in America today. Then the children of the more prosperous classes, at least, were too often hothouse plants, forced intellectually under harsh discipline, dressed like young adults and brought up early to shine in the clever repartee of the salons, with little in the way of games or sports to lighten their daily round of study. Not yet had the "sideshows crowded out the circus," as Woodrow Wilson once charged of our modern schools and colleges.

Goodness is natural, believes Rousseau, while vice is acquired. Hence, the first education should be negative, offering the child chiefly a wholesome environment free from harmful influences. Moral education should come rather from action than from dry precepts. Everything should be done to encourage self-development, which alone takes deep root and becomes effective. We should love childhood, favor its games, make it a period of life, happy in itself, not merely a preparation for a future which, with the high infant mortality of the eighteenth century, might never arrive.

Yet, if Rousseau, in sharp reaction against the confinement and severe discipline of eighteenth-century schools, goes too far at times toward an easy optimism about the supposed "goodness" of human nature, he is by no means so blind to reality as are some of his soft-hearted successors, advocates of a child's complete "self-expression," as it is called, who seem not always actually to have read *Emile* with care. When, for example, the boy breaks a window, his teacher allows the glass to remain out for some days while the rain and the wind drive in. Emile consequently catches cold, but finds through hard experience that windows are not to be broken. We do not need to approve fully of Rousseau's Spartan method in order to see his point. Emile indeed becomes gradually something of a Stoic. He learns to bear suffering as a preparation for the difficult aspects of life. Moreover, though much has been written implying that Jean-Jacques wished to make education easy, he insists to the contrary: "Among so many admirable methods for facilitating the study of the sciences, there is great need for somebody to give us one for acquiring them with effort." Rousseau's statement is of course an intentional exaggeration, but it emphasizes the necessity of hard work. The author realized from his own experience that there is no royal road to learning.

Private property? Emile thoughtlessly plants some beans without permission in ground the gardener was reserving for other purposes. With the tutor's approval, the workman roots up the growing sprigs and the boy, in tears, discovers in a way never to be forgotten his obligations to society. The passage represents a sharp change on the part of Rousseau himself from the bitter tirades of his *Discourse on Inequality*. In the modern world at least, if not in the theoretical Golden Age, ownership has its uses.

Memorizing? Rousseau will have none of it. In the schools of his day, rote learning was no doubt overdone. In violent reaction, Jean-Jacques, like some of his successors, flies to the opposite extreme, overlooking the handicap of a mind which, without a trained memory, lacks materials ready to hand for forming a judgment.

"I hate books," exclaims Rousseau; "they only teach people to talk about what they don't know!" It was a furious attack upon the education of his day. With no laboratories, no field trips, no direct observation of the world, the work of the classroom easily became too much confined to the printed page. The author overstated his case, obviously. The project method is good, but it is not all. The wise reader listens, but without being completely swept away. Rousseau for the moment chose to ignore his own great debt to books.

There is one book only which Jean-Jacques excepts from his indictment. That book is *Robinson Crusoe*. With its vivid narrative of how the shipwrecked mariner little by little learned to do everything for himself with his own hands, Rousseau finds in Defoe's novel the greatest interest and value. It is the boy's book *par excellence*. Emile, too, will learn by doing. In fact, with "the century of revolutions" approaching, as Rousseau prophetically says, Emile will take up the trade of wood work. Voltaire had only contempt for Rousseau's "gentleman carpenter," as he called him, but the vogue of manual training today and its real educational benefits have proved the master of Ferney wrong and the "Citizen of Geneva" right in this matter. It is unfortunate that the child who becomes able to make a stool which will rest steadily on its three legs without rocking is not always taught the even greater necessity of similar accuracy in the crucial field of ideas.

The man of nature, whom Rousseau seeks to form, is not a savage living in the depths of the forest. He is to be in the social whirl, but not of it. He has discovered how not to be carried away by the passions and opinions of men, how to see with his own eyes, to feel with his own heart, to reason with his own mind. The object of education, in Jean-Jacques's opinion as in Montaigne's, is not so much wide factual information as the development of judgment. Emile will learn to be independent, to think for himself. His education, like the self-schooling won with such great effort by Rousseau, will be his alone. He will not be a parrot, but will stand firmly on his own feet.

As for Sophie, her favorite book will be, not *Robinson Crusoe,* but *Télémaque.* The liberal viewpoint and the high moral teaching of the Archbishop of Cambrai had a strong appeal to Rousseau as to many of his contemporaries. But in general, Jean-Jacques, unlike Voltaire or Montesquieu, regarded woman's position as subordinate to man's and withheld from her a broad intellectual training. In this respect, Rousseau lagged behind the *Treatise on the Education of Girls* of his seventeenth-century mentor, Fénelon.

Much of the fourth Book of *Emile* is devoted to religion. Rousseau is so anxious for his pupil to understand his beliefs that he will make no effort to teach him religious concepts before the age of dawning maturity. Doubtful from the standpoint of psychology, the viewpoint is understandable as a reaction against overemphasis on an abstruse catechism in his own early youth.

Rousseau's religion is presented under the title of *Profession of Faith of the Savoyard Vicar.* It is largely the religion of Julie in the *New Heloïse,* but with more place given to philosophy as well as feeling. Rousseau, like Voltaire, believes in "natural religion" in contrast to the fixed creed associated with revelation, but Jean-Jacques's teaching carries with it a more ardent personal note than his rival's. The negative side of Rousseau's position Voltaire admired. In the margin of his copy of *Emile*, as of his adversary's answering *Letter to M. de Beaumont*, Archbishop of Paris, the philosopher of Ferney wrote frequently: "Good," "Bold and Good." But the affirmative side he rejected. *Hors de l'Eglise, point de salut*, was the official doctrine of the established church. How Rousseau could call himself Christian as a mere independent follower of Christ without accepting all items of the orthodox creed, Voltaire could never understand. But Jean-Jacques was only an independent Protestant, a Protestant forming his own new church.

For Jean-Jacques, the *Bible* remained the "pillow-book" which he regularly took to bed with him at night and read throughout later life. It was the unique source of counsel, comfort, and inspiration, which he had first come to know in the intimate family circle of good Pastor Lambercier at Bossey or in the earnest sermons heard in the Protestant Cathedral at Geneva during his early youth. What he did not comprehend, he reserved decision on, treating it with respect rather than with disbelief or scorn.

The sure guide which teaches man to distinguish between good and evil is conscience, that "divine instinct." It will never betray us if we listen honestly. Rousseau's assurance in this respect went back to his own first moral training. If he had often been too weak to follow such teaching, he could not quite efface its precepts from his mind; he could not conceive of conscience as permanently corrupted or non-existent. Prayer, much as for Julie, brings us the necessary strength to resist temptation successfully, he believes. Christ's divinity lies, not in miraculous manifestations, says Rousseau, but in the sublimity of his life and teaching. "The Gospel," he writes, "has characteristics of truth so great, so striking, so perfectly beyond imitation, that its inventor would be more astonishing than the hero."

It is understandable that the Archbishop of Paris quickly found *Emile's* religious teachings heretical. Jean-Jacques, who had moved to nearby Montmorency some years before after an unhappy quarrel with Madame d'Epinay, was informed that the Parlement had ordered his arrest. Under the urging of his friends, Monsieur and Madame du Luxembourg, he hurriedly sorted out his papers, burned some, packed a few belongings, and mounted into a carriage in flight to Switzerland. As he trotted along the road to Paris in the late afternoon, he met four men in black driving in the opposite direction toward Montmorency. They bowed and seemed to smile slightly in recognition, but passed on their way without stopping. Rousseau was convinced that the officers were glad to have him escape, thus avoiding the possible public uproar of arrest. The government had to go through the motions of satisfying the orthodox, but was well content that the embarrassing bird had flown. Jean-Jacques had started on his troubled years of persecution and wandering.

Emile is a truer book than is likely to appear in a brief discussion which so readily makes the faults stand out in relief while obscuring the virtues. How much better to read *Emile* than merely to read about it! On direct acquaintance, its qualities and its shortcomings tend to assume their proper proportions. In the presence of the book as a whole, one is less inclined to take its paradoxes for precepts. Admittedly, Rousseau's errors and extreme statements are many. It was so that he fought the excessive bookishness of the education established in the schools around him. It was so, too, that he compelled the attention of his readers. But, if we do not try to follow *Emile* literally, if we see it rather as a powerful stimulus in the direction of an education more real, more vital, more deeply centered in the needs of the child, than any yet attained, then we discover that Rousseau has proposed an ideal which, though constantly exceeding our limited grasp, is capable of inspiring humanity toward a brighter future. Above all, *Emile* reminds us, as we need always to be reminded, that education is the most important enterprise in the world and that its success depends, not on material surroundings primarily, but on the soundness of the aims in view and on warm human associations between teacher and pupil.

4

Rousseau's book on the *Social Contract* came off the presses of Marc-Michel Rey at Amsterdam near the middle of April, 1762, about a month before *Emile*. Thus these two powerful works appeared almost simultaneously.

Ever since his days as secretary of the French ambassador at Venice in 1743 and 1744, the author had pondered the writing of a comprehensive book on *Political Institutions,* the product of his gradually maturing reflections about the different effects upon a people of a corrupt oligarchy like Venice, of a decadent monarchy as in France, or of a small republic such as Geneva. But the enterprise proved too great for him. Perhaps the publication of Montesquieu's masterpiece, the *Spirit of Laws,* in 1748 made him feel that much of the projected task had already been accomplished. Perhaps the numerous other works of Rousseau which absorbed the busy decade of the 1750s left him neither time nor energy for more. In any case, the little book of the *Social Contract* was only the incomplete result of a long period of meditation on the grave problems of government.

The idea of a social contract was by no means new. Dear to the eighteenth century, the concept raised clearly the question of the basic relationship between people and ruler. Did a king exercise authority by unchallengeable divine right or only by the real or tacit consent of his so-called subjects? In the latter case, obviously, there is implied the right of revolution if the government does not operate in the best interests of the nation.

"Man is born free," cries Rousseau at the beginning of the first chapter, "and everywhere he is enslaved." The sentence is a typical example of the author's remarkable gift for composing a sharp, incisive, passionate phrase calculated to fire men's souls to action or revolt. In a speech on May 10th, 1793, Robespierre, obviously imitating Jean-Jacques, exclaimed: "Man is born for happiness and freedom, yet everywhere he is unhappy and enslaved."

"Might does not make right," continues Rousseau. There is no such thing as a justifiable government resting on force alone. The theory of the social contract is in fact an expression of what Woodrow Wilson, in more recent times, called "government with the consent of the governed."

The right of private property, so angrily assailed in the *Discourse on Inequality,* is now defended, somewhat as in *Emile,* if dependent upon use. Land which is actually worked performs a social function.

Like Montesquieu before him, Rousseau finds weakness in a government which rests on harsh punishments, frequently invoked. Only two years later, the great Italian Beccaria was to attack the whole system of cruel penology then in practice.

With a natural admiration for Geneva, his native city, and with confidence in the sovereignty of the people, Rousseau considers an able and good king more rare than an executive of real merit democratically chosen. Certainly, the examples of Louis XIV and Louis XV were not such as to arouse his enthusiasm. Yet an established government, Jean-Jacques holds, should never be altered unless it becomes absolutely incompatible with the general welfare. Revolutions are terrible crises, he admits, justifiable only in the face of abuses no longer tolerable. Incendiary in his premises, Rousseau, it should be noted, generally draws back conservatively before violent conclusions. His disciples will not always be so hesitant. Although, in *Emile,* the author forecasts the coming of a great upheaval, he, like most of his contemporaries, would have shuddered at the actual course of the French Revolution.

Finally, Rousseau turns to the question of what he calls "civil religion." He states that there should be a minimum code of accepted dogma, including belief in God, in a future life with reward of the good and punishment of the wicked, and in the sacredness of the social contract and the laws. "Without forcing anyone to believe these dogmas," says Jean-Jacques, "the state may banish whoever does not accept them!" In spite of his immediate condemnation of intolerance, here is the paradoxical declaration to which Rousseau has at last been led. Influenced no doubt by his background in the tight little theocracy of Geneva, he had unconsciously worked himself into an indefensible position. Laudable though his intentions were, he was trying, naturally in vain, to reconcile tolerance with coercion of belief. In a marginal comment on this passage in his copy of the *Social Contract,* Voltaire lashed out fiercely: "All dogma is ridiculous, harmful. All constraint on dogma is abominable. Ordering anyone to believe is absurd. Limit yourself to ordering people to behave rightly."

There are evident two antagonistic currents in the *Social Contract,* a strong individualism and an all-powerful government, conceived in the name of the people. The first parts are an eloquent defense of human liberty and the sovereignty of the people; the conclusion, with the intention of protecting the sanctity of the general will, easily becomes a program for the police state. Rousseau had been unable to bring his thought on this complex subject into unity. He admitted as much. His book can readily be invoked in behalf of quite opposite systems. Rousseau's dilemma is not unlike that of some reformers or even so-called liberals, as well as conservatives, today. Believing intensely in the justice of their program, they do not always draw back before its imposition by extra-legal means or perhaps by force. They sometimes forget that the same unfair methods, favorable to their cause on one occasion, may be turned against them on another. It has been said of revolutionaries that "they start out to make everybody happy and end by killing all who disagree with them!" The idea that "the end justifies the means" is an old error which dies hard. The means indeed remain inseparable from the ends and will vitiate the best of good intentions if the methods used are unwise or oppressive. Rousseau's failures are instructive as well as his successes.

But the author of the *Social Contract* has opened up an issue which is becoming more and more urgent. In the face of the complex social, economic, and military problems of the modern world, governments tend toward highly centralized powers in order to deal with these broad problems effectively. There are equal dangers in weakness and in strength, anarchy and despotism. The way of liberty appears as a delicate balance between two extremes. Voltaire found it in the rule of law, not of men. Montesquieu sought safety from tyranny in the separation of governmental powers, the celebrated system of checks and balances, in which, as Madison said, "ambition must be made to counteract ambition." Rousseau obscurely envisaged the problem, though without solving it.

But it was the apparently subversive character of his book which caused it to be promptly attacked and condemned in Geneva and in France. This censorship struck one more blow at the author's peace of mind during his later years. The *Social Contract* was in one of its aspects an eloquent defense of the right of revolution. Yet it seems not to have been widely read or meditated until the approach of 1789. Then, both in its stirring call for freedom and in its unfortunate argument for conformity through the use of force, it fitted in with the trend of the times. There is much of Rousseau's unhappy dilemma in Robespierre, "the incorruptible," the man who dominated France during the Reign of Terror.

CHAPTER XVII

ROUSSEAU AND THE
CONFESSIONS

I

ROUSSEAU SAW HIMSELF AS THE VERY "MAN OF NATURE" WHOM he had so ardently sought to portray in his works. "I am starting an enterprise without precedent and one which will never find an imitator," he wrote at the beginning of his *Confessions*. "I wish to set before my fellows a man in all the truth of nature, and that man will be myself." The book would, he believed, tell for the first time, with the utmost in devastating honesty, the whole story of a man's inner and outer life. It would tear away the veil and show a human being with complete realism.

During the great decade of the 1750s, Rousseau had suddenly taken his stand in behalf of moral progress as against a too exclusive confidence in the development of the arts and sciences; he had violently attacked human inequality; he had poured out his soul in a very personal novel of passionate love; he had drawn up a new program of education in *Emile;* and he had underlined the people's right of revolution against tyranny in the *Social Contract*. It had been a remarkable period of acute intellectual ferment and literary accomplishment. No wonder that he now found himself worn out and, paying the bitter penalty of his disconcerting frankness in social criticism with years of wandering and persecution, wanted at last only peace and no more of the difficult task of writing books!

But there was to be one important exception. He would pass his time looking deeply into himself at the strange man that he was. The reveries of the long walks in the forest of Montmorency, accompanied only by his faithful dog, would culminate in his *Confessions,* which were not to appear until after his death.

A first trial at this self-probing came as early as January of 1762 in four intimate letters to his friend among the nobility, Monsieur de Malesherbes, then Director of Publication, which is to say, of

Censorship. Malesherbes had endeavored to steer a middle course between his duty to the government and a considerate tolerance for Rousseau's startling ideas. Jean-Jacques, in turn, reciprocated by an effort to reveal frankly his inmost being. Finally, about three years later, in 1765, Rousseau began to write the detailed story of his unusual life.

"I venture to believe," continues the author in the second paragraph of the *Confessions*, "that I am not made like any other man in the world. If I am not better, at least I am different. Whether Nature has done well or ill in breaking the mold in which she cast me, can be judged only after I have been read."

Thus Jean-Jacques was filled with pride at being unique. "At least I am different," he insisted. In contrast to the *honnête homme* of the seventeenth century, the perfect courtier, whose constant aim was to conform gracefully with the social ideal of the time, to know always exactly what to say or what to do, to be at all times the gentleman or the grand lady *comme il faut,* Rousseau, the "Bear" of Madame d'Epinay, would stress his complete independence, his sharp departure from society's norm. Thus he typified the individualistic hero of the coming Romantic age. Rousseau was in many ways the literary ancestor of Byron and his often eccentric contemporaries.

In an earlier draft of the *Confessions,* the author had, at the beginning, named Montaigne's famous *Essays* as setting a partial example of the complete human revelation which he sought. Rousseau had long been a devoted reader of Montaigne and was deeply influenced by his vigorous laying-bare of conventional prejudices. Finally, however, Jean-Jacques evidently preferred to acknowledge no predecessors, to emphasize his belief in entire freedom from any model. Even the reference to his favorite Montaigne was dropped from the text.

Before the Judgment Seat of God, Rousseau ventures to say, in continuing: "I have shown myself as I was: mean and contemptible, good, high-minded, and sublime, according as I was one or the other. I have unveiled my inmost self even as Thou hast seen it, O Eternal Being. Gather around me the countless host of my fellow-men; let them hear my confessions, lament my unworthiness, blush at my imperfections. Then let each of them in turn reveal, with the same frankness, the secrets of his heart at the foot of Thy Throne, and say, if he dare: 'I was better than that man.'"

In other words, whatever the reader's final judgment may be about Rousseau, whether we are inclined to condemn or excuse, we need to remind ourselves that he has confessed, not only his committed faults or sins, but at times even the secret thoughts of which he later repented. It is a most exacting standard. Who, even of the best, would be prepared to meet it? Most of us find it terrifying enough to be judged by our acts! Jean-Jacques was indeed the greatest enemy of his own good name before posterity. If many of us estimate him with severity, it is often from information we do not possess about others of his contemporaries who might also be blackened by a like truthfulness. His startling admissions cannot be an atonement for his sins, as he wished and thought, but they did constitute no doubt an important step in his painful moral progress. To preserve a fair balance, we ought at least to ask ourselves how we should probably have evaluated Rousseau's complex character without the harsh brush strokes of the *Confessions*.

How true are the *Confessions?* The problem of sincerity is always a difficult one, whether in ourselves or others. Sincerity is rarely, if ever, absolute. It can easily be obscured by wishful thinking or a human desire for self-apology. In the ascertainable area of dates or bare facts, investigation has sometimes shown Rousseau's memory at fault. This is not surprising in a man often writing about events of twenty, thirty, forty, or even fifty years before. In dealing with the early period of his life, particularly, he had to work without the aid of preserved letters or documents. But corrections of this type, in most cases, do not affect the general interpretation of his character.

There is also a very natural tendency on the part of Jean-Jacques to idealize the remote, seemingly carefree period of his youth. Here, in spite of many troubles, fate appeared in retrospect to have been kinder to him than during the recent days of fame, criticism, and awakened jealousies. The "Golden Age" in his own experience, as in society at large, seemed to have been in the past. The later period of conflict, persecution, wandering, and the half-imagined "plot" against him is in contrast somewhat blacker no doubt than in reality. Yet it is hard to be sure and, though he was ill-fitted for the solitude which he believed to be his favorite state, though his suspicions of friends fed on loneliness and on his misanthropic nature, all was not imagination in his indictment of Diderot, Grimm, Madame d'Epinay, and D'Holbach. There was between them a fundamental disaccord for which the blame rests on both sides.

One more qualification must be noted. "If I have occasionally made use of some immaterial embellishment," observed Rousseau on the first page of his *Confessions,* "this has only been in order to fill a gap caused by my lack of memory. I may have assumed the truth of what I knew might have been true, never of what I knew to be false." Thus Jean-Jacques admittedly fell back at times on the artist's privilege and drew upon his creative imagination for background and color. He told his story vividly. The *Confessions* are certainly Rousseau's best novel, but in no invidious sense. They are of more absorbing interest than any of his other works; they are the most widely read today, even surpassing the *New Heloïse,* which, as we have seen, has long since lost its one-time vogue. Yet, although every detail possible should be carefully checked with available evidence, it does not appear that the author has essentially warped his narrative. Indeed, the reader is still impressed by his remarkable frankness and penetrating self-analysis, which often coincide even with the unfavorable testimony of enemies.

Of course, there is clearly special pleading at times and all of Rousseau's tortured explanations for the abandonment of his children can never wipe out this terrible blot on his character. In confessing himself so boldly, he also laid bare the intimate life of Madame de Warens and that of others who crossed his path. The brush which tarred himself bespattered them as well. It is no wonder that many of his former friends lived in mortal fear of the ultimate publication of the *Confessions,* parts of which Rousseau read aloud to circles of listeners in Paris during the 70s. The power of the author's pen was known and dreaded. Both Madame d'Epinay and Diderot tried with no great success to counteract in advance Rousseau's revelations. The reliability of Madame d'Epinay's *Memoirs* is still in controversy. The self-justification on both sides makes a completely objective decision difficult.

2

One of the important characteristics of Rousseau's *Confessions* is the detailed picture of the games, thoughts, and emotions of his early childhood. In contrast, the great Monsieur de Voltaire contrived to be dull, perhaps for the one time in his life, when he wrote his *Memoirs*. To him, it did not seem worth while to let us see his Jesuit instructors at the College of Louis-le-Grand. We get no intimate portrait of his boyhood friends, nor do we witness the classroom pranks or the eager play which must have gone on in the courtyard during recess, even among these intellectually-minded youths. The day-by-day school life of the son of the notary Arouet has largely disappeared, never to be recovered. That is because Voltaire confined himself to a bare historical narrative in which he presented only the later period of fame. Why try to recapture these childish memories? Probably even the idea of doing so never crossed his mind.

Rousseau thought otherwise. Instinctively, he realized that the child was father to the man, that the early experiences explained and had largely shaped his destiny. His detailed and colorful story has caught the interest of readers from the beginning, and continues to grip them today. With Jean-Jacques, childhood made its definite appearance as a theme in literature, never to leave it. No biography, no self-narrative, can now ignore these formative years. Many a novel today treats fully of life as it first comes to boy or girl before maturity imposes its final mold. Here, too, Rousseau has left a marked impress on later disciples.

In reading the first pages of the *Confessions,* we learn, for example, just what books fell into Jean-Jacques's hands during boyhood days. The same narrative is continued later. It is easy, with these aids, to reconstitute the development of his intellectual life. We witness his first contact with the charm of music. We read the short, sharp sentences which tell of his dismay at being accused of a trivial fault, that of breaking a comb, of the excessive punishment which ensued, and his firm declaration of innocence in writing the *Confessions* nearly fifty years later. "It was a frightful chastisement for a crime which I never committed," cries Rousseau with an over-emphasis characteristic of his susceptible nature. But early impressions bite deep, and what someone else would have quickly forgotten, never faded from Jean-Jacques's memory. The incident remains a lesson in the delicate sensibilities of childhood and the long reach they often have into the unseen future.

Monsieur Lambercier, the good pastor at Bossey, in whose home the young boy was then living, had planted a walnut-tree with a view to needed shade in the afternoon. A kind of basin had been dug at its foot to hold water. The planting and the watering had all been conducted with great ceremony. Impressed by these scenes, Jean-Jacques and his cousin resolved that they too should have the joy of growing a tree of their own. The two children cut a slip from a young willow, "and planted it on the terrace, at a distance of about eight or ten feet from the august walnut-tree." Then they pondered the problem of water which they were not allowed to carry from a distance. For a few days, they made shift, nevertheless, to get some, the shoot began to bud, it started even to put forth leaves, and, although it was still not a foot high, they were convinced that in a short time they would be able to sit down under its shade!

But a fatal drought and certain death for their beloved willow was fast approaching. Under the spur of necessity, they conceived the idea of an underground trench to draw off some of the water from the walnut-tree to the willow. At first, they were unsuccessful, clumsily ignoring the requirement of an even slope. But with experience came knowledge. They dug their basin deeper, lined the trench with narrow planks taken from the bottoms of boxes, formed a kind of latticework at the entrance to prevent the channel from filling with mud and stones, concealed the whole with earth trodden down firmly above, and eagerly awaited the arrival of Monsieur Lambercier for the daily watering of the walnut. The first pail of water was quickly swallowed up by the conduit. Unable to repress their cries of joy, the two children promptly gave away the trick. Monsieur Lambercier exclaimed in astonishment: "An aqueduct, an aqueduct!", ruthlessly broke up their work with his pickaxe, and then walked off with no further word of reproach or displeasure. Afterwards the boys heard him laughing loudly with his sister; they planted another tree somewhere else, and, strange to relate, Rousseau remembered this incident only in terms of light comedy. But who else in his time would have seen the interest in this amusing little tale of childhood.

We have already witnessed the dramatic scene of Jean-Jacques's departure from Geneva at sixteen, his meeting with Madame de Warens, his experiences in Italy, the joyous picnic with Mademoiselle Galley and Mademoiselle de Graffenried which later influenced the *New Heloïse*. These are only a few of the happenings which Rousseau recalls with loving detail and makes vivid to the reader. He too, like the modern Proust, seeks to recapture "times past."

There were the long days of reading and tramping about the countryside at Les Charmettes, less idyllic in actuality than they appeared to Rousseau in retrospect; there was the meeting with the peasant farmer and his fear of the government tax-collector which did much to shape Jean-Jacques's future anger at society; there were incidents which show the precocious influence of sex on the boy's physical and emotional development, forerunner of many a modern portrayal of the storms which sweep adolescence, though they had been long ignored before. Truly youth, too, is life and a very important part of it! Rousseau, instinctively, realized the fact, and over half of his book deals with these significant years of obscurity. His sudden, meteoric appearance before the public in 1750 is now understandable to us, readers of the *Confessions,* as it never was to his astonished contemporaries. Long years of unconscious preparation explain the unique man he had become. Without his frank and detailed revelation, Rousseau's genius would no doubt still remain in many ways a closed book.

It is noteworthy, too, that Jean-Jacques is the father of a whole current of subjective literature in the generations which follow him. Goethe in Germany, Chateaubriand in France, Wordsworth and Byron in England, are only a few of the great writers who lay bare their souls before the world. The French Romantic poets, Lamartine, Vigny, Hugo, and Musset, often trod the same path. For nearly a century, authors would tend generally to occupy the center of the stage themselves, not look out objectively on the varied human scene around them. This viewpoint has its limitations, certainly, but what an intensity of self-revelation it frequently brings! Any type of literature which adds to our intimate knowledge of man has its legitimate appeal, and Rousseau, in spite of his shortcomings and excesses, has enriched our inner experience. The slightest incident, the gentle lapping of the water against the shore, a pleasant odor, some brilliant colors, the physical senses, and the keen emotions that they evoke, all become identified with our own feelings in Jean-Jacques's very personal narrative. Once again we live in and through him, no longer with the life of the intellect alone, but partaking of his whole sentient being.

3

The actual writing of the *Confessions* was completed toward the end of 1770. The story they tell ends with the period of their inception five years before. The First Part was not published until April or May of 1782, four years after the author's death; Part II, the final half, appeared in the autumn of 1789.

The rest of Rousseau's existence had continued, for the most part, to be troubled by his fear of persecution. A revealing, but melancholy work in the form of a dialogue is entitled, *Rousseau Judge of Jean-Jacques*. In his grave mental disturbance, the writer even laid a copy of his manuscript on the altar of Notre-Dame Cathedral at Paris in 1776, hoping in this way to ensure its preservation as a defense against his enemies!

But calm and happiness finally came to Rousseau's tormented spirit. On August 29, 1768, he had tried to regularize his long-standing relation to Thérèse in a kind of civil marriage, which, however, was without legal authority at the time. His literary career terminates in the delightful *Reveries of the Solitary Pedestrian,* divided into ten *Walks,* the last unfinished. The work appeared with the First Part of the *Confessions* in 1782. After several reflective chapters in which the author continues his probing into himself and his complex character, we read, in the *Fifth,* of his happy sojourn in 1768 on the Island of Saint-Pierre in the middle of beautiful Lake Bienne near Neuchâtel.

"The banks of Lake Bienne are wilder and more *romantic* than those of Lake Geneva," writes Rousseau (using a word destined to give its name to a great literary movement) , "because the rocks and woods come down closer to the water, but they are no less smiling."

In this tiny lake, little known or frequented at the time, Jean-Jacques enjoyed the charms of solitude and contemplation, taking refuge, after his supposed stoning by mysterious enemies at Môtiers, in the single house located on one of the small islands. Here he was able to remain for only two months, "but I could have spent two years, two centuries, or a whole eternity without being bored a moment," exclaims Rousseau in dithyrambic exaggeration. After the emotional strains of recent years and the long period of intense literary activity, Rousseau's tired mind was glad to slip gently into the *dolce far niente* of these weeks of peaceful idling. His books and most of his other possessions reposed quietly in their packing cases, undisturbed, unwanted. Instead of occupying himself with his "gloomy papers," he says, he gave his time to the first fever of botanizing which filled his later years with purposeful tramps over the hills and countryside.

"When evening drew near, I descended the island slopes," wrote Rousseau, "and sat down happily on the shore of the lake. There the sound of the waves and the moving water, fixing my attention and driving all agitation from my spirit, plunged it into a delightful revery in which night often surprised me without my noticing it. The ebb and flow of the water, its continuous noise, swelling louder at intervals, ceaselessly striking my ear and my eyes, took the place of the inner movements effaced by the revery and sufficed to make me feel my existence with pleasure, but without the trouble of thought. From time to time there came a feeble and brief reflection on the instability of the things of this world represented by the image of the water's surface, but soon these slight impressions disappeared in the uniformity of the continuous movement by which I was lulled and which, without any active participation of my mind, did not fail to attract me until, summoned by the lateness of the hour and by the signal agreed upon, I could not tear myself away without effort."

"I have always passionately loved the water," said Rousseau in the *Confessions*, "and the sight of it casts me into a delightful revery." Such was his mood of complete fusion with nature, whether he was stretched out flat in his boat drifting idly with the lake currents, his eyes lost in the blue immensity of the sky, or seated on the banks as the waves dashed against the shore, or perhaps beside a brook murmuring softly over its stony bed.

Thought, the concentrated thought which had produced his great books, had always been a painful effort, never a pleasure, Rousseau tells us in the *Seventh Walk*, but unguided revery never failed to bring him relaxation and delight. The eyes themselves found recreation in the forms about him. Colors, agreeable odors even, captured his senses. Jean-Jacques, too, was a man "for whom the external world exists." Even his ideas, he writes, were "no longer more than sensations."

The ninth chapter adds one more fruitless effort to apologize for the tragic abandonment of his children, proving once again how painfully remorse for this irretrievable mistake still gnawed at his vitals.

Finally, in the *Tenth Walk,* we find ourselves with Rousseau on Palm Sunday, April 12, 1778, a full fifty years from his first dramatic meeting with Madame de Warens in Annecy after the boy's impulsive flight from Geneva at the age of sixteen.

This meeting was a decisive turn in his life. Madame de Warens, at twenty-eight, had been attracted by his lively, intelligent, sensitive face. Of his sixty-six years of experience, the few passed with this strange "mother," idealized in retrospect, now seemed the best, the only years, in which he had truly lived. He it was who persuaded her to settle for the summer at Les Charmettes in the country near Chambéry. There he had strengthened his growing taste for solitude.

"I did only what I wished to do," wrote Rousseau. "All my time was filled with affection or with the activities of the country. I wanted nothing but the continuation of so pleasant a state. My only grief was the fear that it might not last for long, and this fear, springing from the financial uncertainty of our situation, was not without foundation. From that moment, I thought of giving myself at the same time some diversions against this uneasiness and some resources to ward it off. I thought that the development of my talents was the surest protection against poverty, and I resolved to use my leisure, if possible, to render back some day to the best of women the assistance which I had received from her...."

The sentence trailed off into nothingness. Rousseau never finished his tenth chapter which he had barely more than begun. The manuscript remains only a rough draft. His reveries and his literary life concluded in a paean of gratitude to Madame de Warens who, with all her grave faults, had rescued him from sordid vagabondage, given him for some years a home, put into his hand books, and drawn him up out of ignorance into a life of thought and gradually increasing knowledge of himself. The first faint stirrings of Jean-Jacques's genius go back clearly to Les Charmettes. Rousseau was not wrong in remembering it so, even if with some exaggeration, as he looked back longingly over the troubled years. We are permitted to doubt whether, without Madame de Warens, Jean-Jacques would ever have succeeded in escaping from obscurity.

4

A little later, in the spring of 1778, Rousseau hesitatingly accepted an invitation from the Marquis de Girardin. Leaving his two-room apartment on the Rue Plâtrière, a prolongation of the already-familiar Rue de Grenelle-Saint-Honoré where he had formerly dwelt, Jean-Jacques established himself in a pavillion of the château at Ermenonville, a little village some thirty miles northeast of Paris. Here there was a beautiful "English garden" with its famous "Island of Poplars." Accompanied by one of the sons of the Marquis or by the local *curé,* Rousseau threw himself eagerly into botanizing tramps under the fir-trees and among the bushes of this delightful country. His habitually nervous movements were temporarily calmed by exercise. At peace with the world, he unbent and entertained the children with amusing stories, or, a "Freshwater Admiral," occupied his leisure by rowing his boat on the lake. There were evenings, too, around the piano at the château when the great man sang, in his now cracked voice, Desdemona's mournful ballad of the willow-tree, which he had recently set to music from the words of Letourneur's translation of *Othello.* His expressive eyes and the lingering traces of his Genevan accent still caught the attention of contemporaries. This charming sojourn was broken for a moment by the sudden news of Voltaire's death at Paris on the 30th of May. In spite of their nearly twenty years of enmity, Rousseau could not view without emotion the passing of his famous rival.

On July 2nd, Jean-Jacques rose, as usual, with the sun, at about five o'clock, and departed for a two-hour walk. At seven, he was back for his cup of coffee with milk. Suddenly, he became ill and dragged himself with difficulty to his bed. Later, trying to get up, he fell to the floor, was raised like a dead weight by Thérèse and the neighbors, and died of a stroke at about eleven o'clock in the morning. The final weeks had been the happiest for many years and he had carried on his regular daily activities to the last. He was buried two days later at eleven in the evening in the midst of his beloved poplars on the island of Ermenonville. On the 20th of Vendémiaire during the 3rd year of the Revolutionary Republic (October 11, 1794), little more than two months after the fall of Robespierre, Rousseau's body was transferred to the Pantheon in Paris, there to be reconciled in death with Voltaire as he had not been in life.

It was a fitting recognition of the powerful influence of these two men on the Revolution which both had in some measure foreseen, yet which neither would have desired in its actual tragic form. Although eighteen years separated them in age, they had died almost within a month of each other in the same year, 1778.

5

There is even today bitter controversy over Rousseau's life and work. This is proof that his ideas live among us. We are far from having solved the crucial problem of moral progress, so vital if we are to survive the threatening achievements of modern science. The issue of economic, social, and racial inequality continues to divide the world. In the midst of constantly increasing speed and the complexities of the machine age, man struggles to find a simpler, more wholesome "life of nature." How to educate the child for greater happiness and self-control remains a largely unrealized ideal. The "social contract," the conflict between individual democracy and increasing regulation by the state, presents a greater and more pressing problem than ever. The *Confessions* and the *Reveries* invite the reader to a deeper exploration of the inner man beneath the froth of surface life. Outdoor nature beckons to a clearer vision of form, color, and sense impression. At the same time, the country may offer quiet peace and relaxation after the city's strident noise and tension. Rousseau, in a host of ways, still speaks to us with a modern voice.

CHAPTER XVIII

DIDEROT THE MAN

I

IT WAS A HOT PERSPIRING CLIMB IN SUMMER UP THE LONG STEEP hill into Langres. Even stagecoach passengers during the eighteenth century had to clamber down from the lumbering vehicle and ease the burden on the puffing horses by making their slow ascent along the circuitous road afoot. The ancient town, situated in the famous province of Champagne, about a hundred and sixty miles southeast of Paris, stands out on the summit of a high plateau which juts up sharply more than fifteen hundred feet above the pleasant valley of the Marne.

There, in the heart of the old walled city, Denis Diderot was born on October 5, 1713, a little more than a year and three months after Rousseau. In spite of a self-confident inscription in gold letters on the marble plaque at Number 6 of what was formerly the Place Chambeau, the house of Diderot's birth has not been positively identified. Only when the child was three or four years old did his family move to the site now indicated.

The boy was of lower middle-class origin, the son of a prosperous maker of that fine cutlery for which Langres had already become distinguished. Today his statue by Bartholdi, creator of the great figure of Liberty in New York harbor, looks down with lively interest upon the little square, which, located near the town's central Cathedral, has rightly come to be named after Diderot.

From the lofty ramparts surrounding this once impregnable city, the view is magnificent out over the broad expanse of fertile plain below. On a perfectly clear day, even the thin white line of Mont Blanc can be picked up faintly on the distant horizon, another one hundred and sixty miles away to the southeast beyond Lake Geneva in Switzerland. The winter winds blow cold over the exposed hill on which Langres is strategically seated; angry storms lie constantly in wait; the weather in all seasons shifts with astonishing suddenness; and the inhabitants themselves, according to Diderot, embroidering on a favorite idea of Montesquieu, are as mercurial as their capricious climate.

"The head of a native of Langres," wrote Diderot later, "is perched on his shoulders like a weather vane on top of a church steeple." He then added: "As for myself, I am characteristic of my country; only residence in the capital and constant application have corrected me a little." Within a single day, he says, criticizing his portrait by the painter, Michel van Loo, "I was calm, sad, reflective, tender, violent, passionate, enthusiastic." His wide forehead, bold nose, flashing eyes, and rapidly changing expression set a difficult task for any artist seeking to catch these mobile features in lifelike fashion on canvas.

A younger contemporary, Garat, offers a vivid, firsthand picture of a typical monologue by Diderot. As he made off with what passed for a two-man conversation, his eyes became far away and absorbed in his own thoughts, his gestures grew ever more frequent and animated, his words turned sad or gay according to the subject. At times, he even enthusiastically acted out a scene from a play or sang the lines of an impromptu song. Eager, talkative, encyclopedic in knowledge and varied interests; visionary often; almost equally ready to discuss the pro or con of any topic; not by nature always persistent in pushing a book to finished perfection, but an extraordinary improviser, gifted with a spontaneity and originality of genius well-nigh unique; with no lack, on the other hand, of dogged determination, industry, and of a certain bourgeois practicality inherited no doubt from his hard-working father—such a complex figure, in sum, was Denis Diderot.

The first thirty years of his life as boy and man remain obscure. He never wrote down the detailed story as did his later comrade, Jean-Jacques Rousseau, in his celebrated *Confessions*. A few bare facts, some more or less unproved anecdotes, and many surmises, based on scattered hints here and there, are all that we can salvage from the darkness today.

Diderot attended the Jesuit college of Langres. He was a brilliant student and made his father proud with the numerous prizes he brought home in composition, memory, and poetry. But the boy, as his daughter, Madame de Vandeul, wrote later, was often careless, inaccurate, and impulsive also, and at times much more interested in hunting small game out in the neighboring fields than in continuing to hitch about on a dull bench in class. What more normal and human! The frequent admonitions of the good priests, his teachers, justified though they doubtless were, irked his independent spirit. One day, in revolt, he told his father he wanted to quit school.

"So you would like to be a cutler?" asked the elder Diderot, proposing at once a practical alternative.

"With all my heart."

"Tying a worker's apron around his waist, the boy set himself to the task beside his experienced father, but botched every knife he tried to make. It was obviously a more difficult trade than he had thought, and one not to be learned in a hurry. Four or five days were enough to open his eyes. Quickly disgusted with the monotony of work in the shop, the youth went shame-facedly back to his attic room at home, picked up his abandoned books again from the table, and returned to the Jesuit college. Life had taught him a first lesson.

"I'd rather be impatient than bored," he admitted frankly to his father, and from then on was content to pursue his studies without interruption. This anecdote narrated by Madame de Vandeul sounds essentially true. In any event, Diderot found he had no taste for being a manual laborer, even a skilled one like his respected father, but he grew in time to perceive the interest of the artisan's complicated processes and described them with painstaking exactness in his great *Encyclopedia*.

In 1726, as he was approaching thirteen, Diderot took the tonsure and indeed, for some two years, wore the gown of a secular abbé. The pious family had long eyed the priesthood as a promising career for their brilliant son. Momentarily, he is said to have been quite narrowly religious; for four or five months, he even fasted, tormented himself with a haircloth shirt, and slept austerely on straw. But the mood quickly passed, never to return. Soon, encouraged by his Jesuit teachers and with the consent finally, if not the enthusiasm of his father, Diderot was off for more advanced study in Paris. Henceforth, except for a few brief journeys, he had left the quiet life of the provinces behind forever.

There is some dispute still as to whether, in Paris, he entered the famous Jesuit College of Louis-le-Grand, where the witty Voltaire had completed his schooling fifteen years before, or the College of Harcourt, or perhaps indeed both, one after the other. A later admiring reference by Diderot to Father Porée's inspired teaching of literature and particularly of Racine seems to point toward Louis-le-Grand. In any case, the boy gained an excellent knowledge of Latin and Greek, a keen appreciation of the ancient classics, a thorough training in the formal arts of rhetoric, and much valuable practice in writing. He was not forced painfully to teach himself the rudiments like Rousseau. But Diderot was too earnestly interested in learning to rely on class work alone. "For several years in succession," he commented later, "I was as religious about reading a canto of Homer before going to bed as is a good priest in reciting his breviary. I was early suckled on the milk of Homer, Vergil, Horace, Terence, Anacreon, Plato, and Euripides, along with that of Moses and the Prophets." Theology and the Bible combined in this way with a broad background in the traditional languages.

On September 2, 1732, Diderot received the degree of Master of Arts in philosophy. He was still only nineteen, but this was not necessarily a precocious age for a bright boy of his stamp, considering the limited curriculum and the hard study required at the time.

For some two years in the office of Clément de Ris, a compatriot from Langres, Diderot, at his father's behest, unwillingly read law and observed the practice of what were for him only the dull forms of legal procedure. The experience was even less successful in his case than it had been with Voltaire earlier. Every minute which Diderot could snatch from his imposed duties, he poured into further study of Latin, Greek, and mathematics. He even, according to Madame de Vandeul, already began to learn the modern languages, Italian and English.

This was all very well from the young man's point of view, eager to broaden and fortify his learning, but the conscientious Clément de Ris felt obligated to inform Diderot's unhappy father of "the bad use his son was making of his time." The good cutler, with a parent's natural preference for what seemed practicality, hoped to see his wayward boy establish himself in a profession where he could be reasonably sure of earning a living. What had been the purpose of all these years of expensive study? Should Diderot become a doctor, a pleader of civil cases, or a criminal lawyer? The son replied facetiously that he had no desire to kill anyone as a doctor; that it was hard to remain scrupulous in civil practice; and that, as for being a criminal lawyer, he did not wish to spend his entire life minding other people's business.

"What do you want to do, then?" asked the much-tried Clément de Ris.

"By my faith! nothing, nothing at all! I like to study; I am very happy, very well satisfied as I am; I ask for nothing better!"

It was a rude awakening for the industrious father, well-meaning, but of narrow experience and outlook. To have this self-willed youngster on his hands was indeed exasperating, after all the money he had spent to keep him studying in Paris! He called upon his son to choose some sort of a profession forthwith or to return that very week to the parental roof at Langres. Diderot refused to do either and the father sternly withdrew his allowance.

We can perhaps today muster a certain sympathy for the unfortunate elder Diderot, as well as for his independent son. Both were right, in their view of things, at the time. The father was looking prudently ahead toward the hard months and years when money would certainly be needed, the brash boy at the necessity of doing no violence to his own richly endowed nature. If this impudent good-for-nothing was in the end to become a genius, who in the early 1730s could foresee so unexpected an outcome? Besides, geniuses are rarely easy to get along with in actuality, interesting as they may appear to posterity in retrospect. Sensitive, recalcitrant, insistent on leaving the clear beaten track for their own uncharted way, they generally make the early years stormy for themselves and those around them. At any rate, the father angrily vowed to let the young man sow his wild oats alone and go to the dogs without financial encouragement from his parents. It was a promise he could not, however, entirely keep when his son recklessly piled up debts which the old cutler was too honest to disown. The story runs, too, that his mother, quite naturally of a softer heart toward her prodigal son than his father, three times dispatched a woman servant on the long trek from Langres to Paris with a few urgently needed gold pieces to which the messenger silently added all of her own meager savings.

2

If the preceding period in Diderot's life is obscure, the next ten years from 1732 to 1742 are almost a complete blank. Only a few anecdotes by Madame de Vandeul and occasional vague hints in his later writings offer us glimpses of a desperately poor and even Bohemian existence. It was far from the gaily romanticized "vie de Bohême" of novel and opera. Not infrequently real hunger dogged his footsteps.

Did Diderot borrow lightheartedly at every opportunity from such family acquaintances as happened to journey up to Paris from Langres? Did he merrily trick a Carmelite monk, Brother Ange, out of a full two thousand francs which the elder Diderot, in his firm bourgeois integrity, felt grudgingly constrained to pay? Did the young man pretend a fervent wish to enter a Carthusian monastery as a novice and perhaps go away with a square meal thanks to the indulgent kindness of the superior? Did he turn his skillful pen to writing six sermons for a missionary to the Portuguese colonies and receive the almost incredible stipend of three hundred crowns, which, for an all-too-brief time, jingled happily in his pocket? Such are the stories of Madame de Vandeul or other contemporaries. "The voice of conscience is feeble indeed when the guts cry out from emptiness!" he exclaimed years afterward with a rough realism springing directly out of bitter experience.

Did Diderot himself, like the strange figure of Rameau's nephew whom he portrayed so vividly later, wake up some mornings with actual wisps of straw clinging to his hair from the stable where he had been reduced to stretching out on the floor with the horses? Did he at times have to pass the night in good weather outdoors under the stars in Cours-la-Reine park near the Seine? No doubt he was glad enough, when days were wet, to find a little less of the damp chill, as well as abundant books for study, in the great crowded hall of the famous Royal Library on the busy Rue de Richelieu. In any case, the description of the meditative student in the Alley of Sighs of the Luxembourg Gardens, with his long gray-plush coat, ripped out at the seams and slit at the cuff, but worn of necessity summer and winter, and the black wool stockings mended awkwardly in back with white thread, sounds like an authentic personal memory.

At times, Diderot tutored mathematics or other subjects. He was obviously far better prepared for teaching than the painfully self-educated Rousseau, but the brilliant Denis soon grew impatient at daily contact with boys too often stupid or lazy. After a few days of good food and warm lodging, he was ready enough to throw over these luxuries for the uncertain freedom of the open street, his bare room under the eaves, or a bench in the park of the Palais-Royal.

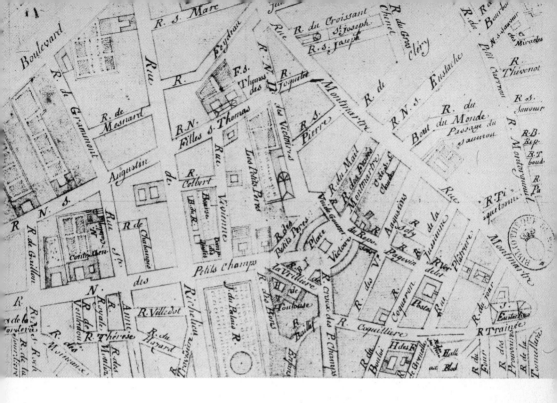

PARIS

Map of central Paris in the 18th century showing streets where Rousseau lived in 1749 and during his last years. See pages 230, 247, and 275.

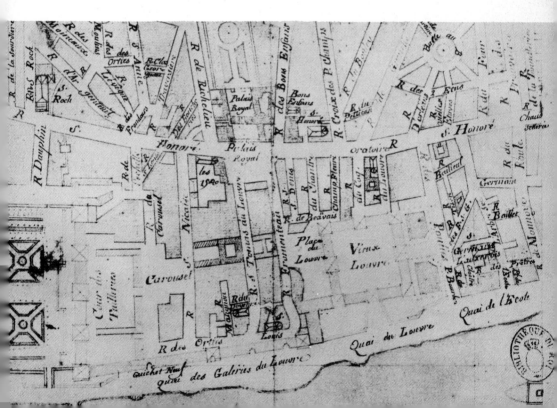

JEAN-JACQUES ROUSSEAU

Portrait by La Tour (1753). See page 324.

DISCOURS

QUI A REMPORTE' LE PRIX

A L'ACADEMIE

DE DIJON.

En l'année 1750.

Sur cette Question proposée par la même Académie :

*Si le rétablissement des Sciences & des Arts a
contribué à épurer les mœurs.*

PAR UN CITOYEN DE GENÈVE.

Barbarus hic ego sum quia non intelligor illis. Ovid.

A GENEVE,

Chez **BARILLOT** & fils.

TITLE PAGE

ROUSSEAU
IN OLD AGE

Bust by Houdon (1778)

ISLAND OF
POPLARS

Where Rousseau was
buried at Ermenon-
ville in 1778.

Once he managed to stick it out for three whole months in the wealthy household of a certain Randon de Boisset. Finally, weary of putting the youngsters to bed at night, getting them up in the morning, and occupying their waking hours during the day, he made up his mind to quit.

"What are you dissatisfied with, Monsieur Diderot? Is your salary too low? I will double it. Is your room uncomfortable? Choose another. Is the food bad? Order any dinner you wish. I'll go to any expense to keep you," offered the prosperous tax-farmer eagerly.

"Monsieur, look at me," replied the young man. "A lemon is not as yellow as my face. I am making men out of your boys, but each day I grow more of a child along with them. I am a thousand times too rich and well cared-for in your house, but I must leave. My object is not to get along better, but just to keep on living."

Such is the vivid story of Diderot's daughter, Madame de Vandeul. It sounds true enough. In any case, mere money would never mean more to him than his basic aims in life.

But there must have been gay moments, too, with other lively young rascals like himself, hopeful writers, musicians, and artists, or the future wife of the painter Greuze, Mademoiselle Babuti, and other bright-eyed girls, with whom he exchanged bold quips as he ranged about the bookstores and small shops of the busy quarter. There were joyous repasts and heady wine in the crowded taverns on days when someone of the party was in funds. Six cents would buy quite a meal in those far-off times, but even six cents was too often lacking! So there were hours of gloom when the stomach seemed to scrape against the backbone and all was gnawing emptiness between. Once he stumbled home so faint that his landlady, in pity, brought out for him some dry toast and wine, while he fell limply into bed in the effort to gain back a little strength.

"On that day," Diderot told his daughter later, "I swore to myself that, if ever I came to possess anything, I would not refuse a poor man help, nor condemn one of my fellows to go through as painful a day as I had suffered." More remarkable is the fact that the vow was actually kept during the more prosperous years of later life.

At such hours of despondency, it would have taken little to drive the young man back in complete hopelessness to Langres or to have set him down again before the dull tomes in the lawyer's office.

Yet there were delightful hours, also, when he could listen with all his ears to the quick repartee and the flashing exchange of literary discussion in the famous Café de Procope opposite the old Comédie-Française on the Left Bank near the modern Odéon theater or Salle du Luxembourg, as it has been recently called. Was Diderot pressing forward from the background to hear the mordant sallies of the already distinguished Monsieur de Voltaire before the latter's hurried departure from Paris in the spring of 1734? We can be sure he was if the opportunity ever came. On other days, the young man was off no doubt to the Café de la Régence on the Right Bank across the Seine near the Palais-Royal to watch Légal play chess, "to push the wood around," as Diderot later facetiously described the game. It was still too early to witness the brilliant moves of the great Philidor.

The publication of Voltaire's *Philosophical Letters* about the end of April, 1734, constituted a literary event of the first water. Their wit, irony, and sharp criticism must at once have aroused the admiration of so omnivorous a reader as Diderot. The little book was certainly a powerful new stimulus to earnest study of the English language and nation, a strong influence toward undermining, in his thought, the existing political, scientific, and religious philosophy of the Old Régime.

Then there was the theater, which drew Diderot like a magnet. While reading the great classic tragedies of Corneille, he gave himself an effective literary exercise. Closing the book suddenly in the midst of a striking scene, he would seek out a suitable reply for the next speaker, but was generally astonished, as he freely admits, to discover how much more logical and vigorous were Corneille's words than the best he could devise himself. Eager as he was, Diderot was never destined to manifest a true dramatic genius, though he undoubtedly quickened his appreciation and understanding of drama by these impromptu efforts.

Or, perched high up in the top balcony, witnessing the masterpieces of the French repertory which he already knew nearly by heart, he would stuff his fingers in his ears in order to concentrate on the facial expression and gestures, only taking his hands away when the movements of the actors on the stage far below seemed out of harmony with the remembered words. What matter that his neighbors looked with surprise at this madman, paying out his good money for a ticket not to hear! Unconsciously, Diderot was even then gathering material for his original observations on pantomime years later.

The young man was enraptured with Mademoiselle Gaussin, with Mademoiselle Dangeville, celebrated actresses of the day. What would he not have done to win their favor? For long hours, even during the bleak days of winter, he haunted the solitary walks of the Luxembourg Gardens declaiming aloud the famous roles of Molière's lively comedies or the sonorous tragedies of Corneille. He even hesitated briefly, he says, between a career as an orator at the then theologically-minded Sorbonne and the glamorous profession of an actor at the Comédie-Française! Needless to say, such public applause was never to be his lot. His real vocation was elsewhere, and the youthful whim passed quickly.

What "a fury for study" Diderot experienced in these days, as he later recalled! Whatever may have been his wild escapades and grievous compromises with conscience, his gay ramblings over the enchanted scene of Paris, his eager listening to the great and the near-great, the whole picture must be completed by ten full years of sober and undramatic reading of everything he could get his hands on—books in the many rich libraries of the capital, books in the shops when he had a few *sous* to spare, books which he could borrow from friends, books received in payment for occasional private tutoring, good books, bad books, old books, new books—so much that the printed word contained of knowledge, of inspiration, of wisdom in the difficult art of life! It is unfortunate that Diderot never gave us, like Rousseau, the detailed story of these formative years. From them came the extraordinary intellectual background of the great Encyclopedist who, in his day, was also to be called the "Philosopher," *par excellence.*

In 1742 Diderot was introduced one day to another young man, poor, but ambitious like himself. This young man, Jean-Jacques Rousseau, after his vagabond years in Italy, in Savoy, and in France, had at last drifted hopefully back to Paris to seek his fortune in the hurrying metropolis which sometimes made, but more often broke, men's reputations. Both were deeply interested in music. In fact, Rousseau had in his pocket a new system of musical notation which, in the end, was to please nobody but himself. Soon, however, he would be on his way to some success as a minor composer. Diderot, on his part, was already curious about many aspects of musical theory. Both men were captivated also by the complex intellectual warfare of chess and, for hours, watched intently each deliberate move of the expert players whose varied games they could follow in the crowded cafés. Jean-Jacques even dreamed of achieving an elusive fame himself by becoming a master, but, study as he would books on gambits and checkmates, he was able to beat only his comrade, the careless and impulsive Diderot. Really skilled antagonists were always too much for Rousseau's poor memory and fatal lack of composure.

Yet what a happy foil the timid, self-educated Jean-Jacques must have been in other ways for the confident, expansive, widely-read student who for ten long years had been piling up knowledge on the firm foundation laid by his Jesuit teachers! For nearly fourteen more years, the two were to be the closest of friends after Rousseau's disillusioned return in 1744 from his post as secretary to the French ambassador at Venice. Undoubtedly, the Genevan needed no effort to draw his Paris companion into enthusiastic monologues which made an important contribution to the former's own intellectual training. But Jean-Jacques had a capacity for stubborn resistance, too, and was by no means inclined to accept without question all of Diderot's bold paradoxes. How often Rousseau's hesitant doubts must have launched the other on an alluring train of thought which might not otherwise have occurred to him!

It was on November 6, 1743, while Jean-Jacques was still in Venice, that Diderot married. The step proved, under the circumstances, unfortunate for his happiness. Antoinette Champion was poor, like the Bohemian student who had attracted her. Moreover, she soon unleashed a shrewish temper, which turned the beginning household into anything but a haven of peace and understanding. This accords with Rousseau's testimony, amply confirmed by days and weeks of implacable domestic silence to which Diderot admittedly was later driven. She was not acceptable, moreover, to the solemn father at Langres, who considered this little seamstress with no dowry and no talents a very bad match for his gifted son. In so reasonable an opinion, the elderly father was undoubtedly right, but Diderot, for the moment, was in no mood to be guided by reason. The new Madame Diderot, besides, was devout, in her narrow and formal manner, while he, for his part, was rapidly becoming more and more of a complete free-thinker. To cap the basic discord, the young husband, so changeable by disposition and impulse, was not likely to be drawn away from other loves, Madame de Puisieux or Madame de Prémontval, by the loud-voiced vixen at home. It was obviously a couple whom a careless fate should never have condemned to be together. The unfortunate Nanette offered in sum, no greater comprehension of Diderot's ideas and complex inner life than did Rousseau's Thérèse of him, while she provoked no doubt more open warfare.

With the reading knowledge of English which he had acquired by hard study over the years, Diderot put into French Temple Stanyan's *History of Greece*. It was mere hack work of course, but there was now a double necessity of earning money to support himself and his wife. The old Bohemian existence could no longer suffice. By the following August, there came a baby daughter, soon to be snatched away by the high infant mortality of the time. Next, with two associates, he plunged energetically into the dull labor of translating the six volumes of Robert James's *Medicinal Dictionary*. The task later served the purpose of providing a broad basis for Diderot's developing interest in biology and science. Before completing this big reference compilation during the following three years, he turned to the pleasanter enterprise of rendering into French Shaftesbury's *Essay on Merit and Virtue* which appeared at Amsterdam in 1745. By this industrious series of translations, Diderot was already becoming known to the publishers. At the same time, he was embarking on his career as a philosophical thinker.

3

In the middle of 1746, Diderot published a little book called *Philosophical Thoughts*. It appeared under the imprint of The Hague. The title, perhaps in part reminiscent of Voltaire's ironic *Philosophical Letters* twelve years before, was in itself an invitation to heterodoxy, though the two works were very different in subject and form. Basically, Diderot set himself in opposition to the austerely religious *Thoughts* of the seventeenth-century Jansenist, Pascal, whose cogent style still presented a sharp challenge to his adversaries. An assiduous reader of Bayle at this time, Diderot remained for the moment ostensibly a deist, but cried to the devout: "Enlarge your concept of God." The author had been well advised, however, in bringing out his book anonymously, for the Parlement of Paris, on July 7th, condemned it to be burned. It is amusing to reflect that in such ceremonies only waste paper was generally consigned to the flames by an easy-going government while the executioner went happily away with a rare copy of a prohibited book in his hands! The *Philosophical Thoughts* no doubt only gained in popularity from such free advertising.

While chiefly occupied during these busy years with the great *Encyclopedia,* Diderot still found time for work of a more personal nature. On June 9, 1749, he brought out a new book entitled, *Letter on the Blind for the Use of Those who See.* In piquant, if somewhat rambling form, it questioned the validity for the blind, and even by inference for others also, of the eighteenth-century's favorite argument for the existence of God, the marvelous order of the universe, the so-called "argument from design." But what of the deformed organisms, the "monsters," which seem not to fit into any over-all scheme? What of the "survival of the fittest" and the disappearance of the "unfit" by evolution through "natural selection"? Such questions had wide connotations for later thinking.

Here was a new application of Locke's widely-accepted theory of sense impressions as the sole source of knowledge. There were also interesting and forward-looking suggestions about the psychology of the blind and on methods to be used in their education, published long before the development of the celebrated Braille system. Diderot's lively curiosity readily leaped over barriers which were impassible to mere routine thinkers.

Diderot had, among other things, been eager to witness and evaluate the first chaotic impressions of a blind woman, seeing the world after an operation for cataract. When the scientist Réaumur chose, rather, to grant this privilege to a feminine friend, Diderot was angry. According to his daughter, Madame de Vandeul, he vented his disappointment in an ironical reference to the preference thus accorded to the "two beautiful, but unimportant eyes" of Madame de Saint-Maur instead of to those of "people worthy of judging the matter," as he put it. The comment naturally rankled.

Now, for some years, Diderot's parish priest had been besieging the police with bitter complaints about the philosopher's pugnacious skepticism. The anonymous publication of the *Letter on the Blind,* the association of the writer's name with the *Philosophical Thoughts,* as with several other printed or manuscript works of an unorthodox nature, and perhaps in the end this over-bold thrust at Madame de Saint-Maur, a lady of rank and influence with the authorities—all these were more than sufficient to endanger Diderot's liberty in the arbitrary eighteenth century. Moreover, it was a time of special nervousness on the part of the government, fearful of sedition and unduly sensitive to mockery of the unpopular terms agreed to in the peace of Aix-la-Chapelle the year before.

"They have arrested in recent days," wrote the Marquis d'Argenson, "a great number of abbés, scholars, and writers, and taken them to the Bastille, such as the man Diderot, several professors from the University, doctors from the Sorbonne, etc."

A "lettre de cachet," written at Compiègne on the 23rd of July and signed with the usual royal flourish, "Louis," was therefore addressed to the Governor of Vincennes, the Marquis du Châtelet. It read as follows:

"I write you this letter for the purpose of telling you to receive in my château of Vincennes the man Diderot and to hold him there until a further order from me. Whereupon I pray God, Monsieur le Marquis du Châtelet, to keep you in his holy care."

Under the forms of absolute government, it was unnecessary to give reasons or to indicate any definite term of imprisonment.

Diderot was thus caught up in a kind of dragnet of repression. In his plain little apartment two flights up at Madame Chatel's in the short, but crowded Rue de la Vieille Estrapade, there was a loud banging on the door one morning at half past seven. It was the 24th of July, 1749. As the door opened, in came a police officer named Rochebrune, accompanied by a certain D'Hémery and two others. After a thorough search of the apartment, they found only twenty-one pasteboard boxes of manuscripts dealing with the *Encyclopedia*, other similar papers on the author's big work-table, and two or three unbound copies of the *Letter on the Blind*. Nothing else incriminating. Madame Diderot either knew nothing or refused to talk. The officer drew forth an order for her husband's arrest, hustled him quickly into a cab, and drove off, not to the neighboring Bastille, already over-crowded, but to Vincennes, six miles east from the center of Paris.

As they approached their destination, the towering Dungeon loomed ahead ominously. There, up the winding stone staircase in the thick walls, Diderot trudged with sinking heart to solitary confinement on the third floor. True, it was better than being in the dampness underground. But it was unusually hot that summer, the narrow slits of windows admitted all-too-little air, and, without books, pen, paper, or companionship, this talkative, enthusiastic, friendly individual, though not physically mistreated, soon found the long days heavy on his hands.

One afternoon a week later, Diderot was officially interrogated. Rashly, he denied authorship of the *Philosophical Thoughts,* the *Letter on the Blind,* and everything else charged. The police knew better after taking also the testimony of a bookdealer. "He'll have to talk," they said of the unhappy prisoner.

Rousseau speaks later of Diderot's "black humor" at this time. The latter, in pleading letters to the authorities, laments the pain in his legs from lack of exercise, mentions his depair, and begs for books and the use of a larger room adjoining. Who knew when he would be released? The "lettre de cachet" was purely arbitrary and always indefinite. A man might remain a prisoner for years awaiting the King's "good pleasure," which sometimes never came through sheer forgetfulness. Rousseau, indeed, wrote a wild letter to the King's mistress, Madame de Pompadour, urging his friend's release or his own incarceration with him. There was naturally no reply. Voltaire prevailed on Madame du Châtelet to intercede with her kinsman, the Governor of Vincennes, apparently to no avail. What did count, however, were the loud outcries of the publishers, threatened with complete loss of the 80,000 livres already invested in the *Encyclopedia* and perhaps of a large slice of the 250,000 which they expected ultimately to spend.

Gradually, Diderot's early confidence began to be worn down by confinement. Realizing at length that he would have to eat humble pie, he signed an admission of most of what had been alleged, and gained permission, after four weeks in the solitude of the Dungeon, to occupy pleasanter quarters in the neighboring château with freedom to receive friends and to take exercise in the unwalled park on his word not to escape.

On August 25th or thereabouts, Rousseau hurried out to visit his friend and found D'Alembert, co-editor of the *Encyclopedia,* already with him. The work could now theoretically go on, but under great difficulties because of the distance from the publishers and contributors in Paris. There was at the time no communication between the two places except afoot or by expensive cab. The big libraries also were far from Vincennes. It was in early October, on one of Rousseau's frequent trips to the château, that Diderot encouraged him to compete for the Dijon prize and write the *Discourse on the Sciences and the Arts,* which made Jean-Jacques famous.

Not until November 3rd, after more than three months of imprisonment, was Diderot finally released. He, too, like Voltaire before him, had experienced at first hand the arbitrary character of the Old Régime. The bitter lesson was no doubt an important factor in leading him to withhold from publication during his lifetime the most original and dangerous of his later works.

Two months before Diderot's departure from Vincennes, his worried father replied from Langres to two letters from the unhappy prisoner. The father still remained without positive information as to his son's marriage and the birth meantime of two children. He ironically expressed astonishment at a request for money from a man engaged in such great literary enterprises and provided with "an honorable subsistance" through the kindness of His Majesty, even though it was at Vincennes! The governmental allowance was indeed four livres a day, but of course gave nothing for his family. Nevertheless, the father yielded slightly in the end and did send a draft for 150 livres. He also invited his son to "make a better use," than in the past, of the paper, pens, and ink which had finally been allowed him in the prison.

At length, during the first half of November, 1750, the *Prospectus* of the *Encyclopedia,* drawn up by Diderot, appeared, describing the general plan and announcing the terms of subscription. Soon there were as many as two thousand subscribers, with more later. In the last days of June, 1751, the first huge folio volume was put on sale, accompanied by an able *Preliminary Discourse* written by the co-editor, D'Alembert. After more than five years of difficulties and obstacles, the prodigious enterprise had been launched. Diderot's public career was now begun. At thirty-eight, he was in the full flower of energy and dawning maturity.

CHAPTER XIX

DIDEROT AND THE
ENCYCLOPEDIA

I

As early as 1728, a certain Ephraim Chambers, an English Quaker, had published in London two folio volumes, entitled, *A Cyclopedia, or Universal Dictionary of the Arts and Sciences*. The idea was excellent, but, like Bayle's famous *Historical and Critical Dictionary* over thirty years before, it was entirely the work of one man and consequently, in execution, left much to be desired. No single author could possibly suffice for so great an undertaking. Nevertheless, in spite of its shortcomings and high price of four pounds, Chambers's *Cyclopedia* proved extremely popular and went through five editions in eighteen years. Though not without numerous predecessors of a sort, it forecast a long series of modern reference volumes in various countries and languages.

On the Continent, there was a Scotchman, an ardent disciple and biographer of Fénelon known in France as the Chevalier de Ramsay. It is interesting to note that on March 21, 1737, Ramsay, who had become Grand Orator of the growing order of Free Masons, called upon "all scholars and artists of the fraternity" throughout Europe "to join in gathering materials for a *Universal Dictionary* of the liberal arts and applied sciences, theology and politics alone excepted. Such a work," he said, no doubt thinking of Chambers, "has already been started in England, but, with the united aid of our fellow members, it can be brought to perfection within a few years. We shall explain," he continued, "not only technical words and their etymology, but also the history of each science and art, its general principles and the manner of working at it." This proposal, in almost identical terms, was echoed in 1740 by the Duc d'Antin, first permanent Grand Master of the Order.

The parallel, except for the prudent omission of theology and politics, is indeed close with the broad program soon to be adopted by the French *Encyclopedia,* including the necessity of a grand collaboration between many minds. A direct connection between the two should, however, neither be too readily accepted nor summarily rejected. There appears to be no evidence that the obscure and individualistic Diderot was a member of the Order in these early years or that, like Voltaire and some other distinguished men of letters, he joined later. It has been maintained that Le Breton, chief publisher of the *Encyclopedia,* and Le Breton, an officer of the Masons, are in fact one and the same, though this has recently been denied. On the other hand, the Masons at this time were torn with internal dissensions and did not become a tightly-knit, influential body until after 1773. Most authorities are therefore inclined to minimize the importance of their support in the inception of the great enterprise. The project of such a great reference work was obviously in the air. Nevertheless, the pronouncements of high Masonic leaders may have aided in turning men's minds in this direction and were perhaps not without effect upon the quick inrush of so many expensive subscriptions, essential to the financial success of the huge publishing venture. The work would no doubt ultimately have come into being without urging from the Masons, but it does not seem farfetched to conclude that their interest, known to the spreading membership, was a significant asset to the *Encyclopedia* throughout the long period of its composition and appearance before the public.

One day, early in 1745, an English bank clerk, John Mills, and a German hack writer, Godefroy Sellius, walked into the office of André-François Le Breton in the short Rue Hautefeuille on the Parisian Left Bank in the midst of the publishers' quarter. They are said to have possessed already in manuscript a translation of Chambers's *Cyclopedia* into French. Here was a wished-for opportunity! Whether because of his possible familiarity with the Masonic project as outlined by Ramsay and the Duc d'Antin or simply on account of his sharp business sense, Le Breton quickly seized upon the unexpected offer. On February 25th, he obtained the required royal "privilege"—but in his own name, exclusively. During the following month, a contract was drawn up between the three to unite in the preparation of four volumes of text and one of plates, the fourth edition of Chambers having already doubled in size from the two-volume original. A *Prospectus* announced the coming publication of an *Encyclopedia, or Universal Dictionary of the Arts and Sciences, translated from the English of Ephraim Chambers.* The great enterprise was beginning to take shape.

But Mills soon protested angrily that he and Sellius were being defrauded by Le Breton's privilege which ignored them completely. On July 7th, therefore, the publisher consented to sign an acknowledgment of the translators' rights. Before long, however, there was a violent quarrel with actual blows between the choleric principals, and on August 8th, at the instance of the aged and respected Chancellor d'Aguesseau, the essential privilege was officially withdrawn. Without this rupture between Le Breton, Mills, and Sellius, it has been suggested, the *Encyclopedia* might have remained a mere translation from Chambers!

Thus freed, by hook or by crook, from the unfortunate originators of the project, Le Breton now began to think in bolder terms. He would publish a great ten-volume work. But such a venture required wider financial backing and a sharing of the tremendous risks. Keeping a half-interest for himself, Le Breton divided the rest among three associates, Claude Briasson, Laurent Durand, and Michel-Antoine David, all of them established publishers in Paris. A new privilege was granted on January 21, 1746.

But who was now to do the basic work of furnishing the text? Mills was paid for some translations repurchased after the termination of the first contract and Sellius continued for several months to provide versions of different articles. As early as December of 1745, the distinguished mathematician, D'Alembert, had been called in as an adviser. About the same time, a certain Abbé Gua de Malves was engaged to direct the work. The Abbé had his moments of brilliance as an economist, but he was visionary and lacked the solid persistence needed for such a difficult, long-term enterprise. The hard-working Diderot was already known to the associate publishers, Briasson, Durand, and David, for whom, with two other men, he was sweating out the slow translation of the six-volume *Medicinal Dictionary* by Robert James. Diderot, too, by February of 1746, was enlisted in the larger cause, though still purely in a secondary capacity.

By the end of the year, it was apparent that the unstable Abbé Gua de Malves was not the man to direct the enormous task. Why not this rising young author, Diderot, so full of ideas, enthusiastic, and at the same time tough-fibered with a rare ability to turn out hour after hour of concentrated work? Diderot was sent to win the approval of Chancellor d'Aguesseau who had already manifested a favorable attitude toward Le Breton's undertaking. The Chancellor "was delighted," we are told, "with several flashes of genius which came out in their conversation" and deigned to accept Diderot as general editor with the famous D'Alembert in charge of the mathematical sections. Prudently, however, the pious Chancellor laid plans for naming reliable censors to insure religious and political orthodoxy.

But the scope of the *Encyclopedia* was growing rapidly. Soon it was proposed to extend the text to seventeen volumes. The idea of a mere translation had already been abandoned. The uninspired work of Chambers would be only a point of departure for a bold effort to gather within covers the essential knowledge of an entire age.

"In fact, the aim of an *Encyclopedia*," wrote Diderot at the beginning of his eloquent article under this heading which was finally to appear in 1755, "is to assemble the knowledge scattered over the face of the earth; to explain its general plan to the men with whom we live, and to transmit it to those who will come after us, so that the labors of past centuries may not be useless to future times; so that our descendants, by becoming better informed, may in consequence be happier and more virtuous; and so that we may not die without having deserved well of the human race."

Here, in a few lines, is the whole program of what was to be called the "Age of Enlightenment." Here is the philosopher's confidence in the beneficent effect of expanding knowledge. Here is a hopeful belief in progress through education. "Ye shall know the truth, and the truth shall make you free," might well have been the challenging text of the *Encyclopedia*. If, as Rousseau saw, humanity too often knows the better and follows the worse, this pessimistic warning only proves the slowness of man's rise from the primeval mire. The pursuit of knowledge offers no easy or quick solution to our human problems, yet to abandon it is to extinguish the one torch which shines feebly in the darkness. Of course, it should be clear that not knowledge of fact alone, but wisdom, judgment, and good will are what is needed. Dispute comes from too narrow a definition of "enlightenment." In spite of vast stores of scientific knowledge, constantly increasing, much of humanity still stands on the shore of a mysterious ocean, reluctant to give over prejudice, self-interest, and vicious propaganda in favor of recognized truth. We cannot say that the program of the Enlightenment failed; we can only say that it has hardly yet been tried.

2

During the next years, the enterprise went slowly forward as manuscripts piled up on Diderot's disorderly table or were filed away in numerous cartons. Through the established prestige of D'Alembert, it had been fortunately possible to enlist also the collaboration of those great figures, Montesquieu and Voltaire, though neither was to do extensive work on the huge undertaking. The still obscure Rousseau, closest friend of the chief editor, was invited to write on music. He was the only one to submit his articles within the prescribed deadline of three months, Jean-Jacques tells us in the *Confessions,* but admits that his work was done badly because of the undue haste. Numerous other contributors were gradually secured, notably at length the Chevalier de Jaucourt, who, as an ardent labor of love, gave over his life to the heavy task.

"This man," wrote Diderot to Mademoiselle Volland in 1760, "has spent the last six or seven years in the midst of as many secretaries, reading, dictating, working thirteen or fourteen hours a day, and such an occupation hasn't yet bored him!" Two weeks later the weary editor, eager to be rid at last of his long bondage, exclaimed, half-humorously: "The Chevalier de Jaucourt? Have no fear that he will tire of grinding out articles. God made him for that purpose! I wish you could see how his face lengthens when we announce the end of his work, or rather the necessity of finishing it. He takes on the most disconsolate look!" Truly, the Chevalier de Jaucourt, in quite a different way from the more original Diderot, was created to carry on the journeyman-work of the *Encyclopedia.*

D'Alembert's *Preliminary Discourse* at the head of the first volume in 1751 was a clear call to the expansion of knowledge through Francis Bacon's experimental method. In this *Preliminary Discourse,* there was moreover a friendly thrust at Rousseau, who, in his recent slashing attack on the sciences and the arts, had accused them of adding to the corruption of humanity while at the same time, by his collaboration with the *Encyclopedia,* "the man of merit of whom we are speaking," observed D'Alembert slyly, "seems to have given his support to our work by the zeal and success with which he has contributed to it." Without such increasing knowledge, concluded the co-editor succinctly, "our vices would remain, and we should be ignorant besides!" Yet it would be difficult to prove, he admitted, that man had become better or more virtuous. Discreetly, he avoided the elusive question of wherein lies the source of moral progress or decline.

In the last days of January, 1752, a second folio volume came out. But by February 7th, the rising opposition of the Jesuits and other orthodox critics, long smoldering, burst into open flame. In the name of the King, the printing, reprinting, or sale of the *Encyclopedia* were all sternly forbidden. The enterprise was assailed as tending "to destroy royal authority, establish the spirit of independence and revolt, and, under obscure and equivocal terms, lay a foundation for error, corruption, irreligion, and incredulity." The revolutionary character of the *Encyclopedia* was thus early recognized.

Monsieur de Malesherbes, director of the censorship, though himself favorable to the *Encyclopedia,* was forced to act. Armed with a "lettre de cachet," he sought out Le Breton in order to seize all the manuscripts and illustrative plates already prepared. With a renewed threat of imprisonment hanging over him, Diderot, according to the *Diary* of the lawyer Barbier, seems to have taken time by the forelock and prudently carried his papers to Malesherbes's own mansion. Who could complain, now that everything had been meekly placed in the hands of the government?

Moreover, with two thousand subscribers and a huge investment by the four publishers, the authorities were inclined to bark, but not to bite. It is noteworthy that further publication of the *Encyclopedia* was not specifically forbidden. More definite measures were merely attempted for future censorship. It was an agreement with tongue in cheek, no doubt. Diderot would certainly endeavor to elude orthodoxy to the extent possible.

Henceforth, publication continued at the rate of one volume a year until 1757. Volume V, in 1755, began with D'Alembert's eloquent *Eulogy of Montesquieu* whose death had come in early February about eight months before. Volume VII, in November, 1757, made considerable noise because of a more provocative article by D'Alembert, this time devoted to Geneva.

The co-editor had recently visited the famous Monsieur de Voltaire at Les Délices on the outskirts of the beautiful Swiss city. There he must have met and talked with some of the Protestant pastors and, no doubt with the urging and encouragement of his host, he put into his descriptive article two challenging points which caused furor. On the one hand, he praised the pastors for a deism and anti-trinitarian theology to which they may indeed have given expression at times in the freedom of private conversations with the captivating heretic who so often entertained them at Les Délices. But it was one thing to speculate between four walls; it was very different to express these ideas publicly to their flocks, all unprepared for such bold philosophy. D'Alembert's second point, certainly welcomed with enthusiasm by Voltaire, was the desirability of abandoning old pro-hibitions and establishing a theater in the Calvinist stronghold.

The latter proposal aroused the opposition, not only of the pastors, but of that erst-while friend of the philosophic party, Jean-Jacques Rousseau, now living at Montmorency north of Paris. In an eager fervor of composition, Rousseau dashed off a long *Letter to D'Alem-bert,* attacking on moral grounds the introduction of a theater into Geneva. The stage must now be tolerated at Paris, he held, since it could not at this late date be successfully forbidden, but, at Geneva, such a change would bring in luxury, a low moral tone, and in every way be harmful to the simplicity and pristine innocence of the Spartan city. It is difficult to do justice to Rousseau's argument in a brief summary which too readily makes his position appear ridicu-lous. Most important, from his point of view, was a continuing emphasis upon the issue of morals, already raised so powerfully in the First and Second Discourses. This is the thread which runs through the heart of all his major works. But his adversaries, too, had their troubles in trying glibly to maintain the Aristotelian thesis that "comedy castigates vice with laughter" and that "tragedy purges the passions." It was obviously inaccurate either to defend, or to attack, the theater in such sweeping terms. Rousseau replied cogently in advance: "The stage purges the passions which we don't possess, and foments those we have!" In other words, we refuse to take a moral lesson unless we wish to.

D'Alembert, selected by Malesherbes *pro forma* as censor, gra-ciously approved the publication of Jean-Jacques's *Letter* against him and wrote a polite, if not very trenchant refutation of his former friend's onslaught. In the *Preface* to the *Letter,* Rousseau had added, in veiled words, an allusion to his unhappy break with

Diderot. The encouragement by Jean-Jacques of a continued ban on the theater at Geneva definitely alienated Voltaire. Henceforth, there would be only violent hostility between the two philosophers who, if at opposite poles of thought largely from the beginning, had up to this time remained on terms of at least outward friendship and respect. The *Letter to D'Alembert,* called forth as it was by the latter's article on *Geneva* in the *Encyclopedia,* stands therefore at the crossroads between Rousseau, Voltaire, Diderot, and D'Alembert. From this time on, Jean-Jacques would diverge completely from the others and pursue his solitary way. Although he could not sincerely, in his new-found views, have refrained from opposing the theater, Rousseau, by the moment chosen for his attack, seemed to Diderot and Voltaire a traitor to the philosophic cause. The "brothers" were now divided. Jean-Jacques was only a "false brother" and his apostasy could not be condoned. In the bitter struggle against censorship and established authority, Rousseau had elected to go on alone, half-radical and half-conservative. Hence, in part, the bitterness of the hostility from what had been for a time his own group. Jean-Jacques, in a moment of crisis, appeared to have joined cause with the enemies of the *Encyclopedia.*

3

For the *Encyclopedia* was shortly threatened as it had never been before. A new upsurge of repression was provoked from numerous quarters. The Encyclopedists themselves were ridiculed under the ill-sounding name of "Cacouacs" which suggested frogs croaking hoarsely in a pond! Finally, on the 8th of March, 1759, the King's Council officially revoked the privilege which had been granted the *Encyclopedia* as long ago as 1746. The enterprise was now definitely at a standstill.

For over a year, ever since the bitter criticism provoked in various quarters by his article on Geneva, D'Alembert had been getting increasingly restive. Indeed, already by the end of January, 1758, he recorded his conviction in a letter to Voltaire that the editors must abandon the *Encyclopedia* and complete it at a more favorable time which, he admitted, "will perhaps never come." Finally, he withdrew in discouragement.

Voltaire, for his part, urged with all his customary vigor that the printing be transferred to Lausanne in Switzerland, but Diderot saw at once the impractical nature of such a move. "The project of finishing the work abroad is a will-of-the-wisp," he replied frankly. The *Encyclopedia* could not be prepared far from the numerous collaborators, far from the rich libraries of Paris, far from Le Breton, Briasson, Durand, and David, who had sunk a huge capital in the venture, far, in short, from the now more than 4,000 subscribers upon whom the ultimate fate of the work depended. Indeed, with remarkable loyalty, not one of the latter had demanded return of his money in spite of the government's injunction to that effect. Moreover, Diderot insisted that "to abandon the work" would be "to do just what the rascals who persecute us desire." Instead, he held, the contributors should go forward with courage and should "profit, as we have in the past, from the imbecillity of our censors." It was a fighting-man's answer.

After the first moments of disarray, it was decided to continue with the volumes of plates to which no one could object. Once the plates were out, there would no doubt be an insistent call for the text which offered the necessary explanations. Soon Diderot and Le Breton agreed to go on also with the basic volumes, printing them in secret without the names of the authors or editors and under a false title page. Instead of distributing them one by one, a method which had provoked continual trouble in the past, the whole would be held back and released at length together. If there was further outcry then, it would be too late for effective opposition. The remaining ten volumes would appear as a final bombshell.

So Diderot, the Chevalier de Jaucourt, and some of the individual contributors toiled on. When others failed, Diderot often stepped into the breach and hurriedly wrote the missing articles himself. By September, 1761, Diderot had delivered the enormous mass of manuscripts to the printer and happily wrote that he was through with the text and could now turn exclusively to the plates. But there was still an exhausting task of revision and slow proof reading.

At one point Diderot needed to consult his article on the Saracens in connection with preparation of the plates. Suddenly he cried out in rage. The publisher, Le Breton, had secretly censored the manuscript, cutting out whole portions of which Diderot was especially proud, for he had hoped to slip into the work his own provocative ideas. But Le Breton was playing safe. He had no desire to be the King's guest in the Bastille and he wanted no further block on the appearance of the final volumes. Diderot wrote a bitter letter to Le Breton. Henceforth their relations would be strictly formal. But the damage was done. The huge volumes had been printed, and the four associated publishers would not retrace their steps.

According to Diderot's daughter, Madame de Vandeul, the angry editor induced Le Breton to print up for him a special copy of the *Encyclopedia* for his own use with the mangled articles restored to their original form. "This copy," she wrote, "is in Russia with his library," which had been purchased by Catherine the Great. Aside from Diderot's well-known tendency to exaggeration and Madame de Vandeul's frequent inaccuracy, the story was long doubted on the basis of its inherent improbability. What publisher would go to the expense of providing a special edition of the *Encyclopedia* for the benefit of one man?

In the spring of 1933, however, Mr. Douglas H. Gordon of Baltimore received a book catalogue, describing a set of the *Encyclopedia* accompanied by an extra volume with more than 300 pages of proof sheets bearing corrections in Diderot's hand. On examination, it turns out that this volume shows the state of the articles before Le Breton's cuts. The set, beautifully bound in red morocco, seems to have come originally from the eighteenth-century library of Le Breton himself. It contains the bookplate of the Russian General Staff. From Russia, it was sold to a group of German dealers whence it traveled ultimately to America and to Mr. Gordon's own private library. A careful study by Mr. Norman L. Torrey, in collaboration with the owner, reveals the nature of Le Breton's excisions, his skill in binding the articles together again, contrary to Diderot's angry charge of bungling, and the way in which, through the cautious intervention of the publisher, the later volumes turned out in the end to be no bolder than those which earlier had run the gauntlet of the official censor. Thus a strange chain of circumstances and a piece of admirably exact research establish the essential truth of Madame de Vandeul's apparently incredible story. It is a lesson on the danger, at times, of too readily rejecting firsthand testimony.

The last half of the *Encyclopedia* appeared at length in the provinces at the end of 1765, ten more big folio volumes of text. There was still hesitation, however, about the risk of releasing them in Paris. In fact, when a few sets were distributed during the following spring, Le Breton saw his worst fears realized and spent an unhappy week behind the dingy walls of the Bastille. Finally, in the summer of 1766, the remaining subscriptions were honored. Although all the work and the printing had been done, as has been indicated, in Paris, the work appeared under the misleading imprint of Samuel Faulche at Neuchâtel, Switzerland. This of course fooled nobody, but offered a respectful sop to the authorities who thus were not openly defied. Such connivance was indeed not uncommon at a time when censorship had already outlived the approval of much liberal public opinion. In 1772, came the eleventh volume of illustrative plates, and the great work was at last done. For twenty-six years, Diderot had bent over the task. His backbreaking labor, his ardor, courage, and persistence had won the long battle.

4

As he looked at the row of huge volumes, sixteen inches high and each one of them nearly three inches thick, standing there in serried ranks on their seven feet of pine shelving in his study on the sixth floor of the apartment building in the Rue Taranne, Diderot must have enjoyed a momentary feeling of relief from pressure and a legitimate pride in his remarkable accomplishment. Seventeen volumes of text and eleven volumes of finely engraved plates with more than 900 double-columned pages per volume! It was the work of a "Society of Men of Letters," as D'Alembert's *Preliminary Discourse* put it, but the enterprise would never have been pushed on to fruition without Diderot's driving energy and determination. These imposing russet-leather tomes with their gilt lettering and decoration on the back were his chief claim to fame in the eighteenth century. Most of his more individual works were to be known only to posterity.

While he joyfully cried out "Land! Land!", did he soon experience a surge of regret, too, and, like Gibbon later, lamenting that there was at the end no more *Decline and Fall of the Roman Empire* to write, think back to the strange gap in his busy days left by the final completion of the great undertaking? It is very possible, and human.

In any event, it has been usual to commiserate with Diderot over these years of literary slavery and to dwell sadly on the more original books he might have written, but for the heavy burden which weighed him down through the best of his life from the age of thirty-three to fifty-nine. Yet this is only speculation and far indeed from being certain.

The *Encyclopedia,* on the contrary, gave Diderot a regular, if modest, income which saved him from a hand-to-mouth existence, relieving him of worry over his livelihood. It took away the dull task of mere translating and inspired him with a broad and definite purpose in warring for the spread of enlightenment. Moreover, his occasional literary excursions into more inviting realms during leisure hours came no doubt with added zest from their very contrast to the daily toil. In great part, as we know, these most original works remained unpublished until after his death. Before receipt of his pension from Catherine II, Diderot would never have been able to afford himself this luxury of independence if he had not possessed the assured income of the *Encyclopedia*—and the generosity of the Empress was a direct tribute to his fame as director of the vast enterprise. Without the *Encyclopedia,* he might, instead, have been driven into a larger number of translated potboilers in place of the masterpieces which have been fondly imagined. So far as we know, Diderot wrote nothing of permanent value during his ten years of precarious freedom from 1732 to 1742.

In sum, the *Encyclopedia* offered him the very human satisfaction of something to excoriate from day to day during the long hours of humdrum labor, but it steadied his roving and mercurial temperament, and turned him from a wandering Bohemian, living by uncertain and perhaps shady expedients, into a hard-working and established man of letters. Without the *Encyclopedia,* there might never have been those other extraordinary flashes of genius which make Diderot most characteristically Diderot today.

In August, 1774, after the death of Louis XV, Voltaire published an entertaining anecdote in praise of the *Encyclopedia.* He claimed that a servant of the late King had told him the story. It seems that one evening the King was supping with a small group in the intimate little palace of the Trianon, adjacent to Versailles. The conversation fell upon the chase, then upon gunpowder, and finally upon the process by which the latter was made.

"It is strange," said the Duc de Nivernais, "that we amuse ourselves every day killing partridges in the park of Versailles, and sometimes killing men or getting ourselves killed on the frontier without knowing exactly what it is we are using."

"Alas! we are reduced to the same pass on everything," replied Madame de Pompadour. "I don't know the composition of the rouge that I put on my cheeks and should be much embarrassed to be asked how they make the silk stockings I am wearing."

"It is too bad," said the Duc de la Vallière, "that His Majesty has confiscated our encyclopedic dictionaries, which have cost each of us a hundred pistoles. We'd soon find the answers to all our questions there."

The King then justified the confiscation, since he had been informed that the twenty-one folio volumes so far published were most dangerous to the kingdom of France. Toward the end of supper, however, he sent out three young men among his servants who came staggering back under the weight of seven of the huge volumes in the arms of each. In the article *Powder,* they discovered that the formula which had been given by the Duc de La Vallière was right. Madame de Pompadour learned the difference between the older rouge of Spain and the modern rouge of Paris. She was told that the ladies of Greece and Rome also used a kind of rouge. She saw how stockings were made, the machine being carefully depicted in one of the volumes of plates.

"What a splendid book!" she exclaimed. "Sire, have you confiscated this storehouse of everything useful so that you alone can possess it and be the only one with all this knowledge in your kingdom?"

Everyone threw himself eagerly upon what interested him most in the great volumes. The King read about the rights of the Crown.

"Truly," he said, "I don't know why they have told me so many bad things about this work."

"Don't you see, Sire," replied the Duc de Nivernais, "it's because it is very good. People never attack the mediocre and the flat in any field. If women make fun of the last lady to arrive, it is certain to be because she is prettier than they are!"

"Sire," said Count de Coigny, "you are most happy to have in your kingdom men capable of knowing all the arts and transmitting them to posterity. Everything is here, from the method of manufacturing pins to that of casting and aiming a cannon, from the infinitely small to the infinitely great. You should thank God for the birth in your kingdom of men who have thus served the entire universe.

Other nations must buy the *Encyclopedia* or copy it in pirated editions. Take away all my goods, if you wish, but give me back my *Encyclopedia*."

"They tell me, nevertheless," replied the King, "that there are a good many faults in this work, necessary and admirable as it is."

"Sire," answered Count de Coigny, "in your supper there were two kinds of stew which failed to come out quite right. We didn't eat them, and yet we had an excellent meal. Would you have thrown the whole supper out the window because of those two unsuccessful dishes?"

The story is told with Voltaire's characteristic brevity and charm. The value of the *Encyclopedia* is shown in vivid dialogue. If any reader should be inclined to accept the narrative as literally true, however, he would do well to hesitate. Madame de Pompadour, who figures so prominently in the anecdote, died in 1764. Volumes XIII and XIV, containing the indicated articles on *Powder* and *Rouge,* appeared only with the last ten folios of the text at the end of 1765 in the provinces, not until 1766 at Paris and Versailles! Unconsciously or with indifference, Voltaire committed an important anachronism. But the moral of this court scene, fictional though it may be, remains. The *Encyclopedia* would survive its shortsighted detractors.

5

One of Diderot's sly methods for transmitting ideas in spite of the watching censor was by means of short, innocent-seeming articles on mere grammatical definitions or synonyms. In a few lines illustrating the use of the word *Anarchy,* for example, he concludes: "We can assert that every government tends toward despotism or *anarchy."* Let the eighteenth century beware of these two extremes in the Old Régime. "When is the *multitude* right?" he asks in an article so entitled. "In everything, but only after a long time," answers Diderot. In the article *Malefactor,* the editor emphasizes one of his favorite ideas. "If there is no such thing as Free Will," he says, "there are only people who do well and those who do ill; but men are nonetheless capable of being changed in the direction of good or evil. Good examples, exhortations, punishments, praise, blame, and laws, all have their effect. The malefactor is the victim of unfortunate heredity." What of *Imposture?* "Nothing is so firmly believed," says Diderot in a sentence worthy of Fontenelle, "as the thing one knows the least about." In other words, the mass of humanity gets on all too well with superstition and credulity. Men seem often to be unhappy with the truth. Many other examples of Diderot's method could be quoted. So he even turned grammar to his purpose in his battles with the censorship. "Strike, and conceal your hand," urged Voltaire. A word to the wise was sufficient.

The article on *Torture* is important. "In England, all torture has been abolished," observed Diderot meaningfully. La Bruyère, the famous seventeenth-century author of the *Characters,* is quoted directly as saying that the use of torture is "a sure means of convicting an innocent man who is physically weak and of acquitting a guilty person born with great endurance." This identical thought was used a few years later by Voltaire in additions to his *Philosophical Dictionary*. It was an effective whiplash against the cruelty of criminal procedure in eighteenth-century France.

We turn to the article on *Sovereigns*. "Men have entered into society in order to be happy," says Diderot, agreeing with his predecessor, Archbishop Fénelon. "But experience always teaches us that the greater the power of men is, the more their passions lead them to its abuse." In England again, Diderot points out, the king is limited by the will of the nation expressed through Parliament. "A sovereign, absolute though he may be, has no right to touch the established law of a state, no more than its religion. . . . He is, besides, always obligated to follow the laws of justice and reason." The unoriginal Louis XV could hardly be expected to welcome this sensible humane dictum. It was a vigorous thrust at tyranny.

On religion, Diderot could not say all that he wished. Yet it is astonishing what he did say. "Religion," he observed under the article *Consecrated Bread,* "does not consist in adorning temples, in delighting the eyes or the ears, but in paying sincere reverence to the Creator, in following Jesus Christ. . . . Let us love our neighbor as ourselves. . . . That is precisely the religion which God prescribes, and it is just the one which men do not practice." Man too readily prefers impressive ceremonies and complex creeds to the difficult task of applying the principles of the Golden Rule in daily life. Diderot, like other leaders of the eighteenth century, preached the simple doctrine of good conduct.

One of the most original contributions of Diderot in the *Encyclopedia,* as has been known from the beginning, is to be found in his detailed descriptions of the processes used in labor and manufacture. These descriptions were supplemented by the many finely drawn plates. Commenting on the work of his English predecessor, Diderot observes in his *Prospectus:* "Chambers added almost nothing to what he translated from our French authors. Everything therefore led us to have recourse directly to the workmen themselves."

"So," he continues, "we turned to the ablest artisans in Paris and throughout the kingdom. We took the trouble to visit their workshops, to ask them questions, to write under their dictation, to develop their own thoughts, to get from them the terms used in their professions, to draw up tables of these words, to define them, to converse with those from whom we had obtained descriptions, and (an almost indispensable precaution) to rectify, in long and frequent interviews with one group of workmen what others had imperfectly, obscurely, and sometimes inaccurately explained. . . . We have seen men who had worked for forty years without knowing anything about their machines. . . . Several times we had to procure machines, set them up, learn to work them, become apprentices, so to speak, and fabricate bad products ourselves in order to show others how to make good ones. . . ."

"We have sent engravers into the shops. They have drawn designs of the machines and tools, omitting nothing which could make them clear to the eyes." In some cases, complicated machines were taken apart, and drawn at different stages of assembly in order to explain them successfully to the uninitiated reader.

We have given the classic account of Diderot's methods, which is his own and has been often cited. Recently, however, Mr. Herbert Dieckmann, from his assiduous studies of the papers in the collection left by Madame de Vandeul, has pointed out that Diderot did not, as has been too readily assumed, do all these complicated articles alone. Quite properly, he often drew upon the descriptions of specialists when such accounts were already in existence. Many processes were much too complicated for any amateur, no matter how clever. It was, nevertheless, a most original contribution which Diderot here made to knowledge and he neglected nothing to bring it to perfection. No wonder Voltaire gave it effective praise when he touched on the articles *Powder* and *Rouge*. It was a new recognition of the importance of the mechanic arts in shaping the material side of civilization.

6

The *Encyclopedia* welded into a vigorous unit its numerous contributors, most of whom, in spite of great divergences in respect to liberal or conservative opinion, were to some degree warring against the *Old Régime*. The so-called "philosophic party" was largely created around these huge folio volumes whose mere publication entailed a long and bitter conflict. And there were the more than four thousand subscribers, each ready to pay the sum, large indeed for the time, of nearly one thousand livres. The *Encyclopedia* built for itself a public, eager in many ways to challenge the existing order of society.

In 1787, on the eve of the Revolution, a lodge of the Free Masons was founded in Toulouse under the very name of the *Encyclopedia*. Daniel Mornet points out how the *Encyclopedia* spread through France. Pirated editions and reprintings even came back from abroad to augment the tide in the country of its origin. Middle-class families read the work together by lamp light in the evening, pored over the unique volumes of beautifully engraved plates. Bankers, lawyers, and priests cherished it in their private libraries. Thomas Jefferson recommended its purchase to his friend in America, James Madison. Reading groups offered it to members who could not readily afford the huge set themselves. Supplementary and index volumes were added by others after Diderot himself had completed his share of the enormous task. A new *Methodical Encyclopedia* appeared slowly during the next half-century, inspired by its famous predecessor, but arranged by subjects instead of alphabetically. The *Encyclopædia Britannica* took its inception timidly in 1771 with a mere three volumes, going only gradually into the many editions and large size which we now know. Springing directly from Diderot's work, authoritative encyclopedias have become standard equipment in any important collection of books today.

The *Encyclopedia* encouraged the use of the experimental method in science and in industry. It stood firmly for the beneficent effect of wider knowledge. Its big folios constituted, first of all, an ardent effort at adult education. But, as we have seen, they represented also, whenever the censor was careless or could be outwitted, an expression of opinion, of an opinion hostile to all that was arbitrary in the thought of Church or State. The *Encyclopedia* struck a powerful blow for liberty, reason, and progress. It could not go as far as it wanted, but, whenever Diderot himself was in control, it went as far as he dared. The wise reader would not fail to see what he meant or, as was so necessary at the time, would quickly learn to read between or beyond the lines. In the eighteenth century, "the celebrated Monsieur Diderot" was everywhere known for his great work on the *Encyclopedia*. Posterity would find for him also a new and still wider fame.

CHAPTER XX

DIDEROT'S CRITICISM OF
DRAMA AND ART

I

LATE IN THE SUMMER AFTERNOON OF AUGUST 20, 1755, A CONFUSED tangle of smart carriages, dingy cabs, even light man-drawn two-wheeled sedans, fought their way slowly into the narrow Rue des Fossés-Saint-Germain, a scant two blocks south of the Seine. There were locked hubs, scratched paint, near-misses of daring pedestrians, frayed tempers! Liveried coachmen on their boxes swore colorfully, flicked their long whips impatiently, reined up their horses sharply. It was the usual uncontrolled theater traffic jam in eighteenth-century Paris.

Bewigged gentlemen with red heels and aristocratic ladies in billowing hoop skirts descended gracefully from their conveyances and swept haughtily past their scraping lackeys toward the open portals of the celebrated Comédie-Française. In the absence of sidewalks, mere foot passengers, dodging as best they could the ugly splotches of mud thrown up from the rough cobblestones, flattened themselves tight against the house walls or picked their steps cautiously on tiptoe in the direction of the crowded entrance. With raucous cries, the indispensable *décrotteurs* plied their trade, darting rapidly hither and yon, polishing slimy shoes in quick brush strokes, skillfully wiping black spots from what were assumed to be white stockings, and pocketing with a grimy hand the two humble copper coins which were the accepted tariff for these daily services. "Ugly hall, . . . ugly sewer of a street!" Voltaire had commented disgustedly to a friend years before.

This was nevertheless a gala occasion. The playbill had announced the first performance of the *Orphan of China,* an exotic new tragedy in the classic manner by the famous Voltaire himself. The patriarch had finally sent it on to Paris from his far-off exile at Les Délices on the outskirts of Protestant Geneva. The great actress of the day,

Mademoiselle Clairon, was to take the leading female role of Idamé, while young Lekain, growing rapidly into dramatic power, would play the part of the conqueror, Genghis Khan. On this particular evening, over thirteen hundred paying spectators, besides an unknown number of deadheads who used their annoying privilege to enter free, crammed the three tiers of boxes around the great ellipse, eagerly pushed into their places on the benches of the raised amphitheater in the rear, squeezed themselves against each others' ribs, under the rude pressure of the soldier guards, amid the sweating standees of the dominant parterre, sat down superciliously on other rows of benches located along the very sides of the stage itself, or even stood in an uneasy mass behind the forthcoming actors in front of the meager painted backdrops.

For more than a century, the hundred and fifty to two hundred gay fops seated or standing on the stage had remained an embarrassment, limiting the free space in front to fifteen feet across at best and the back to a mere eleven! Voltaire had long protested, and for good cause, against this abuse. "Make way for the ghost, make way for the ghost, gentlemen," a herald had pleaded at a production of the author's play of *Sémiramis* in 1748! It is easy to imagine the pitiful impression created by the supernatural apparition under such conditions. Publicly joshing the actors, and especially the actresses, impeding their freedom of movement and sometimes even their entrance, as we have just seen, preventing the development of more realistic sets or the use of effective crowd scenes, these spectators on the stage constituted not only a nuisance, but an insurmountable obstacle to dramatic progress.

Yet the actor-members of the Comédie-Française were naturally loath to give up the extra revenue involved, while the *petits marquis*, for their part, clung smugly to their cherished privilege of seeing and being seen in the forefront of the spectacle. Occasional complaints were without effect although the small amateur stages, which abounded in city mansion as in country château, remained free of these interlopers and thereby offered a visible challenge to a needed reform of the great national theater. So, too, did the colorful Opera in the Palais-Royal which so much attracted the interest of Diderot. With its emphasis on striking and grandiose scenic effects, the Opera persistently refused to tolerate such audience obstruction.

Did Diderot actually attend this important *première* of Voltaire's

Orphan of China? We have no means of knowing positively. Perhaps he was in fact standing eagerly in the center and back of the tumultuous parterre just as he afterwards tells us was to be the case on the occasion of another play in 1759. In any event, he was almost certainly present at a subsequent performance, if not at this first, for the tragedy proved to be long popular in spite of evident defects, and, even though the editor of the *Encyclopedia,* burdened with heavy responsibilities, had for the last twelve years or so since his marriage been much less assiduous in attendance at the theater than in his bachelor youth, it is hard to imagine him missing completely this great moment in the career of the master of French letters. Certain it is, moreover, that Diderot was to comment directly, only three years later, on Mademoiselle Clairon's significant reform of costume in this very *Orphan of China.* He is unlikely to have done so by mere hearsay. In any case, the play was an important part of Diderot's dramatic background.

About five-thirty on this Wednesday afternoon of August 20th, the orchestra struck up its music, imposing gradually an expectant silence on the excited hubbub in all parts of the theater. The curtain was slowly drawn up on pulleys into its slot concealed behind a molding in the ceiling and, in spite of the confused mob of spectators jammed around her, Mademoiselle Clairon made her impressive entrance upon the cluttered stage. To the surprise of the huge audience, she had ventured to abandon the traditional hoop skirts of contemporary fashion. Instead, with arms bare, she wore a gown designed to suggest, however inaccurately, her concept of Chinese dress and, with hands often akimbo or a clenched fist pressed against her forehead in tragic thought, she hinted at something exotic and wholly un-French in pose and gesture. These were important and, for the time, even daring reforms.

Under the influence of Marmontel, another member of the Encyclopedic group, Mademoiselle Clairon had already shown a trend toward more simplicity and naturalness in acting. Three years earlier, she had grasped an opportunity, in the smaller theater of Bordeaux, to try out effectively Marmontel's suggestions and had been impressed by a favorable reaction from the audience. In spite of this illuminating experience, however, she had not yet gone the whole way and seems still to have overplayed somewhat her affecting role of Idamé, the Oriental mother who is torn with anguish at her husband's patriotic willingness to sacrifice their infant son and thus save the royal orphan from a conqueror's vengeance. She probably continued to employ something of the stilted classic declamation popular with the audience and even cherished by the author, Voltaire himself. In any case, her bitter intensity gripped the spectators with a vivid word picture of utter desolation, widespread carnage, a blood-stained palace, and all the frightful horrors which accompanied the Tartar invasion of Peking by Genghis Khan. On the stage, as Diderot testified, Mademoiselle Clairon possessed the mysterious faculty of appearing a full head taller than in real life. In her tragic roles, she was an imposing and even terrifying figure! By comparison, Lekain who, in the masculine lead, had not yet attained to the full maturity of his great genius, admitted with characteristic honesty that she over-shadowed him, out-Heroding Herod, more Genghis indeed than he was! Later, however, he learned to lend conviction to his ungrateful task of playing the cruel barbarian who appears to be too quickly converted to a hardly believable clemency and a chivalrous acquiescence in an entirely unrequited love.

As the spectators with their animated gestures and staccato French accent filed slowly out of the crowded theater about nine o'clock, they were guided, many of them, to their carriages or along the streets by rude-faced lantern-bearers seeking a generous tip in the mild dusk of the late summer's evening. These ladies, gentlemen, and bourgeois had witnessed, without altogether knowing it, an historic occasion. Timidly, but nevertheless unmistakeably, as was presently to become apparent, the stage at Paris had made a definite move toward more realism of speech and costume. Other steps were soon to be taken, and Diderot himself was to play a key part in creating for them a favorable climate of opinion.

2

Early in 1757, Diderot turned aside briefly from the press of work on the *Encyclopedia* to amuse himself by writing a play of his own. It was entitled *The Illegitimate Son*. The result of his efforts was indeed a poor thing, declamatory, unnatural in dialogue, preachy. Not until fourteen years later was it performed at all. Then it was at last dragged painfully upon the stage where it was given once only and without success. But the piece, on publication in mid-February of 1757, was accompanied by three *Conversations* which, by way of commentary, have served to voice Diderot's suggested innovations and to mark a date in dramatic history. Madame d'Epinay, the long-suffering friend of Rousseau, was eager to attract the interest of the mercurial Encyclopedist also. Within two days, she promoted the sale of over one hundred copies of the play with its challenging discussions. The author's closest intimate, Grimm, in his confidential *Literary Correspondence,* enthusiastically informed his aristocratic subscribers in Germany, Scandinavia, and Russia of the philosopher's new claim to fame.

In these *Conversations on "The Illegitimate Son,"* Diderot spoke of his drama as though it were a slice of life and referred to the actors as people to whom the events portrayed had actually happened. By this rather transparent device, he at any rate emphasized his desire for complete realism. French classic tragedy with its three unities of time, place, and action, with its Alexandrine verse, its high-born characters, its nobility of style and feelings, had reached its final climax, he thought, in Corneille, Racine, Voltaire, and even the melodramatic Crébillon. Writers must now seek something different, a bourgeois tragedy in prose which would be nearer to everyday experience.

Let us rid the stage of its embarrassing spectators, he says, and thus find needed space for more realistic scenes, more pantomime, more acting, and less mere declamatory talk. Moments of tense silence, even inarticulate cries, may be utilized effectively, he thinks, forgetting in his enthusiasm how readily either may become ridiculous if carried to excess.

We should depict men as they are, not all black or all white, as in inferior literature, but shot through with the intermingled nuances of good or evil which we actually see in human beings around us, Diderot urges. It was a sound prescription, but unfortunately the author was generally to ignore it in his own stage efforts, though not in the free and easy original tales and novels which occupied the later years of his life. Another concept dear to him was that of portraying men as marked and modified by their professions. The financier, the man of letters, the philosopher, the lawyer, the judge, the merchant, the great noble, he holds, all have their particular characteristics due to their work, their associations, the cast of their daily thought. A whole fertile field of subjects for drama is to be found, Diderot be-

DIDEROT

Portrait by Fragonard

274-1-

ENCYCLOPÉDIE,

O U

DICTIONNAIRE

UNIVERSEL

DES ARTS ET DES SCIENCES,

CONTENANT

L'EXPLICATION DES TERMES ET DES MATIERES COMPRISES SOUS CE TITRE,
SOIT DANS LES SCIENCES DIVINES ET HUMAINES,
SOIT DANS LES ARTS LIBERAUX ET MECHANIQUES;

LA DESCRIPTION

Des Formes, des Espèces, des Propriétés, des Productions, des Préparations, & des Usages

DES CHOSES NATURELLES ET ARTIFICIELLES;

L'ORIGINE, LE PROGRÉS, ET L'ÉTAT ACTUEL DES AFFAIRES
ECCLESIASTIQUES, CIVILES, MILITAIRES, ET DU COMMERCE;
LES DIFFERENS SYSTEMES, SECTES, OPINIONS, &c.

DES

THÉOLOGIENS,	MÉDECINS,
PHILOSOPHES,	ANTIQUAIRES,
MATHÉMATICIENS,	CRITIQUES, &c.

OUVRAGE propre à servir d'un cours d'étude des Anciens & des Modernes;

ET

EXTRAIT des meilleurs Auteurs, Dictionnaires, Journaux, Mémoires, Transactions, Ephémérides,
& autres Œuvres publiées en différentes Langues:

TRADUIT DE L'ANGLOIS

D'EPHRAÏM CHAMBERS,

MEMBRE DE LA SOCIÉTÉ ROYALE DE LONDRES.

Floriferis ut apes in saltibus omnia libant,
OMNIA NOS. —— LUCRET.

CINQ VOL. IN-FOL. AVEC FIG. EN TAILLE-DOUCE,
PROPOSÉS PAR SOUSCRIPTION.

A PARIS,
Chez LE BRETON petit-fils D'HOURY, Libraire, Imprimeur ordinaire du Roy,
rue de la Harpe, au Saint-Esprit.

M. DCC. XLV
AVEC PRIVILEGE DU ROY.

Prospectus of the *Encyclopedia* (1745)

de troisieme guérira; un quatrieme plus sacré les immortalisera par ses chants.

Les Arabes avoient peut-être avant l'islamisme quelques teintures de poésie & d'astrologie, telles qu'on peut les supposer à un peuple qui parle une langue fixée, mais qui ignore l'art d'écrire.

Ce fut un habitant d'Ambare, appellé *Moramer*, qui inventa les caracteres arabes peu de tems avant la naissance de Mahomet, & cette découverte demeura si secrette entre les mains des coraishites, qu'à peine se trouvoit-il quelqu'un qui sût lire l'alcoran lorsque les exemplaires commencerent à s'en multiplier. Alors la nation étoit partagée en deux classes, l'une d'érudits, qui savoient lire, & l'autre d'idiots. Les premiers résidoient à Médine, les seconds à la Mecque. Le saint prophete ne savoit ni lire ni écrire: de-là la haine des premiers musulmans contre toute especes de connoissance; le mépris qui s'en est perpétué chez leurs successeurs; & la plus longue durée garantis aux mensonges religieux dont ils sont entêtés. Car c'est une observation générale que la religion s'avilit à mesure que la Philosophie s'accroît. On en conclura ce qu'on voudra ou contre l'utilité de la Philosophie, ou contre la vérité de la Religion, mais je puis prononcer d'avance que plus il y aura de penseurs à Constantinople, moins on fera de pélerinage à la Mecque. Lorsqu'il y a dans une capitale un acte religieux, annuel & commun, il peut servir de regle très-sure pour calculer les progrès de l'incrédulité, la corruption des mœurs, & le déclin de la superstition nationale. Ainsi, parmi les catholiques, dites, sous telle paroisse on consommoit en 1700, cinquante mille hosties, en 1759 on n'en consommoit plus que dix mille: donc la foi s'est affoiblie dans l'intervalle de cinquante-neuf ans, de quatre cinquiemes, & ainsi de tout ce qui tient à l'affoiblissement de la foi. Je ne doute point qu'il n'y ait un terme stationnaire, une année où la marche de l'incrédulité s'arrête: alors le nombre de ceux qui satisfont à la grande cérémonie annuelle est égal au nombre de ceux qui restent au milieu de la révolution aveugles ou éclairés, incurables ou incorruptibles. Voilà le vrai troupeau sur lequel les ministres de la religion peuvent compter; il peut s'accroître, mais il ne peut diminuer.

Voyez à l'article ARABES *ce qui concerne les Nomades & les Zabiens.*

Mahomet fut si convaincu de l'incompatibilité de la Philosophie & de la Religion, qu'il décerna peine de mort contre celui qui s'appliqueroit aux arts libéraux: c'est le même raisonnement qui a poussé dans tous les tems & chez tous les peuples, les prêtres à décrier la raison.

Il étoit environné d'idolâtres, de zabiens, de juifs & de chrétiens. Les idolâtres ne tenoient à rien; les zabiens étoient divisés; les juifs misérables & méprisés; & les chrétiens partagés en monophysites ou jacobites & orthodoxes, se déchiroient. Mahomet sut profiter de ces circonstances pour les amener tous à un culte qui ne leur laissoit que l'alternative de choisir de belles femmes, ou d'être exterminés.

Le peu de lumiere qui restoit s'affoiblit au milieu du tumulte des armes, & s'éteignit au sein de la volupté; l'alcoran fut le seul livre; on brûla les autres, ou parce qu'ils étoient superflus s'ils ne contenoient que ce qui est dans l'alcoran, ou parce qu'ils étoient pernicieux, s'ils contenoient quelque chose qui n'y fût pas. Ce fut le raisonnement d'après lequel un des généraux *sarrazins* fit chauffer pendant six mois les bains publics avec les précieux manuscrits de la bibliotheque d'Alexandrie. On peut regarder Mahomet comme le plus grand ennemi que la raison humaine ait eu. Il y avoit un siecle que sa religion étoit établie, & que ce furieux imposteur n'étoit plus, lorsqu'on

entendoit des hommes remplis de son esprit s'écrier que Dieu puniroit le calife Almamon, pour avoir appellé les sciences dans ses états, au détriment de la sainte ignorance des fideles croyans; & que si quelqu'un l'imitoit, il falloit l'empaler, & le porter ainsi de tribu en tribu, précédé d'un héraut qui diroit, voilà quelle a été & quelle sera la récompense de l'impie qui préfera la Philosophie à la tradition & au divin alcoran.

Les Ommeades qui gouvernerent jusqu'au milieu du second siecle de l'hegire, furent des défenseurs rigoureux de la loi de l'ignorance, & de la politique du saint prophete. L'aversion pour les Sciences & pour les Arts se ralentit un peu sous les Abassides. Au commencement du ix. siecle, Abul-Abbas Al-Mamon & ses successeurs, instituerent les pélerinages, éleverent des temples, prescrivirent des prieres publiques, & se montrerent si religieux, qu'ils purent accueillir la science & les savans sans s'exposer.

Le calife Walid défendit aux chrétiens l'usage de la langue greque; & cet ordre singulier donna lieu à quelques traductions d'auteurs étrangers en arabe.

Abug-Jaafar Al-manfor, son successeur, osa attacher auprès de lui un astrologue & deux médecins chrétiens, & étudier les Mathématiques & la Philosophie: on vit paroître sans scandale deux livres d'Homere traduits en syriaque, & quelques autres ouvrages.

Abug-Jaafar Haron Raschid marcha sur les traces d'Al-manfor, aima la poésie, proposa des récompenses aux hommes de lettres, & leur accorda une protection ouverte.

Ces souverains font des exemples frappans de ce qu'un prince aimé de ses peuples peut entreprendre & exécuter. Il faut qu'on sache qu'il n'y a point de secte que les mahometans haïssent autant que la chrétienne; que les savans que ces califes appellerent rassemblerent autour d'eux, étoient presque tous chrétiens; & que le peuple heureux sous leur gouvernement, ne songea pas à s'en offenser. Soyez bons, soyez justes, soyez victorieux, soyez honoré au-dedans de vos états, soyez redouté au-dehors; ayez une armée nombreuse à vos ordres, & vous établirez la tolérance générale; vous renverserez ces asyles de la superstition, de l'ignorance & du vice; vous réduirez à la condition de simples citoyens ces hommes de droit divin qui s'élevent sans cesse contre votre autorité; vous reprendrez ce qu'ils ont extorqué de l'imbécillité de vos prédécesseurs; vous restituerez à vos peuples les richesses dont ces inutiles & dangereux fainéans pressentirent; vous doublerez vos revenus sans multiplier les impôts; vous réduirez leur chef orgueilleux à son filet & à la ligne de pécheur, vous empêcherez les sommes immenses d'aller se perdre dans un gouffre étranger, d'où elles ne sortent plus; vous verrez la population & l'agriculture refleurir dans vos provinces; vous aurez l'abondance & la paix, & vous régnerez & vous aurez exécuté toutes ces grandes choses sans exciter un murmure, sans avoir répandu une seule goutte de sang. Mais il faut avant tout que vous soyez bien persuadé que l'amour de vos sujets est le seul appui véritable de votre puissance; & que si dans la crainte que les murs de votre palais ne se renversent en-dehors, vous leur cherchez des étais, il y en a qui tôt ou tard les renverseront en-dedans. Le souverain sage & prudent isolera sa demeure de celle de ses dieux. Si ces deux édifices font trop voisins, ils se prefferont, & il arrivera avec le tems que le trône sera gené par l'autel, & que portés un jour l'un contre l'autre avec violence, ils chancelleront tous...

Mais le regne d'Al-Mamon, ou Abu ... Abdallah ... fut ... Sciences, des A ... Philosophie; il donna l'exemple, il instruisit. Ceux qui

Diderot's article on the Saracens as censored by his publisher, Le Breton. See pages 300-301.

DUNGEON OF VINCENNES

Where Diderot was imprisoned in 1749. See pages 289-291.

MANUSCRIPT

First manuscript page of *Rameau's Nephew* by Diderot. See pages 338-340.

lieves, in the various family relations, the father, the husband, the brother, the sister.

Diderot was right in seeking his people in the ordinary domestic or work-a-day life close at hand, and not alone in the far-off legendary figures of Greece, Rome, or other countries remote in time or space. He was, indeed, following a current which for some years in England and in France had been setting in the direction he advocated. His shortcoming lay in proclaiming a propagandistic moral purpose, which unhappily tends to warp the drama in order to prove a thesis, and in his own inability to draw living, natural human beings for the stage.

During the first part of November of the year following, 1758, Diderot published a second play. This one was called *The Father*. He had already mentioned the theme enthusiastically, as we have seen, in connection with his earlier drama. In fact, the idea may also have been stimulated by the great vogue of a picture, *Father Explaining the Bible,* exhibited in the Salon of 1755 by the newly popular sentimental painter, Greuze.

This play too, like its predecessor, is unconvincing in language, situation, and characters. The moral lesson is preached without finesse. Instead of being implicit, the lesson is too openly shouted from the housetops. The unhappy father drags his parental worries about with him in what appears to us a highly ridiculous manner. In recalling the years of trouble which the younger Diderot had once inflicted upon the elder, in dwelling upon his aged father with more affection, now that the days of authority and attempted discipline were long since over, in meditating on his own growing responsibilities for his one surviving infant daughter, the author has succeeded only in infusing his experiences with mawkish sentimentality, not with the warm breath of family life. There is much excessive gesture and weeping—though this was no doubt in accord with the taste of the time and also a carryover from the traditions of high-flown classic tragedy transported here from Alexandrine verse to such a prose "as never man spake." Played straight as melodrama, Diderot's play would convulse a modern audience with laughter.

Yet it would be a mistake to suppose that this early bungling effort at a new dramatic form was not at least a partial success in its day. From 1761, when it was first produced at the Comédie-Française, to well into the following century in 1839, there were 171 performances in Paris scattered over the years. It was hailed also at Toulouse, Marseilles, and Rouen. The piece was translated into English under the title of *The Family Picture*. Its best year was 1769 when it was revived twelve times at the great national theater in the capital. There Diderot and his affectionate daughter witnessed it, not unnaturally, with tearful emotion. Even the author's unsympathetic wife felt it necessary to view at first hand this unexpected public acclaim for her husband. The actors had at length learned to adapt themselves better than at first to the spirit of this new domestic drama. The parterre in its wild enthusiasm actually demanded two extra performances beyond what had been planned.

Happily, on Monday, April 23, 1759, an important change had already been made in the French stage. During the Easter recess, through the initiative of Count de Lauraguais, who offered to pay the considerable cost of alterations in the theater, the four or five rows of benches on each side of the stage at the Comédie-Française disappeared in favor of a few more boxes, much to the contentment of nearly everyone except the *petits marquis*. The lawyer Barbier commented in his diary: "It's very much better; it seems now as though it never should have been different." Voltaire naturally rejoiced. His new tragedy of *Tancrède,* with crowd scenes and other striking effects, would shortly profit greatly from the reform. Diderot's *Father,* on its first Paris production in 1761, naturally gained a needed freedom of movement which contributed to its success. An important victory had at last been won, in large part through the urging of Voltaire and Diderot.

Accompanying the publication of *The Father* in 1758 there was a long essay entitled, *On Dramatic Poetry*. The term "poetry" is not to be taken literally in the limited sense of verse, but rather in the meaning of high artistic creation. As a matter of fact, Diderot was merely developing in more systematic fashion ideas already sketched out in his *Conversations on "The Illegitimate Son."*

Once more the author emphasizes the essential importance of truth and reality. A new dramatic form with intermingling of tragedy and comedy would be closer to ordinary life than the classic tragedy of the past. Why not now a domestic tragedy in prose? Let us have more pantomime, more action, more development of convincing stage settings. Let us follow the courageous example of Mademoiselle Clairon who, in the *Orphan of China* three years before, had dared to abandon conventional hoop skirts and seek a more appropriate costume. Let us indeed go further than she was able to go in the direction of simplicity and realism. Diderot indicates how the characters of *The Father,* if it should ever be played, ought to be dressed.

The essay is full of penetrating insights which only Lessing in Germany, the nineteenth and twentieth centuries in other countries, would bring into realization. Diderot, in his own time and later, was a great mover of ideas. In his life-long enthusiasm for the theater, he showed himself a stimulating theorist with a remarkable understanding of the possibilities of the stage, even including the interpretive dance and the rich field of opera. But he could not get sufficiently outside of his own personality to create objectively real people speaking and acting like the flesh and blood beings of daily life. "You have the opposite of a dramatist's talent," Abbé Arnaud said to him. "He must transform himself into his characters, and you transform them into yourself."

Only in one late play under the title of *Is He Good or Bad?* did Diderot avoid the undue simplicity of moralizing puppets in favor of the clashing emotions of actual humanity, and in that striking exception the central figure of Monsieur Hardouin was the author himself drawn to the life with his boyish delight in startling paradox and in repeated debates over the complexities of a risqué situation. In spite of distinguished admirers like the poet Baudelaire, the play was never accepted for production by the Comédie-Française. It seems to have remained only a salon diversion of the eighteenth century though it was revived briefly at Geneva in 1928 and in Paris by a group of amateurs in 1951.

One other work deserves special mention in connection with Diderot's discussion of the theater. It is his famous *Paradox on the Actor,* written probably in 1773, but not published until long after in 1830. The great actor, he maintains, has carefully studied every gesture, every movement, every inflection, every delicate nuance of facial or bodily expression until automatically he renders the complex details of his performance. The audience at the end may be torn with tragic emotion or convulsed with comic laughter, depending upon the nature of the play in question. The actor himself is merely tired and goes away hungry to dinner.

Only mediocrity, insists Diderot, relies on feeling. Those who trust to emotion may be on the mountain top today, but tomorrow, and on many other tomorrows, they are deep in the valley of the commonplace. They are unpredictable and uneven. The great actor, on the contrary, controlled by his logical and analytical faculties, is as good, or better, on the hundredth performance as on the first.

There has been much testimony for and against Diderot's thesis. The author had on his side famous eighteenth-century actors like Garrick and Mademoiselle Clairon. "I am convinced," wrote also the modern Frenchman, the elder Coquelin, "that one can only be a great actor on condition of complete self-mastery and ability to express feelings which are not experienced." Other stage celebrities, however, have challenged Diderot's interpretation.

No doubt the latter was intentionally taking an extreme position. In emphasizing the logical faculties, seemingly to the exclusion of feeling, the author admitted freely that he was talking against, and even correcting, himself. Moreover, he was out to astonish the reader. He was writing, as he said to his friend Grimm, "a fine paradox."

In the end, the actor or the actress must certainly be capable of feeling a part, must at sometime have felt it deeply, must then have refined the rendition through intuition, experience, study, reason, all the manifold resources at the disposal of a great talent. It is, as in the case of the poet Wordsworth, "emotion recollected in tranquillity."

The great actor or actress is in sum a very complex being—creature of intense emotion, yes, but guided also by cool and penetrating judgment. When the two are relatively in balance, with the driving force of a powerful feeling controlled by a keen intelligence, plus the mysterious ability to portray vividly the subtlest or the deepest fleeting moods, then a real dramatic genius treads the boards.

In this discussion, Diderot had underlined for his own amusement a great truth, even though, in order to combat the popular fallacy in favor of merely "living a part," he intentionally stressed the "paradox" on the side of the intellect. But no one would have followed with more eager curiosity than the author himself the sharp controversy which his views have provoked since they first became known long after his death. The work is presented, too, with remarkable skill in Diderot's favorite dialogue form and may still be read with much interest today.

3

Three widely separated attempts at exhibitions of painting and sculpture had been made during the reign of Louis XIV. But the public, ill informed, was not yet ready to manifest a continuing interest and the effort was in each case abandoned. Finally, in 1737, there came the first of a long series of biennial "Salons," as they were called, held in the great palace of the Louvre, so conveniently accessible in the very center of Paris. The doors opened for this purpose on the 25th of August and the showing regularly went on through the four weeks of September.

Diderot had consorted with aspiring artists ever since his Bohemian youth. He had expounded theories about the bases of esthetics in an article entitled "Beauty" in the initial volume of the *Encyclopedia* and in the important *Letter on the Deaf and Dumb* as early as 1751. So, in view of this developing curiosity, it is not surprising that the transplanted German Grimm persuaded his friend to write for him a series of discussions of these artistic exhibitions to be inserted in the famous *Literary Correspondence* and distributed confidentially by the editor to aristocratic subscribers throughout central and northern Europe.

The first of these articles, so far as we know, dates from 1759. After that, at two-year intervals, Diderot continued the task down through 1771. Then there was an interruption due to absence in far-off Saint Petersburg whither he had gone to thank in person the Empress of Russia, Catherine the Great, for the purchase of his library and the pension with which, under the guise of appointing him her "librarian," she had graciously made his last years more secure. Two more *Salons* followed in 1775 and 1781, making nine in all.

The *Salons* constitute a very important part of Diderot's literary work during these final decades, but they were not published until shortly after the Revolution or during the course of the century following. Thus, aside from their foreign subscribers, only a few chosen intimates in France could have known them in manuscript at the time they were written although many must have watched curiously in the Louvre while the author rapidly scribbled notes in pencil on little sheets of paper and crammed them into his bulging pockets in preparation for what was to come. Others no doubt listened in amazement on occasion as he poured forth his opinions in those cascades of inspired monologue for which he was already famous. Frequent, too, had been his discussions with the artists themselves who little by little added to his knowledge of technique. Nearly always, however, he insisted that there could be no great art without ideas, intensity of feeling, the ability to see realistically, and an ardent devotion to nature, not convention.

Very characteristic of Diderot was his enthusiastic admiration for that remarkable painter of middle-class and still life, Chardin. It is true that the philosopher by no means had the honor of discovering him, for this great artist had already been placed in the front rank by the public ever since the opening of the biennial exhibitions in 1737. But the intimate friend of Grimm was at one with modern critics in recognizing Chardin's originality, his extraordinary technical skill, and his keen eye for what others so often fail to observe. "His canvases are always inspired by nature and truth," said Diderot as early as 1759. "No one can talk better about painting than he can," wrote the Encyclopedist two years later.

"To view the pictures of others," comments the author of the *Salon of 1763*, "it seems necessary for me to develop new eyes; to see those of Chardin, I have only to keep the eyes given me by nature and use them well." What an understanding he had of colors and reflections! "It's not white, red, black, that you spread on your palette," he says to the artist, "it is the very substance of things; it is the air and the light which you take up on the end of your brush and put on the canvas."

Look at this picture of the ray. "The object itself is unpleasant, but it is the actual flesh of the fish, its skin, its blood. . . . We cannot understand such magic. Here are thick layers of color applied one on top of the other, those below showing through what is above. At other times, you would say a vapor has been blown upon the canvas; elsewhere, it is a light foam. . . . They tell me that Greuze, going upstairs to the Salon and noticing the picture by Chardin which I have just described, looked at it, and walked on with a profound sigh. Such praise is briefer and better than mine," writes Diderot. Indeed, in spite of his admiration for Greuze, the author of the *Salons* admits that Chardin, in this ability to recreate the very reality of ordinary things, "is as far above Greuze as the distance from earth to heaven."

"They say of Chardin," remarks Diderot in 1767, "that he has a technique which is peculiar to him, that he uses his thumb as much as his brush. I don't know whether this is so. What is sure is that no one has ever seen him paint." According to the Goncourt brothers, authorities on eighteenth-century French art, this mystery about Chardin's working methods, his refusal to allow others to observe him, was the result only of his slow thoroughness, his painful, conscientious study of his effects, his lack of the self-confident assurance of Boucher or the facility of a Fragonard.

For a moment, Diderot seemed to think the genius of Chardin was declining. "He is an excellent genre painter," we read in the *Salon of 1767*, "but he is passing." We should not, however, as some have done, make the mistake of considering this remark as Diderot's final word. The old charm soon returned. In 1769 the author observes: "Chardin is not an historical painter, but he is a great man. He is the master of all in the matter of harmony." In 1771, Diderot still recognized Chardin as the artist whom nature seemed to have taken into her confidence. Mercurial though he often was, the philosopher of many moods here remained consistent throughout.

Today we pause with the same admiration as Diderot's before the paintings of still life by Chardin—the atmosphere, the reflections of light upon the different objects, the transparency of glass or of water, the very texture of cloth, the three dimensions which seem to make these inanimate things stand out in the round and infuse into them almost a breath of life. Then there is the scene of the child saying grace at table, the "Benedicite." There is the mother working with her daughter. There is the woman returning with her food supplies from market. Even the children, in the fashion of the time, are clothed like little adults. The faces are serious, intent. This is the life of the hard-working bourgeoisie, so different from the frivolity and gay corruption generally associated with eighteenth-century aristocracy. Chardin himself was a bourgeois of the bourgeois. He stuck constantly to his last. He painted what he knew and he painted with a conviction, a thoroughness, a single-hearted devotion to truth, and a technical skill which were uniquely his own. Diderot also had his roots deep in the middle class. He recognized in Chardin what he himself had tried to do in the field of drama, but without that complete naturalness and sense of reality which distinguished the great painter. Diderot was never more right nor more in accord with modern opinion than in his generally unswerving admiration for Chardin's excellence even though in a limited field.

In the great gallery of the Louvre, the curious public hardly left elbow room before one of the latest paintings by the popular Greuze. It was a struggle to get near and study the canvas closely. "At last I have seen it, this picture by our friend Greuze," exclaims Diderot in 1761. "But it has not been without difficulty. It continues to draw the crowd. It shows a father who has just paid his daughter's dowry. The subject is touching and the spectator feels a pleasant emotion steal over him as he looks at it." So the sensitive Diderot takes on before what we call the "Village Girl Betrothed." Then follow four pages of detailed description intended to give the distant reader as vivid an idea of the scene portrayed as is possible without actually seeing the artist's work. There are only minor criticisms.

Today one is repelled by the overdramatized gestures of the sentimental father. Yet we can understand Diderot's admiration, for these posed figures of the studio are exactly like those he had just incorporated enthusiastically into his mawkish dramas of bourgeois life. They represent his own visions transported to the canvas. The aged head of the family speaks with an inspired expression which seems to us more ridiculous than convincing. There is excessive deference in the bowed head of the groom-to-be. The future bride stands languidly with eyes turned down, too modestly aloof. The mother visibly betrays grief at the coming separation. The hen and chickens in the foreground add a peasant touch but appear also intended to convey the artist's sly hint of the couple's later progeny. Every detail of the numerous other faces is obviously chosen to "say" something, though unfortunately the whole is so artificial as to be far indeed from actually meeting Diderot's insistent appeal for truth and naturalness. Yet, at the time, he thought of the scene as real and so likewise did most of his contemporaries. In this infancy of modern art, the painting told a simple story of commonplace daily life, even though awkwardly and with exaggerated sentiment. In the "Village Girl Betrothed," as in the equally famous pictures of the "Ungrateful Son" and the "Evil Son Punished," which were exhibited in the salon of 1765, untutored people saw a meaning they could easily grasp, and rejoiced accordingly.

In the mid-nineteenth-century play by Augier, Monsieur Poirier looks uncomprehendingly at a delightful depiction of evening with its band of green light stretching out between the orange of the horizon and the cold blue of the rest of the sky. And there is the almost imperceptible shimmer of water in the pool beneath the trees.

"What does that mean?" asks Poirier contemptuously.

"Why, that's nine o'clock in the evening, out in the fields, in the summer time," replies his bourgeois friend, Verdelet.

"That's not interesting, a subject like that," retorts Poirier. "That doesn't say anything. In my bedroom, I have an engraving which shows a dog on the seashore, barking over a sailor's hat. Well, that's something you can understand. That's clever. That's simple and touching."

"Well, Monsieur Poirier," replies his noble, if rather scapegrace son-in-law, Gaston de Presles, "since you like pictures that are touching, I'll have one made for you after a subject that I have taken myself from nature. On a table there was a little onion cut into four pieces, a poor little white onion! The knife lay beside it. It didn't seem to be anything, yet it drew tears from one's eyes."

In Gaston's rather obvious stage persiflage, we see mirrored the modern art-lover's frank mockery of Diderot's admiration for Greuze. In his naïve reaction, the author of the *Salons* showed himself still too deeply immersed in his own time. He earnestly desired a realistic portrayal of ordinary life, but remained blind to the false sentimentality and the strong element of studio pose which the misguided painter offered under that head. Complete naturalness and simplicity, it seems, lie only at the end of a long and difficult road.

In 1769 Diderot exclaims: "I no longer like Greuze." But we should not be misled. It is Greuze the man he is speaking of, not Greuze the artist, as is shown by his continuing admiration for most of the latter's annual product of paintings only a few pages following.

The Mademoiselle Babuti whom we remember from Diderot's free and easy youth had become the Madame Greuze of a later day. As such, she was the subject of a number of half-symbolic portraits praised by the philosopher. She appears also to have inspired several paintings of young girls with sad and haunting eyes in which there is a vague suggestion of deeper grief than is indicated by the would-be innocent title. Diderot does not fail to dwell appreciatively on this *double entente*. In the end, there was to be real tragedy for what at first seemed a happy couple. The bad temper of the artist, the faithlessness of his wife, led to repeated quarrels, culminating in a violent separation which became a matter of legal record. In the hollowness of Greuze's popular preachments and in the sorrow-stricken faces of his not very profound heroines, there is to be found perhaps a hint of the coming break.

4

Anyone who has seen La Tour's pastel portraits on loan at the Louvre or restored to the painter's native city of Saint-Quentin knows the magic of his art. There is D'Alembert with the flashing eyes and the broad smile of the practical joker gaily entertaining society, while masking the open wound of his illegitimate birth. There is the Queen, Marie Leszczinska, in her kindly nonentity. There is Madame de Pompadour, beautiful, surrounded by the books and turning the pages of the music which represented her patronage of literature and the arts. At the same time she looks alertly to one side for the possible appearance of the master, the exacting Louis XV, whose inherent boredom she must be always ready to amuse. There is Jean-Jacques Rousseau, the handsome author of his musical operetta, the *Village Magician,* says Diderot, but not the fierce censor of the sciences and the arts, not the French Epictetus in careless dress and tousled wig, whom one might have expected in 1753 after the startling success of the first Dijon Discourse. The "Citizen of Geneva" had too consciously decked himself out for his portrait on that day.

But for the most part Diderot was caught by the reality of La Tour's paintings. "Flesh and life are in them," he writes. They contain the irregularities of nature itself, one corner of the mouth higher than the other, a slight difference perhaps in the size or position of the two eyes. "I have seen La Tour paint," continues the author of the *Salons.* "He is quiet and composed. He does not torment himself or suffer. He remains cool, and yet his painting is warm." As in his *Paradox on the Actor,* Diderot noted with admiration this astonishing self-control which was so far from his own bubbling excitement, and, in this artist at least, produced such marvelous results. In general, the brusque and independent La Tour penetrated beneath the faces of these men and women who eagerly sat for him, and he laid bare the half-concealed character beneath.

Diderot recognized Boucher's great talents as a painter, but felt

he had prostituted them in his pretty, highly-decorative, lightly sen-
suous nudes. Likewise, although the critic of the *Salons* was much
impressed by the vigorous historical canvas which signalized Fragonard's reception into the artists' academy, he had little use for
the more characteristic works which "le bon Frago" dashed off so
easily for the sly diversion of a gracefully corrupt society.

An artist whom Diderot did, however, praise highly was Claude-
Joseph Vernet, painter of storms, moonlight, landscapes, and French
seaports. With Vernet, something of the Romanticism of Rousseau
and of Diderot takes on form and atmosphere. The latter finds new
methods of varying his discussion in the different *Salons* in order to
interest the reader with a varied approach. In the *Salon of 1767*, for
example, he pretends to have made a trip to the country, describes
the picturesque landscapes seen there, and only after having treated
of his impressions, journeys, and conversations on the subject of
"six sites," does he at length reveal with the seventh that these are
all merely pictures by Vernet. In this last canvas, particularly,
Diderot admires the reflection of the moon on the waves, the dark,
moving clouds, the vessel silhouetted against the silvery disk in the
sky, the blazing torch held by a sailor in the bow of the boat, the
remarkable fidelity of the artist in rendering these contrasting effects
of night over the water. Diderot is no longer a Poirier lingering enthusiastically before the story-telling pictures of a Greuze. He was of
course never solely that, even from the beginning. Now he has
profited from his many intimate talks with artists like Chardin, La
Tour, and Vernet. He has toured the galleries with them or with the
young ex-painter Naigeon, later to become his too faithful disciple
in philosophy. The author of the *Salons* has grown increasingly interested in technique and methods of painting, but he appreciates,
as always, reality, independence, and originality of mind, and above
all the fire of genius. Vernet was of course no Corot, but he was
already pointing the way in that direction.

To a lesser degree, Diderot admired the work of Robert, who
invoked the massive ruins of past civilizations. "What firmness, and
at the same time what lightness, assurance, and facility in the han-
dling of the brush!" exclaims the critic. "But, "Monsieur Robert, you
do not know yet why ruins give so much pleasure. . . . I'll tell you
my own immediate impressions. . . . The ideas aroused in me by
ruins have meaning. Everything is destined to be annihilated, every-

thing perishes, everything passes. Only the world remains. Only time endures. How old this earth of ours is! I walk between two eternities. . . . What is my ephemeral existence in comparison with this disappearing rock, this deepening valley, this decaying forest, these masses tottering above my head? I see the marble of tombs fall into dust, and I do not wish to die. . . . A torrent sweeps the nations one after another into a common abyss, and I alone try to stop on the edge and cleave the flood which runs past me!"

A Montesquieu, meditating over the rise and the striking fall of Rome, a Gibbon, slowly composing his immense volumes on the latter half of the same subject, the increasing number of painters making their voyage of study to Italy and rendering with their palette the picturesque, but melancholy ruins of the ancient world— all these gave added impetus to such reveries over the transitory character of human existence. It was as though, in the midst of a declining eighteenth-century society, the oncoming of violent revolution already cast its lengthening shadows before. Diderot was always one to appreciate such overtones of thought and to see in the painter's canvas more than the artist himself had perhaps put there.

The author discussed also a host of lesser painters, generally with a frank severity favored by the fact that his *Salons* were not to be published during his lifetime. This severity is made more evident still by the growing brevity of his treatment as energy waned with later years, as the task more and more palled on him, and as mediocrity alone seemed to increase. Yet he was naturally inclined to praise if possible.

He remembered what Chardin had said to him and Grimm one day at the Louvre. "Gentlemen, gentlemen, be gentle. Among all the pictures here, pick out the worst, and recognize that two thousand unfortunates have ground their brush between their teeth in despair at ever doing anything even as bad as that. Parrocel, whom you call a dauber and who is one in fact if you compare him with Vernet, is nevertheless a rare artist by the side of the multitudes who have abandoned the career which they entered along with him. Lemoine said that it required thirty years of practice in the profession to learn how to develop a sketch into a painting; and Lemoine was no fool. If you listen to me, you will learn perhaps to be indulgent."

Diderot's *Salons* in 1765 and particularly in 1767 are very long

and detailed. They are extremely personal, filled with digrions
and often with interesting anecdotes of his own life and experience.
Diderot wrote as he wished, letting his pen run and no doubt at
times leaving his coolly practical friend Grimm aghast at the sheer
abundance of material. The author of the *Salons* never got around
to making his long projected trip to Italy. Consequently he was
unable to profit from direct observation of the striking masterpieces
at Rome, Florence, or Venice. But he did know such of the paintings
of Raphael, of Rubens, and of Rembrandt as he could then see in
the nearby gallery of the Louvre. Not infrequently he used them or
the colorful Venetians to measure by contrast the inferiority of too
many luckless contemporaries.

Throughout his *Salons,* Diderot remained primarily a literary
man, quite naturally. This is not the grave defect it was thought to
be by the rabidly hostile critic, Brunetière. It was this fact first of
all which made Diderot an effective link between artist and public.
Moreover, he believed firmly that the artist must do more than show
off technical mastery before his fellows of the craft. He must in some
fashion make a visual commentary on life. Nor should it be forgotten
that, though Diderot was not himself a painter, he learned increasingly from his eager conversations with artists to share their professional viewpoint, to understand their methods and problems.

But Diderot became more and more convinced that the artist
should not let himself be confined within the narrow limits of a
bare realism. Instead, he should dominate subject or model through
his power of intuition, the originality of his creative imagination. A
mere copy of nature could not, for Diderot in his later years, constitute the greatest art. In this too, he looked definitely toward
the future.

Within his own time, many of the paintings admired by Diderot
were purchased on his recommendation in Germany, Austria, or
Russia by wealthy connoisseurs or royal patrons, and in some instances may still be seen in those countries today. His influence in
this respect is readily tangible.

After their long delayed publication at the end of the eighteenth
or during the first fifty-seven years of the nineteenth centuries,
Diderot's *Salons* gradually won growing favor with the public and
helped to stimulate a truer appreciation of art in France. Articles
discussing the annual exhibitions of painting and sculpture became

the accepted thing. The strikingly original painter Delacroix several times records his interest in Diderot. More significantly, the youthful Baudelaire, not yet recognized as a poet, rejecting the commonplaces of contemporary journalism, found support in Diderot for brushing aside mediocrity with a few frank, blunt words. He even called upon his friend, Champfleury, to publish a direct comparison between him and his great predecessor—which Champfleury obligingly did. Particularly in Baudelaire's first *Salon of 1845* and to a lesser degree progressively in those of 1846 and of 1859, we may see, in addition to the profound influence of Delacroix, the clear evidence of Diderot's impact upon the younger man's style and some of his basic standards of judgment.

Thus Diderot left a vigorous impress on the newly developing field of art criticism. Once again he had revealed the astonishing richness of his many-sided genius.

CHAPTER XXI

DIDEROT, NOVELIST AND PHILOSOPHER

I

DIRECTLY WEST OF PARIS, WITHIN ONE OF THE GREAT WINDING loops of the Seine, there lies the beautifully landscaped park of the Bois de Boulogne. Just north of its famous racecourse rise the ancient ruins of an ivy-covered tower. Its crumbling stones are all that now remains of the thirteenth-century Convent of Longchamp. Here, on Wednesday, Thursday, and Friday of Holy Week, the fashionable world of the period before the Revolution streamed out each year in all its finery from the city to thrill at the solemn music of the Tenebrae which commemorated the darkest hours of Christ's sufferings, crucifixion, and death. The impressive setting had not prevented the singing of the sisters from becoming gradually secularized, under pervasive mundane influences, even to the extent of being aided by many professional voices from the quite unreligious Paris Opera.

With his keen interest in music, Diderot undoubtedly knew the Convent of Longchamp at first hand. It was there in any event that he laid the action of a novel, written at white heat during the latter half of 1760 and entitled succinctly *The Nun*. Like nearly all of the author's more original works, this, too, was not destined to be published until years after his death, appearing finally for the first time at the end of the century in 1796.

Diderot's closest friend Grimm is supposed to have related the peculiar circumstances which led to the composition of the novel. It was the unexpected result of a kind of plot hatched up between these two leaders of the philosophic group. The Marquis de Croismare, one of their most delightful intimates, had withdrawn for reasons of practical affairs to his country estate at Lasson near Caen in Normandy. His departure occurred at the beginning of 1759 when the Marquis, born the same year as Voltaire, was sixty-five. As the kindly nobleman, deep in the pleasures of reunion with his children and a friendly local priest, lingered on in the provinces longer than he had originally intended, the two conspirators dreamed up together a complex intrigue which was contrived to play upon his ready sympathies and bring him back to his former associates in Paris.

In the capital, there had recently been much talk about an unhappy nun who was assigned, as it happened, to the very Convent of Longchamp of which we have been speaking. This nun had at last succeeded in bringing legal action to be relieved of the religious vows, forced upon her long ago, as she charged, by her parents for selfish reasons. The Marquis de Croismare had been accustomed to range freely and with democratic understanding among all ranks and phases of life in the great city. He had interested himself in the nun's case and had even, following the accepted practice of the time, endeavored to use his influence in her behalf with the Counselors of the Grand Chamber of the Paris Parlement. But, in spite of his efforts and those of her attorney, the plaintiff in the end lost her suit and her vows were adjudged valid.

Grimm refers to the nun as Suzanne Simonin, the name finally used by Diderot in his novel. Before that, the author had at one time called her Suzanne Saulier. It turns out, however, that a recent student of the subject, Mr. Georges May, has uncovered the files of long-neglected documents recording the arguments, hearings, and appeals in which, from 1752 to 1758, a certain Sister Marguerite Delamarre pleaded to have her unwilling vows lifted in order that she might be freed from Longchamp. The general correspondence in dates, place, and events, leaves no doubt that this is the original source of Diderot's narrative. The author had drawn directly upon life for the inspiration and some of the details of his poignant story. Indeed, to make our assurance doubly sure, he actually, while hesitating about the choice of a name, toyed also with that of Suzanne de la Marre in his manuscript.

The first move of the two plotters, Grimm and Diderot, was to imagine that the nun in question, piquantly younger and more successful in her struggle to escape than Marguerite Delamarre, had managed to scale the walls of her convent and was now imploring the help of the Marquis de Croismare in obtaining some sort of

modest position to earn her living. A series of letters from the fictitious Suzanne Simonin follows. To these, the good Marquis promptly wrote his real replies, the first of them dated "Wednesday, February 6, 1760."

There are many convincing details in the make-believe letters.
Thus the earliest from Sister Suzanne is prudently vague. She refers
to herself only as "an unfortunate woman" without revealing her
name. The brief note is first delivered to an address in the city by
a messenger instructed to wait for an answer. By a shrewd device,
the escaped nun, ignorant of the world outside, has been imagined
as falling into a natural confusion between the very similar names
of a certain Count de Croixmar, Governor of the Royal Military
Academy at Paris, and the absent Marquis. When this mistake has
been cleared up, the writer of the note learns of the Marquis's present
whereabouts near Caen. The next letter is long, factual, and signed. It
indicates the means to be employed in further communication. A
reply should be sent to a Madame Madin, Pavillion of Bourgogne,
"rue d'Anjou," at Versailles. This was the real address of a woman
who had actually been enlisted in the plot, though without being
informed of its nature. The reply, with an identifying cross on its
envelope, was to be inclosed in a second outer envelope directed to
Madame Madin. Thus, through these complex, but plausible precautions, everybody concerned was protected.

The correspondence continued for nearly four months. But when
it became clear that the warmhearted Marquis was even prepared to
install the supposed nun in his château of Lasson as the companion
of his daughter instead of returning to Paris himself, as had been
hoped, the sly intriguers saw that the game was up. Their clever plot
might involve embarrassing consequences. It was therefore necessary
to give the fictional Suzanne an injury attributed to a fall during her
escape from the high-walled convent. Little by little her condition
was made to grow worse. Letters signed with the name of Madame
Madin, though of course not written by her, described the nun's
increasing illness and finally, in early May, her death. The last letter
by the Marquis de Croismare was dated May 18, 1760.

But now Diderot himself was caught in his own trap. He had
become deeply interested in the character created. He had read to
his wife, to Grimm, and to other friends the letters composed
through long mornings of enthusiastic devotion to the fate of the

unfortunate nun. His listeners had insisted on the author's striking out everything exaggerated, everything high-flown, everything which was not straightforward, bare realism. It was essential to convince the Marquis that the letters were true. There must be no slightest trace of fiction, no hint of mere contrivance. Moreover, Diderot's enthusiasm for the English novelist Richardson in his potent use of small details began now to exert its influence. As a result, the Frenchman embarked on what was for him a new way in literature. Gone here was the bombastic preaching of his emotional dramas which had immediately preceded in time the moving tale of Sister Suzanne. Under the impact of the so-called plot leveled at the susceptible Marquis, Diderot learned to compose a novel which seemed to speak with the very accents of life itself. When he came twenty years later to think of possible publication, he even ventured to revise the real letters of Monsieur de Croismare as well as his own fictional ones. By this time, he was evidently looking on the whole enterprise unemotionally from the standpoint of a professional author aiming at a literary effect.

The story is told in the first person by Suzanne Simonin herself. She hates the convent, not, as in many instances, because of irreligion or a thwarted love affair, but from plain revulsion to a cloistered existence. She lacks the vocation necessary for such self-sacrifice. She longs intensely for the freedom of normal living. By bestowing this attitude upon his heroine, Diderot has greatly broadened the effect of his fictional protest. His novel is aimed at all arbitrary abuse of authority. In direct contrast to existing eighteenth-century practice, he holds, it should be difficult to assume the required vows, easy to be relieved of them.

With extraordinary sympathy and insight, the author has entered into the feelings of the nun, so different from those of his own free-thinking self. Memory of one of his sisters who, from very exaltation of religious fervor, had lost her mind after taking orders must have inspired one terrible passage in the novel. Others, more favorable, may have been suggested by recollections of his pious father or by impressions of his devout, if narrow and unsympathetic, wife. But Diderot transcends these limited experiences to depict convincingly Mother Superior Moni, beloved of all around her; he seems himself to share the cold sweat, the trembling body, the weakening knees, of Sister Suzanne; with her, he loses himself completely in a trance of intense prayer for deliverance, stretched out full-length on the steps before the altar in the dark, silent hours between two and three o'clock in the morning.

There are sadistic torments, hysterical and unwholesome episodes in the latter half of the book, as Mothers Superior without the integrity and affection of the deceased Moni set the unhappy tone of their order, but there is nothing pornographic as enemies of Diderot have proclaimed. The story is painful, exceptional in scenes and characters, if you will, but honest, simple, and realistic. In spite of all the obstacles against her, Sister Suzanne marvelously preserves her innate sincerity and innocence throughout. Although nuns in complete revolt were doubtless far from numerous in the rather worldly convents of the eighteenth century in France, the actual case of Marguerite Delamarre is proof that they did exist. The autocratic power of family, church, or state, like all autocratic power, was naturally open to great abuse, and Diderot's narrative is a vivid attack on such attempts to force the human spirit into an unwilling mold. It is also a deeply moving, though of course by no means a literal transcript, direct from life itself.

2

Diderot had always delighted in piquant stories and curious anecdotes. The vivid letters to his mistress, Sophie Volland, abound in them. So also do the frequently discursive *Salons*. Hence it is not at all surprising to find him, in the early 1770s, turning away from the licentious allegories of his youthful years to embark on four short tales strongly marked by this new realistic manner. Many a reader ever since has keenly enjoyed *The Two Friends from Bourbonne*, the *Conversation of a Father with his Children*, *This is no Story*, and *The Inconsistency of the Public's Judgment*.

Let us take as an example the *Conversation of a Father with his Children*. The leading characters in this striking dialogue are the author's own father, his brother (the antipathetic Abbé), his sister, and several neighbors in his native town of Langres. The action occurs in winter before the fireplace in the elder Diderot's home. The old man, mulling over the past, as old men will, drifts into recollection of a certain difficult problem presented when he was called upon to settle the estate of an aged priest who had died in the nearby village of Thivet. The deceased had left numerous relatives, all desperately poor. After careful search among the disorderly papers, Diderot's father unexpectedly came upon a will, drawn so many years before that he wondered if the century-old testator had not himself forgotten the ancient document or considered it long since of no effect. Should the administrator not destroy this clearly unjust will which ignored the penniless members of the priest's family and bequeathed everything to some rich booksellers of Paris named Frémin? Did the father do right in finally deciding to carry out his duties and execute the objectionable will to the letter?

A lively argument ensues. Most of those present stand strictly by the law. Diderot, however, as might be expected, sets his personal concept of reason and human welfare above mere legality. As he bids his father good night, the son bends down and whispers in his ear:

"Father, rigorously speaking, there are no laws for the wise man."

"Speak lower!" enjoined the aged cutler.

"All their provisions being subject to exceptions, he is the one who must decide in which cases to follow the law or to ignore it," continued the son.

"I'd not object," replied the father, "to having one or two citizens like you in a city, but I wouldn't live there if everybody thought that way!"

So the story ends with a pronouncement which is characteristically half against Diderot and half in his favor. In this uncertain world, if all people took on the philosopher's independence, there would soon be no protection of the law at all. Diderot's doctrine, suggests the tale, is valid only for him. To generalize it would call forth a dangerous anarchy in which, as during the chaotic time of the *Judges,* "every man did that which was right in his own eyes." If you must broach such a risky principle, whispers the father to the son, "speak lower!"

As so often in his later years, Diderot relishes any paradox which shows how readily, in the face of human complexities, one may conclude in behalf of either side. "There is no rule for the application of rules," it has been sagely observed. In the doubtful contingencies of life, we are often unable to descry any clear road to the right decision.

The reader of this most original narrative cannot but admire the complete naturalness of tone, the easy flow of conversation from one thing to another, the many realistic details, which all combine to leave us half uncertain when we have finished whether the author is relating an exchange of ideas which actually occurred between him and his father or only the fictional story that it perhaps largely is.

3

Toward 1773 or 1774, during one of Diderot's long pauses in Holland at The Hague on his way to or from Russia, he probably put down on paper a strange work entitled *Jacques the Fatalist and his Master*. Although the episode of Madame de La Pommeraye was translated by Schiller in 1785, while the story as a whole appeared in German seven years later, this novel, like *The Nun,* was not published for a French audience until 1796.

Diderot had read Sterne's whimsical relation of *Tristram Shandy,* which was issued slowly in nine small volumes during the years from 1760 to 1767. The Englishman's book is in many respects very different, but the French writer did use a few phrases and incidents from his contemporary across the Channel. Diderot delighted, too, in following even more than usual his predecessor's extreme discursiveness. In the main, however, *Jacques the Fatalist* is his own and is cast in his own manner.

As the narrative begins, we are introduced to Jacques and his master riding together on horseback along the highway. "How had they met?" asks the author. "By chance, like everybody else. What were their names? What difference does that make to you? Where did they come from? From the place nearest at hand? Where were they going? Does anyone know where he is going? What were they saying? The master said nothing; and Jacques said his captain used to say that everything which happens to us here below for good or evil was written in advance up there in the great beyond."

So Diderot at once sets the unusual tone of his novel, posing in the very first sentences the central question suggested by his title. Do all men's acts spring from the free workings of their own will or are they determined rather by an uncontrollable destiny?

"My captain added," continues Jacques with a soldier's fatalism, "that each bullet fired from a gun had its billet," thus exactly echoing a phrase which occurs late in *Tristram Shandy.*

Like Alexander Pope, Leibniz, or Voltaire's famous *Candide*, Jacques, too, sees all the events of life linked together in an inexorable chain. Had not the boy, at a moment when he was drunk from his father's bad wine, forgotten to lead the horses to the watering trough? Had not his father then become angry and, as his son retorted with a defiant toss of the head, drubbed him a bit roughly over the shoulders with a stick? Wasn't a regiment passing by at that very instant on its way to camp before Fontenoy? Didn't Jacques, out of spite, enlist and arrive just in time for the famous battle? Wasn't it there that he received the bullet with his address on it and the resultant painful wound in the knee just like Sterne's Corporal Trim? Didn't all the later events of his life ensue from this sequence?

"Without that bullet, in fact," he remarks, "I believe I should never have been in love or be walking now with a limp."

Repeatedly, at his master's insistence, Jacques starts to recount "the story of his love affairs," but always it seems to have been "written up there in the great beyond" that interruption after interruption should break off the narrative before it is barely begun. Such a framework, or lack of framework, leaves the easy-going author entire freedom to introduce as many short realistic tales as he pleases, all quite unconnected with the main thread of what we have loosely called a novel. Some of these are masterpieces of their kind. A few are examples of Diderot's never-failing gusto for broad language or Rabelaisian humor. The account of the implacable vengeance of Madame de la Pommeraye is famous and early drew the admiration of Schiller. The character of the vicious, but diabolically shrewd Father Hudson is hardly less noteworthy.

Diderot takes frequent delight in poking fun at the conventional novelist. He points out that the author of *Jacques* could obviously have planned his story differently from the way he did. Certainly he might have manipulated the plot as he wished. But the real events didn't occur in that fashion. Life is by no means so logical as writers of fiction pretend. The realist must tell his tale just as it happened, inconsequential though the incidents may be in sequence or entirely lacking in poetic justice. It was indeed "written up there in the great beyond" that the reader should come in the end to the marriage of Jacques and Denise, but this book is, in modern parlance, only "a slice of life." It might well be the beginning of a whole series of further stories on whether Jacques was fated to become a cuckold or not. As for the author, he professes frankly not to know. Like André Gide's twentieth-century novel of the *Counterfeiters,* the narrative does not conclude; it merely stops, hinting at an equally interesting new succession of episodes not told here.

But what of the fatalistic theme indicated by the title? A rigorous determinism had long since been dear to Diderot. He had indeed already expressed this view clearly in a famous letter to a certain Landois as early as 1756. It is evident to us all that heredity and environment do shape profoundly the whole course of our lives. Such a fact indeed offers the best promise of the successful upbringing of children, of the wholesome effect of good education, of the value of rewards and punishments. If man's deeds are to be looked upon as the result of mere caprice, then there is no way in which we can form the future either for good or ill. The causeless "gratuitous act" holds no appeal to human reason. Contemporary tyrannies, it is true, have callously drawn upon deterministic doctrine in order to create nations of robots trained only to follow their leaders, unthinking. Still, may not a belief in the potency of outside influences be directed also toward more hopeful ends? Obviously, this is impossible except when joined with respect for the individual human personality.

In particular cases, it is clear that we cannot predict the future through belief in determinism. Yet looking backward, one easily traces a pattern of events, perceives that a right or left turning was full of consequences for what came after. Who of the Western World, however, would willingly consent to be bound on the inexorable Buddhist Wheel of Life? Such a fatalism inevitably stifles freedom and initiative. Man feels the need of guarding his sense of personal responsibility. But, if the will is held to be free, what shall we say of previous events or conditions outside of our control which have fixed the character of the will itself and hence determined the nature of its decisions? Such seems to be our philosophical dilemma.

Caught in this age-old labyrinth, we are compelled to make our peace with reality as best we may. It is necessary for us to combine two hostile alternatives, perhaps even in defiance of complete logic, into a working solution for practical affairs. How did the fatalistic Jacques meet the issue? "He conducted himself," says the author with tongue in cheek, "about like you and me. . . . He tried to forestall evil; he was prudent with the greatest contempt for prudence."

337

Diderot himself struggled, half-humorously, in the toils of his own thought-system. "I rage," he wrote elsewhere, "at being enmeshed in a diabolical philosophy that my mind cannot help approving and my heart denying." Similarly old Doctor Johnson, with his dogmatic assurance, laid down the law to Boswell. "All theory," he observed, "is against the freedom of the will; all experience for it."

4

In fair weather or foul, it was Diderot's regular habit to stroll alone toward five o'clock in the afternoon, he tells us, in the then popular garden of the Palais-Royal in the very heart of Paris. If it happened to be cold or rainy outdoors, he found convenient refuge across the street in the famous Café de la Régence, which still stands on the same site today.

Late one afternoon, perhaps in April of 1761, as has been suggested by commentators, Diderot was accosted in the Café by one of the most extraordinary figures imaginable. What "a mingling of elevation and baseness, of common sense and folly!" And "what terrible lungs!" Who could endure such roaring unless fascinated by his originality?

"Today in dirty linen, torn breeches, covered with rags, almost without shoes," remarks Diderot, "he slinks along with his head down. You would be tempted to call him over and give him a handout. Tomorrow, well-shod, his hair curled and powdered, he walks with head high, shows himself off, and you would almost take him for a respected member of society. He lives a day at a time, sad or gay, according to circumstances. His first concern in the morning when he gets up is to know where he will dine. After dinner, he wonders about supper. Night brings its worries too. Either he returns home on foot to the little attic where he lives, unless his landlady, tired of waiting for her rent, has obliged him to give up the key, or else he falls back on a tavern in the suburbs where he waits for the coming of daylight, propped up between a piece of bread and a mug of beer. When he doesn't have six pennies in his pocket, which happens to him sometimes, he has recourse to a friendly cab driver or to the coachman of some great lord who allow him to make his bed on straw with the horses. In the morning he still carries bits of his mattress in his hair! If the season is mild, he often strides the night out restlessly in the park of the Cours-la-Reine or along the Champs-Elysées. . . ."

"I don't have any esteem for these eccentrics," continues Diderot, but "they do break that tiresome uniformity created by our education, our social conventions, and our usual forms of politeness." Such a character appearing in a group of people is indeed a kind of yeast which "restores to each of us a part of his natural individuality. . . . He brings out the truth, helps us to recognize good men, unmasks the rascals; then the man of sense listens and finds out what the world is really like."

"I had known this fellow," observes Diderot further, "for a long time." He even used to borrow a few silver pieces from the author on occasion. Somehow he had wormed his way into a number of respectable houses "where he found a place laid for him at table, but only on condition that he wouldn't talk without permission. He remained silent and ate his meals in a rage. He was a sight to see holding himself in like that! If he took it into his head to break the treaty and open his mouth, all the guests would cry out at the very first word: 'Oh, Rameau!' "

"You were curious to know the man's name," says Diderot now to the reader, "and you do know it. He's the nephew of that celebrated musician who delivered us from the plain-song of Lulli that we had been chanting for more than a hundred years."

In such a casual and seemingly unpremeditated manner has the writer introduced us to the most original of all his creations, the work which goes under the title of *Rameau's Nephew*.

The history of this book is itself extraordinary. Composed apparently for the most part in 1761 or 1762, it was retouched at various times in details up to as late as perhaps 1779. Yet, so far as we know, Diderot never showed or even mentioned it to a single friend or relative. He wrote and kept it for himself. It too, like *Jacques the Fatalist,* was early admired by Schiller who passed it along in manuscript to Goethe. The latter was so impressed by this work of genius that he made a translation which appeared in 1805, but met with little success. In 1821, two Frenchmen retranslated the vivid dialogue from Goethe's German, though without giving any indication of the strange source of their version. Two years later the work was for the first time printed from another copy of Diderot's French text. Finally, as late as 1891, the author's own manuscript turned up along the Quays of the Seine, and was promptly published in its original form. This manuscript is now grandly housed in the magnificent J. Pierpont Morgan Library in New York City.

Rameau's Nephew resembles no other literary work in existence. In a scintillating dialogue between himself and this eccentric, Diderot has offered us a satire of the real Jean-François, scapegrace nephew of his famous uncle, the composer Jean-Philippe Rameau. The author has also pilloried the chief enemies of the philosophic party as well as various other contemporaries, all openly under their actual names. It was no wonder that the writer of this dangerous work made no effort to bring it out during his lifetime!

But, if Jean-François Rameau is brilliantly presented as an utter cynic, a jealous misfit of a musician whose ambitions outran his talents, an unabashed Bohemian living off what he could fawn or flatter from society, a conscienceless rascal indeed, even in theory a procurer who blatantly talks of bartering off his own wife's provocative beauty, had she but lived—there has been much debate as to the reality of Diderot's startling portrait. Cogent evidence has been gathered to show that the younger Rameau was in many ways just as the author pictured him.

Yet we should by no means conclude that Diderot limited himself to a photographic copy of his strange original. Instead, he endowed the extraordinary nephew with a great deal of his own penetrating insight, his own unrestrained joy in smashing conventional idols like the proverbial "bull in a China shop," his own disillusioned feeling on occasion that, absorbed over the years in the painful toil of the *Encyclopedia* and the many favors generously showered upon friends or chance acquaintances, he, too, had never been able to give the full measure of his genius. Rameau's lusty pleasure in shocking his hearers, in throwing himself with complete abandon of gesticulation and mimicry into violent tirades against society, is one aspect also of Diderot's own character as we know from similar passages in other works or the vivid testimony of eyewitnesses.

The "I" of the startling dialogue represents the more conventional side of Diderot, the moralistic preacher of his tiresome plays, the admirer of the painter Greuze, the good bourgeois with "hay" in his boots, as the Nephew so picturesquely puts it, *hay* which amounted to well over four thousand livres of income annually. This was the man who with hardheaded practicality looked out for his financial interest in his father's sizable estate or planned prudently for his daughter's dowry so that she might make what is conventionally spoken of as a "good" marriage. The "He," on the other hand, who plays the big role in the astonishing interchange, is in part the Diderot who reveled in letting himself go like an untamed force of nature, who delighted in laying about him with his bombshells and waiting gleefully for their explosion.

But this does not mean that all the vileness attributed to the real Jean-François Rameau, doubtless with some injustice, is to be charged to Diderot's own account. These are ideas which sprang first of all from painful memories of the author's bitter ten years of Bohemian poverty. They belong also to the later Diderot of uninhibited conversation with his intimate friends and the startling circle grouped about Monsieur and Madame d'Holbach, as portrayed so vividly in the philosopher's remarkable letters to Mademoiselle Volland. The two Diderots, the conservative and the radical, got along very well together, as with many another among us, in the practical affairs of life. After his more than three months of unhappy imprisonment at Vincennes in 1749, the author had good reasons for keeping his most dangerous works safely in manuscript. *Rameau's Nephew,* especially, lay hidden away until long after Diderot's death.

However, this challenging work goes deeper than the half-realistic, half-imaginative portrayal of a breath-taking specimen of depravity. "What a devilish social economy we have!" exclaims the gaunt outcast in a passage which, like the conclusion of Rousseau's famous *Discourse on Inequality,* is directly reminiscent of Montaigne's essay *On the Cannibals.* "There are some men who are gorged with everything while others, who have a stomach just as importunate as theirs, a recurrent hunger like theirs, haven't a bite to put between their teeth!" cries the Nephew furiously. Diderot never forgot that painful day in his own youth when he had with difficulty dragged himself home to fall in a heap upon his bed, faint from hunger.

The worst thing about all this, the cynic Rameau continues bitterly, is "the posture of constraint in which our poverty keeps us. The needy man doesn't walk like other people; he jumps, he crawls, he wriggles, he pulls himself along, he passes his life striking one attitude after another. . . . In the entire kingdom, there is only one man who can walk upright; that is the sovereign. All the rest strike attitudes." But this time Diderot in his own person retorts that even the King has to play a role before his mistress, just as do also the minister and the whole succession of ambitious courtiers before whoever is above them. Only the philosopher who wants nothing and asks for nothing is able to escape this humiliating subservience.

"And where is there an animal like that?" cuts in the Nephew scornfully.

Admittedly, even the independent Diderot has no relish for the life of a Diogenes, naked and cold in his famous barrel, reduced to a diet of raw fish and herbs, and drinking only the unexciting water of flowing streams. The philosopher, too, if he would fain eat from a full table, enjoy clean clothes, and relax comfortably in a good bed at night, must make his reluctant concessions to the power of money, convention, or royal authority. Such indeed is the way of the world, the irksome lot of all humanity.

Thus, in *Rameau's Nephew*, the central issue goes deeper than a mere attack upon the abuses of social organization. In this disintegrating society of France on the eve of Revolution, in any society, can there be effective reform without success in curbing the inherent baseness of human nature itself? Diderot's work, implicitly, goes to the root of man's oldest and most enduring problem.

5

By his eighteenth-century contemporaries, Diderot was commonly nicknamed "the philosopher." No doubt he was no professional originator of new thought-systems, but did he not, like a true Encyclopedist, show himself familiar with every kind of knowledge and always eager to welcome startling ideas? His mind indeed appeared constantly in movement and remarkably free from bondage to past or present. Was it not also his high ideal to be guided by reason and reflection rather than by mere prejudice or passion? Man walks in darkness, but may not the philosopher carry at least a flickering torch to light the way? Such was Diderot's aim and aspiration.

His ostensibly deistic *Philosophical Thoughts* of 1746 and the implied agnosticism of his *Letter on the Blind* of three years later had early won him, as we have seen, a gloomy lodgment behind the thick walls of the Vincennes dungeon. Other challenging works, like the *Skeptic's Walk* or the *Sufficiency of Natural Religion*, more safely gathered dust among those numerous papers which remained unpublished until long years afterwards. *A Letter on the Deaf and Dumb* appeared in 1751, but treated chiefly of sense impressions in relation to esthetics. It was a discussion full of keen, original insights, but not too dangerous for the author's peace.

At the end of 1753, and in more complete form during the first months of the year following, Diderot brought out anonymously an important work entitled, *On the Interpretation of Nature.* It, too, like his provocative little book of 1746, was conveniently, if somewhat disjointedly, arranged in a series of numbered "Thoughts."

"Young Man, take and read," enjoins Diderot earnestly in a brief preface. Inspired by the philosophy of Francis Bacon, the author turns from the abstract world of mathematics, which had so long ruled man's thinking, to urge an experimental approach to all natural phenomena. "We are on the verge of a great revolution in the sciences," he cries.

Stimulated probably by the natural history of Buffon and with a hint of coming Darwinian evolution, Diderot continues: "When we consider the animal world and perceive that, among the quadrupeds, there is not one without its parts and functions, especially those which are internal, entirely similar to those of other quadrupeds, are we not ready to believe that there was originally a first animal, the prototype of all succeeding forms?" At least, this appears to Diderot an essential hypothesis for progress in biological thinking.

Long and painful observation of facts is the prerequisite for scientific advance. "Let us hasten to render such philosophy popular," he counsels. If the reader will turn to Benjamin Franklin's book translated the year before, *Experiments and Observations on Electricity*, he will soon see "how much the experimental method requires of insight, imagination, wisdom, and resourcefulness."

But final causes in the universe, the author believes, will ever remain hidden from man's view. "Who are we to explain the aims of nature?" he asks. Matter appears to be eternal, without beginning or perceivable end. "The physicist, whose profession is to instruct and not to edify," says Diderot, "should therefore abandon the *why* and concern himself only with the *how*."

This is a program in itself sufficient to occupy the investigator for as many centuries as we can now see before us. Let us put aside futile questions of metaphysics in favor of medicine, the properties of common substances, the shape of the plow, and other practical problems which confront mankind, suggests the philosopher. Let us be, as much as in us lies, "the masters of our existence."

Such is the purely rationalistic outlook of Diderot's *Thoughts on the Interpretation of Nature*. It forecasts clearly the astounding developments of research in the natural sciences during the two hundred years which have elapsed since his time. The author appears in this work as one of the most modern of his contemporaries.

6

Yet, try as he would, Diderot, like other thoughtful humans, could hardly limit himself to purely physical science. He was by no means content to turn his back complacently on troublesome philosophical questions. His well-known letter to Paul Landois of June 29, 1756, argues vigorously the case for a strict determinism as against freedom of the will in the puzzling sequence of man's actions. We have already witnessed the same issues entertainingly joined in the half-mocking story of *Jacques the Fatalist*.

Now a startling new work takes form. In two letters of September 2 and September 11, 1769, which seem from internal evidence to have been erroneously inverted by the editor in his arrangement of the author's correspondence, Diderot exclaims enthusiastically to his friend Sophie Volland: "I have written a Dialogue between D'Alembert and me. . . . It is as crazy as can be, and at the same time represents the most profound philosophy." And again: "I think I told you of having constructed a Dialogue between D'Alembert and me. . . . It is impossible to be madder and more profound. I have added in conclusion five or six pages capable of making my sweetheart's hair stand on end; consequently she will never see them. But what will surprise you greatly is that there is not a thing about religion and not a single improper word. After that, I defy you to guess what it can be."

Composed, then, in the summer of 1769, the *Conversation between D'Alembert and Diderot* and that curious mingling of sense and apparent folly known as *D'Alembert's Dream*, were concluded by a briefer exchange of ideas between Mademoiselle de Lespinasse and Dr. Bordeu, which comprised the third part. The whole constituted one more of the author's strikingly original works destined to lie hidden away among his papers throughout his lifetime. Indeed, it did not appear in print until years afterward in 1830.

Diderot had long been keenly interested in physiology, anatomy, and medicine. Early in life, while still only an obscure hack writer, he had toiled for three years or more over the translation from English of James's *Medicinal Dictionary*. It was a labor well fitted to make him familiar with both the technical language and contemporary knowledge of the subject. Later he took extensive notes which have been gathered together under the title, *Elements of Physiology*. In addition, he had studied anatomy under the surgeon Verdier; he had followed the courses of Mademoiselle Biheron, the deviser of vivid anatomical figures in wax; he had attended, along with Rousseau, the popular lectures on chemistry given around the middle of the century by Rouelle; he was intimately acquainted with distinguished physicians like Dr. Petit and Dr. Bordeu, the latter also an important contributor to the *Encyclopedia* and destined finally to be chosen by Diderot for a major role among the three characters in the *Dream of D'Alembert;* finally, the author had read widely along these same lines.

"There are no books I read more gladly than books about medicine, no men whose conversation is more interesting to me than that of doctors," he wrote, adding sagely and not without humor, "but only when I am well."

Convinced that man's conduct can only be explained by an accurate knowledge of his physical origin and existence, he had sought the answers to his questions in a persistent study of biological science. The *Conversation between D'Alembert and Diderot* and the accompanying *Dream of D'Alembert* are therefore the interesting outgrowth of a lifelong interest.

The work opens sharply without preliminaries as though continuing a lively argument already engaged.

"I grant it is difficult," observes D'Alembert, "to accept the existence of a Being so contradictory in nature: a Being which exists somewhere and relates to no particular point in space; a Being which is without space and yet occupies space; which is quite complete in each part of this space; which differs essentially from matter and yet is united to it; which follows and moves matter, while itself remaining motionless; which acts upon it and still is affected by all its changes; a Being of which I have not the slightest conception. Yet quite other difficulties lie in wait for the man who rejects this Being."

But Diderot does not choose to pursue D'Alembert's philosophical summary of the problems in connection with the existence of God. Instead, he moves promptly to the plane of pure biology. The gap between inorganic and organic matter? Why! we bridge it daily in the mere process of eating.

What of the origins of a great mathematician like D'Alembert himself? Here follows a frank passage which could readily have disturbed two of the chief characters in these famous dialogues, Diderot's co-Encyclopedist and the latter's mistress, Mademoiselle de Lespinasse. It is a quick résumé, in scientific physiological terms, of D'Alembert's illegitimate birth as the child of the Chevalier Destouches and Madame de Tencin, of his exposure on the steps of Saint-Jean-le-Rond chapel, from which he took the main part of his name of Saint-Jean-le-Rond d'Alembert, and of his gradual rise through "only material agencies" to become "a passive being, a feeling being, a being who resolves the Precession of the Equinoxes, a sublime being, a marvelous being, a being aging, failing, dying, dissolved, and returned to the leaf-mold." So the inorganic-organic-inorganic cycle is complete.

Diderot by no means holds to the then widely-accepted theory of "pre-existent germs" according to which it was supposed that every sentient being, human or animal, went back pre-formed in each case to a first egg or *ovum*. Our imagination "shrinks," observes the author, "at conceiving an elephant ready formed in an atom, and in this atom another elephant already formed, and so on indefinitely." The great naturalist Buffon had likewise exposed this idea to effective ridicule. It is "contrary to experiment and reason," comments Diderot succinctly. Instead, we must believe in constant change and development of living forms, in a kind of evolution in short. The "order of things" has willed man's existence.

In what does the consciousness of man's identity consist? It is founded "on the memory of his actions" is the reply. How does he think? He is like the wire of a harpsichord which "oscillates and resounds long after one has plucked it." We are "plucked in the same manner by joy, sorrow, hunger, thirst, colic, admiration, terror. . . . But the cause undergoes too many vicissitudes that escape us. Hence we cannot count infallibly on the effect which will follow."

MADAME DE POMPADOUR

Portrait by La Tour (1755). See page 324.

THE VILLAGE GIRL BETROTHED

By Greuze (1761). See page 322.

D'ALEMBERT

Portrait by La Tour
(1753). See page 324.

LOUIS XVI

Portrait by Duplessis.
See page 390.

But D'Alembert's eyes are heavy with sleep. He bids his friend good-night. "You will dream of our conversation on your pillow . . . and you will be forced to adopt hypotheses of a far more ridiculous description," Diderot warns him, thus cleverly preparing the way for the startling paradoxes of *D'Alembert's Dream*. This second and longest section of the work offers the writer a plausible opportunity to say what he wishes without assuming personal responsibility for his bold imaginings. A dream after all is only a dream.

The scene now changes to D'Alembert's apartment. The famous mathematician has been sleeping, dreaming, talking aloud. Is he ill? He appears at any rate to be delirious in the opinion of Mademoiselle de Lespinasse, who has been attending him. But she has jotted down his seeming ravings on paper and submits them to Dr. Bordeu on his arrival. Skillfully, Diderot presents his friend as embroidering wildly on their previous conversation. Mademoiselle de Lespinasse is appalled, but to the matter-of-fact doctor these strange ramblings make sense. In fact, he astounds his feminine companion by even predicting some of D'Alembert's remarks before reading her notes.

"Have you ever observed a swarm of bees escaping from their hive?" reads Mademoiselle de Lespinasse. "Have you seen them go away and, at the end of a branch, form a cluster of little winged animals, all clinging to each other by the feet? This cluster is a being, an individual, an animal of sorts." Thus it is with man and his many different organs. Only, in his case, he has attained unity in his diversity.

Diderot enjoys playing with the then much-discussed idea of spontaneous generation of life. "Why am I what I am? . . . Organs produce needs, and reciprocally needs produce organs." What of the various freaks and monsters such as Siamese twins? "Does one will spontaneously? Will is always born of some internal or external motive, of some present impression, or past reminiscence, of some passion, or plan for the future." Indeed, "try to imagine the occurrence of some other action with the actor remaining the same," Dr. Bordeu challenges Mademoiselle de Lespinasse. In Diderot's thinking, the deterministic explanation of man's conduct will not down.

In the brief third section, the conversation is entirely between the doctor and the young woman. There is some bold interplay on the mingling of species. Bordeu voices, too, the author's keen delight in tilting at conventional morality, though he seems at the same time to underline, as in the *Conversation between a Father and his Children,* the philosopher's right not to generalize the observance of what he so much enjoys discussing. "I should not take my hat off in the street to a man suspected of practicing my doctrine," the doctor candidly admits. Like Diogenes, he warns, "my bark is worse than my bite."

We can hardly, in a few pages, give any adequate idea of this, one of Diderot's most astonishing works. Putting everything on the plane of pure scientific reasoning, he has tried to explain the development and evolution of human and animal life entirely on a naturalistic basis. His philosophy is materialistic in the sense that he considers the universe to be made up only of matter, and this matter, under its multiplicity of forms, is still one. Of course, such a view by no means implies that Diderot is materialistic in the usual colloquial meaning of that term. He does not worship primarily material values and he does not lack an ideal.

In this vivid conversation, Diderot has insights which forecast Darwin's famous theory of the survival of the fittest. There are many passages which would not be disowned by modern biology or psychology. Once more the writer has shown himself master of the dialogue in one of its most original and convincing examples. He was right in being proud of his achievement and expressed a sound judgment when he wrote to Mademoiselle Volland: "It is impossible to be madder and more profound." The so-called madness, indeed, admirably echoed the assumed incoherence of the dream. Diderot had again evidenced a rare determination to write for himself and for posterity alone a book which could not safely be put into the hands of contemporaries.

About three years later another bold dialogue came from his pen. This was the *Supplement to the Voyage of Bougainville.* It too, like *The Nun* and *Jacques the Fatalist,* was withheld from publication until 1796.

Taking as his inspiration a recent account of what moderns have nostalgically called "the mystic isles of the South Seas," the author expressed his delight in the freedom from convention seen in these primitive denizens of a kindly semi-tropical climate. Life came easy here and was lived accordingly. How pleasant for the writer to escape, in imagination at least, from the rush of Paris, the pressing demands of family and friends, the heavy load of the *Encyclopedia,* and dream of dark-eyed beauties who, in dress and in conduct, seemed to follow only the happy liberty of nature, far from civilization's restraints!

But once again, we should not take the philosopher's fond speculations more seriously than they were meant. Diderot dearly liked to shock and astonish, to let himself go to the ultimate conclusion without limit or check. It was true also that he had been the unfortunate victim of a marriage in which love had too soon fled both from him and his wife. Yet, if in consequence he readily permitted himself a license of which he was of course far from being a solitary example in his or any age, we know at the same time how different was his hardheaded counsel to his daughter from the amoral tone of the *Supplement to the Voyage of Bougainville.* The latter was a work quite in the spirit of the startlingly uninhibited conversations so frequent in the circle of his friend D'Holbach, but in actual practice the good bourgeois in Diderot was ever close at hand to check the too daring flights of theoretical reasoning.

7

The roads on this long journey across Europe were terrible. Over the deep ruts and gullies, the carriage rocked and plunged and jumped about like a ship in a rough sea. Serious breakdowns were common. The sixty-year-old traveler suffered also from what he called "a violent colic," which was probably, as an autopsy later seemed to indicate, the painful effect of gall-stones. With each rude jolt, it was like "a knife," he observed, sawing at his intestines. It was indeed an arduous experience in those days to make one's way overland to Saint Petersburg. Yet, ever since 1765 when Catherine II had bought his library and later favored him also with a disguised pension for guarding the books during his lifetime as her "librarian," Diderot had felt a strong obligation to express his thanks to her in person.

He had left Paris on June 3, 1773. After a pause of over two months in Holland, at The Hague, he had begun the major portion of his difficult enterprise on August 20th. Not until October 8th, after forty-nine days on the road, counting occasional stops for interesting art galleries, did he finally come, "more dead than alive," as he wrote home, to his far-off destination.

There he was graciously received in daily audience by the Empress. She appears to have been fascinated by the swift flow of his varied conversation, but promptly found it necessary, if we may believe a well-known story, to place a table between them to protect the imperial thighs from his too eager gesticulation as, forgetful of everything else, he emphasized his arguments in a "man-to-man" interchange of ideas. In any case, Catherine must have been highly astonished at the complete lack of awe manifested by this mercurial Frenchman, in such sharp contrast to the justly fearful courtiers by whom she was surrounded. She was not, however, greatly impressed by the immediate practicality of his notions of government, particularly in what concerned a vast, amorphous, despotic land like Russia.

"Monsieur Diderot," she said to him one day, "I have listened with the greatest pleasure to all that your brilliant mind has inspired in you. But . . . you forget, in your plans for reform, the difference in our two positions. You work only on paper, which tolerates everything . . . while I, a poor Empress, work on the human skin, which is irritable and ticklish to quite a different degree."

"From that time on," according to Catherine, "we talked only of moral and literary questions." Diderot had taken the lesson to heart. Henceforth, he would stick to what he knew at first hand, especially when dealing with a ruler, enlightened no doubt on the surface, but at bottom cruel, unscrupulous, ready to stop at nothing to maintain her power.

The return journey was no less difficult, but was made rapidly in a single month during the early spring of 1774. Diderot appeared impatient to be back in civilization and traveled under forced draught in long day and night stretches. Four times his carriage broke down on the impossible roads. Twice he fell seriously ill. Once he nearly lost his life amid the treacherous ice floes of the Dvina river near Riga. When he had arrived at The Hague, however, he tarried on for six months, busy with literary interests and seemingly in no great hurry to be home. Not until the first days of October, according to his daughter, did the wanderer finally reach Paris again. Humorously he claimed to his wife not to have lost even a "handkerchief" on his difficult travels. He had forgotten to mention that his wig had taken flight in the midst of the jolts and bouncings of the trip out!

Gay as he pretended to be, the trials and fatigues of over 4000 miles on the road had exacted their heavy toll. His legs had weakened from the weeks of no exercise in the confining carriage. His breath came shorter now. He would no longer go on his usual long walks without an unexpected weariness. Old age was beginning to weigh upon him. Yet he still guessed cannily that he had about "ten years of life left in his sack" and, as it happened, his prophecy was to be very exactly realized.

Now, since the previous May, young Louis XVI was King. It looked for a moment like a hopeful reign of good government and reform. Beaumarchais, after his two unhappy attempts to follow in the wake of Diderot's abortive bourgeois dramas, flashed brilliantly across the stage with his two astonishingly witty comedies. At the same time, the far-off American colonies roused the enthusiasm of Europe by their Declaration of Independence and, with French aid, fought out their war at last to its slow conclusion. Meanwhile, shrewd old Benjamin Franklin moved impressively in Parisian society. Voltaire returned briefly from Ferney to the capital and died there, worn out by excitement, public honors, and excessive activity. Hardly more than a month later, Jean-Jacques Rousseau, Diderot's former friend and now his bitter enemy, was gone too, on July 2, 1778. Time was gradually running out, but the Encyclopedist still had energy to resent the tales said to be told at his expense in the still unpublished *Confessions* and half wore himself to exhaustion on a work which was intended to be partly one of personal justification.

More and more Diderot enjoyed his stays in a little country-place at Sèvres just west of Paris. The climb up the four or five flights of the old house on the Rue Taranne was hard on him now. His onetime mistress, Sophie Volland, died on February 22, 1784, but nothing is known of whether Diderot's affection for her had continued during these final years. The last letter in the philosopher's published correspondence with Mademoiselle Volland dates from September a full decade before. An attack of apoplexy struck Diderot down a few days after the death of his beloved Sophie, but he recovered partially in spite of three bleedings in twenty-four hours, which represented the characteristic treatment of the time.

Grimm had already written to Catherine II, urging the need of a new and more convenient apartment for the aged writer. The Empress responded graciously by ordering the preparation of a suitable residence on the centrally situated Rue de Richelieu near the Palais-Royal, the Louvre, and the great Royal Library. On July 17th or 18th, 1784, Diderot was moved from Sèvres to his grand new home. On the 29th, workmen installed a more comfortable bed.

"My friends," he said to them, "you are putting yourselves to a lot of trouble for a piece of furniture which will not be used four days."

On Saturday, July 31st, he got up as usual and, after talking with his son-in-law and his doctor during the morning, ate his mid-day dinner. As he chose an apricot for dessert, his wife for some reason fearfully endeavored to dissuade him.

"What harm do you think that can do me?" replied Diderot.

Still feeling an appetite, he started to eat also a compote of cherries. Suddenly he coughed slightly and, as Madame Diderot addressed a question to him, made no answer. He was dead, leaning there over the table on his elbow.

Previously he had refused the urgings of a priest to make his peace with the church. "Admit," he said, "that I should be telling an impudent lie." He would not at the last go counter to the whole trend of his life since abandoning the early influence of his Jesuit teachers. His philosophy was what it was. He would not pretend to change it.

With Diderot's death, one of the most original geniuses of the eighteenth century had disappeared from the scene. Often he had lacked good taste. His wit was not the polished scintillating wit of Voltaire. He himself frankly lamented the too great hurry in which his works had frequently been composed. "When you write without stopping as the pen runs," he observed, "everything which should be said on a question either doesn't come or else is not expressed the way it ought to be." It was true, especially no doubt of much of what he had prepared under pressure for the *Encyclopedia,* of some purely journalistic works, of things written at the few odd moments when he was free from the daily task. But we have seen also that the masterpieces of his later years are far from being open to this criticism. If the *Salons* sometimes seem too long, the digressions themselves are generally of great interest and there are many other remarkable passages. Above all, *The Nun, Jacques the Fatalist,* the several short stories, *Rameau's Nephew,* and the *Conversation between Diderot and D'Alembert* along with *D'Alembert's Dream,* show what marvels the author could work when he was embarked on a labor of love which gave full expression to his natural bent. Nor did he then hesitate to retouch and revise over the years, but succeeded in doing so without sacrifice of the wonderful spontaneity which was his most engaging trait.

Diderot was deeply interested in drama, in art, in the novel, in science, in philosophy. As an Encyclopedist, he had indeed taken all knowledge for his province. He was as near to being universal as falls to human lot. To sum him up in a brief space is therefore impossible. Moreover, he is known today as he was by no means known in his own time simply because his greatest works did not appear until long after his death. In the best and truest sense of the word, he wrote, just as he would have wished, according to his published argument with the famous sculptor Falconet, for posterity.

PART III

EXPLOSION

CHAPTER XXII

BEAUMARCHAIS ON THE EVE
OF THE REVOLUTION

I

ANDRÉ CARON, MASTER WATCHMAKER.
The large sign was painted in capitals on the low ceiling. For ten years now, people passing by had seen it there through the show-windows fronting on the busy street of Saint-Denis almost opposite the Rue de la Ferronnerie. It was a crowded, most unliterary quarter near the bustling Central Markets in the very heart of Paris. In this plain little shop, which was also the home of the proprietor and his rapidly growing family, a boy was born on the 24th of January, 1732. The infant was promptly christened Pierre-Augustin Caron. Not until the age of twenty-five did he take to himself the more imposing name of Beaumarchais. Altogether there were finally ten children of whom only Pierre and five sisters survived. It was a merry group, and the future dramatist later looked back fondly on what he described as "my youth, so gay, so mad, so happy."

Four years of rudimentary education at Alfort, a few miles east of Paris near Vincennes, were deemed sufficient, and in the spring of 1745 Pierre's industrious father set his son to humdrum work on a bench by his side as an apprentice watchmaker. For the next five years, the boy lingered on unhappily in the dull shop. When he could, he amused himself with the viola, the flute, and later the harp, performed his duties more and more carelessly by day (even slipping into his pocket small amounts of money from his father's till to supplement his meager allowance), ran gaily about town at night, and apparently dreamed for a time of embracing the Bohemian existence of an actor in the broad farces of the Theater of the Fair, so popular then in Paris.

By 1750, all this was more than the exasperated father could longer endure. He expelled, or feigned to expel, his rascally son from home.

But, without funds, the prodigal had no strong urge for the open road. Persuaded by relatives and friends who were perhaps in secret connivance with the elder Caron, the boy humbly signified his willingness to return. The formal "treaty of peace," which the master watchmaker carefully drew up in a long letter containing six numbered clauses, gives striking evidence of an eighteenth-century father's unquestioned authority.

"Monsieur Very Honored Dear Father," replied the son with the ceremonious deference of the period. "I sign all your conditions in the firm will to execute them with the Lord's help. . . . It is fitting for me to suffer a truly merited humiliation, and, if all this, along with my good conduct in other respects, can procure and earn for me a complete return of your good graces and affection, I shall be too happy. In testimony of which I sign everything contained in this letter."

The humble capitulation was not feigned. Surprisingly enough, this austere program resulted in a prompt and radical reform. With sudden industry, the boy devoted himself to his father's exacting trade. So unusual was the young man's natural talent, aided by earnest study of books on mechanics, that, within two years, at twenty, he had invented a new type of escapement to control the movement of a watch. No longer would it be necessary to make these instruments of daily use round and bulbous like an onion! Instead, the Caron device permitted the development of cases which were thin, flat, and handy for the pocket.

But hardly had the escapement been finished when it was fraudulently claimed by a fellow member of the Watchmakers' Guild, a certain Lepaute, in whom the talkative Pierre had unsuspectingly confided. Thereupon, with characteristic boldness, the youth called upon the Academy of Science for an investigation, submitted his preliminary plans and sketches of which his rival had none, proved conclusively his right to the discovery, and was officially hailed as its inventor in a report dated March 4, 1754. Through a direct appeal to public opinion, he had won his first great victory. The "Lepaute affair" was already a beginning of fame.

Indeed, one day, a royal messenger knocked unexpectedly at the plain shop door in the Rue Saint-Denis. The King, Louis XV, commanded young Caron to appear before him amid the august splendor of Versailles! Here was a new rush of excitement in the simple bourgeois household. The last months had been hectic enough with this fight of uncertain outcome over the escapement. Now what an astonishing climax! They must at once fit out Pierre with an expensive costume suitable for his presentation at Court. No doubt father, mother, and sisters smothered him also with sage advice about his conduct under these exciting circumstances.

When at last the inexperienced youth first bowed respectfully before the grand monarch, Louis kindly put him at his ease, plied him with questions about the wonderful escapement, condescended to attach a magnifying glass to his eye in order better to follow the technical explanations, and showed himself frankly amazed to hear that it was now possible to construct a watch small enough to be worn in a lady's ring. No wonder that, in a letter to the well-known monthly magazine, the *Mercure de France,* on June 16, 1755, young Caron spoke with pride of the thin, compact timepiece which His Majesty had been carrying with pleasure for the last year, described the tiny instrument recently mounted in a ring, as requested, for Madame de Pompadour, and signed himself with assurance "Caron the Son, Watchmaker to the King."

2

A year later, Pierre-Augustin Caron married a widow, Madame Francquet, slightly older than himself. Shortly he assumed the more aristocratic name of Beaumarchais from a wooded property belonging to his wife. He began also to frequent the numerous literary cafés of Paris and to strike up a limited acquaintance with Diderot, D'Alembert, and other members of the already famous Encyclopedic group. Under this inspiration, by means of wide and miscellaneous reading, he threw himself into filling the great gaps in his education. But, with the sudden death of his wife, probably from typhoid, in 1757, Beaumarchais was again alone. Later, enemies, without evidence, maliciously concocted the story that he had poisoned his wife. As a matter of fact, far from being an advantage, as some claimed, her death was in every way a heavy blow to him.

To help dispel his grief, he studied intensively the mechanism of the harp, which aroused his eager curiosity now just as the watch escapement had done a few years previously. It was not long before he had devised an improved pedal arrangement destined shortly to be adopted by the harp makers of Paris.

The King's four unmarried daughters, Mesdames Louise, Sophie, Victoire, and Adélaïde, were all in their twenties and infinitely bored by the dull, formal life they were condemned to lead at court. One day they asked Monsieur de La Vallière what had caused the recent vogue of the harp. The Duke did not know, but was sure that his versatile friend, Monsieur de Beaumarchais, would be able to furnish the answer. Why not, then, bring this extraordinary young gentleman to Versailles? So, in 1759, Beaumarchais was presented to the royal princesses; he explained the operation of the harp, and soon consented to teach them how to play the unfamiliar instrument.

One evening, according to Beaumarchais's ardent friend and biographer, Gudin de La Brenellerie, the King himself was standing in the room listening while his daughters gave one of their little concerts. Suddenly, everyone voiced a desire to hear their teacher also. Louis at once pushed his own comfortable chair forward for the harpist, insisting in spite of Beaumarchais's embarrassed refusals that the musician be seated. It was a signal honor which naturally evoked the jealousy of other courtiers.

At about this time Beaumarchais made the acquaintance of an aged financier, the same Paris-Duverney who had long ago helped to enrich Voltaire. Now he was pleased to accept another young man as his protégé. He even advanced Beaumarchais large sums of money, taught him methods of successful speculation, found in the daring, quick-witted youth an apt pupil, and started him also on the road to wealth.

In 1763, Beaumarchais, according to the venal custom of the time, was able to purchase the post of Lieutenant General of the Hunt in the Bailiwick and Captaincy of the Warrens of the Louvre! For nearly twenty-three years, except when absent from the city, he sat weekly as a judge, pronouncing solemnly on violations of the strict royal game laws within a radius of fifty miles from Paris. The procedure was purely formal, decision being always based on the mere letter of the law. Here was a new experience well calculated to reveal the ridiculous intricacies of what, under the Old Régime, was called "justice." It was a schooling which would leave its mark on the scathing satire in his later comedy, *The Marriage of Figaro*.

Two of Beaumarchais's sisters were living in far-away Madrid.

One was married, the other had long thought herself engaged to a rather prominent Spanish journalist named Clavijo. But the latter was evidently in no haste to set up a household. Indeed, after six years, he appeared to have deliberately jilted the unhappy Lisette. Certainly, he was making her the victim of malicious gossip. In early May of 1764, therefore, Beaumarchais climbed into a stage-coach with his baggage and set out for the capital on the other side of the Pyrenees. Traveling night and day, he reached the city, high in the center of the Spanish plateau, on the 18th of the month "at eleven o'clock in the morning," as he carefully noted in his *Memoirs*.

The next weeks offer us, even at this distance, a curious comedy. Beaumarchais promptly sought out the surprised Clavijo, watched his radiant face lengthen and turn to dull lead, coolly browbeat him into signing a confession of his perfidy, even received humble assurances of repentance and an ardent desire to make amends by marrying Lisette whose turn it now was to hesitate. But shortly Clavijo had secretly decamped to another lodging. Beaumarchais tracked him down. Again plausible excuses and fair promises. But, before any action could follow these facile words, Clavijo was once more in hiding. A second time Beaumarchais picked up the trail. The Spaniard, however, had taken medicine. No signing of a contract on a day when one had taken medicine. This alone would nullify it, according to national custom. So at least Beaumarchais was told! In the end, the young Frenchman, after sleepless nights and dire threats, thought himself lucky to escape imprisonment in this foreign country, thanks only to the influence of powerful friends at the Spanish court. He had gained little but a paper victory over the slippery suitor.

Paris-Duverney had entrusted Beaumarchais with two hundred thousand livres in the hope of making some attractive business deals with the Spaniards now that the Seven Years' War had at last dragged to its close. But, in spite of his acquaintance with the French ambassador and with the representative of England, Lord Rochford, in spite of success in gaining the ear of high court circles, Beaumarchais could accomplish nothing. He enjoyed, however, to the full this exciting life of intrigue, of plot and counter-plot. At thirty-two, he was at the height of his reckless energy and handsome charm. With youthful gusto, he donned Spanish sombrero and costume, drove gaily about the city in a carriage drawn by mules to the merry accompaniment of tinkling bells, made love with dashing ardor, plunged into the color and exotic romance of Iberian life. The quick-witted Figaro with his strumming guitar was to spring directly from these vivid months beyond the Pyrenees. Finally, at the end of March, 1765, Beaumarchais left Madrid behind him, stopped over on business in Bordeaux, and was once more back in familiar Paris after nearly a year of absence.

One day the Duc de La Vallière asked the resourceful Beaumarchais for a witty anecdote with which to impress the King, Madame du Barry, and a group of intimates at supper that evening.

"If the King is gay," replied Beaumarchais confidently, "give him this serious moral lesson."

"Sire," he continued by way of example, "while we are laughing here together, have you ever thought that, in virtue of the august rights which the crown has transmitted to you, Your Majesty owes more livres of twenty cents each than there have been minutes elapsed since the death of Christ?"

". . . Here is the calculation. It is now 1768 years since the death of Jesus. . . . Our year is composed of 365 days of twenty-four hours each and every hour of sixty minutes. Counting leap years, you will see that the total makes 929,948,048 minutes, and the King cannot fail to know that he owes more than a billion, in fact almost two billion livres."

But this impressive lesson in the prodigalities of the Court failed to amuse Louis XV as had been hoped. The Duke was queried as to where he had obtained his example. After the reply, someone commented harshly: "That Beaumarchais is a very dangerous man with his romantic ideas of finance and liberty." The figures had apparently been taken from a similar computation by Voltaire a few years earlier, but the King, like his modern counterparts, did not relish so concrete a demonstration of bankruptcy. The witty sally, noted Beaumarchais bitterly, poisoned more than ten years of his life through the loss of royal favor.

3

After the death of Paris-Duverney, Beaumarchais found himself sued by his patron's principal heir, Count de La Blache. According to the curious custom of the time, both sides were expected to visit the judges in order to present the arguments in their own behalf.

The judge who had been selected to study Beaumarchais's case and report on it was named Goëzman. But the defendant had so far been unable to obtain an audience. Finally, it was hinted that Madame Goëzman, with the aid of certain presents, could bring about an interview. Beaumarchais therefore gave her a hundred gold *louis* and a diamond-studded watch. She further demanded fifteen *louis* for her husband's secretary. Beaumarchais protested, but yielded under duress, found the door open at last to Judge Goëzman's chambers, and explained his viewpoint. When the latter, nevertheless, decided against him, the gifts to Madame Goëzman were faithfully handed back with the exception of the fifteen *louis* claimed for the secretary. Beaumarchais insisted on the return of this sum also. Madame Goëzman denied having ever received the fifteen *louis*.

Hereupon Beaumarchais discovered a surprising talent. In a series of *Memoirs,* witty, vivid, filled with conversation and brief vignettes of his antagonists in this hot dispute, he exposed them on the pillory. Thousands of readers snapped up these *Memoirs* eagerly.

"I reply directly and without equivocation," asserted Madame Goëzman confidently, "that never did Lejay speak to me about fifteen *louis* or give them to me."

"Observe, Madame," retorted Beaumarchais suavely, "that there would be much greater merit in saying 'I refused them,' than in maintaining that you didn't know anything about them."

"I maintain, Monsieur," she replied haughtily, "that no one ever spoke to me about them. Would it be common sense to offer fifteen *louis* to a woman of my rank, to me who had refused a hundred the evening before!"

"The evening before what, Madame?"

"Well, Monsieur, the day before the day." (She stopped suddenly and bit her lips.)

"The day before the day," suggested Beaumarchais, "that no one mentioned these fifteen *louis* to you, wasn't it?"

So Beaumarchais suddenly revealed himself a master in ironic cross-examination. Even Louis XV is said to have been secretly amused at this most entertaining of legal arguments. The great Voltaire, far away at Ferney on the Swiss border, gleefully hailed a spirit in many ways like his own.

"What a man he is!" wrote the patriarch to his friend D'Alembert. "He combines everything, wit, gravity, reason, gaiety, vigor, sentiment, all varieties of eloquence, and without seeming deliberately to seek any of them."

In the end, all Paris, as it were, came out to hear the decision in the Beaumarchais case. Madame Goëzman was made to surrender the unfortunate fifteen *louis,* her husband was disbarred from his honorable post in Parlement, Beaumarchais was officially "blamed," as the term went, his four *Memoirs* were condemned to be publicly burned, and he was fined a trifling twelve livres for the sake of the forms. It was an obvious compromise in which the judges timidly straddled the issue and endeavored to censure both sides.

But, from different parts of the city, dignitaries made their way to the house where Beaumarchais was temporarily staying with his friend Lépine and signed their names in the visitor's book. For two days, the narrow street was jammed with carriages. Even the Lieutenant General of Police, Sartine, wrote on the page a large S followed by three stars. His incognito must be preserved, but everyone who counted in society knew his identity. All this honor was of course not for Beaumarchais alone, but fell to him in part as a tribute to his successful struggle against the unpopular new Parlements with which Prime Minister Maupeou had replaced the old courts because of their stubborn, if purely selfish, resistance to royal encroachment.

The Prince de Conti gave a great banquet in behalf of Beaumarchais. As the latter's mercurial temperament radiated triumph, Monsieur de Sartine dropped a humorous word of caution. "It is not enough to be *blamed,*" he warned, "you must be modest besides!"

To be "blamed," however, was more than a mere rebuke. It entailed suspension from his functions as a judge of game laws at the Louvre with loss of his civic rights, and it added grievous obstacles to his already difficult legal battle against La Blache. Beaumarchais's credit as a businessman was also impaired and his whole fortune gravely threatened.

In the effort to win rehabilitation through a renewal of royal favor, Beaumarchais accepted several undercover missions to England. He successfully bought off Théveneau de Morande, who proposed to circulate a salacious pamphlet against Louis XV's notorious mistress, Madame du Barry; he pursued on the Continent a shadowy figure, perhaps of his own invention, named Angelucci, securing in return 72,000 livres in expenses from the government of Louis XVI and a huge diamond, which he wore ostentatiously henceforth, from the Austrian Empress Maria Theresa, mother of Marie-Antoinette; he outwitted that strange figure of disputed sex, the Chevalier d'Eon, and beat down his prodigious demand for 318,477 livres in blackmail against the crown to a paltry 5000.

To occupy his idle moments, Beaumarchais again took up the manuscript of a light comedy which he had been working on from time to time for the last several years. As a result, the *Barber of Seville,* after many postponements, was first performed by the Comédie-Française in its temporary hall of the Tuileries on Thursday, February 23, 1775. But the author had rashly overloaded it with numerous personal references to his recent troubles. The audience, expecting to be amused, was frankly bored. With his remarkable ability to bow promptly before unwelcome facts, Beaumarchais at once tore off the unfortunate additions which he had conveniently pasted on his script, cut his expanded play from five acts to the original four, and three days later was able to rejoice in a striking dramatic success.

4

It was only a few weeks after Beaumarchais's arrival in London during the Chevalier d'Eon affair in April of 1775 that startling news made its slow way across the Atlantic. The American colonists had ventured to fire upon British soldiers at Concord and Lexington!

Beaumarchais again saw frequently his old acquaintance of Madrid days, Lord Rochford. The noble lord talked freely about this grave threat to English prestige. Through his erstwhile enemy, Théveneau de Morande, the secret royal agent met John Wilkes, the fire-eating Lord Mayor of London. The latter was passionately in favor of the Americans and openly violent against King George's seemingly tottering government. At Wilkes's house, the emissary of France became intimate also with an American, Arthur Lee, ambitious, intriguing, and eager to furnish his own impressions of affairs in the unknown country far off on the other side of the Ocean.

The Minister of Foreign Affairs at Paris was the able Count de Vergennes. Vergennes was anxious to combat the hereditary English enemy by helping the American revolt in every way possible. The peace-loving Louis XVI, however, resisted action, being hostile to war on purely Christian grounds. Why, moreover, should he be so rash as to encourage insurrection against royal authority? Such a policy abroad might later have unfortunate repercussions at home. There was also the grave question of ruinous finance piled on top of deficits already dangerous.

The audacious Beaumarchais could perhaps say things which Vergennes himself, as a responsible minister, dared not openly sponsor. On September 21, 1775, the Frenchman addressed from his listening post in London a report of several pages to the King. "All sensible people in England are convinced that the English colonies are lost to the mother country, and this is my opinion too," wrote Beaumarchais confidently. On February 29, 1776, the same observer sent Vergennes a bold letter, headed "Peace or War, For the King Alone." The author of this extensive statement began: "Sire, the famous quarrel between America and England, which will soon divide the world and change the European system, imposes on each power the necessity of examining closely to see how the coming of this separation will influence it for good or ill." In the interest of conserving French possessions in the New World and even peace itself, "we must help the Americans," urged Beaumarchais categorically, supporting his position by a series of numbered arguments.

Back in France, Beaumarchais, on June 10, 1776, over two months before receiving news of the American Declaration of Independence, signed a receipt for an advance of one million livres for which he agreed to be responsible to "the aforesaid Count de Vergennes." This is the famous "million" about which it was long disputed as to whether the money was a pure gift from the French government to the American colonies or merely a loan for business purposes through Beaumarchais. Arthur Lee took particular pains to spread the impression among his friends at home that no repayment was expected. The government of Spain advanced another million secretly and Beaumarchais was expected to raise a third million from private sources.

Under the fictitious name of Roderigue Hortalez and Company, Beaumarchais organized a firm for the purpose of shipping arms and munitions to America. He counted on drawing his cargoes from surplus French stores and on receiving payment in such products as tobacco and rice which would come back in his empty vessels on the return voyage. In an imposing mansion which had once been the Dutch Embassy at number 47 of the Rue Vieille du Temple, he established his headquarters in October of 1776. Soon the Hôtel de Hollande, as it was still called, became a beehive of purposeful activity.

The Americans had urgent need of uniforms, artillery, muskets, and ammunition. Accustomed only to unorganized frontier fighting, they were not experienced in pitched battles or the tactical movements of European troops. They required trained officers, particularly artillery officers and engineers for the planning of entrenched positions. "We need arms, gunpowder, but, above all, we need engineers," cried Arthur Lee from London. "Ah, Monsieur le Comte," wrote Beaumarchais pressingly to Vergennes, "as a favor to me, . . . some powder and a few engineers! . . . But engineers! Engineers and gunpowder!"

The American agent, Silas Deane, had arrived in Paris on July 5th, 1776. Two weeks later, Beaumarchais entered into relations with him, and throughout Deane's stay in France the two got on famously. Arthur Lee, appointed as another American Commissioner on October 22nd after Thomas Jefferson declined to serve, proved, however, a jealous trouble maker. Finally a third representative, the distinguished Benjamin Franklin, drove into Paris toward the end of the same year, on December 21st. His prestige as scientist, diplomat, and world figure, was everywhere immense from the beginning, but, for some reason, he always remained cold to Beaumarchais.

No doubt Franklin had received prejudicial reports from his old friend, Barbeu Dubourg, so promptly supplanted in Vergennes's confidence by the younger man's more energetic and businesslike operations. Moreover, Franklin, calm and poised, was at opposite poles from the mercurial, adventurous Beaumarchais, who had figured in several dubious behind-the-scenes negotiations on behalf of the French government. The aged Philadelphian, unable to fathom the secret intrigues in which the head of the unknown Hortalez and Company had been involved, probably at once made up his mind to follow a safe course and keep aloof. After all, was not Beaumarchais Deane's man? Let Deane, who had entered into agreements before Franklin's arrival, be responsible for him. The wisdom of Franklin's course, from the point of view of his own standing with a suspicious American Congress, soon became apparent, but it was less than just to Beaumarchais's services.

During this and the following crucial year, the latter hurried back and forth from Paris to the various French seaports. At Marseilles, Bordeaux, Nantes, and Le Havre, he was everywhere, driving hard for rapid accomplishment. With the natural decision of a successful man of affairs, he purchased ships, had them equipped, manned with crews and officers, and quickly loaded with barrels, boxes, and huge bales of all sorts. He recruited army officers, including the great Steuben, and arranged for their passage to America.

Silas Deane reported to the Committee of Secret Correspondence which represented the American Congress: "I should never have completed my mission, but for the generous, indefatigable, and intelligent exertions of Monsieur de Beaumarchais, to whom the United States are, on every account, more indebted than to any other person on this side of the ocean." This letter was of November 29, 1776.

Finally, a year and a half later, on March 29, 1778, as Deane was packing up to leave France, he wrote to Beaumarchais himself: "After the perplexing and embarrassing scenes you have had to pass through, it must give you the greatest pleasure to see at last the object of your efforts fulfilled, and a large French fleet ready to sail, which will convince the whole world of the sincere friendship of France and of her absolute determination to protect America's freedom and independence. I once more congratulate you on that glorious event, to which you have contributed more than anybody else."

With naïve and still boyish pride, Beaumarchais made the mistake of showing this letter to Count de Vergennes. He would have done better to keep it to himself. From that moment, the secret agent of the French government found himself out of favor. After all, the King's Minister had no taste for second place in the matter of aid to America.

Portsmouth, New Hampshire, was the main port of entry for Beaumarchais's numerous cargoes throughout the American Revolutionary War. Kegs of gunpowder, lumbering field pieces, heavy cannonballs, thousands of muskets, great bundles of blankets, uniforms, and army shoes, piled up on the docks and then disappeared over rutted roads into the interior. These essential supplies went largely to the army of General Gates in the northern sector. They undoubtedly contributed powerfully to his victory over the English General Burgoyne at Saratoga which, late in 1777, proved a turning point in the war. Meanwhile, Washington's neglected troops, receiving very little of this valuable equipment, struggled to maintain themselves in the middle states of New York, New Jersey, and Pennsylvania. So desperate was the situation after the defeat by Howe on Long Island that Washington wrote at the end of 1776: "If every nerve is not strained to recruit a new army, I think that the game is pretty nearly up."

The American triumph at Saratoga, however, encouraged France to act. With French recognition of the insurgent United States, the unique importance of Beaumarchais's services greatly diminished. Soon French fleets were outfitted, made ready to sail, and set out to combat England on the high seas. An expeditionary force under Rochambeau landed in America and helped win the decisive battle of Yorktown. By 1783, France had lent America, directly or indirectly, thirty-four million livres and had in addition given nine million livres free in cash and supplies. These huge amounts dwarfed even Beaumarchais's contributions, vital as they had been during the crucial period before France's open entry into the war.

The firm of Hortalez and Company existed for seven years from 1776 to 1783. Its business transactions involved the large figure of twenty-one million livres received and an almost equal sum paid out. The profit came only to 51,324 livres, or less than three tenths of one per cent. By dint of feverish energy, business acumen, and additional loans from Vergennes in moments of emergency, Beaumarchais had just barely kept his head above water. But there had been many days and night of deep anxiety.

Vergennes informed the American Congress that "the King had furnished nothing to the Colonies, that he had simply permitted Monsieur de Beaumarchais to take supplies from the King's stores and arsenals, and that he had given obligations for the price of these articles."

Nevertheless, the receipt signed by Beaumarchais on June 10, 1776, for the so-called "lost million" was still kept secret by the French monarchy in order that France's connection with aid to America before the declaration of war against England might not be known. The inability to account for this sum rendered the whole affair suspicious in America.

Yet Silas Deane certified that Congress owed Beaumarchais 3,600,-
000 livres. Barclay, investigating some time later, agreed substantially with Deane. The keen financier, Alexander Hamilton, concluded in favor of 2,280,000 francs which, even if the disputed
million should be further deducted, still represented a large sum
with no account taken of compound interest over the years.

In the end, in spite of Beaumarchais's repeated efforts, no settle-
ment was arrived at during his lifetime. At last, in 1835, thirty-six
years after his death and more than half a century from the end of
the war, a payment, scaled down on a take-it or leave-it basis to
800,000 livres, was made by the American Congress to Beaumarchais's heirs. The whole affair had been one long proof of a debtor's
frequent ingratitude toward his creditor. In the modern world also
examples abound. The millionaire J. P. Morgan is said to have
asked cynically: "Why does that man hate me so? I've never lent
him any money!"

5

As early as 1777, Beaumarchais had first embarked on the writing
of a new comedy, the *Marriage of Figaro*. This sequel to the *Barber
of Seville* involved the same characters, grown older now and more
disillusioned, and it utilized some of the bitter passages which had
finally been rejected for the earlier play. During the next several
years, the work was gradually completed. In the end, it expressed
the author's maturer philosophy of biting satire and incisive criticism of the Old Régime. The *Marriage of Figaro* represents the
height of Beaumarchais's development in the direction of Revolution. It was finally staged in 1784 after years of abortive resistance
on the part of the King, Louis XVI himself.

Jealous enemies had of course made the usual dire predictions of
failure with the general public. The opera singer Sophie Arnould,
however, wittily forecast that the play would "fail fifty times in succession!" As a matter of fact, she was wrong only in the too conservative figure named. Actually, the scintillating comedy enjoyed
a truly formidable run for the time of sixty-eight uninterrupted
performances.

During this active decade preceding the Revolution, Beaumarchais embarked also on the enormous enterprise of republishing
the many-volumed works of Voltaire, whose caustic irony had in such
masterly fashion pointed the way to his own. The indefatigable

editor, overcoming opposition, managed to secure the tacit permission of the French government, bought up masses of his author's manuscripts and letters, obtained the attractive Baskerville type from England, rented an old fortress at Kehl, safely outside of French territory across the German frontier, and finally, between 1785 and 1789, with the aid of co-editors and numerous printers, brought out the seventy volumes of the octavo and the ninety-two volumes of the duodecimo editions. The huge work represented a stupendous literary achievement. This Kehl edition is the most complete collection of Voltaire's works in the eighteenth century and, in spite of shortcomings due to the unscholarly attitude of the time, has remained the basic point of departure for subsequent reprintings. The daring venture was, however, a financial failure which only Beaumarchais's well-lined pocketbook could endure. These years of revolutionary turmoil were far from favorable to so expensive an undertaking and Beaumarchais's tribute to his great predecessor cost him in the end about a million livres!

Yet, although Beaumarchais, like liberal spirits everywhere, welcomed the Revolution when it first broke in 1789, it was not long before he discovered that such long-delayed upheavals are not made in sweetness, light, and "rose water." The great mansion, which late in life he had rashly constructed in the turbulent eastern quarter of Paris facing the somber Bastille, proved a dangerous refuge. In this Faubourg Saint-Antoine, riots roared through the streets daily. With almost two acres of ground and an imposing edifice of two hundred windows, Beaumarchais had ill chosen his time to go up the fool's hill of mad display. To the workmen of the teeming quarter, he appeared a veritable "aristo" and a perpetual object of suspicion. On one occasion, a curious mob swarmed through his house, tracking in mud and dirt, but molesting nothing. On another, hidden in a closet at a neighbor's while a searching party came through after midnight, Beaumarchais dripped cold sweat for four hours. "Upon my word," he wrote when his friend Gudin finally signaled it was safe to come out, "I pressed my forehead in my hands to be certain I was not asleep and dreaming."

In the acute shortage of arms, Beaumarchais was charged with possessing concealed muskets. He was almost completely deaf now and could hardly follow the hostile questioning. At the harsh insistence of the fanatical revolutionary leader, Marat, he was hustled off to prison and crowded into a cell with a group of noblemen. A week later he was called out, to go to his death no doubt. In this moment of nerves strained to the breaking point, he learned suddenly that he was free! He had known the right people at the right time! A former mistress, Amélie Houret, now mistress of the Procurator of the Commune, Manuel, had successfully intervened in behalf of the unhappy victim.

After the terrible prison massacres of early September, 1792, Beaumarchais, in complete disarray, wandered at random through the plowed fields outside of Paris. Finally, mentally and physically exhausted, coated with mud, a picture of dirt and misery, he staggered up to a farmhouse. Indifferent to the vagaries of politics, these peasants brought him a bowl of hot soup and allowed him to spend a peaceful night within the shelter of their barn.

But Beaumarchais's stubborn will was not broken. He insisted on appearing in person before Danton, the powerful Minister of Justice, to prove his innocence in the matter of the muskets! Danton seems to have been amused at the naïveté of this deaf old man, coming out of hiding to demonstrate his good faith in the very face of implacable Revolution. He was actually given the sought-for order to purchase muskets for the French government in Holland! But he was soon proscribed again.

The next years were years of exile and poverty, hardly less filled with movement than any in Beaumarchais's extraordinarily active life. Finally, many months after the fall of Robespierre and the end of the Terror, Beaumarchais was able to obtain amnesty and re-enter Paris on July 5, 1796. His third wife had been obliged to divorce him during the height of the Revolution. It was unsafe then to be married to an exiled *émigré*. Now they were remarried and the family moved back into the huge house, dismal though it was after the long years of neglect, on the Boulevard Saint-Antoine. In spite of everything, Beaumarchais had managed to keep some of his fortune. He died suddenly and quietly of a cerebral hemorrhage without previous illness during the night of May 17-18, 1799. He was sixty-seven years old.

Apprentice watchmaker, teacher of the harp to the four daughters of Louis XV, big businessman, nobleman, courtier, judge, energetic seeker of castles in Spain, undercover emissary of royalty in the less than reputable affairs of Morande, the perhaps fictional Angelucci,

and the controversial Chevalier d'Eon, furnisher of arms to the embattled American colonists and confidant of the King's minister,
Vergennes, author of two brilliant comedies, the *Barber of Seville*
and the *Marriage of Figaro,* publisher of the complete works of
Voltaire, several times a prisoner of abusive power, agent of the
French Revolution and then an unhappy exile, proscribed by it—
Beaumarchais had run the gamut from the lower bourgeoisie high
up the social scale and down again. He had known riches and he
had known poverty. He had tried his hand at nearly everything and
had won success at most. He was goodhearted and generous, clever,
witty, audacious, a shrewd money-maker, and a vigorous defender of
his varied interests before the law. Yet, in his unsurpassed genius for
intrigue, he had been thrown with questionable characters who had
somewhat tarred him with their brush. A certain dignity, a certain
good taste, the wise modesty recommended to him by Monsieur de
Sartine, were always lacking to Beaumarchais. It is this, perhaps,
which accounts for his inability to gain the confidence of Franklin.
At times too, Beaumarchais was incredibly, boyishly naïve. Yet he
possessed so many qualities that it would be unreasonable to expect
him to have all. With his natural human weaknesses, he was a personality unique, it seems, in history. Beaumarchais created the
extraordinary character of Figaro because he was, first of all, to an
unparalleled degree, Figaro himself.

6

The *Barber of Seville,* as we have seen, was first performed at the
Comédie-Française on Thursday, February 23, 1775.

Flitting gaily about the stage at the center of every turn of intrigue, bold, insolent often, yet carrying off each difficult situation
with a ready wit which is never at a loss for a way out of the seeming blind alley, Figaro is Beaumarchais's delightful contribution to
the leading fictional figures of the world. With his colorful satin
vest and breeches, broad band of red silk about his waist, loosely-
knotted neckpiece, white hat with a bright ribbon around the crown,
and a guitar suspended from one shoulder, Figaro, in external appearance, is an obvious product of romanticized memories of Spain,
where the author himself had galloped confidently through top and
bottom of society ten years before.

As the play begins, in the black darkness of a street in Seville, we see a mysterious personage stalking back and forth before the grilled windows. A long brown mantle and a hat with brim turned down before his face are intended to conceal his identity from disturbing prowlers, for this is evidently a "cloak and sword" drama with a comedy twist. The noble lover seeks to win the heart of the beautiful Rosine, held unfortunately incommunicado by her aged guardian, Doctor Bartholo, behind the barred doors and gratings.

Suddenly, Figaro, strumming his guitar and improvising a lively melody to the well-worn themes of love and wine, bursts upon the scene, recognizing almost at once, much to the latter's displeasure, the disguised Count Almaviva.

"Rascal! if you say a word," threatens the angry Count.

"Yes, I recognize you. Those are the kind familiarities with which you have always honored me," retorts Figaro, sardonically, throwing an effective stone into the midst of the nobleman's garden. The wittily impudent servant had long since won a firm place on the French stage, and the aristocratic ladies and gentlemen in the audience were as ready to laugh as the noisy commoners. After all, what were these but amusing plays, and who would be so rash as to connect the bold sallies of an entertaining comedy with anything in real life? Yet less than fifteen years, in 1789, would tell a different story!

Figaro, the barber—Figaro the veterinary—and sometimes the doctor, curing tough customers like Catalans or hardy French mountaineers from Auvergne!—Figaro had already done a little of everything. For, if there exists no universal remedy, bleeding was still considered the nearest thing to it, and this merry descendant of Lesage's Gil Blas was ready to draw his pint of blood or prescribe his horse-doctor's drugs with the best of them! But envy and jealousy lie in wait for all, and who should know this better than Beaumarchais, moving so audaciously among courts and courtiers?

"I thought myself happy to be forgotten," remarks Figaro, "convinced that the great are kind enough to us when they do us no harm!"

"You don't tell the whole story," the Count throws back at him. "I remember, when you were in my service, you were quite a rascal."

"Ah! my Lord, that's because people expect the poor to be without faults. . . . Of the virtues which you require of a domestic, does Your Excellency know many masters worthy to be servants?"

Again Figaro has won the exchange, and the Count can only laugh good-humoredly like the audience and observe: "Not bad!"

But, in this backbiting society torn with envy, where writers are wolves devouring each other, and where critics, publishers, censors, journalists, insects, and mosquitoes all sting, the useful trade of the razor is preferable to the vain honors of authorship, concludes Figaro with what the Count calls the barber's "joyous anger."

"Where did you get your gay philosophy?" asks Almaviva curiously.

"From being accustomed to misfortune. I make haste to laugh at everything for fear of being obliged to weep at it," answers Figaro in a rejoinder famous as the ultimate criticism of a society in mad career toward disaster with no hand to steer or apply the brakes. "Who knows whether the world will last three weeks more?" cries Figaro again later, with cheerful flouting of misfortune.

But crusty old Doctor Bartholo appears at the window in company with the charming Rosine, while the Count and Figaro hurriedly take cover in the darkness.

"It's a barbarous century," mutters the grumbling graybeard. "What has it ever produced to make us praise it? Foolishness of all sorts: freedom of thought, the law of gravitation, electricity, toleration, inoculation against smallpox, quinine, the 'Encyclopedia,' and now these bourgeois dramas!" Bartholo reveals himself promptly as the prince of all reactionaries, a reactionary to bring an end forever to the entire clan of reactionaries, if effective ridicule alone could do it!

"Justice!" cries the doctor to his two comic servants. "Justice is all well enough among wretches like you! But I am your master and am always right. . . . If I don't want a thing to be true, then I say it isn't true. All you need is to let those rascals be right and you'd soon see what would become of authority!"

"Put yourself in my place," Figaro enjoins Bartholo on another occasion.

"Put myself in your place! Ah! I would speak some fine foolishness."

"Monsieur, you're not beginning too badly," retorts Figaro unanswerably.

The two had already crossed swords just previously.

"You carry things with a high hand, Sir," accuses the choleric doctor. "Observe that, when I dispute with a fool, I never give in to him."

Figaro ostentatiously turns his back.

"We differ in that respect, Monsieur," he replies. "I always give in to him!"

But Bartholo's essential ally, Bazile, the unctuous master of calumny, is finally won over to Almaviva by the irrefutable argument of a heavy purse of gold pieces slipped into his outstretched hand at the right moment. Figaro shows himself, as usual, resourceful for every situation. The Count, and the delightful Rosine are married, and the defeated Bartholo is obliged to content himself, after all not too unwillingly, with her extensive property. In this, the wealthy nobleman can afford to be generous without much sacrifice. The subtitle of the "Useless Precaution" underlines the predestined failure of the shrewd, but unamiable Bartholo. With all his penetrating suspicion and careful planning, he and his old age can obviously be no match for the magnetic power of youth and love.

The play is a joyous cascade of intrigue, of plot and counter-plot, of French characters in a colorful Spanish setting. Figaro, throughout, cleverly pulls the strings of action and it is Figaro who makes the telling thrusts at the abuses of rank under the Old Régime. But Beaumarchais was still not in too bad favor at Court. His satire was still given and received with laughter. The latent bitterness of a few years hence was not yet characteristic of the bright and happy *Barber of Seville*.

7

"The King does not want the *Marriage of Figaro* to be played; therefore it shall be played," Beaumarchais is said to have gone on repeating to ready ears.

The comedy had been started in 1777 when many trials continued to plague the harassed author. It was accepted by the actors of the Comédie-Française in 1781, but for three turbulent years of backing and filling by the royal censorship under pressure of the authorities the play could not get on the public stage. Beaumarchais, however, provoked eager interest with the aid of the lively readings which he let himself be persuaded to accord as a special favor to groups beseeching him from all sides. In a society rushing unknowingly toward its doom, there was an avid struggle for the privilege of listening to the forbidden drama.

The Queen, Marie-Antoinette, also had her curiosity piqued. Why could not this diverting comedy be read to her own private circle? Beaumarchais, obligingly enough, furnished a copy of his manuscript, but, when the usually sluggish King heard its alarming contents, he unexpectedly exploded. According to Madame Campan, the royal reader, he cried out angrily: "It is detestable! It will never be played! Why! if this piece were to be performed, the Bastille would have to be pulled down! . . . That man mocks everything which ought to be respected in government." The King, for once, saw more deeply than the superficial courtiers around him, but he had no strength of will to persist in his refusal.

Countess de Polignac, no doubt on behalf of the Queen, made arrangements to have the play presented on the stage of the "Menus Plaisirs" in Paris. At first, rehearsals were kept secret, but many spectators were admitted to the dress performances. The King, however, made no move. The comedy was announced publicly for June 13, 1783. Official silence still. Tickets were issued, bearing a piquant allusion to the provocative popular song, "Mal'brough s'en va-t-en guerre," which Beaumarchais, with his usual flair for the topical, had promptly seized upon and incorporated into his drama. No action yet. Suddenly, between noon and one o'clock on the day of the opening, the Duc de Villequier hurried to the Théâtre des Menus Plaisirs with an order for the actors to cease their plans at once "under pain of incurring His Majesty's anger." There was of course no resisting such a command. Shouts of "oppression" and "tyranny" rose from the disappointed audience.

Count de Vaudreuil was the witty master of court pleasures. In spite of this recent suppression of the "Marriage," he made preparations for a private showing on the stage of his country place at Gennevilliers, only a few miles northwest of Paris. Beaumarchais slyly objected that the royal prohibition had raised an unfortunate suspicion of immorality against his "innocent" play. Such a disastrous reputation could only be removed by a new approval of the censor! A member of the French Academy was thereupon chosen for this task. He bore the appropriate name of Gaillard and with good grace soon did what was expected of him, authorizing the play after some suggested changes. On September 26th of the same year, the *Marriage of Figaro* was at length performed before a select group of three hundred persons, the author himself being invited to witness his triumph. In spite of their open delight in the gay comedy, some spectators were said not to favor a public showing for so dangerous a play. After all, what was entertaining for their "betters" might not be altogether safe for the people at large!

But the people at large were not content to sit silent and take only what was offered them. Besides, there were the energetic whisperings of that chief of intriguers, Monsieur Caron de Beaumarchais. He had habitually overcome opposition in the past. Would he not succeed in doing so again? "All Europe has its eyes on my *Marriage* and on me," he is said to have repeated. "My reputation depends on its being played, and it will be." The King, once more perspicacious, if weak, observed bitterly: "You will see that Beaumarchais will have more influence than the Keeper of the Great Seal." The latter's open hostility to the play was well known. With extraordinary wit, comic verve, and originality, the author actually defended his play successfully in person before the board of three or four censors.

Seven months after the brilliant performance at Gennevilliers, the *Marriage of Figaro* was at last given before the general public at Paris by the Comédie-Française in its grand new building on the site of the modern Odéon theater or present Salle du Luxembourg. It was on Tuesday, April 27, 1784. Never had such a throng been seen under similar circumstances, it was remarked. "Hardly had the doors been opened when the theater was filled. Little more than half of the crowd which had been waiting since eight in the morning managed to squeeze in. Those who did enter crashed their way through the gates, throwing their money at the doorkeepers. . . . More than one duchess was happy that day to find a miserable little stool in the balcony where ladies of rank seldom go." Such was the contemporary report of the journalist Meister. Some grand ladies dined in the dressing rooms with the actresses in order to be sure of seats. Several people were trampled in the wild crowd.

The *Marriage of Figaro* turns about a scabrous subject, the supposed "Right of the Nobleman" to the first favors of Suzanne, who is engaged to be Figaro's bride. In its very central theme, the play is, then, a bold condemnation of the grossest abuses attributed to aristocracy. In blinking that fact, the censorship was obliged in the end to abdicate completely its assumed function.

The leading characters, Figaro, Count Almaviva, the Countess, his wife (who is the piquant Rosine of the *Barber of Seville*), are all

378

BEAUMARCHAIS

Engraving by Saint-Aubin after a painting by Cochin.

FIGARO

Beaumarchais's famous character.

FRANKLIN

Portrait by Duplessis (1783).

TREATY OF FRANCO-AMERICAN FRIENDSHIP (1778).

See page 396.

TRAITÉ
D'AMITIÉ ET DE COMMERCE,
CONCLU
ENTRE LE ROI
ET
LES ÉTATS-UNIS
DE
L'AMÉRIQUE SEPTENTRIONALE,
Le 6 Février 1778.

A PARIS,
DE L'IMPRIMERIE ROYALE.

M. DCCLXXVIII.

older now. The first glamor of youthful courtship and romance which enlivens the earlier play has become tarnished by the disillusionments of a few passing years. The fickle Almaviva casts his wayward eyes in the direction of new conquests, particularly toward Figaro's bride-to-be; the Countess views sadly the ruins of her former love; Figaro, momentarily a bit naïve in preoccupation with his coming marriage, has to be told by his fiancée of the Count's intrigue against him, while Suzanne, the Countess, and the force of accidental circumstances play a major part in averting final catastrophe.

In Beaumarchais's detailed survey of the characters, he carefully warns the actors to avoid all exaggeration in the principal roles. The Count is basically corrupt, it is true, but within the limits of external good manners and the superficial polish of the time. The Countess is deeply wounded by her husband's neglect, yet with an anger which is restrained and with no lessening of her virtuous charm. Figaro is the personification of "reason lightened by gaiety and clever sallies" without any touch of caricature or farce comedy. Suzanne is adroit, witty, bubbling with laughter, though with no trace of stage effrontery. The new character of Chérubin is a young boy in mid-adolescence, timid in the imposing presence of the Countess, but vaguely troubled by her femininity, a person very much, no doubt, like the young rascal Beaumarchais himself at the same age. Bartholo and Bazile are unchanged from the *Barber of Seville,* though here they are only of secondary importance. Brid'Oison, the comic Judge, with a slight stuttering and his emphasis on the pure letter of the law, offers a clear take-off on the author's enemy, Goëzman, but again without slap-stick. The author's own experience in enforcing the ridiculous complexities of the royal game laws in his court at the Louvre had provided him with effective background.

The play abounds in movement. There is a rapid succession of shifting scenes. The plot develops incredibly in sudden turns which Beaumarchais manages with the same extraordinary skill he had shown so often in real life. The audience has reason to be astounded at the color, suspense, and variety of the author's greatest play, a rare instance of a sequel which surpassed even its brilliant predecessor.

The high watermark of revolutionary criticism is reached in the famous monologue of Figaro in the third scene of the fifth act. The speaker is alone, in somber mood, as he muses in the darkness. "Monsieur le Comte," Figaro apostrophizes the absent Almaviva.

"Because you are a great nobleman, you think yourself a great genius! Nobility, fortune, rank, position: all those things make one so proud! What have you done to win so many advantages! You have taken the trouble to be born, and nothing more! For the rest, you are a man ordinary enough! While, as for me, lost in the obscure crowd, I have had to use more knowledge and planning merely to exist than have been expended through the last hundred years in governing all of Spain!"

The reader is reminded of Beaumarchais's own bitterness over attacks on his purchased nobility. "Do you know," he wrote on one occasion, "that I can prove twenty years of nobility? And that nobility is my legitimate property, as a fine piece of parchment adorned with a large seal of yellow wax attests. My nobility, unlike that of so many people, is not uncertain, something for which you have to take somebody's word. No one can challenge its authenticity, because I still hold the receipt for the money I have had to pay for it!"

There follows in the monologue a summary of Figaro's adventurous career which is not without its obvious relationship to the author's extraordinarily varied personal experience. He alludes to his imprisonment at For-l'Evêque. "At once, I see," he says, "from inside a cab, the descending drawbridge of a fortress at the entrance of which I leave behind all hope and liberty," thus concluding with a famous reminiscence from Dante. In an earlier text, Beaumarchais had had the temerity actually to name the Bastille, that hated symbol of autocratic abuse in the eighteenth century. It was perhaps this thrust which particularly angered the generally easy-going Louis XVI.

"How I should like to hold in my hands, at a time when a good disgrace has wiped out his pride, one of those powerful ministers of four days' tenure! I would tell him that, whatever foolishness may be printed, it has no importance except in places where you hinder its circulation; that, without freedom to criticize, there is no such thing as worth-while praise; and that it is only little men who fear little writings."

Figaro sits down and, after a pause, continues:

"Tired of supporting an obscure boarder in prison, they finally turn me out into the street, and, since you have to eat even when not in prison, I sharpen up my quill again and ask everybody what's going on. They tell me that, during my economical retirement from society, there has been established in Madrid a system of liberty in the sale of all products which extends even to the press, and that, provided I speak in my writings neither of authority nor of religion nor of politics nor of morality nor of men in power nor of influential organizations nor of the Opera nor of other public spectacles nor of anyone who has to do with anything, I can print freely whatever I wish, subject to the inspection of two or three censors!" So much for freedom of speech and of the press under Louis XVI! Beaumarchais's long struggle to get his play on the stage had sharpened his irony.

"I was considered for a position," pursues Figaro a little further on. "Unfortunately, I was fitted for it. They needed someone good at figures; it was a dancer who obtained the post! . . . I even began to understand that, to make money, knowing your way around is better than knowledge of the thing itself." It was a piquant thrust at influence-peddlers and inefficiency under the Old Régime.

The long monologue ends in a philosophic revery on the strangeness of destiny. "What a mad succession of events!" exclaims Figaro. "How did all these things happen to me? Why these things and not others? What brought them upon my head? Driven to follow a road on which I entered without knowing it and which I shall leave against my will, I have strewn it with as many flowers as my gaiety permitted. I say my gaiety, but without knowing whether it belongs to me any more than all the rest, nor even what this self is with which I am concerned: a formless assemblage of unknown parts; then a feeble unreasoning creature, next a playful little animal, then an ardent, pleasure-loving young man with every impulse for enjoyment and following all sorts of trades in order to live: a master here, a servant there, depending on the caprice of fortune! Ambitious out of vanity, industrious from necessity, but lazy with delight! An orator under pressure of danger, a poet for recreation, a musician on occasion, in love by mad whims, I have seen everything, done everything, exhausted everything."

Here is a bitter note of skepticism and disillusion. Unexpectedly, Beaumarchais seems to manifest an affinity with Shakespeare's Hamlet whose "To be or not to be" monologue had been widely known in France through more or less faithful translations by Voltaire or others during the last half-century. Figaro speaks, too, with a tone somewhat like Diderot's still unpublished *Jacques the Fatalist*,

D'Alembert's Dream, or *Rameau's Nephew,* though there is no reason to suppose that Beaumarchais, at this time, had had an opportunity to know any of them. Probably, the passage is only the direct reflection of a thoughtful moment in his active and checkered career.

Who has not at some time asked himself these unanswerable questions. Why? what for? what is the meaning of chance, fortune, destiny? Beaumarchais, too, wonders, and his amazement at the wealth and position accorded the corrupt Almaviva by the accident of birth, in sharp contrast to the prodigies of intelligence and wit deployed by Figaro merely to make his way in the midst of an ill-ordered society, constitutes one more fierce indictment of the world around him. It is *Rameau's Nephew* once again, but with only a tinge of the latter's corrosive bitterness.

But could it be that an echo of one of Diderot's eloquent spoken monologues came to Beaumarchais's ears one day as he perhaps passed a vivid hour with the great Encyclopedist in his book-lined study high on the sixth floor of the house on the Rue Taranne or listened to a characteristically brilliant improvisation at the Café Procope or the Café de la Régence? Who now can know?

In any case, only Louis XVI and a handful of serious-minded courtiers or journalists gave signs of being disturbed. The others laughed gaily at Figaro's invectives and went on, unheeding. "After us the deluge?" Perhaps, but who would ever overturn this centuries-old society, seemingly so firmly rooted? The Ancient Régime, said Talleyrand, was a time when living was at its pleasantest—for those of wealth and place and power. Who troubled to think of the rest? Not Marie-Antoinette certainly, not Madame de Polignac, not the Duc de Vaudreuil. And poor Louis XVI was able only to wish timidly for some vague reforms, without knowing upon whom to lean or where to turn for their accomplishment. But Beaumarchais, like Figaro, by wit, industry, versatility, and good fortune, managed finally to ride out the storm. Although sympathetic with the first aims of 1789, Beaumarchais was not at heart a violent revolutionary. We may be sure that the author of the play, desiring only peaceful change and the correction of blatant abuses, hardly realized how potentially dangerous was the gay weapon he had forged. Who, even after the ancient Bastille fell, could yet foresee the emerging Terror?

But the *Marriage of Figaro,* Napoleon is reported to have said, is "the Revolution already in action."

CHAPTER XXIII

LOUIS XVI PAYS THE BILL

I

"Louis XVI appears to promise the French nation a most happy and fortunate reign," wrote the journalist Métra optimistically on June 4, 1774. Less than a month earlier, by his grandfather's death, the young heir to the throne had been unwillingly thrust into power. On May 10th, the very first day of his rule, the new King had addressed to the Controller General of Finance a characteristically well-intentioned letter:

"I beg you," he wrote, "to distribute two hundred thousand livres to the poor of Paris that they may pray for the King. If you find this too much, in view of the needs of the State, you may deduct the money from my pension and from that of Madame la Dauphine." The order was signed, with unconscious irony in the light of what was to come, "Louis Augustus." Meister, secretary to Brimm and his successor in the famous secret *Literary Correspondence,* reading the order, exclaimed with the warm sentimentality of his time: "All Paris has been moved to tears."

"What a burden!" cried the twenty-year-old King, appalled at the weight of his responsibilities. "And I have been taught nothing. It seems as though the universe is about to fall upon me!"

At each public appearance of the two young sovereigns, Louis and Marie-Antoinette, they were enthusiastically acclaimed by a hopeful people. The King was reported to have said to the Lieutenant of Police: "The poor must be able to eat bread at two cents a pound." The new monarch planned important savings in expenses for the royal table, even also in his adored pastime of the chase, and remitted the abhorred tax of the so-called "Joyous Accession to the Throne" which, under his predecessor, had cost a cool twenty million francs. He would no longer tolerate the dissolute morals of the former Court. "I need around me honest men with the courage to warn me of my duty," said the King. Promptly, he exiled the notorious Madame du Barry to a convent and expelled the worst followers of the late royal mistress. A breath of clean air began to blow for a moment over the corrupt circles of Versailles.

In late August of 1774, after less than four months of the King's rule, a new figure stepped into a key position in the government. Turgot became Controller General of Finance. With the enormous debt which had been piling up for over a century during the unhappy reigns of Louis XIV and Louis XV, economy and efficiency of administration were the two great needs of France.

Anne-Robert-Jacques Turgot was at this time forty-seven years old. He had behind him a notable record of reform as Intendant of the southwestern generality, or district, of Limoges which he had made a center of fruitful experiment in improved methods of taxation, construction of roads and canals, freedom of trade in grain and industry, encouragement of popular education, and the organization of government works to aid the poor, in short, a modern and forward-looking program.

The new Controller General attributed his cool rationality to a rigorous Sorbonne training for the priesthood, later abandoned. As early as 1749, while Rousseau was meditating his remarkable attack on the sciences and arts, Turgot demonstrated the liberal trend of his thinking by a Latin essay on the *Progress of the Human Mind.* Influenced strongly by the recent ideas of Quesnay, leader of the Physiocrats or believers in natural economic law, Turgot had already attracted wide attention by his *Reflections on the Formation and Distribution of Wealth,* first published in periodical form during 1769 and 1770. In this work, he emphasized the basic importance of agriculture, argued for a "single tax" on land, and urged the necessity of complete freedom, *laissez faire,* for commerce and industry. Thus Turgot may have helped shape the theories of the Scotch economist, Adam Smith, author of the famous *Wealth of Nations* in 1776.

Turgot had contributed articles to the great *Encyclopedia* edited by Diderot and D'Alembert. He was the friend of Voltaire and of the eighteenth-century philosophic party. When his enemies brought up this incriminating connection, the King is said to have brushed aside the charge with the curt reply: "He is an honest and enlightened man; and that is enough for me." Voltaire wrote hopefully to his old friend, Madame du Deffand: "If anyone can re-establish the finances, he can." Less than a year later, however, the proprietor of

Ferney observed sadly that Turgot "has three terrible obstacles in his way, the financiers, the rascals, and the gout." This last was an allusion to the ill health which did indeed immobilize and handicap him during long periods of his brief term in office.

Turgot was tall, handsome, with an expressive, mobile face. He was serious, a hard worker, well-educated, a keen thinker, and passionately devoted to the public good. Along with these admirable, but by no means popular qualities, Turgot unfortunately was shy, somewhat awkward in society, and a poor speaker in public. Moreover, he possessed the intellectual's tendency to move straight toward his goal regardless of entrenched opposition, seemingly unaware that logic is far from governing the world, ignorant of the practical man's dictum that "politics is the art of the second best," that not what you will, but what you can, is often the wiser, if less inspiring course. Like a man in a hurry, Turgot piled reform rapidly upon reform.

"No bankruptcy," he said to the King, "no increase in taxes, no borrowing." To execute this ideal, but well-nigh impossible program, to save the State solely by stern economy and efficient administration, Turgot besought the youthful monarch, whose dominant weakness he knew only too well, to remain firm. "You must arm yourself," he said to Louis XVI, "against your very kindness, consider where this money comes from which you distribute to your courtiers, and compare the misery of those from whom we are sometimes obliged to take it by the most rigorous methods, with the situation of the people who have the greatest influence on your liberalities."

With driving energy, Turgot attacked the worst enemy, the ever-present deficit. Fearful of an added fatal strain on tottering French finances, he consistently opposed the popular demand for intervention in the far-away revolt of the thirteen American colonies against England. Turgot struck nearly a million livres from the cost of the royal household, nine millions from the military budget, a million from the department of roads and bridges, twelve millions from general operating expenses, and more than a million from other services. On the positive side, he increased retirement allowances, which had fallen several years behind, and gave double payments to those most in need; he applied fifteen millions toward liquidating the huge public debt.

But what could arouse more violent hostility among the greedy than such long-needed, yet always painful economy? On this score, Turgot cherished no illusions. "I shall be feared," he said to the young King, "hated even, by nearly all at Court, by everyone who solicits favors. . . . I shall be vilified, and perhaps in a way plausible enough to make me lose Your Majesty's confidence."

A firm believer in the beneficent effects of free trade, Turgot, on September 13, 1774, removed all restrictions on the buying and selling of wheat within the limits of the kingdom. Here, said the enthusiastic nineteenth-century historian Michelet, thinking of the great battle song to be consecrated by the coming Revolution, "was the *Marseillaise* of wheat!"

It is hard to imagine today the hampering bonds put on the distribution of this basic food throughout fertile eighteenth-century France. Even from province to province, the free movement of grain was generally forbidden for fear of local famine. A secretly-operating government monopoly endeavored to build up a reserve for years of scarcity, but, whether wise or unwise in principle, this measure was widely distrusted in actual practice. Public opinion, in spite of the fervent support of the philosophers, was ill prepared for Turgot's radical change. Even the well-known Swiss banker, Necker, future minister of Louis XVI, issued an attack on it which won many readers.

One of the most hated abuses of the Old Régime was that of the *corvée*. This was a system of forced labor to which were largely due the admirable public roads of France. As the imposed work, varying from six to as much as thirty days a year, was done without pay, it constituted a particularly onerous tax laid upon the already overburdened and desperately poor peasants. They alone were regarded as *corvéables*, or subject to this humiliating and ruinous task. Such days of gratuitous toil were of necessity subtracted from those of productive work, which at best were all too few to offer more than the most meager subsistence.

The abolition of the *corvée* had long been one of Turgot's most cherished reforms. Suddenly, in early January of 1775, the gout struck him down. While he continued to labor incessantly from a sick bed, he had no opportunity for four months to combat directly the intrigues forming against him in the unfriendly and jealous Court. Finally, however, a year later, he issued an edict replacing the *corvée* by a tax in money on all owners of property, "privileged and non-privileged." The justice and impartiality of this tax were actually an added count against it! What! the wealthy, previously exempt from the despised *corvée,* must now, in lieu of it, pay a tax, while the downtrodden peasant went free! This was indeed *lèse-majesté* toward the high in rank and station! Here was an intolerable assault upon ancient and long-established usage, subversive of the very foundations of a still feudal society! Turgot would pay the penalty of such boldness.

As the spendthrift habits of the luxury-loving Court continued, with unceasing demands for exorbitant royal pensions, it became more and more evident that no economy would be possible without the strongest of strong hands on the throne. From nearly all sides, hostility to change increased, and Turgot was again impeded by illness. The well-meaning King, fearful of the growing struggle, remarked sadly: "Monsieur Turgot and I are the only ones who love the people."

A war of libels issued against Turgot rose to greater violence. Vainly, he urged the vacillating King to stand firm. But courtiers, nobility, financial circles, and higher clergy all sought his downfall. Marie-Antoinette joined in pressing for Turgot's dismissal. Only the uninfluential "little people" and the philosophers favored the harassed minister. On the 13th of May, 1776, Louis, unable to screw up courage to the point of telling the disagreeable news to Turgot's face, sent a message to request his immediate resignation. "I hope that time will not justify me," wrote the latter magnanimously but with unavoidable foreboding, as he took leave of his unhappy master.

Turgot had seen clearly the crying need of strict economy and sweeping reforms. He had feared the coming of violent revolution if injustice went too long uncorrected. By constructive measures, he had tried to forestall an upheaval, but with little success. The forces of selfishness and tradition were too strong. Dogmatically, with insufficient allowance for sluggish human nature, Turgot had perhaps tried to accomplish too much in too short a time, compressing into a few months the effort to overthrow the deeply-rooted consequences of centuries of abuse. He had been right in the wrong way. Yet, without the firmest support from the King himself, it is doubtful if anyone could have done better. In less than two brief years, this first hopeful attempt at complete reform had proved abortive. With the fall of Turgot, reaction was once more definitely in the ascendant.

2

The new Controller General, an obscure man named Clugny, when called upon to win the King's favor by good work in his arduous post, answered with cynical frankness: "By my faith, I'm sure the cleverest man in the world wouldn't know how to do it, but, since I need to get myself talked about, I can only upset in one direction what Turgot overturned in the other." The death of Clugny five months later put an end to this crude program.

A heavy-set man, self-confident, somewhat haughty, a bit brusque and stiff, now came into power amid wide acclaim. This was the celebrated Swiss banker, Necker, the opponent of Turgot and of free-trade. For the last thirty years, Necker had been established in Paris where he had grown rich through a combination of business acumen and inside information. The new minister possessed the unhesitating assurance and public reputation which readily accompany such tangible success. He and his wife presided over an influential literary salon where their ten-year-old daughter, the future Madame de Staël, sat eager-eyed on a stool, listening to the brilliant conversation of a brilliant age and sharpening her wits in the most exciting of informal schoolings. As a famous writer of the following century, she was herself to become a powerful mover of ideas.

Necker was a foreigner and a Protestant. He could not therefore assume the post of Controller General of Finance in Catholic France. But new words were conveniently found to solve this dilemma. He was entitled Director General of the Treasury!

Whatever may have been Necker's abilities in the limited field of private business, he possessed no breadth of view, offered no fundamental answer to the desperate plight of the weakening monarchy. Moreover, the government had definitely turned its back on Turgot's thorough-going reforms. Besides, it was now confronted with the huge additional expenses of an imminent American war against the hereditary foe, England. In this difficult situation, Necker, with his great confidence in the power of bank credit, could only propose borrowing and repeated borrowing in one form or another, more or less concealed. By this means, he succeeded in holding on to office for five years.

In February of 1781, Necker published a *Review of Government Finances* which, although not fully frank, since it suggested the existence of a balance instead of the continuing deficit, did throw into bold relief the vicious system of royal gifts and pensions amounting to some twenty-eight millions of francs a year. The popularity of these ordinarily arid figures was immense. On the first day of publication, eager readers snatched up six thousand copies of Necker's summary; soon as many as a hundred thousand had been sold. In this financial report, the Director General of the Treasury had made an unprecedented contribution to the education of the Old Régime.

But on May 19, 1781, Necker was forced to resign. As the news traveled rapidly about Paris the next day, a deep gloom "on all faces" disturbed the Sunday-morning quiet, we are told. Opponents of the dismissed minister of finance were too few not to "blush" at betraying joy. The contemporary observer, Meister, reported in his *Literary Correspondence:* "The sidewalks, the cafés, all public places were thronged, but an extraordinary silence reigned. People looked at one another and shook hands sadly, as though in face of a public calamity, or rather like a family bereaved of its last hope of support."

That evening at the famous Comédie-Française, still in the Tuileries palace, the actors played by coincidence Collé's *Hunting Party of Henry IV,* a revival of fifteen years before. There were allusions to the achievements of Sully at the beginning of the seventeenth century: "Speak with respect of so great a minister," and "I have just seen him enter the Cabinet." There were references to popular King Henry IV, "Sire, with any other prince than you, I should have considered myself lost," or "Ah! what cruel people, how they have deceived me!" Such lines were at once applied by the spectators to the fall of Necker and seemed to offer a criticism of Louis XVI's failure to stand firm in his behalf. Tears of emotion, cries of indignation, wild applause from the mercurial audience, constantly interrupted this topical play. Only the submission of proof that the drama had already been billed a week before anyone knew of Necker's imminent removal, saved the members of the state theater from being severely disciplined. The government promptly prohibited journalists from mentioning Necker in the future either favorably or unfavorably.

So great had been the people's fervent hope for reform of the Old Régime that they had not recognized Necker as only a broken reed. He had at least shown comprehension of the Court's ruinous extravagance and he stood out in happy contrast to all his predecessors in office except Turgot. Necker was destined to return for some moments of abortive power beginning with August, 1788, on the eve of the French Revolution.

3

In these crucial years of the late eighteenth century, the personalities of the King and Queen naturally played a major role.

Louis XVI was thick-set, strong, clumsy, awkward, timid, inclined to be taciturn, with the round face, large nose, big lips, and florid complexion of his German mother. At times of crisis in council, he sometimes, in embarrassment, actually feigned to be asleep! The young man had none of the terrifying majesty of his great ancestor, Louis XIV, none of the handsome mien which in early years at least half-veiled the grievous shortcomings of Louis XV. The appearance of Louis XVI, in short, was commonplace in the extreme. Nature had in no way endowed him to be a king.

The young monarch delighted in heavy manual labor over the forge or anvil, took pride in his skill as a locksmith, threw himself vigorously into the hard cross-country riding of his almost daily hunting parties, strove with sweat to curb his tendency to put on still more flesh. But over-eating, accompanied by frequent attacks of indigestion, largely nullified the effects of exercise. So passionately did he love the chase that, on days when he did not hunt, even on that world-shaking July 14 of 1789, as the grim fortress of the Bastille in wild uproar and murder fell, Louis XVI from long habit prosaically wrote down in his *Diary:* "Nothing." At the formal ceremonies of his coronation on June 11, 1775, the King, like any good bourgeois, found the heavy gold crown uncomfortable on his head. There was no exultation in power for him.

A slight physical defect prevented Louis XVI for seven years from consummating his marriage. The lack of an heir to the throne became the subject of scurrilous popular jokes. The beautiful Marie-Antoinette spoke of her husband in a letter as "poor fellow," thereby recklessly doing further injury to the waning prestige of the young monarch. Finally, in 1777, the Queen's brother, Emperor Joseph of Austria, during a visit to Paris, prevailed upon the hesitant Louis to undergo a minor operation which quickly relieved him of his infirmity. A royal daughter was thereupon born in December of 1778. Three years later the couple had a son, the new Dauphin. In 1785, there came another son who, known later as Louis XVII, disappeared mysteriously during the Revolution. Finally, in 1786, the two welcomed a second daughter who lived, however, only a single year. But the cynical Court refused to believe that Louis XVI had in fact produced heirs. The irreparable damage to the royal reputation had been done.

With all his numerous handicaps and shortcomings, the King was honest and kindhearted, without pride or personal vanity. He had a natural instinct for justice, was a fervent, if somewhat narrow, Christian, and often manifested a shrewd common sense which made up in some degree for his mediocre intelligence. Emperor Joseph, though prepared by the Queen's carping letters for a completely derogatory impression of Louis's capacities, was instead struck by his real grasp of European affairs. The King desired the welfare of his long-suffering people and sought feebly through the good offices of Turgot and Necker to do what was needed. For the graceful and charming Marie-Antoinette, this clumsy and unfortunate man showed a touching respect and affection. Writing from one of his rare tours about the country in June, 1786, Louis, still struggling to modulate the raucous outbursts which irked the polished Queen, said humbly: "You will, I hope, be pleased, for I don't think I have broken out once with my loud voice."

When only a child of twelve, Louis had set up a small hand printing press on which, with the aid of his two younger brothers, he struck off a little volume of *Moral and Political Maxims Selected from "Télémaque."* Twenty-five copies were made, one of which was proudly hurried away to King Louis XV. The latter, however, horrified at this revolutionary doctrine culled from Fénelon, abruptly called upon his too idealistic grandson to break up the offending plates at once.

The then Dauphin, already oppressed by his coming destiny, used often to cry out like Mentor's serious young pupil, Telemachus: "If ever I have the misfortune to reign!" In 1775, near the beginning of his short occupancy of the throne, Louis XVI revealed his enlightened tolerance of bold ideas by having Fénelon's *Examination of Conscience on the Duties of Royalty,* long since available abroad, published even in conservative monarchical France. We have already seen how searching was the thoroughness of the Archbishop's challenge to kingly responsibility and devotion to the people's welfare. Unfortunately, endued with Fénelon's constructive ideas though he may have been, the young sovereign could not gather from his wise counsels the keen judgment and unbreakable will of Monsieur de Cambrai. It was such strength of will, indeed, that Louis XVI most lacked. Without force of character, he could never be an effective king, especially in these days of stress during which his unhappy lot fell.

The Queen, Marie-Antoinette, was the daughter of Maria Theresa, Empress of Austria. The girl had come to France to be married at fifteen in 1770. Only four years later, fate propelled the giddy bride to the throne. Most unwisely, Marie Theresa endeavored to use the young woman in order to strengthen the military alliance between their two countries. The natural result was that the Queen was soon referred to contemptuously by her French subjects as "the Austrian."

A child still in these early years, with little serious education to guide her, yet a "delightful vision" of grace and beauty, as the Englishman, Edmund Burke, saw her on his visit to France, Marie-Antoinette plunged gaily into the whirlwind of pleasure which elevation to her new life made possible. Plays, dances, court *fêtes*, horseback rides, a mad round of frivolity, filled her days. The formal etiquette of the Court at Versailles with the royal levees and the rigid rules of precedence, bored the heedless young girl to extinction. Chafing under these senseless, but long-established restrictions, she flaunted them recklessly in public with consequent gossip and serious damage to her moral reputation. What a relief from the solemn gilded splendor of the great palace to hurry off to the Little Trianon or to play at milkmaid amid the thatched roofs and winding paths of the adjacent "Swiss Village"!

Marie-Antoinette probably never actually made the remark attributed to her about the French peasants: "If they don't have bread, let them eat cake!" The saying had already been quoted by Jean-Jacques Rousseau in the first half of his *Confessions* as referring to an earlier princess. Yet there is no reason to suppose that the young Queen had any greater comprehension of the people's plight than was implied by such a blind or flippant sentence. Neither member of the royal pair had at any time felt obligated to tour the country and study realistically at first hand the life and problems of the nation, as Fénelon would have urged. Installed amid the exaggerated magnificence of Versailles by the unwise decision of Louis XIV, the royal Court was thereby cut off from the teeming, work-a-day world of Paris. If it seemed safer for the moment to be thus aloof from recurrent riots in the tumultuous capital, the danger was only greater and more fateful in the end. Marie-Antoinette was as impractical and shielded from reality by her station as by the broad hoop skirts and towering hair-dos which were the aristocratic fashion of the hour.

Well-intentioned at heart, but fatally ignorant of life about her, the unfortunate Queen quickly became unpopular. On her solemn entry into Paris after the birth of a royal daughter, she heard none of the usual joyous cries of "Vive la reine!" even for the sake of form, but only a stony silence. Why hadn't the police taken the precaution of hiring paid "shouters"? the young woman complained petulantly. Disturbed at times and totally uncomprehending, she cried out at the open hostility of the people: "What can I have done to them?" As the Queen's spendthrift habits and her frivolous companions came more and more to be blamed for all of France's grievous financial woes, the name "Madame Deficit" began to be fastened upon her.

Withal, Marie-Antoinette had a strong will for gratifying her slightest whim, but no thought for reform and efficient administration. To her pouting and cajolery, the King could oppose only a momentary angry stubbornness which weakly yielded in the end. Louis XVI was able to offer neither Queen nor country the firm, wise guidance so much needed. The royal couple themselves were the unhappy decisive causes of the ultimate crash.

4

Surprising news of an American Declaration of Independence reached Europe on August 17, 1776. Liberal minds, prepared by nearly a century of French literature, welcomed with enthusiasm this momentous statement in behalf of human liberty.

Early on the morning of November 28 of this same year, a loud cry echoed down from the sailor on watch high up at the masthead of the small warship. The distant stretch of blue haze in the chill glimmer of the late-autumn dawn was land! As the tiny sailing vessel glided in closer, the foreign-looking pilot jumped, grappled for the swaying ship's ladder, and in the rolling ground swell pulled himself with the seeming ease of long practice over the side to the deck. The land sighted had been that of Belle-Ile off the southern coast of Brittany.

After hardly a month's swift voyage from far-away Philadelphia, the little United States sloop *Reprisal,* mounting sixteen guns, had reached the western coast of France. In the evening, the sloop dropped anchor and prudently lay over night. The next morning she ran on easily into the comparative shelter of the wide blue expanse of Quiberon Bay. There, however, she had to mark time for four tantalizing days while head winds prevented her from making the difficult sail up the mouth of the Loire to the port of Nantes.

At length, on December 3rd, irked by further delay, a rather heavy-set man of seventy, so weak after the voyage that he could hardly stand alone, was lowered painfully into a tossing fishing boat. Accompanied by his two young grandsons, he listened curiously to the Breton sailors jabbering among themselves an incomprehensible jargon allied to the Celtic Welsh. All he could make out was the word for *devil!* No doubt he tried out also such halting French as was still left from his two previous brief visits to this foreign country. By evening, the party had made the twenty miles or so across the bay and up the estuary to Auray, which proved to be "a wretched place" with not even a post-chaise to be hired for the continuation of their journey.

During the four weeks' passage across the Atlantic, rapid as it was for the time, the old man had repeatedly been in danger of capture by English warships. If this had happened, he would almost certainly have been hanged as a most notorious rebel. Indeed, he foresightedly bore with him a sketch of what were then entirely unacceptable peace proposals as a barely possible protection in case he had the misfortune to be taken. Almost exhausted before he left Philadelphia by long hours of trying debate in Congress, tormented with boils, confined to the narrow quarters of a small sloop, he had been further weakened by his limited diet on shipboard. While crossing the ocean, he had been forced to live "chiefly on salt beef, the fowls," as he wrote in matter-of-fact style, "being too hard for my teeth!" Nevertheless, outwardly imperturbable, the scientist that he was at heart had every day dropped a thermometer on a line over the side to take the temperature of the sea water and determine whether they were in or out of the Gulf Stream.

The day after their belated arrival at the inauspicious village of Auray, the party was finally able to procure from neighboring Vannes a "miserable" carriage "with tired horses." By way of cheery welcome in the ominous blackness of the autumn evening, the driver "stopped near a wood we were to pass through," as the indomitable old man recorded with grim humor, "to tell us that a gang of eighteen robbers infested that wood who but two weeks ago had robbed and murdered some travelers on that very spot." The tale was no doubt made the more impressive by difficulty in understanding the rapid foreign speech.

After an enthusiastic banquet in his honor at Nantes and a week of such needed rest as he could get in the midst of numerous visitors, the aged traveler reached Versailles on December 20th. The following day he drove into Paris where he established himself temporarily at the Hôtel d'Hambourg on the Rue de l'Université two or three blocks south of the Seine. Three weeks later he accepted the opportunity to take up a more retired and pleasantly discreet residence in the large and handsome mansion put at his disposal by a warm friend of America, Monsieur Le Ray de Chaumont. This house was situated in the then western suburb of Passy, near the present Palais de Chaillot, the former Trocadéro, and was attractively surrounded with extensive gardens.

But it was not until the 20th of March, 1778, after over a year and a half of wise and patient negotiation, hindered by spies and jealous obstruction even among his closest aids, that the old man was finally received by Louis XVI. On this august occasion, Dr. Benjamin Franklin, true to his popular reputation for democratic simplicity, did not present himself in gay court costume amid the grandeur of Versailles. Instead, he wore plain brown velvet, white stockings, and spotless linen. His long sparse white hair hung loose, steel-rimmed spectacles were on his nose, and, discarding indeed for this occasion his usual fur cap, he followed the custom of the time to the extent of carrying under his arm a white hat.

The King spoke simply and well. "Firmly assure Congress," he said, "of my friendship. I hope this will be for the good of the two nations." Later the Queen desired Franklin, who was all the rage in Parisian society, to stand beside her, and talked to him whenever she could turn her attention distractedly from the usual high stakes of the royal gaming table.

At last a "Treaty of Amity and Commerce" between France and the infant United States had been signed. The accord was now officially acknowledged by Louis XVI in this momentous interview. A great step had been taken toward the ultimate success of the difficult American War of Independence. In addition to Franklin's signal ability and wisdom, several factors especially aided him in his negotiations at Paris. One was the increasing vogue of the Free Masons of which order he was a member. Another was the wide popularity of the Quakers, so effectively furthered forty years before by Voltaire in his *Philosophical Letters*. Franklin was of course no Quaker, but he came from Philadelphia, founded by William Penn. Moreover, he wore the simple dress and cultivated the straightforward manners associated with this strange, but admired sect. Franklin's presence in Paris fitted in also with the increasing vogue of "Liberty, Equality, and Fraternity." In addition, his international reputation as a scientist and experimenter with electricity added greatly to his prestige. Finally, he had the good judgment to improve his oral command of French, mingling easily in the salon society of the time. Even his invention of bifocal glasses aided him in lip-reading of the foreign speech! His engraved portraits were everywhere. While not forgetting American interests, Franklin made himself at one with the people to whom he was accredited.

The King's action, in accepting the treaty after long hesitation, powerfully helped the cause of the thirteen colonies and of humanity in general; at the same time, as Turgot had feared, it further weakened the tottering monarchy which could not indefinitely stand the strain of reckless finance, inept administration, and complete unwillingness to bend in advance of the coming storm, granting long-needed reforms before they were wrested by force from a reluctant government. Moreover, those Frenchmen who most longed for freedom, after formerly looking to England, now found a striking and influential example in the little nation struggling into life far across the stormy Atlantic.

A year later, in February of 1779, the young Marquis de Lafayette, still only twenty-one, returned to France on a six months' mission after a story-book career as a Major-General and friend of the great Washington in America. Lafayette had already become the romantic human symbol of co-operation between the two allied countries. "The Marquis de Lafayette . . . is infinitely esteemed and beloved here," wrote Franklin to the President of Congress on March 4th, "and I am persuaded will do everything in his power to merit a continuance of the same affection from America." Lafayette also enjoyed the confidence of the King's minister, Vergennes, and, like Franklin, helped greatly to stir popular enthusiasm for the cause of liberty. The question of revolution no longer remained in the realm of pure theory. It had entered the field of action aided by a dashing young French nobleman of the highest rank, back now from the foreign wars.

5

In the following years, Calonne, Brienne, then Necker again, became ministers, but were unable to curb the insistent demands of privilege or to reform the vicious system of spendthrift finance. A swifter and swifter current was sweeping the country, fertile and inherently prosperous though it was, toward the brink. The very prosperity of the middle classes made demands for change in the government more imperative. It was no longer possible to resist repeated calls for assembling the Estates General. Finally, these representatives of the country, who had not been summoned for more than a hundred and fifty years, were elected and convoked for May 4, 1789.

The first day was spent in a solemn procession through the streets of Versailles, with the Court and King, to the Church of Saint-Louis where the delegates heard mass. On the second day came the formal assembly. The place was a recently constructed hall in the Rue des Chantiers, behind the Hôtel des Menus Plaisirs, south of the Avenue de Paris.

This hall was a hundred and twenty feet long by about sixty wide within the fluted ionic columns surrounding it. An oval window admitted a flood of light from above, which was softened by a kind of tent of white taffeta. Everything, however, was clearly visible throughout the large room. At one end, an elevated platform for the King and Court was surmounted by a magnificent dais, backed by purple hangings of velvet. These hangings were embroidered with gold *fleurs de lis,* symbols of the French monarchy. Under a superb canopy in front stood the royal throne. At the left of the throne, there appeared a large armchair for the Queen and appropriate stools for the princes with folding chairs at the right for other princes. An armchair for the Guardian of the Seals rested immediately at the foot of the throne, and there were places for still other officials to the right and left. A ceremonious and colorful spectacle!

The representatives of the Clergy sat on benches stretching lengthwise of the hall to the right, the Nobility in the same fashion on the left. The so-called Commons, or Third Estate, occupied seats in the main body of the hall facing the throne. The whole floor was covered with magnificent carpets. More than two thousand spectators watched from raised tiers of benches around the assembly room.

Between nine and ten o'clock on the morning of May 5th, the masters of ceremonies began seating the nearly twelve hundred deputies according to the order of their bailiwicks, each representative being formally conducted to his place by an official usher. Whatever *éclat* this procedure may have been intended to lend to the occasion, it took up more than two wearisome hours. When Necker appeared, he was loudly applauded. The Duke of Orleans, later to be known as Philip Equality in his avid bid for popularity, was likewise hailed by the hand-clapping of the convention. Count Mirabeau, however, violently distrusted for his unscrupulous venality, evoked a hostile murmur as he walked in with the deputies from Provence.

The nobles wore black cloaks with gold embroidery and similarly brilliant vests beneath, white stockings, lace cravats, and hats with white plumes and turned-up brims in the style known as *à la Henri IV*. Among the clergy, the cardinals in red capes, the archbishops and bishops in violet cassocks and square hats, stood out as a mass of color in the front rows. In contrast, the deputies of the Third Estate sat in the center, dressed soberly in the simple black of the eighteenth-century bourgeois, short cloak, muslin neckpiece, and plain three-cornered cocked hat.

When the King entered, the whole assembly rose; the hall resounded with applause and loud cries of *Vive le roi!* Then followed a profound silence, "an august and majestic silence," said the sympathetic Meister, as Louis XVI waited for the princes, princesses, and other members of the Court to find their places about him. The King wore a long royal mantle and on his head a hat with waving plumes. The lower part of this hat was decorated with diamonds among which in the center scintillated the huge Pitt or Regent

Diamond worth even at that time the equivalent of some half-a-million dollars.

The King raised his hat politely in salute to the assembly, then put it on again in accordance with the forms, and read a brief speech from the throne. This speech was received, again in the words of the respectful Meister, with "involuntary" applause. The Guardian of the Seals then proclaimed: "The King permits you to be seated and to put on your hats." Amid a sea of tossing white plumes, the two noble orders resumed their seats to the right and left. The Third Estate, not only followed suit, but audaciously donned their hats also in open sign of equality. The succeeding speech by the Guardian of the Seals, expressive of the King's further program, was badly delivered, and could unfortunately be heard by only a few auditors in the front rows.

Next came the report of Necker, Director General of Finance. His voice likewise was too weak to carry through the hall. He soon asked the King's permission to have the reading continued by a Monsieur Broussonet, Secretary of the Royal Society of Agriculture, who spoke in sonorous tones befitting the importance and size of the assembly. But this report, with its necessarily dull figures, dragged on for almost three hours. The deficit, said Necker, had been reduced from 75 to 56 million livres, not counting payments on the debt, extraordinary expenses, or anticipations! The finance minister thereupon outlined an optimistic program. Amid cries of *Vive le roi! Vive la reine!* the King and Queen made their exit followed by the colorful train of courtiers.

Magnificent as the spectacle may have seemed to Meister and other admirers of the throne, it was too long and badly planned. The delegates were left tired and hungry at the end. The unhappy contrast between the brilliant luxury of the Court and the gloomy state of the country's finances could not fail to drive itself home to the black-garbed members of the Third. The absence of any real program of reform was all-too-quickly apparent. The very choice of Versailles as a meeting place was unwise. The royal splendor underlined the grievances of the masses while the closeness of Paris encouraged them in their violent resistance to privilege.

The original proposal at the assembly of the Estates General had been to continue the traditional vote by separate orders. This obviously would cause the Third to be always outvoted in a proportion

of two to one. The Third Estate had insisted upon double representation, as compared with the other two bodies, and upon voting
by head as individuals. Of the 1165 deputies present at the first
session, about 600 belonged to the Third and almost as many were
distributed between the two other groups. The question of numbers
had therefore been settled, but not the manner of voting. The Third
resolutely declined to organize for business until this crucial matter
should be determined in its favor. The Nobility generally stood firm,
but the Clergy, of whom many were country priests, close to and
sympathetic to the woes of the people, were nearly equally divided.
After many fruitless conferences, lasting over a month, one of the
deputies of the Third Estate, Abbé Sieyès, declared the time had
come for "cutting the cable." On June 10th, he proposed that the
other orders be invited to join with the Third. In case of refusal,
the Third should forthwith, and on its own initiative, regardless of
the King and the other orders, form itself into a national assembly.
This was done.

On June 20th, the representatives of the people suddenly found
their hall of the Menus Plaisirs closed and occupied by workmen.
The obvious intent was to leave them without a room for assembly.
Shortly, however, they located a meeting place not far away in a
bare tennis, or handball, court. Here they swore, significantly, to
"maintain the true principles of the monarchy," and took "a solemn
oath never to separate, but to meet anywhere that circumstances may
require, until the constitution of the Kingdom shall be laid and
established on secure foundations." At once, 577 members signed
this bold declaration which bound the Third Estate firmly into a
body, revolutionary indeed, but still respectful to the King.

On June 22nd, the Assembly obtained a new meeting place in the
Church of Saint-Louis. Here they were shortly joined by most of the
clergy and by some nobles from the provinces of Guyenne and
Dauphiny. The next day the King announced his will. He promised
equality of taxation, if approved by the other two orders, individual
liberty and freedom of the press, and the possible abolition of the
re-established *corvée*. "Never," he asserted, "has a king done so much
for any nation." For the rest, he insisted: "None of your plans or
proceedings can become law without my express approval. . . . I command you to separate at once, and to proceed tomorrow morning
each to the hall of his own order to renew your deliberations." But

it was much too little and too late. Moreover, the veiled threat of dissolution was clear. The Third Estate could only be exasperated by this false assumption of an imperious tone. "The nation when assembled cannot be given orders," replied Deputy Bailly. "We will not leave except by force of the bayonet," cried the strong-willed Mirabeau. "You are today what you were yesterday," Sieyès assured his colleagues.

The government gave orders to clear the hall of the rebellious Third, but some of the liberal nobles persuaded the guards to withdraw. The feeble King was unable to pursue a consistent course either of conciliation or repression. Impatiently, he exclaimed: "Oh well, the devil with it—let them stay!"

On June 27th, the nobles finally yielded and seated themselves with the Third Estate. Thus the "Constituent National Assembly," to draft a constitution for the country, was formed. Lafayette offered his proposal on July 11th for a "Declaration of the Rights of Man and the Citizen."

Meanwhile, the King was gathering troops in the region of Paris and Versailles. But the regular army, recruited by drink, bribery, and impressment, could not be trusted. It was, besides, naturally inclined to sympathize with the people. The militia, conscripted from the peasantry, obviously maintained its memory of the downtrodden countryman. The foreign mercenaries alone could be relied upon to fire in an emergency, and only a strong and ruthless hand, certainly not the hesitant Louis, could have used them effectively to put down a popular revolution.

6

It was about noon on Sunday, July 12, 1789, that Paris again heard of Necker's dismissal. This time the mood of the people was not merely one of sadness, but of open indignation. Young Camille Desmoulins, his habitual stuttering momentarily overcome by excitement, sprang upon a table in the garden of the Palais-Royal and, waving a pistol, with a green leaf as a cockade of Hope in his hat, raised the wild call to arms. Menacing crowds surged through the central streets of the city. The police seemed to have disappeared. A great fear descended upon the capital. On the 13th, at five o'clock, from steeples on every side, the tocsin rang. A huge mass of people pushed its way into the Hôtel des Invalides on the morning of the 14th, collecting 32,000 rusty muskets with the necessary powder and balls.

In the Faubourg Saint-Antoine, the thick walls of the fortress-prison of the Bastille glowered over the eastern quarters of Paris. It stood there, grim and menacing, a symbol of the *lettres de cachet*, of arbitrary imprisonment, of all the abuses of absolute power during the Old Régime. With walls towering a hundred feet high, a moat seventy-five feet wide and filled with water, with cannon protruding from the embrasures, the Bastille certainly seemed safe from any sudden onslaught. The first intention of the men from the Faubourg Saint-Antoine, as they swarmed up to the ancient citadel, was merely to demand arms and a withdrawal of the threatening cannon. But the Governor, the Marquis de Launay, incompetent and hestitant, had seen no reason to provide himself with provisions to withstand a siege. His feeble garrison consisted only of some eighty old soldiers and thirty Swiss mercenaries. The French veterans were on poor terms with the foreigners and were disinclined to fire on their countrymen in the streets.

De Launay, at eleven o'clock, received courteously a delegation of the people, consented to pull back his cannon, not fire unless attacked, and invited the deputies to lunch. The crowd, however, ignorant of what was happening, was disturbed at the failure of their emissaries to return, fearing treachery. They had already pushed into the outer court, undefended and with its drawbridge down.

Meanwhile, two members of the crowd climbed upon the roof of a perfume shop which abutted upon one of the walls of the Bastille. Breaking the chains of the inner drawbridge, they brought it down with a great crash. The unorganized assailants rushed forward into the second courtyard. The Governor, in panic, opened fire. The crowd, on its part, without orders or plan, thought itself trapped by treachery within the walls of the fortress. After several parlays, the attackers had finally consented to withdraw when, in the confusion, several more men fell wounded by a fusillade from the towers. Three hundred soldiers of the French Guards now appeared with four cannon taken from the Hôtel des Invalides. As they were about to fire, De Launay sent a note offering to surrender, but threatening to blow up the Bastille with its powder magazines if his capitulation should not be accepted. The officers of the Guards agreed, but the crowd, exasperated at more losses, shouted: "Lower the bridges! No surrender!"

Rushing into the gloomy interior, the crowd sacked the ancient fortress, liberated the seven prisoners who remained, angrily threw out of the windows the papers from the Archives. A certain young Russian *chargé d'affaires* named Doubrowski, interested in manuscripts and curiously watching the fray, began picking up the papers out of the mud, hired others to assist him, and sent them off to his private collection in his native country. Hence it is that these important records bearing on French history and literature are now in Russia.

The unfortunate De Launay was dragged through the streets, insulted, beaten, finally massacred on the Place de Grève. His aid, Flesselles, was treated similarly. The mob, crazed with emotion, fixed the bleeding heads on pikes and paraded them savagely about the city, a shocking sight to peaceful citizens, who shuddered within their tightly closed houses.

But the victors of the Bastille had lost ninety-eight men killed and seventy-three wounded. They were largely uncommanded and without discipline, ignorant of what was going on in the confused action. De Launay and Flesselles were suspected of a treachery of which they had not been guilty. The work of the mob was the first in a long succession of acts of somber vengeance which stained the next tragic years with blood.

When the Duke of Liancourt talked with Louis XVI, he is said promptly to have disabused the King's slow mind as to the supposed unimportance of the foray at the Bastille on July 14th: "Sire, this is no riot, but a revolution."

CONCLUSION

THE PHILOSOPHERS OF THE EIGHTEENTH CENTURY DID NOT CAUSE the French Revolution as was so bitterly charged by disillusioned *émigrés* after the years of exile and anguish which they had suffered. Daniel Mornet has realistically found the origin of the terrible upheaval primarily in reckless finance and dangerous oppression too long unchecked. In fact, the ideas of the time were themselves formed from the blatant abuses of inefficient and tyrannical government. But the actual shape of the major reforms demanded in 1789 appears already, as Mr. Henri Peyre has well indicated, in the program advanced by the eloquent leaders of French thought. Thus ideas sought at first to guide events.

The black cloud on the horizon appeared to the reflective eye long before the storm broke. "We are approaching a state of crisis and the century of revolutions," Rousseau had exclaimed prophetically in *Emile* as early as 1762. "I see all the nations of Europe rushing to their ruin," he warned ominously ten years later in his *Considerations on the Government of Poland.* More confident apparently of a peaceful outcome, Voltaire wrote enthusiastically to a friend in 1764: "Everything I see sows the seeds of a revolution which will not fail to come, but which I shall not have the pleasure of witnessing. . . . The young are very fortunate; they will see great things." In other passages also, the old man of Ferney saluted hopefully the growth of long-awaited tolerance and reform.

Why did the French Revolution, whose aims were so ardently desired by many, end in tragic bloodshed and at least temporary failure? Revolution is of course war, the most horrible form of war, a bitter civil struggle between citizens of the same country arrayed in hatred against each other. With death and destruction, revolution seeks a solution to abuses which people will no longer tolerate. Through unwillingness to compromise on both sides, a peaceful agreement becomes impossible. As the century wore on, a majority of the "privileged classes" continued their efforts to prevent any change in conditions which so well satisfied and favored them.

Mably, commenting on the conservative lawyers who made up the judicial Parlement, observed: "Occupied with the present moment and with their income from municipal bonds, they do not act except from day to day, they work only to make the machine last out their lifetime; the future disturbs them little." In the face of unbending resistance to union on a wise middle ground, force alone determined the final outcome.

The events of the past too readily look simple to us at a distance. The right decisions appear natural, the errors sheer stupidity. But it was not so at the time. Then the future loomed vague and dark just as before our own eyes today. Alexander Hamilton wrote keenly in the *Federalist:* "We, upon many occasions, see wise and good men on the wrong as well as on the right side of questions of the first magnitude to society." It is a lesson in the difficult conduct of affairs. Good will and prudent restraint are always needed if a dangerous explosion is to be averted. When to act firmly upon principle and when to bow cautiously before expediency remain always delicate questions of judgment for which no set rules can be laid down.

On January 21, 1793, the unfortunate Louis XVI died beneath the guillotine, sincerely protesting his innocence to the last. He had indeed been guilty of no intentional crime, but only of indecision, weakness, and lack of foresight in the presence of the harsh days in which he had been condemned to rule. The 16th of October following, Queen Marie-Antoinette, sitting stiffly upright with her face to the rear of the jolting cart and her hands bound tightly behind her back, traveled the same terrible road through the hostile streets of Paris to the Place de la Révolution. Old and prematurely haggard from recent years of suffering, she offered a frightful change in appearance at a mere thirty-eight from the "delightful vision" of youth and beauty so rapturously admired by Burke at the seemingly auspicious beginning of her brief reign.

Thomas Jefferson, looking back on the grim events which he had observed at first hand as American minister to France, considered Marie-Antoinette primarily responsible for the King's misplaced stubbornness. "He had a Queen," wrote Jefferson, "of absolute sway over his weak mind and timid virtue, and of a character the reverse of his in all points. This angel . . . was proud, disdainful of restraint, indignant at all obstacles to her will, eager in the pursuit of pleasure, and firm enough to hold to her desires, or perish in their wreck. . . . I have ever believed that, had there been no Queen, there would have been no revolution." Certainly her absolutist Austrian background was fatal to any comprehension of the democratic needs of the hour.

Whatever may be one's final estimate of Jefferson's verdict, there can be no doubt that a majority of the Estates General, followers many of them of the relatively conservative Montesquieu, would have been content with the principal reforms suggested in the *Cahiers* which had been drawn up and submitted from all parts of France. The delegates at first would gladly have accepted a limited monarchy with separation of powers after the fashion of England. *Vive le roi* still remained the sincere cry of the day.

But the leaders of the privileged classes, for the most part, would not yield except to superior force, and they hoped to have that on their side. The King and the royal family, in desperation, finally tried to flee the country, but with characteristic ineptitude got themselves caught and were then lodged in prison. Henceforth they could hardly be regarded otherwise than as traitors seeking to enlist the aid of foreign enemies. Indeed, the feeble and stupid intriguers around the King had actually sought to encourage invasion by hostile armies in the hope of overthrowing the new government. Thus the threat of successful counterrevolution appeared always imminent. Should the daring men fighting for long-overdue reforms meekly allow their efforts to be thwarted again as had happened so often in the past?

The First Republic was proclaimed officially on September 22, 1792. It was the Year One of the new revolutionary calendar. The more moderate leaders were at length ruthlessly pushed aside. They were succeeded by chiefs who in their turn dealt also in absolutes, but on the opposite side from royalty. They likewise saw events only in sharply divided terms of black and white with no hint of compromise. All issues appeared to them of a beautiful simplicity. Rigid logic—their logic—seemed to rule human affairs. These savage days of civil and foreign war brought to the front men of unyielding purpose and dogmatic mind, and it is no doubt true that their resistless energy and bold will saved France from being successfully invaded and conquered. But the "Reign of Terror," which indiscriminately sent so many French citizens to the guillotine in Paris and fomented widespread massacres in the provinces, dragged on its terrible way from May 31, 1793, to the fall of Robespierre on July 27, 1794—the ninth Thermidor of the Year Two. Such months of fear and torment left a deep scar upon the French people which still causes a sharp cleavage in their attitudes toward the French Revolution. Indeed, these and other bitter memories of the past seem to have increased the fierceness of their political discussions in general even down to the present day, over a century and a half later.

In the end, the Revolution would in fact "devour . . . its children," as Vergniaud, the great Girondin, forecast sadly a few months before his execution. Camille Desmoulins, Danton, and Robespierre, implacable leaders of the dominant Jacobine party of the Mountain, went in their turn the same way, paying the harsh price of the jealousies, fears, and hatreds which they had inevitably aroused through their arbitrary rule by force. Violence had succeeded upon violence until no one could feel safe. The people wearied at last of long food lines and unceasing bloodshed. They yearned again for tranquillity and the protections of orderly legal procedure.

Soon a new and at first glamorous dictator, Napoleon, burst upon the scene. At the youthful age of thirty, he seized upon the slackened reins of power and held them firmly for a time with all the mighty force of his dominant will and the prestige of his brilliant military victories over a startled Europe. Indeed, he seemed briefly to be exporting the great and longed-for revolution to down-trodden countries abroad. But people were soon undeceived. Napoleon had merely established another and more efficient absolutism of his own. *Plus ça change, plus c'est la même chose,* reads the apt French proverb.

Throughout the nineteenth century, similar struggles between reaction and revolution kept recurring at frequent intervals in France. They continue in many parts of the world today. The effort to establish, maintain, and improve democracy must in the very nature of the case prove never-ending. It is constantly threatened from the two extremes of right and left. To move too slowly or too fast often presents equal dangers. In the complex field of self-government, the necessary balance between many divergent opinions remains always a grievous problem.

But the compromises hammered out by the Anglo-Saxon tradition over the centuries, while always displeasing to doctrinaire minds of whatever color, still offer the surest promise of progress without the tragic price of violence. There can be no democracy unless there is a basic respect for opposing ideas and a mutual willingness on both sides "to live and let live." We need to advance together on all fronts and not to move much faster than the slow march of public opinion.

This is a difficult and often unexciting program, but it is founded on long experience. New republics without deep roots in the past, find it almost impossible to comprehend, let alone to practice. They divide often into numerous splinter parties, ruled by a fixed logic which has little relation to practical affairs and leaves them without a majority to govern. The natural retort to a reactionary absolutism is a radicalism equally intransigent. Under such a bitter struggle between dogmatisms, dictatorship is likely for a time to triumph, just as it did at the end of the eighteenth century in France.

The problems posed by the great French authors of the eighteenth century are still the subtle, difficult, human problems of the present troubled day. Unless we can arm our minds with the insight offered by the literary masterpieces of a former age, which chances in many ways to be astonishingly like our own, we risk repeating against our will an unhappy page of history. As the same scenes flash once more on the screen, who wishes to be forced to say, like the moviegoer, "this is where I came in?" T. S. Eliot has well remarked:

> Time present and time past
> Are both perhaps present in time future,
> And time future contained in time past.

Man's gravest problem remains himself. To throw a vivid light on our human vagaries is the crowning achievement of the best literature. The galaxy of writers presented in these pages have brilliantly held the torch before our feet that we might, by taking thought, tread a bit more surely in the darkness ahead. Without, like some discouraged modern thinkers, despairing of "man's fate," they wrote first of all for their own century, but have much to say for ours as well. War, intolerance, and atrocious cruelty still beset us. Political and religious freedom are far from established. No doubt the hopeful slogan of the French Revolution, "Liberty, Equality, and Fraternity," sounds a bit quaint in the ears of cynics today. Yet the world is never likely to rest until these ideals are achieved much more fully than at present. We should be wise therefore to reopen the instructive book of the past and, reading, take heart, knowledge, and determination for the future.

ACKNOWLEDGMENTS

SEVERAL FRIENDS HAVE KINDLY READ THIS BOOK IN MANUSCRIPT, giving me the benefit of their knowledge and critical judgment in a field so broad as to offer many pitfalls to a writer rash enough to embark on the subject completely by himself.

Thus Professor Henri Peyre of Yale and Professor Robert E. Rockwood of the Ohio State University, deeply familiar with the age of Louis XIV and the transitional period into the eighteenth century which followed, have aided me by reading the first five chapters at a time when the book was only approaching definitive form. The following members of the staff of the Ohio State University have also been of great help. Professors Kenneth Abbott and William McDonald, of the departments of Classical Languages and of History respectively, both at home in the complexities of Roman history, encouraged me by their general agreement with Chapter VII, dealing with Montesquieu and the elusive problem of Rome's Fall. Dean Frank R. Strong of the University's Law School read Chapter IX on "Montesquieu and America," taking a professional look at the much-discussed questions of Constitutional law which are there involved. Professor James Doolittle, a keen student of Diderot, read the chapters which present that many-sided and difficult figure, allowing me to profit from his helpful comments. Special acknowledgment is due Professor David Spitz of the department of Political Science for valuable bibliographical suggestions on some aspects of political theory. My warm thanks are due likewise to Mr. Robert E. Mitchell who has read the manuscript from the point of view of a graduate student, well informed about the men and ideas of the eighteenth century in France. Professor Paul M. Spurlin of the University of Michigan scrutinized the four Montesquieu chapters closely, bringing to them his extensive knowledge of the subject in relation to America and aiding me with constructive suggestions. To Professor Norman L. Torrey of Columbia University, I am under even more obligations since he graciously took time to read the text with great care from beginning to end, helping me frequently with his wide understanding and objective interpretation of the whole complex field.

409

ACKNOWLEDGMENTS

Obviously, however, no one should consider these men as necessarily in full agreement with my book or hold them in any way responsible for such shortcomings or errors as it may still contain. No doubt it could have profited from even further readings by other able scholars, but time imposes stern limits to continued demands upon one's friends, willing to oblige though they may be. The war against mistakes is never-ending, but it is rare that some faults, big or little, do not still manage to slip by in spite of all efforts.

To my wife, as my first reader and penetrating critic, I owe more than I can say. She has patiently borne with this book in many different stages and repetitions, always with interest, understanding, and entire confidence in a final attainment of the right form.

A few chapters have appeared more briefly in several numbers of the *American Society Legion of Honor Magazine.* For welcoming these articles so warmly, I am grateful to the then editor, Mr. W. Francklyn Paris, who took the initiative in first seeking them out and who has each year encouraged me in other similar studies of the eighteenth century addressed to modern readers.

It is more than twenty years ago that the John Simon Guggenheim Memorial Foundation awarded me a six months' fellowship for research on Voltaire and Rousseau in the chief libraries of Europe. While the present book was then unthought of, that experience of travel and study laid the groundwork for much of what appears here in certain important sections. I am glad once again for the opportunity of expressing to this Foundation my appreciation for its invaluable assistance.

To one unnamed collaborator, I am most grateful for his wholehearted belief in this book, even from the time when it was still only a title and a tenuous project in outline form. His firm faith in it has never wavered and has been of the greatest encouragement throughout the long and often painful labor of composition. Without his enthusiastic support and his many fruitful suggestions on matters of detail, it is doubtful whether the book would ever have found its way to publication.

Finally, I am especially indebted to the Ohio State University for a period of three months' assignment to research duty, which made it possible to complete the four chapters on Rousseau much more rapidly than could otherwise have been the case.

To all of these unseen, but always friendly collaborators, it is a special pleasure to renew here my warmest thanks.

January 3, 1955.   G. R. H.

NOTES

This book is not made up of "novelized lives" and no details have been imagined for the purpose of adding fictional color. On the contrary, all statements have been weighed carefully in the light of the best eighteenth-century and modern sources. Lack of space, however, prevents giving references except in those cases most likely to require documentation in the opinion of the scholarly reader, already well informed about the main facts and ideas of the period. The citing below of pages, lines, and key words permits the ready linking of the *Notes* with the relevant passages in the text, while at the same time avoiding the use of superscript figures which might prove of some annoyance to the general reader uninterested in establishing the authenticity of each point.

Additional background material may be easily located by means of David C. Cabeen's *Critical Bibliography of French Literature*, Volume IV, *The Eighteenth Century*, Syracuse University Press, 1951. This volume was edited by George R. Havens and Donald F. Bond with the invaluable help of the General Editor, Mr. Cabeen, and forty-two other American or foreign scholars in the United States.

PRINCIPAL ABBREVIATIONS

USED IN THE

NOTES

Ann. J.-J. Rousseau. Annales de la Société Jean-Jacques Rousseau, Geneva, 1905 ff.

AT. Diderot, *Œuvres complètes,* ed. by Assézat-Tourneux, Paris, Garnier frères, 1875-77, 20 vols.

Corr. inédite. Diderot, *Correspondance inédite,* ed. by André Babelon, Paris, Gallimard, 1931, 2 vols.

Ducros, *Rousseau,* I, II, or III. Louis Ducros, *Jean-Jacques Rousseau de Genève à l'Hermitage (1712-1757),* Paris, Fontemoing, 1908; *Jean-Jacques Rousseau de Montmorency au Val de Travers (1757-1765),* Paris, Boccard, 1917; *Jean-Jacques Rousseau de l'Ile de Saint-Pierre à Ermenonville (1765-1778),* Paris, Boccard, 1918.

Hachette. J.-J. Rousseau, *Œuvres complètes,* Paris, Hachette, ed. by Charles Lahure, Paris, 1885 and various later reprintings, 13 vols.

LSV. Diderot, *Lettres à Sophie Volland,* ed. by André Babelon, Paris, Gallimard, 1930, 3 vols.

MLN. *Modern Language Notes,* Baltimore, Johns Hopkins Press, 1886 ff.

Moland. Voltaire, *Œuvres complètes,* ed. by Louis Moland, Paris, Garnier frères, 1877-85, 52 vols.

PMLA. *Publications of the Modern Language Association of America,* New York, 1884 ff.

RDM. *Revue des Deux-Mondes,* Paris, 1829 ff.

RHL. *Revue d'Histoire littéraire de la France,* Paris, Armand Colin, 1894 ff.

CHAPTER I

Page 3

Line 7, brown: "Il était toujours vêtu de couleur plus ou moins brune," etc. Saint-Simon, *Mémoires,* ed. by A. de Boislisle, Paris, 1879-1930, 41 vols. plus 2 vols. containing the *Table générale,* XXVIII, 371-372. **19, autumn residence:** The King arrived at Fontainebleau from Chambord on September 30th and remained until after All Saints' Day, November 1, 1685. Cf. Marquis de Sourches, *Mémoires,* Paris, 1836, 2 vols., I, 298. **19-20, Fontainebleau:** The Revocation of the Edict of Nantes is dated at Fontainebleau. Ann Maury, *Memoirs of a Huguenot Family,* New York, 1872, p. 510. **25, Wednesday:** Saint-Simon, XXVIII, 343.

Page 4

Line 10, "I am the State." Although this phrase was probably never actually used by Louis XIV, it well summarizes the absolutist viewpoint as expressed in his address of April 13, 1655. Ernest Lavisse and Alfred Rambaud, *Histoire générale du IVᵉ siècle à nos jours,* VI (Paris, 1895), 37, and n.2. **18, a veritable nation apart:** "On lui peignit les huguenots avec les couleurs les plus noires: un Etat dans un Etat." Saint-Simon, XXVIII, 224. **33-34, reluctantly:** Ernest Lavisse, *Histoire de France,* VII (2) (Paris, 1906), 44 ff.

Page 5

Line 4, few: Cf. the words of the Revocation itself: "since the greater part of our subjects of the said pretended Reformed religion have embraced the Catholic." Ann Maury, *Memoirs of a Huguenot Family,* p. 508. **22, the 17th of October:** Henry M. Baird, *The Huguenots and the Revocation of the Edict of Nantes,* London, 1895, 2 vols., II, 25 and n.2. **29, salvation:** *Ibid.,* II, 55. **30, an important part:** *Ibid.,* II, 25, and n.3. **35, The Great Seal:** Ann Maury, p. 510. **38, October 22:** Henry M. Baird, II, 25, n.2.

Page 6

Line 3, temples: Mme de Sévigné, *Lettres,* Paris, Hachette (Grands Ecri-vains français), 1862-66, 14 vols., VII, 470, n.5 (taken from the *Journal* of Dangeau). **5, Bossuet:** Henry M. Baird, II, 55-56. **17, memorable:** Mme de Sévigné, *Lettres,* VII, 470. **18, La Fontaine, . . . La Bruyère:** E. Lavisse, VII(2), 79.

Page 7

Line 20, hypocrites: Mme de Maintenon, Letter to the Comtesse de Saint-Géran, October 25, 1685 (*Lettres,* pub. by Marcel Langlois, Paris, III (1935), 131. **21, Saint-Simon:** *Mémoires,* XXVIII, 226-228, and Notes. **28-29, checking the expansion:** *Mémoires de Louis XIV,* ed. by Charles Dreyss, Paris, Didier, 1860, 2 vols., II, 454, 456, 457. **35, Voltaire:** *Œuvres complètes* (Moland ed., Paris, Garnier, 1877-85, 52 vols.), XXXVII, 557.

Page 8

Line 4, the same decision: "C'est assurément une erreur que d'attribuer à Madame de Maintenon la révocation de l'Edit. Elle ôtée, le cours des choses, qui venait de loin avec une force croissante, aurait suivi son chemin. . . . Mais il est certain que l'instinct de dévotion, qui, joint à l'instinct de galanterie, avait attiré vers Madame de Maintenon le galant assagi fut fortifié par elle." E. Lavisse, VII(2), 60-61. **8-9, a million and a half:** Henri Martin, *Histoire de France,* 4th ed., XIV (Paris, 1859), 54, and n.1. **11, two hundred thousand:** *Ibid.,* XIV, 59. **12, an equal number:** Lavisse and Rambaud, *Histoire générale,* VI, 302. **22, nine thousand:** Henri Martin, XIV, 60. **28, her generals:** Marquis de Sourches, *Mémoires,* II, 5. **37, sixty million livres:** Henri Martin, XIV, 58-59, and n.1.

Page 9

Line 2, two per cent: *Ibid.,* XIV, 59, n.1. **34-35, "dragonnades":** Henry M. Baird, I, 506-07; II, 46-49; James Breck Perkins, *France under the Regency,* New York (1892), reprinted 1920, pp. 180-81.

Page 10

Lines 9-10, nearly the figures: James Breck Perkins, p. 203.

Page 11

Line 11, abominated: Lavisse, *Histoire de France*, VIII(1) (Paris, 1908), 317. 14, October 29, 1709: A detailed account of the destruction of Port-Royal is given by Sainte-Beuve, *Port-Royal*, Paris, 1867-78, VI, 216-40.

Page 13

Line 8, skepticism: "Beaucoup de bruit pour peu de chose, disaient volontiers les sceptiques." F. Brunetière, "La formation de l'idée de progrès," *Etudes critiques sur la littérature française*, 3rd ed., Paris, 1903, V, 218. 26, to buy books: "Elle me légua deux mille francs pour acheter des livres," wrote Voltaire. Moland. ed., XXIII, 512.

Page 14

Line 5, silver plate: Lavisse and Rambaud, VI, 219. 12, Duclos: Quoted by Sainte-Beuve, *Causeries du lundi*, 3rd ed., Paris, 1869, IX, 238, n.

Page 15

Line 14, James Fontaine: Ann Maury, p. 122. 23, La Bruyère: *Les Caractères*, Chap. IX, *De l'homme*, ed. by Servois and Rébelliau, 14th ed., Paris, Hachette, 1920, pp. 332-33.

Page 16

Line 2, In 1675: James Breck Perkins, p. 121. (Cf. Lavisse and Rambaud, VI, 218-20). 11, Fénelon: *Œuvres*, Paris, Didot, 3 vols., 1861, III, 427. 20, Vauban: Lavisse, VIII(1), 271. 24, Boisguillebert: *Ibid.* 27, Racine: Sainte-Beuve, *Port-Royal*, VI, 153-54. 36, fifteen cents: Lavisse, VIII(1), 231.

Page 17

Line 26, admiration: Voltaire, *Lettres philosophiques*, particularly Letters 8, 9, and 10.

Page 18

Line 8, "Strike and conceal your hand": Voltaire, Moland, XLI, 293 (1761).

Page 19

Line 1, support: Saint-Simon, XXVIII, 151. 5, chambermaids: *Ibid.*,

146. 8, cane: Lavisse and Rambaud, VI, 184. 22, mass: Saint-Simon, XXVIII, 364; cf. Lavisse and Rambaud, VI, 203. 26, inconsiderate: Saint-Simon, XXVIII, 266. 36, calm: *Ibid.*, pp. 302-03.

Page 20

Lines 2-3, whom I never see: *Ibid.*, pp. 134-35. 10, having letters opened: *Ibid.*, pp. 138-41. 36, talents: James Breck Perkins, p. 142.

Page 21

Line 14, Gilbert: Saint-Simon, XXVII, 274-75, n.4. 15, My dear child: *Ibid.*, pp. 274-75. 25, September 1st: *Ibid.*, p. 293. 35, the least favorable: Charles Duclos, *Mémoires (Collection des Mémoires relatifs à l'Histoire de France*, ed. by Petitot and Monmerqué, Paris, 1829), LXXVI, 193.

CHAPTER II

Page 22

Line 26, November 18, 1647: Des Maizeaux, "Vie de M. Bayle," *Dictionnaire historique et critique*, Beuchot ed., Paris, 1820, XVI, 43.

Page 23

Lines 11-12, question after question: *Ibid.* 24-25, Plutarch . . . Montaigne: *Ibid.*, p. 44.

Page 24

Line 1, letter: *Ibid.*, pp. 46-49. 37, November 11, 1675: *Ibid.*, p. 58. 38, frontispiece: *Dictionnaire hist. et crit.*, Rotterdam [Geneva], 1715, 3rd ed., 3 vols., folio.

Page 25

Line 12, in 1681: Des Maizeaux, "Vie de M. Bayle," *Dictionnaire*, 1820, XVI, 63. 18-19, in name only: Cornélia Serrurier, *Pierre Bayle en Hollande*, Apeldoorn, Dixon et Cᵗᵉ, n. d. [1913?] p. 37. 21, Geldersche Quai: *Ibid.*, p. 42. 24, seven: *Ibid.*, p. 39. 27, youth: *Ibid.*, p. 35. 38, injurious: *Ibid.*, p. 104.

Page 26

Line 4, disturbed: Des Maizeaux, *Dictionnaire*, 1820, XVI, 162-63. 11, single room: Cornélia Serrurier, p. 126, n.3.

14, puppet shows: *Ibid.*, p. 44 and n. 22, did *not* exist: *Ibid.*, p. 44. 24, fourteen: *Ibid.*, p. 124. 31, West Nieuwland: *Ibid.*, p. 205.

Page 27

Line 17, into view: Howard Robinson, *Bayle the Sceptic*, New York, Columbia University Press, 1931, p. 18. 37, what does not exist: Chapter XLIX, title. 39, History of Oracles: First Dissertation, Chapter IV. "Enfin nous éviterons le ridicule d'avoir trouvé la cause de ce qui n'est point." Critical ed. by Louis Maigron, reprinted, Paris, E. Droz, 1934, p. 32.

Page 28

Line 10, Vanini: *Pensées sur la comète,* crit. ed. by A. Prat, Paris, 1911-12, 2 vols., II, 111 (Chap. CLXXIV).

Page 29

Line 2, of India to Europe: *Ibid.*, II, 316 (final chapter). 3, Oliver Wendell Holmes: *Autocrat of the Breakfast Table*, Boston and New York, Houghton Mifflin, 1894, p. 24. 16, Protestant Inquisitor: Cornélia Serrurier, p. 103. 20, fortnight: Des Maizeaux, *Dictionnaire*, 1820, XVI, 66-67. 30, indifference: Howard Robinson, p. 53.

Page 30

Line 10, conscience: Pierre Bayle, *Œuvres diverses*, La Haye, 1727, folio, II, 77 b. 16, Louis XIV: Howard Robinson, p. 51. 26, father: "Calendarium carlananum," *Dictionnaire*, 1820, XVI, 283. 27, Jacob: *Ibid.* 30, Louvois: Des Maizeaux, *Ibid.*, XVI, 80. 32, ten days: Jean Delvolvé, *Religion, critique et philosophie positive chez Pierre Bayle*, Paris, 1906, p. 76.

Page 31

Line 11, hanged no one: Bayle, *Œuvres diverses*, II, 345 b. 16, tomorrow: Howard Robinson, p. 61. 32, false: Delvolvé, p. 80.

Page 32

Line 12, Christians: Howard Robinson, p. 86. 14, bolder: Voltaire, *Œuvres* (Moland ed.), XLII, 448. 17, Lecky: Howard Robinson, p. 88.

31, two years later: Des Maizeaux, *Dictionnaire*, 1820, XVI, 160-61. 36, as early as 1695: *Ibid.*, p. 176. Described as two tomes, four volumes, in the printed catalog of the Bibliothèque Nationale at Paris.

Page 33

Line 15, private libraries: Howard Robinson, p. 135.

Page 34

Line 18, three articles: "Histoire de M. Bayle et de ses ouvrages," *Dictionnaire hist. et crit.*, 3rd ed., 1715, I, p. xxxiii.

Page 35

Line 15, possible: *Ibid.*, I, p. xxxiv.

Page 36

Line 31, Bible: Emile Faguet, *Dix-huitième siècle*, Paris, Boivin, n. d., p. 1.

Page 37

Line 8, Bibliothèque Mazarine: Howard Robinson, p. 278 (cited from Sainte-Beuve, *Nouveaux lundis*, IX, 26-27).

CHAPTER III

Page 38

Line 3, eyes: Saint-Simon, XXVI, 74. 7, thirteenth: Jules Lemaître, *Fénelon*, Paris, 1910, p. 5. J. Lewis May (*Fénelon*, London, 1938, p. 5) gives the total number of children as *sixteen;* De Broglie (*Fénelon à Cambrai*, Paris, 1884, p. 34) says *seventeen.* 27, Sultan: Letter of October 9 [1675], *Œuvres*, Paris, Didot, 1861, 3 vols., III, 442.

Page 39

Line 19, Bossuet: Lemaître, p. 62. 33, gently: Letter to Seignelay, Feb. 7, [1686], *Œuvres*, III, 445. 37, communion: *Ibid.*, Feb. 26, [1686], III, 446. 39, afar: *Ibid.*

Page 40

Lines 3-4, self-interested: *Ibid.* 5, contemptuous: Letter to Bossuet, March 8, 1686, *Ibid.*, III, 449. 8, attractiveness: Letter to Seignelay, Feb. 7, [1686], *Ibid.*, III, 445; also March 8, [1686], III, 448. 11, gentleness: "Ils nous aiment, et nous regrettent quand nous les quittons." Letter to Seignelay, March 8 [1686], *Ibid.*, III, 448. **14, disillusion:** "quoique nous avancions peu ici et que nos occupations de Paris eussent un fruit plus prompt et plus sensible." Letter to Seignelay, Feb. 26, [1686], *Ibid.*, III, 447. Cf. letter to Bossuet of March 8, 1686, *Ibid.*, III, 448-49. **28, the 4th of October:** E. Carcassonne, *Etat présent des travaux sur Fénelon*, Paris, 1939, p. 108. **30, Duchesse de Béthune:** Paul Janet, *Fénelon* (Grands Ecrivains français), Paris, 1892, p. 66. **39, back to Paris:** *Ibid.*

Page 41

Line 3, unconvinced: *Ibid.*, p. 67. **30, foolishness:** "des rêveries," *Ibid.* **32, disgrace:** Mme Saint-René Taillandier, *Madame de Maintenon*, Paris, 1920, p. 201. **34, ambition:** Saint-Simon, XXI, 297-98.

Page 42

Line 4, correspondence: Letter to Tronson, Feb. 26, [1696], *Œuvres*, III, 479. **6, expediency:** *Ibid.*, III, 480: "Tout le mystère se réduit à ne vouloir point parler contre ma conscience, et à ne vouloir point insulter inutilement à une personne que j'ai révérée comme une sainte, sur tout ce que j'en ai vu par moi-même." **9, more favorable:** E. Carcassonne, p. 51. **11, no wrong:** Letter to Mme de Maintenon, Sept., 1696. *Œuvres*, III, 486: "Jamais je n'y ai trouvé aucune trace de ces maximes infernales qu'on lui impute." **17, a saint:** "une personne que j'ai révérée comme une sainte." *Ibid.*, III, 480. **29-30, tear his body to pieces:** Saint-Simon, XXII, 305.

Page 43

Line 5, the 4th of February: Letter to the Marquise de Laval, *Œuvres*, III, 471. **9, July 10, 1695:** Lemaître, p. 218; Carcassonne, p. 109; Mme Saint-René Taillandier, p. 172. **29, the 2nd of August:** "Je partirai d'ici, Madame, demain vendredi, pour obéir au roi." (Letter of Aug. 1, 1697, from Fénelon at Versailles to Madame de Maintenon, *Œuvres*, III, 519).

Page 44

Line 1, a strange book: Emmanuel de Broglie, *Fénelon à Cambrai*, p. 77. **3, sleepless nights:** E. Carcassonne, *Fénelon l'homme et l'œuvre*, Paris, Boivin, 1946, p. 59. **5, muddy roads:** "des abîmes de boue," De Broglie, p. 42. **13, lax:** *Ibid.*, p. 49, n.1. **21, five to five:** Paul Janet, *Fénelon*, p. 97; [Ramsay], *Vie de Fénelon*, Amsterdam, 1729, pp. 86-87. **24-25, I submit:** Letter to Abbé de Chanterac, April 3, 1699. *Œuvres* III, 544.

Page 45

Line 2, love for his neighbor: Paul Janet, pp. 97-98.

Page 46

Line 13, by force: [Ramsay], *Vie de Fénelon*, p. 239. **14-15, was riding in his coach:** De Broglie, pp. 427-28 (details based on a letter of Fénelon of Nov. 22, 1714).

Page 47

Line 5, great need: *Ibid.*, pp. 435-36. **16, without debts:** Saint-Simon, XXVI, 85. **17, Télémaque:** Letter to Father Le Tellier, probably of 1710. *Œuvres*, III, 631.

Page 50

Line 39, absolute power to do good: *Télémaque*, first part of Book V. Edition by Albert Cahen (Grands Ecrivains de la France), Paris, Hachette, 1920, I, 191.

Page 51

Line 1, Duke of Orleans: Mathieu Marais, *Journal*, Paris, 1863-68, 4 vols., I, 167; Jean Buvat, *Journal de la Régence*, Paris, 1865, 2 vols., I, 494. **8, English Pretender:** [Ramsay], *Vie de Fénelon*, p. 240. **9, Voltaire,** *Lettres philosophiques*, Lanson ed., 2nd ed., Paris, 1915-17, 2 vols., I, 89, 95. **10, Thomas Jefferson:** Marie Kimball, *Jefferson: the Scene of Europe, 1784-1789*, New York, Coward-McCann, 1950, p. 299. **26-27, chimerical spirit:** According to Daguesseau, in Saint-Simon, XXI, 294, n.5. **37, possibly a year earlier:** Majority opinion gives 1694, or thereabouts, as the probable date. Mme de Maintenon, however, writing to Archbishop de Noailles on December

21, 1695, says: "Voicy une lettre, qu'on lui a escrite [à Louis XIV], il y a deux ou trois ans." *Lettres de Mme de Maintenon*, pub. by Marcel Langlois, Paris, IV (1937), p. 475. The median date of 1693 may therefore be the most probable.

Page 52

Line 12, Voltaire: *Œuvres* (Moland ed.), L, 296, 319-20, 334-35. 18, daring letter: For the text, see Charles Urbain, Fénelon, *Écrits et Lettres politiques*, Paris, Bossard, 1920, pp. 143-57, and his *Notes*, pp. 192-94.

Page 54

Line 8, irritate and discourage: Mme de Maintenon, *Lettres*, IV, 475, Dec. 21, 1695. Note also: "Il ne faut ny l'un ny l'autre, mais le conduire doucement, où l'on veut le mener." 25-27, Examination . . . Chaulnes Tables: Text in Urbain, *Écrits et Lettres politiques* of Fénelon.

Page 57

Line 29, burned: Emmanuel de Broglie, p. 360. 32, miss him: *Ibid.*, p. 439. 34, Madame de Maintenon: *Ibid.*, p. 440.

CHAPTER IV

Page 59

Line 8, Voltaire: Moland ed., XXI, 108 *(Micromégas)*; XXXVII, 284 *(Correspondance)*; Trublet, *Mémoires sur Fontenelle*, Amsterdam, 1759, pp. 137-38; Grimm *Correspondance littéraire*, Paris, Garnier, 1877-82, 16 vols., III, 339. 14, universe: Raynal, *Nouvelles littéraires* (Oct. 4, 1751), in Grimm, *Corr. litt.*, II, 102. 18, billiards: Trublet, p. 273. 22, fifty: *Ibid.*, p. 184. 25, sparing: *Ibid.* 28, stomach: *Ibid.*

Page 60

Line 1, gout: Sainte-Beuve, *Lundis*, III, 324. 9, slept: Trublet, p. 216. 17-18, after all: *Ibid.*, p. 215. 26, laughed: *Ibid.*, p. 40. Cf. Sainte-Beuve, *Lundis*, III, 323.

Page 61

Line 2, heart: Trublet, p. 116. 8-9, Mme de La Fayette's: Garat, *Mémoires sur M. Suard*, Paris, 1820, 2 vols.,

I, 115. 13, dragonnades: *Ibid.* 29-30, Chapter: *Ibid.*, I, 116. 39, Ah! you say?: *Ibid.*, I, 118-19.

Page 62

Line 3, only eighty: Grimm, *Corr. litt.*, III, 340; Voltaire, Moland, XLIX, 254. A version with the aged Fontenelle falling flat on his face as he attempted to pick up a lady's glove is found in D'Argenson, *Mémoires*, Paris, Jannet, 1857-58, 5 vols., V, 94. If the latter is the true version, however, it is surprising not to have it reported by the realistic Grimm and the hostile Voltaire. 9, baggage: Trublet, p. 303. 14, Ssh!: Grimm, III, 340. 21, le Bovier: So given by Trublet, p. 273, instead of le Bouvier as often elsewhere.

Page 63

Line 22, existing: Louis Maigron, *Fontenelle*, Paris, 1906, pp. 88-89. Cf. Grimm, III, 340. 28, eighteen more: Cf. *Avertissement* in Fontenelle, *Œuvres*, Paris, 1825, 5 vols., III, 387; Maigron, pp. 32-34; Trublet, p. 278.

Page 65

Line 35, belong: Trublet, pp. 40-41. Cf. Garat, I, 120-21.

Page 66

Line 14, Bayle: Trublet, pp. 24-25, n. 23, imprisonment: Voltaire, Moland, XXVI, 500-01. 27, hand full of truths: Grimm, III, 346, n.3; Voltaire, Moland, XLIV, 314, n.2.

Page 67

Line 2, Mme de La Mésangère: Trublet, p. 128. 11, blond: *Ibid.*

Page 69

Line 24, mud: Voltaire, *Zadig* (beginning of Chap. IX, Moland, XXI, 54). 34, easily: Trublet, pp. 13, 181, 182, 262, 307.

Page 70

Line 29, closing: Fontenelle, *Histoire des oracles*, critical ed. by Louis Maigron, Paris, 2nd printing, 1934, *Introduction*, p.f.; Trublet, p. 154; for a different version, cf. Voltaire, Moland, XXVI, 119-20. 34, according to Voltaire: Moland, XIV, 74; XX, 199; XXVI, 120, 501, and n.

Page 75

Line 29, decade of the 1690s: Trublet, p. 294. 30, before 1680: J.-R. Carré, *La philosophie de Fontenelle*, Paris, 1932, pp. 115 ff. 37, a kind of introduction: Louis Maigron, *Fontenelle*, p. 252.

Page 76

Line 38, Andrew Lang: Cited by J.-R. Carré, pp. 135, n., 137, n.

Page 77

Line 8, did not say: Cf. J.-R. Carré, pp. 651-62, "Les Silences de Fontenelle."

CHAPTER V

Page 81

Line 3, an officer: Jean Buvat, *Journal de la Régence*, Paris, Plon, 1865, 2 vols., I, 47. 13, came out on the balcony: *Ibid.* 19, six o'clock: Clairambault in Saint-Simon, XXIX, 471; Corberon, *Ibid.*, XXIX, 483, says: "six heures et demie." 26, over three thousand: Marais, *Journal*, Paris, 1863-68, 4 vols., I, 183, and n. 28, Sainte-Chapelle: L'avocat Prévot, in Saint-Simon, XXIX, 477.

Page 82

Line 1, ten rounds: Marais, I, 183. 3, the day before the King's death: *Ibid.*, I, 174, n. 5, remonstrance: *Ibid.*, I, 176. 7, lower seats: James Breck Perkins, *Regency*, p. 335. 12, quarter to nine: Corberon, in Saint-Simon, XXIX, 484; Buvat, I, 481, says: "vers les huit à neuf heures." 16, bursting with joy: Saint-Simon, XXIX, 14: "M. du Maine crevoit de joie." 16, bowing: *Ibid.* 22, black: L'avocat Prévot, in Saint-Simon, XXIX, 477, observes: "Je vis arriver vers les neuf heures mondit sieur le duc d'Orléans en habit et manteau noirs." 23-24, raised his hat: Saint-Simon, XXIX, 19-20. 25, read forcefully: "Son discours fut très-éloquent: il le lisoit." (Marais, I, 161.) 26, four or five minutes: See the text in Marais, I, 173-74. 28, ghost-written: "D'Aguesseau et Fleury ont composé les harangues." (Marais, I, 183, n.) 32, change it: *Ibid.*, I, 173. 35, bad handwriting: *Ibid.*, I, 162.

Page 83

Line 3, acclamation: James Breck Perkins, *Regency*, p. 337. 6, at three: Marais, I, 167; "sur les trois à quatre heures," says Buvat, I, 494; Clairambault, in Saint-Simon, XXIX, 475, puts the time "vers trois heures et demie." 8, dismissed: Marais, I, 183, n. 12, Télémaque: Marais, I, 167; Buvat, I, 494; *Télémaque*, Book V. 12, applauded: Marais, I, 167, n. 15, shorn: The word is Saint-Simon's: "Le duc du Maine, se voyant totalement *tondu*, essaya une dernière ressource." (XXIX, 31.)

Page 84

Line 2, owed 2 billion, 400 million: Figures as given in round numbers by Victor Duruy, *Histoire de France*, 20th ed., Paris, 1898, II, 353. 10, Saint-Simon's proposals: James Breck Perkins, p. 353, and n.

Page 85

Line 27, Rue-aux-Ours: (Not Rue-*des*-Ours, as it is sometimes given in English or American books as, for example, in James Breck Perkins, p. 474). 31, hunchback: *Ibid.*, pp. 474-75.

Page 86

Line 5, January 5, 1720: *Ibid.*, p. 476, n.2. 10-11, at 300,000: Henri Martin, *Histoire de France*, XV, 53, n. 16, sold for: Buvat, I, 475-76. 22, pound and a half: Georges Lefebvre, *The Coming of the French Revolution*, Princeton University Press, 1947, p. 102. 26-27, Robbery and murder: "On vole ici et on assassine beaucoup." *Les Correspondants de la Marquise de Balleroy*, Paris, 1883, 2 vols., II, 138. Cf. II, 159-60, 192, 488.

Page 88

Line 7, Madame de Falary: Marais, III, 50; Buvat, II, 460-62.

Page 89

Line 12, Queen of France: Casimir Stryienski, *Le Dix-huitième siècle*, Paris, Hachette, 6th ed., 1923, pp. 68-69.

21, fit to eat: Marais, *Journal*, III, 360 (letter of Sept. 10, 1725). **37, further orders:** Stryienski, p. 85.

Page 90

Line 16, incapable: Voltaire, Moland, XV, 179. **27, two years too long:** Barbier, *Journal*, Paris, Charpentier, 1857-66, 8 vols., III, 179.

Page 91

Line 5, signed: James Breck Perkins, *France under Louis XV*, Boston and New York, 1899, 2 vols., I, 238. **8, chaos:** D'Argenson, *Mémoires*, Paris, Jannet, 1857-58, 5 vols., IV, 269; cf. II, 301, 310; III, 279-81, 300. **10, chase:** *Ibid.*, II, 77 (1739). **17, proficient:** James Breck Perkins, *Louis XV*, I, 255. **19, ravaged:** *Ibid.* **27, condemnation:** *Ibid.*, I, 297.

Page 92

Line 23, Lord Hay: Voltaire, Moland, XV, 240. **27, rolling fire:** *Ibid.* **29, more than six hundred:** *Ibid.*, There are some divergences in details. Cf. Othon Guerlac, *Les Citations françaises*, Paris, Colin, 1931, pp. 263-64, n. **32, Marshal de Saxe:** James Breck Perkins, *Louis XV*, I, 321-22; Stryienski, p. 161. A modern footnote in Voltaire, Moland, XV, 240, n.1, asserts, however, the contrary: namely, that Maurice put blame on the French for this tactic.

Page 93

Line 5, example: James Breck Perkins, *Louis XV*, I, 317. **9, master:** Voltaire, Moland, VIII, 391. **13, cannon:** *Ibid.*, XXXVI, 362-63.

Page 94

Line 4, huntress: James Breck Perkins, *Louis XV*, I, 349. **26, finished:** D'Argenson, *Mémoires*, III, 300. **28, every day:** *Ibid.*, III, 313. **34, revolt:** Stryienski, p. 170. Cf. D'Argenson, *Mémoires*, III, 335-37. **34, revolution:** Félix Rocquain, *L'esprit révolutionnaire avant la révolution*, Paris, 1878, p. 180. **36, deluge:** Othon Guerlac, *Les Citations françaises*, p. 264, and n.1. **39, middle course:** Abbé de Mably, *Droits et devoirs du citoyen*, in *Œuvres complètes*, Lyon, 1796, 12 vols., XI, 403.

Page 95

Line 3, of 1789: Grimm [Meister], *Corr. litt.*, XV, 413 (March, 1789). **5, as best he can:** Victor Duruy, *Histoire de France*, II, 400. **8, stupid:** Félix Rocquain, p. 126. **21, injury:** Barbier, *Journal*, VI, 426-28.

Page 97

Line 7, seconded: Stryienski, p. 230. **21, Here lies Louis:** [Métra], *Correspondance secrète*, London, John Adamson, 1787-90, 18 vols., I, 1; Grimm [Meister], *Corr. litt.*, X, 424, n.1.

CHAPTER VI

Page 98

Line 3, La Brède: Cf. Gérard Pesme, *En flânant chez Montesquieu à La Brède*, Bordeaux, Editions Delmas, 1936, pp. 11-12; Louis Vian, *Histoire de Montesquieu*, Paris, Didier, 1878, pp. 5-6.

Page 99

Line 6, baptismal font: Vian, pp. 15-16. **8, nurse:** *Ibid.*, pp. 16-17. **15, Gascon:** *Ibid.*, pp. 17, 142, 321; D'Argenson, *Mémoires*, V, 87. **17, vine-prop:** Dominique-Joseph Garat, *Mémoires historiques sur la vie de M. Suard*, Paris, A. Belin, 1820, 2 vols., I, 102-03. **21, visiting strangers:** Garat, I, 103. **28-29, composing his book:** Vian, p. 220. **29, intimate circles:** *Ibid.*, p. 219. **32, Oratorians:** Pierre Barrière, *Un grand Provincial: Charles-Louis de Secondat, Baron de La Brède et de Montesquieu*, Bordeaux, Editions Delmas, 1946, pp. 12-18.

Page 100

Line 15, Montesquieu himself: Letter to Solar of March 7, 1749, *Correspondance de Montesquieu*, ed. by Gebelin and Morize, Paris, Champion, 2 vols., 1914, II, 147.

Page 103

Lines 16-17, Amsterdam: Louis Vian, pp. 56-57; Henri Barckhausen, *Lettres persanes*, Paris, Hachette, 1913, 2 vols., I, pp. vii-viii; II, p. 88. For an opinion that another "Amsterdam" edition under the name of Pierre Brunel was the original and was really printed at Rouen, cf. A. Claudin as noted by David C. Cabeen, *Montesquieu: A Bibliography*, New York Public Library, 1947, p. 29. **22, some more *Persian Letters:*** Vian, pp. 62-63. **34, December:** Mathieu Marais, *Journal et Mémoires,* II, 13-14 ff.

Page 104

Line 7, Ambassador of the Grand Turk: *Ibid.,* II, 101-02, 108-09, 112, 118, 162, 165, 172. **11, ten editions:** Montesquieu, *Lettres persanes,* ed. by Henri Barckhausen, I, p. viii.

Page 109

Line 6, Cesare Beccaria: Montesquieu, *Lettres persanes,* ed. by Robert Loyalty Cru, New York, Oxford University Press, 1914, p. 280. **11, Thomas Jefferson:** *The Writings of Thomas Jefferson,* Library ed., Washington, Thomas Jefferson Memorial Association, 1903, 20 vols. I, 67 *(Autobiography).* **12, Voltaire:** Moland, XXV, 539-77; Georges Bengesco, *Voltaire, Bibliographie de ses œuvres,* Paris, 1882-90, 4 vols., II, 173-76.

Page 112

Line 3, boldness: Moland, XXXIII, 365; cf. XXXIX, 520.

CHAPTER VII

Page 114

Line 5, *Persian Letters:* Mathieu Marais, III, 501. **18, Voltaire:** Moland, XIV, 106-07. **27, no public claim:** Vian, pp. 79, 103-04.

Page 115

Line 1, D'Argenson: *Mémoires,* Jannet, V, 88. **13, Make his works public:** Vian, p. 108. **15-16, only three times:** *Ibid.,* p. 109. **22-23, October 31:** *Ibid.,* p. 123. **34, Free Masonry:** Pierre Barrière, p. 193.

Page 116

Line 8, France to live in: Vian, p. 129. **15, Rome *antica:*** *Ibid.,* p. 144; *Corr.,* II, 145.

Page 117

Line 3, Voltaire: Moland, XVIII, 604; XXX, 422-24; XLV, 162. **10, Henry Adams:** *The Education of Henry Adams, An autobiography,* Boston and New York, Houghton Mifflin Company, 1918, pp. 300-03, 382.

Page 119

Line 26, Frederick the Great: Montesquieu, *Œuvres complètes,* Laboulaye ed., Paris, Garnier, 1875-79, 7 vols., II, 149, n.3.

Page 120

Line 19, Lanson: *Histoire de la littérature française,* 12th ed., Paris, Hachette, 1912, p. 713; Laboulaye ed. of Montesquieu, II, 207, and n.1. **33, Lord Morley:** Burton Stevenson, *The Home Book of Quotations,* New York, Dodd, Mead and Co., 4th ed., 1944, p. 1541 (5).

Page 121

Line 21, Voltaire: Moland, XXXVII, 176. **25, Gibbon:** *Encyclopædia Britannica,* 11th ed., XI, 930, Article *Gibbon.*

Page 122

Line 16, perusal of Montesquieu: Ruth Fiske, *Studies on the Rise and Fall of Rome subsequent to Montesquieu,* unpub. M.A. thesis, Ohio State University, 1934, p. 16. **20, causes and effects:** *Ibid.,* p. 22. **22, unknown to the vulgar:** *Ibid.* **26, empires:** *Ibid.* **29, republic:** *Ibid.* **35, the two historians:** *Ibid.,* pp. 28-31. **38, through the centuries:** *Ibid.,* p. 32.

Page 123

Line 14, ill-will: *Ibid.,* p. 78. Cf. pp. 67-78. **19, the Roman fate:** *Ibid.,* p. 87. **26, Simkhovitch:** *Ibid.,* pp. 91-95. **35, Edward Lucas White:** *Ibid.,* pp. 96-101.

Page 124

Line 14, decay: M. Rostovtzeff, "The Decay of the Ancient World and its Economic Explanations," *The Economic History Review,* II, 199 (January, 1930). Cf. also Norman H. Baynes,

"The Decline of the Roman Power in Western Europe: Some Explanations," in *The Journal of Roman Studies,* XXXIII, 29-35 (1943). **25, men's minds:** M. Rostovtzeff, *A History of the Ancient World,* Oxford, Clarendon Press, 1926-27, 2 vols., II, 366.

CHAPTER VIII

Page 126

Line 1, **twenty years and more:** Montesquieu, *Corr.,* II, 147. **7, dictated:** Vian, p. 227. **24, many times begun:** Preface, Laboulaye ed., III, 85.

Page 127

Line 2, **end:** *Ibid.* **5, almost killed me:** *Corr.,* II, 147. **14, the following January:** Clément, *Les Cinq Années littéraires,* La Haye, 1754, 4 vols., I, 171; cf. Raynal, *Nouvelles littéraires,* in Grimm, *Corr. litt.,* I, 231. A review appeared in *Le Mercure de France* for November, 1748. **15, furtively:** Raynal, in Grimm, *Corr. litt.,* I, 265.

Page 130

Line 9, *Persian Letters:* Letter 89.

Page 131

Line 14, **Beccaria:** Cf. above, p. 109, note to line 6.

Page 133

Line 5, **a week:** Unpublished letter of Du Pan to Mme Freudenreich in regard to the Lisbon earthquake of 1755. Bibliothèque de Genève, MSS du Pan, V, f.32 and verso. Cf my *Introduction to Voltaire's Candide,* New York, Holt, 1934, p. xxxviii. **36, early leaders:** cf. the following chapter, below.

Page 135

Lines 6-7, **French parlements:** Sergio Cotta, "Montesquieu, la séparation des pouvoirs et la Constitution fédérale des Etats-Unis," *Revue internationale d'histoire politique et constitutionnelle,* July-December, 1951, pp. 229-33. **23, eternal vigilance:** phrase spoken by Wendell Phillips, and given various unestablished attributions. Burton Stevenson, *Home Book of Quotations,* p. 1106 (2).

Page 136

Line 28, **Mme de Staël:** *De la littérature considérée dans ses rapports avec les institutions sociales* (1800). **36, human geography:** Cf. Jacqueline Berke and Vivian Wilson, *Watch Out for the Weather,* New York, 1951, summarizing in popular form studies on the influence of climate by Dexter, Huntington, Mills, Petersen, and others.

Page 138

Line 18, **end of December:** Vian, p. 325. **21, Number 27:** *Ibid.,* p. 326. **35, Grimm:** *Corr. litt.,* II, 491.

Page 139

Line 1, **Rousseau:** J.-J. Rousseau, *Corr. gén.,* II (Paris, Armand Colin, 1924), 159-60. **3, Raynal:** Grimm, *Corr. litt.,* II, 224-25.

CHAPTER IX

Page 140

Line 1, **1750:** Paul M. Spurlin, *Montesquieu in America, 1760-1801,* Louisiana State University Press, 1940, p. 57. **4, Benjamin Franklin:** *Ibid.,* pp. 58-61. **10, abstract in French:** Gilbert Chinard, *Pensées choisies de Montesquieu, tirées du "Common-Place Book" de Thomas Jefferson,* Paris, Les Belles Lettres, 1925, pp. 21-26. **11-12, bill for books:** Marie Kimball, "Jefferson's Four Freedoms," *Virginia Quarterly Review,* XIX, 204-21 (1943); Marie Kimball, *Jefferson, the Road to Glory, (1743-1776),* New York, Coward McCann, 1943, p. 210; *The Papers of Thomas Jefferson,* Princeton University Press, I (1950), 34. **15, In 1790:** Jefferson, *Writings,* Memorial ed., Washington, D. C., 1903-04, 20 vols., VIII, 31-32. **25, John Adams:** Spurlin, pp. 86-89. **30, James Madison:** George R. Havens, "James Madison et la pensée française," *Revue de littérature comparée,* III, 610-12, 614, 615 (1923); Spurlin, pp. 89-90.

Page 141

Line 1, **Paul M. Spurlin:** *Montesquieu in America,* p. 66. **5, Boston Gazette:** *Ibid.,* pp. 104-05. **13-14, feared authority:** *Ibid.,* p. 117. **15, John and**

Samuel Adams: *Ibid.,* pp. 119-20, 127-29. **21, Spurlin:** *Montesquieu in America,* pp. 133-34. **32, Sir Frederick Pollock:** *Holmes-Pollock Letters,* Harvard University Press, 1946 (2 vols. in one), II, 265-66.

Page 142

Line 5, *Massachusetts Gazette:* Fernand Cattelain, *Etude sur l'influence de Montesquieu dans les constitutions américaines,* Besançon, Millet, 1927, pp. 55 (facsimile), 59; James Truslow Adams, *Revolutionary New England,* Boston, 1923, pp. 387-88, and n.1; Spurlin, p. 143. The date, "October 12, 1772," in the facsimile is the date of the "Proposal," not the date of the number in which it was published. The original is in the Boston Athenæum in a newspaper, bearing the lengthy title of *The Massachusetts Gazette and the Boston Post Boy and Advertiser,* for Monday, October 19, 1772. The long combined title was evidently the cause of confusion and error on the part of Cattelain in reporting the publication. **8,** *Pennsylvania Gazette:* Spurlin, pp. 142-43. **17, 1802:** *Ibid.,* p. 143. **21,** *Maryland Journal: Ibid.,* p. 151. **23-24, James Madison:** *Ibid.,* pp. 165-66. **29, an American classic:** *Ibid.,* p. 177. **35, Madison's knowledge:** *Ibid.,* p. 179. Cf. pp. 89-90.

Page 143

Line 5, Dr. Witherspoon: *Ibid.,* p. 180.

Page 144

Line 7, repair: Quoted by Carl Van Doren, *The Great Rehearsal,* New York, Viking Press, 1948, p. 9. **35, thirty:** *Ibid.,* p. 52. **38, forty-feet square:** Robert Shackleton, *The Book of Philadelphia,* Philadelphia, Penn Pub. Co., 1918, p. 74; Carroll Frey, *The Independence Square Neighborhood,* Philadelphia, Penn. Mutual Life Insurance Co., 1926, pp. 7, 9, 95.

Page 145

Line 1, recent French writer: "Ce furent de magnifiques orateurs qui sauvèrent la jeune République fédéra-

tive: Washington, Madison, Hamilton, Dickinson, Randolph, Franklin." Joseph Dedieu, *Montesquieu, l'homme et l'œuvre,* Paris, Boivin, 1943, p. 198. **4, Jefferson:** Van Doren, p. 28. **12, Madison:** *Ibid.* **32, Washington:** *Ibid.,* pp. 39-40. **39, Madison:** *Ibid.,* p. 30.

Page 146

Lines 21-22, papers of Washington: Sparks, *Writings of George Washington,* Boston, Little, Brown, and Co., 1858, 41 vols. IX, 521-38. Cf. E. G. Bourne, *Essays in Historical Criticism,* New York, 1901, p. 167. **31, James Madison:** Van Doren, pp. 37-38.

Page 147

Line 20, Madison: Spurlin, pp. 186-87. **36, July 17th:** Max Farrand, *The Records of the Federal Convention of 1787,* New Haven, Yale Univ. Press, 1911, 3 vols., II, 34.

Page 148

Line 7, Alexander Hamilton: Spurlin, pp. 185-86. **9-10, James Wilson:** *Ibid.,* p. 186. **11, June 1st:** Farrand, I, 71. **14-15, Edmund Randolph:** Spurlin, p. 187; Farrand, I, 580. **17, James Wilson:** Spurlin, p. 188; Farrand, II, 530. **20, Pierce Butler:** Spurlin, pp. 188-89; Farrand, I, 391. **26, John Adams:** Spurlin, pp. 189-90.

Page 149

Line 8, circumstances of America: *Ibid.,* p. 206. **18, James Bowdoin, Jr.:** *Ibid.,* pp. 209-11. **21, Edmund Randolph:** *Ibid.,* pp. 214-15. **28, Edmund Pendleton:** *Ibid.,* p. 218.

Page 150

Line 12, Madison: *Federalist,* No. 51, Mod. Library ed., p. 337. By Madison, according to Edward G. Bourne, *Essays in Historical Criticism,* New York, Scribner's, 1901, pp. 122-25, 152. **21, Hamilton:** *Ibid.,* No. 1, p. 7. **28, existing confederation:** *Ibid.,* No. 9, pp. 49-50. **33, favor of the Union:** *Ibid.,* No. 9, p. 51. **34, Madison:** *Ibid.,* No. 14, p. 80. **39, roads and canals:** *Ibid.,* No. 14, pp. 80-83.

Page 151

Lines 5-6, Hamilton: *Ibid.,* No. 9, pp. 52-53. 6, Madison: *Ibid.,* No. 43, p. 285. 20, Polybius: Gilbert Chinard, "Polybius and the American Constitution," *Journal of the History of Ideas,* I, 38-58, January, 1940. 21, Locke: John Locke, *Of Civil Government,* Everyman ed., London, Dent, 1924 (reprinted 1947), Chap. XII, p. 190. 28, Burlamaqui: Ray Forrest Harvey, *Jean Jacques Burlamaqui: A Liberal Tradition in American Constitutionalism,* University of North Carolina Press, 1937, pp. 89-90. 35, Madison: *Federalist,* No. 47, p. 313.

Page 152

Line 2, Locke: *Of Civil Government,* Chap. XIII, p. 192. 8, Madison: *Federalist,* No. 48, p. 322. 9, founders: *Ibid.* 14, Hamilton: *Ibid.,* No. 71, p. 466. 18, another passage: *Ibid.,* No. 73, p. 476. 20-21, Thomas Jefferson: Quoted in the *Federalist,* No. 48, p. 324. 29, Madison: *Ibid.,* No. 47, p. 315. 30, Montesquieu: *Esprit des lois,* Book XI, chap. 6, Laboulaye ed., IV, 15.

Page 153

Line 9, Hamilton: *Federalist,* No. 70, p. 455. 16, Montesquieu: Hamilton, *Federalist,* No. 78, p. 504, n. 20, the courts: Hamilton, *Federalist,* No. 78, p. 506. 27, to declare: *Ibid.,* p. 505. 33, Madison: *Federalist,* No. 47, pp. 314-15.

Page 154

Lines 1-2, not a single instance: *Ibid.,* p. 316. 3-4, too great a mixture: *Ibid.,* p. 320. 5, Jefferson: *Ibid.,* No. 48, p. 324. 8, Madison: *Ibid.,* p. 326. 19, ambition: *Ibid.,* No. 51, p. 337. By Madison according to Edward G. Bourne. Cf. above, p. 150, line 12, and Note. 27, Herman Finer: *The Theory and Practice of Modern Government,* New York, Dial Press, 1934, p. 73. 32-33, Charles Evans Hughes: Quoted by Robert H. Jackson, *The Struggle for Judicial Supremacy,* New York, Knopf, 1941, p. 3.

Page 155

Line 5, safety in numbers: Burton Stevenson, *The Home Book of Quota-* tions, p. 726 (20). 18, the ordinary depravity: *Federalist,* No. 78, p. 511. 19, popular assemblies: *Ibid.,* No. 6, p. 30. 22-23, golden age: *Ibid.,* p. 33. 23, government: *Ibid.,* No. 15, p. 92. 26, the simple force of law: *Ibid.,* No. 28, p. 171. 30, ambition: Cf. above p. 154, line 19, and Note. 32, Brandeis: Frank R. Strong, *American Constitutional Law,* Buffalo, Dennis and Co., 1950, pp. 31-32.

Page 156

Line 8, Hamilton: *Federalist,* No. 85, pp. 570-71. 9, Montesquieu: *Esprit des lois,* Book XI, Chap. 4, Laboulaye ed., IV, p. 5. (Nugent translation, Hafner Library of Classics, New York, Hafner Publishing Company, 1949, p. 150.) 21, Madison: *Federalist,* No. 47, p. 320.

CHAPTER X

Page 157

Line 2, November 21: For the detailed story of Voltaire's early life, well documented and only occasionally superseded by later research, see Gustave Desnoiresterres, *Voltaire et la société au XVIIIe siècle, La Jeunesse de Voltaire,* which is Volume I of this important eight-volume series, 2nd ed., Paris, Didier, 1869-76. An excellent brief Life is that by Gustave Lanson, *Voltaire* (Grand Ecrivains français series), Paris, Hachette, 2nd ed., 1910. A single-volume discussion of the Life and selections from the chief Works will be found in my *Selections from Voltaire,* revised ed., New York, Appleton-Century, 1940. The reader may consult David C. Cabeen, *A Critical Bibliography of French Literature,* Volume IV, *The Eighteenth Century,* Syracuse University Press, 1951, pp. 182-207, for the present author's listing and brief evaluation of the principal editions of Voltaire and books and articles about him.

Page 160

Line 38, Ira O. Wade: "Voltaire's Name," PMLA, XLIV, 546-64 (1929).

Page 161

Line 18, Abbé du Vernet: *La Vie de Voltaire,* Genève, 1786, pp. 59-60. 27, Opera: Mathieu Marais, *Journal et Mémoires,* III, 392.

Page 162

Lines 1-2, Marquis d'Argenson: *Mémoires et Journal,* Paris, Jannet, 5 vols., 1857-58, I, 191; Marais, III, 393. 8, Abbé de Caumartin: Marais, *Ibid.* Cf. Desnoiresterres, I, 349. 11, Marais: *Journal,* III, 393. 30, Thieriot: Voltaire wrote to Abbé du Vernet on Jan. 13, 1772, when the latter was already projecting his *Vie* and was seeking first-hand information, referring him to "mon ancien ami Thieriot" and adding: "Il est très-vrai que, dans ma seconde retraite à la Bastille, il me pourvut de livres anglais." Moland, XLVIII, 6.

Page 163

Lines 28-29, Lord Bolingbroke: Letter by Voltaire to Thieriot (Moland, XXXIII, 84-85) the date of which is corrected by Theodore Besterman, in his new edition of the Voltaire *Correspondence* (now in progress), from Jan. 2, 1723, to December 4, 1722 *(Voltaire's Correspondence,* Geneva, Les Délices, 1953, I, 178-80).

Page 164

Line 3, text of the play in hand: Archibald Ballantyne, *Voltaire's Visit to England,* London, John Murray, 1919, pp. 48-49, on the authority of Voltaire's London contemporary, W. R. Chetwood, who for twenty years was prompter at the Drury Lane theater. 5, Edward Higginson: Voltaire, *Lettres philosophiques,* crit. ed. by Gustave Lanson, 2nd ed., Paris, Hachette, 2 vols., 1915-17, I, 19-22. 17, obeying "to" the laws: Moland, XXXIII, 163; Lucien Foulet, *Correspondance de Voltaire (1726-1729),* Paris, Hachette, 1913, p. 138; *Voltaire's Correspondence,* ed. by Theodore Besterman, II, 67. 19, Boswell: *Private papers of James Boswell,* New York, Rudge, IV (1929), 17-18. 32, bombshell: Gustave Lanson, *Voltaire* (Grand Ecrivains français series), Paris, 5th ed., Hachette, n.d., p. 52.

Page 165

Line 2, London: Moland, XXXIII, 373; *Voltaire's Corr.* (Besterman), III, 128; Lanson, *Lettres phil.,* I, p. xliii.

3, April: Moland, XXXIII, 414; *Corr.* (Besterman), III, 229.

Page 166

Line 20, Edward Higginson: Cf. p. 164, line 5, and Note.

Page 167

Line 29, James Madison: *Annual Report of the American Historical Association,* 1901, 2 vols., I, 170. Probable as it is, this statement was unfortunately made by Gaillard Hunt without citing authority.

Page 168

Line 9, Télémaque: Cf. above, pp. 50-51.

Page 169

Line 13, Micah: "Thou shalt sow, but thou shalt not reap." *Micah,* VI, 15. 29, Rousseau: *Confessions,* Hachette, VIII, 116.

Page 170

Line 16, *Persian Letters:* Cf. p. 113, lines 7-13. 20, on chairs: Cf. p. 105, line 38.

Page 171

Line 10, a barbarian of genius: If Voltaire seems nowhere actually to have written the striking words often attributed to him in connection with Shakespeare, he did in several passages express less succinctly the substance of this sharp clash of praise and blame. Cf. particularly Moland, II, 316-17; XIII, 56; XLIII, 140-41. 18, Macaulay: Thomas R. Lounsbury, *Shakespeare as a Dramatic Artist,* New York, Scribner's, 1902, pp. 227-28; George Saintsbury, *A History of Criticism,* Edinburgh and London, Blackwood, 3 vols., II (1928), 397.

Page 172

Line 15, Milton: Milton, *Works,* Cambridge ed., New York, 1899, p. 293. (Introduction to *Samson Agonistes.*) 20, Dryden: *Essays,* Ker ed., Oxford, 1926, 2 vols., I, 165, 224. 25, Pope: Lounsbury, *Shakespeare as a Dramatic Artist,* p. 231. 27, Dryden: Dryden, *Essays,* I, 211. 30, Rymer: Thomas Rymer, *Short View of the English*

Stage, London, 1693, p. 146. **33-34, Julius Caesar:** *Ibid.,* p. 148. **34, John Dennis:** J. E. Spingarn, *Critical Essays of the 17th Century,* Oxford, 1908-09, 3 vols., III, 197; D. Nichol Smith, *Eighteenth Century Essays on Shakespeare,* Glasgow, 1903, p. 26. **37, Addison:** *Works,* Bohn ed., London, 1901, II, 306. Cf. III, 191; II, 316-17, 505.

Page 173

Line 3, Nicholas Rowe: *Shakespeare's Works,* London, 1709, I, pp. xxxiv-xxxv. **3, Charles Gildon:** In Rowe, VII, 397, 404; 347. **10, Pope's Preface:** Works, ed. by Elwin and Courthope, London, J. Murray, 1871-89, 10 vols., X, 334; 534-38. **23, Bolingbroke:** Voltaire, Moland, II, 314.

Page 174

Line 13, Rousseau: *Confessions,* Hachette, VIII, 152-53. **19, "master":** Rousseau, *Corr. gén.,* I, 275-76, 301-02.

CHAPTER XI

Page 175

Line 12, men who had witnessed: Voltaire, Moland, XVI, 132. **16, nineteenth-century historians:** Gustave Lanson, *Voltaire,* (Grands Ecrivains français), Paris, Hachette, 5th ed., n. d., p. 111.

Page 178

Line 3, Thomas Gray: *Elegy Written in a Country Churchyard* (1751), line 36. **3, Napoleon:** Voltaire, Moland, XVI, 115. **31, Lévesque de Burigny:** *Ibid.,* XXXV, 25-26. **34, Abbé du Bos:** *Ibid.,* p. 30.

Page 179

Line 6, Lord Hervey: *Ibid.,* p. 414. **29, Dangeau:** *Ibid.,* p. 30.

Page 180

Line 4, conceals from view: Voltaire, *Siècle de Louis XIV,* ed. with excellent *Introduction* by Emile Bourgeois, Paris, Hachette, 5th ed., 1906, p. xl-xli. **18, man with the iron mask:** Voltaire, Moland, XXXV, 30. **25, clock-making:** *Ibid.,* p. 31. **33, The reader:** *Ibid.,* XIV, 158-59.

Page 181

Lines 5-6, Anatole France: *Le Livre de mon ami,* Paris, Calmann-Lévy, 1925, pp. 127-28. **22-23, Montesquieu,** *Pensées diverses, Œuvres* (Laboulaye ed., Paris, Garnier, 1875-79), VII, 162.

Page 183

Line 13, Joan of Arc: Voltaire, Moland, XII, 49. **20, Christ:** "Et si sur l'imposture il fonde sa doctrine, C'est un bonheur encor d'être trompé par lui." Voltaire, Moland, IX, 361 (*Epître à Uranie,* or *Le Pour et le Contre.*) **24, fanaticism:** Voltaire, Moland, XII, 50. **29, citizens:** *Ibid.* **37, Voltaire:** *Poème sur la Loi naturelle,* Moland, IX, 450; crit. ed. by Francis J. Crowley, U. of California Press, Berkeley, 1938, p. 256. Cf. Diderot, AT, I, 159.

Page 184

Lines 13-14, I should like to discover: Voltaire, Moland, XII, 53. **19, the use of glasses:** *Ibid.,* pp. 53-57.

CHAPTER XII

Page 186

Title, Taking Counsel: I owe this title to that of the Presidential address of my former teacher, the late Edward C. Armstrong, an address given before the annual meeting of the Modern Language Association of America on March 29, 1920, at Columbus, Ohio. Cf. PMLA, XXXV, p. xxiv (at the end of the volume). **10, Micromégas:** Ira O. Wade, *Voltaire's Micromégas,* Princeton Univ. Press, 1950, p. 34; Joe Braden Cox, unpublished Master's thesis on *Micromégas,* Ohio State University, 1942.

Page 187

Line 4, Zadig: For details, see the critical ed. of *Zadig* by Georges Ascoli, Paris, Hachette, 1929, 2 vols. **25, derogatory metaphors:** Voltaire, Moland, XXI, 54, 119; IX, 477; XXV, 108.

Page 189

Line 22, *Essay on Man:* "On life's vast ocean diversely we sail, Reason the card, but passion is the gale." *Epistle II,* lines 107-08; cf. Ira O.

Wade, "A Favorite Metaphor of Voltaire," *Romanic Review,* XXVI, 330-34 (1935).

Page 191

Lines 27-28, some thirteen or fourteen years before: Cf. above, p. 186, lines 6-10. 33, Gulliver's Travels: Moland, XXXIII, 165; Lucien Foulet, *Corr. de Voltaire,* pp. 73-76; Besterman ed., II, 43-44.

Page 196

Line 7, held open: Gustave Desnoiresterres, *Voltaire,* V, 66-67. 10, Rousseau: See below, pp. 222-23. 29, two or three holes: Gustave Lanson, *Voltaire,* p. 133.

Page 197

Line 19, three weeks: George R. Havens, "The Composition of Voltaire's *Candide,*" *Modern Language Notes,* XLVII, 225-34 (1932). 27, *Candide:* Moland, XL, 62. Cf. p. 61.

Page 198

Line 2, thirteen...printings: Voltaire, *Candide,* crit. ed. by André Morize, Paris, Droz, 1931 (reprinting of ed. of 1913), pp. lxv-lxvi. 4, popularity: Daniel Mornet, "Les imitations du 'Candide' de Voltaire," *Mélanges Lanson,* Paris, Hachette, 1922, p. 299. 21, Madame du Châtelet: André Morize, ed. of *Candide,* pp. xv-xviii. 27, a real disciple: *Ibid.,* pp. xxx-xxxi.

Page 204

Lines 29-30, waking his secretaries: Longchamp et Wagnière, *Mémoires sur Voltaire,* Paris, 1826, I, 92. 31-32, Voltaire and Madame du Châtelet: Mme de Graffigny, *Lettres,* pub. by Eugène Asse, Paris, 1879, p. 229. 35, time: *Ibid.,* p. 230. 38, works: André Morize, *Candide,* pp. 223-24, n.; George R. Havens, *Candide,* N. Y., Holt, 1933, pp. 144-45.

CHAPTER XIII

Page 209

Line 1, Colini: Moland, XVII, p. vii; Georges Bengesco, *Voltaire: Bibliographie de ses œuvres,* Paris, 1882-

90, 4 vols., I, 412. 7-8, much in demand: Moland, XVII, p. v.

Page 214

Lines 30-31, Cr. the inf.: Moland, XLIII, 492, 493. Cf. XLV, 507-08, n., for a humorous misinterpretation of this seeming signature, on the part of the postal censors.

Page 215

Line 10, Dom Calmet: Gustave Lanson, *Voltaire,* p. 172. 15, Jesus or Jeanne d'Arc: See above, p. 183, lines 13 and 20. 31, I disapprove: Burdette Kinne, "Voltaire Never Said It!" *Mod. Lang. Notes,* LVIII, 534-35 (1943); Burton Stevenson, *The Home Book of Quotations,* New York, Dodd, Mead and Co., 4th ed., 1944, *Appendix,* p. 2276(1).

Page 216

Line 14, Don Quixote: Moland, I, 410; Grimm [Meister], *Corr. litt.,* XI, 445-46. 15-16, James Boswell: *Private Papers of James Boswell,* New York, Rudge, IV (1928), 17-18. 20-21, Martin Sherlock: Moland, I, 390; cf. p. 398. 26, commonly wore: *Ibid.,* p. 352; cf. p. 395. 30, Madame Suard: *Ibid.,* p. 375.

Page 217

Line 2, Chabanon: *Ibid.,* pp. 361-62. 2, Gibbon: *Ibid.,* p. 335. 6, Boswell, *Private Papers of James Boswell,* IV, 18-19. 10, awake: Longchamp et Wagnière, *Mémoires sur Voltaire,* I, 92. 19, baggage: Moland, I, 387.

Page 219

Line 15, liberalism: Gustave Lanson, *Voltaire,* p. 205.

CHAPTER XIV

Page 221

Line 2, Zion: Pierre-Maurice Masson, *La Religion de J.-J. Rousseau,* Paris, Hachette, 1916, 3 vols., I, 4-5. 5, zigzag walls: Cf. a *Nouveau Plan de Genève,* by Nicolas Chalmandrier, Geneva, 1776. 6, chains: *Ibid.* 9, Escalade: Voltaire, *Essai sur les mœurs,* Moland, XII, 482; cf. G. Desnoiresterres, *Voltaire,* V (Paris, 1875),

66, n. 3.　**18, 20,000 inhabitants:** *Encyclopædia Britannica,* 11th ed., XI, 587 (Article *Geneva*), says 18,500 in 1711 and 24,712 in 1782; Louis Ducros *(J.-J. Rousseau de Genève à l'Hermitage,* Paris, 1908, p. 9) gives the population as "13.000 à peine." In 1757, Voltaire observes that there are about 25,000 inhabitants. (Moland, XXXIX, 268.)　**18, citizens:** There were in Geneva the three categories of *habitants, natifs,* and *citoyens.* (Louis Ducros, *Ibid.,* p. 17, n.1.)

Page 222

Line 8, more of a child: *Confessions,* Hachette, VIII, 3.

Page 223

Line 7, Minutoli: *Ibid.,* **p. 28.** 29, castle: *Ibid.,* p. 30.

Page 224

Line 4, born with the century: *Ibid.,* p. 34.　**27, prolonged struggle:** *Ibid.,* pp. 45, 48.　**34, Pierre-Maurice Masson:** Cf. Louis Courtois, "Chronologie de J.-J. Rousseau," *Ann. J.-J. Rousseau,* XV, 10-11, and notes.

Page 225

Line 6, penny a night: "à un sou par nuit." *Confessions,* Hachette, VIII, p. 49.　**18, Pierre Bayle:** *Ibid.,* p. 78. **22, village priest:** "curé de village." *Ibid.,* p. 79.　**29, such a shivaree:** *Ibid.,* p. 105.

Page 226

Line 8, Faubourg Saint-Marceau: *Ibid.,* p. 113.　**19, peasant's hut:** *Ibid.,* p. 116.

Page 227

Lines 31-32, *Philosophical Letters:* *Ibid.,* pp. 152-53.　**38, some fifteen years:** "Il y a quinze ans que je travaille pour me rendre digne de vos regards." Rousseau to Voltaire, Dec. 11, 1745. *Corr. générale,* I, 275.

Page 228

Line 9, character: *Projet pour l'éducation de M. de Sainte-Marie,* Hachette, III, p. 37.　**26, vainly seeking the right word:** Louis Ducros, I, 109.　**33, eighteen months:** *Confes-*

sions, Hachette, VIII, 228:　**33, records:** Louis Ducros, I, p. 112. Cf. Courtois, "Chronologie," p. 47, n.3.　**37-38, our foolish civil institutions:** *Confessions;* Hachette, VIII, 231.

Page 229

Line 8, Rameau: *Ibid.,* pp. 239-40. **10, gave up:** *Ibid.,* p. 242.　**37, the 24th of July:** Cf. Paul Bonnefon, "Diderot prisonnier à Vincennes," RHL, VI, 204, 1899. The *lettre de cachet* for the imprisonment of Diderot bears the date of July 23rd.

Page 230

Line 8, 25th of August: Cf. Louis Courtois, "Chronologie de J.-J. Rousseau," *Annales J.-J. Rousseau,* XV, 56 (1923).　**11-12, on foot:** *Confessions,* Hachette, VIII, 249.　**12-13, Rue Jean-Saint-Denis:** *Ibid.,* p. 246.　**15, hot:** *Ibid.,* p. 249.　**22, two in the afternoon:** *Ibid.　***27, sparsely built-up:** *Nouveau Plan de la Ville, Cité et Université de Paris avec ses Faubourgs,* Chez C. Roussel, Rue Saint-Jacques, 1713. **39, purify morals:** For a copy of the Program of the Prize Contest, see my critical edition of Rousseau's *Discours sur les sciences et les arts,* New York, Modern Language Association of America, 1946, p. 91.

Page 231

Line 5, pencil: "la prosopopée de Fabricius, écrite en crayon sous un chêne." *Confessions,* Hachette, VIII, 249. For the details of the narrative, cf. my edition of the First Discourse, *Introduction,* pp. 1-9.　**21, account:** Letter to M. de Malesherbes, Jan. 12, 1762. *Corr. générale,* VII, 50-51: Hachette, X, 301-02.　**26-27, Diderot . . . urged:** cf. my edition of the First Discourse, pp. 6-9, 19.

Page 232

Line 6, July 20th: *Corr. générale,* I, 304; cf. my edition of the First Discourse, pp. 27-28 and n.20.　**36, put it into practice:** Louis Ducros, *J.-J. Rousseau de Genève à l'Hermitage,* pp. 230-35.

Page 233

Line 10, Albert Schweitzer: *Out of*

my Life and Thought, New York, Henry Holt, 1949, p. 160.

Page 234

Lines 2-3, Montaigne: *De l'institution des enfants,* Book I, Chap. XXV (or in modern editions, Chap. XXVI), Garnier ed., n.d., I, 116. **7, echoing Plutarch and Montaigne:** cf. my edition of the First Discourse, p. 251.

CHAPTER XV

Page 235

Line 3, oaks: many of these venerable oaks, probably several hundred years old, still stand. Doré Ogrizek, *France, Paris and the Provinces,* New York, McGraw Hill, 1948, p. 202. **12, fine weather:** *Confessions,* Hachette, VIII, 276. "Il faisoit très-beau." **14, primitive man:** "Tout le reste du jour, enfoncé dans la forêt, j'y cherchois, j'y trouvois l'image des premiers temps, dont je traçois fièrement l'histoire." *Ibid.* **22, dealers in old clothes:** Louis Ducros, I, 246.

Page 236

Line 12, Madame de Francueil: *Ibid.,* pp. 244-46; *Corr. gén.,* I, 308, 309.

Page 237

Lines 6-7, Montaigne: *Des Cannibales,* Book I, chap. XXX (XXXI). **20, misery:** *Confessions,* Hachette, VIII, 276-77. **22, prudently rejected:** Roger Tisserand, *Les concurrents de J.-J. Rousseau à l'Académie de Dijon pour le prix de 1754.* Paris, Boivin [1936], pp. 28-30. **31, title page:** see the original edition, or else a facsimile of the title page in Théophile Dufour, *Recherches bibliographiques sur les œuvres imprimées de J.-J. Rousseau,* Paris, Giraud-Badin, 2 vols., 1925, I, p. 57.

Page 239

Line 9, unreliability: *Discours sur l'inégalité,* Notes, Hachette, I, 143-44.

Page 240

Line 26, Voltaire: For a facsimile of Rousseau's page with its marginal notes by Voltaire, see my book, *Voltaire's*

Marginalia on the Pages of Rousseau, Columbus, Ohio State University, 1933, Frontispiece; for a discussion of the passage, see pp. 15-16.

Page 241

Line 17, classical antiquity: Cf. Arthur O. Lovejoy and George Boas, *Primitivism and Related Ideas in Antiquity,* Baltimore, Johns Hopkins Press, 1935, particularly p. xi.

Page 242

Line 19, revolution: Félix Rocquain, *L'esprit révolutionnaire avant la révolution,* Paris, 1878, p. 180; cf. my edition of Rousseau's *Discours sur les sciences et les arts,* pp. 82-83. **24, Abbé Talbert:** The prize-winning discourse may be read in Roger Tisserand, *Les concurrents de J.-J. Rousseau...pour le prix de 1754,* pp. 135-51. **32, I have received, Sir:** Moland, XXXVIII, 446-50; Rousseau, *Corr. générale,* II, 203-05. The latter was printed from the original manuscript; the version in Moland was slightly revised by Voltaire for publication.

Page 243

Line 32, effective reply: *Corr. générale,* II, 206-09.

Page 244

Line 20, bad pleasantries: *Ibid.,* II, 328. **31, harsh, bitter tone:** *Confessions,* Hachette, VIII, 277, n.; *Corr., Ibid.,* XII, 192, n.1, or *Corr. générale,* XIX, 252, n.

Page 245

Line 13, Say not thou: *Ecclesiastes,* VII, 10. **37, Thoreau:** *Walden,* Chap. I, *Economy,* Mod. Library ed., p. 13.

CHAPTER XVI

Page 247

Line 1, the 9th of April: *Confessions,* Hachette, VIII, 287. **1-2, ten in the morning:** *Mémoires de Mme d'Epinay,* Paris, Charpentier, 1865, II, 132. **3, Hôtel du Languedoc:** Louis J. Courtois, "Chronologie de J.-J. Rousseau," *Ann. J.-J. Rousseau,* XV, 58 and n.1 (1923); cf. *Confessions,* Hachette, VIII, 250. **6-7, so much admired:** *Confessions,* VIII, 282. **7, peasant farmer:**

Ibid., p. 287; Mme d'Epinay, II, 132. **11, six flights of stairs:** "au sixième," Louis J. Courtois, "Chronologie," p. 58. **20-21, at the edge of the forest:** Mme d'Epinay, II, 132. **24-25, walking with difficulty:** "une femme de soixante-dix ans, lourde, épaisse et presque impotente." *Ibid.* As a matter of fact, Mme Levasseur, married in 1696 (*Corr. gén.*, II, 395), even if we assume that she was not over fifteen at that time, must have been upwards of 75 or 76 in 1756, not 70. According to Pierre-Paul Plan (*Table de la Corr. générale de J.-J. Rousseau*, Geneva, Droz, 1953, p. 147), Thérèse's mother, born about 1673, would actually have been some 83 years old when Rousseau moved to the Hermitage. **26, armchair:** Mme d'Epinay, II, 132. **27, before noon:** "Nous dinâmes avec lui," writes Mme d'Epinay (II, 132), and dinner came then generally in the early afternoon. The distance from the center of Paris was not more than eleven or twelve miles. **29, Abbé de Linant:** *Ibid.* Cf. *Corr. gén.*, II, 395.

Page 248

Line 4, started to live: Letter of Rousseau to Malesherbes, Jan. 26, 1762 (*Corr. gén.*, VII, 70). **5, cold still:** For the details of this paragraph, see *Confessions*, Hachette, VIII, 288. **17, At last:** *Ibid.* **26, every path:** *Ibid.* **35, chestnuts:** Karl Baedeker, *Paris and Environs*, Leipzig, 1910, p. 401; Morellet, *Mémoires*, Paris, 1822, 2 vols., I, 106. **36, notebook and pencil:** *Confessions*, Hachette, VIII, 288. **38, open air:** *Ibid.*

Page 249

Line 4, Madame d'Epinay: *Ibid.*, pp. 304-05. **8, Bear:** *Ibid.*, p. 282. **8, obsequious politeness:** Grimm, *Corr. litt.*, V, 103. **27, letters:** G. Streckeisen-Moultou, *J.-J. Rousseau, ses amis et ses ennemis*, Paris, Calmann-Lévy, n. d., II, pp. 450-53; *Corr. gén.*, XX, 357 (end of page). **32, time of day:** *Confessions*, VIII, 235.

Page 250

Line 2, dying without having lived: *Ibid.*, p. 305. **6, Mademoiselle Galley:**

Ibid., pp. 95-98, 305-06. **24, pictured himself:** Daniel Mornet, crit. ed. of the *Nouvelle Héloïse*, Paris, Hachette, 1925, 4 vols., I, 112. Saint-Preux was Rousseau's idealization of himself, he told Bernardin de Saint-Pierre. (Bernardin de Saint-Pierre, *Œuvres complètes*, Paris, Dupont, XII, 1826, p. 51.) **26, light-blond:** Mornet, *Nouvelle Héloïse*, I, 115.

Page 251

Line 4, mid-twenties: Rousseau says: "Mme la comtesse d'Houdetot approchoit de la trentaine." (*Confessions*, VIII, 315.) According to Pierre-Paul Plan (*Table de la Corr. gén.*, p. 110), Mme d'Houdetot was born in 1730, making her 26 at the time of Rousseau's infatuation. See the *Confessions* and the *Correspondance* for other details of their acquaintance at this time. For corrections in Rousseau's memory of chronology, cf. Mornet, *Nouvelle Héloïse*, I, pp. 81 ff. **15, Sunday or Monday afternoon:** Louis J. Courtois, "Chronologie," p. 90 and n.2; *Confessions*, VIII, 309-10. "Il étoit tard, elle resta peu." *Ibid.*, p. 310. Cf. Mornet, I, 86. **34, novel:** *Confessions*, VIII, 309. **36, spring:** *Ibid.*, pp. 310, 314-15. But Rousseau, faithful chiefly to his memory of the emotions, not unnaturally found difficulty in recalling the exact sequence of events when writing long afterward and he erroneously put Mme d'Houdetot's second visit a year later. Cf. Mornet, I, 86-87, 90.

Page 252

Line 17, early-June: June 5, 1757. Courtois, "Chronologie," p. 91; Mornet, I, 87. **25, Madame la Comtesse d'Houdetot:** Cf. *Corr. gén.*, III, 99, 129, 161, 171, 264, 292, although a majority of the letters continue to bear a less formal inscription.

Page 253

Line 2, chose the very words: "Mais c'est Mme d'Houdetot même à l'occasion qui écrit comme la Julie de Rousseau, dont elle n'avait pas lu les lettres." Mornet, I, 87. **3-4, end of 1760:** A few copies only circulated in December 1760 (Mornet, I, 237). Rousseau erroneously put the publication as "au commencement du carnaval" *(Confessions,* Hachette, IX, 2). Courtois states that it was on sale by January 28th ("Chronologie," p. 116 and n.2), Mornet in February (I, 147). It was offered to the public in London from the 20th of December *(Corr. gén.,* V, 309). **5, rare copies:** Cf. *Confessions,* IX, 1; Mornet, I, 237-38. **5, lady:** *Confessions,* IX, 2-3. **20-21, over fifty editions:** Daniel Mornet, *Les imitations du "Candide" de Voltaire, Mélanges Lanson,* Paris, 1922, p. 299. **39, nearsighted:** "Ma vue courte me fait mille illusions." *Confessions,* VIII, 25; cf. Bernardin de Saint-Pierre, "Essai sur J.-J. Rousseau," *Œuvres complètes,* XII, 61.

Page 255

Line 11, philosophic party: *Confessions,* Hachette, VIII, 312-13. **36, end of May:** *Corr. gén.,* VII, 232.

Page 256

Lines 1-2, wife of Monsieur de Chenonceaux: *Emile,* Hachette, II, 1, and n.1; *Confessions,* Hachette, VIII, 293. **7-8, moral principles:** *Projet pour l'éducation de M. de Sainte-Marie,* Hachette, III, 37.

Page 258

Line 11, effort: *Emile,* Hachette, II, 147. **28, I hate books:** *Ibid.,* II, 155.

Page 259

Lines 2-3, century of revolutions: *Ibid.,* II, 166. **5, gentleman carpenter:** Moland, XXX, 573.

Page 260

Line 6, Good, Bold and Good: George R. Havens, *Voltaire's Marginalia on the Pages of Rousseau,* pp. 72-73, 146, 147, 148, 151, 154, 155, 158, 170, 172, 181. **9, Christian:** *Ibid.,* pp. 163, 169. **13, Bible:** *Confessions,* VIII, 279; IX, 27. **20, respect:** "respecter en silence ce qu'on ne sauroit ni rejeter, ni comprendre." *Emile,* Hachette, II, 281. **32, more astonishing than the hero:** *Ibid.*

Page 261

Line 2, four men in black: *Confes-*

sions, IX, 30. Cf. Courtois, "Chronologie," p. 129. **31, middle of April:** *Corr. gén.,* VII, 187. Cf. p. 192.

Page 262

Line 22, Robespierre: J. M. Thompson, *Robespierre,* Oxford, 1935, II, 47.

Page 263

Line 25, All dogma: George R. Havens, *Voltaire's Marginalia . . . on Rousseau,* p. 68.

Page 264

Line 21, ambition: *Federalist,* No. 51, Mod. Library ed., p. 337. By Hamilton or Madison according to the editor; by Madison according to Edward G. Bourne, *Essays in Historical Criticism,* New York, Scribner's, 1901, pp. 122-25, 152. **26, The *Social Contract:*** Daniel Mornet, *Les origines intellectuelles de la Révolution française,* pp. 95-96.

CHAPTER XVII

Page 265

Line 21, books: "Quand je vivrois encore cent ans, je n'écrirois pas une ligne pour la presse." *Corr. gén.,* VII, 77. **25, dog:** *Ibid.,* pp. 71-72.

Page 266

Line 5, in 1765: Louis Ducros, *Jean-Jacques Rousseau de l'Ile de Saint-Pierre à Ermenonville (1765-1778),* Paris, E. de Boccard, 1918, p. 257. **17, Bear:** *Confessions,* VIII, 262, 282. **22, earlier draft:** Théophile Dufour, *Ann. J.-J. Rousseau,* IV, 4 (1908).

Page 267

Line 17, true: Cf. Louis Ducros, III, 251, 261-289.

Page 272

Line 2, end of 1770: *Ibid.,* p. 258. **3-4, April or May:** Théophile Dufour, *Recherches bibliographiques,* I, 238. **5, autumn of 1789:** *Ibid.,* I, 239. Cf. Grimm [Meister], *Corr. litt.,* XV, 542. **19, 1782:** Théophile Dufour, *Recherches,* I, 249.

Page 273

Line 23, loved the water: *Confessions,* Hachette, IX. 71. **26, stretched**

out flat: *Rêveries,* Hachette, IX, 363, 362. Cf. *Confessions,* IX, 72-73.

Page 275

Line 1, hesitatingly: Elizabeth A. Foster, *Le dernier séjour de J.-J. Rousseau à Paris,* Northampton, Mass., Smith College; Paris, Champion, 1921, p. 116, and n.6. Rousseau is said to have first gone alone without Thérèse "pour 5 jours" and without papers or baggage. But, according to Mr. Marcel Françon (below, line 6), Rousseau left Paris for Ermenonville about a month earlier than has previously been supposed. **2-3, two-room apartment:** Foster, p. 9. **3, prolongation:** *Ibid.,* p. 12. The eighteenth-century sketch map of the streets in this Paris quarter printed in Miss Foster's book is, however, inverted so that north stands at the bottom. **6, Ermenonville:** The date has usually been given as May 20, 1778 (Louis Ducros, III, 243). Mr. Marcel Françon, however, adduces arguments in favor of about April 18, with Thérèse coming much later. *Ann. J.-J. Rousseau,* XXXII, 191-96 (1950-52). Cf. also a note by the same author, "Rousseau à Ermenonville," MLN, LXIX, 419, June, 1954. **13, Freshwater admiral:** Ducros, III, 243. Cf. letter of René-Louis de Girardin, *Ann. J.-J. Rousseau,* XXIV, 163, (1935). **15, Piano:** "sur le piano-forte." Ducros, III, 243. **16, cracked voice:** Bernardin de Saint-Pierre, *Œuvres,* XII, 64. **16, Desdemona's mournful ballad:** Ducros, III, 243-44. **18, expressive eyes:** Mme de Staël, *Lettres sur les ouvrages et le caractère de J.-J. Rousseau,* n. p., 1789, pp. 105-06; Bernardin de Saint-Pierre, XII, 38; Hippolyte Buffenoir, *Le prestige de J.-J. Rousseau,* Paris, Emile-Paul, 1909, pp. 241, 246. **19, Genevan accent:** Buffenoir, p. 246. **21, Voltaire's death:** *Ibid.,* p. 326. **25, five o'clock:** Ducros, III, 244. **32, two days later:** *Ibid.,* p. 245.

CHAPTER XVIII

Page 277

Title: Diderot: A spirited new book on Diderot by Lester G. Crocker, entitled *The Embattled Philosopher* (Michigan State College Press, 1954)

has recently appeared, too late, however, to be consulted in connection with these chapters. Arthur M. Wilson, 1953 winner of the Oxford Prize awarded by the Modern Language Association of America for his manuscript, *Diderot, the Testing Years,* will publish in the near future, this, the first of a carefully documented two-volume biography—further evidence of the increasing interest in Diderot manifest in this country as in France. **Line 11, October 5:** Although Diderot's birth has been attributed by several biographers and even by the author himself to four or five different dates in early October, the baptismal certificate establishes authoritatively the fact that he was born on the 5th. (Cf. George R. Havens, "The Dates of Diderot's Birth and Death," MLN, LV, 31-32, Jan., 1940). **13, Number 6:** Cf. Chanoine Marcel, *Le Frère de Diderot,* Paris, Champion, 1913, pp. 4-5.

Page 278

Line 3, The head of a native of Langres: *Lettres à Sophie Volland,* ed. by André Babelon, Paris, 1930, I, 67. **8, Michel van Loo:** AT, XI, 21; cf. *ibid.,* XX, 114, XIX, 263-64; LSV, III, 119. **13, Garat:** AT, I, pp. xxi-xxii. **29, He never wrote:** Diderot had projected such an autobiography and took down for the purpose notes of his daily doings. LSV, II, 308, 342. **35, prizes:** Mme de Vandeul, AT, I, pp. xxix-xxx. **39, hunting:** *Ibid.,* I, p. xxx.

Page 279

Line 5, cutler: *Ibid.* **24, tonsure:** *Ibid.,* I, p. xxix; Jean Pommier, *Diderot avant Vincennes,* Paris, Boivin, 1939, p. 7; André Billy, *Diderot,* Paris, Les Editions de France, 1932, pp. 19-20. **28, fasted:** Mme de Vandeul, AT, I, p. lx. **36, Louis-le-Grand:** The reference to Père Porée is in the *Lettre sur les sourds et muets* (1751), AT, I, 383-84. Mme de Vandeul testifies in favor of the Collège d'Harcourt, AT, I, p. xxx. Cf. R. Salesses ("Diderot et l'Université," *Revue universitaire,* XLIV, 322-33, 1935), who likewise argues for the Collège d'Harcourt, considered as a seat of Jansenist influence. Jean Pommier *(Diderot avant Vincennes,* pp. 8-9) favors Louis-le-Grand, but theorizes that Diderot may also have attended the Collège d'Harcourt later. André Billy *(Diderot,* pp. 23-37) holds for Louis-le-Grand. Daniel Mornet, in 1941 *(Diderot,* Paris, Boivin, p. 15), hesitated between the two, but suggested that Diderot's father placed his son "au collège Louis-le-Grand (ou, peut-être, au collège d'Harcourt)." In 1948, however, in his mimeographed course on *Le Neveu de Rameau* (p. 34), Mornet reversed the order of the two institutions: "Il l'emmène au collège d'Harcourt ou peut-être au collège Louis-le-Grand, on ne sait pas très bien, mais cela importe peu puisque les deux collèges étaient entre les mains des Jésuites," thus differing from M. Salesses on Jansenist influence. In spite of Diderot's reference to Père Porée's teaching as of "il y a trente à quarante ans" (AT, I, 384) instead of some twenty years before, I find it difficult not to consider the passage as a real personal reminiscence rather than as a mere fabrication intended to deceive the reader regarding the authorship of the anonymous *Lettre sur les sourds et muets.* Cf. Jean Thomas, *L'humanisme de Diderot,* 2nd ed., Paris, Les Belles Lettres, 1938, pp. 73 and n., 170.

Page 280

Line 8, **Homer:** AT, III, 478. **14, September 2:** Billy, pp. 36-37. **18, two years:** Mme de Vandeul, AT, I, pp. xxxi-xxxii. André Babelon (Diderot, *Corr. inédite,* Paris, Gallimard, 1931, II, 9-10 and n.) cites a letter of Diderot's father to M. Foucou of Paris as evidence that the son left the office of Clément de Ris in the early part of 1736. Mr. Lester G. Krakeur ("La Jeunesse de Diderot: quelques précisions," PMLA, LVII, 133, March, 1942) points out that, accepting, like other critics, the approximate accuracy of Mme de Vandeul's figure of "two years," we must therefore conclude that Diderot probably first entered on the study of law with Clément de Ris during the winter of 1733-34. **26, Italian and**

English: Mme de Vandeul, AT, I, p. xxxii. **28-29, Clément de Ris:** *Ibid.*

Page 281

Line 4, **better:** *Ibid.* **11, allowance:** *Ibid.* **29, mother:** *Ibid.,* pp. xxxii-xxxiii.

Page 282

Line 4, **borrow:** "Lorsque le hasard amenait à Paris quelques amis de son père, il leur empruntait quelque petite somme." *Ibid.,* p. xxxiv. **6, Brother Ange:** *Ibid.,* pp. xxxiv-xxxvi (1200 francs plus 800 or 900 more). **9, Carthusian monastery:** LSV, II, 324. **11-12, six sermons:** Mme de Vandeul, AT, I, p. xxxiii. **15-16, voice of conscience:** AT, V, 422 *(Neveu de Rameau).* **21, wisps of straw:** *Ibid.,* 389. **24, Cours-la-Reine:** *Ibid.* **28, Alley of Sighs:** *Ibid.,* pp. 411-12. **33, mathematics:** Mme de Vandeul, AT, I, p. xxxiii.

Page 283

Line 2, **Randon de Boisset:** *Ibid.,* pp. xxxiii-xxxiv. Cf. the *Salon de 1767,* AT, XI, 274: "Il s'appelle Randon de Boisset. . . . Je l'ai connu jeune; et il n'a pas tenu à lui que je ne devinsse opulent." André Billy, however, connects the anecdote in the text with Elie Randon de Massane and attributes to him Diderot's acquaintance with Randon de Boisset (pp. 43-46). A catalog of the rich library of Randon de Boisset was published in Paris in 1767 after his death. The *Avertissement* reads (p. iii): "La Collection des Livres de feu M. Randon de Boisset mérite à tous égards l'attention des Amateurs." Obviously, however, there is no way of knowing which of these books were in the library during Diderot's youth. **6, dissatisfied:** Mme de Vandeul, AT, I, pp. xxxiii-xxxiv. **20, Mademoiselle Babuti:** AT, X, 349-50 *(Salon de 1765).* **24, six cents:** "Il s'était lié avec l'abbé de Bernis.... Ils allaient tous deux dîner à six sous par tête, chez le traiteur voisin; et je l'ai souvent entendu vanter la gaieté de ces repas." (Mme de Vandeul, AT, I, p. xxxi.) **31, Diderot told his daughter:** *Ibid.,* p. xxxvii.

Page 284

Lines 10-11, to push the wood around: AT, V, 387, 390 *(Neveu de Rameau).* **27, Corneille's words:** AT, VII, 364. **34, stuff his fingers:** AT, I, 359.

Page 285

Lines 3-4, Gaussin…Dangeville: AT, VIII, 398. **7, Luxembourg:** *Ibid.* **14, fury for study:** AT, XX, 80. **19, reading:** Jean Thomas, *L'humanisme de Diderot,* 2nd ed., Paris, Les Belles Lettres, 1938, p. 84. **26, detailed story:** Cf. note to p. 278, line 29. **35, music:** Rousseau, *Confessions* (Hachette), VIII, 202-203.

Page 286

Lines 4-5, elusive fame: *Ibid.,* pp. 157, 203. **6-7, his comrade:** Diderot writes of "Jean-Jacques Rousseau qui me gagnait toujours aux échecs." AT, XI, 127. **24, November 6:** Diderot, *Corr. inédite,* II, 19. **30, Rousseau:** *Confessions* (Hachette), VIII, 246. Cf. Daniel Mornet, *Diderot,* pp. 18-19. **31, domestic silence:** LSV, I, 210, 212; II, 26, 33, 35. **33, father:** *Corr. inédite,* II, 15-19.

Page 287

Line 2, Madame de Puisieux: Mme de Vandeul, AT, I, pp. xli-xlii; p. 125. **3, Madame de Prémontval:** AT, IX, 77-78. *Lettre sur les aveugles,* éd. crit. par Robert Niklaus, Geneva, Droz, 1951, pp. ix-x. **14, daughter:** André Billy, *Diderot,* pp. 73, 83. **29, Philosophical Letters:** Cf. Diderot, *Pensées philosophiques,* éd. crit. par Robert Niklaus, Geneva, Droz, 1950, p. vii. **33, Pascal:** *Ibid.,* pp. viii, xiv. **34, Bayle:** *Ibid.,* p. xxv.

Page 288

Lines 33-34, Madame de Saint-Maur: AT, I, pp. xlii-xliii. Cf. *Lettre sur les aveugles,* Niklaus ed., p. x. **36, parish priest:** AT, XX, 121-22.

Page 289

Lines 9-10, Marquis d'Argenson: *Mémoires,* Paris, Jannet, 1857-58, 5 vols., III, 276 (August, 1749). **26, half past seven:** Joseph Le Gras, *Diderot et l'En-* *cyclopédie,* Amiens, Malfère, 1928, p. 53. Cf. Paul Bonnefon, "Diderot prisonnier à Vincennes," RHL, VI, 204.

Page 290

Line 8, a week later: AT, XX, 122-24. The report is dated: "Du jeudi, trente-un juillet mil sept cent quarante-neuf de relevée." *Ibid.,* p. 122. **11-12, "He'll have to talk":** "Il faudra bien qu'il jase." Paul Bonnefon, p. 208. **13, "black humor":** "Il avait besoin de la société de ses amis pour ne pas se livrer à son humeur noire." Rousseau, *Confessions* (Hachette), VIII, 248-49. **14, pleading letters:** Paul Bonnefon, pp. 210-16. **14-15, pain in his legs:** "J'ai des douleurs de cuisses et de jambes," *Ibid.,* p. 213. **20, Rousseau:** *Confessions* (Hachette), VIII, 247. **23, Madame du Châtelet:** Moland, XXXVII, 38, Voltaire to Raynal, July 30, 1749. **26-27, 80,000 livres . . . 250,000:** Joseph Le Gras, p. 56. Cf. pp. 56-57, 63; Bonnefon, p. 206. **33, pleasanter quarters:** Joseph Le Gras, p. 61. **36, August 25th:** L. J. Courtois, "Chronologie de J.-J. Rousseau," *Ann. J.-J. Rousseau,* XV (1923), p. 56.

Page 291

Line 14, father: André Billy, pp. 142-44. **26, first half of November:** Raynal, *Nouvelles littéraires,* in Grimm, *Corr. litt.,* I, 486; *Mercure de France,* 1er vol. de décembre 1750, p. 130. **29, two thousand:** By February, 1752. Joseph Le Gras, pp. 86-87. **29, more later:** 3,000 subscribers on the appearance of the fifth volume in 1755. Douglas H. Gordon and Norman L. Torrey, *The Censoring of Diderot's "Encyclopédie,"* New York, Columbia Univ. Press, 1947, p. 17; over 4,000 in 1759. *Ibid.,* p. 21. **30, last days of June:** June 28, 1751: "Le premier des dix volumes de l'*Encyclopédie* paraît aujourd'hui." Raynal, *Nouvelles littéraires,* in Grimm, *Corr. litt.,* II, 73.

CHAPTER XIX

Page 292

Line 2, Quaker: John Morley, *Diderot and the Encyclopædists,* London, Macmillan, 1886, 2 vols. I, 121. (Cf.

Billy, p. 88, "fils d'un fermier quaker.") Morley erroneously gives the date of the first edition of Chambers as 1727. **10, five editions:** Morley, *Ibid.* **12, modern reference volumes:** Cf. *Encyclopædia Britannica,* 11th ed., 1910-11, Article *Encyclopædia.* **14,** Ramsay: Albert Cherel, *Fénelon au XVIIIᵉ siècle en France,* Paris, Hachette, 1917, pp. 31-151. **15, March 21, 1737:** Joseph Le Gras, *Diderot et l'Encyclopédie,* Amiens, Malfère, 1928, p. 28. **26, in 1740:** *Ibid.,* p. 29.

Page 293

Line 7, Le Breton: By Jean Gigot, whose conclusions are noted favorably by Jean Pommier in a review, RHL, LI, 378 (1951). There is also a brief discussion of Diderot in this connection. **9, denied:** G.-H. Luquet, *"L'Encyclopédie* fut-elle une entreprise maçonnique?"* RHL, LIV, 23-31 (1954). **11-12, after 1773:** Gaston Martin, *La Franc-Maçonnerie française et la préparation de la Révolution,* 2ᵉ éd., Paris, Les Presses universitaires [1926?], pp. 15-16, 278, though the author seems inclined to exaggerate the influence of the Masons on the Revolution. Cf. on the other side Daniel Mornet, *Les origines intellectuelles de la Révolution française,* Paris, Armand Colin, 1933, Chap. VII, *La Franc-Maçonnerie,* pp. 357-87. **26, Rue Hautefeuille:** Billy, pp. 87-88. Cf. Douglas H. Gordon and Norman L. Torrey, *The Censoring of Diderot's "Encyclopédie,"* New York, Columbia Univ. Press, 1947, p. 9. **34, "privilege":** Joseph Le Gras, p. 32. **35, contract:** Gordon and Torrey, pp. 9-10. **38,** *Prospectus:* A facsimile of the title page is given, *Ibid.,* opposite p. 10.

Page 294

Line 5, July 7th: Le Gras, p. 32. **7, blows:** *Ibid.,* p. 33. **8-9, Chancellor d' Aguesseau:** *Ibid.,* pp. 33-34. **11, suggested:** *Ibid.,* p. 34. **15, ten-volume work:** Gordon and Torrey, p. 10. **20, January 21, 1746:** Le Gras, p. 36. **22, Mills was paid:** Gordon and Torrey, p. 10. **25, D'Alembert:** *Ibid.,* pp. 10-11. **26, Gua de Malves:** Le Gras, pp. 34-35; Gordon and Torrey, p. 11.

33, February of 1746: Gordon and Torrey, p. 11.

Page 295

Line 1, d'Aguesseau: Le Gras, pp. 38-39. **10, seventeen volumes:** Gordon and Torrey, p. 11. **14, the aim:** AT, XIV, 415.

Page 296

Line 5, cartons: Le Gras, p. 53. **11, Jean-Jacques:** *Confessions* (Hachette), VIII, 247. Cf. also Alfred Richard Oliver, *The Encyclopedists as Critics of Music,* New York, Columbia Univ. Press, 1947, on the extent of Rousseau's contributions. **16, 1760:** LSV, I, 322 (No. 10, 1760): II, 11 (Nov. 25, 1760). **34, the man of merit:** D'Alembert, *Mélanges de littérature, d'histoire et de philosophie,* Nouvelle éd., Amsterdam, Zacharie Chatelain et fils, 1763, 4 vols. I, 171, 172.

Page 297

Line 7, last days of January: Le Gras, p. 81. **8, February 7th:** *Ibid.,* p. 82.

Page 298

Line 2, urging: Cf. Margaret Moffat, *Rousseau et la querelle du théâtre au XVIIIᵉ siècle,* Paris, Boccard, 1930, p. 102. Cf. Rousseau, *Corr. gén.,* IV, 91 (Oct. 22, 1758). **32, The stage purges:** Rousseau, *Œuvres complètes* (Hachette), I, 191.

Page 299

Line 25, the 8th of March, 1759: Le Gras, p. 129. **34, "will perhaps never come":** Moland, XXXIX, 384.

Page 300

Line 1, Lausanne: *Ibid.,* 417. **3, will-of-the-wisp:** "une chimère." Diderot, AT, XIX, 451. **7, more than 4,000:** *Ibid.* Also Gordon and Torrey, p. 21. **9, not one:** Le Gras, p. 133. **11, abandon the work:** Diderot, AT, XIX, 451. **30, September, 1761:** Gordon and Torrey, p. 22. **36, secretly censored:** Cf. Gordon and Torrey, particularly pp. 27-64, for this dramatic discovery, which unexpectedly confirms the main lines of Mme de Vandeul's seemingly improbable story (AT, I,

435

p. xlv). For Diderot's angry letter to Le Breton, see AT, XIX, 467-72 (Nov. 12, 1764).

Page 301

Lines 36-37, provinces: Gordon and Torrey, pp. 23-24.

Page 302

Line 2, Bastille: *Ibid.*, p. 24; Le Gras, pp. 160-61. 2, summer: Gordon and Torrey, p. 24. 10, 1772: *Ibid.*, p. 25. 29, "Land! Land!": LSV, II, 273 (Aug. 18, 1765).

Page 303

Line 31, 1774: Voltaire, *Œuvres complètes* (Moland ed.), XXIX, 325-27. Cf. G. Bengesco, *Voltaire: Bibliographie*, II, 305-06.

Page 306

Lines 6-7, "Strike and conceal your hand": "Frappez, et cachez votre main." Voltaire, Moland ed., XLI, 293. 14-15, *Philosophical Dictionary:* Voltaire, Moland, XX, 313 (Article *Question, Torture*). 28, religion: Cf. Joseph Edmund Barker, *Diderot's Treatment of the Christian Religion in the "Encyclopédie,"* New York, King's Crown Press, 1941.

Page 307

Line 30, Dieckmann: " 'L'Encyclopédie' et le fonds Vandeul," RHL, LI, 320-26 (July-September, 1951).

Page 308

Line 11, nearly one thousand livres: John Morley, *Diderot*, I, 176. 14, 1787: Daniel Mornet, *Les origines intellectuelles de la Révolution française,* Paris, Armand Colin, 1933, p. 379. 16, Daniel Mornet: *Diderot, l'Homme et l'Œuvre,* Paris, Boivin, 1941, pp. 195-96. 22, James Madison: "A copy of the old edition of the *Encyclopedia* is desirable for ye reasons you mention, but as I should gratify my desire in this particular at the expense of something else which I can less dispense with, I must content myself with the new Edition for the present." Madison, *The Writings of James Madison,* New York, 1900-10 (ed., by Gaillard Hunt), 9 vols. II, 236-37. Cf.

my article, "James Madison et la pensée française," *Revue de litt. comparée,* III, 610, and n.4 (1923). 26, *Methodical Encyclopedia:* Le Gras, pp. 165-66; AT, XIII, 127. 29-30, three volumes: *Encyclopædia Britannica,* 11th ed., 1910-11, Article *Encyclopædia,* IX, 377.

Page 309

Lines 9-10, "the celebrated Monsieur Diderot": Daniel Mornet, *Diderot,* p. 196.

CHAPTER XX

Page 310

Line 1, Late: H. C. Lancaster says: "As the [seventeenth] century advanced, performances ... began at a late hour, sometimes at five." *(A History of French Dramatic Literature in the Seventeenth Century,* Part V, *Recapitulation,* Baltimore, Johns Hopkins Press, 1942, p. 22.) Speaking of the late eighteenth century, Max Aghion writes: "A cinq heures et demie très exactement, les violons attaquent une ritournelle,... et il faut que le rideau se lève pour qu'un silence relatif se fasse dans la salle." (*Le théâtre à Paris au XVIIIᵉ siècle,* Paris, Librairie de France [1926], p. 120.) 1, August 20, 1755: Voltaire, Moland, V, 292. 1-2, confused tangle: "Sur la chaussée, rasant les bornes, s'avançait une double file de véhicules. L'humble vinaigrette, le cabriolet et le fiacre, voisinaient démocratiquement avec le carrosse à glaces." (Max Aghion, p. 119.) 3, fought their way: Sébastien Mercier proposed that drivers of carriages be obliged "à prendre leur droite" *(La Vie parisienne au XVIIIᵉ siècle: Conférences du Musée Carnavalet,* Paris, Payot, 1928: *La douceur de vivre* by G. Le Nôtre, p. 256), which shows that it was still every man for himself. 5, locked hubs: "Mon cocher prend dispute et voulant passer devant un autre carrosse, il accroche une de ses roues." *L'Amour et la mode* by Raymond Lécuyer. *Ibid.*, p. 140. The coachman thought his master too ambitious to yield the right of way to anyone, no matter of what rank he might be. *Ibid.*, p. 141. 13, In the absence of sidewalks: According to Max Aghion (p. 119), there were no sidewalks in Paris until 1782 when a single one was established in the street leading to the new building of the Comédie-Française. 18, décrotteurs: "On ne sait pas au juste à quelle époque l'industrie enfanta *l'art du décrotteur,* si nécessaire de nos jours dans cette sale et grande ville. On a beau marcher sur la pointe du pied, l'adresse et la vigilance ne garantissent point des éclaboussures." Sébastien Mercier, *Tableau de Paris,* Amsterdam, 1783, Chap. 455, VI, 1. 21, two humble copper coins: "On paie invariablement *deux liards* pour se faire ôter la crotte des bas et des souliers." *Ibid.,* p. 4. 23, Voltaire: "A Paris, vous savez qu'on entre dans une vilaine salle par un vilain égout." Voltaire to D'Argental, Sept. 24, 1742, Moland, XXXVI, 165.

Page 311

Line 4, over thirteen hundred paying spectators: 1308 according to H. C. Lancaster. *The Comédie-Française, 1701-1774,* Philadelphia, American Philosophical Society, 1951, p. 781. Lekain lists the possible free entries, in 1768, as 416. *Mémoires de Lekain,* etc., *Bibliothèque des Mémoires relatifs à l'histoire de France pendant le 18ᵐᵉ siècle,* ed. by F. Barrière, Paris, Didot, 1857, VI, p. 142; cf. H. C. Lancaster, *French Tragedy in the Time of Louis XV and Voltaire,* Baltimore, Johns Hopkins Press, 1950, 2 vols., I, 10. 6, three tiers of boxes: "Il y a trois rangs de loges." Jules Bonnassies, *Comédie Française: Notice historique sur les anciens bâtiments,* Paris, Aug. Aubry, 1868, p. 10. 6, ellipse: "La salle a la forme d'une demi-ellipse." *Ibid.* 7-8, the raised amphitheater: "Au fond de la salle, derrière le parterre: une plate-forme garnie de siéges, nommée *amphithéâtre." Ibid.* 9, soldier guards: "En-dedans, le fusilier vous range comme des oignons, vous fait asseoir, interpelle l'auditeur ventru, le chicane, veut que telle banquette contienne autant de derrières, sans en avoir pris les proportions." Sébastien Mercier, *Tableau de Paris,* VI, 207. Cf. Charles Collé, *Journal et Mémoires,* Paris,

Didot, 1868, I, 310, April 26, 1751. 10, parterre: "Le public était debout au parterre et ne s'assit pour la première fois qu'à la salle construite en 1782." *Ibid.,* p. 11. "It accommodated the part of [the] audience that was usually the largest, the most unruly, and the most influential in determining the fate of the play." H. C. Lancaster, *French Dramatic Literature in the Seventeenth Century,* Part V, p. 16. "On February 19, 1690, no less than 773 persons stood in the parterre." H. C. Lancaster, *The Comédie Française,* p. 594, n.2. 11, the stage itself: "De tout temps, il y a eu sur le théâtre de la Comédie, de chaque côté, quatre rangées de bancs un peu en amphithéâtre jusqu'à la hauteur des loges, renfermés dans une balustrade et grille de fer pour placer les spectateurs. Dans les grandes représentations, on ajoutoit encore, le long de la balustrade, une rangée de banquettes." Barbier, *Journal,* Paris, Charpentier, 1857, VII, 161-62. 12, even stood: "...et, outre cela, il y avoit encore plus de cinquante personnes debout et sans place au fond du théâtre, qui formoient un cercle. Le théâtre n'étoit rempli et occupé que par des hommes, pour l'ordinaire; en sorte que le théâtre étoit très-rétréci pour l'action des acteurs. Pour entrer un acteur sur la scène, il falloit faire place au fond du théâtre, pour son passage." *Ibid.,* p. 162. 16-17, fifteen feet,... eleven: "La scène est loin d'avoir son étendue intrinsèque, étant occupée à droit et à gauche par des spectateurs qui en réduisent le centre visuel à 15 pieds à son ouverture et à 11 à son extrémité opposée." Jules Bonnassies, p. 10. 17, protested: Voltaire, Moland, II, 315; IV, 499; V, 153, n.1. 18, Make way: *Ibid.,* IV, 482. 33, château: "Cette action théâtrale a fait beaucoup d'effet à Versailles, parce que la scène, quoique trop étroite, était libre." Voltaire, speaking of his tragedy of *Oreste* (1750), Moland, V, 153, n. 38, Opera: Yvon Belaval, *L'esthétique sans paradoxe de Diderot,* Paris, Nouvelle Revue Française, 3rd ed., 1950, pp. 30-31, 48-49; cf. AT, VII, 114, and Jean Pommier, *Diderot avant Vincennes,* Paris,

Boivin, 1939, pp. 66-67. "Il y eut un temps où j'aimais le spectacle, et surtout l'opéra," wrote Diderot. AT, VI, 304.

Page 312

Line 3, parterre: "Je serai dans le parterre, vers le fond et dans le milieu," wrote Diderot to Sophie Volland. LSV, I, 43, 4 [2] juin 1759. 8, twelve years: In 1758, Diderot wrote: "Je n'ai pas été dix fois au spectacle depuis quinze ans." AT, VII, 400. This would carry the date back to his marriage in 1743 which, in 1755 at the time of L'Orphelin de la Chine, would have been twelve years before. 13, Mademoiselle Clairon's...reform: AT, VII, 376-77. 17, About five-thirty: Cf. note to p. 310, line 1. 19, curtain: Jules Bonnassies, Comédie Française, pp. 13, 29-30. 24, hoop skirts: "Une actrice courageuse vient de se défaire du panier." AT, VII, 376. 27, clenched fist: "Clairon a affecté même d'avoir des gestes pour ainsi dire étrangers, mettant souvent une main ou toutes les deux sur les hanches; tenant sur le front pendant des moments son poing fermé, etc." Charles Collé, Journal et Mémoires, II, 34. 34, Bordeaux: Mémoires de Mlle Clairon, Bibliothèque des Mémoires relatifs à l'histoire de France, VI, 50-52, and 51, n.

Page 313

Line 3, declamation: Voltaire "est pour la déclamation chantée." Henri Lion, Les tragédies et les théories dramatiques de Voltaire, Paris, Hachette, 1895, p. 237. 5, gripped: Collé, II, 33. 10, a full head taller: AT, VIII, 373, and n. 14-15, more Genghis: "Que veux-tu? lui répondit Lekain, mademoiselle Clairon joue Gengis, il faut bien que je joue Idamé." Mémoires de Molé, Bibliothèque des Mémoires relatifs à l'histoire de France, VI, 252. 15-16, lend conviction: Moland, V, 292; XXXVIII, 453-54. 20, nine o'clock: "Généralement le spectacle se terminait seulement vers 9 heures." Max Aghion, p. 121. 22, lantern-bearers: Mercier, Tableau de Paris, VI, 218, 219, 220.

Page 314

Line 3, Madame d'Epinay: Mémoires, Boiteau ed., Paris, Charpentier, 1863, II, 187. 7, Grimm: Corr. litt., III, 354-57.

Page 315

Line 12, first part of November: Ibid., IV, 47, article dated Nov. 15, 1758. 39, 171 performances: Mary Lane Charles, The Growth of Diderot's Fame in France from 1784 to 1875, Bryn Mawr, Penn., 1942, p. 128. Cf. also H. C. Lancaster, "The Cast and Reception of Diderot's Père de famille," MLN, LXIX, 416-18, June, 1954.

Page 316

Lines 1-2, Toulouse, Marseilles, and Rouen: Corr. inédite, I, 29; LSV, II, 18; Mary Lane Charles, pp. 129-30. 3, The Family Picture: AT, VII, 178. 4, twelve times: Mary Lane Charles, p. 128; 7 times in August, 3 in September, and 2 in December, 1769 (H. C. Lancaster, The Comédie Française, pp. 825, 826). 5, daughter: LSV, III, 198, 199-201. 7, wife: Ibid., pp. 202-03. Cf. pp. 208, 211-12. 10, parterre: Ibid., p. 202. 12, April 23, 1759: Barbier, Journal, VII, 161-63; Grimm, Corr. litt., IV, 111; Collé, Journal et Mémoires, II, 170. 20, Voltaire: Moland, V, 406, and n.3; XXXII, 164; XXVIII, 303; XLIII, 283.

Page 317

Line 14, Abbé Arnaud: Joseph Reinach, Diderot, Paris, Hachette, 1894, p. 146. 23, Baudelaire: AT, VIII, 140-41. 26, Geneva: Journal des Débats, March 25, 1928. 26, Paris: information furnished by Miss Mary Lane Charles of Western College, Oxford, Ohio. Miss Charles witnessed a performance of Est-il bon? Est-il méchant? given by "L'Equipe," an amateur troupe made up of employees of the French National Railways under the direction of M. Demay. The troupe had been organized during the Occupation and gave its performances in a small theater established in the Gare d'Austerlitz. "To this play, seemingly lacking in action," writes Miss Charles, "they lent a vivacity which made it the most attractive of drawing-room comedies."

Page 318

Line 8, Coquelin: "Constant Coquelin: 'France at her Best,'" *The American Society Legion of Honor Magazine*, Winter, 1946-47, p. 591. (Article by the editor, W. Francklyn Paris.) 29, treads the boards: A few sentences are repeated from my article, "Diderot and the Actor's Art," in *The American Society Legion of Honor Magazine*, Winter, 1946-47, pp. 601-608.

Page 319

Line 2, Louis XIV: Louis Gillet, *La Peinture au Musée du Louvre, Ecole Française, XVIII* siècle, Paris, L'Illustration, n.d., *Introduction*, p. viii. 8, the 25th of August: "Désormais, de deux en deux ans, le Salon du Louvre, qui s'ouvrait le jour de la Saint-Louis." *Ibid.* "Le spectacle des tableaux au Louvre a duré tout le mois de Septembre, comme à l'ordinaire." Clément, *Les Cinq Années littéraires*, I, 137. 29, The Salons: The first of four important volumes on Diderot's *Salons* by Jean Seznec, with numerous illustrations, is now in press. It will constitute, no doubt, a definitive discussion of the subject. 35, scribbled notes, LSV, III, 86; Maurice Tourneux, *Diderot et Catherine II*, Paris, Calmann Lévy, 1899, pp. 449-50; AT, IV, 3; Jules Bertaut, *Diderot* (Vie anecdotique), Paris, Louis-Michaud, n.d., p. 132; Herbert Dieckmann, *Inventaire du fonds Vandeul*, Geneva, Droz, 1951, p. xxvii.

Page 320

Line 12, public: Edmond et Jules de Goncourt, *L'Art du XVIII* siècle, Paris, Charpentier, 1906, 1re série, pp. 102, 141.

Page 321

Lines 4-5, Goncourt brothers: *Ibid.*, pp. 155-58.

Page 323

Line 39, wife: *Ibid.*, 2e série, pp. 35-49.

Page 324

Line 16, Jean-Jacques Rousseau: AT, X, 483-84. 24, Flesh and life: AT, XI, 151. 28, quiet and composed: *Ibid.*

Page 325

Line 27, Naigeon: AT, XI, 79-84; LSV, III, 92. 36, Monsieur Robert: AT, XI, 228-30.

Page 326

Line 27, Chardin: AT, X, 234.

Page 327

Line 3, letting his pen run: "J'ébauche, mon ami, au courant de la plume." AT, X, 185 *(Salon de 1763)*. Cf. *ibid.*, p. 226; XI, 333. 15, Brunetière: *Etudes critiques sur l'histoire de la littérature française*, 2e série, II, 261-83, 6e éd., Paris, Hachette, 1904.

Page 328

Line 1, Delacroix: Eugène Delacroix, *Corr. gén.*, Paris, Plon, 1925-38, 5 vols. I, 108, 290-91; II, 32-33, 34, 162. 3, Baudelaire: Cf. André Ferran, *L'esthétique de Baudelaire*, Paris, Hachette, 1933, especially "Baudelaire critique d'art," pp. 377-491; Margaret Gilman, *Baudelaire the Critic*, New York, Columbia Univ. Press, 1943, which gives a penetrating and judicious analysis of the varied influences on Baudelaire of Delacroix, Diderot, De Maistre, and Poe, particularly; Jean Pommier, "Les Salons de Diderot et leur influence au XIXe siècle: Baudelaire et le Salon de 1846," *Revue des Cours et Conférences*, 37²: 289-306; 437-52 (1936).

CHAPTER XXI

Page 329

Line 4, tower: Information furnished by Professor Georges May of Yale University. He refers me also to: Louis Thomas, *Le Patrimoine de la France: le Grand Paris*, Paris, Aux Armes de la France, 1941. "L'Abbaye de Longchamp," pp. 41-49. 14, Opera: Diderot, AT, V, 33, n. (page incorrectly numbered in AT). See also *La Vie parisienne au XVIII* siècle, *Conférences du Musée Carnavalet*, Paris, Payot, 1928, pp. 71-72. 17-18, latter half of

1760: Letter of Diderot to Sophie Volland, Sept. 10, 1760 (LSV, I, 171). Cf. Diderot, *Corr. inédite,* Paris, 1931, I, 192, 193, 250. **23, novel:** Herbert Dieckmann, *"The Préface-Annexe* of *La Religieuse," Diderot Studies II,* ed. by Otis E. Fellows and Norman L. Torrey, Syracuse University Press, 1952, pp. 21-147.

Page 330

Line 23, Saulier: *Ibid.,* pp. 27, 56, 63, 75. **27, Delamarre:** Georges May, "Le modèle inconnu de 'La Religieuse' de Diderot: Marguerite Delamarre." RHL, LI, 273-87, 1951. See also the important book, *Diderot et "La Religieuse,"* by the same author, Paris, Presses Universitaires; New Haven, Yale University Press, 1954. **34, manuscript:** Herbert Dieckmann, article cited, pp. 27, 75.

Page 332

Line 1, listeners: AT, V, 204. **6, Richardson:** Dieckmann, article cited, p. 32. **15, Croismare:** *Ibid.,* p. 31. **31, sisters:** LSV, I, 49, n. Cf. AT, I, p. lviii, where, however, there is no reference to André Babelon's *rapprochement* with *La Religieuse,* probable as it may be.

Page 334

Line 30, eyes: *Judges,* XVII, 6; XXI, 25. **36, rules:** Attributed to Emmanuel Kant, though I am unable to state on what authority.

Page 335

Line 4, occurred: Diderot visited his native town of Langres in the autumn of 1754 (letter of J.-J. Rousseau, Oct. 15, 1754, in the latter's *Corr. générale,* II, 103, Paris, 1924; Diderot, *Corr. inédite,* II, 55, n.). Diderot's father died on June 3, 1759 (cf. my article in MLN, LIX, 33, and n.3, Jan., 1944). Whatever basis of fact Diderot's short-story may contain, should therefore be associated with the visit of 1754. **13, Sterne's:** Diderot and Sterne may have met. (Cf. J. Robert Loy, *Diderot's Determined Fatalist,* N. Y., King's Crown Press, 1950, pp. 39-40, 205, n.27). For the extent and limits of

Sterne's influence on Diderot, cf. *ibid.,* pp. 32-53. See also Alice Green Fredman, *Diderot and Sterne,* New York, Columbia University Press, 1955.

Page 338

Line 2, "I rage," he wrote: LSV, III, 283. M. Pommier believes this undated passage was written to Mme de Meaux rather than to Sophie Volland. Cf. *Le Neveu de Rameau* (Fabre ed., 1950), p. LXXV, n.2, and p. 328. **4, Johnson:** James Boswell, *Life of Samuel Johnson,* Everyman ed., London, Dent; N. Y., Dutton, 1906, and later reprints, II, 210 (1778). **13, April of 1761:** Critical ed. of *Le Neveu de Rameau* by Jean Fabre, Geneva, Droz, 1950. *Introduction,* p. xxxiv.

Page 340

Line 19, the younger Rameau: Milton F. Seiden, "Jean-François Rameau and Diderot's *Neveu," Diderot Studies,* Syracuse University Press, 1949, pp. 143-91. **32, Diderot's own character:** Daniel Mornet, *Le Neveu de Rameau,* mimeographed ed., Paris, Les Cours de Lettres, 1947-48, 3 fascicles, 256 pp. This supplements the same author's earlier article in RDM, Aug. 15, 1927, pp. 881-908. See also Otis E. Fellows, "The Theme of Genius in Diderot's *Neveu de Rameau," Diderot Studies II,* pp. 168-99. A further excellent literary study of *Le Neveu de Rameau* is that by Jean Pommier, "Etudes sur Diderot," in *Revue d'histoire de la philosophie et d'histoire générale de la civilisation,* X, 153-69 (1942). **38, over four thousand livres:** Daniel Mornet, *Diderot l'homme et l'œuvre,* Paris, Boivin, 1941, p. 14.

Page 341

Lines 12-13, uninhibited conversation: Edmond de Goncourt, commenting in his *Journal* (February 24, 1886) on his profound admiration for Diderot, writes: "La grande valeur, la grande originalité de Diderot—et personne ne l'a remarqué—c'est d'avoir introduit dans la grave et ordonnée prose du livre, la vivacité, le brio, le sautillement, le désordre un peu fou, le tintamarre, la vie fiévreuse de la conversation: de la conversation des artistes— avec lesquels il est le premier écrivain français qui ait vécu en relations tout à fait intimes." *(Journal,* Paris, Flammarion, Fasquelle, 9 vols. [n. d.], VII, 81.) **27, Cannibals:** Cf. my edition of Rousseau's *Discours sur les sciences et les arts,* N. Y., Modern Language Association of America, 1946, p. 251, n.309. **29, hunger:** Mme de Vandeul, AT, I, p. xxxvii.

Page 343

Line 16, Buffon: Diderot took notes on Buffon while in prison at Vincennes. Cf. his letter of Sept. 30, 1749, in AT, XIX, 422-23.

Page 344

Line 17, September 11, 1769: Cf. LSV, III, pp. 202-11.

Page 345

Line 11, Verdier, etc.: Cf. the critical edition of *Le Rêve de d'Alembert* by Paul Vernière, Paris, Marcel Didier, 1951, *Introduction,* pp. ix-x. **23, well:** AT, IX, 427.

Page 346

Line 28, Buffon: Cf. Emile Guyénot, *Les Sciences de la vie aux XVII⁰ et XVIII⁰ siècles,* Paris, Albin Michel, 1941, p. 297.

Page 348

Line 32, Bougainville: See the critical edition of this work by Gilbert Chinard, Paris, Droz; Baltimore, Johns Hopkins Press, 1935, and the forthcoming edition of the same work by Herbert Dieckmann.

Page 349

Line 24, colic: Diderot, *Corr. inédite,* II, 242. **26, knife:** *Ibid.* **33, June 3:** André Billy, *Diderot,* Paris, Editions de France, 1932, p. 551. **35, August 20th:** "Nous sommes partis de La Haye, 20 aoust," noted Diderot (Herbert Dieckmann, *Inventaire du fonds Vandeul,* Geneva, Droz, 1951, p. 267, followed by the details of Diderot's itinerary, going and coming, pp. 267-73). This notation of August 20

at the actual moment of departure supersedes Diderot's previous forecast of being on his way "dans quatre jours" (LSV, III, 246) on which are evidently based the two texts of Maurice Tourneux *(Diderot et Catherine II,* Paris, 1899, p. 71) and André Billy *(Diderot,* p. 552), both of whom give August 17th as the date when he left The Hague for Saint Petersburg. **35, October 8th:** *Corr. inédite,* II, 240, and n.

Page 350

Line 1, art galleries: Herbert Dieckmann, *Inventaire,* p. 268. **1, alive:** *Corr. inédite,* II, 242. **6, table:** AT, XX, 138. Maurice Tourneux rejects the story as improbable, though without positive evidence to the contrary. It seems on the other hand quite in accord with Diderot's notable *sans-gêne.* (Cf. Maurice Tourneux, *Diderot et Catherine II,* p. 76, and n.) Cf. also AT, I, p. xxi: "Il frappe sur ma cuisse comme si elle était à lui," (Garat). **15, Monsieur Diderot:** Maurice Tourneux, *op. cit.,* p. 81. **28, month:** "Parti de Petersbourg le 5 mars à 4 h. du soir," notes Diderot. "La Haye… arrivé le 5 avril, le matin." (Herbert Dieckmann, *Inventaire,* pp. 274, 278.) **30, day and night:** "C'était une rude tâche que de conduire un être qui ne voulait s'arrêter ni pour dormir, ni pour manger," writes Mme de Vandeul (AT, I, p. liv). **30, four times:** AT, XX, 58. **33, Dvina:** *Ibid.,* XX, 58, 63. Cf. IX, 28. **36, October:** *Ibid.,* I, p. liv. **38, handkerchief:** *Ibid.*

Page 351

Line 1, wig: *Corr. inédite,* II, 241. **4, legs:** AT, I, p. liv. **6, breath:** *Ibid.* **7, old age:** "Vous me trouverez bien vieilli." (LSV, III, 255.) **8-9, ten years:** "J'ai peut-être encore une dizaine d'années au fond de mon sac" (LSV, III, 260). **27-28, justification:** *Essai sur les règnes de Claude et de Néron* (1778, 1782). Cf. AT, III, 6-8; I, p. liv. **30, Sèvres:** Billy, p. 584 ff. AT, I, p. lvii. **30, four or five flights:** AT, I, p. lvii and n. **36, apoplexy,** *Ibid.,* p. lv. **38, three bleedings:** *Ibid.*

Page 352

Line 1, Grimm: Billy, p. 596.
5-6, July 17th or 18th: *Ibid.*, p. 601.
7, the 29th: *Ibid.* 9-10, four days: AT,
I, p. lvii. 11, July 31st: The date has
often been given as the 30th. For the
correction to the 31st, cf. my article in
MLN, LV, 32-35, Jan., 1940. 19, elbow: AT, I, pp. lvii-lviii. 22, lie:
Ibid., p. lvi. 31, as the pen runs: AT,
XX, 75.

Page 353

Line 6, revise: Herbert Dieckmann,
"The *Préface-Annexe* of *La Religieuse,*" *Diderot Studies II*, p. 35; likewise the same author's *Inventaire, Introduction,* p. xlv, and frequently in
his description of the manuscripts.
17, Falconet: *Lettres à Falconet*, AT,
XVIII, 77-336.

CHAPTER XXII

Page 357

Line 2, ceiling: Georges Lemaitre,
Beaumarchais, New York, Knopf, 1949,
p. 3. 15, happy: *Ibid.*, p. 8.
29, feigned: Louis de Loménie, *Beaumarchais et son temps,* 4th ed., Paris,
1880, I, 72-73.

Page 358

Line 9, I sign: *Ibid.*, I, 76.
33, March 4: *Ibid.*, I, 80.

Page 359

Line 4, costume: Lemaitre, p. 25.
10, magnifying glass: Loménie, I, 82-
83. 14, June 16: *Ibid.*, I, 81-82.
22, Beaumarchais: Lemaitre, p. 32.
28, typhoid: *Ibid.*, pp. 34-35.

Page 360

Line 14, Gudin: Gudin de la Brenellerie, *Histoire de Beaumarchais,* ed. by
Maurice Tourneux, Paris, 1888, p. 20.

Page 361

Line 10, eleven: *Mémoires de Beaumarchais,* nouv. éd., Paris, Garnier,
1859, p. 359. 21, medicine: *Ibid.*, p.
381; Lemaitre, p. 65. 24, sleepless:
Mémoires, pp. 384-89. 38, sombrero:
Loménie, I, 144. Cf. pp. 141-43, 145-
55.

Page 362

Line 8, Duc de La Vallière: Gudin
de La Brenellerie, pp. 54-57. 29, Voltaire: Moland, XLII, 278 (Nov. 1,
1762); cf. p. 281.

Page 363

Line 20, Lejay: Beaumarchais, *Mémoires,* pp. 75-76. 35, Louis XV: Loménie, I, 359. 39, patriarch: Moland,
XLVIII 567 (Feb. 25, 1774).

Page 364

Line 14, signed: Gudin de La Brenellerie, pp. 105-106; Lemaitre, p. 128.
27, modest: Loménie, I, 369.

Page 365

Line 18, pasted on his script: E. Lintilhac, *Beaumarchais et ses œuvres,*
Paris, 1887, p. 251.

Page 366

Line 10, September 21: Loménie, II,
93. 14, February 29: *Ibid.*, II, 99-106.
24, June 10: *Ibid.*, II, 110-11.

Page 367

Lines 4-5, Hôtel de Hollande: Lemaitre, p. 191; Pierre Richard, *La Vie pri-
vée de Beaumarchais,* Paris, Hachette,
1951, pp. 154-55. 13, Arthur Lee: Lemaitre, p. 184. 13, Monsieur le
Comte: *Ibid.* 24, December 21st: Carl
Van Doren, *Benjamin Franklin,* New
York, Viking, 1938, p. 565. 28, Barbeu
Dubourg: Lemaitre, 209-10.

Page 368

Lines 16-17, November 29: Loménie,
II, 140. 18, March 29: Lemaitre, pp.
237-38. 29, Vergennes: *Ibid.*, p. 238.
34, Portsmouth: *Ibid.*, pp. 220-21.

Page 369

Line 8, Washington: *Ibid.*, p. 204.
18, thirty-four million livres: *Ibid.*, p.
294. 24, twenty-one million livres:
Ibid., pp. 250-51. 27, Vergennes, Loménie, II, 181; Lemaitre, pp. 246-247.
35, receipt: Loménie, II, 189. Cf. Lemaitre, p. 333.

Page 370

Line 1, Dean: Lemaitre, p. 264.
2, Barclay: *Ibid.*, p. 293. 3, Hamilton:
Ibid., p. 332. 11, 800,000 livres: Le-

maitre, p. 334, n. **21, rejected:** *Ibid.,* pp. 215-16. **29, Sophie Arnould:** Lintilhac, p. 88.

Page 371

Line 17, a million livres: Lemaitre, p. 268. **32-33, Upon my word:** Lemaitre, pp. 312-13. Cf. Gudin de La Brenellerie, pp. 421-24.

Page 372

Line 5, Amélie Houret: Lemaitre, pp. 314-15, 338-39. **8-9, Beaumarchais:** *Ibid.,* pp. 316-17.

Page 373

Lines 30-31, colorful satin vest: See Beaumarchais's description of Figaro among the Characters at the beginning of the play.

Page 376

Line 26, The King: Lemaitre, p. 275.

Page 377

Line 5, Madame Campan: *Ibid.,* p. 274. **18, Mal'brough:** Grimm [Meister], *Corr. litt.,* XIII, 323. Cf. pp. 321-22. **22-23, Théâtre des Menus-Plaisirs:** located in the "ancien Conservatoire de musique" at No. 2, Rue du Conservatoire. Cf. Lintilhac, p. 84, and n.4; *Paris* (Guide Bleu), Hachette, 1952, p. 191. **24, His Majesty's anger:** Lemaitre, p. 279. Cf. Grimm, XIII, 323. **39, three hundred persons:** Pierre Richard, *Notice: Le Mariage de Figaro,* Paris, Classiques Larousse, I, p. 6. Cf. Grimm, *Corr. litt.,* XIII, 366, 517-18. Cf. Lavisse, *Le Règne de Louis XVI,* IX, 276-77.

Page 378

Lines 1-2, Some spectators: "la plupart des spectateurs," according to Meister (Grimm, XIII, 517), which seems an exaggeration. **9, Europe:** *Ibid.,* XIII, 518. **13, Keeper of the Great Seal:** Loménie, II, 319. Cf. Grimm, XIII, 518. **22, doors:** Grimm, XIII, 517-22.

Page 382

Lines 24-25, Talleyrand: Othon Guerlac, *Les Citations françaises,* p. 274 (quoted by Guizot). **39, the Revolu-**tion: *Encyclopædia Britannica,* 11th ed., Article *Beaumarchais,* III, 590.

CHAPTER XXIII

Page 383

Line 2, Métra: *Corr. secrète,* Londres, Chez John Adamson, 18 vols., 1787-1790, I, 3. **13, Meister:** Grimm, *Corr. litt.,* X, 424-25. **17, King:** Ernest Lavisse, *Histoire de France depuis les origines jusqu'à la Révolution,* IX (*Le règne de Louis XVI (1774-1789)*, Paris, Hachette, 1911), 2. **24, pound:** *Ibid.,* p. 3. **30, duty:** *Ibid.,* p. 4.

Page 384

Line 36, honest: *Ibid.,* p. 31. **37, Voltaire:** Moland, XLIX, 77.

Page 385

Line 2, gout: *Ibid.,* I, 376. **13, second best:** John Morley, quoted by Burton Stevenson, *Home Book of Quotations,* p. 1541 (5). "In politics the choice is constantly between two evils, and action is one long second best." **16, bankruptcy:** Lavisse, IX, 25. **20-21, arm yourself:** *Ibid.*

Page 386

Line 2, feared: Douglas Dakin, *Turgot and the Ancien Régime in France,* London, Methuen, 1939, pp. 133-34 (in a slightly different translation). **9, Michelet:** Lavisse and Rambaud, *Histoire générale du IVᵉ siècle à nous jours,* Paris, Armand Colin, VII (1896), 613.

Page 387

Line 15, Monsieur Turgot: Lavisse et Rambaud, VII, 622. **24, I hope:** Lavisse, IX, 50.

Page 388

Line 3, By my faith: Métra, III, 200; Lavisse, IX, 72.

Page 389

Line 14, Meister: Grimm, *Corr. litt.,* XII, 510-13. **29, emotion:** *Ibid.,* p. 512.

Page 390

Line 25, Nothing: *Encyclopædia Britannica,* 11th ed., 1910-11, XVII, 44, Article *Louis XVI.* **32, poor fellow:**

Lavisse et Rambaud, VII, 616. **36, operation:** Saul K. Padover, *The Life and Death of Louis XVI,* New York, D. Appleton-Century Co., 1939, pp. 98-101.

Page 391

Line 13, Joseph: *Ibid.,* pp. 100-101. **24, loud voice:** Grimm [Meister], *Corr. litt.,* XIV, 422. **31, break up:** Albert Cherel, *Fénelon au XVIIIᵉ siècle en France,* Paris, Hachette, 1917, pp. 386-87. **35, misfortune:** *Ibid.,* p. 388.

Page 392

Line 19, Burke: Edmund Burke, *Reflections on the Revolution in France* (1790). *Works,* New York, George Bell, III (1894), 348. **34, Rousseau:** *Confessions (Œuvres complètes,* Hachette, VIII, 192).

Page 393

Line 15, shouters: Lavisse, IX, 136. **17-18, done to them:** *Ibid.* **30, August 17, 1776:** Georges Lemaitre, *Beaumarchais,* New York, Knopf, 1949, p. 198. **33, November 28:** Benjamin Franklin, *Memoirs,* 2nd ed., London, 1818-19, 5 vols., II, 47.

Page 394

Lines 11-12, four tantalizing days: *Ibid.* **14, December 3rd:** *Ibid.* **20, devil:** *Ibid.* **23-24, wretched place:** *Ibid.,* II, 48. **37, teeth:** Carl Van Doren, *Benjamin Franklin,* New York, Viking, 1938, p. 564.

Page 395

Line 2, Gulf Stream: *Ibid.,* p. 565. **10, that very spot:** *Memoirs,* II, 48. **15, December 20th:** Carl Van Doren, p. 565. **36, King:** Carl Van Doren, p. 595. **38, Queen,** *Ibid.,* p. 596.

Page 396

Line 9, Free Masons: Bernard Faÿ *L'esprit révolutionnaire en France et aux Etats-Unis à la fin du XVIIIᵉ siècle,* Paris, Edouard Champion, 1925, pp. 97-100; Carl Van Doren, pp. 655-56. **11, Quakers:** Bernard Faÿ, p. 94; Edith Philips, *The Good Quaker in French Legend,* Philadelphia, University of Pennsylvania Press, 1932, pp. 92, 123.

18, electricity: Cf. above, Chap. XXI, p. 343, lines 26-29, Diderot's reference to Franklin's book, *Experiments and Observations on Electricity,* published in English in 1751 and in French early in 1752. (AT, II, 39, n., and Carl Van Doren, pp. 162-63.) On the keen interest in electricity at the time, see my edition of Rousseau's *Discours sur les sciences et les arts,* New York, 1946, pp. 212-13. **21, lip-reading:** Carl Van Doren, p. 637; Paul M. Spurlin, "The Founding Fathers' Knowledge of French," *The French Review,* XX, 120-28, Dec., 1946 (pp. 123-24 on Franklin). **36, Lafayette:** *Encyclopædia Britannica,* 11th ed., XVI, 65-66 (Article *La Fayette*).

Page 397

Line 28, hall: Grimm [Meister], *Corr. litt.,* XV, 450-55.

Page 398

Line 39, Regent: *Encyclopædia Britannica,* 11th ed., Article *Diamond,* VIII, 163; Article *Thomas Pitt,* XXI, 667.

Page 399

Line 6, Meister: Grimm, *Corr. litt.,* XV, 452.

Page 400

Line 13, cable: Georges Lefebvre, *The Coming of the French Revolution,* Trans. by R. R. Palmer, Princeton Univ. Press, 1947, p. 81. **39, deliberations:** *Ibid.,* pp. 86, 87.

Page 401

Lines 4-6, Bailly . . . Mirabeau . . . Sieyès: Lavisse, *Histoire de France contemporaine,* Paris, Hachette, 1920, I, 33, 34. **12, stay:** *Ibid.,* I, 33. **27, July 12th:** *Ibid.,* I, 45.

Page 403

Line 6, Doubrowski: L. Léouzon-Leduc, "Rapport sur les papiers de Voltaire conservés dans la bibliothèque impériale et dans celle de l'Ermitage à Saint-Pétersbourg," *Archives des missions scientifiques et littéraires,* I, (1), 54 (Paris, 1850). **28, revolution:** Lavisse, *Histoire de France contemporaine,* I, 53, n.

CONCLUSION

Page 404

Line 4, Mornet: Daniel Mornet, *Les Origines intellectuelles de la Révolution française, 1715-1787*, Paris, Armand Colin: 1933, p. 477: "Assurément, s'il n'y avait eu que l'intelligence pour menacer effectivement l'Ancien régime, l'Ancien régime n'aurait couru aucun risque. Il fallait à cette intelligence, pour agir, un point d'appui, la misère du peuple, le malaise politique." Cf. pp. 1-4. **9, Peyre:** Henri Peyre, "The Influence of Eighteenth Century Ideas on the French Revolution," *Journal of the History of Ideas*, X, 63-87, Jan., 1949: "Pure historical materialism does not explain the Revolution.... Misery in France was no more than relative.... In order to revolt against one's lot, one must be aware of his wretched condition, which presupposes a certain intellectual and cultural level.... Eighteenth-century philosophy taught the Frenchman to find his condition wretched, or in any case, unjust and illogical, and made him disinclined to the patient resignation to his troubles that had long characterized his ancestors. It had never called for a revolution nor desired a change of regime; it had never been republican." (pp. 72-73). On Montesquieu's influence, see pp. 76-77, and on that of Rousseau, pp. 77-87. **14, Rousseau:** *Emile*, Hachette ed., II, 166. **17, Poland:** *Œuvres complètes*, Hachette ed., V, 240. **18, Voltaire:** *Œuvres complètes*, Moland ed., XLIII, 175. Cf. pp. 506, 519-20; XLIX, 483.

Page 405

Line 1, Mably: *Œuvres complètes*, Lyon, 1796, 12 vols., XI, 409. **11, Hamilton:** *The Federalist*, Mod. Library ed., p. 4. **20, innocence:** Ernest Lavisse, *Histoire de France contemporaine depuis la Révolution jusqu'à la paix de 1919*, II (Paris, Hachette, 1920), 23. **24, stiffly upright:** *Ibid.*, p. 166. A contemporary sketch by David is reproduced on the opposite page. **35, Queen:** Marie Kimball, *Jefferson: The Scene of Europe, 1784-1789*, New York, Coward-McCann, 1950, pp. 299-300.

Page 406

Line 12, *Vive le roi*: Grimm [Meister], *Corr. litt.*, XV, 452; Ernest Lavisse, *Histoire de France contemporaine*, I, 17.

Page 407

Line 9, Vergniaud: Lamartine, *Histoire des Girondins*, Livre XXXVIII, chap. XX. (*Œuvres complètes*, Paris, Chez l'Auteur, 1861-66, 41 vols., XII, 306.)

Page 408

Line 21, T. S. Eliot: *Four Quartets*, "Burnt Norton," lines 1-3. **38, book of the past:** It should, however, not be inferred that the present or the future repeat identically the pattern of the past. See a penetrating article by Reinhold Niebuhr "Is History Predictable" in *The Atlantic*, Vol. 194, pp. 69-72, July, 1954.

INDEX

INDEX

Abelard, 253

Absolute government, absolutism, 3-21, 93, 113, 118, 123, 132, 408

Abuses, criticism of, in Montesquieu's *Persian Letters*, 113

Academy (French), 43, 52, 63, 72, 114, 186, 218

Academy of Science, history of, 63, 74

Account of a Journey through Persia and the Orient (Chardin), 102

Acton, Lord, 54

Adams, Henry, 117

Adams, John, 140, 141, 148, 151

Adams, Samuel, 141

Addison, Joseph, 172

Adélaïde, daughter of Louis XV, 360

Aesop, 64

Age of Louis XIV (Voltaire), 160, 181, 182, 183, 197

Aggression, multiplication of means of, 134

Agriculture, 123, 125

Aguesseau, Chancellor d', 294, 295

Airvault, in relation to Voltaire's name, 160

Aix-la-Chapelle, Treaty of, 27, 95; peace of, 289

Albigensian, Albigensians, 22, 34

Alembert, D', 32, 36-37, 52, 208, 232, 290, 291, 294, 295, 296, 297, 298, 299, 302, 324, 344, 346, 359, 363, 384; see *Dream of D'Alembert,* or *D'Alembert's Dream* (Diderot)

Alexander the Great, 64, 182

Alfort, Beaumarchais's education at, 357

Allain, Maître, 159

Almaviva, Count, character by Beaumarchais, 374, 375, 378, 379, 382

Almaviva, Countess, character by Beaumarchais, 378, 379; see Rosine

Ambition to counteract ambition, Madison's dictum, 154, 155

America, 9, 128, 133, 135, 141, 153, 159, 185, 219, 369; arms and munitions shipped to, by Beaumarchais, 366

American colonies, 96, 121, 351, 385; colonists at Concord and Lexington, 365, 373

American government, 148, 154

American Indians, 74, 76

American Revolution, 141, 142, 143, 366, 368, 388

Amsterdam, 237, 261

Anacreon, 64, 280

Anatomy, comparative, 239

Ancients and Moderns, Quarrel of, 72, 73, 74

Ange, Brother, 282

Angelucci, 365, 372

Anglican Church, 167

Anglo-Saxon tradition, 407

Annecy, 224, 225, 227, 235, 250, 274

Anthropocentric or man-made concepts, 112

Anthropology, 239

Anti-clericalism, 219

Antin, Duc d', 292, 293

Antiquity, classical, 241

Aquinas, Thomas, 195

Arabian Nights, trans. by Galland, 102

Archives of the Bastille, 403

Argenson, Marc-René, (the elder) Marquis d', 11, 70, 71, 75

Argenson, René-Louis, (the younger) Marquis d', 91, 93, 94, 115, 158, 162, 289

Argental, d', 158

Aristotle, 64, 133, 136, 151, 156, 194, 239; Aristotelian thesis, 298

Armies, mercenary, 210

Arnaud, Abbé, 317

Arnould, Sophie, 370

Arouet, François, father of Voltaire, 169, 269

INDEX

Gates, General Horatio, 369
Gaussin, Mademoiselle, 285
Gautier, Théophile, 26
General Criticism of the *History of Calvinism by Father Maimbourg* (Bayle), 29
Generalization, Montesquieu's liking for, 119, 120, 136
Genesis, 238
Geneva, 6, 24, 131, 196, 206, 221, 222, 223, 224, 235, 243, 260, 262, 263, 264, 270, 274, 297, 298, 299, 310, 317; article on, 299; Citizen of, 259; Lake, 250, 253, 272, 277; a Protestant Zion, 196, 221, 233, 243
Genevan accent, Rousseau's, 275
Genghis Khan, 311, 313
Gennevilliers, 377
"Gentleman in Ordinary of the King's Bedchamber," Voltaire's position as, 186
Geoffrin, Madame, 60, 61
Geography, human, 136
George III, King of England, 153, 365, 369
Georgia, 146
Germany, 9, 197, 207, 271, 317, 327
Gibbon, Edward, 121, 122, 123, 185, 217, 302, 326
Gide, André, 337
Gildon, Charles, 173
Girardin, Marquis de, 275
Glasses, use of, 184
"God," article by Voltaire, 213; belief in, 263; existence of, 346; remunerative and avenging, 213; Supreme Being, 190, 213; see Religion
"God and Liberty" (saying of Voltaire), 218
Goethe, Johann Wolfgang von, 271, 339
Goëzman, Louis-Valentin, 363, 364
Goëzman, Madame, 363, 364

"Gold Tooth," story of (Fontenelle), 71-72
Golden Age, 48, 49, 76, 155, 233, 237, 241, 255, 256, 258, 267
Golden Rule, 207, 212, 213, 215, 306
Goncourt brothers (Edmond and Jules de), 321
"Goodness" of human nature, Rousseau's opinion on, 231, 257; Voltaire's opinion of, 211
Gordon, Douglas H., 301
"Government with the consent of the governed," 262
Government, American, 148, 154; despotic, based upon fear, 130; national, 149; representative, 150
Graffenried, Mademoiselle de, 250, 270
Graffigny, Madame de, 204
Grand Turk, Ambassador of, 104
Grant, General Ulysses S., 48
"Gratuitous act," 337
"Grave-diggers" in *Hamlet,* 171, 173
Gravitation, 171
Gray, Thomas, 178
Greece, xii, 237
Greek city states, 133
Greeks, ancient, 76
Grenelle-Saint-Honoré, Rue de, 236, 247, 275
Greuze, Jean-Baptiste, 283, 315, 320, 322, 323, 324, 325, 340; Madame, 323
Grimaud, Madame, 62
Grimm, Frédéric-Melchior, 138, 249, 267, 314, 318, 319, 320, 326, 327, 329, 330, 331, 352, 383
Gua de Malves, Abbé Jean-Paul de, 294
Gudin de la Brenellerie, Paul-Philippe, 360, 371
Guillotine, 406
Gulliver's Travels (Swift), 191, 192
Guyon, Madame, 12, 40, 41, 42, 43

INDEX

INDEX

Physicians, 170, 345
Physiocrats, 384
Pierce, William, 146
"Pimpette" Dunoyer, 159
Pinckney, Charles, 146
Pitt or Regent Diamond, 398
Place de la Révolution, 405
Plates, illustrative, 302, 307
Plato, 73, 280
Plâtrière, Rue, 275
Plurality of Worlds, see *Conversations on the Plurality of Worlds* (Fontenelle)
Plutarch, 23, 116, 233, 234
Poirier, Monsieur, character by Emile Augier, 322, 323, 325
Poitou, 157, 160
Police state, 263
Polignac, Countess de, 377, 382
Pollock, Sir Frederick, 141
Polybius, 116, 151, 156
Pompadour, Madame de, 93-94, 96, 290, 304, 305, 324, 359
Pontverre, Monsieur de, 223, 224
Pope, Alexander, 172, 173, 189, 191, 198, 336
Pope, the, 13, 44, 47
Population, representation in proportion to, 151
Porcelain, replacement of, 184
Porée, Father, 158, 279
Port-Royal-des-Champs, 10, 11, 12
Portsmouth, New Hampshire, 368
Potomac river, 143
Potsdam, 181, 191, 197
Powder, article, 304, 305, 308
Power politics, 55
Prayer, 255, 260
Precession of the Equinoxes, 346
"Pre-existent germs," 346
Preliminary Discourse of the *Encyclopedia* (D'Alembert), 291, 296, 302
Prémontval, Madame de, 287
Prepositions, intricacies of, 164
Presbyterians, 167

Presles, Gaston de, character by Emile Augier, 323
"Pretended-Reformed Religion," 9
Pretender, English, 46, 51, 168
Prévost, Abbé, 85
Prices, rise in, 86
Prie, Madame de, 88
Prime Minister, diminishing power of, 135
Primitive man, 235
Primitivism, 49, 76, 235
Princeton (formerly College of New Jersey), 140, 142, 143
Principles of Natural Law (Burlamaqui), 151
"Privileged classes," 15, 169, 404, 406
Proclivities, stoic, of Montesquieu, 132
Profession of Faith of the Savoyard Vicar (Rousseau), 259
Professions, Diderot's desire to portray men in, 314
Profiteering, 107-08
Progress, xi, xii, 72, 183, 309, 407; modern, 231, 232; moral, xii, 65, 74, 110, 233, 234, 265, 276; progress through education, 295
Progress of the Human Mind (Turgot), 384
Project method in education, 258
Propaganda, 220
Property, 241, 242; private, 211, 240, 258; right of private, 262
Prophets, Old Testament, 280
Protestants, 4, 7, 8, 10, 12, 15, 30, 31, 39, 40, 66, 113, 121, 163, 206, 207; see Huguenots; see Protestantism
Protestantism, 9, 22, 24, 224
Proust, Marcel, 271
Providence, 117, 190, 191
Provincial Letters (Pascal), 10
Ptolemaic theory, 66
Puisieux, Madame de, 287
Punishments, harsh, 262; moderate

INDEX

Saint-Lambert, Jean-François, Marquis de, 251, 252, 254
Saint-Louis, Church of, 400
Saint-Marceau, Faubourg, 226
Saint-Maur, Madame de, 288, 289
Saint Petersburg, 319, 349
Saint-Pierre, Abbé de, 180
Saint-Preux, character by Rousseau, 250, 252, 256
Saint-Quentin, 324
Saint-Simon, Duc de, 7, 18, 21, 38, 41, 42, 82, 84, 178
Salente (ideal country in Fénelon's *Télémaque*), 49, 50
Salon of 1845 (Baudelaire), 328
Salon of 1846 (Baudelaire), 328
Salon of 1859 (Baudelaire), 328
Salon of 1763 (Diderot), 320
Salon of 1765 (Diderot), 326
Salon of 1767 (Diderot), 321, 325, 326
"Salons" (Diderot), 66, 99, 319, 323, 326, 327, 352
Santayana, George, 118
Saracens, article on (Diderot), 300
Saratoga, battle of, 369
Sartine, Monsieur de, 364, 373
Saturn, 192, 193, 194, 195
Saulier, Suzanne, 330; see Simonin, Suzanne
Savoy, 221, 226, 250, 285
Savoy, Duke of, 221
Saxe, Maurice de, 92, 93
Scarron, Paul, 41
Scellières, Abbey of, 219
Schiller, Johann Christoph Friedrich von, 335, 336, 339
Schomberg, Marshal, 8
Schweitzer, Albert, 233
Schwetzingen, castle of, 197
Science, 63, 74, 179, 233; biological, 345; modern, 276; natural, 100, 101, 194; political and social, 128; research in, 344; role of science, 171; scientific experiments, 117; scientific rationalism, 77
Science, Academy of, 63, 74, 195
Scientist, Franklin, 396; see Franklin, Benjamin
Secondat, Charles-Louis de, see Montesquieu
Secret Literary Correspondence (Métra), 383
Sects, 167; multiplicity of, 207
Sedan, 24, 25, 26
"Self-expression," 257
Sellius, Godefroy, 293, 294
Sémiramis (Voltaire), 311
Seneca, 233
Separation of Church and State, 121, 167, 219
Separation of governmental powers, 120, 134, 135, 141, 142, 147, 151, 152, 153, 154, 155, 156, 264; see Church and State, separation of
Serious and Comical Amusements of a Siamese at Paris (Dufresny), 102
Servetus, Michael, 6, 207
Sétoc (in Voltaire's *Zadig*), 188
Seventeenth Century, appreciation of nature in, 67
Seven Years' War, 95, 96, 200
Sévigné, Madame de, 6, 61
Sèvres, 351, 352
Sexes, equality of, 109
Shaftesbury, *Essay on Merit and Virtue,* 287
Shakespeare, William, 164, 171, 172, 173, 174, 216, 381
Shays's rebellion, 151
Sherlock, Martin, 216
Shoemakers, in Shakespeare's *Julius Caesar,* 171
Short and Easy Means to Prayer (Madame Guyon), 41
Short stories of Diderot, 353
Sidney, Algernon, 149
Sieyès, Abbé Emmanuel-Joseph, 400, 401

INDEX